Sports in American History

From Colonization to Globalization

Gerald R. Gems, PhD
North Central College

Linda J. Borish, PhD
Western Michigan University

Gertrud Pfister, PhD
University of Copenhagen

Human Kinetics

Library of Congress Cataloging-in-Publication Data

Gems, Gerald R.
  Sports in American history: from colonization to globalization / Gerald R. Gems, Linda J. Borish, Gertrud Pfister.
    p. cm.
  Includes bibliographical references and index.
  ISBN-13: 978-0-7360-5621-2 (hard cover)
  ISBN-10: 0-7360-5621-1 (hard cover)
  1. Sports--United States--History. 2. Sports--Social aspects--United States--History. I. Borish, Linda J., 1961- II. Pfister,
Gertrud, 1945- III. Title.
  GV583.G46 2008
  796.0973--dc22
                            2008015955

ISBN-10: 0-7360-5621-1
ISBN-13: 978-0-7360-5621-2

Acquisitions Editor: Myles Schrag
Developmental Editor: Amanda S. Ewing
Assistant Editor: Jillian Evans
Copyeditor: Tom Tiller
Proofreader: Kathy Bennett
Indexer: Gerry Lynn Shipe
Permission Manager: Dalene Reeder
Graphic Designer: Nancy Rasmus
Graphic Artist: Patrick Sandberg
Cover Designer: Bob Reuther
Photographer (cover): see page xi
Photo Asset Manager: Laura Fitch
Photo Office Assistant: Jason Allen
Art Manager: Kelly Hendren
Associate Art Manager: Alan L. Wilborn
Illustrator: Greg Maxson
Printer: Sheridan Books

Printed in the United States of America   10 9 8 7 6 5 4 3 2 1

Human Kinetics
Web site: www.HumanKinetics.com

United States: Human Kinetics
P.O. Box 5076
Champaign, IL 61825-5076
800-747-4457
e-mail: humank@hkusa.com

Canada: Human Kinetics
475 Devonshire Road Unit 100
Windsor, ON N8Y 2L5
800-465-7301 (in Canada only)
e-mail: info@hkcanada.com

Europe: Human Kinetics
107 Bradford Road
Stanningley
Leeds LS28 6AT, United Kingdom
+44 (0) 113 255 5665

e-mail: hk@hkeurope.com

Australia: Human Kinetics
57A Price Avenue
Lower Mitcham, South Australia 5062
08 8372 0999
e-mail: info@hkaustralia.com

New Zealand: Human Kinetics
Division of Sports Distributors NZ Ltd.
P.O. Box 300 226 Albany
North Shore City
Auckland
0064 9 448 1207
e-mail: info@humankinetics.co.nz

Contents

Preface

The intense media coverage of sport in American culture in the twenty-first century, highlighting issues such as professional players' salaries, amateurism, gender equity, scandals, and nationalism, has developed out of the rich and complex history of sport from early America. The study of American sport history provides a critical context for understanding how sporting activities have changed and how various factors have shaped them. The investigation of topics such as sport in Native American cultures, the growth of modern sport, gender perspectives on sport, and religious influences on sport shows the importance of sport in society. *Sports in American History: From Colonization to Globalization* provides a comprehensive, new approach to examining underexplored issues and groups in American sport history.

This text resulted from friendships involving diverse circumstances. To some degree, two of the authors experienced and have studied the historical ethnic, religious, gender, and social-class factors that affected the assimilation of immigrant groups and the nature of sport for more mainstream groups. The third author, a non-American with expertise in the study of international sport history, has been able to cast a critical eye on American society from the perspective of an international scholar affected by the globalization of American culture. Their education in related fields (although with PhDs in different academic programs) and their interdisciplinary scholarly endeavors involving mutual interests have brought them together in a common quest to increase understanding of the ways in which sport shapes American history, and in turn how the context of American history shapes sporting practices. This book explores the process of Americanization and resistance by some newcomers to America through the eyes of those who have often been forgotten, or whose stories have been considered unimportant, or in some instances whose stories have been invisible in American sport history. It is the sport history of those diverse Americans as well as the stories of the authors as they have experienced it in academic and athletic contexts. The collaborative process of developing and writing this book began in conversations at a sport history conference in 2003, and it required knowledge from all of the authors' areas of expertise and the respect and cooperation needed to produce such a comprehensive book.

This book is a core text for undergraduate courses in American sport history, American studies, and sport studies, but it will also be useful for graduate students and scholars in sport history and sport studies. The book not only provides a narrative history of sport in the United States but also challenges and enables students to address difficult and controversial issues as they study sport and history in their diverse contexts in culture. For students in the fields of American history, sport history, American studies, gender studies, and other areas of study, this book provides a framework for understanding how and why sport intersects with many facets of American society. To that end, evidence-based insights and primary sources are provided in order to explain the role of sport in the social construction of American culture over time. Sport is not just a reflection of the larger society; therefore sport is examined as an agent of change. Even the term *sport* changes in meaning over time and particular events, and its uses are traced by the various peoples in the regions that came to make up the United States.

This text draws attention especially to women, minorities, and the multitude of ethnic and religious groups that have composed American society—and to their historical role in the construction of sport culture. Whereas most American sport history texts are written by men and about men—especially white men—this book is more inclusive of women and nonwhites because they, too, have shaped the meaning of sport in the United States. Various peoples in the past have influenced concepts of sport as played by white men in the integration of gender, ethnicity, race, and religion of diverse groups. Therefore, this historical study delineates that the designation of whiteness has itself been a contested issue not only for African Americans but also for Asian Americans, Native Americans, and Hispanic Americans, who may now take their whiteness for granted. Such insights will allow students to develop new and alternative perspectives, examine sport as a social and cultural phenomenon, generate better understandings of current sport practices, reflect on future developments, and engage in lively discussions.

Throughout much of the text, the authors illuminate the struggles that resulted in the ongoing construction of American culture and the central place of sport in that culture. Any society will involve the norms, values, and behaviors of one dominant group that subordinate or alternative groups may challenge. In sport history, sport becomes part of this contested terrain of a dominant group seeking to establish the norms, values, and standards for the community. That is, immigrants and ethnic groups, as well as white Protestant mainstream Americans, influence sport in American history. Women, too, influence sport in American society through their struggle to gain access to sport and values associated with sport, typically the prerogative of white men. Diverse primary sources about sport are featured in this text, beginning with the colonization of American society and continuing through recent times of globalization of sport. Showing how individuals of ordinary and extraordinary circumstances played, promoted, criticized, capitalized on, or fought for human rights and equality in sport and society, this text offers a more complete rendering of sport in the experiences of American peoples.

The book also provides context about certain historical years and eras in which particular conditions affected the course of events involving sport. For example, the reform movements in pre–Civil War years played a key role in the expansion of sport and changing attitudes about sport for men and even some women. Certain conditions in the aftermath of World War I enabled Adolf Hitler to assume leadership of Germany, and that influenced political and sporting events in the United States and in the Olympic Games. Hitler's ascent to power would be impossible—even unthinkable—in Germany today but sports still involve politics, as discussed in the concluding chapter. The authors carefully note the conditions and context of each era in order to inform readers about the factors that spurred or impeded change over time. For example, the concept of quantification—and the compilation of records and statistics that so fascinate American sports fans—were unnecessary and virtually unheard of before the advent of technological advances and industrialized urban centers. Likewise, the invention of the bicycle during the 19th century elicited wholesale reforms not only in women's dress but also in courtship patterns and in a quest for greater independence. The athletic successes of female and black athletes fostered scientific investigations of evolutionary theories and the social stratification that divided and continues to divide American society. Such contextualization encourages students to question gender roles as well as racial and ethnic stereotypes, consider cause-and-effect relationships, and examine the role of sport in social processes and social change in American society.

The book is divided into sections based on historical periods, providing context for each era, from the indigenous tribes of premodern America through colonial societies to the global dominance of modern American popular culture. A handy time line is provided for ready reference. Chapters are arranged both chronologically (by eras) and topically (by issues or concepts). The ebb and flow of history and the ways in which people participate in sport and society at times mean an overlap in critical time periods in American sport history; factors that influence social history and sport history persist in some chapters so that discussion of issues may refer to events that occurred prior to the chronological span covered in a chapter. Readers might trace the influence of the Puritans in colonial America and later other majority white religious groups who exercised power and, in turn, ascertain their lasting influence on American culture. Students also learn about the challenges to that power that resulted in a more heterogeneous, pluralistic society and grasp this connection to sport. Thus particular attention is drawn to the factors of race, religion, ethnicity, gender, social class, the economy, and politics in the social developments in American culture.

Each chapter includes objectives, an introduction, a summary of points covered, and discussion questions to aid students and instructors in class preparation. Unique features include the use of primary documents from each era, including photographs, posters, and quotations. Students will notice that many of the historical quotations derived from primary sources retain their original spellings, which may look like misspellings to modern readers. For example, "ſ" indicates a long s, so "ſo" is pronounced "so." Other sections of the text retain the original vocabulary and grammar used in a particular period, such as the reference to "woman's rights" in the nineteenth century. The text also contains two types of sidebars. People and Places sidebars offer glimpses into the lives of those people who as individuals or as part of institutions affected, or were affected by, sport during a historical period. International Perspective sidebars, written by European scholar Gertrud Pfister, offer innovative comparisons at a time when Americans seemingly lack knowledge of other cultures and globalization issues. The features might prompt discussions about how sport may be viewed from national perspectives and from international perspectives, or how some groups within a society perpetuate their power and status by invoking sport, as in the current construction of sport stadiums and museums as sites of remembrance, nostalgia, and enactment of particular views about a sport hero or event in a nation's history.

Of course, no book can provide all the answers—or all the questions. This book is a starting point and entry into the fascinating field of sport history for furthering students' journeys on their own path to inquiry, reflection, contemplation, and research. The authors incorporate the latest scholarship to facilitate students' understanding of sport and history. This book contains an extensive bibliography of sources and primary documents and a determined focus on and broad coverage of the less-known or untold stories of sport—those of the nonwhite, the middle and lower ranks, the less powerful, the working class, and the various "others" whose histories are no less important to the ongoing construction of sport in American culture.

This book is the result of a cooperative venture over several years. The authors have developed a stronger spirit of friendship and scholarly inquiry rather than a competitive spirit that at times has dominated sport in American history. As intellectual teammates, the authors offer an innovative, lively, and inclusive book on sports in American history.

Acknowledgments

This book emanated from discussions about a new and comprehensive study in American sport history and what such a book might look like when Amy Clocksin of Human Kinetics approached Linda Borish and Gerald Gems at a sport history conference. These fruitful discussions yielded an exchange of ideas, and Amy spearheaded our book proposal through the initial review process at Human Kinetics, after which we began working with other dedicated colleagues in developing our book; we are grateful to Amy for her assistance, enthusiasm, and guidance. In supporting the development and completion of this collaborative book project, we are indebted to the excellent editors at Human Kinetics. We wish to deeply thank Myles Schrag and Amanda Ewing for their diligence, tact, patience, and expertise. They offered terrific assistance in providing insights and answering our queries with helpful information, making this a wonderful academic experience. We also acknowledge the contributions of these Human Kinetics colleagues, who assisted us in the different phases of our work: Dalene Reeder, Laura Fitch, Jillian Evans, Patrick Sandberg, Nancy Rasmus, and Bridget Walczak. Despite the geographic distances among the coauthors while writing the book (being in different U.S. and international locales posed a challenge at times), the ongoing efforts of the editors spurred us to work together in a truly joint endeavor. We acknowledge the critical comments offered by the anonymous reviewers, whose own expertise and suggestions have made our book a better product; their knowledge aided us in our efforts to create a new American sport history book, and we are grateful for the time they devoted to the review process.

Our colleagues in the North American Society for Sport History, the International Society for the History of Physical Education and Sport, and others in American Studies organizations have shared their vast knowledge with us over the years, and they encouraged us to develop a book in American sport history that integrated the experiences of many diverse Americans. In formal sessions at conferences or in informal gatherings, many of our colleagues aided us in creating a more complete book, and we deeply thank them. The research pursued for this endeavor could not have occurred without the outstanding assistance of numerous archivists and librarians in various locales who, as caretakers of the past, make our work possible. For the written and visual evidence in our book, we are indebted to the many people who helped us acquire the historical materials that appear throughout our work.

The coauthors each acknowledge the valuable help provided to them in their individual work on this project:

I would like to acknowledge Kim Butler, archivist, and the librarians of Oesterle Library at North Central College for their research assistance and the provision of photos.

—Jerry Gems

I wish to acknowledge the valuable contribution of the Burnham-Macmillan History Endowment Grants I received at Western Michigan University, which allowed me to travel to national and international conferences and to share research with colleagues. I would like to acknowledge the importance of a sabbatical leave taken during the 2005-2006 academic year at Western Michigan University in order to devote necessary time for research, writing, and acquiring images and primary sources for this book.

I thank Marion Gray, professor and chair of history, and Thomas Kent, Dean of the College of Arts and Sciences, for their support in providing a sabbatical award. Thanks, too, to my colleagues in the department of history who have viewed American sport history as a valuable part of our curriculum and encouraged my research in the field. In addition, I thank The Hadassah-Brandeis Institute, Brandeis University, for granting me a Research Associate position to continue my ongoing research on gender issues, sport history, and American Jewish women. Thanks to my parents Hope and Philip Borish whose love and encouragement in this and other intellectual endeavors, and previous sporting ones, provide guidance. And thanks to my identical twin sister, Anne, during all of those years of playing doubles together, for helping me learn about cooperation, not solely competition, as a necessary component in completing significant work with good colleagues.

—Linda J. Borish

I would like to acknowledge Henriette Arnoldus, librarian at the Department for Exercise and Sport Sciences at the University of Copenhagen, for research assistance.

—Gertrud Pfister

Credits

Cover Images

Exercises of the Youths courtesy of the Library of Congress, LC-USZ62-371
The Futurity Race at Sheepshead Bay courtesy of the Library of Congress, LC-DIG-pga-00720
Brown vs. Hamill in rowing match courtesy of the Library of Congress, LC-DIG-pga-00798
Babe Didrikson, Babe Ruth, Billie Jean King, Bobby Jones, Four Horsemen, Michael Jordan, and Muhammad Ali © Associated Press

Time Line Photos

Page 3: Christopher Columbus courtesy of the Library of Congress, LC-USZC2-1687
Page 7: Governor John Winthrop courtesy of the Library of Congress, LC-USZ62-120506
Page 41: Signing of the Declaration of Independence courtesy of the Library of Congress, LC-D419-181
Page 43: Eli Whitney courtesy of the Library of Congress, LC-USZ62-8283
Page 45: Battle of New Orleans courtesy of the Library of Congress, LC-USZ62-7809
Page 67: Andrew Jackson courtesy of the Library of Congress, LC-USZCN4-189
Page 69: Battle of the Alamo courtesy of the Library of Congress, LC-USZCN4-23
Page 71: Samuel Morse courtesy of the Library of Congress, LC-D429-29975
Page 73: Yankee Sullivan courtesy of the Library of Congress, LC-USZ62-920
Page 105: Dred Scott courtesy of the Library of Congress, LC-USZ62-5092
Page 105: Abraham Lincoln courtesy of the Library of Congress, LC-D416-16462
Page 139: Alexander Graham Bell courtesy of the Library of Congress, LC-G9-Z1-14931-A
Page 141: Great Railroad Strike courtesy of the Library of Congress, LC-USZ62-125624
Page 141: Thomas Edison courtesy of the Library of Congress, LC-D414-K3490
Page 175: James Naismith courtesy of the Library of Congress, LC-USZ62-115891
Page 177: Robert Garrett © Getty Images
Page 181: Model T Ford courtesy of the Library of Congress, LC-USZ62-118659
Page 183 (top to bottom): Ray Harroun © Associated Press, Francis Ouimet © Associated Press
Page 185: Ethelda Bleibtrey © Associated Press
Page 229: Helen Wills courtesy of the Library of Congress, LC-USZ62-115647
Page 231: Sonja Henie and Gilles Grafstrom © Associated Press
Page 233: Amelia Earhart courtesy of the Library of Congress, LC-USZ62-110822
Page 235: Jay Berwanger © Associated Press
Page 239: All-American Football Conference game © Associated Press
Page 273: Althea Gibson courtesy of the Library of Congress, LC-USZ62-114745
Page 275: Alan Shepard © Associated Press
Page 277: Malcolm X © AP Photo/Eddie Adams
Page 279: Mark Spitz © Associated Press
Page 281: 1980 U.S. men's hockey team © Associated Press
Page 307: Joan Benoit © AP Photo/Lennox McLendon
Page 309: Summer Olympics in Beijing, China © AP Photo/Herbert Knosowski

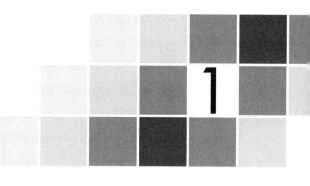

Sporting Experiences in Colonial America
1400–1750

CHAPTER OBJECTIVES

After reading this chapter, you will have learned about the following:

- The foundations of sport in colonial America emerging from the peoples of various cultures

- The significance of sporting practices and recreation for diverse groups of Native Americans

- The attitudes of various European colonists about sport and physical exercise and how these attitudes shaped sport patterns in American colonies

- The influence of religion on sport throughout the American colonies

- The importance of social class, race, and gender in the growth of sport in colonial America

- The types of sports played in colonial America, as well as regional variations in sport

In the 1500s, the Aztecs played tlachtli, a Native American ball game. Such sporting activities drew the attention of white settlers and missionaries, who viewed Native American sports based on their own conception of sport from their white European heritage. In describing the game, Spanish missionary Fray Bernardino de Sahagún noted distinctive features of the game's players, equipment, and victory prizes:

> They [the rulers] played ball. There were his ball-catchers, and his ball-players. They wagered [in this game] all [manner of] costly goods—golden necklaces, green stone, fine turquoise, slaves, precious capes, valuable breech cloths, cultivated fields, houses, leather leg bands, gold bracelets, arm bands of quetzal feathers, duck feather capes, bales of cacao—[these] were wagered there in the game called tlachtli.

> On the two sides, on either hand, it was limited by walls, very well made, in that the walls and floor were smoothed. And there, in the very corner of the ball court, was a line, drawn upon the ground. And on the walls were two stone, ball court rings. He who played caused [the ball] to enter there; he caused it to go in. Then he won all the costly goods, and he won something from all who watched there in the ball court. His equipment was the rubber ball, the catcher gloves, girdles, and leather hip guards. (449–450)

Three groups of people shaped the sporting heritage in colonial America: Native Americans (the original inhabitants of North America), Africans (forced against their will to come to the New World as laborers and slaves), and white Europeans (especially those from Great Britain). All played a role in the patterns of sport that developed in colonial America, and the cultural worlds of Native Americans and Africans collided with those of European peoples colonizing North America in the 1500s and 1600s. The religious patterns, social-class structures, race, gender roles, ethnicity, and regional environments of these three peoples all contributed to colonial America's sporting traditions.

Before Christopher Columbus reached the New World in 1492, several million Native Americans lived in North America, and they maintained cultural worlds distinct from the European cultures, including Native American ball games and ceremonies related to their sporting activities. Thus European colonists did not, as some have maintained, discover a "virgin wilderness," lacking settlements and peoples. Rather, Europeans encountered cultures, environments, and societies quite different from what they left behind in such countries as England, Spain, France, and Portugal.

Historian Carl Guarneri has explained that early encounters between Europeans and Native Americans "illustrated features that would characterize the collision between European and North American peoples of the next two centuries: the quest for riches, the exchange of goods, the power of legends about the New World, clashes of religious worldviews, the impact of disease, technological gaps in warfare and food production, and the violence of exploitation, enslavement, and resistance" (29). In this period of early contact between Native Americans and Europeans, various societies of Native Americans existed in the New World. Despite the European perception (which would become a stereotype) that "typical" American Indians all shared certain characteristics, the fact is that "native societies of North America were enormously varied. Their practices ranged from hunting and gathering to farming and craft production, and their languages and religions were more varied than those of Europeans" (32). Indeed, the inhabitants that Europeans desired to colonize and conquer in the sixteenth and seventeenth centuries were not undiscovered—they were merely new to the Europeans, and the Native Americans embraced their own religious, economic, political, and social beliefs.

On the eve of the European colonization, the North American continent featured varying tribes in the North, the Midwest, and the Southwest. Guarneri has identified six broad groups of native peoples, indicating the diverse nature of Native

American societies: the Anasazis, peoples of the Great Plains, the Mississippians, the Eastern Woodland peoples, the Hunter-Gatherers of the North and Northwest, and other variations of Native American societies demonstrating varying patterns and links with other tribes.

The Anasazis resided in the dry American Southwest and used complex systems of irrigation to grow corn, beans, and squash. Later, due to drought, they resettled in areas now known as Arizona and New Mexico, and they developed the Acoma, Hopi, and Zuni pueblos. These Native Americans were later encountered by Spanish conquistador Francisco Vásquez de Coronado, who termed them the Pueblo Indians (Guarneri 30–31). Other indigenous peoples lived in the Great Plains and pursued buffalo as a main source of their way of life. These seminomadic tribes included the Cheyenne, Arapaho, Pawnee, and Sioux, and their people exhibited warrior skills and hunted on the Plains (Guarneri 29, 31). Another group of native inhabitants, known as Mississippians, lived in the Mississippi and Ohio River Valleys. They established societies in the American Midwest and Southeast, cultivating crucial foods such as corn, beans, and squash. The Cahokia mound builders developed a large society of more than thirty thousand people near present-day St. Louis, with temple mounds, orderly cornfields, and structures (Guarneri 31; Rader, *American Ways* 4).

Other tribal societies included the Eastern Woodland peoples, who inhabited the Atlantic seacoast in parts of what is now the United States, as well as parts of what is now southeastern Canada. Tribes in this region pursued hunting, fishing, and agriculture at various times, with farming and fishing in the summer, and moving in smaller bands for hunting in the winter. This group included the Iroquois nation, a league of six tribes covering the areas now known as northern New York and Pennsylvania. Iroquois culture included participation in physical activities and sport. Furthermore, "because of their unity and physical prowess, and because their territory was between French and English zones of settlement, the Iroquois would figure primarily in colonial wars" (Guarneri 32). As discussed later in this chapter, such collisions between Europeans and Native Americans would influence the nature of sport in early America. Another of the tribal societies was the Hunter-Gatherer group of the North and Northwest. These tribes engaged in hunting and gathering and in fishing in the waterways of California and the Pacific Northwest. Inhabitants remained in their small villages, away from colonizing European settlers, until the late eighteenth century. According to Guarneri, the sixth group of Native American peoples consisted of "Variations and Connections." This refers to the diversity of native peoples. The native groups of North America had widely varying practices, languages, and religions (Guarneri 32).

These diverse peoples and landscapes of North America influenced the nature of sport in the early decades of the New World and—along with the varying attitudes about sport (both those that favored and those that were critical of certain types of games and pastimes)—formed the basis of early sporting experiences. Experienced by a range of men and women in diverse Native American, slave, and colonial communities, sport thus became part of colonial society, with different meanings for different peoples amidst the debates and challenges of settling the New World.

Native American Pastimes and Sports

Long before Europeans colonized the New World, Native Americans led physically active lives in pursuits necessary to their sustenance and religious beliefs. They used their fishing and hunting prowess, as well as their expert knowledge of the land and water, for field sports. Colonists in the various regions might adapt these sporting practices in their own outdoor excursions in hunting, fishing, and fowling. Indigenous peoples in their native societies swam and canoed along waterways as a means of passage, and children learned to swim at an early age. Fishing, as well

Pre-1492

- Native American games played

1492

> Christopher Columbus lands in America

1492

- Spanish expel Jews and Moors (Muslims) from Spain

1517

- Martin Luther begins Protestant Reformation and attacks Catholicism

1530s

- John Calvin launches religious reform

1558

- Elizabeth I crowned Queen of England

1565

- St. Augustine, Florida, founded by the Spanish (first permanent European settlement in the New World) as hunting with a bow and arrow, provided food, and hunting also served military purposes in times of war. The practice of archery also involved training games and competitions.

Other games, such as hoop-and-pole contests, provided additional training, as well as opportunities for wagering. In such contests, played throughout the North American continent by all tribes, males rolled a hoop along a flat field, and individuals or teams attempted to pierce the hoop with spears, darts, or arrows (King 18, Koppedrayer 21–22, Dyson 148–149). Indeed, indigenous peoples in America played a wide variety of games, including marbles and shinny, a game similar to hockey. The latter could be played on the ice during the winter and was enjoyed by men, women, and children. Tribes of the Northwest and Southwest played shuttlecock, a game similar to badminton, in which an object (sometimes a corn husk with feathers) was kept aloft with paddles or hands. For the Zunis of the New Mexico region, it also held deeper religious meanings, signifying spiritual power or favor and often involving wagers (Meneses 280–281).

Archery

For Native Americans, archery was a utilitarian necessity. Among the Sioux tribes of the Western plains, boys shot arrows through rolling hoops that approximated the moving targets presented by animals. In the Mandan tribe of the Dakotas, men practiced a form of speed shooting in which they competed to see who could keep the most arrows aloft at one time. In the Southeast, Cherokees held contests—for men, women, and children—in which cornstalks served as targets.

Early accounts by white European travelers reported the athletic skills of the indigenous peoples in archery. James Rosier, a British explorer, noted (ca. 1605) the archery equipment of Native Americans in New England: "When we went on to ſhore to trade with them, in one of their Canoas I saw their bowes and arrows, which I tooke up and drew an arrow in one of them, which I found to be of strength able to carry an arrow five or six score stronglie" (Rosier, qtd. in Altherr, Part 1 38). The

Archery was an important aspect of many Native American cultures, as George Catlin, noted researcher and painter of Native Americans, shows in his painting *Archery of the Mandans*.

Denver Public Library, Western History Collection, George Catlin, photographer. B-926.

proficiency of Native American archers was also noted by British clergyman Charles Wooley, who traveled in colonial New York in about 1678 and wrote about the indigenous peoples in the New York area: "Before the Christians especially the Dutch came amongst them they were very dexterous Artists at their bows, insomuch I have heard it affirm'd that a Boy of seven years old would shot a Bird flying" (Wooley, qtd. in Altherr, Part 1 39).

Running

Running also served utilitarian purposes, as when messengers needed to search for food, deliver goods, or carry news of war or other important events between tribes. Iroquois runners in the Northeast could cover 240 miles (385 kilometers) of their tribal network over a three-day period. In the Southwest, Native American tribes integrated running into cultural practices. The Aztec relay runners of Mexico brought news of conquistador Hernán Cortés' arrival to King Montezuma in 1519 by rushing 260 miles (420 kilometers) in only 24 hours. In 1680, the Pueblo tribes of New Mexico organized a successful revolt against their Spanish overlords by means of a system of running messengers that coordinated their attacks. Running also held particular religious significance for the tribes of the Southwest. Religious rituals, rites of passage in puberty, fertility ceremonies, and competitive contests all involved running activities, some of which required phenomenal displays of endurance. Both males and females engaged in kickball races that required the continuous propulsion of a ball over a long course in a contest of skill and stamina. Sometimes sticks were substituted for the balls, and stick races, serving as fertility rites, covered distances as long as 25 miles (40 kilometers). Not unlike the artifacts and memorabilia of modern sports halls of fame, favorite sticks, believed to possess magic, were treasured by runners for many years (O'Fearghail 29–30, Meneses 168, Collier 262–266).

Horse Riding

Humans' need to deliver messages on foot diminished when European explorers introduced the horse to North America in the Columbian Exchange. (The Columbian Exchange was when Europeans and Native Americans interacted in a mutual transfer of animals, plants, and diseases. Since this transfer of products and diseases continued long after 1492 for centuries, Guarneri suggests it is more accurate to call it the "Post-Columbian Exchange.") In fact, "first brought to America by Columbus, horses helped the Spanish conquistadors to overpower native peoples"; however, with the use of horses spreading "through Spanish outposts, Native Americans acquired them by trading, raiding, or rounding up runaways" (Guarneri 56, 65). Native Americans considered the horse to be a sacred animal and treasured it accordingly as a prized possession. Members of tribes of the Western plains became skilled equestrians, and both men and women engaged in horse races within their own tribes and against other clans. Races often covered 3 or 4 miles (about 4.5 to 6.5 kilometers), and winning riders gained considerable prestige and material goods. In 1806, Nez Perce riders even challenged members of the Lewis and Clark Expedition to a horse race as they explored the northwestern territory of the newly acquired Louisiana Purchase, which doubled the size of the young United States (Johnson 105–106).

The Shoshone Indians of northern Utah participated in horse races as part of their sporting heritage, having worked along with Eastern Shoshone Indians to develop their herds of horses for hundreds of years. For the Shoshone people of the Washakie colony in northern Utah, breeding horses provided a step "to developing a horse racing tradition." Horse teams of the Washakie farmers were skilled at breaking horses. "Their ancestors had raced horses for pleasure as well as for purse by wagering on outcomes, and the Washakie residents of the early twentieth century rekindled the earlier flame by competing with their white neighbors at horse racing" (Kreitzer

◄ 1585
• First English settlement founded on Roanoke Island off North Carolina coast

◄ 1586-1588
• English settlers founded other settlements on Roanoke Island

◄ 1588
• Defeat of the Spanish Armada by the English

◄ 1607
• Jamestown Colony founded in Virginia (first permanent English settlement in North America)

◄ 1609
• Santa Fe, New Mexico, founded by the Spanish

◄ 1618
• King James I proclaims the Book of Sports in England

237). Thus, the rich tradition of horse racing for the Shoshone Indians persisted over the centuries as recalled by ancestors as they raced horses against nonnative peoples. The enthusiasm for horse racing also took hold among Shoshone peoples in other areas, such as Owyhee, Nevada; Fort Washakie, Wyoming; Fort Hall, Idaho; and Skull Valley, Utah. In each of these areas, tribes held "horse races that coincided with other holiday celebrations such as the Fourth of July and county fairs. These races were well organized, right down to the monitoring of track sizes, specific distances to run and other regulations" (Kreitzer 237). Clearly, then, the horse influenced the sporting traditions of diverse Native American tribes.

Lacrosse

The most prominent competition in Native American culture was lacrosse. Played throughout the North American continent, lacrosse went beyond Native American everyday life as a magical, religious, ritualistic activity—and as a pragmatic one (providing training for war). Funerals and memorial ceremonies included lacrosse games. Top lacrosse players won esteem, and upon death some were even buried with their lacrosse sticks. North American Indian cultures played versions of lacrosse in various regions, and "in playing lacrosse, the name given by the French to a stick-and-ball game, groups of both men and women engaged in a far more vigorous sport" than games of chance (Rader, *American Ways* 8). Lacrosse required teamwork yet allowed for individual brilliance on the playing field. The popular game had flexible rules. There were no out-of-bounds lines, fields were irregularly constructed, and games were played with varying numbers of players (sometimes in the hundreds). Players wore no protective equipment and sometimes competed in the nude, like ancient Greek Olympians. The Choctaw tribes of the Southeast even allowed players to use two sticks. Goals were set at great distances, depending on the number of players; in fact, in one game played in 1721 by the Miami Indians of the Midwest, a European spectator judged the goals to be as far as 2 miles (3.2 kilometers) apart (Vennum 237). Lacrosse games tended to be a communal activity, with participants encouraged by drummers and chanting women (Twombly 35–36). Gambling on games involved

George Catlin painted this horse-racing scene of the Minatarees in the mid- to late 1860s.

George Catlin, *Horse Racing— Minatarees*, Paul Mellon Collection. Image courtesy of the Board of Trustees, National Gallery of Art, Washington.

◆1619

• First slaves imported
  to Virginia from Africa

◆1620

• Pilgrims founded
  Plymouth Colony

◆1630

› Massachusetts Bay
  Colony founded by
  Governor John
  Winthrop and the
  Puritans

INTERNATIONAL PERSPECTIVE

Folk Football Games in Preindustrial Europe

The immediate forerunners of the game of football were ferocious folk games that had been played in European countries including Denmark, England, and Italy since the Middle Ages. As a rule, they took place on religious holidays ("holy days") and were played on the streets, squares, and fields of villages and towns. The rules were simple: A ball had to be taken to a previously arranged "goal," in the course of which violent disputes arose. There was no fixed number of players, and mostly large groups—sometimes even whole villages—played against each other. Sport historian Allen Guttmann has described the game as follows: "When village competed against village, kicking, throwing, and carrying the ball across fields and through narrow streets . . . into the portal of the opposing village's parish church, every one was involved."

In Belgium, for example, football games were played between married versus unmarried men. The group which succeeded in getting the ball to a prearranged place was rewarded with beer. In one source, a statement of claim submitted to a magistrate in Brabant, it was recorded that more than a thousand people, both players and spectators, had gathered before the start of the game, and more than four hundred took part in the fight for the ball. In the event, many players were injured, fields were trampled underfoot, fences were torn down, and irrigation ditches were destroyed. The surrounding land looked as if a huge army had camped there. Little wonder that the authorities repeatedly tried—in vain—to prohibit the games.

These folk games survived because they were part of the festival culture; they strengthened the sense of community and allowed people to give vent to their emotions and needs, which was otherwise forbidden. At the beginning of the nineteenth century, the game, considered rough and unrefined, was played in the upper-class public schools of England. With the introduction of rules, the game was "tamed," and with it the pupils.

Information from Dunning, Eric. Ed. *The Sociology of Sport: A Selection of Readings.* London: Cass, 1971; Mangan, J.A. *Athleticism in the Victorian and Edwardian Public School.* Cambridge: Cambridge University Press, 1981; Renson, Roland. "Leibesübungen der Bürger und Bauern im Mittelalter [Physical Exercises of Townsmen and Peasants in the Middle Ages]." Ed. H. Ueberhorst. *Geschichte der Leibesübungen* [History of Physical Exercises]. Vol. 3:1. Berlin: Bartels & Wernitz, 1980. 97–144.

◆1632

• George Calvert
  (Lord Baltimore)
  developed
  Maryland with
  grant of land

◆1636

• Harvard College
  founded

◆1664

• English capture
  New Netherland
  from the Dutch,
  renaming it New
  York

substantial wagers. In 1794, the Seneca and Mohawk tribes (members of the Iroquois Confederacy) settled a land dispute by means of a lacrosse game. A 1797 rematch featured 500 players per side, with 60 from each tribe engaged in the game at one time. In the Huron tribe of the Northeast, players bet not only their material goods but also their own wives, children, and personal freedom. Losers might also forfeit their hair or even their little finger. Not surprisingly, such conditions led to furious and sometimes deadly contests. The Algonquians considered the game to be sacred; the Cherokees of the Southeast blamed the outcome of lost games on powerful medicine men who influenced tribal fortunes. Players cleansed their bodies by means of fasting and laxative use before games, as well as sexual abstinence. Southeastern tribes conditioned their players for the rigors of the game by performing painful scarification rites to enhance their powers of endurance (Vennum 28).

The Choctaw Indians' playing of lacrosse also drew interest from Europeans. George Catlin, noted researcher and painter of Native Americans, described a Choctaw lacrosse match: "Each party had their goal made with two upright posts, about 25 feet [7.6 meters] apart, set firm in the ground, with a pole across at the top. These goals were about forty or fifty rods [220 to 275 yards, or 200 to 250 meters] apart," and at "a point just half way between, was another small stake, driven down, where the ball was to be thrown up at the firing of a gun, to be struggled for by the players. . . . The sticks with which this tribe play, are bent into an oblong hoop at the end, with a sort of slight web of small thongs tied across, to prevent the ball from passing through." The ball players held the stick in one hand and leaped in the air to catch the ball in the webbing of the stick or to throw it to a fellow player. The players did not wear moccasins or, for that matter, any clothing except the breechcloth around the waist, along with "a beautiful bead belt, and a 'tail,' made of white horsehair or quills, and a '*mane*' on the neck, of horsehair dyed of various colours." A score was made when "the ball was passed between the stakes of either party, or was counted for their game, and a halt of about one minute; when it was again started by the judges of the play, and a similar struggle ensued; and so on until the successful party arrived to 100, which was the limit of the game, and accomplished at an hour's sun, when they took the stakes," as the sunlight ended. At the end of the ball game, the players, "by a previous agreement, produced a number of jugs of whiskey, which gave all a wholesome drink, and sent them all off merry and in good humour, but not drunk" (Catlin, qtd. in Riess, *Major Problems* 27–30). Catlin's writings and paintings provide a European American view of this Native American sport. Catlin described the ball playing of the Choctaws as "most beautiful sport," and his paintings of it outnumbered all of his other paintings of the Choctaw tribe (Goodyear 139). This team game of lacrosse played by Native Americans in colonial America changed over time as other peoples adopted it as part of American society.

European travelers in colonial America were often fascinated by lacrosse, and they provided numerous descriptions of the game, though, as in the following account by Baron de Lahontan, a French traveler in the Northeastern region in about 1703, they sometimes used derogatory language for the players, representing their white European perceptions of the ball play of Indian tribes:

> The Savages, who commonly play at it in large companies of three or four Hundred at a time, fix two Sticks at five or six Hundreds Paces diftance from each other; They divide into two equal Parties, and tofs up the ball about half way between the two Sticks. Each Party endeavour to tofs the Ball to their side; fome run to the Ball, and the reft keep at a little diftance on both fides to affift on all Quarters. . . . [T]his Game is fo violent that they tear their

Ball Playing Among the Sioux Indians by Seth Eastman.

In the Collection of the Corcoran Gallery of Art. Accession number 69.63. Artist: Seth Eastman, title: *Ball Playing Among the Sioux Indians*, 1981. Oil on canvas, 28 1/4 × 40 3/4 inches. Corcoran gallery of Art, Washington, D.C. Gift of William Wilson Corcoran.

Skins, and break their legs very often in ſtriving to raiſe the Ball. All theſe Games are made only for Feaſts or other trifling Entertainments; for 'tis to be obſerv'd, that as they hate Money, ſo they never put it in the Balance, and one may ſay, *Intereſt is never the occaſion for Debates among them.* (Baron de Lahontan, qtd. in Altherr, Part 1 439; italics in original)

Such curiosity doomed the British soldiers of Fort Michilimackinac in 1763, when the Ojibwa and Sauk tribes of the Midwest used lacrosse as a subterfuge for retaliation. They initiated a lacrosse game outside the walls of the fort and even threw the ball inside on occasion to test the garrison's response. When soldiers opened the gates and ventured outside to become spectators, the Native American bystanders, who harbored weapons under their cloaks, attacked to avenge their people and lands lost at the hands of the white invaders. Those in the fort who survived the carnage faced slavery at the hands of the Native Americans (Vennum 88–103).

Later, in other parts of the continent, white spectators traveled to watch the games without serious repercussion. In 1765, a game between Cherokee women drew great interest, and Ojibwa games featured both boys and girls. The Dakota people even played men against women, though the latter enjoyed numerical superiority, with five women for every male opponent (Vennum 184). The incursion of whites into native lands, and their consequent appropriation of land, had inevitable repercussions. Differing moral attitudes and the imposition of white standards led to bans on gambling, the required wearing of Western-style clothing, and harassment by Christian missionaries of native tribes who played lacrosse on Sundays rather than attend church services (Vennum 104–117).

Shinny and Double Ball

Shinny—a sort of field hockey using decorated, curved sticks to propel a ball—was played throughout the continent, mainly by women in some tribes (such as the Crees), but only by men in others (such as the tribes of northern California). The Crows even had mixed teams. Double ball, on the other hand, was played almost exclusively by women. Similar to lacrosse, the game involved two balls strapped together and thrown using sticks, and it served as a test of endurance—a decidedly different quality than those expected of white women. As with men's games, women gambled on double ball, marking another big difference between native women and colonial Anglo women (Keith 101–102). As Oxendine has pointed out, the important role played by women in American Indian societies was reflected in sporting activities: "North American Indian women participated in ball games as active, agile players and as avid, ardent spectators" (22). He wrote that women played all known games, albeit often with different rules.

Toli and Other Forms of Stickball

In the Mississippi region of North America, the Choctaws played a traditional native game called toli (more commonly known as stickball), which derived from roots in pre-Columbian times and eventually developed into lacrosse. Many variations of toli were played by Native American tribes (Stepp 285). An early account of the Choctaws playing stickball was provided by a Jesuit priest around 1729, but the game had likely been played by the tribe even earlier. It exhibited aspects of warfare and was used to settle disputes. A single game might "last for days with almost no boundary on where it [the game] was played and teams could number in the hundreds" (Stepp 287). A description of the toli game played among the Choctaws in the pre-Columbian period conveys the physical nature of the sport:

> The rules of the game were minimal. . . . Defensive tactics were varied and often brutal. Preventing opponents from scoring often meant tripping, tackling, or striking the head or body of a foe with the hand or an unyielding hickory

◦1665
- Horse racing appears in New York Colony

◦1692–1693
- Salem Witch Trials conducted

◦1676
- Bacon's Rebellion in Virginia

◦1681
- William Penn establishes Pennsylvania with grant of land

◦1690s
- Shift in labor practices from white indentured servitude to black slave labor in the Chesapeake region

◦1732
- Schuylkill Fishing Co. established in Philadelphia

racket. As a result, injuries were frequent, and some games were actually terminated before a winner was determined owing to casualties that decimated one or both ranks. (Stepp 287)

Betting on the outcome of a toli game played by the Mississippi Choctaws by non–Native Americans became commonplace with increased white and Native American interactions in the late nineteenth century. Yet some white settlers wanted to curb the violence of the game, as deaths occurred in high-stakes matches, and in 1889 the Mississippi legislature banned gambling at stickball games (Stepp 287).

Varied stick-and-ball games drew the interest of other Native Americans in the Mississippi region, with some being played by both men and women. In 1700, a Jesuit missionary, Father Paul du Ru, witnessed a type of stickball played among the Muskogees; he noted that they gambled on the outcome, and he described differences between the men's and women's versions:

> We walked to the village where there were games and a great dance. The men play in pairs; one of them has a ball in the hand and throws it ahead. Both of them run as fast as they can, throwing a big stick after this ball, and as well as I could make out, the one whose stick is closest to the ball wins the play. Then the one who wins throws the ball next time. This is a rather strenuous game; nevertheless it is played by both old and young. . . .

> [The women] separate into two parties between two large posts in the square. Somebody throws a little ball in the center, and the one who seizes it first tries her best to run around the post on her side three times, but she is prevented by the women of the opposite party who seize her if they can. When she can no longer resist them, she throws the ball to her people who make a similar effort to run around their posts. Sometimes the ball falls into the hands of the other side which then tries the same manoeuvre. The games are very long and ordinarily when they are over the women plunge into the water to refresh themselves. Sometimes the men play this game also. (455)

White settlers also wrote journal accounts of other sporting activities pursued by Native Americans. Englishman William Wood described Native American sports in New England in his *New England Prospect* in 1634, noting that the indigenous inhabitants played soccer (or football, as he termed it), along with other active sports:

> For their ſport activitie they have commonly but three or foure; as footeball, ſhooting, running and ſwimming: when they play country againſt country there are rich Goales, all behung with Wampompeage [shells], Mowhack-ies, Beaver skins, and blacke Otter skinnes. . . . Their Goales be a mile [1.6 kilometers] long placed on the ſands, which are as even as a board; their ball is no bigger than a hand-ball, which ſometimes they mount in the Aire with their naked feete . . . ſometimes alſo it is two dayes before they get a Goale, then they marke the ground they winne, and beginne there the next day. Before they come to this ſport, they paint themſelves, even as when they go to warre. (qtd. in Altherr, Part 1 160–161)

Although Wood appreciated the vigorous soccer played by the indigenous peoples in Massachusetts, he claimed that English people were superior: "[O]ne English . . . [is] able to beate ten *Indians* at footeball" (161).

As with other sports and pastimes, Native American peoples often bet on these games, and, as sport historian George Eisen has commented, "We must remember that gambling in Indian cultures was both a pastime in itself and an activity that accompanied all sport events" ("Early" 10). For example, the Iroquois and Seneca Indians played a ball game and "the teams were composed of phraties, a unit established partly for social and partly for religious purposes." At the game played at tribal councils the "ball was made of stuffed deerskin, about the size of a soccer ball. Before the game started, members of each phraty placed bets, consisting usually of articles of personal property, thus adding to the general excitement of the contest" (Dewey 736). The attitudes of white settlers viewing Native American sports, however, often reflected the religious perspectives of Europeans about sport and society as they embarked on settling North America.

Influence of Religion on English Colonists

In Europe, on the eve of cultural contact with the New World, the ongoing clash between Catholics and Protestants continued. Spain was unified under the Catholic monarchy of Ferdinand and Isabella, which resulted in the Inquisition against Jews, Muslims, and false converts, and the Spanish conquest of Granada in 1492 ended the Muslim presence in southern Spain. In coming to America, Columbus and other Spanish conquerors "believed that the new lands had been opened to them by God as a reward for their religious zeal and a challenge to expand Christianity's domain." Other European colonists in the New World, such as French Jesuit missionaries and English Puritans, "shared the desire to establish godly realms [there]. . . . In their case, religious expansionism received an additional push from the Protestant Reformation, which after the 1520s produced an all-out contest between Protestants and Catholics for minds, hearts, and territory in the Christian and 'heathen' worlds" (Guarneri 38).

These religious tensions influenced European colonists' views of the appropriateness of physical exercise and sport. Europeans came to the New World both for religious reasons and in a quest for wealth, and both religious and profit motives influenced the types of physical activity and sport that they accepted or prohibited in establishing colonies in North America. Several colonists desired to perpetuate their own cultural and economic ways, and this influenced their descriptive accounts of Native American sport. The colonists' "approach toward Indian culture and recreation, biased as it was, indicated their general attitude toward man, God, and society. . . . [T]hese early Pilgrims in some ways predetermined modern American attitudes toward sports and specifically ethnic sports" (Eisen, "Early" 15).

Calvinism

In the 1530s, John Calvin called for religious reform in Europe. "Reform" Protestants, as Calvinists were often known, spread their religious beliefs throughout the sixteenth century to England, Scotland, France (French Protestants), and the English colonies. Calvinists preached a doctrine of predestination—that one's fate was known by God and that only a select few would be chosen by God for salvation, while all other souls would be damned. In Calvinism, society was theocratic, and God was sovereign. The struggle to be a good Christian, to believe one would be one of the "saints" rather than one of the "sinners," permeated all aspects of life. Calvinist authorities "insisted upon personal austerity, public fasting, evening curfews, and intensive religious instruction. They prohibited dancing, card playing, heavy drinking, and fashionable dressing" (Rader, *American Ways* 32). Calvin made little distinction between body and soul in seeking salvation; both needed to be free of sin. In fact, "of all the leaders of the Protestant Reformation who held, at best, an ambivalent attitude toward amusement and games, John Calvin was the most important." He promoted a strict doctrine, and, in Geneva, Switzerland, from 1541 to 1564, "he attempted to construct a 'theocracy,' a reign of godliness. Amusements and games took a beating" (Baker 74). The most ardent followers of Calvinism, the English Puritans, would bring this scrutiny of pastimes and

How Religion and Sport Are Related

In the United States, a considerable number of studies emphasize the close connection between sport and religion. However, most of these studies focus on Protestantism and men's sport in the U.S. If one takes other cultures, other religions, and women's sport into consideration, the complex and ambiguous relationships between sport and religion can be observed.

Religions and physical cultures are linked by numerous processes of interaction, although evaluations and judgments depend to a large extent on the perspective. Followers of a particular religious creed will look at things differently from those who take a critical view of the creed or are indifferent to it.

The link between world view and physical culture can clearly be observed, for example, in the spread of modern sport, which from the end of the nineteenth century evolved into the dominant form of physical culture all over the world but did not meet with the same measure of acceptance in all societies. This is revealed, for example, by an analysis of participants and sporting success at the Olympic Games. The countries with the highest numbers of participants and victories are countries in which a "Protestant ethic" and a large degree of secularization go hand in hand with a high level of industrialization. Societies that by contrast have shown, or still show, little interest in sport are those with a contemplative or fatalistic world view.

Since religions invariably prescribe codes of conduct, and since these codes of conduct invariably include rules on the use of the body as well as on the use of one's leisure, sport has always been explicitly or implicitly a matter of concern for religion—and vice versa. Numerous examples may be cited to illustrate that attitudes toward the body, body ideals, and cultures of movement are correlated with religious convictions. The Olympic Games of Greek antiquity and the Greeks' belief in their gods, for example, are grounded in the same basic philosophy.

This is equally true of modern sport. Religions, which regard the body as the servant of the soul or as the door through which evil enters, or both, reject the cult of the body which is demanded by sport. By contrast, the ascetic ideals and deferred gratification patterns inherent in many religions (in which rewards are deferred until after death) are beneficial for meeting the demands made on the body in training and contests. Religions measure sporting activities by the extent to which these are compatible with their axioms and rules. Apart from religion, however, traditions, conditions of life, political and social circumstances, and numerous other factors exercise an influence on the diffusion as well as the forms and levels of sport in a society.

The faith or creed a woman adheres to affects the opportunities she has to participate in sports much more than a man's religion determines the extent of his participation, since religions—at least the monotheistic world religions—assume a masculine/feminine dichotomy of tasks and responsibilities as well as a polarity of men's and women's natures. From this they derive a hierarchic ranking of gender and prescribe different ideals, norms, and behavioral patterns for men and women. Since religions control and regulate the relations between the sexes and sexuality in particular, numerous rules and prohibitions are connected with the body, and since the female body is considered to be seductive, weak, and in need of protection, it is covered by numerous taboos. For this reason, women's sports attire and coeducational sports, for example, posed a problem for Catholic bishops and popes right up to World War II. Even today religious precepts greatly restrict the sporting activities of women in Islamic societies.

Information from Magdalinski, Tara, and Jim Chandler. *With God on Their Side: Sport in the Service of Religion.* London: Routledge, 2002; and National Institute of Sport Sciences. Ed. "Sport and Religion." Proceedings of the IX International HISPA Congress, Lisbon, 1982.

sport—in their view, physical exercises and amusements lacking positive attributes for health and well-being—to the English colonies. During the late sixteenth and early seventeenth centuries, Puritans railed against various "devilish pastimes," and this outlook influenced the nature of sport and physical activities when Puritans immigrated to the New World. As Baker has stated, "In North America, as well as in England, the age of Puritan prohibitions is an important chapter in the history of sports" (72).

Church of England

During the Protestant Reformation, King Henry VIII of England divorced Catherine of Aragon without Pope Clement VII's consent and created and proclaimed himself head of the Church of England (also known as the Anglican Church) in 1534, thus ending the ancient ties between England and Rome. In doing so, Henry "inadvertently opened the door to centuries of religious strife" (Rader, *American Ways* 32). Henry died in 1553, and religious affiliations of the crown crossed from Protestantism to Roman Catholicism during the reign of Queen Mary (daughter of Henry and Catherine of Aragon), who adopted her mother's religion. Protestants persecuted during Mary's reign desired to escape to places adhering to Calvinism. Upon Mary's death in 1558, the state religion shifted back to Protestantism with the accession of Queen Elizabeth I (Henry VIII's daughter) to the throne.

The rule of Queen Elizabeth I influenced religious viewpoints about sport in the new colonies. King Henry's support of horse racing, for example, was endorsed by Elizabeth, and, while jousting contests declined for young gentlemen, horse racing appealed to the court of ladies and nobility: "Despite the demise of the armored knight the horse remained essential not only for mobility on the field of battle but also for transportation, the pleasures of hunting, and competitive sports" (Baker 62). Tennis also became popular among the royal ranks. Henry VIII had owned seven rackets, had built a tennis court at Hampton Court (now purportedly "the oldest in the world still in use"), and had constructed two indoor and two outdoor courts at the Palace of Westminster. He had even played a doubles match with the Emperor, the Prince of Orange, and the Margrave of Brandenburgh in 1522 (Baker 62; Gillmeister 79). Queen Elizabeth continued this support for tennis; she "refrained from playing tennis but loved to watch matches involving the leading nobles of the realm" (Baker 66).

In 1588, England defeated the Spanish Armada in a battle on the high seas, and Protestant England triumphed over Catholic Spain, freeing itself from Spanish expansion. English colonists then pursued their expansion overseas with "Westward Fever," looking to the New World to carry their religion and values around the world, which of course included converting Native American peoples to their faith. Protestant attitudes of English men and women in the upper ranks of society extended into the world of play and sport in English colonization efforts. Sports for the royals of England, however, did not transfer to different social ranks that emerged over time in early colonial America as colonists in the early settlements faced the quest for survival in the New World.

Puritanism

During the Protestant Reformation, the strict religious doctrine upheld by the English Puritans prohibited sports and games that they saw as immoral or failing to serve any useful purpose. Yet when Puritans immigrated to the New World, various communities and religions that developed over time incorporated some sporting practices. The banished activities included improper dancing, drinking, prostitution, violent sports, games, and wild festivals. Puritans believed that such physical exercises and sport detracted from their devotion to God and from community building. In fact, most Protestants frowned upon amusements as "idle" use of time, rather than useful activity to improve physical and moral health. Yet for instruction of youth, Calvin believed that certain recreations were acceptable, including archery, swimming, walking, fishing, and hunting.

The English men and women who followed the rigid tenets of Calvinism, with its intent to do away with the rituals and hierarchy of the Church of England, desired to reform Protestantism in the late sixteenth and early seventeenth centuries, and they became known as Puritans. They wanted to "purify" Protestantism during the reign of King James I, who led the kingdom upon Elizabeth's death. The King's dislike for the Puritans was reciprocated by them (Rader, *American Ways* 34). English Puritans wanted to curtail popular recreations and maintain Sabbatarianism, or the keeping of the Sabbath (Sunday) as the Lord's day of prayer. They disapproved of the sporting activities of the English aristocracy, who often engaged not in productive hard work but in games and popular amusements that, to the Puritans, represented idleness. The Puritans objected to the supremacy of the wealthy class in England and to their way of life, which included playing such sports as tennis, fencing, bowling, and quoits (a kind of ring toss). In condemning such pursuits, English Puritan Philip Stubbes, critic of popular pastimes, wrote in 1581 in *The Anatomy of Abuses*, "Any exercise which withdraws us from godliness, either upon the Sabbath or any other day, is wicked, and to be forbidden." Stubbes also railed against the popular sport of football, or soccer, as did other critics who viewed this game as a violent sport of peasants that was connected with gambling. Stubbes deemed football as "a friendly kind of fight [rather] than play or recreation, a bloody and murdering practice [rather] than a fellowly sport or pastime" (qtd. in Baker 75). Thus both religious and class conflict emerged over Sabbatarianism.

English Puritans also attacked the popular recreations of the lower ranks. They considered gambling on sports and games by either class to be a sin and a squandering of resources. The Puritans also attacked the activities of the English masses that they linked to Catholic festivals and pagan rituals as occasions to engage in frivolous contests and to gamble on "blood sports," such as bullbaiting, bearbaiting, cockfighting, and ratting. These violent sports, where animals mauled one another until one was victorious, would be a target of Puritans both in England and in the American colonies. In sum, the Puritans criticized those who spent their days in gambling, drinking, merriment, blood sports, pastimes, and games for living an immoral and undisciplined way of life rather than serving the Lord in the Church of England.

The battle between Puritans and non-Puritans (of various classes and moral persuasions) over "time to play" and "time to pray" was addressed in an important declaration by King James I in the *Book of Sports*, issued as a royal proclamation in 1618. It stated that sport embodied social purposes, such as military and political uses, and, predictably, this stance taken by the King and his Anglican majority generated conflict with the Puritan minority. In part, it read as follows:

We heard the general complaint of Our people, that they were debarred from all lawful Recreation, and exercise upon the Sundayes afternoone, after the ending of all Divine Service, which cannot but produce two evils: The one, the hindering

King James I and the Puritans differed greatly in their views of recreation on the Sabbath.

Hulton Archive/Getty Images

of the conversion of many, whom their Priests will take occasion hereby to vexe, persuading that no honest mirth or recreation is lawful or tolerable in Our Religion, which cannot but breed a great discontentment in Our people's hearts. . . . The other inconvenience is, that the prohibition barreth the common and meaner sort of people from using such exercises as may make their bodies more able for warre, when Wee, or our Successors, shall occasion to use them. And, in place thereof, sets up filthy tiplings and drunkennesse, and breeds a number of idle and discontented speeches in their Ale houses, For when shall the common people have leave to exercise, if not upon the Sunday and holy daies, seeing they must apply their labour, and win their living in all working daies? (qtd. in Riess, *Major* 22–23)

The King declared that certain sports promoting health were acceptable:

Our pleasure likewise is, Our good people be not disturbed . . . or discouraged from any lawfull recreation. Such as dancing, . . . Archery, . . . leaping, vaulting, or any other such harmlesse Recreation, nor from having of May Games, Whitson Ales, and Morrisdances, and the setting up of Maypoles, and those sports therewith used so as the same be had in due and convenient time, without impediment or neglect of Divine Service. . . . But withall we doe here account still as prohibited all unlawfull games to bee used upon Sundayes onely, as Beare and Bullbaitings, Interludes, and at all times, in the meaner sort of people, by Law prohibited, bowling. (qtd. in Riess 23)

This declaration by King James I challenged the devout Puritans seeking to uphold their religious codes. The King ordered his proclamation to be published throughout the country, and the asserting of such political positions about sport, labor, religion, and social class prompted some devout Puritans to seek a new location where they could worship and enforce their religious tenets as they saw fit. In 1633, the Declaration on Sports was reissued by King Charles I—again casting traditional sport as beneficial to the well-being and military readiness of the people. The Puritans who viewed sport as a profane undermining of religion "gritted their teeth about such a prospect and whenever possible tried to undercut the proclamation in England and New England" (Altherr, Part 1 1). In the American colonies, then, the settlers developed a sporting heritage drawing on their attitudes from Europe.

Sport in American Colonies

The changing cultural, religious, and economic landscape in England during the authority of King James I prompted English Puritan leaders, as well as leaders of what was known as the Virginia Company of London, and the English men and women forced to labor in the New World as indentured servants, to colonize North American regions. The cultural traditions these colonizers brought with them—and their interactions with the indigenous peoples and Africans in North America—shaped the development of active recreation, physical exercise, games, and sport in colonial American society. Immigrants' reasons for coming to the colonies varied by region, and a range of physical activities and sporting pursuits emerged in the various colonies. The rest of this chapter explores how peoples, places, and beliefs shaped colonial sports in the South, the North, and the Middle Colonies.

Jamestown, Virginia

Differences between traditional British culture and that of the American colonies became apparent in the first settlement at Jamestown, Virginia, founded in 1607. Jamestown became the first permanent English settlement in the New World. Rather than a colony governed as a political unit of England, Jamestown was founded as a business enterprise, owned by the Virginia Company of London, answering to King James I. The primary purpose of the Virginia Company from the beginning was to make a profit for shareholders, merchants, and political officials investing in their colony in the New World, with King James as head of the enterprise. While initially the King granted a charter to the Virginia Company with a desire to Christianize the Native Americans, the greater goal was a quest for profit by the King and his supporters in England.

Captain John Smith, the military commander of the settlement, arrived in Jamestown to find a harsh environment and climate in the early years. Colonists faced death and hardship, and Smith had to enforce strict laws requiring that all contribute to the colony's welfare. Yet the uneasy combination of gentlemen seeking wealth and gold in the venture and lower-ranked unskilled servants (some with criminal backgrounds) needing to perform manual labor, instead of men like farmers and blacksmiths, represented a challenge to the intense work required to sustain James-town in the initial years. Lack of supplies, conflict between men of the upper rank and those of the lower rank over labor, with young men resisting hard physical tasks while some of the English settlers engaged in hunting and fishing for their sustenance, disease and malnutrition—all led to a struggle to survive, known as a "starving time" in Jamestown. Between 1607 and 1609, only about 60 of the approximately 900 set-tlers sent to Jamestown survived. John Smith, the first strong leader of the Virginia colony, stated that unskilled servants "never did know what a day's work was" (qtd. in Nash et al., Brief 5th ed. 52).

The settlement did, of course, survive, and tobacco became the cash crop of Jamestown and of other settlements in Virginia and Maryland. Strong demand for the "jovial weed" back in England motivated English planters to seek cheap labor to grow this work-intensive crop, and initially most of the labor was done by lower-ranked and unemployed immigrants who became indentured servants, selling their labor for four to seven years in return for passage across the Atlantic Ocean to the American colonies. English colonists did try to enslave American Indians and force them to do the hard work of planting crops. The Powhatan Confederacy of the Chesapeake region, led by Opechancanough, resisted the English planters' incursion into their lands, but a war in 1622 failed to halt the growth (Nash et al., Brief 5th ed. 56–57). In 1619, the first Africans were forced to come to the British colonies in North America when 20 blacks arrived in Jamestown as captives of Dutch privateers. This unfortunate group marked the beginning of the shift to slavery that would transform the labor force in the colonial South by the end of the seventeenth century. Through much of the 1600s, however, Southern gentry depended primarily on indentured servants, who made up 75 to 80 percent of Chesapeake laborers during this period.

This changing population in the Virginia colony during the 1600s would shape an ethic of leisure for wealthy Chesapeake planters bent on finding other persons to perform grueling physical labor in the fields while they themselves enjoyed pastimes and sport. Southern gentry—young, white noblemen who would acquire large tracts of lands and were averse to manual labor—frittered away their time at bowling, cards, horseback riding, and gambling, while forcing physical labor first by new immigrants and servants, then by black slaves. This powerful Southern gentry would display its cultural values and social status in the sporting practices of the Chesapeake region.

Southern Colonies

The colonies in the Chesapeake region of Virginia and Maryland, as well as the colony of South Carolina developed with different motives and populations than the Ameri-can colonies in other regions. These Southern colonies played a pivotal role in the sporting traditions and pastimes in the early decades of colonial America. The wealthy white Southern gentry, the indentured servants (men and women) who worked for years under harsh labor contracts, the black slaves, the single male laborers, and the

Native Americans—all shaped the work and sport patterns in these colonies. Key factors included social class, race, gender, and religion in the diverse mix of peoples in the region. At times, sport divided groups, serving as a site of conflict between slave owners and slaves, or between lower-class laborers and plantation owners; at other times sport united peoples of the same race or class in maintaining their power and status over other groups in colonial American society.

On plantations, masters used horses to traverse their land holdings, to oversee their slaves and crops, to travel to other locales, and to engage in sporting contests. Horse racing, card playing, and gambling went hand in hand with the status of a wealthy planter in the Southern colonies. In 1724, a Virginia writer remarked, "The common planters, leading easy lives, don't much admire labor or any manly exercise except horse-racing, nor diversion except cock-fighting." The Virginia legislature ruled cockfighting illegal by 1740, but the law had little influence on residents' sporting habits. The Southern colonists even imported fighting cocks from England and Ireland (qtd. in Guttmann, *Sports: The First Five Millennia* 120).

Many wealthy Southern planters used sport as a way of asserting and enjoying their socioeconomic status, and the development of horse racing and cockfighting were in turn intertwined with socioeconomic developments. One of the biggest changes, of course, was the shift to black slaves as the dominant force of labor in the South. The major shift to black slaves occurred first in Virginia, the leader both in slavery and in Southern sporting traditions, and after 1660 the slave population increased. As the supply of indentured servants (from the surplus of unemployed lower-class young white men, the poor, and the "undesirables" from England) decreased, the English entered the African slave trade in the colonies—in New England and in the South. Southern planters justified their forcing of Africans into chattel slavery by means of their ethnocentric belief in white superiority and in the Englishman's superior culture. In short, the planter elite wanted slaves in order to maintain their wealth and power in the South, and they increasingly codified the racist structure of slavery in the form of laws that defined slaves as legal property bound to a life of enforced labor.

The planters' perceived need to enforce the slavery of Africans intensified after class conflicts in Virginia pitted wealthy white planters against lower-ranked white farmers seeking to advance in their mobility. In 1676, farmer Nathaniel Bacon desired more land to increase his social status, and, along with other white farmers, demanded that Native Americans be driven off or killed in order to free the land they coveted. They fought not only against native tribes but also against Governor William Berkeley's militia and the gentry in the government. This violence of white farmers against white militia and upper-rank colonists led to a civil war of class and race conflict in Virginia, and, though Bacon's Rebellion dissipated quickly upon his death from dysentery, the Southern gentry moved forcefully to reestablish the unity of white Southerners of different social classes. Wanting to quell the growth of a rabble-rousing class of poor whites, they embraced slavery in order to solidify the lower and upper white ranks to dominate over black slaves. In this way, whites of various social classes could join in controlling blacks in a hierarchy of power dependent upon the notion of a superior white race. In this social structure, even poor white farmers might aspire to own slaves, and while many could not afford to do so, they could still believe in their racial superiority over blacks. Thus "a racial consensus, uniting whites of different ranks in the common pursuit of a prosperous slave-based economy, began to take shape" (Nash et al., Brief 5th ed. 59–60), and the introduction of slavery into agricultural life in the Southern American colonies would have an impact on race, society, and sport—especially on the increasing popularity of horse racing.

Horse Racing and Gambling in Southern Gentry Culture

Horse racing prospered throughout the colonies, especially in the Southern region. Rationalizing it as a necessity for the improvement of breeding, colonists built horse-racing tracks in areas that were home to plantations and horse owners in

Virginia, Maryland, and South Carolina in the 1660s. As historian Timothy Breen has explained, "The great planters' passion for gambling, especially on quarter-horse racing, coincided with a period of far-reaching social changes in Virginia," and, "by 1700, the ruling gentry . . . [were] united as they had never been before" (31).

The horse racing and gambling highly identified with these influential Southern gentry consisted of contests on the racetrack as well as between only those planters with enough money for the high-stakes wager on the horse race. Tobacco plantation owners embraced the values of materialism, individualism, and competition in sport and everyday life, and their practice of horse racing and high-stakes gambling visibly

INTERNATIONAL PERSPECTIVE

Horsemanship: Haute École and "Horse Ballet"

In many epochs and cultures, horse riding has been a means to an end: Horses have been put to use for transportation, for hunting, and in war. In the European Middle Ages, riders in armor on powerful horses were the main contestants on the battlefield. These elite warriors formed a new order of nobility, the order of knighthood, which lost its importance in the thirteenth century with the introduction of new weapons and new methods and tactics of warfare. During the Renaissance, horse riding grew into an amusement of the aristocracy and served thenceforth as an element of noble presentation in courtly festivities. The art of horse riding for its own sake—horsemanship—reached its apex in the Baroque Period (1600 to 1750).

Riding belonged to life at court, embodying as it did the principles and ideals of courtly society, in which importance was attached not so much to quantitative performance or contest but to the proper measure and the proper form. Gentlemen members of court were well acquainted with poetry, art, and music, and were proficient in mathematics, dancing, horse riding, and fencing. Horsemanship thus played a major role in an education at court.

In accordance with the refined habits and tastes of the court, the ideal of education was that of the "cavalier," who stood out on account of his extravagant dress, noble manners, and strict adherence to the code of conduct of courtly society. On horseback he was an artist, molding the horse into a work of art and accentuating the aesthetic dimensions of horse riding. The object was to master the skills of the "high school" (haute école) of horsemanship, that is, the highest level of dressage, which aimed not to tame but to train the animal systematically and progressively over many years. In the haute école, the natural gait of the horse is altered—for example in the piaffe, in which the horse trots without moving forward, and in the capriole, in which the horse jumps in the air and lands again on the same spot. The haute école was indispensable for the many different riding and horse shows, such as the "horse ballet" and the "carrousel." These displays—as well as school riding generally, with its predetermined configurations—necessitated a move to special outdoor and indoor arenas.

During the Renaissance, this new form of horsemanship spread from Italy to France and later to England and Germany. An important role in this process was played by textbooks and manuals, which appeared in numerous editions and were translated into various languages. Italian and French riding academies served as the centers of horsemanship, where young aristocrats from all over Europe were trained in the art of the "high school."

The great role played by horsemanship at European royal courts is revealed in sources relating to life at the court of Louis XIV, the Sun King, who kept about six hundred riding horses at Versailles. Louis himself was out on his riding courses every day with his courtiers, accompanied by orchestral music and devoting his time to the art of riding.

A royal birth or wedding prompted extravagant festivities which lasted for several days and involved music, dancing, theatrical plays, and horse carrousels and horse ballets. The term *horse carrousel* covered a variety of performances, including a kind of polonaise (dance) on horseback and exhibitions of groups of riders (quadrilles) in splendid costumes who enacted a set subject. It also included forms of tilting, in which the galloping rider had to insert his lance through a small ring or knock a helmet off a wooden stand. In 1662, for example, a carrousel with five hundred noblemen on horseback was performed at the Louvre for the French royal court on the occasion of the birth of one of Louis' sons. The colorful costumes represented various nations.

Even more artistic than the carrousel was the "horse ballet," a dance on horseback in which a group of riders executed figures to music. The largest known horse ballet was performed at the wedding of Leopold I with the Spanish Infanta, Margarita Teresa, in 1667. A total of 1,700 riders rehearsed for an entire year before the event, with the emperor himself executing the most complex of figures. At the actual performance, 600 riders "danced" on horseback to the music of 100 instrumentalists.

Thus knights' tournaments in the sixteenth to eighteenth centuries were no longer contests but shows, in which, with regard to decoration and costumes, no limits were set on either fantasy or wealth. The monarch's prestige rested on the success of such extravaganzas. Social changes in the eighteenth century—above all the French Revolution and the ensuing wars—marked the end of the "high school" of horsemanship. The ostentatious royal courts vanished, and along with them the studs and stables, the riding academies, and the cavaliers and the ladies of court who had admired the skills of horse riding.

A reminder of this bygone age can be seen in the Spanish Riding School in Vienna (founded in 1572), which preserves and cultivates the haute école of horsemanship. It is the best-known home of classical equitation and a magnet for tourists who flock to see the exhibitions of haute école performed by magnificent Lippizaner stallions.

Information from Spanish Court Riding School. <http://www.wien-vienna.com/hofreitschule.php>; Horsemanship. 2008. Encyclopædia Britannica Online. <http://search.eb.com.ep.fjernadgang.kb.dk/eb/article-9106288>; Sports. 2008. Encyclopædia Britannica Online. <http://search.eb.com.ep.fjernadgang.kb.dk/eb/article-253555>

displayed their unity and power over the women in the family (who were typically spectators rather than competitors), the lower-ranked white farmers and workers, and of course the black slaves in colonial American society. The quarter-horse races of Virginia "were intense contests involving personal honor, elaborate rules, heavy betting, and wide community interest," and this "deep play" exclusive to the Southern gentry demonstrated that a "horse was an extension of his owner; indeed, a man was only as good as his horse" (Breen 32, 34). The power of the male gentry, along with the deference they garnered from the less powerful members of society, were apparent at horse-racing events. Only those planters of great means could afford the privilege of gambling for large sums at these public spectacles. One such was William Byrd II (1674–1744), owner of one of the earliest Virginia plantations (Westover plantation in Charles City). The Byrd family participated in the gentry culture as enthusiastic horse racers and breeders. By the 1720s and 1730s, for planters like William Byrd and Robert "King" Carter, quarter-mile (0.4-kilometer) racing was "*the* sport in Chesapeake" (Struna, *People* 98). Byrd, writing in his diary, documented horse races in the summer and fall of 1740:

1 May 1740 After dinner we walked to the race but were soon forced to retire for the rain.

8 May 1740 About 12 the company went to the race and so did my family and I gave them all money and sent a pistole myself by Mr. Hall who brought back two about 4 o'clock.

7 August 1740 My son was gone to the race. . . .

30 October 1740 After dinner we had a race which I went not to but won
20 shillings (qtd. in Altherr, Part 1 249).

The horse racing of the Southern elite planters enabled these powerful men to display their status and authority, while the lower sorts in colonial society—women, poorer planters, servants, and slaves—stood at a distance, watching the races rather than participating, thus reinforcing the prominence of the male gentry in both sport and society. After the race, the tavern, or ordinary, as it was called, provided a venue for sports, drinking, and gambling by common planters who lacked the wealth and status of the gentry.

The races also involved legal contracts in Virginia courts and maintained that gentlemen and their horses raced and gambled only against their social peers. An order from the York County Court on September 10, 1674, proclaimed that

> James Bullocke, a Taylor, haveing made a race for his mare to runn w'th a horse belonging to Mr. Mathew Slader for twoe thousand pounds [907 kilograms] of tobacco and caske, it being contrary to Law for a Labourer to make a race, being a sport only for Gentlemen, is fined for the same one hundred pounds [45 kilograms] of tobacco and caske.

> Whereas Mr. Mathew Slader & James Bullocke, by condition under the hand and seale of the said Slader, [agreed] that his horse should runn out of the way that Bullocke's mare might win, w'ch is an apparent cheate, is ord'ed to be putt in the stocks & there sitt the space for one houre. (qtd. in Altherr, Part 1 242)

Records from Henrico County in the late 1600s show the importance of gentlemen appearing as witnesses in cases about horse races and wagers:

> William Randolph, aged about 38 years, Deposeth: That about Saturday last was a fortnight this depon't [deponent] was at a race at Mawvern hills [Malvern Hill] at w'ch time Mr. Wm. Epes and Mr. Stephen Cocke came to this depon't and desired him to take notice of ye agreem't: w'ch was That ye horse of ye s'd Epes and the horse of Mr. Wm. Sutton was to run that Race for ten Shillings on each side, and each horse was to keep his path. . . . (qtd. in Stanard 296)

Thus the races at the numerous courses in the Chesapeake region held cultural, monetary, and legal significance. Wagers served as badges of honor for the gentlemen planters who owned the horses and needed to uphold their social status by putting large stakes on the races. No race could be cancelled under the rules of the competition unless one of the horses died between the date of the wager and the time set for the contest (Carson, *Colonial* 51).

Public notices of upcoming horse races appeared in town newspapers and gazettes. One Joseph Butler advertised his willingness to race in this announcement on September 10, 1744, in the *South Carolina Gazette*:

> *Joseph Butler of Charles Town* will run his Gelding CHESTNUT, from the Quarter Houſe to Charles Town, with any Horſe, Mare, or Gelding that can be brought againſt him by the firſt Day of *December* next, for 500 or 1000 *l.* Inch Weight, the loweſt Horſe carrying 13 Stone. Enquire of the Printer, w[h]o will inform you of one in Charles Town that will enter into the Articles, upon the above Terms, in the Subscriber's behalf. Joseph Butler (qtd. in Altherr, Part 1 238)

Another advertisement in the *South Carolina Gazette* publicized a race to be run in April 1747 by "any Horſe, Mare or Gelding" at the house of Isaac Peronneau, with the winner garnering the prizes of "a handſome quilted Buck-ſkin ſeat ſaddle, Bridle and Houſing, Value 30 *l.* Alſo a handſome ſilver Watch and ſeveral other Things To be raffled for" (qtd. in Altherr, Part 1 239).

The sport of horse racing persisted as a favorite recreation of Southerners. Gentry and plantation owners continued to race in contests in Maryland and Virginia and in Charleston, South Carolina, as well as in less formal contests. Near Charleston, wealthy South Carolinians constructed a horse-racing track as early as 1665. The state's diverse population of white Christians, Jews, free blacks, and slaves may well have prompted a range of people to watch the races at the course. Jews settling in Carolina, along with Huguenots (French Protestants), desired freedom of worship and rights to trade in Charles Town (later, Charleston): "Gentiles and Jews raised their voices in protest" against England, and, in "aspiring to higher status, Jewish men and women sought the same marks of social standing that gentiles were seeking" (Rosengarten and Rosengarten 75, 88). As a symbol of gentility, horse-racing contests drew Southerners of distinction, and Massachusetts lawyer Josiah Quincy Jr., visiting Charleston in 1773, noted the popularity of the races:

> March 16th. Spent the morning ever since five o'clock, in perusing public records of the province; . . . am now going to the famous races.
>
> The races were well performed—but Flimnap beat Little David (who had won the last sixteen races) out and out. The last heat the former distanced the latter. The first four mile [6.4-kilometer] heat was performed in eight minutes and seventeen seconds, being four miles. Two thousand pounds sterling were won and lost at this race, and Flimnap sold at public venue the same day for 300*L* sterling! . . .
>
> At the races I saw a fine collection of excellent, though very high-priced horses, and was let a little into the singular art and mystery of the turf! (qtd. in Altherr, Part 1 240–241)

Other Southern Outdoor Pursuits

The planters of both the wealthier and the poorer ranks hunted birds, squirrels, and other animals using various hunting equipment such as pistols and bows and arrows. Fishing was a popular pastime on the waterways in the South, as in colonies throughout British North America. The sports that Southern planters and their children participated in often took place at their plantations, meaning that only those of the upper rank had the opportunity to do so. In 1721, at the Westover home of Virginia planter William Byrd II, located on the James River, he set to constructing a bowling green, noting progress in diary entries. On March 16, he "began to turf the bowling green." On March 24, he "walked about the garden" to see his "people lay the turf." And by May 10, the green appeared ready for use in a game with the Reverend Peter Fontaine. Guests of the Byrd family at Westover continued to bowl on pleasant summer afternoons 20 years later. In another volume of Byrd's diary, he recorded 10 games in August 1739, when he played with neighbors, business agents, and his 11-year-old son, William. His interest in bowling persisted during the following summer, when he noted 32 pleasant evenings when guests bowled with him, and in the last summer of the diary, 1741, Byrd played a bowling game almost every July afternoon. He and his friends also played cricket at Westover in the early 1700s (qtd. in Carson, *Colonial* 77, 81).

Though faced with a shorter winter season than their Northern counterparts, Southern colonists also engaged in ice skating on ponds. Men and women might seek to skate for fresh outdoor air, and even ice skating could involve wagering for Southern sportsmen. Byrd's companions at Westover enjoyed skating when the weather permitted. On a cold December day in 1709, after having skated with friends the previous day, Byrd took again to the ice and "slid on skates, notwithstanding there was a thaw." That same evening, Byrd and his friends "gave Mr. Isham Randolph two bits to venture on the ice. He ventured and the ice broke with him and took him up to the mid-leg" (qtd. in Carson, *Colonial* 86). Other Southern colonists skated, walked, hunted, fished, rode horses, had cockfights, and gambled away from plantations over time. "For gentleman, slaves, and all in between, cockfights, horse races, and even fox hunts had become regional passions" (Gorn and Goldstein 27). Still, access to sports by mainly the white, wealthy, landowning gentry persisted, and they exercised their prerogative in playing sport and displaying their control over landholdings, slaves, and public competitions.

Those Southern colonists who wanted to uphold religious propriety with Sabbath Day observance supported statutes prohibiting sport on the day of rest. In the territory of colonial Carolina, set up by the English King Charles II, the promise of religious freedom and the lure of free land attracted people seeking to establish a settlement for the upper classes to maintain hold over the land and colonial government. In 1701, North Carolina and South Carolina became separate colonies, with South Carolina relying heavily on slave labor for the grueling work of cultivating rice on plantations, while North Carolina practiced slavery but also developed other economic industries. A North Carolina provincial law circa 1741 urged colonists to maintain the Sabbath as a day of religious reflection: "*An Act, for the better Obſervation and keeping of the Lord's Day, commonly called Sunday, and for the more effectual Suppreſſion of Vice and Immorality.*" This law called for people on Sunday to "carefully apply themſelves to the Duties of Religion and Piety; and that . . . no Perſon whatſoever, ſhall upon the Land or Water, do or exerciſe any Labour, Buſineſs or Work, of ordinary Callings . . . nor employ themſelves either in hunting, fiſhing or fowling, or uſe any Game, Sport or Play, on the Lord's Day." Anyone fourteen years of age or older in North Carolina caught violating this prohibition on sport or pastimes "ſhall forfeit and pay the Sum of Ten Shillings, Proclamation Money" (qtd. in Altherr, Part 1 9).

The promise of religious tolerance in Carolina's Fundamental Constitutions of 1669 brought Christian dissenters and Jews from England to the Carolinas, and in the new British settlement of Charles Town religious dissenters conducted business and practiced their religions (Rosengarten and Rosengarten 60). The prohibition on sport and recreation on the Sunday Sabbath remained the custom in colonial South Carolina, and a provincial law enacted in about 1712 sustained observation of "the Lord's Day, commonly called Sunday" and listed prohibited activities: "No public ſports or paſtimes, as bear-baiting, bull-baiting, foot-ball playing, horſe-racing, interludes or common plays, or other unlawful games, exerciſes, ſports or paſtimes whatſoever shall be used on the Lord's-Day" (qtd. in Altherr, Part 1 7). Violators were subject to a monetary fine. Despite such efforts, the impulse to play even on a day of rest persisted, although legal efforts of colonial governments strived to curtail sporting activities. Laws passed by colonial governments suggest that some colonists wanted to play sport on their day off from regular labor.

On other days the residents of South Carolina of upper social status might play sports such as tennis, and other South Carolinians might participate in foot races as well as the sporting practices identified like ball playing, horse racing, and pastimes. Eliza Lucas Pinckney, on her Charleston plantation, refers to the sport of tennis in her letter book in 1742, offering insight into the game in her own writing. In one passage, she made an intriguing reference to another socially charged activity, that of diving: "But if the diver should pretend each of these perls as Big as a Tennis ball . . ." (qtd. in Altherr, Part 1 108). In fact, on plantations in South Carolina and the

Chesapeake region, swimming and diving in deep waterways for such treasures as pearls marked physical and racial divisions between white slave owners and their enslaved swimmers, as explored in the next section.

Slaves and Plantation Realities of Play

When plantation slaves were not toiling in the fields from sunup to sundown, they enjoyed some free time to indulge their pleasures or engage in sporting activities that provided sustenance. Plantation masters dominated slaves in forcing them to perform hard physical labor, but when slaves were in their own quarters, away from the master, in the evenings or on the Sabbath or holidays, they wanted diversions from their work. "Regardless of how cruel the plantation became for slaves, their struggle for survival never became so severe that it destroyed their creative instincts or prevented them from establishing their own way of life" (Wiggins, *Glory* 3). Slaves engaged in their recreation in the confines of their physical environment. Fishing supplemented their diets, but only the most trusted slaves were allowed guns for hunting. Slaves maintained elements of African cultures in their dances and music, and in such performances they might also play the role of the trickster, mimicking or mocking their white owners in the form of pretentious caricatures unknown to the masters. "It was generally on Sundays, when there was little work, that the slaves both young and old would dress up in hand-me-down finery to do a high-kicking, prancing walk-around. They did a take-off on the high manners of the white folks in the 'big house,' but their masters, who gathered around to watch the fun, missed the point" (Wiggins, "Sport and Popular Pastimes" 74). At times, slaves also had to entertain their masters as jockeys in horse races, and they sometimes worked as horse trainers or as boxers or wrestlers in rough physical contests wagered upon by their owners. Slaves themselves gambled at bowling, cards, and dice games, though Southern legislatures tried to ban such activities by the 1830s (Wiggins, "Sport and Popular Pastimes" 74).

With their lives inevitably rooted in physicality, slaves took pride in their physical prowess. They competed in horse and boat races, foot races, and jumping contests; utilitarian sports such as swimming also proved useful. Since many plantations and fields were located near waterways, African slaves used swimming skills learned in their native homelands. As historian Kevin Dawson has explained, "From the age of discovery up through the nineteenth century, the swimming and underwater diving abilities of people of African descent often surpassed those of Europeans and their descendants. Indeed, most whites, including sailors, probably could not swim" (1327). According to Dawson, from the medieval period through the late nineteenth century, most whites could not swim, and in the Middle Ages, "numerous factors caused a devaluing and discarding of swimming," including religious reasons, concerns by doctors about the effect of immersion in water, and beliefs about the dangers of bodies of water, uncertain elements, and creatures contained within bodies of water (Dawson 1333). Whites' reluctance to swim compared to the skills in swimming exhibited by blacks persisted; in the "late nineteenth century, westerners were evidently adverse to the freestyle because it generated more splashing than the breaststroke," though "blacks, Asians, and Native Americans had demonstrated its speed and strength to them for centuries" (Dawson 1334). Slaves used their swimming ability in the rivers and ponds on or near plantations for both competitive and practical purposes. On one South Carolina plantation,

> John Clinkscales contended that in the antebellum years one of his father's slaves . . . named Essex was "by odds the best swimmer on [his] father's place" and possibly even the county, suggesting his reputation was perhaps earned in interplantation contests. In the seventeenth century Richard Ligon observed a planter-organized contest in which Barbadian slaves had to catch a duck placed in a large pond. The captor was awarded the duck, presumably to eat or sell it. The proprietor of these Sunday "recreations,"

> Colonel Drax, "calling for some of his best swimming *Negroes*, commanded them to swim and take this Duck; but forbad them to dive, for if they were not bar'd that play, they would rise up under the Duck, and take her as she swome, or meet her in her diving, and so the sport would have too quick an end." (Dawson 1341)

Many slave women on Southern plantations had also learned to swim in their African cultures, and they used that physical ability in antebellum slave life. "Whether organized by slaves themselves or by slaveholders, contests probably offered the winners prestige in the slave quarters. They indicated that bondwomen could beat their male counterparts. In addition to providing enslaved participants and observers with merriment, the communal nature of such contests, as of other recreations and sports, probably enhanced slaves' sense of community" (Dawson 1341).

The physical prowess that slaves displayed in their swimming feats stood in contrast to the reluctance of white colonial men and women to engage in swimming activities. Furthermore, "Western women probably refrained from swimming because most people swam nude, and western standards of modesty did not tolerate public disrobing by white women" (Dawson 1341). In a 1696 treatise on swimming, the author stated that "it is most certain that the Indians, and the Negroes, excel all others in the Arts of Swimming and Diving. It is to them the Ladies are obliged for their Ornaments of Pearl; they are the Divers who fish for them; they are also very useful for recovering Anchors and Merchandizes that have been cast away" (qtd. in Dawson 1333).

Moreover, in a physical test of vigor and swimming agility, slaves also encountered creatures of the sea in "blood sports" differing from those engaged in by white Southerners in animal contests on land. Slaves in bondage engaged in these physical activities while the master often kept a watchful eye on their swimming pursuits. Slaves "fused swimming to blood sport when they fought sharks, alligators, and manta rays to amuse themselves and to demonstrate their skill and strength—and perhaps their manhood" (Dawson 1341). In one instance in the Carolinas in 1700, a slave adeptly wrestled with a shark, and John Lawson reported that "some Negro's, and others, that can swim and dive well, go naked into the Water, with a Knife in their Hand, and fight the Shark, and very commonly kill him, or wound him so, that he turns Tail, and runs away'" (qtd. in Dawson 1342). While such displays of bravery in the water—along with diving for pearls, an arduous and dangerous task—challenged the health and physical strength of the slaves, such pursuits also enabled them at times to display prowess and work away from the harsh labors and strict supervision of the fields. In diving for pearls, especially, slaves might earn material rewards, though slave masters demanded most of the finds; divers were frequently forced to sell them to their owners (Dawson 1348, 1349).

Yet the competitions of slaves in some sporting activities revealed the realities of their harsh lives of bondage. Drawing on their parents' experiences, slave children often played games that emphasized the need to cooperate with, rather than eliminate, one another. "Even the various dodge ball and tagging games played by the children contained designed stratagems within the rule structure that prevented the removal of any participants." The devastating loss of a father, mother, brother, uncle, grandparent, or other family member sold by a plantation master meant that the pastimes of children emphasized loyalty and solidarity in slave quarters (Wiggins, *Glory* 11). The time that children and parents might spend together in pastimes proved precious, and it became a valuable reprieve from the cruel institution of slavery.

New England Colonies

Sport in colonial America was also shaped, of course, by those English colonists who immigrated to New England—a much different environment—with their own particular ideas about family and religion. New England colonists initially strived to maintain their devout religious outlook in their everyday lives, and this stance shaped attitudes about sport and, in turn, the patterns of sport pursued in these colonies. The sports that New Englanders deemed most valuable offered practical and healthful benefits in accordance with the colonists' views on mind, body, and soul.

Pilgrims in Plymouth

In 1620, William Bradford founded Plymouth Colony in Massachusetts. A discontented Englishmen, Bradford wanted to practice religion as a Separatist, that is, separate from the Church of England. He and his Pilgrim followers wanted to determine the religion, laws, and social customs of their new colony. The rigors of survival efforts—building houses, clearing land, making clothes, planting crops, and preparing food—left little time for play, and Bradford and his followers held an attitude toward diligence that was duly summarized in the phrase "in detestation of idleness." Thus when Bradford, on Christmas Day of 1621, witnessed a group of newly arrived immigrants at play in the streets of Plymouth, their decision to engage in pastimes rather than work (on a day not supported as a holiday of the Pilgrims) generated tension between the immigrant laborers and Bradford, who was intent on implementing his religious codes. Bradford wrote about the incident in his account of Plymouth Plantation:

> On the day called Christmas day, the Governor called them out to worke, (as was used,) but the most of this new company excused them selves and said it was against their consciences to work on that day. So the Governor tould them that if they made it a matter of conscience, he would spare them till they were better informed. So he led-away the rest and left them; but when they came home at noone from their worke, he found them in the street at play, openly; some pitching the barr, & some at stoole-ball, and shuch like sports. So he went to them, and tooke away their implements, and tould them that was against his conscience, that they should play & others worke. If they made the keeping of it a mater of devotion, let them kepe their houses, but ther should be no gaming or revelling in the streets. (82–83)

Thus Bradford viewed the pastimes as idleness and attacked such amusements as counter to the religious observances of the colonists in Plymouth.

Similar tensions were stirred in a 1627 incident wherein Thomas Morton wanted to celebrate the naming of the colony by erecting an 80-foot (24-meter) Maypole at Merry Mount, similar to one he had seen in England. Bradford was not pleased to see youth dancing at the Maypole and participating in what he considered immoral behavior. He claimed that Morton and his fellow merrymakers were engaged in "drinking and dancing aboute it many days together, inviting Indean women for their consorts, dancing and frisking together . . . and worse practices." Bradford deemed these actions to be pagan celebrations, like "the feasts of the Roman Goddes Flora, or the beastly practices of the madd Bacchinalians." To halt such revelry, Bradford sent Morton to England and made "that May-polle to be cut down," ending these celebrations in the colony (Bradford 141–142).

Puritans in New England

Although the Pilgrims wanted to separate themselves from nonbelievers in their Plymouth Colony, Puritans in England at the time fervently wanted to establish a godly community and practice their religious tenets free of opposition, and so they began immigrating to New England, where they soon outnumbered the Pilgrims. During this Great Migration, more than twenty thousand Puritans came to the United States between 1629 and 1640 (Rader, *American Ways* 34). As part of this wave, John Winthrop led a group of Puritan immigrants to the Massachusetts Bay Colony in 1630. Winthrop, a devout religious leader, desired to found a new religious colony in contrast to what he saw as lax religious laws in England. Winthrop and his followers of men and women in families sailed to the New World to found a utopian community, "a City upon a Hill," as a model for the world to imitate in reforming society. Indeed, Winthrop believed that the Puritans had made a covenant with God and that God would watch over them if they strictly followed God's laws. Winthrop emphasized the need for conformity in order to fulfill the utopian mission of church, family, and state linked together in a Puritan community of religious codes, and this covenant or contract with God shaped the Puritan perspective on sport and the body during the initial period of the Great Migration.

The Puritan beliefs upheld and enforced by Winthrop, who served as both the Puritan head of the church and the governor of Massachusetts Bay, dictated the religious creed of the colony, the basis of all activities in the Puritan community. Puritans believed in predestination, with no free will for persons—only God knew which souls were to be predestined for heaven or hell—and in the Covenant of Grace, which held that only by God's grace can one be saved or become one of the elect, one of the "visible saints" of the community. Puritan religion challenged what they termed the Covenant of Work, which was the belief that one's own hard work, or human ability, conveyed a sign of God choosing those who were saved. Nonetheless, the Puritan Work Ethic meant that all persons needed to contribute to the community for its service to the Lord. In Massachusetts Bay Colony, every person was to pursue a "calling" to serve God and work for the well-being of the community, rather than for individual achievement and glory. In keeping with this tenet, Puritan attitudes espoused by the leaders on sport and recreation emphasized that sport as a lawful activity must serve a useful purpose for one's health, whether physical or moral, in the community. Winthrop even wrote in his diary of the need for replenishment of mind and body to offset the labors of physical and spiritual pursuits in building the New England colony: "I examined my heart, and findinge it needfull to recreate my minde with some outward recreation, I yielded unto it, and by a moderate exercise herein was much refreshed" (qtd. in Gorn and Goldstein 32). Thus Puritans in colonial America, with their emphasis on spiritual vigor, may be viewed perhaps as "the moral athlete of yesteryear" (Lucas and Smith 113).

Puritan restraints on sport, games, and popular amusements stemmed from moral and religious convictions that also shaped their political, social, and economic considerations in colonial life. Rigid rules of conduct prohibiting sports (for example, laws in Massachusetts, Rhode Island, and Connecticut) banned activities including dice, card games, quoits (a ring-toss game somewhat similar to horseshoes), bowls, ninepins, and other games. Puritans viewed gambling as evil and frivolous, and it also ran counter to their focus on productive activity that was necessary for the colony to survive and maintain the social and economic basis of communal activities. The Puritan belief in lack of free will to change one's situation in society meant that if one experienced a change in status, it was the result of religious conversion, not human ability to change one's economic standing. Sabbatarianism remained important for the Puritans. They protected Sunday, a day of prayer and rest, with their "blue laws" that restricted popular recreations, sports, games, and pastimes, and Puritan officials punished violators. In a 1630 incident in Massachusetts Bay, when one John Baker failed to uphold the Sabbath, court officials ordered that he "be whipped for shooteing att fowle on the Sabbath day" (qtd. in Guttmann, *Sports: The First Five Millennia* 118).

Puritan leaders did allow sports such as fishing, fowling, archery, and hunting, which they viewed as useful since they provided food and wholesome bodily recreation for church authorities and residents in the community. However, to uphold the Sabbath and curtail blood sports, some colonial New England newspapers published announcements intended to stop such behaviors. The *New England Weekly Journal*, for example, printed an article on September 25, 1732, addressing cruelty to animals:

A Sportſman's Dog or Horſe are his Boſom Friends; he is fonder of them than his Wife, would ſerve them ſooner than his Brother, had rather feed them than the Poor, and is more ſolicitious for their Education and preſerving the

Breed, than for the Heir of his Family and Fortune; But when grown old or difabled, they are both neglected and treated with Cruelty and Contempt.

. . . *Horfes*, in particular, frequently die under the Tyranny of their Drivers, and the Hardfhip of their Toil, and we even make a Sport of their Miferies.

Throwing at *Cocks* is an annual Inhumanity. *Bull-baiting* is a ftanding Diverfion, and the Pain of the Creature at the Stake, and the Wounds of his Enemies the Dogs, is fometimes Sport to the Great and Polite, as well as the Butcher and Carman. *Duck-hunting* is another of the fame Kind, and an *Owl* is often joyn'd to double the Cruelty and Entertainment together. *Cock-fighting* and *Horfe-racing* are Barbarities in the higheft Vogue, and Ladies are now as fond of the laft, as the moft favage amongft us.

But who or what are they which we treat in this inhuman Manner? Why Part of the Works of the Deity we worfhip, Creatures made like our felves,

PEOPLE & PLACES

Cotton Mather

Cotton Mather of Boston, Massachusetts, was the leading Puritan minister in New England in the late seventeenth century and early eighteenth century—a third-generation Puritan clergyman. He expressed firm attitudes about the type of sports he deemed healthful and beneficial to Puritans, as well as those he deemed sinful and to be prohibited. Mather pronounced that the observance of the Sabbath meant to serve the Lord and pray, rather than to play sports, as in this 1703 statement from *The Day Which the Lord Hath Made:* "Sports on the Lords Day! Never did any thing found more forrowfully or more odioufly, since the day that the World was firft blefs'd with fuch a day" (qtd. in Altherr, Part 1 7). Mather also preached against mixed dancing, drinking, violent sport, and other physical exercises he viewed as harmful to the body and soul. He especially identified youth as straying

Photo courtesy of Library of Congress, LC-USZ62-92308.

from the Puritan codes in engaging in sporting pursuits: "Some of our Rising Generation have been given up to the most abominable Impieties of Uncleaness, Drunkenness, and a Lewd, Rude, Extravagant sort of Behavior. There are the Children of Belial among them, and Prodigies of Wickedness" (qtd. in Dulles 20).

At the same time, he declared that outdoor physical exercise—such as walking, hunting, fishing, boating, and other diversions he termed innocent—could fortify the mind and body for work. Mather chronicled his own experience with such healthful sport, though acknowledging an accident in his 1716 fishing excursion:

This Day a singular Thing befel me. My God, Help me to understand the Meaning of it! I was prevailed withal, to do a Thing, which I very rarely do, (not once in Years) I rode abroad with some Gentlemen, and Gentlewomen, to take the country Air, and to divert ourselves, at a famous Fish-pond. In the Canoe, on the Pond, my Foot slipt, and I fell overboard into the Pond. Had the Vessel been a little further from the Shore, I must have been drown'd. But I soon recovered the Shore, and going speedily into a warm Bed, I received no sensible HARM (qtd. in Altherr, Part 1 201).

as fond of Pleafure and as fenfible of Pain; only rang'd in a lower Rank in Life, perhaps to try how we fhould deferve more Happinefs, by being ftudious to preferve theirs. ("Cruelty to Animals" 1)

The only organized spectator sport in New England in the eighteenth century was horse racing. "More formal horse racing began in two areas of Rhode Island: Newport and an area called the Narragansett country." In the 1720s, "both of these towns began to provide horse racing not only to local residents but also to other New Englanders willing to travel to see organized, high-quality racing." By the 1730s, racing promoters hired professional riders, advertised horse matches weeks in advance, and held dozens of races in a single day (Daniels, *Puritans* 173). Horse racing also began to expand in Massachusetts. Boston newspapers carried advertisements for horse races as early as 1715, and in the 1720s advertisements announced races held a few miles outside the city. A typical notice in May 1721 offered a punch bowl valued at 10 British pounds as prize for a 3-mile (4.8-kilometer) race on Cambridge Heath. Interested parties could enter any horse not higher than 14 hands and carrying a jockey of nine stone (about 125 pounds or 57 kilograms) after paying the entry fee of 20 shillings (Altherr, Part 1 287). By the 1760s, horse races were staged frequently at several sites in eastern Massachusetts, close to Boston and near some of the urban regions of Connecticut (Daniels, *Puritans* 173).

Yet the Puritan utopian vision encountered challenges as new immigrants brought their own ideas about labor, leisure, sporting activities, and religion to the New World. Many newcomers rejected the rigid Puritanism, and change during the second generation of Puritans weakened the hold of religion on the New England way of life. A decline in church membership reflected New Englanders' need to address how to maintain adherence to Puritan beliefs, and the Halfway Covenant of the mid-seventeenth century diluted the religious experience necessary for becoming a Puritan. The Puritan leaders—that is, the New England Congregational clergy—adopted the Halfway Covenant that "allowed for children of church members, if they adhered to 'forms of godliness' to join the church even if they could not demonstrate that they had undergone a conversion experience" (Nash et al., Brief 5th ed. 115–116). In addition, mid-seventeenth-century colonists in New England often rejected the stricture against sport and games and felt an interest in achievement in their work and social

PEOPLE & PLACES

Harvard College

Young men from prominent New England families who attended Harvard College (founded in 1636 in Cambridge) faced Sabbath laws in their time away from classes. Puritan minister Thomas Shepard Jr. wrote a letter to his son at Harvard to give his opinion on his son's use of time, telling him to pursue serious study and to "recreate your Self a little, and so to your work afresh; let your recreation be such as it may stir the Body chiefly, yet not violent." He also urged him to let the recreation "be never more than may Serve to make your Spirit the more free and lively in your Studies" (ca. 1670, qtd. in Altherr, Part 1 14). The effort to curtail drinking, gambling, and rowdy activities fit with the religious orientation of the college; according to historian Bruce Daniels, "Even at places like Harvard, even during the militia gatherings that offered the greatest opportunities for young men to indulge in disreputable behavior, one does not find accounts of ball games occurring." Sports deemed more appropriate for young men in the outdoors offered benefits to refresh the mind and body. Fishing was perhaps the most popular and accepted colonial sport, and the Harvard administration officially approved of "fishing and fowling" for Harvard students (Daniels, *Puritans* 167, 169).

roles. Yet, despite some challenges, ordinances to preserve the traditional religious outlook and limit recreation and sport persisted, such as one that a clerk in Boston proclaimed in the *Boston Weekly Newsletter* in August 1736:

> *Whereas there are several good and wholsome Laws of this Province made to prevent the Prophanation of the Lord's-Day, forbidding the Exercise of any Labour, Work, or Business, or the use of any Game, Sport or Recreation, Swimming in the Water, unecessary Walking or Riding in the Streets, Lanes, Highways, Common-Fields or Wharves on said Day, the Evening preceeding, or Evening following: Notwithstanding which many Persons do transgress in the above Particulars;*

> *Resolved*, That for the future more effectual Care be taken for the punishing those who shall offend against any of the aforementioned Laws; also that the Disorders and Breaches of the Laws respecting Licensed Houses be duly Prosecuted. And the Clerk of the said Court is herby directed to publish this Order in the publick Prints. Attest. Byfield Lyde, Cler. (Lyde 2; italics in original)

As religious adherence waned and New Englanders of the next generation in the seventeenth century increasingly wanted to obtain economic improvement and enjoy amusements, games, drinking, and gather in places for social and leisure pursuits in the community, the places for public meeting expanded beyond the traditional church as the center of the Puritan community.

As the number of taverns in colonial America increased, they became a locus for amusements and sporting pursuits popular among colonists of various social classes. Some wealthier men gambled on sport, while others came as spectators, and some lower-rank colonists brought their skills for a contest in cards or the blood sport of animal baiting or cockfighting. In the growing cities of the Northeast, such as Boston, New York, and Philadelphia, taverns became widespread as places for colonists and travelers to meet for respite from travel, enjoy food and beverage, participate in sport and games, and communicate with each other; indeed, taverns became nodes

Drinking and other amusements began to gain ground in the seventeenth century, as illustrated by *Stolen Frolic in a Puritan Farmhouse.*
© Bettmann/CORBIS

City Tavern

in a network of venues for the exchange of information. In Massachusetts, some moral codes remained in force, so that tavern keepers were to prohibit shuffleboard, bowling, and dancing, which the authorities believed led to gambling, illicit sexual activities, and lack of productivity. In tavern culture, card and dice games were commonly played, and many taverns also provided space for ninepins alleys or bowling greens (Struna, *People* 70). Rather than adhering to the preaching of Puritan ministers, some colonists recognized taverns as a site of profit making, and demonstrated their human ability by competing at sport and gambling in order to gain money in their own version of the work ethic. From about 1700 to 1749, the Black Horse Tavern in Old Saybrook, Middlesex County, Connecticut, regularly featured tavern sports, card games, drinking, and gambling, particularly for the rowdy young men who worked in the town's maritime and shipbuilding industries. This tavern also served as an inn, where travelers coming to New England might stay and partake of food, beverage, and sport as a diversion from their tiring travels and tasks. The tavern welcomed travelers and townspeople with the sign "Entertainment," clearly marking a shift away from the strict earlier codes constraining sport and amusement in New England society.

Public gatherings—not only in taverns but also in the public square and common grounds in New England towns—brought colonists together in militia drills, training exercises, and amusements. Young men engaging in militia training gained wide acceptance, and New England officials allowed men to wrestle (Daniels, *Puritans* 168). Sometimes entire troops "took part in sham battles and shooting contests," displaying their skills for spectators gathered specifically to watch the event (Struna, *People* 79).

Middle Colonies

In 1681, King Charles II of England conferred on William Penn, a reformer and ardent Quaker, the proprietorship of Pennsylvania in the middle region of colonial America. Penn received the land in lieu of payment for large debts that the King owed him, and, like other Protestant reformers in colonial New England, he put forward his religious views as the basis of the new colony. He wanted to provide Quakers with a colony where they could practice religious freedom and establish a model community in the New World. He wanted to base this "Holy Experiment" on the teachings of radical seventeenth-century preacher George Fox. As a follower of Fox, Penn belonged to a particular religious sect in England in the 1640s and 1650s known as the Society of Friends, or Quakers. Fox's theology—based on a belief in the Holy Spirit or "Inner Light"—shaped Penn's leadership in instituting codes about religion, recreation, the Sabbath, and interactions with Indians in the colonies. His passionate focus on the Quaker faith allowed little tolerance for sport in the middle colony of Pennsylvania. William Penn established an earlier colony in North America in 1674, "West New Jersey that sputtered at first," but then it waned; for the Quakers, therefore, when Penn received the royal charter for Pennsylvania in 1681, they reestablished their place in colonial North America (Nash et al., Brief 5th ed. 76–77).

Sporting Pastimes in Colonial Pennsylvania

In the Pennsylvania colony, William Penn and the Quakers promoted a religious outlook dissimilar to that of the Puritan men and women who settled in the 1600s in British North America. Quakers trusted direct inspiration, a special communication with God, rather than the rigid institutional church and the strict power of men as ministers and heads of the colony. Quakers believed that by intensive searching and discussion with ordinary laypeople, known as "Public Friends," they could understand the Inner Light. In their distinctive beliefs in creating the colony as a refuge from persecution and open to different religious backgrounds, the Quakers accorded colonial women in the community extraordinary equality at a time when other colonists upheld patriarchal domination in family and society. According to Fox, the Inner Light could be communicated to females as well as males, and Penn established his colony in Pennsylvania in accord with this religious principle and the attending views of men's and women's roles in public activities.

Not surprisingly, Penn's Quaker beliefs influenced the nature of sport and recreation in the new colony. Quakers believed in simplicity and virtue as the path to God, marking quite a contrast with the conspicuous consumption of Southern gentlemen and planters, with their horses, plantations, slaves, sporting equipment for billiards and other pursuits, and games of chance such as dice. Such diversions and recreations—and the ornamentation and materialism pertaining thereunto— drew criticism from the colony's officials as potentially interfering with Quaker worship. Their focus was firmly on the spiritual well-being of individual men and women, rather than on building wealth and social status in order to garner respect and gain control in the hierarchical structure over common and lower-rank farmers, women, servants, and slaves, as was characteristic both of colonial Southern sportsmen and of the wealthy men and merchants of colonial New England. Quakers refused to tip their hats to their social betters in deference or wear fancy clothing as a display of social status. Of significance for the place of sport in Pennsylvania, the Quakers also refused to bear arms or fight in military campaigns, as their colony was known as a "Peaceable Kingdom." As a result, they did not engage in public sporting displays of manly prowess on muster days or in military training as was done in Massachusetts, or hold shooting matches as other colonies did. Physical, violent sports linked with guns—as well as competitions in boxing, bullbaiting, and revelry—held no cultural significance for Quaker men and women in colonial Pennsylvania and New Jersey.

William Penn.
Photo courtesy of Library of Congress, LC-USZ62-106735.

Penn and his Quaker followers addressed the issue of sport and recreation explicitly. While their laws generally promoted religious freedom, some laws mandated strict adherence to the Sabbath, thus limiting sport and recreation. Quaker leaders declared Sunday a day of religious meetings and rest from daily work, and blue laws prohibited card games, cockfights, bearbaiting, gambling, drinking, carousing, and other amusements deemed offensive. Friends did allow participation in sports recognized as wholesome and in innocent pastimes for health benefits and practical recreation. Colonists in Pennsylvania and New Jersey could enjoy ice skating, sleighing, walking, swimming, fishing, and hunting. And, as in other colonies in American society, horse racing took place in Pennsylvania because of the importance of horses in colonial American transportation and agriculture. Gambling on races, however, was prohibited.

Sporting Interests and Challenges to the Quakers

Quaker ministers and authorities faced a challenge in trying to enforce regulations that barred illegal amusements. As the population of Pennsylvania increased, many non-Quakers came to the colony in the early eighteenth century with their own values and motives for settling in the area, and from 1715 through 1740 Pennsylvania underwent political, social, and economic changes. Quakers' control over laws and social customs weakened. New immigrants, including Germans, Scots-Irish, and nonbelievers from England settled into the colony and challenged the stern moral codes and blue laws that restricted sport and recreation. Some of the newcomers formed lower classes of laborers and enjoyed tavern sports, drinking, gambling, and boisterous social gatherings. Other new Anglicans who did not share Quaker religious ideals—such as merchants who possessed wealth and power—desired to partake of sports and display their social status. Philadelphia became a hub of political, business, and social activity, with some residents engaging in increased recreation and sporting pursuits that included physical exercise in horse racing, bowling, and skating, as well as the pastimes of billiards and card playing and the drinking and gambling that often accompanied them. Even blood sports such as cockfighting and bullbaiting grew more popular.

Eventually, organized elite sports clubs were founded, though Quakers heard their leaders instruct them to stay away from the sports, diversions, and amusements available in such associations. Upper-class gentlemen and politicians established the social and sports organizations to foster their interests in common pursuits and sporting endeavors—for example, "the Colony in Schuylkill, founded in 1732, for its fishing, hunting, and dining pleasures" (Jable, "Pennsylvania's" 119), and the Philadelphia Jockey Club, organized in 1766 to provide a venue for horse racing. Thus the Quaker faith gave way to other leisure and consumer interests of colonists. While William Penn's Holy Experiment faltered with the diversity of the Pennsylvania population and the rise of secular institutions such as the tavern, the early blue laws "revealed the existence of sports and pastimes in a society where the dominant political and social force shunned these activities." It turned out that "many early Pennsylvanians had a strong need to play, and sports and amusements fulfilled that need" (Jable, "Pennsylvania's" 119, 121).

New York Colony

Dutch settlers came to New Netherlands in the New World in 1624, where in New Amsterdam (later named New York City) a trading post drew newcomers to the colony. The Dutch people brought sport and pastimes to the new colony as part of their culture and social customs. In the Dutch settlements along the Hudson River, taverns served as the principal site of recreation. There, both men and women played a game similar to handball. The Dutch also introduced a game called kolf, which bore some similarity to both golf and ice hockey in using a ball and a club to project the ball. Stray balls that hit persons or property proved harmful in the colony, and in order to regulate game play, an ordinance was put in place in 1656 at Fort Orange and Beverwyck. It stated that magistrates, "having heard divers complaints from the burghers of this place against the practice of playing golf along the streets, which causes great damage to the windows of the houses and also exposes people to the danger of being injured," thus determined that this "is contrary to the freedom of the public streets." Therefore, "their honors . . . hereby forbid all persons to play golf in the streets, under penalty of forfeiture of fl.25 for each person who shall be found doing so" (qtd. in Altherr, Part 1 158).

More popular was the game of skittles, a form of bowling. Patrons also found laughter in scaring cats caged in a barrel. The cats were released by throwing the bowling pins at the cage, which was broken open. Geese suffered a more drastic fate, as they were hung from ropes or trees, and the rider who could pull off the greased neck won the animal for dinner. The popular "gander-pulling" contest could also be played with the greased live goose suspended on a wire stretched between two poles, as an adventurous, active person attempted to pull down the geese while riding on horseback or moving through rapid water in a boat.

Rather than catering to a rigid religious vision that tended to constrain colonists' sporting activities and diversions, the New Netherlands settlement harbored various religious and ethnic groups. The heterogeneity of New York City included a range of religious and ethnic customs, along with diverse sporting practices. In 1654, the first Jewish settlers came to America when 23 Jews, including women and children, emigrated from Brazil to New Amsterdam. This marked the beginning of Jewish life in America, and, like other immigrants, they came for the promise of freedom of religion in the New World. The lack of rigid Sabbatarianism in New Amsterdam made it a logical starting place for such immigrants. Still, as in other colonies, strict observance of the Sabbath on Sunday remained a pronouncement of New Amsterdam's public officials. To uphold observance of the Sabbath, the Governor, Peter Stuyvesant, banned sporting and other physical activities deemed counter to the spirit of the Lord's Day. In January 1656, Stuyvesant proclaimed the rules for adherence to the Sabbath, announcing that Sunday was a day of "fasting and prayer for God's blessing[,] protection[,] and prosperity in trade and agriculture but principally for a righteous and thankful use of his blessing and benefits." The language of his order, however, shows very well what people actually did on Sundays! "We interdict and forbid, on the aforesaid day

Gander-pulling, a Dutch pastime, was a contest that involved pulling a greased goose from its hanging place.

Reprinted from J.A. Lucas and R.A. Smith, 1978, *Saga of American sport* (New York: HarperCollins), 546.

of Fasting and Prayer during Divine Services, all labour, Tennis-playing, Ball-playing, Hunting, Fishing, Travelling, Ploughing, Sowing, Mowing and other unlawful games as Gambling and Drunkenness, on pain of arbitrary correction and punishment already enacted against the same" (qtd. in Altherr, Part 1 5). Dutch officials enforced the Sabbatarian law once again during the following year, when records of a court case stated, "The officer, plaintiff, against Claes Hendericksen Meeuwes Hoogenboom defendants Gusbert van Loenen. The plaintiff says that Jan Daniel, the under-sheriff, reported to him on the 7th of March, being the day of prayer ordered by the honorable director general of New Netherland and proclaimed here, the defendants played hockey on the ice, demanding therefore that said defendants be condemned to pay the fine indicated in the ordinance." The defendants, however, gave a different view of events. "The defendants, appearing, maintain that they did not play hockey and promise to prove it. The parties having been heard, the court orders the defendants to produce their evidence on the next court day" (qtd. in Altherr, Part 1 462). When the British captured New Amsterdam in 1664, they renamed it New York. The Dutch pastimes, however, continued.

The colony's outdoor environs provided venues for men and women to participate in winter sports on the snow and ice, such as skating, sleigh riding, and hockey. British clergyman Charles Wooley observed the skating in New York City and noted it in his journal in about 1678. He commented on the lively skating: "And upon the Ice its admirable to see Men and Women as it were flying upon their Skates from place to place, with markets on their Heads and Backs" (qtd. in Altherr, Part 1 462–463). As late as 1748, a British subject claimed that "[t]he Dutch are a most unusual breed. They construct sleighs in the most fanciful fashion, some of them in the shape of swans and other water birds. They race them on the frozen ponds and they pretend that winter is not a season of cold and death. They also erect booths on the ice and spend endless hours skating and quaffing warm liquid out of pewter cups. Their penchant for racing on even the most fragile ice quickens the blood. They fly with great swiftness, mindless of the dangers to themselves and their horses" (qtd. in Twombly 22.) The Dutch enthusiasm for ice skating, experienced by women and men skaters, would later appear evident in the success of female Dutch ice skaters in the modern Olympic Games, and in this middle colony the Dutch demonstrated great love of sport and amusements for men, women, and children.

Horse racing was established in America in 1665 when Governor Richard Nicholls founded the Long Island Course in New York.

© Bettmann/Corbis

Men and women of the New York colony also took part in bowling, ninepins, a variety of ball games using stakes or rackets, marksmanship, fishing, hunting, and archery. Thus, like other groups of colonists in British North America, the Dutch colonists made sport part of their experience. In more favorable climates in New York, horse racing gained popularity, as it did throughout colonial America. In 1665, Governor Richard Nicholls announced a horse race to occur near Hempstead, New York. While the race was mainly for improving the breed of horses, rather than amusement, it proved popular, and the swiftest horse was rewarded with a silver cup. More generally, horse racing gained popularity in various regions of the country. As it persisted in locales like Philadelphia (with its Philadelphia Jockey Club), men of gentility and high social status patronized clubs for horse racing throughout the Northeast. By the nineteenth century, racing became widespread in American culture, and in both "North and South, there were racecourses on the outskirts of most large towns and many in smaller communities" (Larkin 283).

Summary

People of diverse backgrounds—Native Americans, Europeans, and Africans—inhabited settlements in the New World and engaged in sporting forms and pastimes during the colonial years. The presence of peoples of various religious, economic, social, and political perspectives, with their diverse racial, ethnic, and gender identities, meant that colonists participated in a range of recreations and amusements in their patterns of work and play. Sporting activity was often engaged in informally, but for colonists of higher status and wealth sporting pursuits also took place in more formal incarnations.

DISCUSSION QUESTIONS

1. How do the concepts of sport in the precolonization period and the period of American colonial development differ from current or more recent concepts of sport?

2. What are some of the characteristics of Native American sport?

3. In what ways did religion affect the growth of sport in the early American colonies?

4. Explain some of the similarities and differences between the sports played in various colonies.

5. What were the sporting experiences of African Americans in early colonial America?

6. Explain the ways in which men and women of various groups of colonial Americans participated in sport and how sporting practices illustrated gender differences.

Sport and Pastimes in the American Revolutionary Era and Early National Period

1750–1820

CHAPTER OBJECTIVES

After reading this chapter, you will have learned about the following:

- How some traditional sports served practical purposes and persisted from the earlier colonial American period

- The Great Awakening's role in shaping attitudes about sport in various parts of colonial American society

- The importance of Enlightenment ideas in American sport, physical exercise, and care of the body

- The meanings of sport in frontier society

- How economics, consumer changes, and social rank shaped access to sport for Americans of diverse backgrounds

- The place of sport in the American Revolutionary era

- The role of sport and active recreation for women in the New Republic

- The nature of ongoing interest in the various uses of horses and horse racing

Revolutionary leader, diplomat, and inventor Benjamin Franklin (1706–1790) of Philadelphia embodied the characteristics of a self-made man. He stressed virtue and self-help—as well as physical and mental vigor—as American values. In both his thinking and his sporting pursuits, Franklin displayed colonists' increasing emphasis on individualism and on the practical education of mind and body through mental and physical exercise. He wrote in his autobiography about his belief in the importance of "Bodily Exercise":

> [As a young boy] living near the Water, I was much in and about it, learned early to swim well, & to manage Boats. . . . [I]n a Boat or Canoe with other Boys I was commonly allow'd to govern, especially any case of Difficulty. . . . [U]pon other Occasions I was generally a Leader among the Boys. (9–10)

During a sojourn in England, Franklin recollected his impressive swimming ability:

> I stripped & leaped into the River, & swam from near Chelsea to Blackfriars, performing on the Way many Feats of Activity both upon & under Water, that supris'd and pleas'd those to whom they were Novelties. I had from a Child been ever delighted with this Exercise, had studied & practis'd all Thevenot's Motions & Positions [in *The Art of Swimming*], added some of my own, aiming at the graceful & easy, as well as the Useful. All these I took the Occasion of exhibiting to the Company, & was much flatter'd by their Admiration." (53–54)

His triumphant swimming display prompted a British noble to ask Franklin to teach his two sons to swim. Sir William Wyndham "wish'd to have them first taught Swimming; and propos'd to gratify me handsomely if I would teach them. . . . [I]f I might remain in England and open a Swimming School, I might get a good deal of Money" (Franklin 55). He declined and returned to the American colonies but continued to pursue his interest in swimming, developing a wet suit for skin diving and, at age 25, writing a book on swimming and the buoyancy of water (Twombly 39).

In a shift from earlier colonial culture, an increasing number of colonists in the eighteenth century stressed proper care of the body to uphold physical and moral health by using their own abilities rather than succumbing passively to God's will. In developing American society during a time of growing challenges to the bonds of the British empire, some colonists asserted the place of human and individual agency rather than the view of God as all-powerful as asserted by earlier colonists. Franklin proved to be perhaps the most famous swimmer in American colonial history, and his experiences as a printer, statesman, reformer, civic-minded leader, and American revolutionary figure offered a shift from Puritanism by expressing confidence in human ability in endeavors ranging from physical activity to politics. These changed beliefs about the human body were joined by new attitudes toward the use of science and intellectual inquiry, all of which fed into new views of physical health and sport in colonial American culture.

In the 1700s, a growing quest for economic and political opportunity, and a desire to have a voice in colonial affairs in pursuit of democracy, brought about a change in the outlook of colonists on the eve of the

Benjamin Franklin, colonial American printer, became a leading statesman and gained fame as an inventor, scientist, and promoter of moral virtues, as well as an advocate of physical ability.

Photo courtesy of Library of Congress, LC-D416-29337. Prints and Photographs Division, Detroit Publishing Company Collection.

colonies' fight for independence from England. Many colonial North Americans of varying social rank began shaping an American identity based on their experiences of religion, politics, sport, economics, and work. With many colonists focused increasingly on the quest for material wealth and status—catalyzed by growing individualism and faith in human ability—diverse views of sport and physical activity arose among the heterogeneous groups of colonists. Religious leaders, however, expressed deep concern about many colonists' pursuit of economic status and desire for material rather than spiritual wealth, and they worried that the rising values of freedom, self-improvement, and upward mobility threatened the fabric of American society. Thus, debate over the place of sport in this period of tremendous economic and population growth pitted certain colonists against others; the assorted viewpoints on sport and physical activities also played a part in the growing tension between individualism and maintenance of a rigid sense of community in American life during the revolutionary era.

Stated more generally, changes in colonial American life in the middle decades of the eighteenth century prompted a clash between "old" and "new" cultural values. Growing emphasis on science and reason, for example, conflicted with the Northeastern Puritans' emphasis on religion and Biblical codes. Some colonists purported their belief in deism, the notion of God as a sort of clockmaker, the original supreme creator of the universe who set events in motion and then stepped away. These cultural and religious changes in colonial American life, along with colonists' experiences during the American Revolutionary Period, altered ideas and activities related to sport in these decades when colonists shaped a new American society.

The Great Awakening and the Place of Sport

Amid the tensions between old and new values in the middle period of the eighteenth century, religious revivalism swept the colonies. This movement, known as the Great Awakening, involved not only religious inspiration but also a general ferment of new ideas about colonial American society, power, equality, and individualism. It produced a widespread experience—with religious revivals in all colonies touching all classes, ages, and races—and as the first intercolonial event the Great Awakening bound the colonies together in one step of a process that would culminate in the American Revolution. From 1730 to 1760, throughout the American colonies, "this quest for spiritual renewal challenged old sources of authority and produced patterns of thought and behavior that helped fuel a revolutionary movement in the next generation" (Nash et al., Brief 3rd ed. 101). The consequences of the Great Awakening in colonial America reached far beyond the religious sphere, and colonists' changing cultural values also affected sport. The call to colonists to awaken from their religious slumber came together with the clergy's powerful mid-eighteenth-century message that people should engage in moral pastimes and sport instead of vulgar and frivolous activity. Popular revivalism thus carried social and political implications that were reflected, among other things, in viewpoints on sport and the use of leisure time.

New England Colonial Awakening, Faith, and Pastimes

Religious and civic leaders in New England worried about the decline in Calvinist thinking and adherence to religious principles. The Puritan elite were alarmed by the increasing emphasis placed on good works and human reason by Benjamin Franklin, Thomas Jefferson, Dr. Benjamin Rush, and other colonial leaders who employed new scientific and intellectual approaches to understanding their world. In his famous 1741 sermon *Sinners in the Hands of an Angry God,* Jonathan Edwards, of Northampton, Massachusetts, used a fire-and-brimstone approach to urge young people to seek salvation only through God's grace, rather than through the notions of human ability and good works. Edwards' forceful urging to those people straying from congregations and ignoring God's power, justice, and fury at sin, awakened listeners and spread to other locations throughout New England; clergy members intensified their calls to curtail boisterous pastimes and

1730s–1773

1730s–1750s
- First Great Awakening of religious revivals in American colonies

1750s
- The Enlightenment in American colonies shaped new ideas about reason, the body, and science

1756–1763
- Seven Years' War fought (also known as French and Indian War); ends with the signing of the Treaty of Paris

1764
- Sugar and Currency tax acts imposed by England

1765
- Stamp Act and other taxation acts; colonists resist Stamp Act

1766
- Jockey Club founded in Philadelphia

1770
- Boston Massacre occurs

1773
- Boston Tea Party occurs

unwholesome sports. George Whitefield preached to large audiences as an English believer of the Methodist branch of the Anglican Church, and he proclaimed a "new life" for colonial Americans in his tour of the colonies in 1739 and 1740. His emotional appeals in open-air revivals reached thousands of colonists, and he stressed that all souls—no matter one's status, race, gender, or age—could achieve conversion. This kind of public preaching to large audiences expressed democratic rather than traditional messages of faith, with the emphasis on devoting time to the soul rather than to amusement and sport. The clergy frowned upon horse racing, whether with white or black jockeys, as they did with other forms of frivolity. One itinerant Methodist minister in Virginia in 1772 complained to another about horse racing and black jockeys: "[A]s there was to be a horse-race that afternoon, I began to speak freely of the absurdity of it, and shewed [sic] how rediculus [sic] it is for gentlemen of sense to ride many miles to see two or three horses run about a field with Negroes on their backs" (qtd. in Altherr, Part 1 281).

Indeed, zealous clergymen such as Jonathan Edwards generally viewed sport and recreation, tavern activities (gaming, gambling, drinking), and animal sport as sins. Their admonition to colonists to uphold the Protestant work ethic, rather than waste time in such frivolous pursuits, spread throughout town and countryside. In passionate sermons appealing to the congregants to seek moral salvation, Edwards exclaimed, "Are there not some here who have debased themselves below the dignity of human nature by wallowing in sensual filthiness, as swine in the mire . . . ?" (Nash et al., Brief 3rd ed. 102). This intense call to conversion entailed spending time on church-going rather than tavern-going, and even elite New Englanders and leading citizens of the Northeastern cities needed to heed the religious message of the Great Awakening if they "awakened" to the societal changes after hearing such sermons.

The moral campaign of the Great Awakening also included efforts to enforce Sabbath codes and close taverns on Sundays. A Boston law specifically ordered that "[t]he Lord's Day not be prophaned [sic] by boys, or idle persons swimming or skating thereon, &c." Likewise, a Vermont statute of 1787 stated that no one "shall upon land or water, do any labour, business or work . . . of any kind whatever . . . nor use any game, sport, play or recreation, on the first day of the week or Lord's day. . . ." Such offenses were punishable by a fine of 10 shillings. In 1797, in Maine, one of the itinerant missionaries, Paul Coffin, a Congregationalist, assessed the residents as follows: "The people here are much reformed. Formerly, they lived in strife, excess in drinking, shooting on the Lord's day, &c. These vile practices are now forsaken" (qtd. in Altherr, Part 2 2–3). Traditional utilitarian sports touted as appropriate for health and exercise—such as fishing, hunting, and horseback riding—were still accepted.

Southern Colonies, Critics of Sport, and Social Elites

By the Revolutionary Era, the distinct development of regional cultures was clearly in evidence in the South, in New England, and in the Middle Colonies. The climate, soil, landscape, and slave labor that supported profitable tobacco and sugar crops in the South differed from those of the North, with its greater diversity of agricultural and industrial development (Cobb, *Away* 9–10). In 1785, Thomas Jefferson remarked upon what he saw as the differing demeanors of the newly independent residents of the United States: "In the North they are cool, sober, laborious, independent, jealous of their own liberties, and just to those of others, interested, chicaning, superstitious and hypocritical in their religion. In the South they are fiery, voluptuary, indolent, unsteady, jealous for their own liberties, but trampling on those of others, generous, candid, without attachment or pretensions to any religion but that of the heart" (qtd. in Cobb, *Away* 10).

In the Southern colonies and rural areas, traveling or itinerant preachers rode on horses to bring their message of religious conversion to the varied population throughout the region. Such circuit riders appealed to diverse open-air crowds of Southerners, exclaiming that no social distinctions existed in the eyes of God and that all people—white and black, rich and poor, women and men—needed to engage in the religious experience. New denominations of Baptists and Methodists gained converts, and a growing number of colonists heard the message of equality and individualism in the circuit riders' sermons. By 1860, approximately 75 percent of Southern churchgoers adhered to the Baptist or Methodist traditions (Cobb, *Away* 48).

These "New Lights" preachers challenged traditional authorities and their mandated sporting patterns, and, foreshadowing ideas of the Revolution, focused on individualism rather than deference to the Southern elite. When these calls to resist the authority of one's "betters" were heard at revival meetings by ordinary white men and women, free and enslaved blacks, and lower-rank farmers, they accepted and applied them to the sports, gambling activities, and other trappings of leisure practiced by plantation owners and other Southern elites. Benjamin Latrobe, an architect who traveled throughout the new country, remarked upon his experience of a gentry gathering at a Virginia horse race on April 21, 1796: "Everybody here is so engaged in talking of Lamplighter, the Shark mare, the Carolina horse, etc., that I am as much at a loss for conversation as if I were among the Hottentots. . . . The concourse upon the race ground was very great indeed—perhaps fifteen hundred person. It cannot be of much interest to know that Lamplighter, the favorite of the field, upon which all the odds were laid, was beaten two successive heats, and came in only third. . . . I have now got into Mr. Shore's house for the day, and feel a little more at home than in the buzz of betting on the course" (qtd. in Altherr, Part 2 303). Supporters of the Great Awakening desired to severely decrease just this kind of intense enthusiasm for sport and gambling expressed by Southern genteel society and upper-rank sportsmen in the region.

Thus the ministers and followers of the evangelical religious movement challenged the Southern gentry's control of the lower-rank colonists and slaves with their message of people of diverse backgrounds joining their crusade, as well as their displays of public prowess and shows of wealth in the form of sports and recreations. The religious leaders criticized the sporting activities and public recreations typically involving drinking and frivolity, such as horse racing, gambling, court day, cockpits, the muster field, and election day. The New Lights challenged both these social and sporting practices of Southern gentry and the traditional hierarchy they controlled: "Against the system in which proud men were joined in rivalry and convivial excess was set a reproachful model of an order in which God-humbled men would seek a deep sharing of emotion while repudiating indulgence of the flesh" (Isaac 168). Thus the rigid deference previously accorded to the Southern elite demonstrated at the race track, or in watching these gentleman planters as they engaged in field sports, gave way to newer values of equality and the fellowship of believers. By seeking to include lower-rank whites as well as slaves among their brothers and sisters, then, religious dissenters challenged not only the conspicuous display of sport and recreation exhibited by the Southern gentry but also the very order of traditional Virginia itself. As Isaac has stressed, "The social world of the Baptists seems so striking a negative image of gentry-dominated milieus that it must be considered to have been shaped to a large extent in reaction to the dominant culture" (163–164).

Elkanah Watson, an agriculturist and advocate of improved farming who promoted the benefits of practical competitions for American farmers (as discussed in chapter 3), criticized the behavior he witnessed at a bloody cockfight during a trip to Virginia with a prominent planter. He noted that "the moment the birds were dropped bets ran high," and he commented on the vicious battle between the birds and the animated responses of the crowd:

> The little heroes appeared trained to the business, and not the least disconcerted by the crowd or shouting. . . . [A]dvancing nearer and nearer, they flew upon each other at the same instant with a rude shock, the cruel and fatals gafts being driven into their bodies, and at times, directly through their heads. Frequently one, or both were struck dead at the first blow, . . . and in the agonies of death would often make abortive effort to raise their heads and strike there antagonists.

1774–1788

•1774
- First Continental Congress held in Philadelphia

•1775
- Second Continental Congress convenes
- Battles of Lexington and Concord

•1776
› Declaration of Independence signed

•1776–1783
- American Revolutionary War fought

•1783
- Peace treaty signed with England in Paris

•1787
- Constitutional Convention held
- Northwest Ordinance begins; expansion of land in the old Northwest

•1788
- Constitution ratified
- Messenger (top racehorse) imported from England

I soon sickened at this barbarous sport, and retired under the shade of a wide-spread willow, where I was much better entertained in witnessing a voluntary fight between a wasp and spider. (qtd. in Riess, *Major* 27)

Watson was not only alarmed by the deadly fight between the birds but also found his moral character jarred by the crowd of both genteel people and lower-rank spectators of the blood sport. He was "deeply astonished to find men of character and intelligence giving their countenance to an amusement so frivolous and scandalous, so abhorrent to every feeling of humanity, and so injurious in its moral influence," and he loathed the accompanying habits of "gambling and drinking, in the waste of time, and often in the issues of fighting and duelling" (qtd. in Riess, *Major* 27).

Despite moral criticisms, however, animal blood sport continued, as did unusual forms of hunting animals for sport rather than for food and healthful exercise, and accounts of such activity appeared in newspapers. Consider an article titled "Country Sport," reprinted in several newspapers (among them the *Commercial Advertiser,* the *Hampden Federalist,* and the *Columbian Centinel*), which described a sporting event for men in Canton, Ohio, that took place on December 26, 1816:

About the 1st inst. according to previous notice, a company of about 700 Men collected from different parts of Worthington, Ohio, where they organized themselves: had their hunting ground particularly marked out in a hollow square of an oblong from 5 miles wide by 8 long [8 by 13 kilometers]. In the centre of which was a mile [1.6 kilometers] square—They formed round the oblong and commenced their march toward the centre square about sunrise; and astonishing as it is not the less true, the result was in killed—2 Wolves, 3 Bears, 33 Deer, and 117 Turkeys. ("Country Sport" 3)

Thus traditional sports and social gatherings for men continued even as some Americans questioned the value of such activity in the new society.

Cockfighting drew spectators who gambled and enjoyed rowdy behavior at the matches.
© Getty Images

Consumerism and Changing Patterns of Colonial Life

In the 1760s, colonial Americans increasingly realized that their cultural world seemed to be differing from that of England, and they would soon seek to break away decisively from the English monarchy and English identity. Prior to that, however, as historian Carl Guarneri has discussed, the Atlantic system of trade "transmitted religious ideas as well as material goods" to the American colonies. The trends of the Great Awakening and increasing production of consumer goods traveled across the ocean together as American colonists began to acquire materials and goods beyond those needed for survival: "Without intending to, the Great Awakening aligned religion with the consumer revolution." It was only in 1763—and "[o]nly after Britain began reorganizing imperial relations" (Guarneri 86–87)—that Great Britain and the North American colonies moved toward armed conflict. The end of the Seven Years' War with the Treaty of Paris signed in 1763 initiated the taxation on the American colonies imposed by Great Britain to raise money for its war debts, and these economic restraints and severe political acts of taxation by England limited the colonists' economic and political freedom in American society.

At the time of the Great Awakening, the prominent role played by the British in the colonies and in Atlantic trade spurred changes in colonial American economic and cultural life. These shifts originated in Britain, where "the combined forces of urbanization, rapid population growth, and increased workshop production sparked a 'consumer revolution' that made more and more goods available to families above the poverty line. The Atlantic trade exported this consumer revolution by showcasing an 'empire of goods' to colonists" (Guarneri 85–86). Thus, in this period preceding the growth of tensions between the British Empire and the American colonists in the Revolutionary Era, an Anglo-American culture arose based in part on newly developing British practices and customs adopted by colonials aspiring to middle-rank status. The combination of rising incomes among colonial American families and decreasing prices of British manufactured goods meant that more material objects now found their way into American life. Items such as English teapots, cups, silverware, furniture, and clothing marked the new consumerism of middle-class American colonists. "Social occasions such as tea drinking and card playing became consumption rituals as well as opportunities to use special accessories or show off new possessions" (Guarneri 86). During economic hard times, this consumerist seeking of British goods would decrease and be manifest in strained relations between the colonists and the British Empire.

While some lower-rank colonists strived via the consumer revolution to obtain the trappings associated with the wealthier colonists, cultural and sporting trends were defined in no small part through the specification of certain places for given social classes to perform their sport and leisure activities. Historian Richard Bushman has suggested that those classed as ladies and gentlemen required appropriate environments for asserting their gentility and pursuing their pastimes: "Gentility did not suggest new activities for people; it elevated old ones. Singing, cardplaying, eating and drinking, conversing went on in every tavern. All that distinguished genteel drawing rooms was the manner of the people and the style of the objects that surrounded them" (xviii).

Taverns for refined men conducting business, politics, and social activities served different purposes than did the taverns for ordinary laborers, sailors, travelers, and other men seeking gaming, drinking, and sporting pastimes. Many taverns—sites of consumerism where patrons enjoyed food, beverage, hospitality, games, and sport—catered to colonists in the lower and lower-middle ranks of colonial America. They were frequently associated with men engaging in rowdiness, drunkenness, blood sport, and gambling. Such taverns became a target of reform and refinement by middle- and upper-class colonial officials. Massachusetts politician and patriot John Adams expressed deep concern about the rise of taverns, pronouncing them "the eternal Haunt of loose, disorderly People." Adams described the colonists who frequented taverns thusly: "Young People are tempted to waste their Time and Money

1789–1806

- **1789**
  - First U.S. Congress; George Washington elected president

- **1791**
  - Bill of Rights ratified

- **1793**
  - Cotton gin invented by Eli Whitney

- **1800**
  - Washington, D.C., becomes U.S. capital city

- **1802**
  - National Race Course opened near Washington, D.C.

- **1803**
  - Louisiana Purchase made

- **1804–1806**
  - Lewis and Clark Expedition conducted

- **1806**
  - American trotter Yankey runs a mile (1.6 kilometers) in 2:59

The Man Full of Trouble Tavern in historic Philadelphia is the only surviving tavern building from pre-Revolutionary Philadelphia.

Photo courtesy of Library of Congress, HABS PA, 51-PHILA, 276-5.

and to acquire habits of Intemperance and Idleness that we often see reduces many of them to Beggary, and Vice" (qtd. in Bushman 161). In contrast, the City Tavern of Philadelphia, which opened in 1773, appealed to refined gentlemen such as Adams and other leaders of the Revolutionary Era. Adams met there with other delegates for the First Continental Congress in 1774, and it provided a place to honor patriotic leaders including George Washington at the end of the Constitutional Convention in September 1787. Other taverns, however, continued to attract a less refined sort of patron, and the boisterous crowd's drinking, gaming, and gambling formed the heart of tavern culture. In this light, perhaps another colonial Philadelphia establishment, the Man Full of Trouble Tavern, was aptly named.

In urban areas with many taverns, some supporters of wholesome recreation urged curtailment of the drinking and amusements typical in taverns and encouraged steps to honor the Sabbath with worship rather than the sport of boys or youth pursuing outdoor physical recreation. On May 13, 1789, in Philadelphia, one correspondent begged

> leave, through the channel of the *Federal Gazette,* to recommend to the *Corporation,* to LESSEN the number of taverns, huckſters, and dogs, in the city of Philadelphia and to paſs laws, to PREVENT the following evils. . . .
>
> 1. The noiſe of carriages from diſturbing places of public worſhip on Sundays.
>
> 2. The ſports of boys on Sundays every where, and of every kind, eſpecially ſuch of them as are carried on near places of worſhip. Swimming and ſkeating on Sundays, are improper. They corrupt our youth, and expoſe our city to the contempt of ſober foreigners.
>
> 3. The practice in ſome taverns of entertaining citizens on Sundays, eſpecially in the evenings.

4. Drunkenefs, and profane fwearing, by punishing both in the moſt exemplary manner.

5. Galloping horſes, through our ſtreets, whereby many children have been killed, or had their bones broken.

6. *Firing out the old year*, as it is called, whereby much miſchief has been done, and ſick people greatly diſturbed and injured. ("Philadelphia" May 13, 1789, n. pag.)

In the rural areas of the Midwest, with population increasing in lands acquired via the Northwest Ordinance under President Thomas Jefferson, laws enacted to address gambling and sport in tavern culture cast such practices as immoral. An Ohio law of February 1, 1805, pronounced in one section

> [t]hat if any perſon licenſed to keep a tavern, or any retailer of wine, ſpiritous liquors or ſtrong drink, ſhall knowingly permit or allow of any ſporting or rioting in ſuch houſe, or on the premiſes, on the ſabbath, or at any time knowingly allow or permit any kind of betting or gaming for money or an other value, either at cards, dice, billiards, bowls, hovel-board, fives, or an other game of hazard or chance . . . , every ſuch tavern-keeper or retailer, on being thereof legally convicted before any court having cognizance thereof, ſhall, for every ſuch offence, be fined in any ſum not exceeding twenty dollars, at the discretion of the court, with coſts, . . . (qtd. in Altherr, Part 2 19).

While many in the elite class forwent tavern visits in favor of their own leisure outings, they did not necessarily give up the sporting pursuits typically associated with these venues. As Bushman has explained, "Tavern life seemed degrading to the elite, yet they played cards and drank in their own parlors. Elegant tables, finely finished chairs, and the attire and posture of the players transformed the meanings of these activities" (53). In contrast to rural farmers and lower-rank people, colonial elites believed their amusements to be appropriate in their genteel culture as markers of their consumerism and leisure apart from ordinary folks.

The Enlightenment in America and Ideas of Sport and the Body

The Enlightenment drew on the seventeenth-century scientific investigations by thinkers who emphasized belief in human reason and the scientific method. Two such men were John Locke, who developed influential theories of the human mind and of political philosophy, and Isaac Newton, whose work on the laws of nature advanced the scientific revolution. The intellectual movement forged an age of reason and pursuit of progress and scientific discovery. In America, the gentry and well-educated colonists began to focus on rationalism and science rather than on Calvinist doctrines of faith. The Enlightenment also influenced thoughts about sport and how the human body functioned.

In this vein, Benjamin Franklin hailed the advantages of turning to strategy and reasoning, rather than divine influence, in one's pastimes. In his 1779 essay "The Morals of Chess," Franklin wrote, "For life is a kind of chess, in which we have often points to gain, and competitors or adversaries to contend with. . . . [I]ts effects on the mind, be not merely innocent, but advantageous, to the vanquished as well as the victor" (Franklin 233). Thus adherents of the American Enlightenment combined intellectual and physical culture in order to delineate a rational mode of inquiry to investigate the world and human beings.

1807-1819

•1807
- First agricultural fair (Berkshire, Massachusetts) founded by Elkanah Watson with horse races and contests of physical skills and rural skills like plowing

•1810
- Tom Molineaux, a freed black man, loses English championship boxing match to Tom Cribb

•1812
- War of 1812 fought against Great Britain

•1815
- Battle of New Orleans fought

•1816
- First American yacht, *Cleopatra's Barge*, built in Salem, Massachusetts

•1819
- *American Farmer* magazine founded by John Stuart Skinner to cover outdoor sport and rural health

Dr. Benjamin Rush

Dr. Benjamin Rush, Philadelphia physician and writer of medical and health books in the mid-1700s, and a signer of the Declaration of Independence, commented on sport and physical health based on his medical knowledge of the body. Using Enlightenment thinking, he combined scientific, medical, and moral stances in advocating practices to support a healthy mind and body. Rush urged Americans to pursue forms of exercise and sport that he deemed healthful, and his numerous sermons and books gave recommendations for physical education for students.

Photo courtesy of Library of Congress, LC-USZ62-97104.

In 1772, Rush wrote *Sermons to Gentlemen Upon Temperance and Exercise,* in which he encouraged young men to pursue horseback riding, noting the significance of such sporting activity for the well-being of the gentlemen:

> RIDING ON HORSEBACK is the moſt manly and uſeful ſpecies of exerciſe for gentlemen. Biſhop Burnet expreſſes his surprise at the lawyers of his own time, being ſo much more long-lived . . . than other people, conſidering how much thoſe of them who become eminent in their profeſſion, are obliged to devote themſelves to conſtant and intenſe study. He attributes it entirely to their RIDING the circuits so frequently, to attend the different courts in every part of the kingdom. . . . But we ſhall hereafter mention another cauſe which concurs with this, to protract their lives. It may be varied according to our ſtrength, or nature of our diſorder, by walking-pacing-trotting- or cantering our horſe. . . . In riding, to preſerve health, eight or ten miles a day are ſufficient to anſwer all the purpoſes we would wiſh for. (qtd. in Altherr, Part 1 15–16)

Rush also joined fellow Philadelphian Benjamin Franklin in recommending that Americans of various ages engage in swimming:

> Too much cannot be ſade in praise of SWIMMING, or as the poet of Avon expreſſes it—"buffeting the waves with lofty sinews." Beſides exercising the limbs, it ſerves to wash away the duſt, which is apt to mix itself with the ſweat of our bodies in warm weather. . . . I would strongly recommend the practiſe of bathing, and ſwimming, frequently in the ſummer ſeaſon. (qtd. in Altherr, Part 1 29)

Rush commented on swimming for students in an essay he presented at a Methodist academy on August 2, 1790. He noted that because the Methodists banished every "ſpecies of play from their college . . . the healthy and pleasurable exerciſe of swimming, is not permitted to their scholars, except in the preſence of one of their maſters" (qtd. in Altherr, Part 2 22). He proposed what he viewed as appropriate physical activities for male youth in his 1790 essay "On the Amusements and Punishments Proper for Schools." Lamenting that many youth had sedentary habits, he urged that "the amusements of our youth shall consist of such exercises as will be most subservient to their future employments in life," in particular supporting outdoor exercise and agricultural pursuits (qtd. in Hartwell 24). Rush's 1772 sermons gave a list of other sporting activities he also deemed healthful for males: "To all theſe ſpecies of exerciſe which we have mentioned, I would add, SKEATING, JUMPING, alſo, the active play of TENNIS, BOWLES, QUOITS, GOLF, and the like" (qtd. in Altherr, Part 1 224–225). Rush also encouraged appropriate education of women at the

Young Ladies' Academy of Philadelphia. He suggested that "dancing might be pursued as a form of healthful activity" (Park, "'Embodied Selves'" 71). Other health and physical education writers offered advice about appropriate physical activities for women, which is discussed below.

Rush also advocated temperance and proper diet as part of his health reform program informed by the Enlightenment. In 1784, in his *Inquiry into the Spirituous Effects of Liquor on the Human Body and Mind,* he addressed the potentially horrible impact of hard liquor on physical and mental health. He said that beer, wine, and cider may be used for medicinal purposes but distilled spirits prove harmful to one's physical well-being. He urged Americans to alter their diets and to exercise to improve their physical health. The pamphlet "was a masterpiece. Its rational arguments, logic, and incisive examples made it both the century's most effective short piece and also a model for later temperance publications." In fact, by 1850 "more than 170,000 copies had been circulated" (Rorabaugh 40–41). Rush's widespread influence on eighteenth-century attitudes about physical exercise, sport, and care of the body persisted into the following decades.

In 1810, a children's advice book titled *Youthful Recreations* stated that "it must be confessed, that youth is the time to obtain a stock of health, and that is best promoted by moderate exercise." The text continued:

For he who fits by the fire all day,
And Never goes abroad to play
May keep himself from being cold,
But may not live till he is old.

The author of *Youthful Recreations* also promoted other advice and sporting activities: "To prevent *bodily weakness and infirmity,* exercise is necessary. . . . To play with *battledore* [bat or racket] and *shuttlecoc*k or with a *trap and ball,* is good exercise." Furthermore, good physical health was not the domain only of wealthy children: "Children of the affluent, but even such of the poor who are impelled by necessity to pick cotton, card wool, to sit and spin or reel all day, should have at least one hour, morning and evening, for some youthful recreation. . . . [T]hey should at least play *Hop-Scotch*" (qtd. in Altherr, Part 2 17).

Physical education became part of the effort to train white Protestant American boys and young men of the upper class to fulfill their prescribed gender roles in the mid-eighteenth century. These boys, sons of better-educated fathers and members of genteel families, learned about health of mind and body as part of the Enlightenment mind-set. Due to their privileged way of life, many of these males did not perform physical labor in agriculture or other manual tasks to exercise their bodies. Supporters of physical education in the private schools for boys included Noah Webster and Dr. Benjamin Rush, both of whom were "decidedly favorable to bodily exercise of certain kinds." Webster, author of a hugely influential American dictionary, gave a speech on physical training for young men in Hartford, Connecticut, in 1790. In his "Address to Young Gentlemen," Webster stated that it "should be the business of young persons to assist nature, and strengthen the growing frame by athletic exercises." He urged that when "it is not the lot of a young person to labor, in agriculture or mechanic arts, some laborious amusement should constantly and daily be pursued as a substitute, and none is preferable to fencing. A fencing skool iz [sic], perhaps, as necessary an institution in a college as a professor of mathematics." Webster recommended, too, that these well-to-do young gentlemen partake of such sports as running, football (soccer), quoits, and dancing to offset their lack of physical training (qtd. in Hartwell 23–24).

INTERNATIONAL PERSPECTIVE

GutsMuths and the Beginning of Physical Education

Johann Christoph Friedrich GutsMuths (1759–1839) has exerted a great and enduring influence on the development of physical exercise throughout the world. People from many countries have visited Schnepfenthal, Germany, where he lived and worked, and his writings have been translated into many languages. In 1802, an American edition of his *Gymnastik für die Jugend* (*Gymnastics for Youth*) was published in Boston but wrongly attributed to Christian Gotthilf Salzmann. The curious spelling of GutsMuths' name, incidentally, was his own invention.

After GutsMuths' studies, it was chance that brought him in 1785 to Salzmann's Philanthropinum in Schnepfenthal (Thuringia, Germany), a school which was to become the center of GutsMuths' activities for 50 years. The philanthropists—literally, "friends of mankind"—were committed to the ideas of the Enlightenment and conceived a revolutionary pedagogy based on the responsibility of individuals for themselves, their potential for development, and their striving for perfection. Their (utopian) aim was to create a new kind of human being: an enlightened citizen guided by reason. A further revolutionary idea was that of a holistic education to improve the body as well as the mind. The philanthropists were of the opinion that reason could develop only through practical experience and cognition—that is, through the senses—and consequently that physical education and bodily exercise were indispensable. The Philanthropinen were boarding schools in which these ideas were put into practice.

In Schnepfenthal, GutsMuths developed the first systematic form of physical education based on the new pedagogy and named it after the gymnastics of Greek antiquity. In his most important work, *Gymnastik für die Jugend* (1793), GutsMuths expounded on the significance of physical exercise in an education founded on reason and intended for practical use. At the Philanthropinen, the (male) pupils were taught a wide variety of physical exercises ranging from running, lifting, and carrying to balancing and climbing. The program of the pupils' physical activities included not only games but also gardening and hiking. Nearby lakes provided opportunities for swimming in the summer and skating in the winter. Assuming that one's surroundings could be taken in only through the senses, the philanthropists schooled their pupils' faculties of seeing, hearing, and feeling. The philanthropists' ideas of respecting childhood, self-fulfillment, and the importance of play and games were based on notions of utility: From their perspective, play meant "work under the mantle of youthful joy" (GutsMuths, "Gymnastik" 209).

After the turn of the century, GutsMuths was increasingly influenced by nationalistic political ideas. In his last book on gymnastics, a manual for the "sons of the fatherland" appearing in 1817, he tried to achieve a synthesis of his gymnastics system and that of Friedrich Ludwig Jahn's Turnen, which aimed at the liberation of Prussia from the French occupation and the unification of Germany as a nation-state (Pfister, "Cultural").

Young white men of privilege in the United States received their training for political and business careers at institutions of higher education such as Harvard, Yale, Princeton, Brown, King's College (now known as Columbia University), William and Mary, and Thomas Jefferson's University of Virginia. These institutions were created to develop an educated male citizenship for democratic and public positions. Their curricula included proper care of the body, mind, and soul, and they integrated physical activities into academic life to help students maintain a wholesome mind and body. The athletic pursuits, however, lacked the organizational and competitive structure of modern sports. At Yale, for example, a school law enacted by the college president and fellows on October 6, 1795, restricted sporting activity near the campus: "If any Scholar ſhall go a-fiſhing or ſailing, or more than two miles (3.2 kilometers) from the College, upon any occaſion, without leave from the Preſident, a Profeſſor, or a Tutor, shall undreſs himſelf for ſwimming in any place, expoſed to public view, he may be fined not exceeding thirty four cents." Princeton student James Garnett wrote about the sports he played in March 1813: "With respect to our amusements we have had a great many since the good weather commenced; in the vacant hours we exercise ourselves by running, jumping, throwing quoits and pitching." Timothy Dwight, Yale president, noted the sports played on campus by students in the early 1800s as part of his observances about learning and morals in New England: "Boys and men play at football, cricket, quoits, and at many other sports of an athletic cast; and in the winter are peculiarly fond of skating. Riding in a sleigh, or sledge, is also a favorite diversion in New England" (qtd. in Altherr, Part 2 25, 103).

The expansion of sport for male students at colleges would not occur until the early decades of the nineteenth century. In 1826, Harvard would become the first American college to start a gymnasium, and organized competitive sports would follow even later (as is explored in subsequent chapters). For now, the select young men in these academic and social contexts might heed the advice given on sport and culture by John Adams to his son John Quincy Adams: "I would advise you, my Son, in Skating, Dancing, and Riding, to be always attentive to this Grace," to perform such activities as skating not just with vigor but with "an Elegance of Motion" (qtd. in Bushman, 200–201). In the new nation, for the sons of republican men to achieve manly vigor, "economy, industry, and hardihood" must go together with grace and refinement (Bushman 201). As part of the cultural matrix in which these elite young men assumed their gender and socioeconomic privilege, then, certain kinds of sporting activity signified civility versus vulgarity and helped mark one's place in the new democracy.

Frontier and Backcountry Sport

In contrast to citizens of the growing cities and rural communities witnessing the resurgence of religion and morality—as well as the urban centers disseminating new scientific ideas, inventions, and views of health and the body—those living in the less populated frontier or backcountry areas, with their harsher landscapes, faced a different set of physical demands in daily life and in sporting activity. House or barn raisings brought frontier settlers together in a communal purpose and provided opportunities for sport. An Illinois resident in the first decade of the nineteenth century asserted that "The whole neighborhood assembled and split rails, cleared land, plowed up the field, and the like. In the evenings of these meetings, the sports of throwing the mall, pitching quaits [quoits], jumping and the like, generally closed the happy day" (qtd. in Altherr, Part 2 20).

Historian Elliott Gorn has analyzed this rough-and-tumble way of life for frontiersmen and the physical, brutal sports these men embraced as a demonstration of their honor in rural areas. No-holds-barred fighting held an important place in the culture of the Southern backcountry. Gorn has explained that contestants began their brawl in an outdoor space that the spectators surrounded, and "fighters battled each other until one called enough or was unable to continue. Combatants boasted, howled and cursed" (Gorn, "Gouge and Bite" 36–37). The pummeling, gouging, and pulling of the opposing fighter's eyes, hair, or other body parts demonstrated the physicality of the fighter who withstood the violent battle to claim victory. These fierce fights were viewed as a way for rough-and-tumble fighters to defend their honor and physical skills in rural Maryland, Virginia, and Georgia and in frontier regions of Kentucky, Alabama, and the Carolinas, where the harsh environment forced inhabitants to struggle for existence through hunting and subsistence farming. Thus, rather than the work ethic, temperance, and moral

The Yankee's Bar Room....continued from page 29.

Rough fighting in the Southern backcountry enabled men to show their physical skill and pride by incurring and inflicting bodily injury in these brutal sporting contests.

Photo courtesy of Lilly Library, Indiana University, Bloomington, Indiana.

and religious values touted by government officials and clergy in colonial towns and settled communities, the back-woods culture of frontiersmen and their families exalted other values and skills. As Gorn has remarked, "eye-gouging matches were focal events in the culture of lower-class males who still relished the wild ways of old"; whereas the upper-class or educated "gentleman's code of honor insisted on cool restraint, eye gougers gloried in unvarnished brutality" (Gorn, "Gouge and Bite" 39, 49).

Numerous accounts of the violent sport described the bloody and brutal fights witnessed by spectators in the backcountry. Travelers from other countries were astonished by these sporting brawls, and their recordings of what they witnessed in their journeys through the American backcountry vividly expressed their wonder at such fights. A French traveler to Virginia in 1791 detailed the frontier style of fighting: "The manners of the poor people of that region are rude and violent. They swear, get drunk, gamble and fight often. They have a way of fighting which is not in use among the Americans in the East. The fighters use their fists, feet, and teeth. They are of one mind to gouge each other's eyes out." He also noted that the spectacle took place "amid applause from the ferocious circle urging them on." A traveler in Virginia in 1796 claimed that "[i]t is by no means uncommon to meet those who have lost an eye in combat, and there are men who pride themselves upon the dexterity with which they can scoop one out. But what is worse than all, these wretches in their combat endeavour to their utmost to tear out each other's testicles. Four or five instances came within my own observation, as I passed through Maryland and Virginia . . . [and] in the Carolinas and Georgia . . . the people are still more depraved in this respect than in Virginia." He concluded "that in some particular parts of these states, every third or fourth man appears with one eye" (qtd. in Altherr, Part 2 135–37).

In recounting what they saw during travels in the backcountry, some critics noted gender-related and socioeconomic aspects of these rituals in which rural men fought against other men to degrade each other's honor and body. Men exhibited their physical courage and pride in these sporting brawls and defended their own honor and the honor of family members in their violent clashes. One 1798 account claimed that

> [t]he citizens of North Carolina, who are not better employed, spend their time in drinking, or gaming at cards and dice, in cock fighting or horse-racing. Many of the interludes are filled up with a boxing match; and these matches frequently become memorable by feats of gouging. . . . The victor for his expertness, receives shouts of applause from the sporting throng, while his poor, eyeless antagonist is laughed at for his misfortune. . . . [T]his more than barbarous custom is prevalent in both the Carolinas, and in Georgia, among the lower class of people. (qtd. in Altherr, Part 2 135)

INTERNATIONAL PERSPECTIVE

Boxing and the Civilization Process

Norbert Elias (1897–1990) was one of the most distinguished sociologists of the twentieth century. In his major two-volume work *The Civilizing Process*, he emphasizes the links between social conditions and the human psyche, taking as his example the changes in both rules and behavior in post–Middle Age Europe. The growth of towns and the establishment of royal courts and aristocracies led to increased "chains of interdependence," which led to the concentration of power in the sovereign state and to the internalization of control in individual subjects.

Elias is one of the few eminent sociologists to have dealt with sport in his writings. In "The Genesis of Sport as a Sociological Problem," he applied the basic principle of his civilization theory to sport, demonstrating that the norms and rules of physical activities, along with their structures and patterns of interpretation, are dependent on the particular level reached in the civilization process. Elias constructed a link between the brutality of the sport of pankration (similar to ultimate fighting) in Greek antiquity and the idealization of the warrior, and the dependence on nature and the inability to plan ahead and the way that war and violence were taken for granted in this period of history.

Pankration was reportedly invented by the heroes Hercules and Theseus, who fought using a combination of wrestling and boxing. In antiquity, pankration was part of the Olympic contests and was also used in training soldiers. Many different forms of combat were involved, and everything was allowed with the exception of biting and gouging out the opponent's eyes. The match ended when one of the contestants conceded defeat, was knocked unconscious, or was dead, and deaths were a regular occurrence. If the match had not been decided by sunset, the contestants struck each other alternately with their fists until one of them gave in.

According to Elias, contact sports with rules governing the way they are carried out reflect the "standards of civilized behaviour" in modern societies. In wrestling, and especially in boxing, rules were successively introduced to reduce the dangers to life and limb and then later to prevent injuries altogether. Numerous rules and regulations—addressing, for example, which areas of the body one is allowed to hit, as well as weight classes, ring dimensions, number and length of rounds, rest breaks, gloves, mouthpieces, head protection (in amateur boxing), and, last but not least, the role of a referee, who can end an unequal match—transformed boxing from a fight to the death into a sport which meets the standards of civilized conduct in industrial nation-states. Whether the various subcultural "ultimate" combat sports with "no holds barred" signify a regressive step in civilization is a point of discussion, not the least because civilization processes are not linear but occur in long-term surges and waves (Elias and Dunning).

The practice of gouging spread throughout the backwoods areas of the frontier. Some Easterners believed that half of the residents of Kentucky no longer had eyes by 1793 and that, a decade later, nearly a third of the Pennsylvania Germans had only one eye. A Connecticut resident traveling through the Pennsylvania area wrote that he "saw one day a horse with one eye, carrying on his back the husband, wife and child, each with only one eye" (qtd. in Altherr, Part 2 138). A few years later, in Ohio, a traveler tried to comfort a man whose nose had been bitten off in a fight, but the victim replied, "'Don't pity me, pity that fellow over there,' pointing with one hand to another who had lost an eye, and showing the eye which he held triumphantly in the other" (Altherr, Part 2 141).

Despite laws against maiming or gouging in New York, New Hampshire, Pennsylvania, Kentucky, Illinois, Indiana, Louisiana, Tennessee, Georgia, and Missouri, the practice persisted. In the frontier areas, and especially in the South, rough-and-tumble fighting held cultural significance; men expressed their honor and physicality in their efforts to be the victorious combatant. A South Carolina backcountry judge aptly summarized the sporting practice of gouging and fighting in the American backcountry in this declaration: "Before God . . . I never saw such a thing in the world before. There is a plaintiff with an eye out! A juror with an eye out! And two witnesses with an eye out!" (qtd. in Rader, *American Ways* 77).

Though this fighting without rules between fellow frontiersmen of equal or similar status was commonplace, other types of fights were staged at times to highlight social class and race differences. Southern sportsmen who owned plenty of land and slaves and thus assumed elite status in their patriarchal, hierarchical culture would sometimes stage boxing matches that pitted slaves against one another, and this ritual carried its own meanings, as explored in the next chapter.

Women's Active Recreation in the Revolutionary Era and Early National Period

Gender prescriptions defining white women's roles remained in force in the early eighteenth century. Whereas upper-class white males might participate in some sport and physical exercise at the new colleges, such as Harvard and Princeton, young women were barred from attending such institutions. Indeed, women at this time in colonial American society faced restrictions imposed by a patriarchal culture and religion, including gender expectations assigning them to roles in the domestic realm as wives, mothers, daughters, sisters, and upholders of moral values which they were expected to share with the family at home and in places of worship, rather than attending facilities of education that seemed suited only for men and boys. During this time, women possessed no legal, political, or economic rights, though many were keenly aware of the rights, privileges, and legal standing of their husbands and brothers of the middle and upper classes who garnered social and political positions and public deference. During the Enlightenment in America, a few eighteenth-century writers posited that, "[s]ince the limbs and organs of both sexes are basically the same," there "must be one best diet, regimen and type and amount of exercise to develop the human body regardless of the sex of the individual" (Park, "'Embodied Selves'" 71–72). But such viewpoints remained far from the mainstream commitment to separate educational, social, and sporting behaviors for women and men. Women's domestic responsibilities, along with society's prohibition of travel by morally upright women without chaperones or families, limited their chances of partaking in the popular recreations of Southern gentry or Northern gentleman in billiard halls, cardrooms, and taverns.

The noncompetitive physical activities of walking, gardening, bathing, and even horseback riding—practical, active recreations deemed healthful for the female constitution and for supporting the domestic care of children—might be pursued by some women, depending on their age and status and the urban or agricultural setting in which they lived. As distinguished historian Allen Guttmann has written, "None of the contests that we commonly classify as sports was thought suitable for women"; in fact, in early America, women's sports "were limited to husking bees, quilting contests, and other competitions directly related to women's domestic labor" (Guttmann, *Sports: The First Five Millennia* 119). Women who attended public sporting displays might contribute their domestic skills in providing food, but their status apart from the male participants in the active recreations reaffirmed the gender differences enforced at the time. The social interchange at public gatherings such as shooting matches, muster days, court days, and the like did at least offer some relief from women's mundane daily tasks. Women of lower rank might support their husbands or brothers embattled in the rough and brutal fighting on the frontier by joining spectators who witnessed the public contest. In the early national period, observer Daniel Drake noted that these civil affairs typically gave way "to a heterogeneous drama of foot races, pony races, wrestling, fighting, and general uproar" (qtd. in Larkin 274).

In society's genteel ranks, the rowdy and gambling crowds of young men, male laborers, and travelers seeking respite from the road at taverns were deemed inappropriate company for women of religious faith and middle- and upper-rank social status. Thus, while taverns might accommodate women as travelers in appropriate quarters, "their barroom clienteles were almost exclusively male" (Larkin 282). Those places setting themselves apart from the slew of typical taverns in early American cities—"a tiny handful that polite society called their own"—hosted dinners and balls for the leading political figures and the social elite. Taverns for genteel entertainment contrasted with those catering to the "lower-class vices—cursing, fighting, lewdness, and drunkenness" (Bushman 161, 164). In these finer taverns, no bearbaiting, gambling, or vulgar behavior greeted the women, who instead enjoyed refined social events. So too, card games played by young women in the refined environments of their private homes contrasted with such games played in the public gathering spots. Bushman has described differences in the pastimes of the higher and lower socioeconomic classes in early American culture: "Cards played on a mahogany table by the light of candles in silver holders, the genteel must have believed, was different than cards in the greasy hands of a day laborer in a dark tavern with a mug of beer at his elbow." Elite women, like their male counterparts, could enjoy their leisure activities in a beautiful environment that in their view "helped to change ordinary forms of vulgar entertainment into cultivated expressions of enlightenment and civilization" (Bushman 52).

The daily lives of children were similar during the 1700s, before they learned tasks to perform along gender lines. Young girls might enjoy some of the same recreations and pastimes near their home environs that young boys engaged in. For example, girls and boys both enjoyed playing games such as hide-and-seek and tag, and they pursued outdoor sporting activities such as sledding and skating. The physical activities of "both sexes mixed competition with collaboration but the boys placed a stronger emphasis on their rivalries and the girls stressed their cooperation more heavily" (Rotundo 34). As girls got older, their play diminished, while boys pursued more physically rigorous sports and games, and at that point gender identity in sport manifested the separate gender roles in American society. Some American women and men, however, probed the physical capabilities of women to participate in sport and active recreation, and in the early decades of the nineteenth century some women began to engage in more physical activities and sport. Even in the last decades of the eighteenth century, "an increasing number of American men and women argued that women were far more capable, stronger, healthier—and even wiser—than they were customarily pictured to be; or at least they could become so if their development were not arrested by social customs and false and limiting conceptions of their abilities" (Park, "'Embodied Selves'" 91). The social activism of women and men seeking to expand sporting and physical activities for women is addressed in following chapters.

Native American Sport

While the white male citizens of the new republic struggled with the meanings of democracy and the quest for social mobility, and females, too, sought to identify their place in the new republic, the indigenous tribes contended with the usurpation of their lands, the imposition of an alien culture, and pressure to assimilate to the white world. By 1791, a French noblemen who observed Native Americans in the Northeast claimed, "The games of their children are those of ours; they have ball and tennis, racing and shooting with the bow, for youth. . . ." (qtd. in Altherr, Part 2 66). By the turn of the nineteenth century, the Oneida tribe of western New York had adopted quoits while continuing the sport of archery. Fur trader Daniel Williams Harmon observed the Assiniboine archers of the Northern American (Canadian) plains in the early 1800s and remarked, "Their youth, from the age of four or five to that of eighteen or twenty years, pass nearly half of their time in shooting arrows at a mark; and to render the employment more interesting, they always have something at stake, which is generally nothing more than an arrow, or something of small value." He judged the archers to be "the best marksmen, perhaps, in the world. Many of them, at the distance of eight or ten rods [44 to 55 yards, or 40 to 50 meters], will throw an arrow with such precision, as twice out of three times, to hit a mark of the size of a dollar" (qtd. in Altherr, Part 2 66). But not all tribes assimilated willingly or peacefully. On the Western frontier, the Apaches of Arizona resisted white incursions throughout the nineteenth century, and as early as 1807 U.S. soldiers feared their bowmen. Writing in about 1807, Lieutenant Zebulon Pike stated that their arrows were more than a yard (or meter) long: "With this weapon they shoot with such force as to go through the body of a man at a distance of 100 yards [91 meters], and an officer told me that in an engagement with them, one of their arrows struck his shield and dismounted him in an instant" (qtd. in Altherr, Part 2 66).

The most popular indigenous sport continued to be lacrosse. Throughout the 1780s and 1790s, white observers wrote accounts of games they witnessed among the Iroquois Confederacy in New York, the Shawnees of Kentucky, the Creeks of Alabama, the Cherokees of Tennessee, and the Chickasaws of the Mississippi Valley, as well as the Ottawas of the Lake Superior region. The Corps of Discovery, sent by President Thomas Jefferson to explore the lands of the Louisiana Purchase from 1804 to 1806, witnessed a game among the Mandans of the Dakota region. Zebulon Pike, who explored the Great Plains and the Rocky Mountains, also wrote of seeing a lacrosse game: "[T]his afternoon they had a great game of cross on the prairie, between the Sioux on the one side, and the Puants (Winnebagoes) and Reynards (Fox) on the other." The wagers reached sums up to the amount of some thousand dollars at that time, Pike reported, and the game featured 200 to 300 participants. Pike stated that "the Sioux were victorious—more I believe, from the superiority of their skill in throwing the ball, than by their swiftness, for I thought the Puants and the Reynards the swiftest runners" (Altherr, Part 2 422–427, 427–428 [quote]).

Sporting Practices During the American Revolutionary War

The changing cultural, social, political, religious, and economic landscape in the American colonies was marked by a series of moves and countermoves leading to the heightened tensions of the 1760s and 1770s, when the colonies sought independence from the English crown. The fight for freedom and democratic principles of equality, however, did not extend to blacks, indigenous peoples, women, or poor whites. During the American Revolutionary Period, ideas about tempering sport and leisure pursuits revealed the serious nature of the impending political, social, economic, and military challenges in the young nation. The shift in the colonies toward challenging the social and political power of the elites who controlled resources and property—and the joining together of colonists to battle England in the Revolutionary War—generated a cautious view of sport during the war and in the new nation at the end of the eighteenth century.

As the American Revolution approached amid increasing tensions with England—linked to the monarchy's decision to impose harsh taxes and curtail political freedom and assemblies in the colonies—the moral and political rhetoric of colonial patriots allowed little room for gaiety, popular recreations, and sport in forging an independent American nation. The work ethic, rather than a play ethic, pervaded the colonial struggle for independence in the 1770s and 1780s. In struggling to implement the possibilities of democracy, individualism, liberty, and political freedom to dissolve the ties of empire with England, colonial advocates of independence called for diligence, morality, and hard work. Political and religious leaders gave little opportunity for the luxuries of leisure and sport, instead urging the American people to unite in the arduous struggle for freedom from England and establish a republican form of government in the new nation. The patriotic leaders and political thinkers in the new republic believed the inhabitants of the nation needed to pursue virtue and self-improvement in moral activities rather than indulge in offensive and wasteful pastimes.

The American colonists convened the First Continental Congress in 1774 in Philadelphia to respond to increasing hostilities with Britain, and in this step toward establishing a democratic governing body the place of pastimes and sport became part of the deliberations. A resolution passed that the colonies "discountenance and discourage every species of extravagance and dissipation, especially all horse-racing, and all kinds of gaming, cock-fighting, exhibition of shows, plays, and other expensive diversions and amusements" (qtd. in Rader, *American Sports* [2004] 16). In these tumultuous years leading to the colonists' rebellion, the focus on the national crisis curtailed the time and means for engaging in sport. When the Congress ratified the Declaration of Independence of the 13 colonies on July 4, 1776, however, the grand celebration did allow for sport and amusement. Indeed, on July 3, in Philadelphia, patriot John Adams had written to his wife Abigail in Massachusetts about the momentous occasion: "I am apt to believe that it will be celebrated by succeeding Generations, as the great anniversary Festival. . . . It ought to be solemnized with Pomp and Parade, with Shews [sic], Games, Sports, Guns, Bells, Bonfires and Illuminations from one End of this Continent to the other from this Time forward forever more" (Adams 115). Of course, this tradition of celebrating American independence with games and sport persisted, and in 1816, the *New Hampshire Patriot* published an article describing events that took place on the 40th anniversary of the nation's founding: "Salutes of artillery were fired at sunset, and sports, festivity, and fireworks, closed the evening. . . . Independence was proclaimed on every hill and reverberated on every valley. It was as if all had sworn a confirmation of freedom before gods and men" ("Fortieth Anniversary" 2). American celebrations of Independence Day would include different activities as new sports were developed in the early nineteenth century.

In the newly formed republic, politicians and other authorities continued to mark out a place for moderate and useful sport, the value of which had been manifested in the sporting skills and physical vigor displayed by many soldiers and generals during the American Revolution. Virginia planter George Washington, a key Revolutionary War general whose

George Washington helped to foster the idea of physical fitness and military might as exhibited in his physical stature and prowess on horseback.

Photo courtesy of Library of Congress, LC-USZ62-72497.

considerable physical ability had served as a model for his men in the Continental Army, later did the same for all citizens as president of the United States. Washington "set an example for his men by taking part in sports when he could find time in his busy schedule." He played ball games and wicket, a form of cricket. Moreover, Washington's physical health and commanding public presence, exhibited in his magnificent patriotic leadership, also popularized his favored pursuits of horseback riding and foxhunting. Other soldiers played "fives," a variation on handball, as well as the bowling game of ninepins, familiar to many colonists (Ledbetter 30–32), and of course the physical abilities displayed in horsemanship and swimming proved useful in various wartime situations. Washington promoted sports in correspondence in 1777 in Norristown, Pennsylvania: "Games of Exercise for amusem't, may not only be permitted but encouraged" (qtd. in Altherr, Part 1 16). In his diaries, he recounted foxhunting outings in Virginia in several entries:

> 19 March 1773: "Went a hunting. Found a Fox by Muddy hole Plantation and killdit after a chase of two hours 3 Quarters."

> 5 October 1773: "Went a hunting in the Neck with Mr. Custis & Lund Washington. Found a Fox & after runng. it two hours & half lost it."

> 5 December 1785: "It being a good scenting morning I went out with the Hound. . . . Run at different two foxes but caught neither. My French Hounds performed better today; and have afforded hopes of their performing well, when they come to be a little more used to Hunting and understand more fully the kind of game they are intended to run."

> 10 January 1786: "Rid to my Plantation in the Neck, and took the hounds with me. About 11 Oclock found a fox in the Pocoson at Sheridens point and after running it very indifferently and treeing it once caught it about one Oclock." (Altherr, Part 1 378, 387; Part 2 354–355)

Washington also helped publicize the specific need for physical fitness for military might: "Bodily accomplishments have ever been assigned a prominent place in the codes of the soldier and the gentleman; and every outburst of military ardor in our history has led to attempts to engraft certain kinds of technical training upon the general training of the rising generation" (qtd. in Hartwell 24). Both the Revolutionary War and nineteenth-century wars in the United States followed this pattern.

Use of Horses

The practicality and popularity of the horse in American life persisted after the Revolutionary War. Thomas Benger of Pennsylvania took steps to improve the breeding stock of American horses by importing a famous British racehorse, Messenger, to Philadelphia. Derived from Arabian thoroughbreds, Messenger produced a line of great champions that included American Eclipse, Whirlaway, Man o' War, Swaps, and Secretariat (Twombly 29). An American breed known as the Morgan horse also emerged in the post-Revolutionary era in Vermont. The breed originated with a small horse, owned by Justin Morgan, that "had the strength of a beer-wagon brute and the style and speed of a thoroughbred." The horse worked the field during the week, reputedly hauling loads greater than his own weight, while winning races in Vermont and western Massachusetts on weekends. With such remarkable qualities, the horse was prized as a stud, and he fathered a line of horses that dominated harness racing throughout the nineteenth century (Twombly 33–34).

Various forms of horse racing spread throughout the United States, and early U.S. presidents demonstrated their horsemanship. "George Washington and Thomas Jefferson took immense pride in their horses and bred them to improve the bloodlines of saddle, work, carriage and racehorses." Washington helped organize races in

Alexandria, Virginia, and was recognized as an excellent horseman himself. While Jefferson was president, he frequently rode horses for exercise, and he "rarely missed the meets at the National Race Course in Washington, D.C., which opened just outside the city boundary two miles [3.2 kilometers] north of the White House in 1802" (White House Historical Association n. pag.).

Racecourses also appeared elsewhere in the new nation and drew keen interest. In 1806, the American trotter Yankey covered a mile (1.6 km) in just under 3 minutes. Organized horse racing in the South was centered in New Orleans, where a racetrack was constructed on the nearby Hampton plantation by 1815. That venue was supplanted by the Metairie track in 1837, as New Orleans became the hub of modern sport in the region (Guttmann, *Sports: The First Five Millennia* 121). The following advertisement from the *City Gazette* in Charleston, South Carolina, on February 26, 1816, gave racegoers the list of horses for the day:

> *Sports of the Turf.*—This day, at 12 o'clock, will be run for, over the Washington Race Course, the Proprietor's Purse of *One Thousand Dollars*. For this race, which, it is supposed, will be the best contest during the week, the following horses have been entered:
>
> Mr. Winn's r. h. Ringleader, 5 years old, 95 wt. pink dress.
>
> Col. Richardson's s. m. Miss Fortune, 6 years old, 95 wt. blue and red.
>
> Mr. Singleton's s. g. Little John, 5 years old, 95 wt. black and red.
>
> Commodore Dent's Rattler. (*Sports of the Turf*, n. pag.)

Horse racing would continue as a popular sport, and new forms began to develop, as explored in subsequent chapters.

Sport for Exercise

Political officials in the new republic urged people to engage in sport for physical well-being and invigorating exercise, rather than for wagers or profit seeking. As John Adams engaged in his patriotic duties in the American Revolutionary Era, he offered the following thought to his learned, independent-minded wife Abigail on raising their children in their Massachusetts home: "[M]ake your children *hardy*, *active* and *industrious*"—qualities viewed as virtues for this next generation of Americans in the early Republic (qtd. in Bushman 199). Those sports deemed valuable for moral and physical health gained the approval of republican leaders, even as they criticized what they saw as the idle amusements, sports, and vices current in European powers. Toward the goal of promoting healthful exercise, "what may well have been New England's first sports association, the Shad and Salmon Club of Hartford, [was] organized in the 1780s to promote outings and a series of fishing contests" (Daniels, *New England* 170). For yeoman farmers, gentlemen, and patriots, these outdoor sports invigorated the body and engaged one in nature rather than in violent activity, and, while they had been popular for some time, they now featured an organized format in which upstanding male New Englanders could partake of outdoor excursions enabling appropriate exercise in their communities.

The growth of outdoor sports for white middle- and upper-rank men continued in the Philadelphia area with the establishment of organizations for sport and physical recreation. One of the long-standing and influential fishing clubs of the United States, the Schuylkill Fishing Company, was founded in 1732 and expanded in the latter decades of the eighteenth century. In promoting exercise, sport, and sociability, the "Schuylkill Fishing Company of the State in Schuylkill," known also as "The Colony of Schuylkill," was founded by followers of Philadelphia Quaker William Penn. The club linked its fishing privileges to Native American inhabitants (the Quaker faith the CASTLE of the STATE in SCHUYLKILL.

Members of the Schuylkill Fishing Company met in the Castle near the Schuylkill River and enjoyed fishing outings on the river.

The Library Company of Philadelphia

called for peaceful relations with the Indians) who lived along the Schuylkill River by paying homage to Tammany or Tamamend, "a band chief of the Delaware or Lenni-Lenape Indians," whose name meant "the affable" or "the worthy one" (MacGregor 393). To honor Tammany as its patron and saint, the sportsmen of the Schuylkill Fishing Company "established a saint's day for the Indian chief—the first of May, the day that marked the official opening of their fishing season"—a ritual that "was celebrated to assure a successful season of fishing" (MacGregor 393–394). Members of this club enjoyed catching fish and partaking of other recreations on the water, as well as hunting in the woods. After the American Revolution, the company became known as the State in Schuylkill.

Records of the Schuylkill Fishing Company reveal the sports that its members enthusiastically pursued in the Philadelphia area through the nineteenth century. Earning membership in the club was "by no means easy," as no gentleman was "placed on the roll of probation until eight members signif[ied] approval." After then serving an apprenticeship for at least six months, the candidate had to be supported by a majority of club members in order to gain admission and join other members in pursuing "on the banks of the river the fishing, fowling, and feasting." Each member of the club was "provided with his own bateau, tackle and bait, apron, hat, etc." In the eighteenth century, the club's officers met regularly in the building known as the Castle near the Schuylkill River (Watson 291, 293–294, 296–297). Members wrote about their sporting experiences, as in this communication from William Parsons to Thomas Stretch, governor of the Schuylkill Fishing Company, regarding fishing by the club on May 7, 1775: "And as to what relates to the Fishery of the several Waters within the limitts of their Embafsy they have been very afsiduous not only in searching for and catching but in drefsing and eating of Fish" (qtd. in Altherr, Part 1 214). In addition, the group's records indicate the types of fish these sportsmen encountered in their outings. In *A History of the Schuylkill Fishing Company of the State in Schuylkill, 1732–1888* a member chronicled the following:

Circa 1789: "That Mr. Benjamin Scull, the *Prince of Fishermen*, produced a Trout, which he this day took in Schuylkill that measured *fifteen inches*" [0.4 meter].

15 September 1791: "Be it remembered that on the fifteenth day of September last, a *Sturgeon* of four feet [1.2 meters] in length, leaped on board one of the vessels belonging to the fleet, opposite to the Castle, of which the company then present, made a delicious repast." (qtd. in Altherr, Part 2 233)

The men in this club also enjoyed engaging in other upper-class sports with leading citizens of Philadelphia. Several members also held membership in the elite Gloucester Fox Hunting Club—for example, Samuel Nicholas, admitted to the Schuylkill Fishing Company as member No. 102 on May 1, 1760, who was among the 27 founders of the Gloucester club in 1766, as well as First Officer of the American Marines in 1775. Gloucester members marked their covenant this way: "We the subscribers, being about to provide and keep a kennel of Fox Hounds, do mutually agree with each other in the manner following . . . ," with further text outlining the amount to be paid as well as rules and regulations that members would follow. Members of both the Schuylkill Fishing Company and the Gloucester Fox Hunting Club included leading Philadelphians such as John Dickinson, Levi Hollingsworth, Thomas Mifflin, Robert Morris, and Samuel Morris Jr. (Fagan 3, 9, 11–14).

Republican Motherhood

For white American women of the new republic, the Revolution's promise of freedom failed to include them, and the gender-based constraints they faced in many areas of life extended to sporting endeavors and pastimes. Abigail Adams, wife of Revolutionary patriot John Adams, urged her husband in her correspondence in 1776: "In your new code of Laws, I pray you remember the Ladies." Moreover, she remarked pointedly on the authority of men in the patriarchal system: "Do not put such unlimited power in the hands of the Husbands. Remember all Men would be tyrants if they could" (qtd. in Kerber 12, 23). During the Revolutionary War, women participated in political acts such as staging boycotts, signing petitions, and aiding husbands and sons in managing businesses, but they did not gain suffrage or other rights in the new republic, as the Revolution fell short of extending equality and freedom to women. Instead, a new ideology developed regarding women's relation to the political sphere with a particular focus on the prescribed roles for the female gender. In this young democracy, the notion of women's roles in the republic emerged to praise the value of mothers as educators, nurturers, and child bearers who raise sons to be virtuous, active citizens in a democratic society. Their Revolutionary War experiences prompted some women to consider the male, public, political sphere as not solely isolated from their domestic sphere, since, as "Republican Mothers," (Kerber 146-147) they could be involved in the republican society by utilizing their domestic skills as guardians of the home, thus imparting virtue and morals to their children for participation in democracy.

Abigail Adams of Massachusetts wrote about women's experiences in the American Revolutionary Era, supported women's expanded opportunities, and reminded her husband, patriot John Adams, to consider the role of women in the new nation.

To fulfill these gender-specific domestic roles in helping to shape public affairs in the new nation, some women argued for access to education in female academies, since better knowledge and skills in reading, writing, and caring for the health of family members could prepare women to be better mothers. This would expand white women's influence beyond the home, but such influence stemmed from their gender-based domestic role—women's sway in the public would be derived from domestic power rather than equality in the American republic. The education in female academies emphasized female attributes in training young women to became mothers and wives. In the idea of Republican Motherhood, supporters "at least recognized the importance of health as the state in which women must exist to fulfill that ideal." At this time in the early republic, however, "they had not . . . moved concertedly to link physical performance and sport and health" (women would do this in the early nineteenth century). Women in various regions continued to engage in walking, riding, and gardening; after 1790, therefore, "the everyday sporting life of 'republican mothers' changed little" (Struna, "'Good Wives'" 247, 249). At the end of the eighteenth century, gender lines remained in force in American society in sporting practices and political customs.

White women of the middle and upper classes might participate in some of the acceptable sports for health and outdoor exercise. In the Northeast, winter sports included sledding, with women and men sometimes participating together. In 1794, British traveler William Priest described sledding in Philadelphia:

> The chief amusement of the country girls in winter is sleighing, of which they are passionately fond, as indeed are the whole sex in this country. I never heard a woman speak of this diversion but with rapture. . . . The tavern and innkeepers are up all night; and the whole country is in motion. When the snow begins to fall, our planter's daughters provide hot sand, which at night they place in bags at the bottom of the sleigh. Their sweethearts attend with a couple of horses and away they glide with astonishing velocity; visiting their friends for many miles round the country. (qtd. in Altherr, Part 2 441)

Abigail Adams expressed her viewpoint on hunting, a typically male sport, in a letter to Thomas Brand-Hollis on September 6, 1790:

> A lovely variety of birds serenades me morning and evening, rejoicing in their liberty and security; for I have as much as possible, prohibited the grounds from invasion, and sometimes almost wished for game laws, when orders have not been sufficiently regarded. The partridge, the woodcock, and the pigeon are too great temptations to the sportsman to withstand. (qtd. in Altherr, Part 2 330)

A woman in Philadelphia who recorded her own experiences with sleighing in wintertime expressed her displeasure at the amusements that took place in taverns after a sleighing excursion for outdoor exercise. Ann Warder, wife of a British merchant, wrote in her diary on December 7, 1786:

> After dinner Jerry Parker took Sally, Lydia, and myself and son, out sleighing, which I found much more agreeable than expected. We met several parties starting out as we returned. This pastime is abused; large parties collect and riotly go together to taverns where they sup and return at all hours of the night. (qtd. in Altherr, Part 2 440)

For Republican Mothers, the public sphere of taverns and rowdy sport went against the moral and gender codes of the late eighteenth century.

The manly worlds of politics, sport, and public institutions remained generally off limits for women in the gendered structure of early American life. The opening of early educational academies to middle- and upper-status women, however, would be part of a long path toward defining women's roles in American society and sport in the next century. The emphasis on the heroism and physical skills demonstrated by men in the Revolutionary War—and on the strength and courage possessed by male leaders of the government—indicated in negative fashion the limitations on freedom and equality for women in American society generally and in sporting experiences particularly. As historian Linda Kerber has explained about the Revolutionary Era and the early republic, "Men took pride in qualities that distinguished them from women." Men such as George Washington, John Adams, and Thomas Jefferson, "who remodeled the American polity after the war remodeled it in their own image. . . . Women's weakness became a rhetorical foil for republican manliness" (11).

Turn of the Nineteenth Century and Societal Patterns

The passion for sport demonstrated by some citizens in both the urban and rural areas of American society in the eighteenth century may have been tempered by the realties of the Revolutionary War and the ensuing need for the American people to focus on building the new nation. In the early decades of the nineteenth century, however, changing economic, social, political, and cultural contexts in both city and country life shaped new forms of sport and physical activity, examined next in chapter 3.

The War of 1812, known as the Second War for American Independence, again called on the military and physical strength of American soldiers to defeat the British. The use of the horse by such military heroes as Andrew Jackson, a future president of the United States and a skilled horseman, added to a spirit of optimism and growth in the nation. The victory by the United States ushered in rapid economic, social, cultural, technological, and population changes in the first half of the nineteenth century. Such changes influenced viewpoints on sport and transformed the types and organization of sport experienced by men and women in American culture.

Summary

As the colonial society matured into a new republican nation, breaking its bonds with England, the physical activity evident in American life involved traditional sports that were often organized locally in informal contests. Yet several sports came under fire from religious proponents of the Great Awakening and from genteel political leaders who challenged them as immoral and impractical in the expansion of a new American society. On the frontier, at the horse track, and in the tavern, competitive forms of sport were often accompanied by gambling and consumerism that contrasted with the moral and religious pursuits encouraged by preachers. In addition, amid intellectual trends of the Enlightenment, economic trends of the consumer revolution, and the vicissitudes of the American Revolutionary Era, sport in the early national period was also shaped by the realities of social class, race, gender, and locale, with white men being the main partakers of sport and public culture.

DISCUSSION QUESTIONS

1. Why does sport have a place in American culture during times of economic, political, or military conflict, as occurred during the American Revolutionary Era?

2. On what basis did religious critics and preachers of the Great Awakening argue the need for American colonists to abstain from certain sports and activities?

3. Why was the Enlightenment important in promoting sport and physical education in the young nation, and who were some of the leaders in this promotion of sport for exercise?

4. Explain differences in men's and women's sport and leisure activities during this period. How were these differences influenced by traditional gender roles?

5. What sporting activities seemed important in forging the new republic, and why?

Antebellum Health Reforms and Sporting Forms

1820–1860

CHAPTER OBJECTIVES

After reading this chapter, you will have learned about the following:

- The importance of antebellum health reformers in promoting a positive attitude about exercise and sport

- The role of both women and men in advocating sport and physical education for women

- Views of rural health and sport for women and men in the Antebellum Era

- The development of sporting journalism and its influence on antebellum American culture

In his widely acclaimed article "Saints, and Their Bodies" (first published in *Atlantic Monthly* in March 1858), Thomas Wentworth Higginson, health reformer and advocate of vigorous sporting activity, proclaimed the moral and physical benefits of sport for Americans in the vibrant period of change in antebellum American culture. Higginson linked morality and muscles, especially for men, as key preparation for filling their roles in a democratic nation: "There is in the community an impression that physical vigor and spiritual sanctity are incompatible" (583). To counter that prevailing attitude, Higginson urged a new outlook on sport for a strong nation of sturdy men and moral vitality:

> Physical health is a necessary condition of all permanent success. To the American people it has a stupendous importance, because it is the only attribute of power in which they are losing ground. Guarantee us against physical degeneracy, and we can risk all other perils. . . .

> . . . We love to encounter in the contests of manhood those whom we first met at football, and to follow the thoughts of those who always dived deeper, even in the river, than our efforts could attain. . . . [W]e may hope for a reaction in favor of bodily exercises. And when we once begin the competition, there seems no reason why any other nation should surpass us. . . .

> But even among American men, how few carry athletic habits into manhood! . . . Full grown men are, of course, intended to take not only as much, but far more active exercise than boys. . . .

> Passing now to out-door sports (and no one should confine himself to indoor ones,) we . . . rank water first. A square mile even of pond water is worth a year's schooling to any intelligent boy. A boat is a kingdom. . . .

> . . . [M]eet Nature on the cricket ground or at the regatta; swim with her, ride with her, run with her, and she gladly takes you back once more within the horizon of her magic, and your heart of manhood is born again. . . . ("Saints" 585–586, 589, 591, 592–593, 595)

Thomas Wentworth Higginson, health reformer and advocate of physical activity.

Image courtesy of Library of Congress, LC-USZ62-73367.

Higginson and other like-minded antebellum reformers campaigned for causes including education reform, abolitionism, women's rights, and temperance. These reformers expressed nationalism in seeking to establish a populace made up of strong, vital, and moral citizens—after the War of 1812 and especially during the antebellum years—in order to advance the young democratic nation. To counter criticism that the United States was a nation of weak, puny, nonathletic citizens when compared with those of England and other countries, activists like Higginson touted health reform and strove to promote gender-based physical training for men and women. Higginson, especially, posited that these reform movements must rest on the sound moral and physical health of individual citizens, and, in this time of rapid change, a large portion of the white middle class in urban and rural settings placed increasing emphasis on physical exercise: "A restlessness and a slowly growing desire for physical freedom and expression seemed near. The apostle for this new awareness was Thomas Wentworth Higginson" (Lucas, "A Prelude" 54).

Overview of the Antebellum Period

The process of transformation in the first half of the nineteenth century in the United States involved social, economic, geographic, technological, and religious changes, and, in turn, these changes shaped the health and sport movement of antebellum America. The United States strove to define itself as a separate nation, with its own customs and culture, and sport became a part of this cultural expression. While the English language was retained, many British customs and practices, as well as forms of governmental organization and democracy, took on a very different cast. The nature of the American people and society was also brought into question by the continuing development of differing regional lifestyles within the expanding country. The regulation of the physical and spiritual body emerged as central concerns in the largely white, Protestant, slaveholding republic, which of course was also populated by Native Americans, free and captive African Americans, Hispanics, an increasing number of newer European immigrant groups, and groups of Asian immigrants coming to the western United States. The transformation of a traditional, rural, agricultural society into a modern, urban, industrial one in the North—through the application of science and technology from the early 1800s to the eve of the Civil War—shaped the twin movements to pursue physical health and sporting forms for diverse groups of people in the young nation. In this chaotic period, rural–urban interactions and inevitable tensions between rural and urban values came to light in ideas put forward about sport by many voices (both male and female) for reform.

In other facets of culture, citizens of the new republic strove to carve out a clear sense of what it meant to be an American. U.S. authors created literature with a specific focus on distinctly American stories, such as "Rip Van Winkle," *The Last of the Mohicans*, and *Moby-Dick*. Some women, including Harriet Beecher Stowe, author of *Uncle Tom's Cabin*, questioned the patriarchal nature of American society, with its ongoing practice of slavery and the domination of political and economic life by white men. A small group of particularly articulate woman's-rights supporters called for equal rights and suffrage in their "Declaration of Sentiments," modeled after the Declaration of Independence, at the 1848 woman's rights convention held in Seneca Falls, New York, marking the beginning of the woman's rights movement in the United States. Noteworthy American women Elizabeth Cady Stanton and Susan B. Anthony led this effort in the antebellum years. During these decades of active social reform and social change, groups of ethnic and religious immigrants also sought to establish their place in the American polity and society.

In the Antebellum Period, the United States expanded both in population and in territory, and this growth influenced sport in various parts of the nation and for sundry groups of Americans. After 1820, a growing number of immigrants made the hard journey to America. German, Irish, Jewish, and English immigrants, as well as some Asian immigrants to the West Coast, swelled the population and typically migrated to the burgeoning cities. In the 1830s, about six hundred thousand immigrants came to the United States, and during the 1830s through the 1850s, five to six million people had immigrated to America (Walters). In 1815, 18 states existed in the Union, and Louisiana was the westernmost of them. By 1860, the nation included 33 states, including California and Oregon on the Pacific coast. This expansion of land and people was marked by growing belief in "Manifest Destiny" by white, middle-class Americans. This ideology held that westward expansion revealed the destiny of Americans to succeed and fulfill God's plan for the American

1819-1830

- *American Farmer* edited by John Stuart Skinner

1820

- Missouri Compromise passed

1820–1860

- Antebellum reform movements: health reform, physical exercise, publications on sport and health for men and women, critics' attacks on sporting activities deemed immoral

1821

- First public high school opened in Massachusetts

1823

- Catharine Beecher founds Hartford Female Seminary, offering physical and domestic education for females

- Monroe Doctrine proclaimed

- Round Hill School founded (Massachusetts) and included physical education as an integral part of the curriculum

- North–South horse races staged: American Eclipse defeats Sir Henry nation, which gave them a divine right to conquer the land and its native inhabitants. Manifest Destiny provided a moral mission for expansion from the East to the West and encouraged land-hungry settlers to move ever westward, creating a frontier society even as urbanization took hold in the Northeast. Many American families in the Midwest left places like Missouri to seek a better life and acquire farm land in the West, and some went west to a region they thought might improve the health of family members. They crossed the Overland Trail in the 1840s in an arduous journey to new lands.

Manifest Destiny led American settlers into Texas, at the time still a territory of Mexico, in the early nineteenth century. There, white settlers mixed with Mexicans in another frontier society, and their labor and leisure intertwined as Mexican vaqueros' work skills of riding and roping evolved into the sport of rodeo. Hunting and fishing provided both sport and sustenance, and gambling at cards, billiards, and horse racing consumed hours for many men. At least three horse tracks existed in Texas by the early 1830s (Dyreson, "Sporting" 278). For women, quilting remained both a pastime and a necessity, and community dances sometimes lasted through the night. Despite such pleasures, frontier life proved difficult and violent. Both white and Tejano (denoting a Texan of Mexican descent) settlers in Texas revolted against their government in 1835, producing the independent republic of Texas, which was annexed by the United States in 1845. Continued conflict with Mexico erupted into the Mexican-American War from 1846 to 1848, which resulted in the U.S. acquisition of California and the Southwest.

The Gold Rush of 1848 brought fortune seekers, most of them single men, to California from around the world (including China), creating a polyglot society of immigrants of different backgrounds and faiths, such as Jews, Protestants, and Catholics. Among the varied recreational pastimes introduced were bull-and-bear fights and snow skiing. The latter proved practical for mail delivery during the winter. Downhill skiing was popular in the mountainous regions of the western United States, and, as farm families began emigrating from the Midwest to the western frontier along the Overland Trail in search of better land and economic opportunities, women joined in this sport as well.

BULL AND BEAR FIGHT.

Bull-and-bear fights in the early nineteenth century proved a popular pastime in frontier communities.
CULVER PICTURES

During the Antebellum Era, reform campaigns were fueled by the Second Great Awakening, a spiritual fervor spread in revival settings in which many Americans experienced a zeal for religion. In this religious movement, antebellum health reformers usually linked physical health with moral and spiritual health. One's spiritual well-being went hand in hand with one's physical well-being in the tenets of the Awakening's millennialism; that is, belief in a thousand-year reign of peace and prosperity starting with Christ's return to earth required citizens to possess good moral and physical health. During the Awakening, Baptists and Methodists made particularly strong gains in the South, and by 1860 almost 75 percent of Southern Christians adhered to one of the two denominations (Cobb, *Away* 48). Despite such religiosity, however, different regions of the country continued to disagree over the issue of slavery.

Views of human variety were affected by efforts throughout the nineteenth century to establish the nascent field of anthropology's scientific credentials by means of racial studies and analyses of ethnic, socioeconomic, and gender groups. White American scholars studied Native American tribes and noted physical, social, and cultural differences. They generally deemed Native Americans to be heathens or, at best, "noble savages." Ventures into pseudoscience in the early decades of the nineteenth century, at a time when doctors and medical professionals had not yet articulated professional standards, also included those who claimed to determine one's interior make-up from physical characteristics. Phrenologists studied the structure and bumps on human skulls in order to judge mental faculties, and physiognomists examined facial features in order to judge character. The mid-nineteenth-century scientific revolution set in motion by the works of Charles Darwin provided greater impetus to the focus on differences and classifications. Scientists generally debated the number and types of races but labeled the various cultural groups as savage, barbarian, or civilized. Theories of evolutionary progress put forward by Anglo-Saxon scientists typically placed Anglo-Saxon Protestant groups at the apex of a proposed racial hierarchy. The stereotypes associated with such rankings became rationalized, justified, and entrenched, as the general public assumed the legitimacy of this purportedly scientific research. Belief in the survival-of-the-fittest paradigm was used to rationalize the continual westward expansion of the country and the related taking of Native American land and Mexican territory. With backing from the government, U.S. settlers considered it their God-given right, and their country's Manifest Destiny, to spread their particular form of civilization to supposedly less-advanced peoples. While the skin color with which one was born served as a major determinant of social acceptability, other qualities—middle-class social values and aspirations, standards of decorum, and a particular brand of morality—required diligence.

Some scholars have used the term *whiteness* to describe this standard of acceptability in the new American society. Whiteness afforded particular rights and privileges in American society, which generated a quest for it that persisted into the twentieth century. But whiteness in this sense meant more than skin color. Poor or working-class whites also lacked social capital, and Catholics, Jews, and other non-Protestants failed the test due to their religious convictions. The southern and eastern European immigrant groups that followed the Irish to the United States faced similar strident discrimination: One New York commentator stated, "It is no uncommon thing to see at noon some swarthy Italian . . . resting and dining from his tin kettle, while his brown-skinned wife is by his side" (Jacobson, *Whiteness* 56). Slavs worked the blast furnaces in factories, "which were too damn dirty and too damn hot for a white man" (Arnesen 18). Some Americans described Jews as lecherous peddlers with high-bridged noses, thick lips, and bulging eyes, and regular newspaper cartoons reinforced such stereotypes in the form of caricatures (Diner).

This myriad of changes in the United States altered culture, landscape, and sport and pastimes. While Americans overwhelmingly worked the land on their own farmsteads or as farm laborers in rural areas, an increasing number of people flooded into

1825
- Erie Canal opened
- First trotting track opened (Long Island, New York)

1828–1836
> Andrew Jackson serves as U.S. president

1830s–1840s
- Second Great Awakening occurs

1831
- *A Course of Calisthenics for Young Ladies* published
- *Spirit of the Times* founded by William T. Porter published sports results

1832
- Black Hawk War fought

1833
- Oberlin College founded (first coeducational college)

urban areas of the North to pursue new forms of labor in an industrial context. Thus even as the rural agricultural society persisted in some regions of the country, people in the growing Northeastern cities developed new modes of manufacturing products and new ways of making a living, and these changes provided the context for new sporting forms and consumption of information about sporting activity.

Amidst massive changes in population, land expansion, immigration, and new forms of transportation (such as turnpikes and the first railroad—the Baltimore and Ohio in 1828), white middle-class Americans often looked around and saw problems to solve in order to ensure the growth of American society. Reformers, those men and women who sought to improve society by working both with individuals and with social structures, contemplated new ways to shape American society. Reform movements—such as the antislavery crusade, temperance campaign, the woman's rights movement, education and health reform, and sport campaigns—held some characteristics in common. Antebellum reformers believed in the new beginnings of their democratic society, and no problem was so great that it overwhelmed their optimism. The evil of slavery could be abolished; women could win the right to own property, vote, and earn a living wage; the sin of drunkenness could be eradicated; education for the young could be provided in public schools to develop an educated citizenry for democracy; and physical weakness and bad diet could be mended through appropriate health practices, sport, and exercise.

Health Reformers

As reform activists sought to improve the physical constitution of antebellum Americans, the historical context of the health and sport movement was shaped by gender, socioeconomic, and rural-versus-urban distinctions. In their critique of the social, physical, and moral condition of American citizens, reformers such as Catharine Esther Beecher, Thomas Wentworth Higginson, Sylvester Graham, Dr. William Andrus Alcott, and Mary Gove Nichols—along with other white, middle-class activists—envisioned an ideal society in which robust individual and collective health would serve as the basis of American culture. These reformers found plenty of problems to address in the changing cultural conditions of the urban environment.

In their campaign to save American society by resolving the ill health of its citizenry and providing suitable sporting activities, antebellum health reformers advocated a plan for self-help. Thomas Wentworth Higginson, a soldier and minister who graduated from Harvard Divinity School, supported athletics, favored abolition and woman's rights, and promoted the value of robust health and the benefits of sport in articles published in popular magazines and books. He stated in 1859: "Health is the central luminary of which all the stars that spangle the proud flag of our common country are but proud satellites" (Higginson, "The Murder of the Innocents" 355). Like-minded reformers of health and physical well-being presented good hygiene as a moral obligation and bad hygiene and disease as evil; whether the obligation was to God, the race, the nation, or oneself, failure to fulfill the laws of health constituted immorality. The gospel of health exemplified the religious zeal of antebellum reform activism (Borish, "The Robust Woman"; Cayleff; Whorton).

Dr. William A. Alcott (1798–1859) wrote numerous books and manuals urging both men and women to reform their ways in order to achieve bodily health and pursue sports that he deemed morally appropriate. His popular works—including *The Young Man's Guide* (published in 1833 and in many later editions), *The Young Woman's Guide*, the *Library of Health*, and *The Laws of Health: Or, Sequel to The House I Live In*—addressed health, hygiene, sport, and recreation. In these self-help manuals, Alcott proclaimed his view that for Americans "healthy bodies meant healthy spirits" (Park, "'Embodied Selves'" 88). In *The Young Man's Guide,* Alcott denounced gambling as immoral and clearly identified the sporting activities he viewed as useful: "Gaming is an evil. . . . Let me warn you, then, my young readers,—nay, more, let me *urge* you never to enter this dreadful road." Alcott further asserted that gaming led to a horrible alliance: "I mean gambling, intemperance, and debauchery." Instead of these unwholesome practices, Alcott recommended selected recreation and sporting activities for young men: "Recreations they must have; active recreation, too, in the open air. . . . Some of the most appropriate are playing ball, quoits, ninepins, and other athletic exercises; but in no case for money." He also listed skating as a good outdoor sport (qtd. in Menna 15–17, 19). He also wrote manuals about physical health addressed to young women, which are discussed later in this chapter.

Other health reformers in middle-class antebellum culture urged urbanites to partake of wholesome exercise and pay attention to their stomachs in seeking a healthy diet. Sylvester Graham postulated a more radical idea known as the vital force theory. Graham believed that particular foods excited the nervous system, leading it to possible temptation. He thus linked food and nutrition to morality and declared that people ought to abstain from alcohol, coffee, tea, spices, meat, and other foods that might excite the stomach and harm digestion. To combat the perceived effects of such unhealthy foods, he invented a bland substance known as the Graham cracker. Another reformer interested in improving the body, Mary Gove Nichols, promoted hydropathy, or the water cure, as a means to vigorous health and care of women's health ailments. She described hydropathy in her *Experience in Water-Cure* (1850), asserting that immersing the body in water baths and using cold water to clean the body provided refreshment, and that appropriate exercise and loose-fitting clothing enabled a woman to pursue better health (Cayleff 36).

PEOPLE & PLACES

Almira Phelps

Almira Hart Lincoln Phelps (1793–1884) promoted female education and advocated physical education in her curriculum. Phelps wrote several textbooks and essays that were influential during the nineteenth century, beginning with *Familiar Lectures on Botany* (1829). One of her most significant books, *The Female Student, or Lectures to Young Ladies on Female Education*, first published in 1833, emphasized the importance of physical exercise in addition to academic exercises in the classroom for white middle-class students. Like her counterparts (male and female) in the health reform movement, Phelps included gymnastics for women in her recommended program (Chisholm 738). The following excerpt from *The Female Student*, titled "Health [and] Neatness," suggests Phelps' view of physical education and female gymnastics:

> The term physical education is used in reference to the improvement which can be effected in the human frame and the senses, by a proper system of discipline. . . . The body is an instrument which the mind directs; and as in this state of existence they must dwell together, it becomes of great importance that they should mutually promote the welfare of each other. . . .
>
> Calisthenics [from two Greek words, signifying grace and strength], or female gymnastics is very properly becoming a branch of education. I have, however, seen with regret, that many of you appear to engage in physical exercise with reluctance, as if every moment taken from your studies were time lost. With the view already given of the intimate connection between the mind and body you must be convinced that the latter cannot with impunity be neglected. (qtd. in Menna 20, 21–22)

1835–1841

•1835
• The Great Foot Race (international pedestrian race) is sponsored by John Cox Stevens and held at Long Island's Union Course

•1836
› Battle of the Alamo fought

•1837
• Mount Holyoke (all-female school) requires student exercise
• Financial panic of 1837 occurs

•1837–1838
• "Trail of Tears" (forced relocation of Cherokee tribe) occurs

•1841
• Catharine Beecher publishes *A Treatise on Domestic Economy, for the Use of Young Ladies at Home, and at School*; best seller on women's domestic activities and need for physical health

Proponents of the health and sport movement concluded that the poor habits of urban men and women—be they horrible eating practices that led to dyspepsia, or a failure to practice invigorating outdoor exercise—led to their lack of physical vigor. Instead, activists argued, city folks should pursue the kind of activity that (so the reformers believed) farm folks of the past had engaged in. Higginson had the following to say about his middle-class contemporaries who exhibited frail health: "Dolly the Dairy-Maid is becoming to our children as purely ideal a being as Cinderella" (qtd. in Borish, "Benevolent America: Rural Women" 949). Recurring images appeared during the nineteenth century of the healthy farm family partaking of fresh air and wholesome physical activity; in contrast, urban health reformers decried the physical weakness of contemporary Americans in cities. Higginson concurred with Catharine Beecher's findings in assessing the serious problem of female ill health, but he focused primarily on males in diagnosing the poor health of Americans in the antebellum era. Yet it was not just urbanites and males alone who succumbed to dyspepsia. A farm journalist in *The Plow: A Monthly Journal of Rural Affairs* in 1852, queried, "Who Has Got The Dyspepsia?" and berated, "Don't all speak at once. We know most of you have got it"(qtd. in Borish, "Benevolent America" 321).

Muscular Christianity

In his famous 1858 article "Saints, and Their Bodies," Thomas W. Higginson argued that energetic health went hand in hand with men's productive activities and religious beliefs. A sound mind and body would enable white, urban, middle- and upper-class men to pursue important opportunities in business and politics. Physically and morally fit men could support their families with economic gains and achieve respected positions in a young democracy. In lauding the benefits of wholesome sport for young men, Higginson drew on English sporting traditions. "This powerful and pervasive English love of athletics, first noted in the exclusive public schools, was intensified and gained international fame by the publication of the phenomenally popular *Tom Brown's Schooldays*" (Lucas 51–52). Written by Thomas Hughes, this 1857 work featured young men being instructed in classics for the mind, religion for the spirit, and athletics for the body, based on the positive role assigned to athletics at Rugby School by headmaster Thomas Arnold. Hughes' book "became an instant success on both sides of the Atlantic," and American reformers embraced in this "idealized picture of vigorous boy-life" the benefits of competitive sport, marking a shift in outlook on the body and religion in antebellum American society. The concept of the "noble, idealized Christian athlete" became

Tom Brown's Schooldays, the popular book written in 1857 by English author Thomas Hughes, influenced antebellum American reformers to promote wholesome sport along with spiritual and academic training for young men.

From T. Hughes, 1857, *Tom Brown's Schooldays* (Adamant Media Corporation).

THE CONVERSATION DURING THE MATCH.   P. 342

part of the reform message of those Americans urging sport and physical activity as acceptable and healthful for youth in American culture (Lucas 52). Therefore, white men in positions of political and religious leadership ought to make physical culture part of their own training, according to this outlook on health, sport, and antebellum American life.

For Higginson and like-minded reformers, men ought to be "Muscular Christians," engaging in certain behaviors deemed appropriate for their gender. Muscular Christianity referred to the belief that the body was the temple of God and that cultivating one's body for the glory of God developed morals and built character. The Muscular Christian embodied the best of physical culture and moral virtue in a trilogy of mind, body, and spirit. Higginson's concept, like Beecher's "cult of domesticity" (which prescribed virtue for women, as discussed later in this chapter), revealed the workings of gender ideology. Muscular Christianity embraced muscles, morality, and manliness in athletics. In spreading the gospel of health, Higginson emphasized the need for men to be physically fit in order to pursue their proper roles, and the movement constituted a considerable part of the health reform crusade, in which cultivating the body for a strong constitution and cultivating the mind for knowledge went together. Higginson himself was "America's version of the [M]uscular Christian," reaching a wide audience with his writings and lectures. Indeed, Higginson was a model of the antebellum social-reform outlook. Influenced by "the optimism of the period," he became "a symbol and a champion of the newer and better day and an especial apostle of the new crusade for health and happiness" (Lucas 55).

Higginson posited alarming consequences for men if they ignored the laws of health, and he detailed how sports could resolve this problem. In particular, he criticized the terrible eating and sedentary habits of middle-class urban men, whom he believed were suffering from dyspepsia. Higginson's letters in the 1850s to an archetypal urban businessman, Dolorosus (sad one), elaborated the drastic consequences of this dreaded malady on men's careers. Based on his gendered perspective, Higginson linked Dolorosus' dyspeptic plight to his having to give up his business at age 35 due to ill health. Puny, sickly men, Higginson believed, could not fulfill their roles in the world, and, in place of such supposedly effeminate businessmen, he articulated a vision of hearty men pursuing their career interests. Whether a businessman, politician, or conqueror of the West, success depended on male physical health, and sport promoted the necessary vigor and vitality (Borish, "The Robust Woman").

Proponents of Muscular Christianity touted sport as essential for building character, leadership, competitiveness, courage, teamwork, and discipline. Thus they emphasized sport as a kind of positive training for manhood, one that helped men develop physical and moral fitness that they could transfer into their appropriate pursuits in American society. Reformers such as Higginson, Oliver Wendell Holmes, and Henry David Thoreau (who lived in a small hut at Walden Pond, near Concord, Massachusetts, and authored *Walden*) believed that outdoor sport for boys promoted physical strength and prepared them for manhood (Gems and Borish, "Sports, Colonial Era" 637–643). Holmes encouraged men to engage in sport into their older age. He commented on physical activities in his 1858 series of articles titled "The Autocrat at the Breakfast Table" in the *Atlantic Monthly*. In the following excerpt, Holmes described particular sports that he believed were invigorating for American men and acknowledged the positive view of sport expressed by "a young friend" who had recently written "an admirable article in one of the journals"—a direct reference to Higginson's "Saints, and Their Bodies." Holmes described how sport could play a vital role in a man's life, and he identified his own love for

> one particular form of active exercise and amusement, namely *boating*. For the past nine years, I have rowed about, during a good part of the summer, on fresh or salt water. My present fleet on the river Charles consists of three rowboats. . . .

• **1840s**
  - Immigrants moving westward on Overland Trail

• **1843**
  - First collegiate rowing club formed at Yale

• **1844**

  › Telegraph invented by Samuel Morse; enables rapid communication of news and sporting results
  - New York Yacht Club founded

• **1845**
  - Texas annexed

• **1846–1848**
  - U.S. fights war with Mexico

• **1848**
  - Seneca Falls Woman's Rights Convention held in New York; right to vote for women first proposed
  - German American immigrants founded the first Turner society in the United States
  - California Gold Rush occurs

When I have established a pair of well-pronounced feathering-calluses on my thumbs, when I am training so that I can do my fifteen miles [24 kilometers] at a stretch without coming to grief in any way, when I can perform my mile [1.6 kilometers] in eight minutes or a little less, then I feel as if I had old Time's head in chancery, and could give it to him in my leisure. . . .

I do not deny the attraction of walking. . . . Walking is an immeasurably-fine invention, of which old age ought constantly to avail itself.

Saddle-leather is in some respects even preferable to sole-leather. . . . Riding is good. . . .

Boxing is rough play, but not too rough for a hearty young fellow. . . . I dropped into a gentleman's sparring exhibition only last evening. . . .

But boxing you and I are too old for, I am afraid. I was for a moment tempted, by the contagion of muscular electricity last evening, to try the gloves. . . . (qtd. in Kirsch, *Sports* [Vol. 3] 22, 23–24, 26, 27)

Reformers generally viewed the outdoor sports of rowing, swimming, and vigorous horseback riding as properly manly pursuits for males of various ages. Higginson went so far as to say, "Without a boat one is so much the less a man," and, knowing that owning a boat might pose an economic challenge, he also said, "To own the poorest boat is better than hiring the best" ("Saints" 593). Team sports, including baseball, cricket, and football—"contests of manhood"—were also deemed beneficial to men ("Saints" 594).

Thus Muscular Christianity combined manly athleticism with the quest for fulfillment in the world. Sport became both a training ground for men and, thanks to the reform movement, a more widely accepted form of leisure activity. This program, spearheaded by white, middle-class reformers, stressed physical vigor, moral courage, and religion, and it provided advice to male youth on the healthfulness of sport as an antidote to urban temptations and sedentary ways. Institutions were formed in the burgeoning cities of the Northeast—including the Young Men's Christian Association (YMCA), which appeared in the United States in 1851—to combine muscles and morals in building physical and spiritual health based on Muscular Christianity. The concept of bringing youth under the arm of a religious organization also took hold among Jewish men, who founded the first Young Men's Hebrew Association in the United States in 1854. These influential organizations, and women's roles in them, are given attention in the next chapter, which addresses the expansion of organized sport and the new cultural and physical spaces developed to foster it.

Women and Physical Activity

Everywhere they looked in the burgeoning Northeastern cities (in contrast to the countryside), white, middle-class, Protestant social reformers witnessed an alarming degeneration of female health. As a result, women were failing to fulfill the gender-based urban ideal of "the cult of domesticity" or "the cult of true womanhood" (discussed later in detail). Women's primary role in urban antebellum culture was a multifaceted one as wife, mother, moral guardian, and nurturer, and to fulfill this (biological and social) reproductive role they needed vigorous health. How could a mother make her home a loving haven and train her children to live in an active democracy if she were a perpetual invalid? Female sickness was antithetical to domestic tranquility and child rearing. It took a robust woman to properly inhabit her assigned arena—the domestic sphere—and fulfill her roles in the cult of true womanhood.

Catharine Beecher, a white, middle-class reformer who wrote widely on women's issues in antebellum society, lamented in 1856 that city women were pursuing a path of physical and mental destruction that resulted in "a race of *sickly and deformed pigmies*" ("Health" 400), whereas country women sustained their hardy well-being through domestic labor. Beecher wrote many of her important works during this time—including *A Treatise on Domestic Economy, for the Use of Young Ladies at Home, and at School* (1841), *Letters to the People on Health and Happiness* (1855), and *Calisthenic Exercises for Schools, Families, and Health Establishments* (1856)—and founded the Hartford Female Seminary in 1823 as a forum for disseminating her ideas on domestic and physical education. Beecher set the tone for discussion of the debilitating effect of city life on women's health. Though she saw the urban environment as detrimental to the health of both men and women, in her comments on city life she particularly perceived women's health as "precarious" and demonstrated "the ubiquity of the image that linked women with infirmity in the middle decades of the nineteenth century" (Sklar 205). Thus a sense of urgency pervaded the gospel of health as preached by antebellum American health reformers.

In rhetoric infused with religious fervor and a perfectionist creed, Beecher and other urban reformers urged Americans to heed "the laws of health and happiness." Beecher's deep concern about female health registers in the following pronouncement:

> You, my female friends, may I enter your nursery, your parlor or your kitchen? I have matters of interest to present in which everyone of you have a close personal concern. . . . [I]f a plan for *destroying female health* in all the ways in which it could most effectively be done were drawn up it would be exactly the course which is now pursued by a large portion of this nation. . . .
>
> The *standard of health* among American women is so low that few have a correct idea of *what a healthy woman is.* (*Letters* 7–8, 122)

Health reformers such as Beecher and William Alcott, who wrote self-help books on health and contributed articles to antebellum periodicals on health and exercise, paid particular attention to social class as a factor in the poor health of city women. In Beecher's ideology, health was a problem both for wealthy, leisured women and for poor, working women. The urban environment of both groups threatened their well-being.

In Beecher's view, upper-class ladies rejected productive housework as a means of sustaining physical vigor, choosing instead to employ domestic servants, and as a result they were afflicted with sickly constitutions due to a lack of physical activity. Beecher tried to dispel the prejudice, rooted in social-class mores, against middle- and upper-class women performing their own housework. She advocated domestic work as one possible cure for female maladies. What better way to strengthen the muscles and invigorate one's body than through active domestic exercise? Daughters gained physical fitness in the employments of "sweeping, dusting, care of furniture and beds . . . and nice cooking." According to Beecher, a young lady who "will spend two hours a day at the wash-tub, or with a broom, is far more likely to have rosy cheeks, a finely-moulded form, and a delicate skin, than one who lolls all day in her parlor or chamber, or only leaves girt in tight dresses to make fashionable calls." In sum, Beecher praised "the gentle exercise and *amusement* of housekeeping" (qtd. in Borish, "The Robust Woman" 143). Beecher gathered anecdotal evidence to support her case. She asked married ladies she met in her travels to list the names of women in their community who were healthy. The sad picture that emerged showed few if any healthy women. Yet her findings were based on upper-class, urban women,

1849

> Tom Hyer fights Yankee Sullivan (pictured) in bare-fisted boxing match

1851

• Young Men's Christian Association appears in United States

1854

• Young Men's Hebrew Association founded in Baltimore

• Gadsden Purchase made

1858

• Muscular Christianity movement in the United States emerges with Thomas W. Higginson writing famous article, "Saints, and Their Bodies," promoting moral and physical health

Catharine Beecher promoted health reform and physical education at her female schools, emphasizing women's proper gender role in antebellum American culture.

Harriet Beecher Stowe Center, Hartford, CT.

who devoted little time to physical exercise. Moreover, some women may not have volunteered information about their own health. For some upper-rank women, so-called fashionable diseases of ill health may have served at times as a way to escape domestic duties.

Working-class women, on the other hand, endured horrible conditions detrimental to their well-being. Their bodies were debilitated by long hours spent working in noisy, unventilated rooms. Indeed, factory life proved disastrous for female fitness. Thus, Beecher's message was that all ranks of women in the city seemingly faced health complaints and needed healthful physical activity to improve their physical well-being. In her view, urban female physical weakness required a female solution—a gender-based program of sport and physical exercise.

In contrast, health champions Beecher and Higginson idealized the health of farm men and women. Farm women, in particular, embodied perfect health, according to these reformers, who envisioned farm life as bucolic and health-promoting for females, particularly when compared with the lives of sickly urban women. Hence, a rural–urban dichotomy emerged in the beliefs of these reform-minded advice givers, who lamented the perceived passing of a golden age in America's agricultural past. They posited a clear difference—in terms of health and happiness—between the active, outdoor life of rural farm families and the sedentary life of urban folks in their own generation.

Not all, however, believed that farm life was ideal. In their urban boosterism touting the technological, commercial, and sporting advantages of the city, some journalists criticized farm life as inferior to modern city life. Farm journalists vigorously responded by expressing their disdain for the corruptions and wealthy trappings of the city that enticed farm youth and jeopardized their moral and physical health. The farm press constructed positive images of rural women's health, such as an 1868 description in the *Massachusetts Ploughman* of a farmer's daughter with "the glow of health upon her cheek" ("The Farmer's Daughter" n. pag.).

In particular, the home-leaving of farm boys and girls alarmed reporters of New England agriculture, and the farm press emphasized the well-being of daughters as a factor in rural depopulation. Many rural daughters welcomed the chance to leave the farm, with its fatiguing domestic work, seeking instead to gain access to middle-class urban cultural experiences. The agricultural press featured common farmers who defended their agricultural way of life and wanted young women to remain on the homestead, but many young women wanted to escape the countryside. Rural women who gave advice in farm journals tended to side with farm girls who portrayed the health-depleting tasks of their life on the farm. This view of farm life stood in stark contrast to the idealized myth of farm life filled with health-giving physical exercise, as envisioned by urban health reformers such as Beecher and Alcott, and in contrast to the image of farm daughters' vim and vigor endorsed by farm men. Writing in 1846 for the *American Agriculturist,* a woman correspondent advocated that these girls "need reforming mentally and physically" (Borish, "Benevolent America: Rural Women" 950). Yet in the debate on the physical condition of farm daughters, farmers wanted to maintain the status quo. While more progressive farm men and journal editors promoted improved farming methods to enhance farm life, they criticized the rising expectations of farm girls who sought cultural options, as well as better physical health and physical recreation, away from their domestic labors. Some farm girls did leave the countryside to work in the newly established textile mills such as those in Lowell, Massachusetts, to earn some money for their families or themselves and gain some freedom from the rigors and restraints they faced as farm daughters in everyday rural life. Historian Thomas Dublin noted that between 1830 and 1860, "tens of thousands of young, single women . . . left their hill country farms in northern New England and sought employment in the expanding factory towns" (3). Some New England farm daughters worked in the mills for only a few years until marriage, and others left the mills to find better employment opportunities in the city. For young farm women, the mills "offered individual self-support, enabled women to enjoy urban amenities not available in their rural communities, and gave them a measure of economic and social independence from their families" (Dublin 23–24). Farm women who stayed behind in the countryside were often aware of the tensions between the rural and the urban worlds as written about in letters by their female kin and friends who worked in the mill towns, as well as in the rural and urban periodicals addressing the physical condition of women in antebellum American culture.

Physical Education

Physical education became an integral component of the curriculum at Catharine Beecher's schools for young women. The prescribed gender roles for young middle-class women and girls contoured the remedy of sporting activities and physical exercise promoted by Beecher and her fellow female education reformers. In 1831 a treatise titled *Course of Calisthenics for Young Ladies*, "purported to have been written by an American mother, was published in Hartford, Connecticut" with the author "designated only by the letter 'M'" (Park, "'Embodied Selves'" 77). Some chroniclers of physical education have attributed this volume to Catharine Beecher; in the book, she urged young women to participate in "free and light gymnastics and musical drill" (qtd. in Hartwell 29).

Beecher introduced calisthenics at her first institute, Hartford Female Seminary, in 1823, and girls at her schools generally performed calisthenics for improving physical health. Taught by a female physical education instructor, such exercises were often designed with a therapeutic orientation to strengthen specific parts of a woman's body.

Beecher's *Calisthenic Exercises for the Schools, Families, and Health Establishments* featured many descriptions and illustrations of exercises appropriate for women.

Reprinted from C. Beecher, 1856, *Physiology and calisthenics for schools and families* (New York: Harper & Brothers).

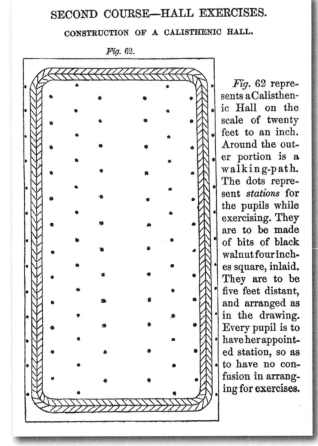

SECOND COURSE—HALL EXERCISES.

CONSTRUCTION OF A CALISTHENIC HALL.

Fig. 62.

Fig. 62 represents a Calisthenic Hall on the scale of twenty feet to an inch. Around the outer portion is a walking-path. The dots represent *stations* for the pupils while exercising. They are to be made of bits of black walnut four inches square, inlaid. They are to be five feet distant, and arranged as in the drawing. Every pupil is to have her appointed station, so as to have no confusion in arranging for exercises.

Design of a Calisthenics Hall in Beecher's *Calisthenic Exercises for the Schools, Families, and Health Establishments*

Reprinted from C. Beecher, 1856, *Physiology and calisthenics for schools and families* (New York: Harper & Brothers).

Beecher assured critics that this regimented form of activity would not injure women's health, and she also faced ideological hurdles in promoting calisthenics and sport for women. Contemporary definitions of femininity included a lack of robustness and physical vigor, which limited female participation in sport and public activities. To put it another way, the kind of physical strength needed in order to achieve total health and autonomy in the public world was viewed as an unnatural condition for women and one incompatible with femininity (Verbrugge; Vertinsky, *The Eternally Wounded Woman*). Beecher's program of activity went in tandem with acceptable gender views of women's physical well-being for white, middle-class, urban Protestant females. As part of reform in the Antebellum Age, such physical activities for women as those endorsed by Beecher did not challenge gender prescriptions of woman's sphere. Later women's schools would build on Beecher's model of sport and physical education in advocating appropriate gymnastic training and calisthenics as suitable for the female gender, such as the early sport programs at Smith College, Mt. Holyoke, Vassar, and other educational institutions for women.

Outdoor Sports

Health advisors proclaimed that outdoor sporting forms offered important benefits to women who were supposedly lolling in their urban households. They praised walking and horseback riding, for example, for their power to invigorate women in the fresh open air. So, too, gardening provided health and aesthetic dividends for the woman and her family. Catharine Beecher advised women to maintain their physical vigor as well as to engage in sporting forms fitting for the female gender. Beecher urged women to exercise outdoors in what she termed a "Temple of Health," with "a variety of pleasant walks, and shades, and flowers, to attract and please in the summer months, and other arrangements provided for outdoor sports and exercises in winter" (*Letters* 169). Ice skating in public parks and private ponds proved a popular sport and an invigorating pastime for women and girls (as explored later in this chapter).

At times, those of middle- and upper-rank status enjoyed games of croquet, which offered healthy and social interactions in a coeducational setting. By the 1860s, in fact, croquet had become a fashionable recreational craze, but rampant cheating by women who moved or concealed the ball with their hoop skirts apparently diminished the pleasure for male players who played to win (Sterngass). The middle-class press wrote about croquet and noted the appeal of the sport for women, as in the following humorous poem published in *Harper's Weekly* in 1867:

Women's Physical Education in Early Nineteenth-Century Europe

The European "grandfathers" of gymnastics (among them Johann Christoph Friedrich Guts-Muths, Friedrich Ludwig Jahn, and Per Henrik Ling) focused exclusively on physical exercises for the male sex, but women and girls were increasingly being discovered as target groups for physical education from the 1820s onward. Amid the political and social changes that followed the French Revolution—including the growing gender-based division of labor (ascribing to women the role of housewife and mother and to men the role of breadwinner employed outside the home)—the health of the supposedly "weaker sex" began to attract the interest of male doctors and educators. Since women were barred from higher education and academic professions, however, they took virtually no part whatsoever in professional discussions about education and physical exercise for the female sex.

Among the first to champion physical exercise for girls was Phokion Heinrich Clias (1782–1854), who trained Swiss troops, worked for three years as a captain in the British Army, and became superintendent of physical training at the royal military and naval schools. In 1841, he was invited to France to work with schools and the military in Paris. Clias conducted numerous courses of physical training, including courses for girls and women. His book *Kalisthenie* (1829), in which he wrote about his experiences in London, was a landmark in the history of women's physical education. Its influence can be attributed in large part to the emphasis Clias placed on gentle exercises to enhance female grace and beauty.

Clias' successor in London was Gustavus Hamilton, who had already published his "Elements of Gymnastics for Boys and Calisthenics for Young Ladies" in 1827. That year also saw the publication of G. P. Voarino's "A Treatise on Calisthenic Exercises, Arranged for the Private Tuition of Young Ladies," which may well be the first book exclusively devoted to women's physical exercise. Like other educators, the author emphasized that gymnastics could improve the shape of the body as well as prevent and even cure "bodily infirmities" and deformities (Todd 11).

J. A. Beaujeu prescribed for his female pupils much more complex and strenuous exercises than Clias and Voarino. His motto was "Head up, legs down," and exercises such as the "flying course" required considerable strength and effort. In his "Treatise on Gymnastic Exercises, Or Calisthenics for the Use of Young Ladies," published in 1828, he described exercises that had been introduced at the Seminary for the Education of Young Ladies in Dublin in 1824. Besides his work at the Royal Hibernian School, where the sons and daughters of military personnel were educated (and where the curriculum included physical education), Beaujeu and his wife ran a "female gymnasium" (Todd 11). Madame Beaujeu also took calisthenics to the United States, where she opened a school in Boston in 1841.

In the 1830s, additional works appeared (including that of Johann Adolf Ludwig Werner in Germany) which stressed grace and graceful exercise. By contrast, the French doctor Antoine Bureaud-Riofrey laid emphasis on strength and stamina. In his "Physical Education Especially Adapted to Young Ladies" (published in Paris in 1835, in a German edition in 1837, and in English in 1838), he recommended 10 hours of daily exercise for 7-year-old girls and 5 hours daily for 14-year-old girls. Exercises included walking, dancing, and swimming, as well as free exercises, weight training, and activities with batons or dumbbells or on the horizontal bar.

European literature on girls' and women's physical exercise and education was also read with interest in America, with calisthenics finding especial favor. The more vigorous physical activities, however, such as those recommended by Beaujeu and Bureaud-Riofrey, were suited to neither the ideals of femininity nor the notions of propriety and decorum to be found in the New World.

Information from Todd, Jan. "The Classical Ideal and Its Impact on the Search for Suitable Exercise: 1774–1830." *Iron Game History* 2.4: 6–16.

Given—the smoothest of lawns,

With the turf closely cut and elastic;

Given—the fairest of girls,

With spirits enthusiastic;

Given—a number of swells,

Of the type most delightful and pleasing;

Given—sides made up of these,

With the usual chaffing and teasing;

Given—the hoops duly placed,

And the mallets and balls all selected;

Given—the game has commenced,

Then this to find out you're expected:

What length of time will it be—

Allowing for feints and pretenses—

Ere, in the course of the game,

"Spooning" in earnest commences?

("A Croquet Problem" 583)

For the most part, however, reformers put forward noncompetitive individual sports as the favored therapy to correct the health problems of women and girls. For many women linked to the domestic arena, sporting activities such as walking and

A game of croquet, a popular sporting pastime and social outing for middle-class Americans.

Photo courtesy of *Harper's Weekly*, Sept. 8, 1866.

gardening could be enjoyed within the domestic context—a crucial factor in antebellum American culture, with its gender ideology holding that women should not participate in the public, male world of competition and spectators.

Bloomer Costume

Whether in urban or rural life, some women asserted their right to wear the new "bloomers" sporting costume to improve their health and participate in outdoor exercise for increased mobility and health. Elizabeth Smith Miller introduced the costume in the spring of 1851 for comfort while gardening. She wrote that "Turkish trousers to the ankle with a skirt reaching some four inches below the knee, were substituted for the heavy, untidy and exasperating old garment" (i.e., her long skirt). After adopting this costume, Miller went to Seneca Falls, New York, to visit her cousin Elizabeth Cady Stanton, a woman's rights activist. Stanton "had so long deplored with me our common misery in the toils of this crippling fashion that this means of escape was hailed with joy and she at once joined me in wearing the new costume" (qtd. in McClymer 47).

Also joining in was Stanton's friend and neighbor, Amelia Jenks Bloomer, editor of the reform newspaper *The Lily*, who advocated the costume in her paper, after which, as Smith recalled, "the dress was christened with her name." However, while wearing the bloomer costume, Elizabeth Smith Miller and Mrs. Stanton endured ridicule, as Smith Miller recounted: "We endured, in various places much gaping curiosity and the harmless jeering of street boys." She asserted, "All hail the day when we shall have a reasonable and beautiful dress that shall encourage exercises on the road and in the field—that shall leave us the free use of our limbs" (qtd. in McClymer 47–48). Thus bloomers became a key issue in the movements for woman's rights and dress and health reform. Amelia Bloomer wore the new costume and published an image of herself wearing it in 1851. It avoided the risks of tight-laced fashions (such as corsets which restricted waistlines to a mere 17 inches) that injured women's bodily health, as well as the typical skirts sweeping the ground. Appropriate shoes—rather than fashionable, painful ones—also formed part of the looser-fitting costume, which became increasingly popular. An item published in the *Granite Farmer* in 1851 informed readers that "[t]he Bloomer style of ladies' dresses, which consists of a short frock and Turkish trousers, seems to be gaining ground fast in all directions" (qtd. in Borish, "Benevolent America: Rural Women" 954).

Woman in the bloomer costume, designed to promote freedom of mobility in physical activity for women.
CULVER PICTURES

The bloomer costume spurred heated discussion about the appropriateness of antebellum women wearing a male garment (trousers) in public view, and, more broadly, about women's health, physical emancipation, and power in farm life. Several farm women offered an endorsement of bloomers, joining their urban sisters in wearing this new kind of clothing that challenged male authority. Wearing the new outfit, farm women conveyed their desire to engage in physical activity with suitable attire for sturdy health and greater mobility.

Rural Sporting Practices

Sport and physical recreation for rural men and women went hand in hand with physical health within a gendered context. Some physical amusements on the farm proved practical for both men and women, such as swimming, walking, and horseback riding. In other sporting forms, farm men and women might participate in gender-separate recreation, such as fishing and the winter sports of skating and sledding. Yet leisure time to pursue such physical activities often belonged more to the farm men, who, unlike farm women, were not tied to the domestic labors of the farm (indoors and out), including child-care responsibilities and household tasks that often lasted late into the evening. Farm men typically spent their day outdoors working at hard, dirty, physical tasks, but they were at least outside in the fresh air and away from the domestic work spaces that were often sloppy, odorous, and full of kitchen refuse. Farm women, on the other hand, spent long hours at indoor tasks, shut up in the farmhouse, which restricted their opportunity to partake of the same pure outdoor air. A farm woman contributing to the agricultural press acknowledged that many farm women typically remained tied to indoor and smelly domestic chores. She commented on the gender-related dimensions of the fresh-air question, asserting in 1845 that "it was the height of folly for a farmer's wife to think of rambling in the woods for flowers, and that it was perfectly useless to inhale the air . . . unless she ran out in a great hurry to see what was the matter with the chickens, or to look up eggs for some purpose of cookery" (qtd. in E. M. C. 287–288).

Rural health reformers in antebellum New England argued that farm dwellers needed certain kinds of physical exercise in the open air, not health-depleting labors, to better their physical vigor. One journalist, writing in the 1852 *New England Farmer*, declared, "It is quite a mistake to consider the labor of the day as equivalent to exercise." He believed that "[a]thletic sports and out of door exercises, of every description, are no less conducive to the morals, and happiness, than they are necessary to the perfect health of the young of both sexes" ("Physical Recreation" 483–484). In fact, health reform that valued healthful physical exercise and sporting activity became part of the larger reform activism in both rural and urban areas as several health proponents participated in other reforms of the antebellum era.

In some areas, baseball bridged the gap between urban and rural life due to its being played in the open air, on green pastures, with no industrial clock to determine the length of the game. Canadians in the Ontario region recorded baseball games as early as 1838, and by the 1840s baseball clubs proliferated throughout the eastern United States, competing against each other despite a variety of rules and field configurations. The growth of baseball, explored in the next chapter, would accelerate by 1858, when clubs formed the National Association of Base Ball Players and adopted the New York version of the rules.

Agricultural Fairs

In the early 1800s, in order to prepare them as future farmers, boys in rural areas competed in contests at agricultural fairs by demonstrating their farming skills. The first agricultural fair was held in 1810 in Pittsfield, Massachusetts, and others soon followed. New England agricultural societies initially sponsored local fairs, originated by gentleman farmer Elkanah Watson, "father of the agricultural fair," who wanted to spread agricultural improvement to ordinary farmers of Massachusetts. In 1807, after Watson exhibited two merino sheep, he recalled that "[m]any farmers, and even women, were excited by curiosity to attend this first novel, and humble exhibition." By 1811, the Berkshire Agricultural Society incorporated in order to foster the interests of common farmers (Neely 21, 61; Borish, "'A Fair'").

The public spectacle of the agricultural fair—a special leisure event on the farm family's calendar—featured men and boys, and women and girls, engaging in certain recreations compatible with gender-based expectations in field events (plowing and mechanical arts) and domestic arts, respectively, though at times women bucked conventions in their sporting behavior. Farm women and men, as well as agricultural reformers and male promoters, all participated in agricultural fairs, which provided a venue for leisure, sporting events, and celebration of agricultural pride. Thus these annual fall exhibitions, lasting three or four days, served as social, educational, and recreational events for the farming community as part of the agricultural reform movement in the early and middle nineteenth century. Fairgoers enjoyed the break from their laborious routines and the chance to display their physical skills. By the middle decades of the century, country fairs flourished at the county, state, and regional levels in what constituted a "golden age of the agricultural fair" (Butterfield 289–297). Male and female participation in New England agricultural fairs changed over time—from the inception of the fair in the early nineteenth century as a practical event for the farming community to a more complex leisure- and profit-oriented event in the century's middle years—along with shifts in the workings of gender in rural society.

In the context of the fair, farm women participated as both spectators and competitors in public leisure activities that were usually the prerogative of men in the gendered conventions of farm life. In the pattern of activities at the fair, women's integrated work and leisure experiences persisted when they displayed their domestic products. Farm men, however, claimed power as judges at the fair, conferring awards of excellence to farm women who displayed their cultural power in bread and butter making, home manufactures, and fine arts. Some women challenged male authority at the fair and competed in nontraditional contests, such as female equestrianism, thus extending their interest in competition to the horse track. Such contests placed women in forms of competition that contrasted with the socially constructed images of feminine sporting behaviors; women's physical recreations deemed controversial at the agricultural fair clashed with the kinds of physical activities deemed appropriate for them in rural health-reform campaigns. Juxtaposing domestic arts competitions with the physical display of the female body in horse racing generated controversy about gendered recreational practices in rural New England. Rural improvers wanted women to compete publicly for prizes only through the display of domestic skills. Such competitions integrated work and recreation yet extended farm women's proficiency in the domestic sphere to the public sphere, where they could gain social prestige and recognition. One rural New England booster encouraged farm women in this way: "[F]air ones of the dairy, and all ye tidy housewives, that give honor and reputation to Yankeedom, the time draws near for you to show *your* prowess; yes, to exhibit to the world how important to the farmer is the farmer's wife" (Thomas n. pag.). In contrast, women who raced horses around the track, as men did, were criticized by agricultural traditionalists.

More generally, the agricultural press exhibited divided opinion on the "Horse Question" at the fair. Some farmers worried that farm men and women attending the horse track were faced with temptations that should be challenged in the age of antebellum reform, such as gambling, drinking, and other immoral behaviors. Agriculturists preaching improvement in exhibitions of farm life clashed with profit-seeking fair promoters who wished to capitalize on the popularity of horse races, which lured large crowds, often at the expense of more mundane exhibitions of large pumpkins, plump cattle, and horticultural splendors (Borish, "'A Fair'"). The addition of women's horse races increased the number of patrons at the fairgrounds and fanned the controversy for some farm progressives who believed it was not a woman's right or place to ride horses for prizes.

One critic who joined the chorus condemning the appearance of women on the racecourse put it this way: "Horse-jockeys, horse-fanciers, fast horses and 'fast women' have been the most conspicuous objects on most of the 'fair grounds,' the present season." He went on to compare the parade of female equestrians to the parade of domestic animals:

Our daughters as well as our horses, girls of tender age, girls of larger growth, and even wives, as well as fillies, pacers and breeding mares, are brought on to the course for exhibitions, and gazed at, and criticized by thousands, and praised and flattered, and caressed, for the same reasons as the animals which they drive, beauty of skin, and form and limb, and grace of action. ("Cattle Shows" 14–15)

One racing opponent put it this way: "Will not these females soon answer the description of a 'fast woman'?" Such advice givers deemed horseback riding beneficial to women's health and acceptable within their gender conventions but clearly drew the line at seeing women ride competitively for premiums ("Female Jockeys" 142). Female horse racers at the agricultural fair paraded their bodies in sport, which in many advisors' minds pushed too hard against the usual gender dimensions of women's contests in rural society.

Despite these concerns, women persisted in taking part in such public contests. In California, women displayed their equestrian skills in races and exhibitions, even flouting convention by riding in the straddle position common to males, rather than sidesaddle as expected of women. By 1858, a national equestrian convention for women was held at Union Course on Long Island, and four thousand spectators attended. Substantial prizes included a $500 piano for the winner of one race (Kirsch, *Sports* [Vol. 3] 187–191). Thus horse racing not only questioned gender roles but also highlighted regional differences as discussed in the next section.

Horse Racing and Harness Racing

Southerners bred their horses for speed, while Northerners favored endurance, but the two regions disagreed, of course, on far more than horse breeding, as abolitionism and industrialization threatened the plantation lifestyle of the South. Such differences played out in the sporting world in 1823, when Northern industrialist Cornelius Van Ranst, owner of the racehorse American Eclipse, accepted a challenge from North Carolinian William Ransom Johnson, owner of Sir Henry, to pit the two horses against each other in a best-of-three match over a 4-mile (6.4-kilometer) course for a purse of $20,000. A betting frenzy ensued, as supporters of each horse wagered astronomical sums. One Virginia plantation owner bet five years of cotton production on the

Agricultural fairs in the nineteenth century provided a place for agricultural contests and festivities for farm families.

Image courtesy of Library of Congress, LC-DIG-pga-00607.

Southern champion, while a Northern cotton mill owner countered with three years of his profits on American Eclipse. Congressman John Randolph wagered $10,000 and his entire wardrobe on the Northern horse (Twombly 40). The contest took place at the Union racetrack on Long Island before a reported sixty thousand spectators, with the horses splitting the first two heats before American Eclipse emerged as the winner. In the following years, such intersectional horse races intensified, as did the North–South regional conflict.

Harness racing also emerged as a significant sport in antebellum American culture. Historian Melvin Adelman judged harness racing to be the first modern sport in America, due to its organization and commercialization, which began in the New York metropolitan area: "Sportsmen began racing their 'roadsters' (as street trotters came to be called) because it provided them with an amusement which was convenient, participatory and relatively inexpensive. Third Avenue quickly emerged as New York's major trotting area. . . . Early nineteenth century trotting consisted almost exclusively of . . . impromptu contests, [but] permanent structures began to emerge" ("The First" 8). Horse racing became so popular that newspapers, such as William T. Porter's *Spirit of the Times,* began reporting the results in 1831, and race results and statistics from the harness track became a key component of modern sport during the antebellum period.

The interest in trotting races intensified with the formation of the New York Trotting Club in 1824 and 1825 on Long Island as the first organized trotting club in America. The press reported on techniques used by the club to improve the breed, efforts to promote the sport, the construction of a course for harness racing sponsored by the club, and racing matches between the New York club and groups from other Northeastern locales (Adelman, "The First" 9). In a November 17, 1847, trotting race, Black Hawk faced Jenny Lind in a match involving $500 mile (1.6-kilometer) heats at the Union Course. Trotting races in the Northeast generated interest among horsemen and race fans alike, and, in a distinct departure from thoroughbred racing, which was steeped in the wealth of the elite men and families who owned thoroughbreds in the United States, "[m]ost of the owners of trotting horse and the proprietors of trotting tracks, however, appear to have been middle class in origin. The different social origins affected the entire tone of the two turf sports . . . [, and] harness racing enticed a broader segment of the populace" (Adelman, "The First" 13).

The middle-class status and decorum of the gentlemen who owned the trotters increased the visibility of harness racing and spectators enjoyed watching the trotters race at the tracks. Thoroughbred horse racing faced hard times during the economic depression that began in 1837, and harness racing tended to generate new sporting interests in American horses. Adelman has stated, "As thoroughbred racing collapsed

Advertisements for harness-racing matches informed spectators of upcoming races and purses for the winning horse.
© CORBIS

The race between trotting horses Black Hawk and Jenny Lind, 1847.

Image courtesy of Library of Congress, LC-USZ62-7745.

throughout the North in the decade following the Depression of 1837, the sporting press took increasing note of the activities of the trotting horse. . . . In contrast to the aristocratic and foreign thoroughbred, the trotter was perceived as the democratic, utilitarian, and, by logical extension, the American horse" ("The First" 10). Owning trotters for the harness track symbolized a middle-rank businessman's respectability and social standing in the community. In Bridgeport, Connecticut, Nathaniel Wheeler, who gained his middle-class position as an industrialist in the sewing machine industry, owned trotting horses and underscored the importance of the sport for gentlemen.

The growth of harness racing after the economic depression increased the popularity of sport in the middle of the nineteenth century. Observers of the races included rural and urban sport enthusiasts. As Adelman has explained, "Harness racing surged to the forefront of not only the turf world, but modern sport in general, because more than any other sport of the day it captured the flow of the American experience. In common with other forms of popular entertainment, the emergence of trotting as a spectator sport was a product of the two dynamic forces—urbanization and economic expansion—transforming and modernizing American life" ("The First" 14).

Rise of Agricultural and Sporting Journalism

The United States was a mostly agricultural nation in the antebellum period, and the focus on betterment of farming spurred development of the agricultural press, with attention to the health of farm families and improved techniques for farming. One such publication, the *American Farmer*, was founded in 1819 in Baltimore, Maryland, by John Stuart Skinner, "the pioneer and father of American farm journalism" (Demaree 23). Devoted to improving agriculture, the journal covered numerous aspects of agriculture and rural economy. Of particular note, Skinner developed two special departments in the *American Farmer:* a sporting section and a women's section. Skinner regularly included articles and advice on sport, recreation, and physical health for farm men and women, and his propensity for exercise, recreation, and sporting pursuits—along with his own belief that such activities were essential to the well-rounded American—led

PEOPLE & PLACES

Nathaniel Wheeler

Nathaniel Wheeler cofounded the Wheeler and Wilson Manufacturing Company and served as company president. Wheeler was a self-made man in the nineteenth century, using technological know-how from his work as a carriage manufacturer in Watertown, Connecticut, to build a very successful business in the sewing machine industry. Wheeler and inventor Allen B. Wilson established their company in Watertown with patents for a sewing machine, and in 1856 the company moved to Bridgeport and expanded its sewing machine production.

Wheeler lived in his spacious home with his wife, Mary Crissy Wheeler, and their children. In her domestic activities and philanthropic work, Mary Wheeler exemplified the "cult of domesticity" in antebellum American life for middle- and upper-class women, while Nathaniel Wheeler embodied the sporting gentleman displaying his wealth in business and leisure. Nathaniel Wheeler owned several trotters in his stable at the Bridgeport home and also possessed carriages. As Wheeler and Wilson Manufacturing Company continued to make profits, Wheeler could enjoy various leisure activities, such as harness racing and sleigh and carriage racing (*Communities*). Thus Wheeler and Wilson Manufacturing Company (later taken over by the Singer Company) provides an example both of the prosperity that the owners and managers of new technology possessed in the nineteenth century and of the display of status through sporting activity.

him to increase the coverage of sport in the *American Farmer* between 1819 and 1824, and eventually (in 1825) to launch a section titled "Sporting Olio"—that is, sporting miscellany (Berryman). The column proved popular, and, in a representative sentiment, Skinner opined in 1825, "How much better to repair to the fields, the woods or the neighbouring streams, at the close of a week of hard study or sedentary labour, and there spend the afternoon in gunning, fishing, swimming, bowling at ninepins, pitching quoits, etc., according to one's fancy and the season, than to abuse whole days in *militia mustering!* frequenting gaming-houses, whiskey drinking, etc." (qtd. in Demaree 33). In "Sporting Olio," Skinner shared his love of outdoor sport, covered horse racing, and gave information on breeds of animals of interest to agriculturalists.

Skinner also established the "Ladies' Department" in the *American Farmer* as a place to deliver articles and practical material for rural women—farm mothers and farm daughters—in order to make his journal of interest to the whole farm family. In this department, Skinner wanted to present "subjects for the rational amusement and instruction" of feminine readers (qtd. in Demaree 33). Skinner printed articles on rural women's health, recipes and food preparation for the family, outdoor exercise, and recreation. The *American Farmer* published articles on reform issues "and the rise in popularity of outdoor sports" (Berryman and Brislin 60). Later in the antebellum period, other farm journals followed his lead by introducing their own columns of advice on the physical health and exercise of farm women as well as men. Thus Skinner provided an important forum for rural Americans and others who paid attention to the condition of farming in antebellum American society and integrated information about good health and good farming for rural readers in the pages of his magazine.

Skinner eventually sold *American Farmer* but continued to capitalize on his sporting and horse-racing interests by creating *American Turf Register and Sporting Magazine* in 1829. This sports journal became the first of its type in the United States. In fact, Skinner's magazine "was more influential than any other factor of its day in improving the breed of American horses" (Demaree 36).

The editors of the *Homestead* agricultural journal in Connecticut sought to address the needs of rural, middle-class supporters of what they called "improved farming." As agricultural historian Sally McMurry has explained, progressive farm men and women of the rural middle-class read agricultural journals for "book farming," to gain the advice of agricultural reformers promoting scientific and profit-oriented farming. These rural journals "aimed for an audience of practical farmers" (McMurry 1–2). In this vein, *Homestead* proprietor Mason C. Weld and his fellow editors wanted to dispel prejudice against book farming and communicate information to genuine farm men and women. The magazine aimed to help farmers "put the farm in trim and the cattle in good case, and [make] the door yard bloom with flowers and the garden laugh with vegetables" ("To Our Friends" 787).

Practical farming information was accompanied by material on physical health and sporting activity, as well as advertisements of products intended for use in work and play. Advertisements (pitching items such as horse-keeping gear) and horse-racing results appeared alongside entries with titles such as "On the Preservation of Health," "Bathing or Washing in Winter," and "Recreation." Another topic was the well-known Sylvester Graham diet of brown bread, debated by both rural and urban folks. One reader of the *Yankee Farmer* declared his distaste for the touted Graham diet: "Where are the *Grahamites*? frozen, starved or grown so lean that they have been blown away" ("Where are the *Grahamites*?" 2–3). In short, some viewed it as anything but a useful diet for sport and physical activity.

Thus the printing press made it possible for sports journalism to reach both city residents and those in outlying rural regions. Agricultural journals provided a forum for discussing sport and physical education, and their editors wished to promote American nationalism by boosting the well-being of the nation's citizens, many of them residing in rural areas. In addition to *American Farmer* and *American Turf Register,* information about healthful sports was spread by such publications as *Spirit of the Times, American Agriculturist,* and regional periodicals including the *New England Farmer* and the *Boston Cultivator.* These publications formed the beginning of what sport historian Stephen Hardy has described as "an industry of providers, even though the production of sporting goods appears to have lagged behind the production of formal ideology." As part of larger commercial trends in sport and leisure in the early decades of the nineteenth century, these periodicals were important in promoting the practice of sporting pursuits and the associated economic activity: "Consumers who could *read about* sports in specialty publications tended to *play* sports with goods furnished through homecrafting, merchant importers, or local artisans" (Hardy, "Adopted" 134).

As Americans moved increasingly to urban regions, so did the providers of sports information in an expanding market and a culture ripe for communications about sport and sport-related products. Immigrants to the city continued to read magazines, including newer urban ones. Numerous city newspapers provided coverage (listing statistics and records and recounting noteworthy feats) of horse racing, harness racing, ball games, pugilism matches, and other sporting pastimes. Such publications in the early and middle decades of the nineteenth century included the *New York Herald* and the *New York Times.* During this period, "The editors of the major sports journals wielded enormous power over the antebellum sporting scene. William T. Porter, editor of the *Spirit of the Times,* and John Stuart Skinner, editor of *American Turf Register and Sporting Magazine,* influenced the nature and direction of sport reporting and writing, cultivated a sporting audience, and shaped the development and appeal of sport prior to the Civil War" (Menna 35).

Sports journalism of the early and mid-nineteenth century included articles that advocated development of a more robust American citizenry though exercise and sport. This attitude went hand in hand with the growth of modern sport, as discussed in chapter 4. For example, here is an excerpt from an article in the *American Turf Register and Sporting Magazine* titled "On Exercise" (November 1838):

Exercise prevents disease, or rather perhaps fortifies the body against it. If good health were a commodity that could be brought like a box of "Morrison's pills" or other health-conferring nostrums, who is there that would not hurry to the mart and purchase eagerly, even though they were obliged to swallow that box as well as its contents at one unsavory mouthful? . . . [T]ake exercise at least once a day, so as to excite the natural heat, and other functions of the body; take that exercise which has the most general effect upon the system, and which induces you to be in the open air; *be regular* in taking exercise. . . . [W]hen you do eat you may be assured that exercise adds more relish to your food than "the King of Oude's Sauce" or any other condiment of that diction that ever was invented. (qtd. in Menna 33–34)

Magazines such as *Atlantic Monthly, Harper's Weekly*, and *Frank Leslie's Illustrated Newspaper* also published articles on the benefits of good health and physical exercise and sport.

Sporting Practices of the Middle and Upper Classes

While the antebellum agricultural and sporting press promoted benefits of physical exercise and of certain sports, some middle- and upper-class urbanites, along with men seeking to expand their business activities in growing rural towns and cities, pursued sports affiliated with higher socioeconomic status. In the South, still rural in many areas and generally less urbanized than the North, certain sporting practices persisted from the early nineteenth century. In places where new technology was more readily available, middle- and upper-class men in particular integrated it into sporting contests to promote their visibility as higher-ranked sportsmen and businessmen.

Dueling

The more sophisticated gentlemen of the South settled their disputes of honor by means of dueling, usually with swords or pistols. Used in Europe for centuries, the practice had migrated to America with the colonists. A duel could be staged when the honor of a white upper-rank male was challenged by another man in the form of an insult to his character, honesty, wife, or even mistress. The loss of one's honor from not defending oneself might affect family pride, status, and social esteem for years. Even prominent Americans engaged in the practice. Stephen Decatur, an American naval hero in the War of 1812, fell mortally wounded in an 1820 duel. Before becoming president in 1828, Andrew Jackson fought numerous duels, allegedly killing several men in the process. South Carolina even had a dueling club, and such confrontations occurred on a regular basis at a selected site in New Orleans. Although Virginia outlawed dueling in 1809 and other states followed (including New York in 1828), duels continued legally in Washington, D.C., for another decade. The U.S. Navy permitted dueling as late as 1862, and as late as 1870 residents of Savannah, Georgia, dueled over the results of a sailboat race (Holland 142, 149, 272). Practice of this ultimate form of competition perplexed religious reformers, and itinerant ministers traveled the backcountry on moral crusades to preach against such uncivilized transgressions against the human body. Such developments signaled the imposition of a middle-class culture and standards of decorum in American life.

Steamboat Races

Along the waterways, steamboat races were thrilling passengers and onlookers by the 1830s. These events were dangerous, as overheated boilers sometimes exploded with fatal consequences, but such risks failed to quell the activity. Steamboats transported spectators to sporting events, carried passengers to clandestine boxing matches or steamboat races, and, in the absence of or before the invention of the telegraph, communicated news of the results of contests. In particular, steamboats competed in the

1830s on the Mississippi and Hudson rivers, showing off the new steam technology of the antebellum era (Menna 87). By the 1850s, steamboats were also racing on the Great Lakes and on the Sacramento River in California. The following description from the *Spirit of the Times* conveys the excitement of an 1832 race along the Hudson River between the steamboats *Erie* and *North America*:

> At the hour of starting, our wharves were crowded by multitudes of interested spectators, all eagerly watching the busy preparations for the coming contest. The North America shot away from the dock first, but being compelled to sweep around a vessel laying in her course, she gave the Erie an opportunity to come along side and thus it is said, they left the city neck and neck. Now came the tug of war, and none could witness the contest between these two perfections of art, without emotions of awe and sublimity.
>
> The tide was favorable and they scud away with almost terrific rapidity—now one and now the other ahead; but at no time was the distance between them sufficient to give alarm or hope to either. . . .
>
> A few short hours decided this closely contested race. The North America arrived at the foot of State street dock eight minutes ahead of the Erie, making the passage from New York to Albany in the extraordinary short time of nine hours and thirty minutes. (qtd. in Menna 88)

The most famous steamboat race was the exciting contest between the *Robert E. Lee* and the *Natchez VI* in July 1870, spanning 1,278 river miles (2,056 kilometers) from New Orleans to St. Louis and finally won by the *Robert E. Lee* after three days of action.

Yachting

In New England, wealthy Boston merchant George Crowninshield built a yacht for the then-princely sum of more than $50,000. Dubbed *Cleopatra's Barge* and launched in 1816, Crowninshield's vessel embarked on a European voyage in 1817. He raced and defeated continental yachtsmen and intended to return in 1818 to challenge sailors of the Baltic countries but suffered a fatal heart attack in the interim. The magnificent yacht was sold for a pittance and turned into a trading ship in Hawaii.

It took three more decades before those of similar interests founded the New York Yacht Club (in 1844), and the first America's Cup yacht race was staged in 1851, as discussed in the next chapter.

Public Spaces for Health and Sport

For New Yorkers of various social classes, ethnicities, and races, the creation of Central Park (the first landscaped public park in the United States) in the 1850s provided a place to play sports and enjoy fresh air in natural environs within a major city. With the increased pace of urbanization in the antebellum era, sports played in city streets came under criticism as a potential threat to persons moving about in the walking cities, as they were known, including businessmen, clerks, and the residents and visitors attending stores and buildings. In the early decades of the nineteenth century, New York city officials had wanted to keep sport out of the parks in busy areas where working-class men and youth playing games sent errant balls—or ran—into busy streets, thus perhaps endangering city folks who were passing by. For example, in 1816, the *New York Courier* addressed the passing of a park-related law which legislated

> that no person or persons shall play at ball, quoits, or any other sports of play whatsoever in the public ground, commonly called the Park, in the third and sixth wards, of the said city, nor in the Bowling Green, nor on the Battery, in the first ward of the said city, nor throw stones, nor run foot races, in, over or upon either the said Park, Bowling Green or Battery; under the penalty of five dollars for every offence.

> A fit and proper person shall be appointed to be called the keeper of the Park, whose duty it shall be to see the provisions of this ordinance are observed, and also to prevent all riots and noise, in or adjacent to the said Park, Battery and Bowling Green, and to report all offenders to the Attorney of the Board. ("A Law" 3)

The appeal of city parks as potential sporting areas for working-class and young people was reflected in a statement by one J. Morton, the Clerk of the Common Council: "[I]f any offence shall be committed against this ordinance, by any minor, apprentice, servant or slave [many slaves were still held in the antebellum North], the penalty in such case be paid by the parent, guardian, master, or owner (as the case may be) of the person so offending" ("A Law" 3).

Providing appropriate grounds for sport and play in growing urban areas thus became a key issue for civic-minded public officials. Eminent white, middle-class New Yorkers, as well as reformers such as writer Walt Whitman, educator Horace Mann, and journalist Sarah Josepha Hale, championed the need for a public park in New York City. Mayor Ambrose Kingsland's 1851 proposal of a 160-acre (65-hectare) space started the necessary political process for establishing Central Park. Built to promote the moral and physical health of urban residents in a wholesome natural setting—and to promote political power, urban boosterism, and real estate, among other motives—Central Park provided the framework for creation of other public parks in the United States. The park's famous designer, Frederick Law Olmsted, and his codesigner Calvert Vaux, allotted space for sporting activities in the open air to serve the youth of the city, but the park became a contested space, as various public groups expressed claims to it, often clashing over whether park grounds should be used for active sports and ball games or reserved for less boisterous recreations such as enjoying nature through walks and rambles. Sporting events usually attracted rowdy crowds, as well as gambling and fast horses and carriages, whereas city officials believed that park grounds were best used for calmer recreations, more fitting for elite groups strolling in the park (Rosenzweig and Blackmar). Rules instituted by park supervisors initially restricted sporting activity in the park and instead encouraged visitors to partake of the fresh air and scenery through more peaceful kinds of recreation.

Olmsted and Vaux's vision of Central Park relied on their "Greensward Plan" for controlling the types of activity and movement in the park. "In an effort to keep out sporting men and trotting matches, the Greensward plan had omitted long, straight drives; some newspapers worried that Central Park might turn into an 'aldermanic commons for fast driving'" (Rosenzweig and Blackmar 244), and, given the growing popularity of harness racing, such concerns seemed realistic. Park commissioners determined speed limits for carriages and horses, though debate usually ensued. The speed limits and absence of straight roads failed, however, to keep out those wanting to race, and arrests for speeding initially occurred as part of the "ban on fast driving" that park officials "intended to ensure not only safety but gentlemanly refinement." Class-based tensions in the park persisted, as park and city officials wished to maintain the park as a place of beauty and quiet recreation and to keep out those visitors deemed undesirable to gentlemen (Rosenzweig and Blackmar 245–246).

Early on in the history of Central Park, lower-rank groups wanting to play sports and ball games prompted the park board to at least consider their interests, or, perhaps more accurately, consider how to prevent them from being realized. Central Park historians Rosenzweig and Blackmar have researched park visitors' use of the grounds, as well as the class bias displayed by the refined gentlemen of the park board. Even before the park opened to the public, some of the early baseball clubs in New York (baseball is discussed further in chapter 4) asked the board to provide ball grounds for their use. Clubs for baseball, cricket, and other sports followed with their own petitions to park commissioners. As Rosenzweig and Blackmar have written, "The ball clubs saw the new park as the answer to their dreams, but Olmsted and the board began to wonder whether their presence might prove instead to be a nightmare" (249). Ball games, with their large teams and crowds and boisterous activities, worried park commissioners and like-minded park visitors from the upper class, who envisioned the park as a place of more refined recreation.

In an annual report about Central Park, the class issue surfaced in the restrictions that board members wanted to enforce on the behavior of people playing sports. It would not be possible "to satisfy the requirements of the numerous cricket, ball, and other adult clubs within the area of the Park, and at the same time preserve in the grounds an appearance that would be satisfactory to the much more numerous class that frequent the Park for the enjoyment of the refined and attractive features of its natural attractions to those that visit it merely as a picture." Park commissioners felt that sport and other vigorous physical activity that threatened the "picture" portrayed by natural scenery in the park needed to be curtailed. The officials supervising Central Park in the 1850s and 1860s believed that excluding ball games was an effective means to prevent "'match games and the objectionable features that have been the frequent attendant of these games'" (qtd. in Rosenzweig and Blackmar 249). Similar concerns surfaced about the use of public space at the playgrounds and rural scenery in the park—and about the type of sporting behavior exhibited by schoolboys. To limit activity by working-class youth, park authorities required boys to show a certificate from a teacher confirming their good attendance and character, but many working-class boys during this period did not attend school beyond their early years. Schoolgirls, too, gained access to the fields for certain sporting games like croquet. "The park would be open to women's recreation, but only to those genteel and restrained forms of exercise that the park's male manager deemed appropriate" (Rosenzweig and Blackmar 249, 251).

One of the most popular sports pursued by women in Central Park was ice skating, which gave them an outdoor pastime on the frozen waterways to promote health and enjoyment. Whether skating with other women or girls or in a mixed-gender skating party, women turned increasingly to ice skating during the antebellum period. Writing about the rage for skating in Central Park, a *Harper's Weekly* journalist noted that park commissioners had provided good ice for the skaters, who had "turned their ponds and

Women ice skating on the ladies' pond in Central Park, displaying their skills beside the other skaters.

Image from *Harper's Weekly*, 1860.

swamps for good use, by flooding them every cold night, and inviting skaters to try them every morning. The idea has been a hit." The winter sport attracted "thousands of persons of both sexes" at Central Park, and, "[t]hroughout the North and East, skating . . . [had] long been a favorite amusement with ladies as well as men" ("Skating" 101). Skating not only drew both sexes but also young and old alike, and young children just learning joined more experienced skaters in having their share of slips. One humorous illustration of the day showed a youngster observing the skating mishap of a policeman.

In warmer weather, women and young girls turned to swimming for healthful exercise. Women learning to safely care for and avoid the drowning of their children near waterways might swim in the public baths of Central Park. Swimming provided a means for women to achieve physical health and to prevent horrible drowning of family members, frequently reported in urban and rural newspapers of the day. While private baths were enjoyed by women of higher social status and means, public baths with a swimming pool provided a place where city women of modest means could learn to swim. A *New York Times* account of a bathhouse swim school in Central Park Garden indicated that visitors "would not only have witnessed feats of skill and endurance performed by women and girls. . . [b]ut by atoms of humanity not more than 4 to 5 years old" (qtd. in Johns and Farrell-Beck 55).

Tensions also arose in other cities, such as Boston and Chicago, over the number and types of participants engaging in sport in public spaces. As early as 1851 in Chicago, an ordinance was enacted to prohibit ball playing in parks. City fathers reasoned that such a law might dispel the image of the rapidly growing city as a frontier community. Then, as now, public amenities attracted the middle class and businesses to the city. By that time in burgeoning Midwest cities where urban men and women might partake of sports, games, and the beauty of park grounds, Chicago vied with St. Louis, Cincinnati, and Milwaukee for commercial dominance in the West.

Sporting Pastimes of African Americans and Native Americans

While middle- and upper-class white Americans touted the benefits of sport and exercise for health and desired to engage in new sporting experiences, the white Protestant majority held sway over the minority groups of African Americans and

Native Americans. African Americans in Northern urban areas faced severe restrictions on their sporting experiences due to discrimination in public parks and facilities, and enslaved African Americans in the South confronted the shackles of bondage enforced by owners as they sought to create their own sporting and recreational activities within the slave community. Both free and enslaved African Americans sought the rejuvenation and toughness they might gain through sport and exercise to withstand both Southern white masters and powerful Northern whites who held economic, political, and social power. As a result, separate African American sporting organizations began to develop in the North, as free blacks continued to pursue their sporting heritage. Native Americans, on the other hand, were increasingly forced off of their lands in the East and moved to the West due to political decisions (i.e., Manifest Destiny) in order for white families and land seekers to gain new and better land for settlement. Native Americans tried to maintain their cultural and sporting practices, such as lacrosse, but the forced western migration altered some of their sporting experiences.

African Americans

The white South's increasing dependence on slave labor to grow the tobacco, rice, and cotton that supported its agricultural way of life led to a growing population of slaves. Inside the slave community, from sundown to sunup, away from the harsh rigors of grueling labor and the master's watchful eye, slaves created their own world of culture and recreation to survive the brutalities of slave life. Slaves desired to gain some autonomy over their own lives in the time away from the fields and houses where they were subjected to the daily regimen of hard labor. In addition to singing, making music, and dancing, they used their physical skills in various sporting forms.

In the Southern plantations of the gentry, an informal boxing match between slaves was a common occurrence, and wealthy planters would also "frequently organize formal boxing contests and pit their slave champion against other slave champions from

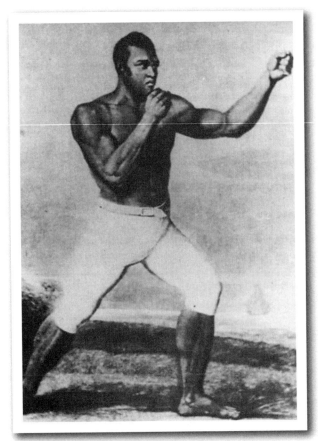

Tom Molineaux (pictured) lost to Tom Cribb in a championship boxing match in England.

From B. Spears and R. Swanson, 1988, *History of sport and physical education in the United States* (Dubuque, IA: Wm. C. Brown), 153.

different plantations of the community." Historian David Wiggins has remarked that slave owners often won more on their wagers during these fights than on horse races. According to some accounts, once extremely good "boxer-slaves" earned fortunes "in bets for their masters, [they] were given their freedom and moved away from the South so they could ply their fistic trade to better financial advantage for themselves" (Wiggins, "Good" 273).

To meet that goal, the earliest black athletic stars had to travel abroad. One who did was Tom Molineaux, and it is not clear whether he was born to freedom or secured his liberty through his athletic skills. In any case, he embarked in 1809 for England, where he met another American-born black fighter, Bill Richmond.

The latter became his trainer, and a year later Molineaux fought Tom Cribb for the championship of England before a hostile crowd. Molineaux disputed his loss to the champion but suffered the same fate in a rematch. He later turned to wrestling and died in Ireland in 1818.

Slaves enjoyed horse racing and often staged spontaneous and very informal races on the plantation. They would also accompany their masters to other plantations, and when the master rode, the slaves might do so as well, perhaps sharing in some of the excitement. Often they went simply as spectators, but frequently they were trainers or jockeys as well, and they did participate in racing contests, wherein skilled black jockeys earned pride in their horsemanship. A slave named William Greene was a jockey for several years on Edward Hamilton's plantation. "I remained with him [Hamilton] from nine years old until I was twenty," explains Greene. "He then took me to be a race rider. He kept a number of fine noble horses, with a number of race horses; and being of the right size for a rider he took me to ride races." Similarly, Jacob Stroyer, who lived on a South Carolina plantation, was first employed as a trainer of racehorses and then became a jockey (Wiggins, "Good" 273–274).

African Americans in the North, who generally worked manual-labor and low-paying jobs due to racial discrimination, might participate in horse-racing activities, though sometimes it took a bit of cleverness to pull off. The following account from the black press revealed how one black servant outwitted his master and displayed athletic prowess in his riding skills despite Sabbath restrictions on sport. In "An Unexpected Race," a story published in the 1855 *Provincial Freeman*, in a large town in Worcester County, Massachusetts, a clergyman named Ridewell owned a cherished horse. Of Baptist sentiment, Ridewell was "very rigid in his ideas of moral propriety. He had in his employ an old negro, named Pompey, and if this latter individual was not so strict in his morals as his master, he was . . . very cunning. . . . Pomp was a useful servant, and the old clergyman never hesitated to trust him with the most important business." Yet in this town, several individuals feared not what Mr. Ridewell preached, and instead of attending Sabbath church service they would gather on Sunday evenings upon a piece of land "in the outskirts of the town, and there race horses." This place, hidden from view by woods, allowed the participants to hold horse races without the knowledge of officers or others who might have stopped them. Here, the African American servant manifested his cleverness. Pompey's knowledge of horses came into play, as "the good old clergyman owned one of the best horses in the country. This horse was of the old Morgan stock, with the mixture of the Arabian blood in his veins, and it was generally

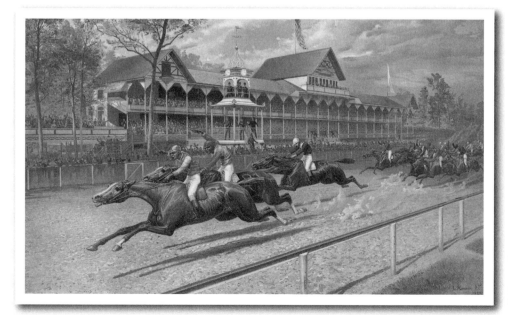

The Futurity Race at Sheepshead Bay by Currier & Ives shows black jockeys racing.

Image courtesy of Library of Congress, LC-USZ62-14022.

known that few beasts could pass him on the road." Mr. Ridewell as a preacher took no worldly pride in his horse, and in fact "stoutly declared that the fleetness of his horse never afforded him any gratification." Pompey knew that this valued horse remained in the pasture, because the clergyman lived close to the church and thus always walked to meeting. Pompey discovered that the horse races were on tap and decided to enter his master's horse on his own,

> for he felt sure that old Morgan could beat anything in the shape of horse-flesh that could be produced in that quarter.

> So on the very next Sunday evening, he hid the bridle under his jacket went out into the pasture and caught the horse, and then off to the spot where the wicked ones had congregated. Here he found some dozen horses assembled, and the races were about to commence. Pomp mounted his beast, and at the signal, old Morgan entered into the spirit of the thing, and came out two rods [11 yards, or 10 meters] ahead of everything. So Pomp, won quite a pile, and before dark he was well initiated in horse-racing. . . . He did so again, and again he won . . . [and so] for two months, [could be seen] making his appearance upon the racing ground every Sunday afternoon. . . . And during this time Pompey was not the only one who had learned to love the racing. No, for old Morgan himself had come to love the excitement of the thing, too, and his every motion when upon the track showed how zealously he entered into the spirit of the game. (Cobb, "An Unexpected Race" n. pag.)

Yet the racing by Pompey and his cohorts did not remain secret to a deacon viewing it from a distance, and developments eventually led to an "unexpected race" involving the minister. Reverend Ridewell, morally outraged at such Sabbath races, thought he, fellow deacons, and others shocked at the races might catch them in the act by going to the spot. On the following Sabbath evening, he ordered Pomp to bring up Morgan and put him in the stable. When the clergyman and his horse then came upon the race scene, "The horses of the wicked men were just drawing up for a start as the minister approached, and some of the riders who at once recognized 'old Morgan' did not recognize the reverend individual who rode him." One of the jockeys asked the minister if he was there for the first race, and the stunned clergyman responded, "Wicked men!" Just at that moment, the race leader shouted, "And off it is!" and Reverend Ridewell was drawn into the race: "Old Morgan knew that word too well, for no sooner did it fall upon his ears than he struck out his nose, and with one wild snort he started, and the rest of the racers, twelve in number, kept him company." The minister's efforts to halt the fast-racing Morgan were futile, and those present admired what appeared to be his riding skill. One approached him afterward and said, "'[Y]ou ride well. . . . We had not looked for this honor'" (hence the name "Ridewell"!). The matter was then resolved, as Pompey informed his master that "[s]ome of those wicked men had been in the habit of stealing old Morgan from the pasture, and racing him on Sabbath afternoons. Pomp found out this much—but he could not find out who did it." The whole incident was resolved such that Reverend Ridewell was cleared, with no immoral actions on his part, and he could finally "laugh with right good will when he spoke of his unexpected race. Be sure there was no more Sabbath racing in town," by Pompey or others (Cobb, "An Unexpected Race" n. pag.).

In the South, slaves' swimming skills, utilized by masters for work on the waterways near plantations, could also be displayed in informal swimming pastimes. Bill Crump, a slave in antebellum North Carolina, remarked that he worked in the fields from sunup to sundown (as quoted in Dawson with the dialect spoken): "we had a couple of hours at dinner time tar swim or lay on de banks uv de little crick an' sleep. . . . 'bout sundown master let us go swim ag'in iff' ne we anted to do it" (qtd. in Dawson 1340).

At other times, plantation masters organized formal swimming contests. As with similar owner-organized competitions in boxing, wrestling, and racing on horseback or on foot, swimming races gave slaves a chance to display physical prowess and gain self-esteem. These contests pitted the best swimmers of one planter against those of another planter (as discussed in chapter 1), and, as with other staged slave sports, plantation owners often wagered on the outcome. Victory in such a contest likely provided slaves with prestige among their fellows in the slave quarters.

Some enslaved swimmers also participated in blood sport in the water. Slaves who showcased their stamina and swimming skills in battling sharks, alligators, and other dangerous sea creatures might find masters wagering on their athletic exploits. Whether the slaves who defeated such sea animals were allowed to keep them for their own use as food, as was sometimes the case when slaves went fishing or hunting, may not be knowable. In either case, such displays of fierce aquatic skills may have enabled slaves to express some strength and pride within the slave institution that was designed to fully crush their humanity and independence. Indeed, "bondmen may have used aquatic blood sports to display and affirm their masculinity" (Dawson 1341).

Throughout the South, African Americans faced strict segregation, and the vast majority remained slaves throughout the antebellum period. Although some slaves were forced to become boxers, wrestlers, or jockeys for their owners' amusement, many slaves created and enjoyed their own diversions, such as singing and dancing at parties, hunting, and fishing. Josiah Hanson, a slave who later became a minister, remarked that "[t]he sternest and most covetous master cannot frighten or whip the fun out of us" (Wiggins, "Sport and Popular Pastimes" 62).

Even in areas of the country where slavery was not practiced, rigid racial segregation in rural and urban locales in early nineteenth-century America still made it unlikely for free blacks to integrate into sporting facilities. Still, free black men and boys were united in lively activities such as boxing, track-and-field events, hunting, and fishing. In antebellum cities like Boston, free blacks formed their own churches due to exclusion from white churches and the desire to have black preachers leading their important meeting and spiritual space. Free blacks also desired to have their recreational space safe from racial discrimination.

Native Americans

Native American inhabitants battling white encroachment in the Midwest and Southeast were often forced to move westward to lands less populated by white settlers. In their still-unconquered western lands, Native Americans continued to practice their rapidly vanishing pastoral and, for some such as the Plains Indians, nomadic lifestyle of following the buffalo herds. In addition to hunting, they engaged in dances and stickball games (particularly lacrosse), and tribes of the Southwest practiced long-distance running rituals. Lacrosse seemed to be inherent in most Native American cultures, and the contest often involved masses of players. White missionaries, however, railed against the gambling and nudity that accompanied some games. An 1825 game in Georgia drew a crowd of three thousand people and bets of $3,500 total (Vennum 111, 277). By the 1830s, Eastern tribes who had more exposure to white society adopted more formal rules, enforced by referees, and whites became commonplace as spectators at games among the Iroquois Confederacy in New York. By 1848, the Cherokees of the Southeast adorned themselves in their best clothing for such matches.

The interplay of Anglo and Indian cultures inevitably produced a hybrid population and sporting culture. The nascent field of anthropology took great interest in physical differences, socially constructing the concept of race in the process. Within that context, footracing gained great favor in the 1830s, and professional runners competed for stakes and publicized their efforts with pseudonyms meant to draw attention, such as the "American Deer," the "Boston Buck," and the "Yankee Clipper." The racialization of bodies produced stereotypes, and it was widely believed that Native

Americans were more powerful runners. Louis Bennett, the product of a mixed union between a Scotsman and a Seneca woman, capitalized on this notion by adopting the name "Deerfoot" and running in a loincloth and moccasins with a feather in his hair. He became a national sensation when he succeeded in breaking the record for a 10-mile (16-kilometer) run. In 1835, Henry Stannard, a Connecticut farmer, had been the first to run 10 miles in less than an hour (59:48). Deerfoot embarked on a tour of Great Britain in 1861, where he lowered the record to 51:26.

Immigrants and Sporting Cultures

Immigrants to the United States in the middle decades of the nineteenth century brought their cultural, linguistic, religious, culinary, and athletic practices to their new country. To maintain their ethnic identity and form a community with their fellow immigrants amidst the larger white, Protestant, and often elite population, immigrant groups created their own cultural and physical spaces to experience sporting forms brought over from their homelands. In ethnic-minority athletic clubs, newly arrived immigrants organized leisure activities to promote their own language, values, and cultural traditions among their youth. Newcomers to American cities encountered a cultural and physical environment of people, surroundings, and behavior considerably different from those of their homelands, and sport became a way for men and women to foster a sense of fellowship with those of similar ethnicity, race, social class, or experience. Indeed, "[s]port clubs, as one type of voluntary association, became one of the basic means by which certain groups sought to establish subcommunities within the larger society." These subcommunities allowed members to participate in sport and maintain their cultural identity (Rader, "The Quest" 356–357). Ethnic sporting, social, and drinking practices—especially those of young men—sometimes clashed with the interests of white, educated, middle-class social reformers and their agenda of promoting physical activity and sport linked with good health, proper morals, and preferred gender and behavioral codes. Over time, however, ethnic sporting clubs would influence the sporting habits of native-born Americans (as discussed in the next chapter).

German American Turners

Germans were among the first immigrants to the new United States. Charles Beck, a member of the German Turner gymnastics movement, traveled to Massachusetts in 1825. There he was employed at the Round Hill School, founded two years earlier in Northampton by Joseph Cogswell and George Bancroft. The school introduced physical education to its curriculum, and Beck instituted an outdoor gymnastics site. Charles Follen, another German Turner, was employed as an instructor at a Boston gymnasium and instructed students at Harvard University in gymnastics in 1826. Yet another Turner, Francis Lieber, arrived the following year to direct the Boston gym and operate its swimming pool.

Many Germans migrated to America in 1848 during a time of political revolution in Germany. These immigrants formed voluntary associations modeled on those in their native country, known as Turner societies. German immigrants founded the first Turner society in the United States in Cincinnati, Ohio, in 1848, followed by a Turner society located in New York, and then one in Philadelphia in 1849. In 1851, a group of German immigrant men in Indianapolis formed a new organization to foster athletic and cultural activities from their homeland and called it the Indianapolis Turngemeinde. This Turner society, referring to the German word *turner*, meaning a tumbler or gymnast, was founded by August Hoffmeister, Jakob Metzger, Alexander Metzger, Clemens Vonnegut, John Ott, and Karl Hill (Stempfel 5). These German Turners in America endorsed gymnastics for attaining physical fitness as part of their educational emphasis, encapsulated in the motto "a sound mind in a sound body" (from the Latin "mens sana in corpore sana"). German immigrants of some of the Turner societies joined together to establish the national Turner organization in America in 1850 to nurture their cultural practices, language, and beliefs. They wished to promote the German gymnastic system, focused on a program of marching, free exercise, and gymnastics drills, as well as dancing for girls, and they promoted apparatus-based exercise using equipment such as the balance beam, rings, horse, parallel bars, and vault, as well as games and play. These early German American Turner societies drew on the philosophy of Friedrich Ludwig Jahn (1778–1852), known as the father of German gymnastics, and they merged athletic interests with ethnic interests in seeking fellowship with other German newcomers to American cities.

The same year the Indianapolis Germans founded their Turner society (1851), the German American sports event known as the National Turnfest took place in Philadelphia. Featuring gymnastics, disciplined physical exercises, and athletic endeavors such as running and jumping, the National Turnfest is the oldest ongoing amateur athletic contest in America. Thus the German Americans who founded the first Turner society in 1848 became pioneers in physical education in the United States; additional Turner societies followed in Milwaukee, Chicago, Louisville, and other cities with large German immigrant populations. Until the mid-1850s, when there were established German populations in various cities, all of these Turner societies owed their organization and growth to the numerous German immigrants who came to the United States to escape the revolutionary uproar in Germany in 1848 and 1849 and to pursue their political views in freedom (Hofmann; Barney).

The Turners of Indianapolis included gymnastics from their earliest days, when they used founder John Ott's furniture factory. "The front yard was used for physical exercises. The gymnastics apparatus consisted of a horizontal bar; later money was raised among the members for a set of parallel bars" (Stempfel 5). The Indianapolis Turngemeinde, known as the Gymnastic Community, merged with the Indianapolis Socialistischer Turnverein, and the new organization became known as the Social Gymnastic Club. These German American Turners joined together to build their first Turnhalle, or Turner Hall, which remained a hub of German life for immigrants, offering the use of gymnastic apparatus, a library, lectures, and musical and theatrical performances. The start of the Civil War, during which many German Americans joined the Union Army, led to inactivity and the eventual closing of the Turnhalle.

The German Turners in Milwaukee also played an active role in gymnastics and competitive exercises in implementing the Turner philosophy of "a sound mind in a sound body." Business leaders in the German American community founded the Milwaukee Turners in July 1853. Led by George Brosius, known as the American Turnfather, the Milwaukee Turnverein emphasized the German gymnastic system of using apparatus and physical exercise drills. Brosius had come to Milwaukee in 1842 with his family, and he began teaching physical instruction at the Turnverein Milwaukee in 1854. Milwaukee Turners who were physical education instructors promoted the introduction of physical education and gymnastics in public schools in Wisconsin and the nation. German American Turners formed communities throughout the United States, from the East Coast to the West Coast, and spread their intellectual and sporting ideas to men and women.

Scottish Caledonian Clubs

Scottish settlers perpetuated traditional Highland games in New York as early as 1836; they formed the first Caledonian club in Boston in 1853 and went on to form numerous Caledonian clubs in various areas during the 1850s. These Scottish newcomers to America wished to sustain their language, native costume, music, dance, foodways, games, and athletics in their new home. The many Caledonian clubs that followed typically limited their membership to those of Scottish lineage. At their athletic meets, they competed in several events: long jump, high jump, running, sack races, blindfolded wheelbarrow races, vaulting, putting heavy stones, caber (pole) tossing, and tugs-of-war, as well as dancing Highland flings and a gambol with broadswords. In the late 1850s, the New York Caledonian Club began to commercialize and professionalize its annual games by charging admission fees and offering cash prizes to winning competitors. Widespread interest in the events drew as many as twenty thousand spectators at the games in New York City, and Caledonian clubs eventually opened their competitions to non-Scottish athletes of various races or ethnicities (Rader, *American Sports* [2004] 69). Some of these Caledonian contests also drew the

INTERNATIONAL PERSPECTIVE

Turnen: On Politics and Bodies

The system of exercise known as *Turnen* originated in Prussia in the early nineteenth century in a period of social changes initiated by the Enlightenment, the French Revolution, the ensuing wars and subsequent restructuring of Europe, the technological revolution, and the rise of the bourgeoisie or middle class. In this period, ideas of national education arose, especially with regard to training bodies able to take up arms and defend the homeland. So it was with German *Turnen*, which was developed to a large extent by Friedrich Ludwig Jahn (1778–1852). The aim of the *Turner* was to liberate Germany from French occupation, to overthrow the feudal order, and to form a German nation state.

　　Turnen was a comprehensive concept of games, exercises, and physical activity, ranging from climbing and balancing to running and throwing, and from wrestling to playing games. The principles of *Turnen*, though, differed fundamentally from those of the kind of sport that was developing in England. The *Turner* did not attach any importance to records and abstract performance; instead, they used a person's height, for example, as the criterion for judging a high jump. They preferred all-round exercising of the body to specialization, and they strove to improve the "nation's strength" rather than individual performance. The *Turnen* grounds, incidentally, were no place for girls and women, who could only admire the bold feats of the *Turner* as spectators.

　　In the Restoration period after Napoleon's defeat, *Turnen* was banned for being part of a seemingly dangerous nationalist movement, and in 1820 the *Turnen* grounds were closed down by order of the Prussian cabinet. Twenty years later, *Turnen* enjoyed a revival, when the *Turner* played a vital role in the bourgeois revolution in 1848 and 1849. The majority of them stood up for freedom and civil rights, as well as for a unified Germany. When the revolution collapsed, many of the *Turner* who had taken an active part in it emigrated to the United States.

　　With the founding of the German Empire in 1871, the *Turner* dream of a united Germany had come true, and they placed themselves wholly under the command of God, the Emperor, and the homeland. In this period, the Turner Federation was the largest "sports" organization in Germany, although English sports began to compete with *Turnen* for members. Despite fierce resistance against sport and its supporters, *Turnen* lost adherents and public attention after World War I. Following World War II, *Turnen* developed into a "sport for all" movement and attracted more and more girls and women, and today more than five million Germans are members of the Turner Federation, and 70 percent of them are girls and women. Until World War II, the *Turner* had seen themselves as a political movement, and they fought against the spread of Anglo-American sport and also viewed the internationalization of *Turnen* with skepticism (Pfister and Hofmann). After the war, the *Turner* movement lost its political emphasis and increasingly adapted to the principles of modern sport.

Information from Pfister, Gertrud. "Physical Activity in the Name of the Fatherland: Turnen and the National Movement (1810-1820)." *Sporting Heritage* H.1 (1996): 14–36.

attention of American-born athletes and spectators, and the running, jumping, and weight-throwing contests were eventually adopted as modern track-and-field events by young, white, upper-class men.

Irish Americans

Antebellum Irish taverns and boxing clubs in the Northeast became popular sites for young, working-class Irish men to sharpen their pugilistic skills and enjoy beer, gambling, and camaraderie with each other. In the gender-divided social world of Irish men and women in the nineteenth century, the physical space of the tavern and the sporting behaviors associated with it were clearly marked as male terrain. Approximately 70 percent of prizefighters in the antebellum era were Irish or Irish American, and pugilism fostered a rising nationalism in the United States, as Irish newcomers, stridently opposed to the British overlords who occupied their ancestral homeland, challenged English fighters (Riess, *Sport* 87). The adoption of British prizefighting rules, which forbade hitting below the belt or punching a downed fighter and provided for referees or umpires, signaled a further transition to regulated, middle-class standards of sporting decorum, in contrast with the no-holds-barred practices typical on the American frontier. Before the new rules took effect in the United States, a New York boxing match in 1842 had produced a fatality, as Thomas McCoy bled to death.

In 1849, Tom Hyer, backed by nativists, defeated Irish immigrant Yankee Sullivan in a bout that portrayed internecine social tensions between the native-born and newcomers. At the same time, John Morrissey (1831–1878), another Irish immigrant, exemplified the possibility of ascendance from street brawler to respectability. One of eight children born to a poor family in Ireland, Morrissey emigrated to Troy, New York, then traveled to New York City to test his toughness. In 1853, he defeated Yankee Sullivan under British rules and claimed the American boxing championship. He successfully defended his title in 1858 against American John C. Heenan in a fight held in Canada. Morrissey retired with fame and fortune as proprietor of a gambling establishment, as explored further in the next chapter.

Heenan, however, challenged Tom Sayers, the British champion, in 1860. The fight, staged in Great Britain, lasted 43 rounds over a period of 2 hours and 20 minutes but produced no decision, as both men claimed the championship. The fight carried great cultural significance, as the young United States was divesting itself of British influence in search of its own identity. Sport thus assumed the role of surrogate warfare, as the U.S. moved toward international prominence throughout the remainder of the century (Kirsch, *Sports* [Vol. 3] 142–147).

Meanwhile, the Irish presence in boxing remained prominent in the antebellum era. Morrissey's postretirement ventures as a gambling-hall proprietor included building a lavish parlor at Saratoga Springs, New York, and his political connections allowed him and his business associates to construct a racetrack there. More generally, the boxing bouts of the middle nineteenth century manifested the ethnic and cultural conflicts of the larger society, as Yankee (typically Protestant) fighters sparred against Irish Catholic fighters, thus highlighting anti-Irish sentiment and concern about the thousands of new immigrants entering many of the cities and organizations in the Northeast.

Asian Americans

Most immigrants to America in the early and middle nineteenth century came from European groups; however, after the discovery of gold in 1848 in Sutter's Mill, California, some Chinese immigrants began to appear. Asian immigration—that is, "meaningful Chinese immigration to the United States[,] begins roughly with the California gold rush of 1849. . . . Between the beginnings of the Chinese migration in 1848 and the passage of the Chinese Exclusion Act in 1882, perhaps three hundred thousand Chinese entered the United States" (Daniels, *Coming* 239). During the Gold Rush, these were mostly single young men; the larger period of Chinese immigration to the western United States, mainly California, occurred after the Civil War. Most of the sporting organizations formed by Chinese people in California, in response to the racial discrimination they faced, arose in the latter part of the nineteenth century. Some Chinese Americans participated in sports by the 1890s in the San Francisco Bay Area, including "hundreds of contests ranging from boxing and cycling to Caledonian games, baseball, football, and more" (Park, "Sports" 446). Organizations designed to promote sport for Chinese American youth began to emerge in the early twentieth century.

Summary

The antebellum period marked a time of widespread change for Americans in rural and urban life—and for immigrants coming to America. From the 1820s through the 1850s, health reformers and advocates developed a positive outlook on the need for vigorous exercise and sport in order to advance a nation of sound American men and women. Yet not all inhabitants of the United States gained access to sporting opportunities or were included in the programs touted by reformers and sports journalists. Increased attention by people of diverse backgrounds to sport, along with the growth of industrialization, urbanization, and technological innovation—as well as the influence of social-class distinctions and gender and race lines that remained in the culture—provided the framework for modern, competitive sport in the nineteenth century, as discussed in the following chapter.

DISCUSSION QUESTIONS

1. Compare the influence of sports journalism on attitudes about exercise and sport in the antebellum period and in the present period of the twenty-first century.

2. Why did exercise and sport form a focal point for many male and female antebellum health reformers during the decades of the 1820s through the 1850s? Identify some of these reformers and compare their recommendations.

3. Explain the ways in which rural and urban tensions influenced health and sport movements in the antebellum period.

4. What factors affected the development of women's sport and physical education in antebellum American culture?

5. How did sport become part of the cultural experience of white Americans in the emerging middle class? Of immigrants? Of other minorities in antebellum American culture?

Rise of Rationalized and Modern Sport

1850–1870

CHAPTER OBJECTIVES

After reading this chapter, you will have learned about the following:

- Factors shaping the rise of modern sport in the middle years of the nineteenth century in the United States

- Specific ways in which social class shaped the organization of sports clubs and associations

- The importance of the sporting fraternity to competitive sport and economic interests in sport

- The establishment of rationalized recreation and sport, as well as the ways in which this process was affected by issues related to gender, race, and ethnicity

- The effect of nationalistic beliefs on the emergence of American team sport

- Issues related to the development of the first intercollegiate contest in the United States

- The effect of the Civil War on sporting experiences in the United States

The basis of modern organized team sport emerged in the early days of American baseball, which gained popularity in the mid-nineteenth century, as described by Charles Peverelly in his *Book of American Pastimes* (1866):

> The game of Base Ball has now become beyond question the leading feature of the out-door sports of the United States, and to account for its present truly proud tradition, there are many and sufficient reasons. It is a game which is peculiarly suited to the American temperament and disposition; the nine innings are played in the brief space of two and one half hours, or less. From the moment the first striker takes his position, and poises his bat, it has an excitement and vim about it, until the last hand is put out in the ninth inning. . . .

> It is also, comparatively, an economical recreation; the uniform is not costly, the playing implements, colors, and furnishing of a neat club-room, need not occasion an extravagant outlay when divided, pro rata, by the members of the full club. . . . [T]he great mass . . . can participate in this healthgiving and noble pastime.

> The game stands today in a proud and fairly-won position—scarcely requiring eulogy from any source. Dating from the years when the Knickerbocker Club [1845], closely followed by the Gotham, Eagle, and Empire, gave their colors to the breeze as rallying points for the lovers of the game to muster at, it has grown with giant strides until its organizations are the pride of numberless villages, towns, and cities, all over the land. . . . Having no debasing attribute, and being worthy of the presence of the good and the refined, it has everywhere been countenanced and encouraged by our best citizens; and of the thousands who gather at important matches, we have always noted with sincere gratification that the ladies constituted an honored proportion. (qtd. in Levine, *American* 35–37)

In the middle decades of the nineteenth century, the growth of sports such as baseball accelerated in American society, and a variety of perspectives were forwarded on the meanings of sport as an expanding form of cultural activity in the United States. Some advocates touted the benefits of American sports during this time period—one of intellectual, technological, scientific, and social changes, as well as continued population growth. In the decades preceding the Civil War, sport grew rapidly; during the years of brutal fighting, sport was of course affected by the war but continued to be played at various times and places throughout the conflict.

The reasons for modern sport's rapid development during this period were various, and the growth was of course affected by larger issues of gender, race, and social class. The gendered aspect of baseball was noted by William Wood, physical education instructor and author of physical training and athletic manuals, who wrote in 1867 that, "Base Ball [may be] truly called the American National Game. There is scarcely a city or town or village in the United States where this invigorating and manly exercise is not to some extent enjoyed" (*Manual* [Vol. 1] 14). Yet other commentators on American life expressed concern that giving too much time and emphasis to playing and promoting sport detracted from appropriate values of a work ethic, especially for those in the lower and middle classes. After traveling to communities in the northeastern United States, correspondent William Clift, authoring his columns using the name Timothy Bunker, wrote an essay titled "Base Ball Clubs," in which he countered the view of many antebellum health and sport reformers: "Base ball, as it is played now, is getting to be a great nuisance," because it "makes good ball players, but bad farmers and mechanics, bad husbands and fathers. I am not ready to have the plow beams whittled into ball clubs just yet" (Clift 304, 306).

This chapter examines the development of various sports and the wide attention generally paid to sports between 1850 and 1870, as the popularity of sports intensified and sporting journalism and commentaries on sporting activities continued from the ebb and flow of the antebellum years, examined in Chapter 3. Sports that were either emerging or growing considerably during this period included early forms of baseball, horse racing, footracing, yachting, rowing and crew, boxing, gymnastics, and racket sports. These years also brought the country's first intercollegiate sporting action and, more generally, saw sport become a major part of popular culture for diverse peoples in the United States. The various rationales for organizing sports during this time period evoked an assortment of viewpoints on sports.

Concept of Modern Sport

From the 1840s until the eve of the Civil War, the number of American city dwellers increased due to immigration, industrialization, and the growth of new occupations. The stream of people—from overseas and from rural America—pouring into factories in increasingly cramped cities such as New York, Boston, and Chicago prompted concern about the need for urbanites to engage in physical exercise and sport in order to offset their otherwise sedentary routines. The development of sport in this urban American culture was also influenced by technological innovations in home and work life, along with changes in communication and transportation. As historian Steven Riess has explained, "The evolution of the city, more than any other single factor, influenced the development of organized sport and recreational athletic pastimes in America. Nearly all contemporary major sports evolved or were invented in the city" (Riess, *City* 1). The city served as the locale for key moments in the development of American sporting culture; it was the site of the first organized, rationalized (i.e., justified with beneficial reasons for playing sport in the eyes of supporters and played with rules), commercialized, and professional sports. In the process of urban cultural expansion, sporting culture also expanded, due to changes in the city's physical environment and structures, increases in urban population, and the circulation of fresh perspectives on sport expressed by people of varied social class, race, gender, and ethnicity.

Indeed, the city became the focal point of modern sport. As discussed in chapter 3, health and sport reformers during this period called on citizens to engage in healthy activity as a way to provide the incipient nation with a population marked by sound moral and physical strength. These proponents saw modern American sport and physical recreation as an antidote to the enervating effects of long hours of work, school study, and intellectual business pursuits for many white Americans of the middle class. Whether performing exercises with an "Indian club" (a bottle-shaped club of varying weight) for increased strength and vigor or participating in rowing, ball games, or gymnastics in newly formed athletic clubs, urban dwellers increasingly made sport a central part of urban American life in the middle decades of the nineteenth century.

This crucial period brought the development of new sporting forms, as well as the continuation and growth of previously practiced physical recreations, all of which were part of a transition from premodern to modern sport in American culture. Sport historian Allen Guttmann has articulated key characteristics of the nature of modern sport: secularism, equality, rationalism, bureaucratic organizations, quantification, and the quest for records (*From Ritual to Record*). Drawing on this framework other sport historians have examined how these modern forms of sport were characterized. As historian George Kirsch has explained it, "Democratization, rationalization, bureaucratization, specialization, regional, national, and international competition, extensive media coverage, and fascination with numbers all characterized the new style of athletics." In addition, as modern sport emerged in the mid-nineteenth century, "Sporting clubs and associations of organizations [voluntary associations] scheduled matches

Fig. 13.

Fig. 14.

Indian club exercises were designed to develop a healthy body.

Reprinted from W. Wood, 1867, *Manual of physical exercises: comprising gymnastics, rowing, skating, fencing, cricket, calisthenics, sailing, swimming, sparring, baseball. Together with rules for training and sanitary suggestions* (New York: Harper Brothers).

and legislated regulations to govern play on and off the fields" (*Sports* [Vol. 3] xiv). The nature of urban life, in which work and leisure patterns were increasingly regulated by the clock and by social stratification, led to an increasing emphasis on outcomes of sporting contests and on recording performance statistics and breaking records. Other elements of modern sport include equality of opportunity for all players (in theory, as players in a given competition played by the rules have a fair chance to win), competition as a key factor in American culture at a time when many male leaders and politicians viewed competition as a means to achieving success and victory, and codification of rules. The emergence of these attitudes influenced the growth of sport in the middle of the nineteenth century. As Kirsch has said, "Professionalism and commercialism inevitably followed as the mania for sports spread throughout society. . . . Spectators paid to see their heroes in action; the telegraph and printing press kept millions abreast of the latest results" (*Sports* [Vol. 3] xiv). Similarly, historian Melvin Adelman has posited six main characteristics that differentiate modern sport from premodern sport: organization, rules, competition, role differentiation, public information, and statistics and records. Although the transition may not have occurred in one swift line of change, the rise of modern sport was marked by clear movement toward these characteristics ("The First" 6–7).

The modern sporting boom in America was initially a male-dominated movement, with men serving as the players, managers, and, in many sports, the spectators. Women did of course participate in this cultural development in their own ways, though as in earlier times (covered in preceding chapters) gendered ideology and customs meant that women's sport and other recreational physical activity developed in different ways from men's.

Influence of Transportation on the Development of Modern Sport

Major urban centers that served as hubs for railroad routes became key cities in the rise of sport in the mid-nineteenth century. Railroads such as the Baltimore and Ohio (begun in 1828) replaced transportation by boats and barges, moving goods and humans faster over long distances and playing a crucial role in bringing people together to play and watch urban sports in larger numbers. By 1840, 3,000 miles (4,828 kilometers) of track had been laid, mainly in the Northeast. By 1850, some 30,000 miles (48,280 kilometers) of track linked the Eastern and old Northwestern (lower Midwestern) sections of the country (Nash et al., Brief 5th ed. 283), and cities such as New York, Boston, Philadelphia, Chicago, Baltimore, and St. Louis became known for their rich sporting cultures for the upper, middle, and lower classes.

The railroad expanded the city from a local walking environment, with close proximity required in order to secure sites for sporting activity, to a larger setting where participants could travel to other destinations in order to watch or compete in

INTERNATIONAL PERSPECTIVE

England as the Cradle of Modern Sport

Games and dances, physical activities, performances and movement cultures have always existed in all societies. On closer scrutiny, we detect that the multifaceted world of sport and games has culture-specific patterns, and from the nineteenth century onward a specific form of physical culture developed in England. This was modern sport, which is characterized by the (theoretical) equality of opportunity and an orientation toward performance and competition. The most important trait of modern sport is its orientation toward the setting and keeping of records. In this way, performances in running, for example, can be compared with each other even though they take place at different times and in different places, without the runners ever having met each other. As Guttmann has emphasized, the principle of competition and the pursuit of records have had numerous consequences, including quantification of performance, standardization of apparatus and facilities, bureaucratization, specialization, rationalization (i.e., a logical relationship between means and ends), and professionalization (*Games*). Thus it is not a specific movement or pattern of movements that makes a physical activity a sport but the principles and intentions underlying it. Even if abstract performances and records may have existed in other epochs and cultures, the combination of the principles just enumerated is typical of sport in industrialized Western countries.

In considering why England became the cradle of sport, a number of theories have been put forward, ascribing the origin of sport variously to Puritanism or the Enlightenment and the world views associated with these movements. In addition, aside from its social structure and relatively high level of industrialization, one must also take into account the country's protected position as an island, its political system of constitutional monarchy, its imperialist policies, and the power it derived from the British Empire at large.

According to Dunning and Sheard, rugby, cricket, pedestrian races, and especially boxing matches were organized before the Industrial Revolution. Boxing developed from fist fighting to a sport based on rules and regulations in which younger members of the aristocracy and gentry also participated in the middle of the eighteenth century. Besides boxing, the struggle for yards (meters) and against seconds also became fashionable and was enthusiastically taken up in rowing, running, and horse racing. Originally, members of the English upper class used their watermen or footmen in order to compete; later, gentlemen themselves competed against each other. Part of the attraction of these competitions lay in the betting that accompanied them; in turn, betting made regulations and standardization necessary to ensure that money changed hands only after a fair competition.

Dunning and Sheard explain the development of modern sport with England's distinct social configuration. The early dissolution of feudalism gave peasants the opportunity to play their rough games, and the relative independence of the aristocracy from the monarchy opened the way for a wide range of rural pastimes.

The emergence of modern sport is not only an outcome of the specific socio-economic conditions in England but also a part of the modernization processes which took place in Europe during the transition from the eighteenth to the nineteenth century. There is undoubtedly a connection between the rise of sport and the adoption of the values, standards, and structures of industrialization—including rationality, technological progress, the abstract organization of time, and an economy aimed at the accumulation of capital.

Sport was initially restricted to the English upper class, then to the upper and middle classes, before it finally reached the workers. Moreover, the rise of sport was closely connected with the educational system. During the nineteenth century, sport

>> continued

> U.S. Supreme Court decides Dred Scott case regarding slavery and citizenship

1858

• National Association of Base Ball Players founded

1859

• First intercollegiate baseball game played (Amherst over Williams 73-32)

• U.S. championship regatta in Boston won by Joshua Ward

1860

> Abraham Lincoln elected as president

• South Carolina secedes from the Union

1861

• Amherst College offers nation's first male physical education program

• U.S. Civil War begins with shots fired at Fort Sumter, South Carolina

1861–1865

• U.S. Civil War fought

>> continued

gained new importance and a new meaning in English public schools (Mangan). Headmasters used games, especially football and cricket, as a form of social control in the belief that the wild folk football games had to be regulated and thus tamed in order to discipline the players. Between 1850 and 1890, sports and games became compulsory in the leading public schools. Competition also arose between schools and universities, the best example of which is perhaps the famous boat race between Oxford and Cambridge, held for the first time in 1829.

By the end of the nineteenth century, sport in England had developed into an established system, with national and international associations, well-defined rules, and enormous popularity.

sport. Some towns aided railroad companies in securing passengers when sport teams and their followers traveled to neutral destinations for competitions in locales served by a railroad line. In the summer of 1852, Harvard and Yale competed in the first intercollegiate athletic contest when a railroad company sponsored a race to promote its resort at Lake Winnipesaukee in New Hampshire (as explored in some depth later in the chapter). Thus cities featuring railroad hubs gained economic and promotional advantages, since trains could both bring sport teams and spectators into the urban culture and transport them away from the city to other sport sites.

After the Civil War, the growth of sport was also influenced by completion of the transcontinental railroad, linking the East and the West, in 1869. The railroad provided a critical mode of transportation for moving people, both as sportsmen and sportswomen and as spectators, along with sporting goods and products. The transcontinental railroad would play a major role in the growth of travel by professional sport teams to California and other Western regions. It also enabled the staging of national sporting events that brought together sports journalists, promoters, urban boosters, and thousands of spectators to watch boxing matches, baseball games, and other contests.

Manuals written about sport and physical exercise popularized sport in American culture and informed the public about a range of sports such as cricket.

Reprinted from W. Wood, 1867, *Manual of physical exercises: comprising gymnastics, rowing, skating, fencing, cricket, calisthenics, sailing, swimming, sparring, baseball. Together with rules for training and sanitary suggestions* (New York: Harper Brothers).

The Cut.   The Drive.

Railroads thus provided new opportunities to city politicians, capitalists, civic leaders, and boosters. City builders developed and promoted commercial amusements and amenities, bringing new sporting structures and venues to the urban masses. The invention of the telegraph in 1832 by Samuel F. B. Morse, which was in operation by 1844, improved communications and made railroad travel more efficient thanks to its capacity to disseminate information about schedules. Thus in the booming city life of the mid-nineteenth century, entrepreneurs and transportation managers who were increasingly aware of the expansion of sport could now cater to those men and women with sufficient wealth and leisure time to take part.

Influence of the Media on Modern Sport

As sport coverage grew in newspapers and sporting journals (as discussed in chapter 3), manuals and advice books also increased the dissemination of sport-related information. In cities and towns, men and women reading about sport at home and in educational institutions found new books touting positive effects of sport, describing rules, and introducing new sports equipment. Typical publications included *The Book of Sports* by Robin Carver (first published in Boston in 1834); *Athletic Sports for Boys: A Repository of Graceful Recreations for Youth* (1866), which described boxing, fishing, rowing, sailing, fencing, skating, gymnastics, and other sports; and Dioclesian Lewis' book about his system of exercises in *New Gymnastics for Men, Women, and Children* (1862). In 1867, William Wood published his well-illustrated *Manual of Physical Exercises, Comprising Gymnastics, Calisthenics, Rowing, Sailing, Skating, Swimming, Fencing, Sparring, Cricket, Base Ball, Together with Rules for Training and Sanitary Suggestions.* Wood later penned *The Law of Athletics, Showing How to Preserve and Improve Health and Beauty, and to Correct Personal Defects Caused by Want of Physical Exercise* (1880), which included material on sports he deemed health building.

Writings by health reformers and sport enthusiasts such as Thomas W. Higginson, Catharine E. Beecher, Almira Phelps, and Dr. William A. Alcott (discussed in chapter 3) offered rationales and positive creeds about exercise and sport for a nationalistic spirit, for religious reasons, for the sake of individual good health, and for provision of a citizenry fit to perform its roles in the young democratic society. In addition, as sport became more organized, rationalized, and popularized, advertisers fanned and tapped into Americans' enthusiasm for sport by promoting sports equipment, publicizing sport competitions, and selling fashions and products to an expanding market of consumers in the urban economy.

Other forms of communication were used to disseminate scores and circulate accounts of athletic performances. The telegraph provided a means for sports and newspaper journalists to report on the results of athletic contests for an increasingly sports-hungry urban public, which feasted on news of intercity competitions in cricket and baseball, as well as results from the horse track, the boxing ring, and, later, international competitions that tested American nationalism in the arena of sport.

Subcommunities and the Growth of Modern Sport

Subcommunities based on social class and status played a key role in the new forms of sport that emerged in antebellum America, as many middle- and upper-class white citizens wanted specifically to separate themselves from the immigrants and poor workers crowding into the cities. The elite sports played by the upper classes, and the sports clubs organized to help the wealthy play and socialize with each other, introduced new sporting contests to American culture. Historian Benjamin Rader has investigated the evolution of subcommunities and elite sport in the experiences of white, native-born Americans of the upper class. These groups "tried to cope with the new urban-industrial society by forming subcommunities based on status. The socially

1862
- Morrill Land Grant Act passed for development of public universities

1863
- President Abraham Lincoln issues Emancipation Proclamation

1865
- Lee surrenders at Appomattox
- President Abraham Lincoln assassinated
- Thirteenth Amendment passed by Congress, abolishing slavery

1866
- Ku Klux Klan formed
- New York Athletic Club founded

1868
- Fourteenth Amendment ratified, providing citizenship to freedmen

1869
- Transcontinental railroad completed
- First intercollegiate football game played (Rutgers vs. Princeton)
- Knights of Labor workers' union founded
- Cincinnati Red Stockings become first pro baseball team

exclusive club became the main agency of status ascription" (Rader, "The Quest" 361). Membership in these clubs—which depended on wealth, gender, and race—served as a badge of exclusivity for the men who joined them for sport and leisure pursuits. These elites participated in aquatic sports such as yachting and some rowing events, as well as racket sports, in the latter part of the century.

Yachting

John Cox Stevens founded the New York Yacht Club in 1844, establishing himself as the premiere yachtsman in the country. As a prestigious, socially acceptable sport, yachting linked Stevens with New York City's elite citizens. To foster his passion for sport and American exceptionalism (i.e., his belief in American superiority due to its democratic principles and moral and physical vigor), Stevens wanted to show the supremacy of American yachtsmen by taking on the mighty British yachtsmen of the 1850s. Specifically, he wished to build a yacht to dethrone the British, and his boat, the *America*, handily defeated 18 British rivals in 1851 (a trophy was not awarded until 1857), thus earning him an onboard visit from Queen Victoria.

The exclusive nature of the New York Yacht Club required would-be members to possess money and social status; it was an elite group, and participating in it carried considerable prestige. Each member paid $40 in dues for the first year and $20 annually thereafter. Of course, members also owned high-priced yachts, and "the club prescribed expensive uniforms . . . and sponsored regular balls and social cruises to Newport, Rhode Island, Bar Harbor, Maine, and other nearby wealthy summer resorts" (Rader, "The Quest" 362). The 1857 *Constitution of the New-York Yacht Club*, based on the original rules drafted in 1844, indicated the strict requirements for membership, as well as the money needed for owning a yacht suitable for the club:

PEOPLE & PLACES

John Cox Stevens

Courtesy of the New York Yacht Club.

The sporting career of John Cox Stevens (1785–1857) shows the critical place of sport in the 1840s through the 1870s for elite white men in America. Stevens initiated spectacles of sport to enhance his own status as a wealthy businessman and as a promoter of American cultural values in competition with international rivals. Stevens was a leading patron of sport in the Antebellum Era, using his wealth to support such sports as horse racing, yachting, and pedestrianism (walking for competition) and to secure fields for ball games. To maintain some social and moral distance from sportsmen of lower socioeconomic rank, he did not patronize boxing matches. In 1831, working with his brother, Stevens established the park of Elysian Fields in Hoboken, New Jersey, across the river from New York City. As historian Benjamin Rader has noted, "In establishing Elysian Fields, nurturing the turf, and sponsoring pedestrianism, John Cox Stevens displayed a typical range of interest for a wealthy antebellum sportsman" (*American Sports* [2004] 37). Stevens' participation in the elite sport of yachting, however, reinforced his lofty position in the incipient nation.

Each candidate for admission must be proposed and seconded in writing; the name and address of the candidate, with the names of the members proposing and seconding him, must be sent to the Secretary. Members shall be elected by ballot. A quorum to consist of representatives from five Yachts, and two black balls shall defeat an election. . . .

All voting to be by representatives of Yachts; each Yacht to be entitled to one vote. . . . No yacht shall be presented unless she has been launched and a certificate signed by the Measurer, filed with the Secretary, specifying her tonnage and rig; and no representation shall be admitted upon any Yacht not now represented in the Club, smaller than twenty-five tons. (qtd. in Kirsch, *Sports* [Vol. 3] 60–61)

Prompted by Stevens' success, other elite yachting clubs entered races in various cities and maintained their associations for elite urban men (Gorn and Goldstein 78). Northerners, such as James O. Nixon, who purchased the *New Orleans Crescent*, helped found the Southern Yacht Club in New Orleans in 1849 (Guttmann, *Sports: The First Five Millennia* 121). The organization owning Stevens' *America* boat (a syndicate he established) presented the trophy cup to the New York Yacht Club, stipulating that international yachtsmen should compete for it in future races, and the success of the America's Cup continues today.

Rowing and Regattas

As with other sports during the growth of organized, commercialized sport and rationalized recreation, boating and rowing were typically seen as male pursuits. The vigorous and physical nature of rowing drew praise from antebellum health reformers, sport boosters, sports journalists, advice givers, and city leaders. Thomas Higginson, perhaps, expressed this view most succinctly when he claimed that rowing a boat went together with developing manliness, as noted in chapter 3. Similarly, physical education instructor and sport advocate William Wood declared, "Rowing is popular because it is a manly and healthful sport and pastime. . . . There is perhaps no sport or exercise in the world which affords a fairer or better trial of the finest qualities of manhood" (*Manual* 92).

The nation's numerous waterways—harbors, rivers, and canals—made rowing available to many of the workers in the maritime trades, and to the middle- and upper-income men in rowing clubs. In the mid-nineteenth century, both amateur and professional rowing matches and regattas were staged at city waterfronts in places such as New York City (as well as various localities in upstate New York), Boston, Philadelphia, and Washington, D.C. Sport historian Ronald Smith has determined that, aside from thoroughbred and harness racing, rowing gained more attention than any other sport in the 1830s (*Sports* 27). Men from the middle and upper classes established the earliest rowing clubs, amateur boat clubs established for the enjoyment of the sport, to provide opportunities for what they viewed as a recreational activity appropriate for their status:

Many clubs were being organized in New York, such as the Wave, Gull, Cleopatra, Pearl, Halcyon, Ariel, Minerva, and Gondola, and they, in 1834, formed the Castle Garden Amateur Boat Club Association, with a boathouse at Castle Garden; this was the first association of the kind in the United States and it had as objects both rowing and recreation. Among the members were many of the fashionable young men of the time, and the barge parties from Castle Garden were recognized among the pleasures of New York. But they were famous racing clubs as well, and the *Wave* was known to all oarsmen. . . . The Rollins brothers were members of the *Wave* crew and had a considerable reputation as amateurs. The Gazelle and the Gull were other noted clubs, the beautiful blue *Gull* finishing second to the *Wave* in several regattas. (Crowther and Ruhl 7–8)

A regatta held by the New York Amateur Boat Club in September 1837 drew a throng of at least ten thousand people (Rader, *American Sports* [2004] 40), and rowing also gained interest in other cities, including Boston, where, on August 5, 1842, the first regatta took place over the Chelsea course. The next year, New York oarsmen came to row against fellows enthusiasts from Boston (Crowther and Ruhl 12–13). Two other prominent clubs were the Narragansett Boat Club (1838) of Providence, Rhode Island, and the Detroit Boat Club (1839). The Narragansett club, now the oldest boat club still existing in the United States, grew steadily: "As the 19th century matured, so did the Narragansett Boat Club. It became a premier social and athletic organization of Providence's East Side" (Crowther and Ruhl 10–11; Narragansett Boat Club n. pag.). The Detroit club, also one of the oldest continuous boat clubs in the United States, served as both a boating and a social club for men. In one of the early contests, the club brought a "four-oared clinker from New York, and in the next year bought a Crolius boat and got it around the Erie Canal. With these craft a two-mile (3.2-kilometer) race was pulled from Hog Island (now Belle Island) to the boat-house on May 24, 1843—the first race in Western waters." A fire in 1848 destroyed the boat house and all but one boat, but the club reorganized and built other clubhouses (Crowther and Ruhl 11).

In the decades preceding the Civil War, both society and sport confronted the issue of slavery, and rowing at times dealt with rising intersectional tensions in boating matches between Northern and Southern clubs. As rowing was developing into a more modern sport—with organized clubs, rules, competitions, and improved equipment and techniques—regional pride in winning a match on the water appealed to socially respected young men. In December 1837, an article in *Spirit of the Times* referred to slavery in discussing a proposed match between a New York City boat club and one from Georgia:

> The Aquatic Club of Georgia has not yet withdrawn its challenge to our New York cracks, to row a straight mile (1.6 kilometers), for $10,000 aside, $2,000 ft. The Georgia boat is named *The Lizard*, and it will be observed by the following from *The Advocate*, published at Brunswick, Ga., that our Clubs cannot take the exception raised last Fall on account of the color of the crew of the Georgia boat. . . .

> "THE AQUATIC CLUB OF GEORGIA.---The challenge which this club published to the New York boatmen has never been noticed in any official manner. A gentleman of this city met some of the Whitehallers during the summer, and learned from them that they would not consent to row against black servants; but if the gentlemen of Georgia would row their boat, the case would be different. The challenge of the Georgia Club says nothing of the rowers, and the New Yorkers would have avoided the injury their reputation has suffered had they made inquires of the proper persons. We are authorized to say that the Lizard shall be manned by gentlemen, who, we warrant, shall, be the equals of Knickerbockers in bone and muscle, blood and sinew." (qtd. in Menna 107)

It seems that the race never did occur, but of course the intense debate on slavery continued in various arenas in antebellum America.

In 1851, rowing expanded in Boston, and the Union Boat Club, "which has always contained men who stood for the best in the sport, was formed." At first, the club did not hold races, but in 1854 the city of Boston "decided to make the regatta part of the Fourth of July Celebration"—that is, part of the tradition (as we have seen in earlier time periods) of engaging in sport and other active pastimes on Independence Day. The Boston regattas "were open to both professional and amateur oarsmen," yet the line "was being drawn between amateurs and professionals, [though at this point] . . . it was still a very hazy one." Professional rowing would take off in the late 1850s and the 1860s, but it was in these earlier years that questions about amateurs and professionals competing in the same match (whether in rowing or other sports) began to be part of modern sport (later chapters address challenges to the amateur code). In 1857, the Union Boat Club became a key association in the formation of the Beacon Cup Regatta for amateur oarsmen, and they performed well in these rowing contests, wherein they competed against various other clubs organized in the 1850s (Crowther and Ruhl 22–23).

The rich history of rowing in nineteenth-century American sport involves another important rowing club, the Potomac Boat Club in Washington, D.C., which participated in many regattas on the Potomac River. Initially founded as the Potomac Barge Club in 1859, the club attracted male citizens of good social and economic standing to its membership ranks. Along with other Washington, D.C., area rowing clubs, the Potomac club formed the Potomac River Rowing Association. At the time, rowing enjoyed widespread popularity and drew huge crowds of spectators, and performances by professional rowers stimulated young males and older amateurs to form rowing clubs in locales with good waterways. The Potomac Boat Club competed against other clubs and hosted athletic and social events for the middle- and upper-rank men of the club and their families; the clubhouse later hosted other sports, too, such as swimming and canoe races (Gems and Borish, "Sports, Colonial" 639). The club also hosted national regattas. In June 1859, the *Washington Star* hailed the rowing and athletic activities of the club: "We are glad to know that some of our prominent citizens have turned their attention to this pleasant and healthy exercise; for certainly there is no city in the Union where this exercise is more needed and can be so successfully prosecuted as in this, where there are so many engaged in sedentary pursuits and where we have such a magnificent stream as our broad Potomac" (qtd. in Proctor 8). Over the years, the club continued to draw elite Georgetown members to participate in rowing and social events. Professional rower Charles Courtney competed in matches on the Potomac River and later became coach of the Potomac Boat Club before going on to establish the rowing team at Cornell University. In fact, in the 1850s, amateur rowing—the first intercollegiate sport in the United States (as explored later in this chapter)—continued to be part of the growth of modern sport in colleges and other institutions. Professional rowing, however, gained prominence beginning in the late 1850s, with the physical prowess of oarsmen generating matches for money and drawing numerous spectators.

The rapid spread of rowing clubs in the 1850s ground to a halt when the Civil War began in 1861. Until then, races to determine the champion sculler of the United States generated strong interest among spectators and gamblers. One such was the Championship Regatta held in Boston on October 24, 1859, featuring six scullers and won by Joshua "Josh" Ward of Newburgh, New York: "A few vigorous strokes to close with, and Joshua Ward, still the champion, made his boat fly rapidly along, and crossed the line first, amid ringing cheers!" Ward beat out Thomas Doyle of Boston by 10 seconds. "Ward is the best man, and this year, at all events, is not likely to deprive him of the laurel he has so worthily won," reported the *New York Clipper* (qtd. in Kirsch, *Sports* [Vol. 3] 48, 49).

Josh Ward continued his rowing success in professional matches in the early 1860s. He and his siblings, known together as the Ward Brothers, competed against the Biglin Brothers, with "the more important races . . . [being] those for money," according to rowing chronicler Samuel Crowther Jr.:

> Josh Ward stands out as the old rugged type of oarsman,—big, muscular
> and possessed of remarkable power and endurance; he could row a race

at any distance, but was especially good on the longer courses, and his time of one hour and twenty-three minutes in the ten-mile (16-kilometer) match . . . on the Hudson at Poughkeepsie, has never been equalled; in his prime he held the records for nearly every course. The Ward family was then coming into rowing, and as it is undoubtedly the most famous of all the old rowing families, a word should be said of them. (Crowther and Ruhl 148–149)

The family lived at Cornwall on Hudson, and the brothers' father, a hotelkeeper and fisherman, brought the boys up on the water. Several of Josh's brothers also became outstanding oarsmen—John, Ellis, Gil, Charles, and Hank—and "Josh and Ellis had almost perfect sculling form." In August 1862, Josh Ward was challenged by James Hamill, a champion rower who won "sculling matches about Pittsburg"; Hamill surprised the country by defeating Ward on the Schuylkill River to win the national professional sculls title. Ward regained his title in a much-ballyhooed rematch at Poughkeepsie in 1863 (Crowther and Ruhl 148–149, 150). *Frank Leslie's Illustrated Newspaper* reported on the race and declared Ward to be "The Champion Sculler of America":

> *The* great race between Ward and Hamill, at Poughkeepsie, on the 23d of July, has restored to the brows of Ward the chaplet of Champion which he saw so suddenly and unexpectedly wrested from him last September by James Hamill, of Pennsylvania, when, over-confident of his superiority, he allowed his young antagonist to win the two successive races on the Schuylkill. ("Joshua Ward" 315)

The rematch paid each rower $500 a side to row a 5-mile (8-kilometer) course on the Hudson beginning at Newburg. The competitors had trained intensely, and the spectators were eager for the race. Here is part of the account from *Frank Leslie's Illustrated*:

> Poughkeepsie on the day of the race was crowded with strangers from Boston, New York, Philadelphia and Pittsburg, and betting on the result was quite animated and exciting. . . .
>
> At every stroke his [Ward's] success became more a matter of certainty, and, without relaxing his exertions, he continued to pull as strong and regularly as he had done at the first, the firing of the signal gun of victory proclaiming him the winner of the race by 10 lengths, and restoring to him his forfeited title of Champion Oarsman of America. ("Joshua Ward" 315)

The 1860s saw additional keenly fought rowing matches between professionals, and in 1867 James Hamill again competed for big money and a championship title, facing

The Biglin Brothers, rowing champions of the 1870s.

Image courtesy of Library of Congress, LC-USZ62-85536

Walter Brown of Portland, Maine, with a $4,000 purse at stake for the 5-mile (8-kilometer) race on the Hudson River. More than fifty thousand spectators gathered on the banks to watch the evenly matched oarsmen, "and the betting was larger than on any previous race in this country" (Crowther and Ruhl 156). This heated contest was distinguished by the fact that each sculler had a barge with oarsmen behind him, and questionable tactics included the brandishing of pistols:

GREAT FIVE MILE ROWING MATCH FOR $4000 & THE CHAMPIONSHIP OF AMERICA.

A professional rowing match for a championship between James Hamill and Walter Brown with the racers vying for the $4,000 purse.

Image courtesy of Library of Congress, LC-USZ62-684.

In Hamill's [barge] was John Biglin, and Charlie Moore steered for Brown; Biglin and Moore flourished each a pistol, and every moment one or the other was threatening to shoot as the opposing barge happened to come too near the rival sculler. Amid such a volley of curses the two rowed on. Brown was a very fast starter, and he at once took a couple of hundred yards' [183 meters'] lead and attempted to give Hamill a wash, but Hamill, though slow at the start, came up, passed Brown, and reached the stake-boat four lengths ahead. At that time only one stake-boat was provided for a race, and the boat that first reached it had the right of way, and the other man must go around him. Hamill attempted to make a close turn, and the strong ebb-tide took him hard on the boat and he could not get loose. Brown was close behind him, and seeing the predicament, headed directly for Hamill, broke his boat and put Hamill, who could not swim, into the water to be picked up by his pilot. Then Brown went on down and claimed the race; Stephen Roberts, the veteran oarsman, was referee; Brown's people claimed that no foul had occurred, and, of course, Hamill's backers asserted their rights. . . . [T]o increase the excitement, the dock, on which the crowd stood, fell in, and about half of them went into the water. When all had been calmed, the referee gave the race to Hamill on the foul. (Crowther and Ruhl 156–157)

These two outstanding rowers continued competing in races in the latter 1860s.

Racket Sports

In addition to aquatic sports, wealthy men in metropolitan areas also used racket sports in reinforcing their elite status. Sports clubs offered indoor racket sports for elite and upper-class men seeking healthful exercise during the winter season. Racket (or *racquet*, as it was often spelled then) sports gained popularity in the mid-nineteenth century, especially in New York City, where wealthy gentlemen formed the Racket Court Club on Broadway in 1845. The club "soon became one of New York's most prominent social clubs. . . [and it] remained exclusive into the 1850s, when it banned tradesman from membership" to prohibit middle- and working-class men from becoming members, preserving membership only for the very rich men of the city (Kirsch, *Sports* [Vol. 3] 297, 298). *The Constitution and By-Laws of the Racket Court, Adapted 7th May, 1845* codified the club's intention of maintaining certain standards for members:

> [Club members wish] to keep a place where they and their friends can have the benefits of taking athletic exercise, and enjoying judicious recreation and relaxation of both body and mind, without being compelled to mix with uncongenial associates; and aware that the permanent existence of such an establishment can only be secured by a strict adherence to the restrictions upon gambling, and rules governing the admission of members, and strangers to be introduced by them . . .

> Besides the game of Racket, requiring a court of 40 by 120 feet [12.2 by 36.6 meters], and a Bowling Saloon in the rear, the premises on Broadway, covering a space of about 55 feet [16.8 meters] square, will contain a Reading Room well supplied with newspapers and periodicals, a Billiard Room, two Whist and Chess Rooms, a Refectory, and if approved of by the members, a Gymnasium. (qtd. in Kirsch, *Sports* [Vol. 3] 298–99)

Indoor sport was also offered by a number of public racket clubs in the 1850s. As with many of today's public tennis courts, players had to sign up for a court, and rules sometimes depended on the size of the court. Following are excerpts from "Rules of the Game in a Close Court," printed in the *New York Clipper* on January 7, 1860:

> 1. Subscribers who agree to Play together must subscribe their names on a Slate placed near the Marker, they can then take the Court in the order their names are inscribed. . . .

> 3. To secure the Court for a Double Match, it is requisite that three of the persons who are to play should have their names inscribed; two for a single match. . . .

> 10. Person playing Matches of general interest, may play FIVE Games, whether there *two, three, or four* players ….

> 4. In serving, the server must stand with one foot within the compartment allotted for the server, the out player into whose court the ball is to be severed, may stand where he pleases ; . . .

> 5. The ball must be served above and not touching the cut line on the front wall, and it must strike the ground (before it bounds) within, and not touching the line enclosing the Court opposite to where the server stands. (qtd. in Kirsch, *Sports* [Vol. 3] 304–5)

These early forms of racket sport would evolve into indoor rackets and tennis in the latter years of the nineteenth century. The Racquet Court Club Building (New York City), built in 1875, served as an urban recreational and commercial building for wealthy businessmen. This athletic club was one of the first in New York City and housed one of the earliest indoor tennis courts.

Sporting Fraternity

Various groups, usually composed of men, influenced the rise of sport in urban America. The group referred to as the "sporting fraternity" engaged in sports of various moral and physical dimensions, often in marked contrast to the supposedly healthful and status-building (and more rationalized and organized) physical activities espoused by educated, middle-class, civic-minded Victorian men, who viewed wholesome sport as crucial to building the vigor and high moral character called for in citizens of the new urban culture and economy. Also known as "the fancy," the sporting fraternity consisted of an informal brotherhood of men sharing values and interests—a sort of solidarity, involving a passion for drinking, gambling, talking, fisticuffs, and social get-togethers associated with their preferred sports (Rader, *American Sports* [2004] 32). The so-called "rowdy bachelor culture" featured young unmarried men acting as pleasure seekers, gamblers, drinkers, and competitors, and shaping a sporting culture quite at odds with that favored by those who sought to create what they saw as an upstanding culture of physical activity. The sporting fraternity—which included working-class men, ethnic minorities, bachelors, saloon and tavern keepers seeking profit, city dandies, and members of the middle and elite classes desiring pleasure and profit for themselves in sporting enterprises—engaged in an array of antebellum urban sports, which linked these groups of men in expressions of masculinity. American studies scholar Simon J. Bronner has explored "manly traditions" and how highly gendered exhibitions of manliness occur in various ethnic and class contexts. He writes that "gender display is . . . a range of identities variously expressed and negotiated" (Bronner xii). In antebellum America, men's sporting behavior took place largely in locations separate from the daily living areas inhabited by both sexes together, and it involved symbols and activities intended to demonstrate participants' manliness. Young middle-class and wealthy men seeking adventure in the bachelor subculture of saloons found a place for the shared pursuit of hedonism, dissipation, and masculine prowess.

Notable in the sporting fraternity were Irish immigrant men, who brought their sporting and drinking traditions to America as part of the largest immigrant group in the mid-nineteenth century. Historian Steven Riess has noted that in the urban sporting fraternity, "all part of the male bachelor subculture, these sportsmen measured manliness by skill at wenching, drinking, gambling, and fighting" (*City Games* 15). The sporting fraternity's particular choice of sports left its imprint on the physical spaces and events of modern sport as it expanded in the middle decades of the century.

Boxing

The sporting fraternity relished the pugilism found in the taverns, gambling institutions, and other facilities of the Victorian underworld. In particular, bareknuckle fights (i.e., without gloves) at this time were frequently bloody confrontations between young urban males seeking money from the gamblers who bet on their physical prowess. A fighter's courage was challenged by the typically brutal fighting of his opponent, and, in sharp contrast to the relatively wholesome self-defense art of boxing or sparring, the prizefighting of this sporting fraternity emphasized not developing health and agility but gaining pride and victory through the gambling. In his manual on physical exercise and sport, William Wood illuminated the perceived difference between boxing or sparring as a respectable sport and the vicious bareknuckle boxing practiced by the working-class and ethnic-minority groups of tavern culture: "This manly exercise has no necessary connection with the brutal and disgusting exhibitions of the 'Prize Ring.' An accomplished sparrer is as such, no more a vulgar bruiser than an elegant penman is a forger or counterfeiter, or a clever gymnast, who can climb a ladder 'hand over hand,' is a burglar" (*Manual* 238).

As with billiard contests in this Victorian counterculture, bareknuckle boxing matches drew spectators from across the spectrum of society. The antiboxing legislation of the Antebellum Period meant these illegal boxing matches were staged in the secluded rooms of the sporting fraternity's saloons, in rural locations, or on seafaring vessels in order to escape the notice of legal authorities. Such settings highlighted the underworld aspect of these gatherings of bachelors and fancy men of Victorian culture, and the swearing and drinking, the gambling, the bloody violence, and the pleasure seeking all emphasized the supposed manliness of the world of boxing. Some boxers and saloon keepers achieved a kind of success in this world of physicality and illegal sport, rather than in the rationalized, middle-class, Protestant world of the work ethic promoted by many male Victorian leaders. As historian Benjamin Rader has observed, "The prizefighter, with his immense strength, muscular body, and swift, decisive answers, represented [for some] an appealing alternative to the effeminate self-effacing Victorian idea of manhood" (Rader, *American Sports* [2004] 44).

Taverns and Billiard Halls

The rapid growth of sports in antebellum urban cities took place in a variety of venues supported by the sporting fraternity. The saloons and taverns fostered competitive games, sports, and drinking, especially for working-class men, whose brand of billiards was marked as different from the billiards played in the homes of the wealthy, sober, and elite in Victorian America. Saloon billiards, taking place amid the usual gambling, drinking, and bantering of working-class men, often took the form of highly competitive contests. A description of the billiard table by James Hall in 1828 noted characteristics seemingly fitting for the sporting fraternity gathered in the saloon:

> The stained and dirty floor was strewed with fragments of segars [cigars], playbills, and nut shells, the walls blackened with smoke seemed to have witnessed the orgies of many a midnight revel. . . . A set of benches attached to the walls, and raised sufficiently high to overlook the table,

CRUELTY TO ANIMALS—"WHICH ARE THE BRUTES?"—[Sketched by A. R. Waud.]

Such criticism of animal cruelty did little to curtail the staging of animal blood sport in the nineteenth century.
© Corbis

accommodated the loungers, who were not engaged at play . . . [and who] sat or reclined solemnly puffing their segars, idly sipping their brandy and water, or industriously counting their chances of the game. (qtd. in Riess, *Major*, 51–52)

In the 1850s, with billiard halls accessible to working-class men in the cities where they worked and lived, the sporting fraternity played billiards frequently. In 1858, Michael Phelan of New York defeated Ralph Benjamin of Philadelphia to win $1,000 in the first major billiard contest in the United States (Kirsch, *Sports* [Vol. 3] 283). Phelan, a major promoter of billiards, competed against John Seereiter in Detroit the following year for a large sum of money. The bets of their boosters also loomed large at the table. The billiards play engaged the audience of men and women from 7:30 one evening until 5:00 the next morning. Phelan emerged victorious and supposedly earned $15,000 for his effort. With the bachelor subculture supporting billiard halls and taverns that showcased the sport, a talented player might earn considerable money through gambling and plying his skills before spectators (Rader, *American Sports* [2004] 41; Riess, *City* 17).

To the delight of gamblers, billiard halls sometimes staged animal contests as well—cockfights and rat fights, for example. In response, sport and health promoters who were developing a positive philosophy about the value of sport and exercise offered their moral outrage, as captured in 1867 in a *Harper's Weekly* illustration with the title *"Cruelty to Animals—'Which Are the Brutes?'"*

Pedestrianism

The spectators and gamblers affiliated with pedestrianism (professional footraces) in the mid-nineteenth century played a key part in the recreational culture of the sporting fraternity; in fact, only horse racing drew larger crowds than this test of individual physical achievement. In this period of early commercialized sport, pedestrianism was a sport with more modern characteristics than mere impromptu footraces, and it provided early opportunities for working-class athletes to earn an income with their physical prowess. For example, John Cox Stevens—famous sportsman and promoter of upper-rank Victorian sporting culture as a way to demonstrate American identity and nationalistic spirit against mighty British competitors—offered a $1,000 purse to the winner of an 1835 event heralded as the "Great Foot Race." The race intensified sporting fever for footracers and competitive race walkers and attracted spectators to watch these athletes perform. This "great trial of human capabilities," as described in the *American Turf Register and Sporting Magazine*, drew a field of international competitors vying for the cash prize offered by Stevens for the successful racer who completed the 10-mile (16-kilometer) course in less than an hour; he would add to the purse another $300 for the triumphant pedestrian who outraced all his competitors in the allotted time and thus earned all the prize money. The race was held at the Union Race Track in Long Island, where fans cheered the nine competitors. American farmer Henry Stannard of Killingsworth, Connecticut, won the race, finishing in 12 seconds less than an hour—among those he defeated were an Irishman and a Prussian who covered the 10 miles but took more than the hour allowed—and the American crowd lauded their countryman's victory. In "The Great Foot Race" the *American Turf Register and Sporting Magazine* provided the following coverage:

Stannard, the winner, we understand, has been in good training for a month. He is a powerful stalwart young man, and did not seem at all fatigued at the termination of the race. He is greatly indebted to Mr. Stevens, for his success; Mr. S. rode round the course with him the whole distance, and kept cheering him on, and cautioning him against over-exertion in the early part of the race; at the end of the sixth mile [roughly the 10th kilometer], he made him stop and take a little brandy and water, after

Can That Be Called Sport? Mensen Ernst and His Incredible Walking Feats

Mensen Ernst (1795-1843) was a Norwegian adventurer and globetrotter who gave up his occupation as a merchant sailor in order to pursue a "sporting career" as a runner. His "Sea, Land and Fast Journeys on All Five Continents," which made him prosperous and well known throughout Europe, are described in detail in a biography published in 1839.

As in the United States, pedestrianism had also become fashionable in Europe, and runners, or race walkers as they were also called, competed for the favor, as well as the money, of the curious public. In contrast to modern sport, there was no standardization of distances, conditions, or styles of running. Consequently, it was impossible to compare performance or establish records. But that was of no great importance to the runners, whose aim it was to increase suspense among the spectators—and thus the entertainment value of their performance—by thinking up ever greater sensations. To supplement their earnings, the runners took jobs as couriers or footmen, whose task it was to clear the way for noblemen's coaches. Mensen Ernst, for example, was in the service of Prince Pückler-Muskau for a time.

Like other race walkers, Mensen Ernst organized his runs himself. He wagered that he would cover a certain distance in a certain time and encouraged spectators to place bets. He also competed against dogs, horses, and other runners, and in most cases he won. From 1820 onward he staged his "productions" in numerous cities all over the European continent, for example in Copenhagen, Rome, Venice, and Constantinople. His spectacular performances attracted great crowds everywhere.

An extraordinary aspect of his achievement is to be seen in his ultra-long distance walks, in which he crossed deserts, climbed mountains, swam rivers, and had to overcome all manner of dangerous encounters with people and wild animals. In 1828, for example, he walked from Egypt to Germany via the Balkans, and in 1832 he wagered that he would cover the 2,500 kilometers from Paris to Moscow in 15 days. He managed the journey in 14 days, thereby earning 4,000 francs in prize money.

Ernst's most amazing achievement was his walk from Constantinople to Calcutta, which took him 59 days. In order to appreciate this achievement, it must be remembered that in those days there was neither motor transport nor telecommunications such as the telegraph or telephone. Ernst was completely on his own, having to rely on inadequate mapping to find his bearings and having to communicate with the inhabitants of the countries he traveled through. Besides having incredible stamina, he was endowed with little need for either sleep or the pleasures and comforts of life.

His wish to reach the source of the Nile prompted Mensen Ernst's last walk. He set off from Muskau in Upper Lusatia (Prussia) and, via Constantinople and Cairo, arrived at Aswan, where he fell ill with dysentery and died.

Was Mensen Ernst the greatest pedestrian of all times? Or was he also endowed with sharp business acumen, ably marketing his talent for race walking by embellishing his memories and exaggerating his adventures? It is entirely possible that hyperbole was an integral part of the business. After all, it was about public performance rather than sporting contest. However, the numerous newspaper reports that have survived clearly illustrate that there was a core of truth in the legend of Mensen Ernst.

Information from Wolfert, Raimund. *Globetrotter and Kosmopolit: Schnelläufer Mensen Ernst (1795-1843).* <http://www.fuerstpueckler.de/zeitungsartikel/laufer.htm>.

which his foot was on the mile [1.6-kilometer] mark just as the thirty-six minutes were expired; and as the trumpet sounded he jumped forward gracefully, and cheerfully exclaimed, 'Here am I to time;' and he was within the time every mile. . . . He was called up to the stand and his success (and the reward of $1,300) was announced to him, and he was invited to dine with the Club [New York Jockey Club]; to which he replied in a short speech thanking Mr. Stevens, and the gentlemen of the Club for the attention shewn to the runners generally throughout the task. . . . (qtd. in Riess, *Major* 52–54)

The popularity of the Great Race of 1835 led to other pedestrian races at the Beacon Race Course in Hoboken, New Jersey, in the 1840s. These races, featuring professional American pedestrians competing against their British counterparts, drew spectators eager to see the quest for American supremacy played out in sport. In 1844, one of these international races attracted a crowd of thirty thousand, who saw racers from England, Ireland, and the United States, as well as a Native American competitor. However, such events—usually accompanied by betting, drinking, rowdiness of spectators, and suspicion of fixed races—did not gain the support of health and morality-conscious Victorian sportsmen, and the growth of other sports (including team sports, as discussed later in this chapter) dampened enthusiasm for pedestrianism by the eve of the Civil War. Nevertheless, Edward Payson Weston gained acclaim in a failed attempt to walk from Boston to Washington in 10 days in 1861, and six years later he successfully finished a 26-day marathon from Maine to Chicago (Kirsch, *Sports* [Vol. 4] 335).

During pedestrianism's heyday, American champions often found competition in the international ranks. One such runner, George Seward, "the champion Sport runner of the world, better known as the American Wonder," left New York by boat to compete in England in 1843. William Wood provided the following account in his 1880 manual *The Law of Athletics*: "On September 30th, 1844, he [Seward] ran 100 yards [91.4 meters] in 9 £ seconds; this record has stood the test of time." Seward not only excelled "at this distance, but also in 'Hurdling,' from one hundred and twenty to three hundred yards [110 to 274 meters]; hurdles regulation height, three feet six inches [1.1 meters]" (Wood 36). Seward practiced a serious physical training routine as a champion runner:

Rise between 6 and 7 A.M.—Pass the sponge over the body and rub dry.

Exercise.—A brisk walk of from three to five miles [4.8 to 8 kilometers] according to the weather; wash, rub dry, and good hand friction.

Breakfast at 8 or 8.30 . . .

Exercise 10.30.—Starting on a slow walk, increase the pace, coming in on a sharp run; go a good distance if the condition and weather will permit.

Dinner at 1 P.M. . . .

Exercise 3.30.—Walking and running moderately with a light dumb bell in each hand; dropping the bells with a spurt of a hundred yards [about 91 meters] or so.

Supper at 7. . . .

Bed at 10.

(Wood, *The Law* 36–37)

Horse Racing

Horse racing expanded in the mid-nineteenth century as a sport popular with both owners and the spectators who gathered at the track, and the sporting fraternity patronized the races. Horse racing, as a favorite sport for the upper class—especially thoroughbred horse racing—involved the promoters of the sport seeking to engage the interest of the broader public. The supporters of horse racing like horse breeders and track managers strived to diminish the religious and other objections to their racing. In addition, horse-racing enthusiasts needed to solve numerous practical and financial problems so that they might make their events both entertaining and profitable. Organizers of the horse races needed to offer substantial prize money to draw quality horses for lively contests, and they needed to find suitable space and construct amenable facilities for horse owners, trainers, attendants, horses, and spectators (Kirsch, *Sports* [Vol. 3] 180–181).

Horse racing engendered the systematic breeding of horses during this period. As noted in chapter 2, the importation of the British racehorse Messenger in the post-Revolutionary years produced a series of championship horses. Messenger sired numerous offspring, including Abdullah, who birthed Hambletonian, who in turn emerged as the harness-racing sensation of the 1850s, when interest in that form of racing swelled (see chapter 3). Hambletonian raced for eight years, then produced 1,331 foals as a stud, earning his owner a sizable fortune in fees and considerable fame (Twombly 31). Meanwhile, harness racing developed a good following at the track. Lady Suffolk (known as "the Old Grey Mare") raced 162 times, and in 1859 Flora Temple defeated Princess, a California horse, in an intersectional race between East and West (Kirsch, *Sports* [Vol. 3] 214, 217).

In the growth of organized sport forms like horse racing, distinctions of social rank were clear between those men of wealth and means and those of the lower ranks. For example, John Cox Stevens, a leader in the antebellum turf network, served as president or vice president of the New York Jockey Club for more than 22 years. While spectators of all classes might enjoy watching horse racing, only the wealthy ran the sport and owned the expensive animals.

Highly publicized antebellum races covered by the general and turf press included an important series of intersectional contests between North and South to determine supremacy on the racetrack. From 1821 through 1845, five horse races, known as the North-South races, or "The Great Intersectional Races," took place at the Union Race Track, opened in 1821 on Long Island. These races drew large, lively crowds, and the increasingly distinct cultural and economic characters of the North and South spurred heated debates on issues such as slavery, agricultural tariffs, and temperance that formed bones of contention between Northerners and Southerners in the decades preceding the Civil War. Crowds included both elite and lower-rank spectators, many of whom took a train to the racetrack.

In 1823, much to the delight of Northerners, the Northern champion Eclipse defeated the Southern horse Sir Henry for a $20,000 prize, and the North rejoiced again in 1842, when Fashion defeated Boston, the Southern favorite. In 1845, the Southern horse Peytona, from Tennessee, and the Northern horse Fashion faced off before a grandstand crowd numbering thirty thousand, with another twenty thousand amassed in hopes of getting a glimpse. Much to the displeasure of the Northerners at the track, Peytona triumphed over Fashion to win a purse of $20,000. The *New York Herald* covered race day, noting not only that the huge crowd added to the excitement but also that "the sectional feeling and the strong rivalry of sportsmen, and in one sense partizans—the vast sums of money pending on the race, attached a degree of absorbing interest to the result, quite proportionate to the great demonstration that took place." And on the makeup of the large crowd: "We saw many distinguished sporting characters, politicians, editors, reporters, managers, actors, devils, &c.," all of whom cheered the horses to the finish when "Fashion appeared to have the lead, but on approaching the draw gate[,] . . . not withstanding the mob closing on the track, Peytona led a way clear length in advance in 7.45.1/4" (qtd. in Riess, *Major* 57–61).

PEYTONA AND FASHION.
IN THEIR GREAT MATCH FOR $20,000.
OVER THE UNION COURSE L. I. MAY 13TH 1845, WON BY PEYTONA

The famous North-South horse race in 1845. Peytona, the Southern horse, triumphed over Fashion, the Northern horse.

Image courtesy of Library of Congress, LC-USZ62-14099.

The economic gains by some of the boosters of the horse races, such as horse trainers or track managers, waned as mainly economic investments of the affluent horsemen yielded dividends. The economic and status benefits in the horse-racing industry were secured by the elite owners in the "sport of kings." By the advent of the Civil War, thoroughbred horse racing declined in the North because of such factors as the high amount of money needed to maintain horses, poor track management at facilities, meager attendance at regular horse meets, and decline in the breeding industry in the North. For some Americans, horse racing had served as a surrogate form of warfare, perhaps dissipating interregional tensions between the North and South until mid-century as debates intensified on slavery. In any case, the end of the contest for dominance on the track did not, of course, put a stop to the political, economic, and moral arguments that persisted about slavery and states' rights as the two regions moved toward war. Racing could not stem the tide of intersectional crisis in the United States, and instead of battling on the turf of the track for supremacy determined by the speed of a horse, the North and South moved inexorably toward fighting it out on the turf of the nation as a whole for supremacy determined by the bloodshed, victories, and losses of human soldiers in the Civil War.

Horse racing did, however, continue after the war. In 1866, affluent members of the American Jockey Club opened Jerome Park in the Bronx as a racetrack for thoroughbreds. Wealthy businessman Leonard W. Jerome and his capitalist friends August Belmont, William R. Travers, and James R. Hunter had founded the American Jockey Club as an exclusive club, and the track they built, situated on valuable land in Westchester County, was an impressive sporting venue for the elite sport of thoroughbred racing, with a luxurious clubhouse, amenities, facilities for other sports, and sleeping quarters. To foster the respectability of horse racing, and to counter the negative image given by the drinking, gambling, and vice associated with the turf course, Jerome instituted rules and regulations to uphold his sense of proper moral and social-class conduct. No alcoholic beverages were to be sold, gamblers were to be prohibited, and appropriate decorum was encouraged (Riess, *City* 25; Rader, *American Sports* [2004] 49). The *New York Clipper* wrote about the new park, noting its elite aspect: "The attendance was very large, it being estimated that thirty thousand spectators were present . . . as well as many ladies." To popularize horse racing, it reported, "the public should be permitted to enjoy the privileges of our race tracks at a small charge for admission, say fifty cents," rather than the $2 and $5 admission fees that were charged. The report concluded, "Very few except the wealthy classes can afford to indulge in the 'luxury of horse racing'" (qtd. in Riess, *Major* 143). Thus for the ordinary masses wanting to attend sporting contests, other sports would have to satisfy their desires.

Growth of Sports Clubs and Advancing Rational Recreation

The rise of American sport in the nineteenth century was shaped considerably by the interest of citizens (especially men) of differing social, ethnic, racial, and religious groups. While some single and young men pursued the sports favored in the rough settings of the sporting fraternity, many other men of the middle class decried those pursuits as immoral and wasteful of time. As an antidote, they touted a different version of sport deemed appropriate for respectable, disciplined, and hard-working "Muscular Christians." These men, seeking to participate in sport to achieve muscular and spiritual rectitude, wished to form voluntary associations for organizing appropriate sporting activity and rational recreation—robust physical exercise with the purpose of securing the health of the mind and body—to integrate into their urban experiences. These voluntary associations—formed by men with similar backgrounds, occupations, social classes, or ethnicities—served athletic interests centered on a particular sport or social club. The rise of sport during the mid-nineteenth century (1840 to 1870) was apparent in the number of sporting clubs organized for men and boys and in the spectators they often attracted to their competitions.

Gymnastics and Active Bodies

The extensive material published during this period on improving health and maintaining a sturdy body through physical exercise posited gymnastics as a powerful way to offset the ill effects of sedentary urban life, and gymnastics became part of a physical education movement featuring various forms of physical exercise promoted by instructors. German gymnastics, introduced by the German American Turners and intended to invigorate the body, was pursued in gymnasiums and YMCAs built in urban areas and in the schools. Dr. Dioclesian Lewis, a Harvard-educated teacher and medical practitioner, founded his New Gymnastics to appeal to men, women, and children and promoted his program through lectures, publications, and direct instruction. Lewis "borrowed lavishly from German sources so that his 'New Gymnastics' were in the main neither new nor his own," but he did help publicize the usefulness of light gymnastics and popularized gymnastics for schoolchildren (Hartwell 31). The system promoted by Lewis involved the use of hand apparatuses, such as wooden dumbbells, wands, beanbags, and small rings, with appropriate sizes and weights for men and women. The exercises were performed to music and arranged so that both sexes could participate, using lighter apparatus suitable for women.

In addition to ardently promoting his New Gymnastics in numerous publications, Lewis put his regimen into practice as founder and proprietor of the Normal Institute for Physical Education in Boston in July 1861. This influential school provided teacher training, introducing gymnastics to instructors who then promoted the sport in programs across the United States (Park, "'Embodied'" 89). Here is Lewis in his *New Gymnastics for Men, Women, and Children* (1862): "This book describes and illustrates a new system of physical training. Like air and food, its exercises are adapted to both sexes, and to persons of all ages." He asserted the positive outcomes for people doing his gymnastics. "This system of exercises will correct drooping or distorted shoulders, malposition of the head, and many other common defects." Lewis described numerous exercises with clubs and dumbbells that a person could undertake in specific positions to strengthen particular parts of the body, and he eagerly encouraged both adults and children to engage in the sport.

Lewis also supported Catharine Beecher's introduction (discussed in chapter 3) of calisthenics and physical education for women at her female institutions, and he recommended a gymnastics costume for women resembling the bloomer costume that Amelia Bloomer endorsed in the interest of woman's rights and physical mobility. Catharine Beecher had organized the Milwaukee Female College in 1851 as a venue for implementing her philosophy of women's physical and domestic education, and the institution offered sporting activities like gymnastics and horseback riding early on its curriculum for women's physical well-being. Beecher wanted to improve the physical education department in the 1860s with the construction of a calisthenics hall. Gender ideology at the time constrained women from playing more vigorous sports or competing in sports. Beecher included some of Lewis' gymnastic exercises in the program as gender-appropriate sporting activity to build the health of the women at the college.

Harvard College continued its educational program for physical and mental well-being for young men in the collegiate setting; it offered gymnastics and physical training to its students, and in the North a few educated free blacks might gain access to noteworthy educational institutions. Aaron Molyneaux Hewlett became the first African American on the Harvard staff, serving as the first director of the Harvard College Gymnasium, built in 1859, and as an instructor in physical education and curator of gymnastic equipment at the gymnasium from 1859 until his death in 1871. Hewlett's physical education instruction included the use of exercise equipment and clubs to strengthen the body and improve the form of male students. Hewlett's position on the Harvard staff contrasted sharply with the status of enslaved blacks during the Antebellum Era and with that of Southern blacks during the Civil War. Hewlett was predecessor to Dr. Dudley Sargent, director of the Hemenway Gymnasium and later director of the School of Physical Training at Harvard (discussed in chapter 6).

Instructors and authors touted a less vigorous form of physical exercise for the young American women attending female educational seminaries or reading health and domestic advice manuals about gymnastics. At Vassar, Mt. Holyoke, and Elmira Female College, young women used light handheld clubs or beanbags in their gymnastics. In fact, Dioclesian Lewis' "gymnastic regimen eventually found its way to female seminaries, to early women's colleges, as well as to a few early, private coeducational colleges." Lewis' nineteenth-century gymnastics for women usually included a greater percentage of calisthenic exercises for female students than gymnastics exercises appropriate for male students, as the gendered reference to the name calisthenics suggests, and he stressed the need for female students to better their health by developing sturdy bodies and a capacity for agile physical movement. Advice givers on sport and physical education for women generally approved of gender-specific activities for women, rather than the energetic sports pursued by men, and many nineteenth-century gymnastic

Aaron Molyneaux Hewlett served as the first director of the Harvard College Gymnasium.
Photo courtesy of Harvard University Archives.

regimes "directed U.S. women to self-consciously cultivate bodies comprising impeccable thoraxes and rounded chests buttressed by straightened spines" (Chisholm 738, 744, 751).

Young Men's Christian Association

For men in the cities, appropriate cultural environs in which to participate in sport began to be constructed specifically for their gender and dominant religious practices. The Young Men's Christian Association (YMCA), founded in England in 1844, developed in the United States in 1851. In the 1850s, especially in urban areas such as Boston, New York City, Washington, D.C., and other places teeming with young single men and working-class laborers, the YMCA promoted a particular Protestant brand of Christianity and later began offering gymnasium facilities as an inducement to attract patrons to its cause. Before the Civil War, "the original purpose of the YMCA had been to offer spiritual guidance and practical assistance to the young men who were flooding into the nineteenth-century cities" (Rader, *American Sports* [2004] 106). To offset the lure of urban amusements such as dance halls and billiard halls, and to provide a safe place away from crime, vice, drinking, and gambling, the YMCA became a site of moral and physical activity for young urban men. Thus the gymnasium, appealing to the athletic interests of young men in search of leisure pursuits, became an arm of the church, as YMCA facilities meant that young men might learn about both Christianity and sport, engaging in reading, recreation, and fellowship in a moral and safe environment. During the period of 1851 to 1870, as one historian has explained, the YMCAs "were trying to find a pattern of physical education that would meet existing needs and suit the era: physical work, as it was called at first, was not always seen as a legitimate function of the association" (Johnson xiii–xiv). In later decades, and with the pioneering leadership of Dr. Luther Halsey Gulick Jr., sport was given a larger place in YMCA programs (as discussed in chapter 6).

By the 1870s, several YMCAs were equipped with weight-lifting apparatus and offered some sports programs to induce the practice of Muscular Christianity, which signaled a transition in the relationship between the spiritual and secular worlds. Whereas clergy had previously shunned physical pursuits as a possible sinful temptation or a frivolous pastime, the new perception of the body as the housing for the soul required physical strength, maintenance, and well-being. Racial divisions, however, remained in force in the YMCAs in many cities. Washington, D.C., was home to the first YMCA branch organized for African Americans, providing a place where black men and boys could engage in social and recreational activities. The branch was founded in 1853 by Anthony Bowen, a former slave. Thus, the YMCA became a venue where the pursuit of sound health through exercise and sport was a wholesome form of recreation that bridged the sacred and the secular for whites and some blacks, albeit in separate facilities.

Young Men's Hebrew Association

In 1854, in Baltimore, Maryland, a group of Jews established the first Young Men's Hebrew Association (initially called the Young Men's Hebrew Literary Association), marking the beginning of the YMHA movement in America to promote literary, social, moral, and athletic activities for Jewish youth. Since Protestant social clubs often excluded them due to anti-Semitism, German Jews organized YMHAs in other areas as well. The YMHAs patterned themselves after the Young Men's Christian Association (YMCA) in offering facilities for reading and recreation and promoting spiritual values for Jewish youth. After this early phase, the YMHA movement expanded greatly following the Civil War, and YMHAs in late-nineteenth-century cities offered educational classes, athletics, lectures, and social programs in an effort to assimilate young, male Jewish immigrants into American life.

As YMCAs promoted "Muscular Christianity," YMHAs wanted to promote "Muscular Judaism," as termed by Max Nordaux who founded this movement, for Jewish youth by integrating physical fitness with spiritual values; they encouraged athletics along with spiritual development in order to counter stereotypes of Jewish people as weak and scrawny. There was also the question of participating in sport on the Sabbath, which of course was Sunday for the Christian community and Saturday for the Jewish community; playing sport on their respective Sabbath days was initially prohibited by both Christian and Jewish Ys. As the number of YMHAs increased, a national governing association emerged for the YMHAs and for arranging sport and cultural programs. Later, plans developed to merge Young Men's Hebrew Associations and Young Women's Hebrew Associations, creating the forerunner of the Jewish Community Center movement in the twentieth century.

YMHAS developed permanent facilities in cities including New York, Philadelphia, Louisville, and New Orleans in order to attract new members and advance the pursuit of athletics for young men. Many YMHAs expanded from rooms for libraries and social clubs to include gymnasiums, swimming pools, bowling alleys, billiard rooms, and other recreational facilities. The New York YMHA featured gymnasium equipment in 1875 and opened a full gymnasium in 1877 (Kirsch, "Young Men's"; Borish, "Young Men's").

Ladies Auxiliaries of Sporting and Religious Associations

For Protestant and Jewish women, membership opportunities in their respective Christian or Jewish Ys for spiritual and sporting activities remained limited. Initially, in the 1880s, women typically formed Ladies' Auxiliaries of the YMCA or YMHA, an arrangement that withheld full membership from them and thus denied them full access to the organization's buildings and physical education programs. When women formed their own Young Women's Christian Association (YWCA) in Boston, they offered calisthenic classes for women. As women's roles expanded in this association, and others formed their own YWCAs or YWHAs, women's involvement in various sports increased. Ethnically specific religious organizations such as the Young Men's and Young Women's Hebrew Associations paralleled the white, Anglo-Saxon, Protestant programs in serving their own needs. Thus sport became a tool for conversion in the contest for souls and ethnic identity.

Growth of American Team Sport and Competition

The expansion of modern sport by the mid-nineteenth century, especially for men and boys, also took the form of a rise in team sports marked by emphasis on competition, rules, associations of clubs, interest in performance and the keeping of statistics and records, and the spread of information about sports and the players. Moreover, spectators crowded the playing fields to watch men play team sports, and boys too began to learn the rules of the games. In particular, the team sports of baseball and cricket thrilled sports enthusiasts, journalists, and health-minded advice givers who heralded the value of team sports for men and boys. Baseball, in fact, became an American pastime, and nationalism surfaced in the attitudes toward it, especially in comparison with the British favorite of cricket.

Emergence of Baseball

The tradition of bat-and-ball games played by young men and boys prior to the 1840s and 1850s evolved into the popular pastime of baseball, which emerged as the premier sport in the United States by the latter part of the nineteenth century. Alexander Cartwright, a bank clerk and secretary of the New York Knickerbockers baseball club, recorded the rules in 1845 and as a result has been accorded the title "Father of American Baseball." The pioneering role of the Knickerbocker Base Ball Club was chronicled by Charles Peverelly in *The Book of American Pastimes* (1866):

> During the years 1842 and '43, a number of gentlemen fond of the game, casually assembled on a plot of ground on Twenty-seventh street . . . bringing with them their bats, balls, etc. It was customary for two or three players, occasionally during the season, to go around in the forenoon of a pleasant day and muster up players enough to make a match. The march of improvement made a "change of base" necessary, and the following year they met at the next most convenient place, the north slope of Murray Hill, between the railroad cut, and Third avenue. Among the prominent players were Col. James Lee, Dr. [Franklin] Ransom, Abraham Tucker, James Fisher, and W. [William] Vail, the latter better known in later years of the Gotham Club as 'Stay-where-you-am Wail.' In the spring of 1845 Mr. Alex. J. Cartwright, who had become an enthusiast in the game, one day upon the field proposed a regular organization, promising to obtain several recruits. His proposal was accorded to, and Messrs. W. R. Whea-ton, Cartwright, D. F. Curry, E. R. Dupignac Jr., and W. H. Tucker, formed themselves into a board of recruiting officers, and soon obtained names enough to make a respectable show. . . . [I]t was suggested that as it was apparent they would soon be driven from Murray Hill, some suitable place should be obtained in New Jersey, where their stay could be permanent; accordingly, a day or two afterwards, enough to make a game assembled . . . [and] marched up the road, prospecting for ground on each side, until they reached the Elysian Fields, where they "settled." Thus it occurred that a party of gentlemen formed an organization, combining together health, recreation, and social enjoyment, which was the nucleus of the now great American game of Base Ball, so popular in all parts of the United States, than which there is none more manly or more health-giving. (qtd. in Levine, *American* 37)

This "manly" game, as it came to be heralded by followers, was played by fellow clerks, tradesmen, and laborers, but not, at this time, by professional baseball players. The early rules of baseball, as codified by the Knickerbocker Base Ball Club, established in baseball a key element of modern sport, and some other teams adapted the club's rules. Cartwright put forward the field for baseball in the shape of a diamond and placed bases 90 feet (27.4 meters) apart at the corners. The full set of rules, adopted in 1845 and printed in *Spirit of the Times* in 1855, included the following:

> RULE 1. The Bases shall be from 'Home' to second base 42 paces; and from first to third base 42 paces, equi-distant; and from 'Home' to pitcher not less than 15 paces; . . .
>
> 2. The game to consist of 21 counts or aces, but at the conclusion an equal number of hands must be played.
>
> 3. The ball must be pitched, not thrown for the bat.
>
> 4. A ball knocked outside the range of the first or third base is foul. . . .
>
> 5. Three balls being struck at and missed, and the last one caught, is a hand out; if not caught, is considered fair, and the striker bound to run. Tips and foul balls do not count.
>
> 6. A ball being struck or tipped, and caught either flying or on the first bound, is a hand out.

7. A player must make his first base after striking a fair ball, but should the ball be in the hands of an adversary on the first base before the runner reaches that base, it is a hand out; . . .

8. Players must make the bases in their order of striking, and when a fair ball is struck and striker not put out, the first base must be vacant, as well as the next base or bases, if similarly occupied. . . .

9. A player shall be out if at any time when off a base he shall be touched by the ball in the hands of an adversary. . . . [But] if the ball drops it is not a hand out. . . .

10. A player who shall intentionally prevent an adversary from catching or getting a ball is a hand out.

11. If two hands are already out a player running home at the time a ball is struck cannot make an ace if the striker is caught out.

12. Three hands out, all out.

13. Players must take their strike in regular rotation. . . .

14. No ace or base can be made on a foul strike.

15. A runner cannot be put out in making one base, when a balk is made by the pitcher.

16. But one base allowed if the ball, when struck, bounds out of the field.

17. The ball shall weigh from 5 1/2 to 6 ounces [156 to 170 grams], and be from 2 3/4 to 3 1/4 inches [7 to 8.25 centimeters] in diameter.

(qtd. in Kirsch, *Sports* [Vol. 3] 73–74)

Various versions of the baseball rules abounded, with the Knickerbocker Rules or others (such as the Massachusetts rules) being played in baseball games in sundry towns and cities, especially in the Northeast. Sport historian George Kirsch has

An image of Base Ball, illustrating this popular, outdoor manly sport in the mid-nineteenth century.

Image courtesy of Library of Congress, LC-USZ62-640.

determined that the "New York game" won out over other versions of baseball because "[w]herever New York businessmen and newspapers appeared, they carried with them their local sport," and with New York gaining prominence as "the largest and most powerful city in the Untied States, it was also exporting and promoting its native sport as the American national pastime . . . The 'Massachusetts game' was not as attractive and could not compete with the game from Gotham" (Kirsch, *Sports* [Vol. 3] 71–72). Massachusetts rules games were played on an irregularly shaped square field, which meant different distances between the bases. By turning the field diagram to create a diamond shape, Cartwright created equal distances between all bases. In the Massachusetts version of baseball the batter stood midway between first and fourth— that is, home base—and tried to hit the ball. A batter, after hitting the ball, ran around the bases until safe at a base or was put out. The ball player was retired from the side "if the catcher caught three missed balls, or if a hit ball was caught on the fly, or if he was struck by a thrown ball while running the bases (called 'soaking' or 'burning' a runner)" (Kirsch, *Baseball and Cricket* 54–55). One out typically ended the inning, and the first team that scored an agreed-upon number of runs won the baseball game.

From the 1850s through the early 1860s, the New York rendition of baseball gained traction, and the codified rules circulated among ball players. Acceptance of the New York rules set the number of players at nine and fixed the design of the field, with a base positioned at each corner of a diamond-shaped infield. A batter still got nine pitches, delivered underhand and designated as above or below the waist by the batter himself into the 1870s. In 1858, 22 clubs in the New York area organized an affiliation grandiosely titled the National Association of Base Ball Players, which adhered to amateur guidelines. The association included the Knickerbocker, Gotham, Eagle, Empire, Baltic, Harlem, Independent, Metropolitan, Champion, St. Nicholas, Excelsior, Star, Enterprise, Union, Liberty, and other clubs. These class-based gentlemanly clubs gradually gave way in the face of recruitment and professionalism as rivalries (and wagering) between clubs, neighborhoods, towns, and various occupations fostered a greater attention to winning. In August 1860, *Wilke's Sprit of the Times* reported on the excitement about a championship game to be played between two rival teams:

The Grand Base Ball Match.

The "rubber" or third trial between the Atlantic and the Excelsior Base Ball Clubs, for the honor of the championcy, will, we learn, be played sometime in the first week of September, and will, without doubt, attract the most numerous assemblage which ever gathered to watch a baseball championship in the United States.

In regard to the grounds, we have heard several named, we know of but one which appears appropriate and suitable, and that is the East New York Parade Ground, adjoining the Howard House. There is here some beautiful field of thirty acres. The ground is as smooth as a floor, and upon it some twenty or thirty thousand spectators may enjoy an uninterrupted view of the entire contest. The facilities for reaching this locality are unsurpassed, there being three railroads . . . [which] will [be], for a trifling fee, depositing passengers directly upon the grounds. We will feel positive that the committees of the respective clubs can do no better than to immediately secure the Howard House grounds. ("Base Ball" 389)

The formation of more and more baseball clubs—made up of clerks, artisans, shopkeepers, and laborers—in both urban and rural areas soon meant there were plenty of teams to compete against one another for laurels and team pride. The spread of baseball also kept the game in the public eye and attracted more spectators. And, as

PEOPLE & PLACES

Henry Chadwick

One of the most influential early sports journalists was Henry Chadwick, who began his career in 1843 and by the 1850s was the leading sportswriter on cricket for the *New York Times*. Increasingly, however, he promoted the American game of baseball. As a sportswriter, he incorporated the baseball box score, previously used for cricket matches, and initiated the statistical categories of batting average, hits, total bases, and home runs. In 1858, Chadwick became a member of the National Association of Base Ball Players Rules Committee, and as committee chair he engineered a number of rule changes that modernized the game: the requirement of catching the ball on the fly to achieve an out (first-bounce catches had previously counted as outs), the switch from underhand to overhand pitching, and the establishment of a fixed distance between the pitcher and batter. The National Baseball Hall of Fame elected Chadwick to membership in 1938 in recognition of his important contribution to baseball and to sports journalism.

an alternative to the tough, bloody, and often immoral sports found in saloons and commercial amusement halls, and to offset the physical weakness of businessmen occupied in sedentary jobs and lacking exercise in the fresh air, health and sport advocates promoted baseball as especially useful in helping middle-class Victorian men and their sons become Muscular Christians. Thomas W. Higginson offered his own experience of baseball in the 1850s in an *Atlantic Monthly* article written for his accountant friend "Dolorosus" ("sad one"). Higginson believed that the outdoor competitive sport of baseball enhanced the physical fitness of businessmen, and he supported his case by citing a game between his friends of the Excelsior and Union baseball clubs: The players displayed "manly figures and handsome, eager faces," in contrast to Dolorosus, who featured a "meager form and wan countenance," thus prompting Higginson to announce, "I am satisfied that no description can do justice to your physical disintegration." Rather than criticizing baseball players as idly wasting time, Higginson and fellow sport advocates urged the physically weak man who overused his brain and shunned physical activity to go outdoors to a baseball field (Higginson, "A Letter" 467–468).

Baseball gained a hold on the sporting practices of Americans of different social ranks, races, and ethnicities. In short, as sport and baseball historians have emphasized, baseball "may well have been the most important sport in the antebellum era. Although some Victorian critics condemned the game for the usual offenses, it was much less raucous than the old sports of the bachelor subculture" (Gorn and Goldstein 79). By 1866, at the Tenth Annual Convention of the National Association of Base Ball Players, held in New York City, 212 baseball clubs, hailing from numerous states, were members (Wood, *Manual of Physical Exercises* [Vol. II] 191–192). Historian Ronald Story has explored the cultural appeal of baseball in early American society and found that it was viewed as "a superb outlet for boisterous young males in a way that languid pursuits—fishing or the saloon games or backyard games such as horseshoes or marbles—were not." Moreover, playing baseball could serve men and boys well, insofar as "a reputation for baseball excellence carried over in other areas, lending status to players in a brawling era that held physical prowess and 'grit' in high regard" (Story 123).

Baseball led an emphasis on American team sport for men and boys that continued throughout the nineteenth century. Even during the Civil War, when other major sports events were drastically slowed by the brutal conflict raging at myriad sites in the

INTERNATIONAL PERSPECTIVE

Why Baseball Had No Chance in Germany

After the end of the eighteenth century, several related games developed in Europe in which the ball had to be hit with a bat or club. Rounders and cricket were played in England, and *Schlagball* ("hit the ball") was played in Germany. Cricket and a similar "German ballgame" are described in the famous book *Games*, published by Johann GutsMuths in 1796. European emigrants took these games to North America, where they became the roots of baseball. American soldiers reimported baseball to Germany after World War II, but without any great success.

At the end of the nineteenth century in Germany, Schlagball was a game for youngsters, flourishing in the context of the German games movement, which influenced the playground movement in the United States. With the arrival of modern sport and its focus on performance and competition, Schlagball became "sportified," meaning that new rules made the game faster, more difficult, and more competitive.

The Prussian authorities and the German Gymnastic Association propagated the game for physical education in schools and clubs because it was looked upon as a German game which could counteract the growing popularity of soccer (which had English roots). From 1898 onward, Schlagball was played during the German Turner festivals, and the first German championships in Schlagball took place in 1913. Schlagball was even included in the program of the Olympic Games planned for 1916 in Berlin, but World War I prevented the holding of the Games and therefore also the Olympic blessing of this German game. Still, Schlagball became increasingly popular in the 1920s; besides being played in many clubs, it was also a popular and widely played school sport. Girls and women, too, played Schlagball and had their own competitions and championships.

After World War II, however, the number of players and teams decreased continuously, and the game nearly disappeared from the sporting landscape. Identifiable reasons for this decline include its numerous and difficult rules, as well as the permanent changes to them caused by the need to adapt them to the increasing skills of the players. This often led to unclear situations and controversies. Schlagball thus did not fascinate spectators. Additionally, in the 1920s the Germans had already opted for soccer as their national game, one which closely mirrors the principles of modern sport: it emphasizes the fight of player against player; it has a continuous flow of action; it has a single criterion for success; it is easy to understand; and the rules, as well as the state of the game, are transparent even for spectators who do not play the game.

Information from GutsMuths, Johann Christoph Friedrich. *Spiele zur Übung und Erholung des Körpers und Geistes* (Games for exercise and recreation of the body and the mind). Schnepfenthal, 1796; "Historie—anno dazumal bis heute (History—from the past to today)" <http://www.schlagball.com/cms/index.php?option=com_content&task=view&id=13&Itemid=27si>; Pfister, Gertrud. "Sozial- und Kulturgeschichte der Sportspiele (Social and cultural history of games)." Eds. A. Hohmann, M. Kolb, and K. Roth. *Handbuch Sportspiel* (Handbook Sport Games). Schorndorf: Verlag Karl Hofmann, 2005. 31–46.

United States, the popularity of baseball increased among the soldiers in the military fields far from their native cities or farms. Military regiments from numerous states played baseball during the war, and both Northern troops and Southern troops (who learned the sport from Northern prisoners of war) found the game a most welcome respite from the horrors of war. After the war, these troops helped to spread baseball across the nation, and as an indication of the growth of the game, especially as promoted by Union veterans, representation of baseball clubs in the National Association of Base Ball Players increased from 62 clubs in 1860 to 91 clubs from 10 states at the end of the war in 1865 (Rader, *American Sports* [2004] 54).

The Champion Nine of the Union Base-Ball Club of Morrisania, New York.
© Bettman/Corbis

Historian George Kirsch has studied the growth of baseball in the middle decades of the nineteenth century and commented on the strength of its fandom even in its early years: "The vicarious involvement of the spectators in the thrill of victory was as obvious in the 1850s and 1860s as it is today. Every team had its 'club followers,' who identified with their heroes and came to root them to victory." This keen "partisanship intensified after the Civil War, especially among the fans of the leading nines" (qtd. in Riess, *Major* 104). *Frank Leslie's Illustrated Newspaper* reported on the exciting scene at a championship game played just months after the war ended:

> The Elysian Fields in Hoboken, New Jersey, were crowded on the 3rd. inst. [of this month] to witness the grand contest of the United States, between the Mutual Club of New York and the Atlantic Club of Brooklyn. Never before was there a vast assemblage of people gathered together for a similar occasion, and never has there been known in the annals of our national sports, such a closely contested game of base-ball, as that which took place on Thursday. ("Base-Ball Match for the Championship" 356)

The Atlantics won by a score of 18 to 12, and baseball would continue its ascent to the status of national pastime. It still had to compete, however, with the widely popular British sport of cricket for the leisure time of young men, and cricket prevailed in cities like Philadelphia during the mid-nineteenth century.

Cricket

For sport-minded British immigrant men in the United States, the English sport of cricket proved immensely popular as part of their sporting heritage. Cricket, in fact, preceded baseball as a team sport followed by spectators, and it provided for the English what baseball provided for a growing number of Americans—a "national pastime" (in a phrase coined in 1856 by the New York Mercury baseball team). "Before 1860 (and to a limited extent afterwards), cricket enjoyed its own popularity in the U.S. and the question as to whether cricket or baseball would ultimately capture the American sporting heart was still unanswered" (Majumdar and Brown 142). In the 1850s, the rise in nationalistic spirit in the United States fueled the sport press covering baseball and cricket; the increased interest in American identity at this time spurred baseball to wider appeal, and baseball would surpass cricket as an expression of national strength in sport.

Cricket was considered the first major organized American team sport, and it saw an upsurge in players in the 1840s. The St. George Cricket Club, for example, was formed in Manhattan in 1839. Cricket teams consisted mainly of middle- and upper-class men, and as many as four hundred cricket clubs, with ten thousand members, were playing matches by 1860, sometimes in intercity matches as far west as Chicago and Milwaukee (Riess, *City* 33). International competition began as early as 1840, with a match between the United States and Canada, and an English all-star squad defeated the North Americans in 1859. Cricket differed from baseball in equipment (e.g., wickets, bails, stumps, and flat bats), field dimensions, and rules (for example, 11 players per side). Before the Civil War, cricket clubs proved popular in several American cities. Philadelphia became a leading cricket center, with wealthy Victorian men playing the sport to reinforce their social class and privileged position. Such elites might join the Philadelphia Cricket Club or other groups, as the city was home to some of the oldest cricket clubs in the United States. Club members in the Victorian era favored the "widely-held belief that moral, social, and vocational values could be developed through cricket. As a consequence, certain Philadelphians steered their sons toward the game with the intent of socializing them to be productive and successful adults" (Jable, "Social" 205–206). In suburban areas such as Germantown, cricket clubs offered a rural, outdoor setting comfortably removed from the chaotic city. The Germantown and Philadelphia Cricket clubs played important roles in the success of cricket in nineteenth-century America, and cricket clubs were the precursors of the prominent country clubs built by the turn of the century, when sports such as tennis and golf, played by both men and women, surpassed cricket among the elite (as explored in subsequent chapters).

For most Americans, however, baseball seemed more appealing than cricket, since men played baseball at a swifter pace, and it gained popularity both among young men seeking athletic activities and among their supporters who came out to watch. A *New York Herald* journalist in 1859 addressed the lack of interest in cricket as compared with the enthusiasm for the American game of baseball:

> [Cricket] is too slow, intricate and plodding a game for our go-ahead people. . . . In cricket a very smooth ground is wanted on account of the bowling as the ball must strike the ground before it reaches the batman or strikes the wicket. . . . In base ball very smooth ground is not required, but a rather larger space is necessary for cricket. . . . It occupies on an average about two hours to play a game of base ball—two days to play a game of cricket. (qtd. in Riess, *Major* 90–92)

As cricket's star faded, baseball's fortunes rose. "As American nationalism emerged and strengthened, baseball, continually forged and molded to suit the needs of Americans, began to assert a stronger hold on the American public, eventually pushing cricket forever into the margins of American sporting life" (Majumdar and Brown 143). Baseball, a faster, rougher sport that featured striking displays of men's physical skills, captured the attention of American men. Compared with cricket, baseball was "aggressively physical"; it was also "simple to learn and unlike . . . cricket, easy enough to play to accommodate a range of ages and skills." Moreover, baseball offered "endless bursts of action and limitless quick sprinting with very little dead time in between" (Story 122–123). By 1860, baseball had become the preferred team sport of the nation, and its dominance continued during and after the Civil War.

Rise of Intercollegiate Sport

By the mid-1840s and 1850s, the sport of rowing enjoyed considerable popularity. Rowing clubs were formed for middle- and upper-class men and their sons, and rowing matches began to play a significant role in athletic life for young white men at some of the elite Eastern universities. Sons of the wealthy organized a collegiate rowing club at Yale College in New Haven, Connecticut, in 1843: "William J. Weeks, '44, purchased a four-oared Whitehall boat in New York, and bringing it to New Haven formed with Henry W. Buel, John W. Dulles, John McLoud, Virgil M. D. Marcy, John P. Marshall, and William Smith the first boat club at Yale, and which was also the first rowing organization at any American college" (Crowther and Ruhl 14).

Spurred by Yale's club and by the Chelsea regattas of the 1840s, Harvard College followed suit by forming its own rowing club in 1844. "Yale oarsmen had their eyes on" the progress of Harvard's club, which in time led to a challenge to Harvard "'to test the superiority of the oarsmen of the two colleges,' and a race was arranged for August 3, 1852" (Crowther and Ruhl 16, 17). This crew race marked the first intercollegiate sporting contest in the United States. A railroad company carried the athletes, supporters, and spectators to the regatta as a way to promote both its railroad line and a resort in New Hampshire. Railroad Superintendent James Elkins "offered to pay for the transportation and lodging of the Harvard and Yale crews if they would race at Center Harbor on Lake Winnipesaukee, New Hampshire. Forty-one students from the two colleges accepted the proposal," and thus commercialism and sport meshed in this first intercollegiate sporting contest (Kirsch, *Sports* [Vol. 3] 40). Harvard, in the Oneida boat, defeated three Yale crews in the 2-mile (3.2-kilometer) race to win the first prize—silver-mounted, black walnut oars. The *New York Herald* described the race as follows:

> On the day of the regatta, the boats came crowded to overflowing with passengers, and these, together with the people from the villages around, lined the wharfs and shore for some distance. The scene was extremely fine, as the boats lay all abreast, waiting for the sound of the bugle. The beautiful lake . . . the unruffled smoothness of the water, and the perfect silence of the throng around—all added to the beauty of the scene. . . .
>
> The prize regatta came off at four in the afternoon. The boats were towed off to a starting point upon the lake, two miles [3.2 kilometers] distant from the shore, in order to row towards the shore. It was almost precisely a reenaction of the scene of the morning, save, perhaps, that the oarsmen bent somewhat more lustily to their oars. The result was the same as in the first race, there being nearly the same space between the boats. A pair of fine black walnut oars were presented, as the prize, to the Oneida. . . . The crowds dispersed highly gratified with the performance, the performers meanwhile adjourned to a very welcome repast at the Senter House. (qtd. in Kirsch, *Sports* [Vol. 3] 40–42)

This flyer promoted the race between Harvard and Yale in 1852.

www.rowinghistory.net

The enthusiasm for this first collegiate regatta led to another rowing match, when Yale issued another challenge to Harvard in 1855. The race took place on the Connecticut River at Springfield, Massachusetts, and once again Harvard triumphed. In 1858, *Harvard Magazine* "suggested that an association of colleges should be formed to hold annual regattas, . . . and on May 26 delegates from Harvard, Yale, Brown, and Trinity met at New Haven and evolved the College Union Regatta" (Crowther and Ruhl 28–29). Members raced on Lake Quinsigamond near Worcester, Massachusetts, and again Harvard proved victorious in 1859 (the race was cancelled in 1858 due to the death of a Yale oarsman who drowned during an outing). Yale would beat Harvard in another regatta, but Harvard triumphed in the regatta last held before the Civil War. The advent of the Civil War in 1861, however, halted the regattas, and many of the young men went off to war. When intercollegiate regattas resumed in 1864, the increasing rivalry between Yale and Harvard, along with Yale's intense desire to win, brought about a shift in tactics, as Yale students hired a professional coach. The Yale crew featured its six best oarsmen to date, and they came ready to compete despite Harvard's great confidence. In the event, "the championship was taken from Cambridge, [with] Yale taking the lead soon after the start, and keeping it during the whole race" (Crowther and Ruhl 32–33). Other elite colleges and schools then adopted the same strategy, and, though initiated and organized by students without institutional sponsorship, boat clubs assumed affiliation with their schools, and heated challenges spurred competition in intercollegiate rowing.

In addition to matching skills with oarsmen from other colleges, rowing teams vied with international teams as well. In 1869, a four-oared crew from Harvard competed in England against the Oxford University rowing team in the first of several intercollegiate competitions between American and English rowers. The scene was the Thames River in London, where, in a hard-fought race, Oxford, familiar with the river from their numerous runs on the Thames and cheered on by local spectators, emerged victorious. In covering the contest, the *New York Times* conveyed the keen attention increasingly being paid to such vigorous competitions between groups of young men: "The two greatest commercial nations of the world were engaged yesterday, not in the usual pursuit of gain, but in watching an extraordinary trial of strength between eight young men." Though Harvard lost, the contest evoked enthusiasm in America both for the sport and for such international matches: "An international boat race between nations like the American and English cannot, therefore, be regarded as a trivial incident," the *New York Times* reported, and these competitions challenge "the world to admire physical pluck, endurance, hardiness, a sound constitution, and other gifts, which we were intended to cultivate and rejoice in no less than in the pretentious intellectual forces" ("The *New York Times* Reports" 113–114).

The first intercollegiate baseball game was played in Massachusetts in July 1859, with Amherst College defeating Williams College by a score of 73-32. Because the game was being played in Massachusetts, the teams decided to use Massachusetts baseball rules. High scores were commonplace at that time as batters could call for the pitch to their liking, above or below the waist. Williams and Amherst agreed on the rules, including that each team would use its own ball, "which could be batted in any direction as in cricket, and they decided that the team which garnered 65 runs would be a victor." An issue in baseball rules at this time centered on catching the ball—if the player caught the ball on the fly or the first bounce, a batter was considered out. Catching the ball on the fly "was considered more 'mannish'" and the two "schools decided to do the masculine thing" (Smith, *Sports and Freedom* 54). College baseball, however, did not take off as fast as other collegiate sports, such as rowing and, later, football and track and field. College football (that is, one version of the game as played before the rules became standardized and modernized) was first played in the United States in 1869 by Rutgers and Princeton. The origins of these intercollegiate sports, as well as associations and mechanisms designed to organize college sports, are explored in later chapters.

Currier & Ives print of the 1869 Harvard versus Oxford international boat race.

Image courtesy of Library of Congress, LC-USZ62-847.

The Civil War and Sporting Experiences

As the chaos and carnage of the Civil War dominated Americans' lives between 1861 and 1865, the growth of American sport was of course greatly slowed. The Northern states, transformed by industrialization and urbanization and critical to the sporting boom in the mid-nineteenth century, now turned the full attention and capacity of their large populations toward providing the resources and products necessary to defeat the Confederacy. Sport did persist, however, and, in addition to baseball (discussed earlier in this chapter) other sports were engaged in whenever a soldier secured a few moments for diversion. Thus boxing, horse racing, wrestling, swimming, hunting, and fishing continued to be pursued to varying degrees during the war. Soldiers' desire to participate in sport, rather than just watch, meant that many men also wanted to play sport after their wartime days were done: "Both Johnny Reb and Billy Yank were by nurture and by inclination participants. . . . Watching with no prospect of joining was like being shot and having your name spelled wrong in the newspaper" (Fielding 156). As a result, sport clubs developed throughout the country, as former soldiers continued their interest in athletic activities, which, free of the horrors of the Civil War, offered a pleasant way to engage in competition against other men.

The Civil War also had another effect on American sport in the 1860s. The deaths of millions of white soldiers as well as free and enslaved blacks—due to military battles as well as disease and infection on the battlefield—generated a desire for robust military officers and troops trained for war in order to preserve the United States. In response, military leaders and the federal government moved to provide support for agricultural, land-grant colleges to train physically sound and mentally prepared men for military and other forms of service crucial to the nation's growth and development. These colleges, established with support from the Morrill Act of 1862, provided students with education in agriculture, engineering and mechanics, and home economics (for women admitted to colleges). Over time, educational institutions such as Penn State University, originally founded in 1855 and part of the growth of land-grant institutions, the University of Michigan, the University of Maryland, and Ohio State University integrated athletics and academics for young men in various regions of the country. These institutions provided the community structures and resources necessary to develop major athletic programs in the nation and promote sport for training a sturdy, physically energetic, male student body (as discussed further in the intercollegiate sport section of the next chapter).

Summary

For individual athletes and teams in American sport from 1850 to 1870, the values linked with sport continued to form a critical component of American identities. The growth of modern sport provided competitive, rationalized, organized, and publicly recognized contests, with sports information disseminated through the press. These early modern sports often utilized new forms of technology, both for playing the game and for transporting players and supporters to competition venues. As specialized skills emerged in athletic performances, and as victories and records gained prominence in defining the sporting experiences of participants, betting persisted in several sports, meshing easily with early commercialism. As part of the rise of modern sport, specific social classes often formed their own subcommunities, such as yachting and rowing clubs, in order to separate themselves from immigrants or persons of different races or backgrounds. The so-called "sporting fraternity" spurred the growth of certain sports, including boxing, billiards, pedestrianism (footracing), and horse racing, and infused betting into its sporting culture. Sport also registered gender ideology—that is, ideas of what it meant to be a man or a woman—and an emphasis on using one's body in rational recreation and sport in order to fulfill the ideal of a healthy and physically vigorous citizen of the United States. Rivalries—for example, between associated baseball teams or collegiate rowing clubs—quickened the quest for supremacy in American sport, and team sports such as baseball meshed with the increasing nationalistic spirit. At the local and national levels, sport became increasingly integrated into everyday life for participants, managers, and spectators. It also occasioned debates about codes of conduct for fair play, and in the following decades the continuing rise of modern sport would sometimes generate criticism, as issues of amateurism and professionalism surfaced more vividly in the playing and marketing of sport (as explored in the following chapters).

DISCUSSION QUESTIONS

1. How did modern sport change with advancements in athletic performance, competition, technology, and sporting organizations?

2. What factors were critical to the shift from premodern to modern sport during the middle decades of the nineteenth century?

3. Why did certain groups of men and women affiliate with, and support, specific types of sport?

4. What role did spectators play in the various forms of sport and in advancing the boom in sports during this period?

5. How did members of the "sporting fraternity" participate in sport, and in what ways did they challenge the moral and health-related rationales for sport in the mid-nineteenth century?

6. Why did some sports develop as amateur pursuits, while others involved professionals?

7. Why did baseball emerge in the mid-nineteenth century as an especially popular team sport in America?

8. How did the first intercollegiate sport develop, and why was rowing such a popular sport from 1850 to 1870?

5

New Identities and Expanding Modes of Sport in the Gilded Age

1870–1890

CHAPTER OBJECTIVES

After reading this chapter, you will have learned about the following:

- The relationship between urbanization and sporting culture
- The development of sport forms specific to social class and ethnicity
- The development and growth of intercollegiate sport
- The development of commercialized and professional sports
- The role of sports entrepreneurs and the media in the promotion of sport
- The relationship of sport to the bachelor subculture and concepts of masculinity
- The burgeoning of sport as a liberating experience for women

In November of 1869 the Rutgers student newspaper reported that the second of the three games of Foot Ball between Princeton and Rutgers was won by the former at their ball-grounds, on Saturday, the 13th inst. [of this month]. Eight out of fifteen was the game, but as Princeton won the first eight the other innings were not played. The style of playing differs, materially, in the two Colleges. A fly, or first bound catch, entitles (sic) to a "free kick," a la Princeton. We bat with hands, feet, head, sideways, backwards, any way to get the ball along. We must say that we think our style much more exciting, and more as Foot Ball should be. After the regular game two innings were played after our fashion, and we won them. It is but fair to our twenty-five to say that they never have practiced the "free kick" system. At half-past six we sat down to a very fine supper, prepared for us by our hosts. Speeches and songs, accompanied, of course, by the study of practical gastronomy, passed the time pleasantly until the evening train bore us Brunswickwards. We hope soon to welcome Princeton to New Brunswick for the third game, and beat them. Their cheer, sounding as if they meant to explode, but for a fortunate escape of air, followed by a grateful yell at the deliverance of such a catastrophe, still sounds in our ears as we thank them for their hospitality. If we must be beaten we are glad to have such conquerors. (qtd. in Kirsch, *Sports* [Vol. 4] 234)

So began the game that would overtake the national pastime of baseball on college campuses by the end of the nineteenth century. It more resembled the British game of soccer, but, with rule modifications and a greatly diminished spirit of cordial hospitality, it would come to define the American character in the ensuing years. Indeed, American sport would be distinguished from British practices by a win-at-all-costs attitude, intense competition, and a thwarting of amateur ideals prevalent at American colleges and high schools by the end of the century.

In the ensuing years, American sport forms and practices increasingly diverged from the British models. The regulation of sport emanated from urban processes as the United States experienced a social transformation throughout the nineteenth century. The gradual transition from rural, communal, and agricultural society occurred more abruptly in some localities. Chicago, for example, erupted from a frontier outpost to a city of more than a million inhabitants in one lifetime. The new urban environment housed various ethnic, religious, and racial groups, each with its own interests, values, and recreational practices. This sometimes volatile stew combined with industrialization to produce social inequalities; various tensions and conflicts between races, ethnicities, and classes; and political struggles. All of these developments influenced sport in various forms and American society in numerous ways. They produced class-based sport forms and associations that unified some ethnic, religious, or class-based factions while excluding others. In all groups, however—regardless of class, race, ethnicity, gender, or religious affiliation—sporting practices moved from premodern to modern status, characterized by greater organization, rationalization, quantification, commercialization, and professionalization. While sport in some respects unified particular groups and divided others, sports such as baseball and football began to establish particular national cultural characteristics.

The evolving nature of American society presented cultural dilemmas in the years following the Civil War. The carnage that eventually resulted in the emancipation of the slaves seemingly resolved the greatest cleavage in the American polity, and held promise for the realization of a classless democracy. During the Reconstruction period following the war, education became somewhat available to freedmen, and some African Americans even won election to Congress. Their ascendancy proved short-lived, however, as the political compromises of the Republican and Democratic parties eventually undermined black gains. The disputed presidential election of 1876 resulted in the victory of a Republican, Rutherford B. Hayes, on the condition that he restore white Democratic power in the South, thus negating the Reconstruction advances of African Americans. While technically they were still free, the resolution doomed generations of blacks to poverty as sharecroppers in the agricultural economy of the South.

The Civil War had been more than a battle over slavery. It resolved the question of the economic nature of the republic, which had lingered since its inception, and Thomas Jefferson's independent yeoman farmer gave way to Alexander Hamilton's capitalist entrepreneur in the era known as the Gilded Age. In the industrial North, the unbridled pursuit of wealth, combined with growing acceptance of the Social Darwinist tenet of survival of the fittest, rationalized the plight of the poor as inevitable due to their own character weaknesses. Large corporations and trusts dominated the economy, and individuals such as Andrew Carnegie, Cornelius Vanderbilt, J.P. Morgan, and John D. Rockefeller amassed enormous fortunes. Bribery and corruption ran rampant in business matters, and U.S. senators also became millionaires in a modern secular world that distanced itself from the moral prohibitions of earlier eras. Sport, too, moved away from its premodern traits to assume modern characteristics. As described by Allen Guttmann, the practice of sport became rationalized and more secular. Bureaucratic governing bodies emerged to regulate competitions, as winning assumed greater importance. Professional athletes enhanced the probability of success (for example, a professional pitcher could easily make the difference between winning and losing), and performances became quantified in the form of records that might allow for scientific measurement of human progress. Clubs and business owners sponsored events and teams to promote their identity or products; thus sport acquired commercial aspects and generated profits (Guttmann, *From* 62, 73).

Sport and Social Stratification

The highly visible accumulation of wealth and privilege upset notions of the United States as a utopian democracy. Within this context, sport and leisure practices both reflected and confounded American social ambiguities. While some sporting practices and their attendant crowds transcended class lines to present an egalitarian image, other sport forms reinforced class distinctions. Despite working-class roots, the Biglin Brothers reached championship status as professional rowers, and both baseball players and their fans often came from the lower and middle rungs of the social ladder. Thoroughbred and yacht owners, however, operated in distinctly different and separate circles, espousing a particular value system. Victorian decorum stressed the virtues of sobriety, dignity, self-control, and a white Protestant religiosity. Yet sporting ventures of wealthy and middle-class young men led some to seek adventure in a bachelor subculture centered in the saloons. In such environs, men shared in the pursuit of hedonism, dissipation, and masculine prowess. In such ways, sport both separated and united the distinct social groups in America.

Religion and Sport in the Gilded Age

Sabbatarian laws, evident in earlier periods of American sport history and discussed in previous chapters, continued to impede sporting developments in the South, and white middle- and upper-class Protestants still regulated Sunday contests well into the twentieth century in the Northeast. Heavy concentrations of Irish and German immigrants, however, fostered liberalization in the Midwest, especially in the urban areas. As early as 1855, Germans in Chicago erupted in the Lager Beer Riot when the nativist mayor attempted to prohibit consumption of their favorite beverage. A death, injuries, and the imposition of martial law resulted in a referendum that overturned the legislation.

1869-1876

1869
- Fifteenth Amendment passed by Congress prohibiting denial of the right to vote based on race
- National Woman Suffrage Association founded by Elizabeth Cady Stanton and Susan B. Anthony for suffrage and other woman's rights
- American Woman Suffrage Association founded to promote suffrage

1874
- Tennis introduced to United States

1875
- First Kentucky Derby held

1876

- Telephone invented by Alexander Graham Bell
- National League (baseball) founded
- Battle of Little Big Horn fought
- Intercollegiate Association of Amateur Athletes of America founded
- Westchester (New York) Polo Club founded
- First national track-and-field championship held (New York Athletic Club)

The Young Men's Christian Association expanded in the 1870s and offered physical training and sport programs to induce (as examined in the preceding chapter) the practice of "Muscular Christianity" among young, single men in various cities. Railroad companies hired the YMCA to provide wholesome forms of leisure to their employees, and the recreational link between railway firms and the YMCA became more pronounced after the national strike of 1877, when employees crippled and even destroyed much of the system in a violent confrontation over wage cuts. That same year, the YWCA, the female counterpart to the male organization, offered calisthenics classes for women in Boston, where in 1884 the YWCA even constructed a gymnasium for the females of the city.

Minority ethnic religious groups, such as the Young Men's Hebrew Association (discussed in chapter 4), also added new locations and increased sporting programs, countering the Protestant orientation of the YMCAs. The "Jewish Ys" initially (before the turn of the century) catered to the athletic interests of Jewish men, with women becoming auxiliary members rather than forming (as they would later) separate Young Women's Hebrew Associations. At the YMHA of Louisville, organized by well-established Jews primarily to assist Eastern European immigrants, Isaac W. Bernheim, a Kentucky distiller and philanthropist, completed the gymnasium in 1890. One year later, the Louisville YMHA conducted separate classes for women. In the late nineteenth century, at both Jewish and Christian Ys, sport became a tool in the contest for souls and sport took on a larger significance.

American Protestantism espoused individualism, a concept alien to the communal lifestyles of many immigrant groups, and, as industrialization and urbanization transformed American society in the post–Civil War era, ethnic groups maintained their alternative customs and practices in urban enclaves, homogeneous rural communities, and church parishes dominated by Old World clergy. Sport provided one means of assimilation and acculturation, but the process proved uneven.

Urbanization and the Continuing Promotion of Sport

Cities fostered the growth of sport, and technology sped its pace. The inventions and technological innovations detailed in chapter 4 gave way to other types of mechanization in the latter decades of the nineteenth century, and these, too, altered sport in American society. Electricity replaced gaslights in urban establishments, and sports clubs and entrepreneurs offered more commercialized entertainment for members and the general public. The growing manufacturers of sporting goods used the faster process of mechanization to produce sports equipment, making sporting products available for home consumption in rural and urban houses as well as for use in organized sporting associations. Mail-order businesses sent advertisements and sports manuals to people in large cities, small towns, and rural areas alike. In the 1880s, sporting goods manufacturers such as Spalding, Rawlings, Reach, Meacham, and McClean promoted their wares to the public, as documented by sports historian Stephen Hardy: "Wherever or however the consumer might purchase an article of sporting goods—through the mail or at a hardware store, general store, department store, or the sportsman's 'depot'—the manufacturer wanted him to buy a specific brand." In developing and standardizing sports products, "[t]he marketing efforts of sporting goods firms clearly expanded opportunities and interest in active play among a wide range of Americans" ("Adopted" 141, 146). Thus sporting practices continued to become more organized, rationalized, and quantified, a process initiated (as analyzed in chapter 4) in previous decades, and in the Gilded Age sport more markedly took on the characteristics of capitalist enterprise.

Capitalism bred an unequal distribution of wealth, however, and as the fortunes of working-class employees diverged from those of their bosses they took notice and began forming unions to gain rights and better working conditions. Wage labor dictated long hours and minimal leisure time for workers, but sport sometimes masked the growing development of distinct social classes. Particular sport forms, such as billiards,

PEOPLE & PLACES

Alfred J. Reach

Allegedly the first openly acknowledged professional baseball player, Alfred J. Reach first starred as a catcher for the Philadelphia Athletics in 1865. He continued to play as an infielder through 1875. Reach also opened a store in which he sold baseballs, bats, and other equipment, and as the business prospered he took on a partner in 1881, Ben Shibe, who later owned the Philadelphia franchise in the American League. Shibe's leather works began manufacturing baseballs and gloves, and the American Association (a National League rival from 1882 to 1891) adopted the Reach baseball as its official game ball in 1882. By 1883, Reach owned the Philadelphia Phillies of the National League, and the Reach ball and the Reach baseball guide became the official American League standards after the turn of the century. The Reach Company patented a cork-centered ball in 1909, which was subsequently adopted to replace the rubber-centered ball, fostering a livelier game. The company expanded to manufacture other sporting goods, including golf equipment, and was eventually bought by the rival Spalding Company.

Information from <www.baseballlibrary.com/ballplayers/player.php?name=Al_Reach_1840>.

might be played both in the parlors of the wealthy and in working-class saloons, and boxing matches drew spectators from across the spectrum of society.

Sport for the Elite

More often, sport forms distinguished between the social classes. While spectators of all classes might enjoy horse racing, only the wealthy could own the expensive animals. Affluent members of the American Jockey Club opened Jerome Park in New York as a racetrack for thoroughbreds in 1866. Monmouth Park was established in 1870, and the Brighton Beach course in Brooklyn followed in 1879. A coalition of Democratic Party politicians and rich socialites controlled the sport in New York state throughout the remainder of the nineteenth century. Outside the Northeast, Pimlico commenced operations in Baltimore in 1870, and Churchill Downs opened in Louisville, Kentucky, in 1875, with the running of the First Kentucky Derby, which established the state as another racing hub.

Railroad magnate Cornelius Vanderbilt favored harness racing, and his support lent a measure of prestige to the sport. The National Trotting Association was formed in 1870, and a national breeders' association followed in 1876. Harness racing remained a staple at rural county fairs, and the running of such contests at city tracks somewhat bridged the growing urban–rural divide. Venues such as ball parks and horse tracks provided an open-air, pastoral setting within the bustling cities as the urbanization process began to transform the economy from agriculture to industry.

Horse racing was democratic at least in the sense that spectators represented all classes, but racetracks began to construct specialized clubhouses with amenities for wealthy clientele. In 1871, the Metairie Racetrack in New Orleans designated a segregated section for African American patrons. Similarly, though racetracks organized betting that welcomed all comers, some required a minimum bet of an amount that excluded those with less disposable income. Independent bookies who operated at the tracks did accept small bets, and, in the cities, illegal poolrooms and bookmakers catered to less savory customers and urban workers unable to attend the events at the track. Such operations, protected by underworld figures and their allied politicians, formed

1880
• League of American Wheelmen founded
• Laws instituted to enforce the segregation and disenfranchisement of Southern blacks

1881
• United States Lawn Tennis Association founded

a criminal nexus in many American cities, and they remained a focus of crusaders over the next 25 years, as moral reformers and clergy attempted to banish gambling from American society.

While horse racing transcended class lines in some ways, yacht racing necessarily attracted only the wealthiest sportsmen. The Southern Yacht Club, founded in New Orleans in 1849, enrolled elites as members and conducted its regattas on Lake Pontchartrain and the Gulf of Mexico. The Civil War interrupted such excursions, but the club reorganized and resumed operations after the hostilities ceased. For the wealthy, sport and leisure practices transcended regional boundaries as they traveled to warmer climates. Northern elites traveled south in the winter and established yacht clubs. In the North, James Gordon Bennett Jr. assumed leadership of the New York Yacht Club. His daring victory in 1866 in the first transatlantic race, during which six lives were lost, garnered increased media attention for the sport, and new yachting clubs soon appeared in New York, San Francisco, Chicago, and Detroit (the Great Lakes provided suitable basins for competition in the Midwest).

In 1875, Bennett traveled to England, where he watched British army officers engage in a game of polo. The next year he introduced the game to his wealthy friends in New York, who formed the Westchester Polo Club. During the summers, they retired to their palatial retreats in Newport, Rhode Island, but continued their equestrian interests. Wealthy adherents disseminated the game in their travels, and polo clubs emerged throughout the United States and its colonies, in such places as New Orleans, San Antonio, Colorado Springs, Los Angeles, and Hawaii. West Point taught the sport to its cavalry officers, who then practiced it at their diverse duty stations. Like yachting, polo became a marker of social distinction in the form of a sport unavailable to the masses.

Bennett, perhaps the first great sports promoter in the United States, engaged in several other sporting ventures during the period. He sponsored Daniel O'Leary, a professional pedestrian (footracer), who competed for prize money:

> Great preparations are in progress and nearly completed for O'Leary's grand test race, the 156 hours "go-as-you-please," in which men and horses are to compete on equal terms for a purse of $4,000 . . . . The inclosure, grand stand, and other buildings . . . will be in readiness . . . when the tournament will be inaugurated with a match race for $500, in which Daniel O'Leary himself is to ride thirty miles . . . against three runners who are to go ten miles each. The runners are James McLeavy, the Scotch champion; White Eagle, the fleetest of foot of the Caughnawaga tribe of Indians from Canada; and Charles Price, the champion ten-mile runner of England. ("O'Leary's Tournament" 3)

Bennett also supported the first intercollegiate track meet in 1871, promoted foxhunting in Virginia, and built the attractive Newport Casino in Rhode Island in 1880, commissioning the famed architectural firm of McKim, Mead, and White to build and design the Victorian club. The Newport Casino provided a playground for the wealthy in New England, with spaces reserved for billiards, dancing, dining, bowling, lawn bowling, horse shows, archery, and lawn tennis. By this time, the eccentric Bennett had left for exile in Paris, having been ostracized by the moneyed social set for his vulgar behavior in polite company. His crudeness had degraded his privileged status. Still, he managed to implement increased sports coverage as heir to the *New York Herald,* and he later awarded prestigious international trophies to winners of auto and airplane races.

Other wealthy young men formed the New York Athletic Club (NYAC) in 1866 to participate in physical activity with like-minded counterparts. Two years later, the club was incorporated and commenced track-and-field competition. Club members distinguished between their own amateur pastimes and the practices of the professional pedestrians who pursued the sport for remuneration. Following the lead of the NYAC, numerous other elite and middle-class organizations formed metropolitan clubs. Adopting the British amateur code, they restricted membership by excluding all who gained compensation from their physical abilities. The ruling was meant to ensure equal competition and fair play, but a broad interpretation even eliminated many craftsmen and laborers of the working class who earned their wages by physical labor. It was a controversial issue. Many clubs only allowed amateur competition. "Open" competition allowed anyone to compete, but some amateurs lost their amateur certification if they competed in such affairs. Some clubs that sought competitive advantages used alleged amateurs but paid them in cash or kind clandestinely.

The NYAC assumed leadership of the amateur movement over the next decade by building a cinder track, introducing the use of spiked track shoes, and offering the first amateur national track-and-field championship (in 1876). It sponsored a national swimming championship for amateurs a year later, and both wrestling and boxing tournaments in 1878. By the end of the decade, amateur clubs had proliferated as far as the Midwest. As modeled in the sporting practices of the English aristocracy, amateurs were prohibited from competing against professionals or accepting compensation for their efforts, and the concept of amateurism permeated interscholastic and intercollegiate athletics thereafter. By the 1880s, the NYAC limited its membership, thus devoting greater attention to maintaining its elite social status than to its athletic endeavors, and other aspiring "athletic clubs" soon established restrictive covenants to assure the desired constituency. Such clubs, marked by social status and prohibitive membership fees, fostered a tight network of financial, commercial, social, and religious contacts that controlled the business economy of many American cities. Such practices and associations created social divisions within the society quite at odds with notions of equality and a classless democracy.

In Philadelphia, the wealthy emulated the British in their adoption of cricket. Featuring leisurely contests that sometimes took two days to complete, played in pristine white uniforms, and interrupted by breaks for tea, the British game carried distinct symbols of the aristocracy. English immigrants brought the game to the area in the 1840s, and young Americans adopted it as their own, even excluding foreign-born citizens from the best clubs. Five socially exclusive clubs emerged in Philadelphia as high-status communities, and after the Civil War each group built an extravagant clubhouse on lush grounds to distinguish itself from clubs of more moderate means. In 1874, a Philadelphian all-star team traveled to Halifax, Nova Scotia, where it defeated British and Canadian teams.

Maintaining Ethnic Forms of Leisure

As the upper classes established clubs and sporting practices that reinforced their elevated social status in American society, a number of ethnic groups sought to retain their European cultures. The German Turner associations, described in chapter 3, were the most prominent, with 317 clubs and nearly forty thousand members by 1894 (Hofmann 22). Other groups emulated the well-organized Germans.

Czechs

The Czechs organized nationalistic clubs known as Sokols based on the German Turner model in Prague in 1862. Like the Germans, they emphasized patriotism and gymnastic training to develop sound bodies as a bulwark against the Austrian Habsburg empire that imposed itself on local cultures. By the middle of the nineteenth century, Czechs began immigrating to the United States, where many took up residence in the Midwest, and in 1865 they established a Sokol in St. Louis. Like the German associations, the Czech Sokols faced division over issues of religion, splitting into contentious freethinkers (the

◄ 1882

• Chinese Exclusion Act passed

• Pullman industrial recreation program launched

• First country club established (Brookline, Massachusetts)

• John L. Sullivan defeats Paddy Ryan for heavyweight boxing title

◄ 1883

• New York Athletic Club holds first national swimming championship

◄ 1886

• American Federation of Labor organized

• Haymarket Affair occurs in Chicago

◄ 1887

• First women's amateur golf tournament held

◄ 1888

• Amateur Athletic Union organized with national championships in boxing, fencing, gymnastics, swimming, track and field pseudonym used at the time to designate atheists) and their Catholic opponents. Still, both factions stressed adherence to Czech culture and gymnastics, and they often performed mass drills. Such ethnic clubs maintained their communal societies and resisted assimilation into the American mainstream.

Poles

The Polish Falcon clubs followed the models of the Germans and Czechs, establishing similar units in the United States by 1887. The number of clubs, known as nests, reached a dozen within seven years, most of them in Chicago, which became the favorite American city for Polish immigrants. Like the Germans and Czechs, they promoted gymnastics, as well as their own language and culture, but the assimilation of second- and third-generation Poles brought a greater emphasis on American sport forms, such as baseball and football, by the twentieth century (Kirsch et al. 368–370). Poles developed particular skill in bowling, producing many champions in later years.

African Americans

While European clubs fought inclusion, African Americans sought integration, only to be denied. In the South, African American boxers and pedestrians did compete in New Orleans before the Civil War. Others played a game called raquette, similar to lacrosse, which drew large, integrated crowds, and interracial gatherings also witnessed the horse races at the Metairie Track in that cosmopolitan city. Throughout the rest of the South, however, African Americans faced strict segregation, and during Reconstruction even the more liberal city of New Orleans began enforcing Jim Crow conditions by segregating beaches and refusing to admit blacks to white athletic clubs.

In the North, free blacks generally enjoyed greater freedom than blacks in Southern states, but in 1867 the amateur National Association of Base Ball Players voted to exclude black players and clubs from membership. By 1876, the National League of professional players banned African Americans as well, and after the 1884 season

PEOPLE & PLACES

Moses Fleetwood Walker

Photo courtesy of National Baseball Hall of Fame Library.

Born in Ohio in 1857 to a black father and white mother, Moses Fleetwood Walker attended Oberlin College and the University of Michigan before earning his fame as the first African American professional baseball player in a major league. In 1884, Walker played catcher for Toledo of the American Association, and his brother Weldy also played for the team during part of the season. Toledo released the Walkers after that season, and Moses Fleetwood Walker then played for minor league teams through the 1889 season. He later became a successful entrepreneur, newspaper editor, author, and inventor of an artillery shell as well as improvements for motion picture projectors. In his writings, he advocated emigration of black Americans to Africa, a radical reaction to racism later adopted by Marcus Garvey, a black activist.

Moses Fleetwood Walker, a mixed-race (black and white) catcher for Toledo of the American Association, lost his job when management failed to renew his contract, allegedly because Cap Anson, player-manager of the Chicago White Stockings, had refused to play games with an African American. Other white racists sided with Anson, and by the 1890s black ball players faced exile from major league teams, a condition that would persist for the next half-century. As a result, they resorted to playing in minor leagues and semipro circuits and joining barnstorming clubs. The Philadelphia Orions had already assumed the latter status as early as 1882.

In the longer run, black athletes responded to this racism by forming their own parallel organizations and institutions in pursuit of sport and recreation. Blacks founded their own YMCAs in Richmond, Virginia, and Nashville, Tennessee, in 1867. In that same year, African American women, despite their relatively powerless position in society, founded their own baseball team, known as the Dolly Vardens, in Philadelphia. In the South, blacks were segregated into separate institutions, forced to play sports only among themselves, and in 1892 the first football game between black colleges was played by Biddle University (now Johnson C. Smith University) of Charlotte, North Carolina, and Livingstone College of nearby Salisbury.

Two years later, the League of American Wheelmen banned black cyclists from its ranks in order to appease its Southern members. Because black athletes were largely neglected, sport had little assimilative value in terms of general social acceptance and economic opportunity for African Americans during most of the nineteenth century.

Boxing remained one of the few sports open to blacks, because white spectators enjoyed watching the brutalization of African Americans. Whites developed stereotypes of blacks as cowardly, lacking manly courage and toughness, unable to sustain punishment, and therefore unfit to meet the standards of whiteness. Whites claimed that blacks were particularly susceptible to blows to the stomach, and they questioned blacks' endurance at a time when bouts might endure for a hundred rounds or more. White male southerners corralled black boys (whom they sometimes blindfolded) and made them engage in battle royals for the whites' own amusement so that they might wager on the last one standing.

Billiards was another sporting activity of African American males during this time, as reported in *The Spirit of the Times*:

> Let it be known that our colored citizens are not without ambition in a billiardistic way, and the balls, propelled by cues in ebony hands, are wont to echo muchly in the purlieus of the Eighth Ward of this city. Evening following evening the two tables in the room kept by Major Pool, at 149 Wooster Street, are nightly invested by a small brigade of negroes, and the balls are kept in lively agitation. Parties awaiting their turns, too, are numerous, and, with feet elevated before the fire, and reclining at an angle of about fifteen degrees, remind one forcibly of certain positions which were said to be assumed by certain Congressmen during parliamentary discussions. The room presents the appearance of a colored paradise, and the *habitues* seem perfectly at their ease, and undoubtedly regard their present *otium cum dignitate* as a faint reflex of the good time coming, and not far distant in the future. As we are of the humanitarian sort, we heartily wish them godspeed; but trust that their newly acquired importance may not be used as a means of inciting them to act of lawlessness and violence.

> During the fall of 1870 considerable feeling was manifested between certain of the colored citizens who had acquired some knowledge of the game, and for the purpose of settling the point Major Pool procured a handsome cue which he offered as a prize to be contended for by the players who were so inclined, and which was to be symbolical of the Colored Championship. The

1889

- Hull House settlement opens in Chicago; offers sport and athletic programs for immigrants
- First All-American football team selected
- Boston Athletic Association introduces water polo to the U.S.
- First U.S. speedskating championship held

1890

- Wyoming grants women suffrage
- Sherman Antitrust Act passed
- Polo Association (later called the United States Polo Association) founded
- Brotherhood League (baseball) founded
- National American Woman Suffrage Association is organized, combining the two woman's rights groups of 1869

cue is valued at $50. There were seven entries, consisting of J. Vaughn, C. Marsh, R. Huclus, William Miller, J. Joseph, W. Jackson, and the proprietor of the room, Major Pool. During the tournament, W.S. Widgeon of this city acted as referee, and J. Sands of Savannah and W.T. Jones of Philadelphia as scorers. The games were of 1,000 points each, at American four-ball caroms, each carom to count 3. The first game was between Vaughn and Marsh, the former winning by 244 points; highest run, 63. In the second game Huclus beat Miller by 196; highest run 54. Jackson and Joseph contended in the third game and the former was vanquished by 199; highest run, 39. The fourth game produced a lively display between Pool and Joseph. Pool finally won by 135 points, his highest run being 39. The contestants in the fifth game were Huclus and Pool. Won by the former with a majority of 235, he having again scored 54 as his highest run. (Wouldn't that be a good number to play first in the lottery?) The struggles finally narrowed down to a contest between Huclus and Vaughn. After a long contest of one hundred and ninety one innings, Huclus pulled out ahead, by a score of 1,000 to 963. His highest run was 36, as against 27 by his opponent. Huclus was then amid much excitement, proclaimed champion. But we are told that "uneasy lies the head that wears the crown," and it has been again verified in this instance; for on Tuesday last the Championship Committee were handed the appended document, which shows that Vaughn does not consider the results of the last game as a true index of the comparative abilities of himself and Huclus:

NEW YORK CITY, Feb. 14, 1871

To Messrs. Wm. T. Widgeon, Wm. T. Jones, and S. Ellis, Committee for Colored Amateur Championship—*Gentlemen:* This is to notify Mr. Robert H. Huclus, Amateur Champion of New York City, that I hereby challenge him to play a match-game of billiards for the Championship and Champion cue at the earliest possible time allowed by the regulations. As I desire to play the first game according to the conditions of the tournament, an early answer is solicited.

Yours sincerely, John H. Vaughn (qtd. in Kirsch, *Sports* [Vol. 4] 314)

Irish

Irish immigrants during this period were considered to be among the lowest on the social scale. In the South, Irish laborers performed the most difficult tasks since slaves, who were property, were considered more valuable. By 1850, Irish women composed 75 percent of the house servants in New York City. In 1874, an African American doctor described the Irish as

remarkable for open, projecting mouths, prominent teeth, and exposed gums, their advancing cheekbones and depressed noses carry[ing] barbarism on their very front. . . . [D]egradation and hardship exhibit themselves in the whole physical condition of the people . . . giving such an example of human degradation as to make it revolting. They are only five feet two inches, upon an average, bow-legged, bandy shanked, abortively featured, the apparitions of Irish ugliness and Irish want. (qtd. in Roediger, *Black* 56–57)

The Irish gained a measure of whiteness and entry to the mainstream culture as they proved their mettle in the boxing ring and on the baseball field. Their social capital also rose with their eventual domination of the Democratic party, and the linkage of sport and politics allowed some, particularly Irish Americans at first, to earn a measure of social and economic mobility. Politicians often sponsored working-class sporting clubs, whose toughs supplied political muscle as shoulder-hitting intimidators at the polls on election days. Irish political bullies acted as enforcers or protectors in rivalries with other urban and ethnic gangs. Such activities provided a foundation for the Democratic Party political machines that ruled big cities, most notably the Tammany Hall group in New York. In such an environment, boxers earned respect and even prominence.

In Chicago, Tom Foley, a member of the city's professional baseball team and an expert pool player, earned enough money to finance a large billiard hall. His physical abilities enabled him to assume entrepreneurial and political opportunities (much as John Morrissey used his success in boxing, as discussed in chapter 3). Foley won a seat on the Chicago city council as a member of the Workingmen's Party. Such advances fueled perceptions of sport as a meritocracy and as a means to socioeconomic mobility for poor Americans and the ethnic immigrant groups who flooded American shores from 1880 to 1920.

Boxing did, in fact, produce numerous heroes in specific ethnic groups, including the biggest sport star of the nineteenth century in bareknuckle fighter John L. Sullivan. Born in 1858 to Irish immigrant parents, Sullivan, known as the "Boston Strong Boy," earned his initial notoriety by challenging saloon patrons, boasting that he could beat any man in the house. In 1882, Sullivan easily defeated then-champion Paddy Ryan at a clandestine spot in Mississippi. By 1885, he was popular enough to draw ten thousand spectators for a New York City bout, and his performances established his status as the world's toughest man. In 1889, in the last of the bareknuckle championship fights, Sullivan conquered Jake Kilrain in a contest that lasted 75 rounds. Sullivan toured the country in theatrical performances and boxing exhibitions, and his picture adorned countless saloons as a working-class hero. As champion from 1882 to 1892, Sullivan imposed a color ban, refusing to fight black boxers, thereby asserting the whiteness of the Irish and marking the symbolic prize as one for whites only. He lost his title to another Irish American, "Gentleman Jim" Corbett, in New Orleans in 1892 under the new Marquis of Queensberry rules. The new rules prohibited wrestling, required boxing gloves rather than bare knuckles, provided for timed 3-minute rounds, and declared a knockout after a 10-second count by the referee. Sullivan's career thus witnessed the transition from the bareknuckle brawl (similar to saloon or back-alley fights) to a regulated, more strictly governed competition. In the process, working-class toughness and physicality merged with middle-class order and bureaucracy to produce a sport amenable to different layers of the social strata (Gorn, *Manly*).

The most famous of the nine-teenth-century Irish baseball play-ers, Mike "King" Kelly, exemplified the merger of sport, working-class masculinity, and the perception of meritocracy and social mobility. Born

John L. Sullivan: King of the bareknuckle boxing champions and the first great American sports hero.

Mike "King" Kelly in his Boston uniform after being traded by A.G. Spalding in 1886.

Photo courtesy of National Baseball Hall of Fame Library.

to Irish immigrants on the last day of 1857 in Troy, New York, Kelly began a pro career with Cincinnati in 1878 but reached stardom with Chicago from 1880 to 1886. He led the league in batting during the 1884 and 1886 seasons and scored the most runs in each of those years. A fast runner, Kelly was an expert base stealer, and his prowess was hailed in a popular song titled "Slide, Kelly, Slide." Stories abound about his legendary trickery, as well as his adherence to the lifestyle of the bachelor subculture. On one occasion, when the umpire's back was turned, he allegedly sprinted across the pitcher's mound from first to third base and the distracted official assumed he had stolen two bases. Another time, too hungover to play, he rested on the bench until a pop fly traveled toward him. Realizing the fielders could not make a play, he jumped up and announced his substitution as catcher before snaring the ball. As an outfielder, he supposedly ended a close game in the dusk when he leaped into the dark fog to grab a long drive with the bases loaded. The umpire called the batter out, and his teammates heartily congratulated him on the amazing catch, whereupon he admitted that the ball had traveled well over his head but that he had a spare in his pocket.

Such antics endeared Kelly to his fans, and he engaged in theatrical tours, supposedly being the first to sign autographs for admirers. His ghostwritten autobiography, released in 1888, helped to create the genre of sports autobiography, as many players would follow his lead over the next century. By this time, Albert Spalding, head of the White Stockings team, had less enthusiasm for Kelly's off-field gambling and drinking. Spalding had a Pinkerton detective follow Kelly, and the spy reported that Kelly stayed out until 3 a.m. drinking lemonade and that his leadership, as it were, proved detrimental to younger players. When confronted with the charges, Kelly's only amendment was that he drank straight whisky, not lemonade; he did not want his masculinity questioned. Spalding soon sold Kelly to the Boston club for the then-astronomical sum of $10,000. When the players revolted over the reserve clause—which allowed a team to renew a player's contract at will, thus preventing players from moving freely from team to team—to form their own league in 1889, Spalding, as head of the National League, offered Kelly $10,000 and a guaranteed contract to return. But Kelly, loyal to his coconspirators, maintained solidarity by stating that he "could not go back on the boys" (Pearson 199). Kelly's steadfast adherence to the honor code and the norms of the bachelor subculture contrasted with the values of those in the upper classes who saw drinking and carousing as immoral, unwholesome, and unproductive.

ABSORPTION OF A BASEBALL PLAYER.

This cartoon portrayed the negative image of baseball players in the late nineteenth century.
Image courtesy of Library of Congress, LC-USZ62-42416.

Development of an Intercollegiate Sporting Culture

As African Americans struggled for opportunities and other ethnic minorities distanced themselves from the mainstream culture, the children of the upper classes established the early norms for intercollegiate sport. In 1869, Harvard's crew journeyed to England for a match with Oxford on the Thames River. Although Harvard lost, the adventure stimulated interest in rowing, and other colleges formed rowing associations in 1870. Sixteen schools competed in the regattas, and smaller colleges managed to triumph over prestigious institutions such as Harvard and Yale. In 1873, as the nature of fair competition became a greater issue, the association banned the employment of professional coaches. The regattas of 1874 and 1875 drew large crowds and national media attention at Saratoga Lake, New York. Crew members followed a strict training regimen in the quest for victory, as American competitive spirit and greater emphasis on winning began to be felt on college campuses. Such traits emerged in other competitions and soon marked the national character. The events of the mid-1870s represented the heyday of collegiate rowing, as other sports began to gain importance.

Rowing was for a time the most popular intercollegiate sport; in fact, intercollegiate track-and-field competition served as a sidelight to the 1873 regatta, when the *New York Herald* offered a trophy for a two-mile (3.2-kilometer) race. Five track-and-field events appeared on the program the following year, and in 1876 the Intercollegiate Association of Amateur Athletics of America (IC4A) assumed authority for the track-and-field races. The open competitions offered by the New York Athletic Club, however, soon attracted college athletes and surpassed the allure of the regatta games. Track-and-field competition eventually gained ascendance and popularity and no longer needed an attachment to the crew races.

Four schools formed the College Union Regatta Association in 1858, and the regatta of 1859 also featured an intercollegiate baseball contest, in which Amherst beat Williams 73-32. (The rules of the game at that time greatly favored the batters and such high scores were not unusual.) Throughout the 1860s, Harvard fielded an exceptional baseball team, with an undefeated string that lasted for seven years, and by 1870 home games drew as many as ten thousand fans. That summer, the team embarked on a tour through the East and Midwest, playing against both amateur and professional teams. After the Civil War, baseball spread to Southern college campuses, but Northeastern schools first formed the American College Baseball Association in 1879. A loosely run league, it tried to enforce weak eligibility rules, which allowed part-time students and faculty members to play on school teams. In many cases, colleges even employed professional players to enhance their chances of winning. Such developments blurred the distinction between elite sports and gentlemanly behavior, constituting a further departure from the traditional and aristocratic sporting practices of British schools.

Rowing became a major collegiate sport in the latter nineteenth century and fostered modern training devices such as sliding practice seats, as shown in this Muybridge photo series.

Image courtesy of Library of Congress, LC-B2-963-11

INTERNATIONAL PERSPECTIVE

Fencing at European Universities

The *Mensur* fencing practiced by students is neither a sport nor a duel, but it has something in common with both. *Mensur* properly means *measure* and refers to the predetermined distance between two fencers. Mensur fencing is still practiced today in Germany, Austria, Switzerland, and Belgium.

The roots of Mensur fencing can be traced back to the Middle Ages, when students were permitted to carry weapons in order to defend themselves against attack on their journeys to and from the towns in which their universities were situated. The growing number of students in the early modern period led to the rise of a student culture, in which class affiliation, prestige, honor, and the ability to defend oneself all played significant roles. Students formed loose groups consistent with their social provenance; they lived in private lodgings and, not infrequently, caused trouble in the university towns. Insults or attacks on their honor were immediately avenged, weapon in hand, and fierce duels with no regard for rules became an integral part of student life. The object of a duel was to seek redress for a real or imagined insult. Here, it was not a question of victory or defeat but of proving that one was "man enough" to defend one's honor or the honor of one's class.

Over the course of the eighteenth century, specific dueling rituals had developed, and insults were no longer avenged immediately. Instead, such redress took place at a later time at a prearranged place, with seconds taking care of the organization and watching over the procedure of the confrontation. The dueling weapon of choice was customarily the sword or pistol. The duel ended when the prearranged number of pistol shots had been fired or when one of the two opponents was wounded. Unlike the Mensur, then, duels quite frequently led to severe wounds or even death.

The great significance of fencing in wars, as well as in everyday life, led to a demand for fencing instruction. In those days, in addition to dancing teachers and riding instructors, a university's staff also included fencing masters. From about 1800 onward, students started to form *Verbindungen*, or student corporations, which often had an anti-Semitic and nationalistic orientation. Perceived as lifelong alliances, these hierarchically structured groups imposed strict rules on their members' conduct at the university and were aimed at forming character and personality. Numerous emblems and rituals—for example, insignia, badges, drinking rites, and, above all, fencing—bonded the members of these corps together. Fencing was learned and trained in specific training halls. The acquired skills were used in Mensurs with sharp weapons. The opponents stood facing each other in a circle of limited circumference, and evasion was deemed dishonorable. Even so, student fencing was not (and still is not) dangerous, due to the protective clothing worn and the strictly obeyed sequence of the blows. The head was the preferred target, and scars on the face were cherished badges of honor.

From around the middle of the nineteenth century onward, participation in the Mensur became compulsory for all student corps members. This led, among other things, to the staging of Mensurs between the members of different corps. Subsequently, the Mensur lost its dueling character, though motives for fighting duels continued to exist. A growing distinction was made, however, between dueling and fencing among students, since, like the aristocracy and military officers, they continued to have the right to seek satisfaction, as well as the obligation to give it.

At the end of the nineteenth century, student corps enjoyed a further boost in popularity, since corps members were admired and acknowledged as being a cut above the rest. Mensur fencing played a significant role in this distinction of status as an initiation rite and as an anchor for member identification. Fencing is a ritual, a trial of courage and an entrance billet to a community that is proud of its exclusiveness and which conveys this pride to its members who have conquered their fear in order to be accepted in this male bonding activity. The Mensur and dueling signaled social status, as well as attributes of character such as courage and manliness, thus underscoring students' claim to positions of leadership.

In the second half of the nineteenth century—quite independently from students' Mensur fencing at universities—fencing was established as a sport. Here, as in other sports, the sole criterion was the sporting skill of competitors. As early as the first Olympic Games of the modern era in 1896, fencers took part in competitions with foil and saber, and in 1900 with the épée as well. In 1924, foil fencing was added to the list of women's Olympic disciplines.

The German National Socialists prohibited student corps, and after the Second World War neither corps nor Mensur fencing was deemed to be in keeping with the zeitgeist of the postwar years. The few student corps that have been either newly founded or refounded play no role whatsoever at universities today.

Information from McAleer, Kevin. *Dueling: The Cult of Honor in Fin-de-Siècle Germany.* Princeton, NJ: Princeton University Press, 1994.

Winning assumed its greatest importance in the sport of football, where victory carried great symbolic weight in the context of Social Darwinist notions of masculinity and physical prowess. With no war being fought during the Gilded Age other than frontier skirmishes with Native Americans, young white men had few venues in which to develop and display such courage, and football provided the physical contact and martial strategies not found in other team sports. The roots of the game lay in English peasant soccer games. By 1827, Harvard students engaged in a general melee at the start of the school year in order to brutalize freshmen as a rite of passage. Yale took up the harsh welcoming ritual in 1840 and continued it until school authorities banned it in 1860. Boston schoolboys continued the roughness, but by 1868, Princeton student William S. Gunmere had adapted the London Football Association's rules for games at the New Jersey college. The regulations allowed for 25 players per team in a soccer-style contest, and on November 6, 1869, Princeton traveled to Rutgers for the first intercollegiate match, won by the home team 6 to 4. Columbia joined in a triangular fray (a series of matches between three schools playing each other) in 1870, as rules became negotiable. In 1872, Harvard adopted rugby rules that allowed running with the ball. Harvard, not wanting to defer leadership to Yale or Princeton and favoring its own rules, declined to attend a rules convention the next year in which American schools began to depart from the British version of the game (Gems, *For Pride* 12). By 1876, other schools adopted the rugby rules, changing the emphasis from kicking to running.

In the Midwest, students at the University of Michigan took up the game and arranged a contest with Cornell to be played in Cleveland in 1873, but Michigan president Andrew White interceded, stating, "I will not permit 30 men to travel 400 miles [about 645 kilometers] merely to agitate a bag of wind" (Nelson 32). For the most part, however, school administrators exercised little control over student activities at the time; students arranged their own rules conventions, games, and training, and accounted for their own expenses. They held their first official intercollegiate football championship in 1876. Yale defeated Princeton in a wild game featuring 11 players per side, but Harvard disputed Yale's claim to the title, as it adhered to 15-man teams. The athletic rivalry exposed deeper sentiments harbored by the Boston Brahmins, who sent their sons to Harvard, and the nouveaux riches, who sent their offspring to Yale. Such social tensions would be played out on the gridiron thereafter at the risk of societal and institutional pride, resulting in greater involvement and support by alumni, trustees, and other benefactors.

The 1877 championship was marked by greater commercialization, as the New York Polo Club offered a trophy and its grounds for the game. The location, in the nation's media capital and largest city, heightened expectations for profit and publicity, as well as the perceived importance of winning. During the 1877 season, the *Tufts Collegian* complained about Yale's tactics: "[T]he gentlemen who compose the Yale team have cultivated a habit of losing their tempers, and mauling their antagonists with doubled fists. . . . [L]ookers-on, mostly students . . . showed their magnanimity by facetiously pelting our men with pebbles and second-hand tobacco quids" (*Harvard Advocate* 49).

Early football games were compared with boxing matches, and serious injuries were rampant.

Image courtesy of Library of Congress

PEOPLE & PLACES

Walter Camp

This athletic pioneer played five sports at Yale but earned his fame in football. After serving as both player and coach on the Yale football team, he took on a larger role as Yale's supervisor of athletics from 1888 to 1906, in which position he raised money, generated alumni support, recruited top athletes, and developed training systems that led Yale to dominance on the gridiron in the Gilded Age. Camp garnered the accolade "Father of American Football," however, for his work on the rules committee, a loose association of schools and coaches, on which he served from 1878 through 1925. Among the most drastic changes, Camp advocated the introduction of a line of scrimmage, a limit of 11 players per side, a system of downs and distances, scoring changes that reduced reliance on kicking, and the practice of tackling below the waist. Along with sportswriter Caspar Whitney, Camp also created the first All-American team in 1889.

The team captains at Yale and Harvard still differed over the number of players allowed to participate in the game for each side. Yale agreed to use 15 in 1878 but wanted a $100 guarantee for a Thanksgiving game, indicating a greater sense of commercialization. That year, Princeton emerged as the champion by beating Yale before a crowd of two thousand at Hoboken, New Jersey. Woodrow Wilson, future president of the United States, served as secretary for the Princeton coaches' board. Walter Camp, a pioneer of American football as player, coach, and sports journalist, captained Yale and became secretary of the rules committee, a position he held until his death in 1925.

By the latter 1870s, Harvard, Yale, and Princeton had adopted durable canvas jackets and pants, which replaced the tights previously worn by players. Evolution of clothing and equipment provided not only greater protection but also competitive advantage. Players greased their pants to hinder would-be tacklers, but the ongoing brutality of the game proved evident in numerous accusations of throttling (choking), kicking, and slugging of opponents. Frederic Remington, a Yale player and later a famous artist, allegedly dipped his jacket in slaughter-house blood in order to make it more "businesslike" for the 1878 contest with Harvard.

The game further deviated from soccer in 1880, when Camp introduced the scrimmage line; as in warfare, the game was thus increasingly marked by specific maneuvers (plays), concerted strategy, and territoriality. Two Kentucky teams, Centre College and Transylvania, played the first intercollegiate game in the South, which readily took to football's militaristic features.

When the overemphasis on ball control produced boring (often scoreless) contests, Camp introduced (at the 1882 rules convention) the concept of downs and yardage to be gained. Attempts to limit eligibility often faced disregard, and scoring still emphasized kicking, with 5 points awarded for field goals and 4 points given for kicks after touchdowns. Still, players and fans were drawn to a game featuring relative carnage that asserted one's masculinity. The 1883 rules still allowed for hacking, throttling, butting, and tripping. One might punch an opponent three times before being ejected from the game. The heartiest young men were drawn to the bloodbath, and football grew rapidly into the Midwest. By 1886, it had reached California.

The organized violence drew increasing numbers of spectators, further commercializing the game. In 1885, an impartial referee replaced the alumni who had previously officiated the games. Another umpire was added in 1888 to deter brutality, but spectators continued to fill the competitive venues. The 1893 Princeton–Yale

THE TWELFTH PLAYER IN EVERY FOOTBALL GAME.

A newspaper cartoon portrayed the figure of Death hovering over any football game as casualty rates escalated.

Image from *World*, November 14, 1897.

game, billed as the national championship, attracted forty thousand spectators, including New York residents, alums, and spectators from as far as Oregon and Texas. A 4-hour parade preceded the contest, despite a severe economic depression. Opponents characterized the intercollegiate frays as "the playful gamboling of twenty-two prizefighters" (Gems, *For Pride* 25–26), and faculty members at the elite institutions attempted to intercede, with little success.

By this time, football had assumed particular characteristics that many Americans perceived as defining the national character. Walter Camp claimed that "our players have strayed away from the original Rugby rules, but in so doing they have built up a game and rules of their own more suited to American needs." Another proponent extolled the activity that "embodies so many factors that are typically American . . . [. V]irile, intensive, aggressive energy that marks for progress is the root which upholds and feeds American supremacy and American football" (Gems, *For Pride* 20).

Throughout the 1880s, new rules sparked specialization on the football field that resembled its counterpart in industrial factories. Players assumed particular roles for greater efficiency, as linemen and backs were assigned distinctive positions with specific duties. Before the end of the decade, football had surpassed baseball in popularity on college campuses.

INTERNATIONAL PERSPECTIVE

The Soccer Craze in Europe and Beyond

Soccer was "invented" in England but soon became popular in Europe and South America. The soccer craze spread in two primary ways. First, it was exported to different countries by Englishmen who were not willing to forgo their leisure activities while living abroad, and second, it was imported to countries by travellers returning home from England, where they had seen and fallen in love with the game.

Ports such as Le Havre and Gothenburg were typically the places where English soccer enthusiasts first got together to play. English sailors took the game to Genoa and Naples in the 1880s, and British businessmen introduced it to Turin and Milan.

Teachers from various European countries such as Belgium and Switzerland were sent to England to familiarize themselves with the country's education system. Enthralled by the soccer craze they experienced there, they took it back with them and sparked the craze in the schools of their home countries.

In the Netherlands, sport was "the work of Englishmen resident in the Netherlands and of the Dutch who had been in England" (Guttmann 46). Here, however, sport met with strong resistance since physical education teachers rejected competition-oriented sport and favoured German *Turnen*.

One of the countries that promptly imported the game of soccer in its early years was Denmark, which had close economic ties with Great Britain. In 1889, the first national soccer association on the European mainland (the *Dansk Boldspil Union*) was founded there.

The British "colony" in Vienna "started the ball rolling" by forming the first soccer clubs in Austria in 1894, made up of factory and office workers of English firms. Soccer developed from a subculture of Vienna's "English community" into a cultural mass-market product capable of gratifying different groups of the population at the same time.

Thus, soccer had spread across the whole of Europe in the form of an association game even before the turn of the century.

At the start of the twentieth century, British soldiers and sailors, followed by British entrepreneurs, exported soccer, along with their culture, to other continents. Soccer thrived best in South America, where British capital and know-how dominated the markets and the British way of life served as a model for the upper classes. Britain's influence was especially strong in Argentina—most of all in the city of Buenos Aires, which had the largest British community outside of the Empire and subsequently developed into soccer's first stronghold in South America. In much the same way the sport also spread to Uruguay and Chile. In Brazil soccer was first played almost exclusively by British citizens of the middle and upper classes. After the turn of the century, the game rapidly became popular among all classes, including the black population. Generally, it can be said that "English commercial houses and colleges were the great propagandists for the sport that, in time, became the passion of the multitude" (Guttmann 61).

In contrast to its development in Europe or South America, sport spread to Africa under conditions of imperialism and colonization. The colonial powers took their values, norms, customs, and habits—along with their physical activities—to the regions they governed and controlled. In Kenya, for example, British officers and colonial government officials established a sport culture that was almost exclusively for the benefit of Europeans. Nevertheless, pupils at missionary schools also had physical education and sport lessons, which included soccer, and it was from these pupils that the "black elite" was recruited. In spite of this, soccer spread slowly in Africa, with a soccer association being founded in Kenya in 1922 but not until 1945 in Nigeria.

1904 saw the founding of the Fédération Internationale de Football Association (FIFA), which controls and guarantees international standards in soccer as well as its rules and its language. However, each country has its own history of soccer, and cultural differences can be observed, for instance, in the speed at which it spread, in the way it became anchored socially, in the extent and rate of its professionalization, in the styles in which it is played and, finally, in its myths. However, no studies have so far been undertaken to analyze and explain these differences against the backdrop of the social developments of each particular country.

Information from Guttmann, Allen. *Games & Empires: Modern Sports and Cultural Imperialism*. New York: Columbia University Press, 1994.

Male Sporting Culture

The bachelor subculture of the nineteenth century (explored in the previous chapter) maintained its male gender identity and transcended class lines during the Gilded Age. Men of the bachelor culture shared a sense of physical prowess, toughness, and physicality as marks of masculinity. As modernization and increasing industrialization diminished the need for independent craftsmen and farmers throughout the nineteenth century, men gradually lost the sense of self-esteem and the social identity previously tied to occupations and physical labor on farms. Nine of every ten men were self-employed before the Civil War, but fewer than one-third enjoyed such status in 1910 (Gems, *For Pride* 5). The shoemaker, for example, lost his independence in becoming a wage laborer in the shoe factory, tied to a particular capitalistic work ethic and time discipline. He could no longer hunt or fish according to his will, set his own work pace, or even his own schedule. Industrialization robbed him of his former sense of self and the discipline of the clock reigned.

To compensate, men turned to the homosocial environment of the sporting world. Immigration demographics were skewed toward men, and the early American republic was largely a male society. During the Antebellum Period, five million immigrants, mostly young males, journeyed to the United States (Foner and Garraty 534), and, with limited opportunities for marriage many men remained bachelors. By the mid-nineteenth century, 40 percent of young men between the ages of 25 and 35 remained single, and many of them found a sense of inclusion and camaraderie in the company of like-minded males, often joined by married men who sought refuge from the domesticity of the home. On occasion, the wealthy, too, entered the sports netherworld, courting social ostracism to maintain their identification with the cult of masculinity. But for the most part, these "sports," or "the fancy," as they were known, included craftsmen, volunteer firemen, working-class laborers, gamblers, petty criminals, and Irish immigrants who did not subscribe to the moral, religious, and social tenets of decorum and respectability that held sway among middle-class whites.

These men congregated in billiard parlors, theaters, brothels, and urban saloons to tell stories, brag, drink, smoke cigars, gamble, and seek the carnal pleasures offered by prostitutes or "sporting ladies." The urban saloons offered the male fraternity a club-like atmosphere where they might indulge themselves in luxurious surroundings. In New York City, Kit Burns' Sportsman's Hall offered seating for four hundred, and Harry Hill's Dance Hall, another of New York's more popular establishments, featured multiple bars for hard spirits, beer, and wine. It also included a concert hall and a stage for boxing and wrestling matches. At the Prairie Queen in Chicago, the winner of the boxing match received a house prostitute as a prize.

Saloons often included a back room where illegal boxing matches were staged (which had also been a practice in some antebellum establishments). Proprietors skirted the law by staging "exhibitions," for which no decision was rendered. Patrons paid an entrance fee to become "members" in such "clubs," and betting on the participants provided a sense of adventure and risk in otherwise mundane lives. Harry Hill won national fame as a boxing referee and as a repository for large bets. Billy McGlory, a New York underworld figure, charged 15 cents for entry at his promotions. His Grand Scarlet Ball, held at Armory Hall in 1883, included a cakewalk by African Americans, boxing matches of men fighting women, a beauty contest, and a masquerade ball (Gilfoyle 115).

Until 1882, when the Marquis of Queensberry rules gained ascendance, bareknuckle prizefights (i.e., boxing without gloves) proved to be the most popular form of entertainment in the country. By the 1880s, good bareknuckle fighters could earn as much as $500 for a single bout—equivalent to a laborer's annual wage. Boxers became heroes, rivaled only by top billiard players, and spectators paid as much as a week's wage to view and gamble on championship matches. Even before the Civil War, New York billiard parlors averaged annual revenues surpassing $10,000 each, and in 1865 billiard tables in Chicago were rented at a rate of $4,000 per day. Pool hustling became a tenuous occupation for many who were unable or unwilling to submit to the dictates of the industrial workplace. In the Midwest, however, John Brunswick, a Swiss immigrant, found lucre in business as a manufacturer of billiard tables. After starting in Cincinnati in 1845, he opened a Chicago office in 1848 and by 1879 had merged with the Balke and Collender companies to promote tournaments and sell his products to saloons. The manufacture and sale of sporting goods became a booming business.

While the bachelor subculture and the sporting fancy continued to enjoy blood sports such as cockfights, dogfights, and rattings that thrilled spectators and offered myriad options for gambling, white middle-class moralists and reformers remained adamant that these sporting practices were unacceptable in mainstream culture. In ratting contests, for instance, gamblers bet on the number of rats killed by a dog in a stipulated time or on the amount of time it would take for the canine hunter to accomplish the grisly task of extermination. At Kit Burns' establishment, onlookers even paid to watch a local human celebrity known as Jack the Rat bite off the heads of the rodents (Riess, *Sport* 17).

Professional pedestrian races, which (as noted in chapter 4) had gained popularity in the Antebellum Era, continued to stimulate gambling by the sporting fancy. The walkers or runners competed in endurance races at indoor venues; some races, in which either individuals or teams attempted to outlast or outdistance their competition, lasted as long as six days. Both men and women vied for prizes, sometimes in mixed-gender (men vs. women) encounters. By 1870 in New York, female swimmers were competing for prizes that included jewelry. Five years later, British swimming champion J. B. Johnson defeated the local champion in a 13-mile (21-kilometer) race in Philadelphia for $1,000, as international competition drew increasing attention (Kirsch, *Sports* [Vol. 4] 46).

More often, the sporting fraternity's "cranks" (serious fans), as they were known, wagered on horse racing with offtrack bookies, who accepted small bettors. Larger cities also had established poolrooms where laborers and white-collar clerks might place bets. Telegraph reports of race results at such places allowed nonspectators to participate in the speculation. For those who were less advantaged but still had some recreational time, unregulated outlaw tracks outside the jurisdiction of local authorities attracted patrons with low entry fees and access to independent bookies, some of whom even extended credit. Middle-class Americans viewed such operations with disdain, but violent incidents in Chicago did little to encourage change. There, George Trussell, a professional gambler who owned a champion trotter, engaged in shootouts on city streets with his rival, Cap Hyman. The violent confrontations ended when Trussell's girlfriend, "Irish Mollie" Cosgriff, killed him, allegedly for spending more time with the horse than with her.

Rowing and pedestrianism also provided early opportunities for working-class athletes to earn an income with their physical prowess. Among rowers, the Ward Brothers and Biglin Brothers became household names, and the artist Thomas Eakins portrayed the latter in several paintings during the 1870s. By that time, however, baseball had emerged as the premier sport in the United States, outdistancing the popularity of regattas, though nostalgic paintings and serene images of rowers on the waterways continued to interest American artists.

Business of Sport

In 1858, 22 clubs in the New York area established an organization presumptuously titled the National Association of Base Ball Players, which adhered to amateur guidelines. The class-based gentlemanly clubs gradually gave way to recruiting and professionalism as club, neighborhood, town, and occupational rivalries spurred greater attention to winning.

Various versions of baseball rules still abounded in the mid-nineteenth century, but the Civil War gave priority to the New York rendition (New York rules superseded Massachusetts rules in the military camps and were carried back to veterans' hometowns), which set the number of players at nine and established the diamond-shaped infield with four bases equally aligned at its corners. As commercialization and club sponsorship assumed greater prominence, clubs attracted paying spectators to finance their operations. For important games, which might involve gambling or just club pride, individual stars might be paid for their services. The Brooklyn Excelsiors recruited young James Creighton, a star pitcher, with such inducements in 1860, and he is generally acknowledged as the first professional player. Al Reach became an openly acknowledged pro in 1865.

Professional Baseball Teams

Civic pride and commercial rivalry led Cincinnati to form the first known fully professional team in 1869. Cincinnati businessmen competed with those in Chicago, St. Louis, and Milwaukee for the hinterland trade, and baseball provided a means to publicize the municipality. Cincinnati hired the best players from Eastern clubs and sent them on a national tour from coast to coast. Salaries ranged from $600 to $2,000, and the professional Red Stockings returned undefeated, winning 58 contests and tying once. Chicago countered the next year with a professional team of its own. Merchants raised $15,000 in a joint stock company to field the White Stockings, with city leaders serving as the primary stockholders. The squad embarked on a campaign against other commercial centers and quickly proved their mettle. A crowd of 100,000 welcomed them home after a 157-to-1 win over Memphis.

The National Association of Base Ball Players split over the issue of professionalism at the 1870 rules convention. As a result, the National Association of *Professional* Base Ball Players (emphasis added) was formed in 1871, and it survived until 1876 as a loosely organized federation. Teams did not always play scheduled games, and players repeatedly broke their contracts when another team offered a better salary. A town of any size might buy entry into the league for a mere $10.

In 1876, that unwieldy arrangement gave way to a much more tightly structured organization known as the National League. William Hulbert, a member of the Chicago Board of Trade and president of the Chicago White Stockings, wrested control of baseball from the Eastern establishment by proposing an association run by club administrators rather than players. Hulbert cajoled other owners to reorganize the league based on sound business principles in order to maximize their profits, as the following document shows:

FIRST NINE OF THE
CINCINNATI
(RED STOCKINGS) BASE BALL CLUB.

The first professional baseball team hailed from Cincinnati.

Image courtesy of Library of Congress, LC-USZ62-32016.

Chicago, Jan. 23, 1876

The undersigned have been appointed by the Chicago, Cincinnati, Louisville and St. Louis clubs a committee to confer with you on matters of interest to the game at large, with special reference to the reformation of existing abuses, and the formation of a new association, and we are clothed with full authority in writing from the above named clubs to bind them to any arrangement we make with you. We therefore invite your club to send a representative, clothed with like authority, to meet us at the Grand Central Hotel, in the city of New York, on Wednesday the 2d day of February next, at 12M (sic). After careful consideration of the needs of the professional clubs, the organizations we represent are of the firm belief that existing circumstances demand prompt and vigorous action by those who are the natural sponsors of the game. It is the earnest recommendation of our constituents that all past troubles and differences be ignored and forgotten, and that the conference we propose shall be a calm, friendly and deliberate discussion, looking solely to the general good of the clubs who are calculated to give character and permanency to the game. We are confident that the propositions we have to submit will meet with your approval and support, and we shall be pleased to meet you at the time and place above mentioned.

Yours respectfully,
W.A. HULBERT.
CHAS. A. FOWLE.
(Kirsch, *Sports* [Vol. 4] 84)

The thought was that if owners projected a more wholesome (and therefore more acceptable) white, middle-class, Protestant image that would appeal to like-minded middle-class citizens and families, they would also forbid gambling and Sunday games. They limited membership to assure a greater potential for profit. The initial membership consisted of larger cities: Boston, Chicago, Cincinnati, Louisville, Hartford, St. Louis, Philadelphia, and New York. The owners eventually regulated team schedules, ticket prices, and officiating, but labor problems persisted, as players known as "revolvers" jumped teams for better pay. Individual owners accommodated such moves when they placed their immediate self-interest and their desire to win above the interests of the league. In 1879, the owners agreed to a strategy designed to rectify this divisive issue—they employed a "reserve clause" in player contracts, which retained or "reserved" an athlete's service explicitly for one team only. Without constant bidding for players, owners held down their costs and increased their profits. Players lamented their lost freedom to negotiate their services but still enjoyed salaries that were three or four times higher than those of average working men. William Hulbert lorded over the league, enforcing his edicts in a dictatorial manner—including expulsions of New York, Philadelphia, and Cincinnati for violations of league policies—until his death in 1882. Thus, much like industrial magnates, baseball owners consolidated their resources in the face of rival leagues and maximized their profits at the expense of their employees.

The following is the extraordinary rule adopted by the American Association at its schedule meeting: "And in case any player under reserve shall willfully hold off and refuse to sign a regular contract with the club that has him reserved, for the purpose of harassing the club, or compelling it to increase his salary, or who shall by any means, directly or indirectly, endeavor to attempt willful extortion from the club which has him reserved, he shall, on satisfactory evidence being furnished from the club so engaged, be placed upon the black list by the President and Secretary and notices issued to all clubs as provided by the constitution and the National agreement." (*Chicago Tribune* 9)

Employer–employee labor differences erupted in 1889, as labor relations in professional baseball reflected similar tensions in the industrial workforce throughout the United States. The players' revolt of 1889, led by John Montgomery Ward, the New York Giants' shortstop and a lawyer, started with the organization of the Brotherhood of Professional Base Ball Players in 1885. As with other early labor unions, the players banned together as workers in an attempt to win greater freedom and better salaries from their employers. The restrictive reserve clause allowed no opportunity to negotiate their contracts or seek better offers. When owners failed to address their concerns, players formed their own Brotherhood League (also called the Players' League) in 1890, competing for fans against both the National League franchises and the teams of the American Association (formed as a rival organization after the National League expelled Cincinnati in 1881). The American Association clubs, run mostly by brewery owners, used baseball as a means to sell their products but adhered to the same employment practices of the older National League.

The Players' League attracted most of the top players and found sponsorship from prospective owners who had been locked out of the National League oligarchy. The teams operated under a socialistic arrangement, whereby players and owners shared profits and club management, thus mounting a direct economic and philosophical challenge to the capitalist sport structure. They scheduled their teams in seven National League cities, forcing baseball fans to make a choice. Led by Albert Spalding, the National League retaliated by bribing star players to return, offering free tickets to its games, and providing franchise inducements to the players' sponsors. Both leagues absorbed financial losses in the cutthroat competition, but the established National League maintained greater resources. The Brotherhood League collapsed after a year, and the American Association lasted only until 1891. The National League then absorbed four of the American Association franchises and faced no further threats until the organization of the upstart American League in 1901.

Sport Entrepreneurs and the Making of Sporting Culture

Sport afforded entrepreneurial opportunities not only to players and owners but also to sports journalists. As discussed in chapter 4, Henry Chadwick, an English immigrant, found a career as a sportswriter, and in the 1860s he expanded his sports journalism by covering baseball for the *New York Herald*. He also served as editor of the *Beadle Base-Ball Player,* an early guide to the game, for more than 20 years. In 1867, Chadwick founded the *Chronicle,* a weekly paper that promoted baseball as a character-building influence on young men. Chadwick also established the box score and the batting average, an early means of quantification and analysis that heightened fans' interest in the game, and, as a member of the rules committee, he suggested a new rule requiring a batted ball to be caught on the fly, which was implemented after 1864 (Rader, *American Sports* [1983] 111).

Irish immigrant Richard Kyle Fox, another journalist who shaped modern American sport, assumed control of the *National Police Gazette* in 1877. Printed on pink paper, the *Gazette* offered salacious material that emphasized theatrical news, scandals, crimes, sports, and scantily clad women. The formula attracted a large working-class readership and could be found in all haunts of the bachelor subculture. Anthony Comstock and his Society for the Suppression of Vice campaigned to silence the publication but succeeded only in enhancing its notoriety. Fox promoted numerous pseudosports (such as ratting and clog dancing), as well as female weight lifting and cycling, but he proved most successful as a boxing promoter. He not only provided in-depth and sensationalized coverage of pugilistic events but also sponsored bouts of great interest. Fox created the system of weight classes and awarded bejeweled belts to the champions of each category. By the 1880s, his publication reached a weekly circulation of 150,000, nearly double that of the respectable middle-class *Harpers' Weekly.* The *Gazette* became the Bible of boxing, and by 1883 Fox's enterprise operated out of a $250,000 seven-story headquarters in New York City (Reel).

The *National Police Gazette* attracted readers with sensationalized stories of crime, sport, and sex.
Image courtesy of Library of Congress, LC-USZC62-63903

Another successful sporting entrepreneur was Albert Pope, who made his mark as a manufacturer of bicycles. Crude forms, propelled by riders who sat astride a framework over two wheels and walked, appeared early in the century. These velocipedes were replaced by the so-called English ordinary, introduced to the United States at the 1876 Centennial Exhibition held in Philadelphia and featuring the innovation of a large front wheel (four or five feet high) coupled with a small rear wheel. The rider perched on a small seat and steered with handlebars. Balancing atop the frame required considerable skill, but having mastered it the cyclist might achieve considerable speed. Speeding cyclists, known as "scorchers," raced in parks and on city streets, posing a danger to pedestrians and those on horseback. The ordinary proved dangerous to riders as well, when the front wheel encountered rocks or holes, catapulting the rider over the front wheel—a fall known as a "header."

New cycles cost $100 each, and even a used one would bring $35. Pope's mass production lowered the costs, but the sport remained largely a middle-class pastime. Pope promoted the sport through magazines and cycling clubs, and he organized the first cycling club, in Boston, in 1878. The Chicago Cycling Club, founded a year later, became the largest of many in that city, and cycling organizations soon proliferated throughout the country. The activity proved especially attractive to young men and women who used cycles to elude their required chaperones in a break from the strict moral courtship regimen of the Victorian Era.

The large number of cycling clubs banded together in 1880 to form the League of American Wheelman (LAW). With an extensive and growing membership, LAW gained considerable political clout. Candidates courted their vote, and officeholders catered to their demands, including requests for paved roads and parkways where enthusiasts might avoid the dreaded "header." Clubs provided road maps and organized "century rides" of 100 miles (161 kilometers). In turn, middle-class cyclists in cities such as Boston influenced the Better Roads Movement, and their desire for resting spots along the way during excursions outside the city helped promote middle-class tourism through the rise of new businesses offering places to eat, sleep, and repair bicycles en route. Bicyclists also formed a community of consumers purchasing products for their bicycles, as well as sportswear for their journey (Hardy, *How* 148,

The bicycle offered new patterns of socialization and courtship as young men and women sought greater freedom from the restrictive etiquette of the Victorian Era.

Image courtesy of Library of Congress, LC-USZ62-28614.

160–163). Cyclists thus affected urban transportation networks and the early tourism industry even before the advent of the automobile.

Perhaps the most successful of the early sports moguls, Albert G. Spalding first earned fame as a player. Born the eldest of three children in a well-to-do Illinois family in 1850, Spalding found his boyhood abruptly changed by his father's death in 1858. The family soon moved to the town of Rockford, and by the age of 15 Spalding starred as the pitcher on the Forest City baseball club, Rockford's finest. At an 1867 baseball tournament in Chicago, Spalding garnered national attention when he pitched his club to victory over the Washington (D.C.) Nationals, considered the best team in the country.

The Chicago Excelsiors, another noteworthy team, promptly offered Spalding a spot on its roster and a job in Chicago with a substantial income. When his employer's business failed, he promptly returned to Rockford and the Forest City team. The Rockford contingent's tour of the Midwest and East in 1870 included a victory over the Cincinnati Red Stockings. Harry Wright of the Boston Red Stockings, newly acquired as player-manager from Cincinnati, then offered Spalding $1,500 to join his club, and Spalding soon became the dominant pitcher in the newly formed professional baseball players association.

The following year, Spalding accepted an offer to play for the Chicago White Stockings, where he rose from player-manager to owner and then assumed leadership of the National League after the death of William Hulbert. In conjunction with the organization of the National League in 1876, Spalding and his brother had launched their own enterprise that same year. The Spalding Brothers sporting goods firm, headquartered in Chicago, soon reached national proportions with its marketing and manufacture of sports products and made him a millionaire.

In its first year, the Spalding firm produced the official league book and a baseball guide. By 1879, the business had acquired a bat factory in Hastings, Michigan, near a forest that supplied its materials and thus minimized production costs. It was the first of many such plants that even employed workers in Scotland, Leeds, and London, and branch offices reached as far as Egypt. Its publications increased in the 1880s and produced Spalding's Library of American Sports. Spalding's sporting ventures eventually fostered a separate company that included 300 sports titles in Spalding's American Sports Publishing Company. These guides and books touted a range of sports and, of course, promoted Spalding sporting goods throughout the country (Hardy, "Adopted" 139, 146).

As Spalding further expanded his offerings, he sold products through mail-order catalogs to consumers across the nation. Product endorsements by professional athletes and company-sponsored "Spalding teams" enhanced belief in Spalding's wares

RHODE ISLAND.—FIRST NATIONAL MEET OF AMERICAN BICYCLISTS, AT NEWPORT, MAY 31st—THE PARADE OF THE CLUBS ON BELLEVUE AVENUE. FROM A SKETCH BY CHAS. UPHAM.—SEE PAGE 263.

Media images, such as this one of the first national cycle meet at Newport, helped to popularize the sport.

Image courtesy of Library of Congress, LC-USZ62-32016.

as superior and "official" sports products. Spalding also enhanced the brand name by selling sports equipment supposedly used by big-league players and other successful athletes, and men, women, and children could be found using his sporting goods for their own use and enjoyment. The Spalding line of goods included virtually all sports, as he bought out competitors and manufacturers of golf, tennis, football, basketball, and general exercise equipment, as well as uniforms. He produced gear for field sports, boats for outdoorsmen, and bicycles for urban cyclists. As his biographer Peter Levine has observed, his competitive drive eventually prompted him to seek a monopoly in the sporting goods market (*A. G. Spalding* 71–96).

By 1880, Spalding held the contract for the official league ball to be used in all games, and he declared other products produced by his firm to be "official" as well, regardless of whether they were actually so designated. In later years, he offered trophies to public school athletic leagues in big cities such as New York and Chicago, and even as far away as the U.S.-occupied Philippines, in order to gain players' and administrators' brand loyalty. In the 1888–1889 off-season, he organized a worldwide baseball tour intended to bring the American game and American ideals to other nations and, of course, expand his markets, but stops in Hawaii, Australia, Ceylon (now Sri Lanka), Egypt, Italy, France, England, Ireland, and Scotland produced only limited success and failed to supplant cricket within the British Empire. Nevertheless, Spalding gained an international presence, and the Spalding brand achieved wide visibility.

The presumptuous Spalding even attempted to rewrite history. Unwilling to accept the notion that his beloved game of baseball originated in Britain, he insisted that it evolved from American colonial practices. In 1905, he organized the Mills Commission, a group of former baseball administrators and associates, as well as two United States senators (but no historians) to determine the origin of the sport. After a two-year study, the group determined that Abner Doubleday created the game at Cooperstown, New York, in 1839. At the time, few doubted the findings, though proof for such an allegation rested with a specious letter sent to Spalding. In 1911, Spalding produced his own history of baseball, a year after he failed to gain a U.S. Senate seat from California, which reinforced the nationalistic myth of the American birth of the game. Though thoroughly refuted, the creation myth persists among many Americans (Block 16–17).

As entrepreneurs such as Spalding made their fortunes, other employers tried to maximize their profits by controlling their employees' leisure time through wholesome sport offerings. Employees who were hung over often didn't report to work on Mondays, or they were unproductive. Some of the employee teams (e.g., the Chicago Bears and Green Bay Packers) would eventually become fully professional.

Industrial Recreation Programs

In the aftermath of the Great Railroad Strike of 1877, employers tried to gain greater control over largely immigrant and ethnic-minority workforces. Many employed the YMCA without success to initiate recreation programs and proselytize a particular brand of Protestant Christianity. In Chicago, George Pullman, builder of railroad sleeping cars, constructed an entire town south of the city to house his laborers and manufacturing plant. Pullman made sure that his company town was far enough from the temptations of the big city, and his only saloon, in the company hotel, prohibited all but corporate officers. Pullman did, however, provide magnificent athletic facilities for track and field, rowing, soccer, cricket, tennis, baseball, football, ice skating, billiards, boating, and riflery. He reasoned that such amenities would provide wholesome leisure alternatives to the saloon and serve as a means of social control to produce reliable and efficient employees. The Pullman Athletic Association (PAA) was incorporated in 1882 as the first industrial recreation program in the United States.

Spalding's baseball tourists at the Sphinx, February 9, 1889. A.G. Spalding, wearing a pith hat, is in the middle of the picture.

National Baseball Hall of Fame Library

The PAA produced several sport spectacles that brought fame and publicity to the company. The national rowing championship of 1883, held at Pullman, drew a crowd of 15,000 people, and newspapers provided extensive coverage of the annual road race for cyclists. Pullman hired professional coaches and top athletes, and some of the PAA's competitors earned national prominence. Pullman also offered a library, stores, and a total of 40 organizations to meet workers' needs, but the owner also served as landlord. Wages reverted back to the owner for rent, food purchases, and fees for use of the facilities. When the Depression of 1893 forced pay cuts, reduced working hours, and layoffs, the alienated workforce went out on strike, led by Eugene Debs, a prominent socialist. The threat of violence required U.S. Army troops to quell the confrontation.

Despite the hostility engendered by employer–employee confrontations, workers maintained their interest in sport. Labor unions began to organize their own baseball teams and provided billiard rooms and other facilities to enhance camaraderie. Companies, too, promoted similar programs for workers that became known as welfare capitalism. Extensive recreational programs were offered by, among others, the National Cash Register Company in Dayton, Ohio; the Pennsylvania Railroad; the Heinz Company of Pittsburgh; Hershey Chocolate Company; and United States Steel.

Gendered Sport, Class, and Social Roles

Men such as Spalding and Pullman established the forms and practices of modern American sporting culture with little regard for women's participation as workers at their companies in the years following the Civil War. However, in a gradual departure from the Antebellum Era, when their gender-prescribed role of sedentary urban living undermined their physical health, women did begin to assume a more active role in physical recreation and sport. For rural women, new forms of physical recreation might alter their physical condition in farming communities, while women who left the farmstead were introduced to new urban modes of sporting and leisure pursuits. White middle- and upper-class women with more leisure time and access to some educational institutions—in contrast with their working-class counterparts—now found that some sporting practices seemed gender-appropriate within society's moral and social codes. And all women, in pursuing their physical and sporting activities, had to navigate relations with men within their class and ethnic contexts, even as challenges to constraints in women's dress (which typically limited physical mobility) and the desire to engage more actively in sport prompted several women reformers to more directly challenge the male hierarchy in American sport and culture by the late nineteenth century.

Pastimes for Working-Class Women

Working-class women competed as professional rowers as early as 1867, and in the 1870s they attracted attention as paid pedestrians and boxers. In 1871, five women competed in the regatta of the Empire City Rowing Club on a 2-mile (3.2-kilometer) course. Amelia Shean took the singles crown in a 17-foot (5.2-meter) workboat in a time of 18 minutes and 32 seconds. In 1876, Mary Marshall defeated a male opponent in a best-of-three walking race in New York City. Marshall competed against Bertha von Hillern, a German immigrant who became a celebrity as a pedestrian and who advocated exercise for women during 1876 and 1877. The following year, Ada Anderson arrived from England and drew thousands of spectators to her endurance walks. In 1878, she walked daily for a month and, on another occasion, covered 2,700 quarter miles (i.e., a total of 675 miles, or about 1,085 kilometers) in 2,700 quarter hours, sleeping on cots as needed (Kirsch, *Sports* [Vol. 4] 350). Her exploits prompted a surge of female pedestrians, with more than one hundred competing professionally by 1879 (Shaulis 39).

With such competition, some female walkers turned to other pursuits to earn a living—Louise Armaindo, May Stanley, and Elsa Von Blumen, for example, became endurance cyclists—while still others entered the harsh world of pugilism (Shaulis 43). Cycling enjoyed such popularity that it spawned early globalization efforts:

THE WHEEL.
MATTERS OF INTEREST TO DEVOTEES OF THE SILENT STEED.
A NEW COMBINATION.
PROFESSIONAL BICYCLING STARS GO ON A TRIP AROUND THE
WORLD.

A combination of bicycle riders, to be known as "The League of Champions," was formed in Chicago week before last. Chicago's favorite, Mlle. Armaindo, the champion long-distance rider of America, heads the list. John S. Prince, short-distance champion; Henry W. Higham, long-distance champion of England; Fred S. Rollinson, ex-champion, and Thomas W. Eck, professional, comprise the party. All are under the management of Fred J. Engelhardt, the well-known manager of sporting celebrities. It is the intention of the "League" to give exhibitions and races in the leading cities throughout the West, thence to Australia and England. Armaindo, with a record of 843 miles in 72 hours, Price, with 486 miles to his credit at the end of 30 hours; Higham, with 1,040 miles in 72 hours; and Rollinson with 50 in 3 hours, is a sufficient guarantee of the strength of this organization. The "League" has entered into an agreement, a portion of which is decidedly novel. A pool is made of the earnings from which the expenses are paid. From what remains of any and all earnings of any member or the League collectively, 10 per cent shall be paid into a racing fund, which shall be used only for stake-money with outside challengers and for the expenses incident to a preparation for a race if no challenges are received from persons outside the League within a reasonable time, then the amount on hand will be put up to be contested by Armaindo, Higham and Prince in a six day race. Even then any outsider can by depositing a third of the amount on hand, enter and start in the race, the winner to take the entire stake. On the evening of Nov. 16th this combination left Chicago for Kansas City. At San Francisco Prince is to meet Charles Smith, champion of the Pacific slope, still a six days match will take place there for 10 percent of the gross receipts of the tour, which will be contested for by Prince, Higham, and Armaindo. They expect to sail for Australia on February 1, where Higham will try conclusions with Rolf, an Australian champion. Each one of the party takes two machines on the trip. The return home will be by way of England. (qtd. in Gems, *Sports* 155–156)

Nell Saunders won a silver butter dish by beating Rose Harland in a boxing match. The middle class deemed such pastimes unseemly and unladylike. A Chicago reporter averred that "prize fights between men are beastly exhibitions, but there is an unutterable loathsomeness in the worse brutality of abandoned, wretched women beating each other almost to nudity, for the amusement of a group of blackguards, even lower in the scale of humanity than the women themselves" (Pierce, *A History* [Vol. 2] 468).

Middle-Class Sporting Pursuits

For middle-class white women, participating in pastimes that were more genteel allowed for a greater measure of acceptance. Women of the middle and upper classes played many sports, including croquet and tennis, that were deemed appropriate for their social position and gender. Women at the Staten Island Cricket and Baseball Club also engaged in archery and darts, and by 1880 archery clubs that accepted women could be found from coast to coast. In August 1879 in Chicago, 20 women competed in the first national archery tournament, with Mrs. Spalding Brown of Hastings, Michigan, crowned the champion. Women's fashions, however, greatly restricted their mobility and sporting opportunities, especially for middle-class and wealthy women who adhered strictly to the prescribed fashions of the age. Confined by corsets and bustles that accentuated gender differences, women competed mainly in relatively passive sports that did not infringe on masculine spheres or challenge displays of manly prowess. Women of this period who did engage in more active pastimes—on the tennis court, the golf links, or the water (rowing), or in collegiate sporting pursuits—paved the way for an increasing number of women to participate in more vigorous and competitive forms of sport in the decades to follow.

Croquet

Croquet became a fashionable recreation in America during the 1860s because, when played publicly on the front lawn of a family home, it allowed young, white, middle-class women to congregate with young men in a public group setting without the necessity of a chaperone. The croquet craze that began in the 1860s prompted women to play the game at home, as well as on their holidays at Gilded Age resorts that typically featured croquet lawns along with amenities for other sports such as swimming, tennis, and boating. Catharine Beecher played croquet with her sister Harriet Beecher Stowe on the lawn at Nook Farm, near Hartford, Connecticut, where Harriet lived. For middle-class women like those of the Beecher family, croquet provided not only a pleasant outdoor sport but also a time for social gatherings of family and friends. A croquet rules book, *How to Play Field and Parlor Croquet* (1865), gave a sense of how to approach the game:

> While men and boys have had their healthy means of recreation in the open air, the women and girls have been restricted to the less exhilarating sports of indoor life. . . . Grace in holding and using the mallet, easy and pleasing attitudes in playing, promptness in taking your turn, and gentlemanly and ladylike manners throughout the game, are all points which it is unnecessary for us to enlarge on. (qtd. in Dulles 191)

The publication of rule books and the manufacture of croquet equipment by sporting goods companies helped generate enthusiasm for the game among women, as they purchased croquet equipment for family use.

Croquet held popular appeal for women during this period when middle-class Americans' lives were greatly affected by the gendered ideal of "separate spheres" of men's and women's endeavors. Generally, middle-class women pursued domestic and female-oriented activities, though at times women expanded their role in public sporting pastimes. Though viewed as a sport, croquet "was not [deemed] 'manly' like baseball; it did not demand physical strength and stamina; it was neither fast-paced nor highly competitive." As a family game, "[i]t was inclusive and sociable, gentle and genteel," and playing croquet "compensated for the stresses and strains of modern life by uniting all, young and old, male and female, on 'common ground'" (Lewis, "American" 373). On family lawns and resort grounds, women playing croquet partook of nature in a wholesome setting, and often in a mixed-gender context, but, it was thought, in such a way as to protect them and their families from rougher sporting scenes and activities deemed harmful, such as urban street life, saloons, gambling, drinking, and immoral and commercial amusements (Lewis, "American" 377).

During the croquet fad, women increased their participation in sport and sometimes tested traditional gender roles. Historian Jon Sterngass has investigated the nineteenth-century croquet craze in terms of gender roles and such behaviors as cheating: "Female grace and good manners may have been the ideal for the rule- and taste-makers, but on the croquet ground, a peculiar sort of gender reversal enabled women to temporarily jettison their passive role and dominate, if not humiliate, men. Women played the game seriously, enjoyed matching skills with men, and often emerged victorious." This image of women in croquet, of course, counters Victorian gender stereotypes, and thus the sport "challenged the superiority of males and undermined the concept of separate spheres" that was so prominent in nineteenth-century American culture (Sterngass 399, 405). Women might outwit men in a game of croquet, and they could use their long clothing to disguise shots by keeping the mallet hidden from the sight of other players or by using their hoop skirts to surreptitiously move the balls during the game. Some actions by women carried sexual connotations, as when they lifted their long skirts, thus displaying their feet to male players. On some occasions, a male may have picked up a ball to set it in place for the croquet shot, showing his courtesy. A female player striking the ball with her mallet to direct it through the croquet hoop, demonstrating athletic skill, undermined the notion of separate spheres. Women hitting men's balls with a mallet, a symbolic reversal of gender power, presented a challenge to traditional roles while occurring in the mixed company of men and women. At times, women propelled their balls against those of male contestants, an act with implied sexual meanings. On croquet played in the nineteenth century, historian Jon Sterngass described how when female croquet players had their ball next to their opponent's ball, "the tight croquet stroke could be interpreted as an act of symbolic castration. Men were 'forced' to look on helplessly as their female opponent lined up the two balls, lifted her skirt, placed her dainty foot on her own ball, and with a resounding thwack, hammered the other ball to parts unknown" (Sterngass 403). Such suggested sexual behaviors stirred up the moral and gender codes of the day.

Participants and observers commented on the cheating that seemed commonplace in croquet. In these situations, gender identity held no sway, as both middling women and men may have sometimes bent the rules to their own advantage. In his reminiscences about American summer resorts in the 1870s, William Dix noted that most Gilded Age resort hotels had croquet lawns, where "people wrangled and bickered and—let it be whispered—sometimes cheated over that effete game" (qtd. in Sterngass 402). Women also commented on their own cheating in the quest for victory at croquet. Katherine Rice, who attended Albany Female Seminary in New York and enjoyed playing croquet at the school, "complained in her diary in 1873 that in an unspecified game, 'Mattie cheated! cheated! cheated! cheated! cheated!!!!!! But no one seems to think that very unusual in her'" (qtd. in Sterngass 409; exclamations in original). The game itself involved competition, and as a result conventional gender roles could be contested as part of the action in the cultural space of the croquet lawn.

Lawn Tennis

In the spring of 1874, Mary Ewing Outerbridge introduced the game of lawn tennis to members of the Staten Island Cricket and Baseball Club after she had learned to play the popular English sport in Bermuda. She brought back a set of tennis equipment to show her brothers, who were also interested in sport. "Having gained the permission of her brother, A. Emilius Outerbridge, director of the [club] . . . she rigged up the net in a remote corner of the cricket ground without much ado. It was thus for the first time that lawn tennis was given the attention of a sports club and thus attracted public attention" (Gillmeister 209). One of Mary's brothers, Eugenius H. Outerbridge, suggested that the club hold a tennis tournament, and thus the first lawn tennis tournament in America took place on September 1, 1880, at the Staten Island Cricket and Baseball Club, in what reporters hailed as a national tournament. Doubles competitors included the team of Richard Dudley Sears and Dr. James Dwight, who later won five U.S. doubles championships as partners; Richard D. Sears later became seven-time U.S. singles champion (Gillmeister 208).

This tournament led to the organization of the United States National Lawn Tennis Association (USNLTA) in May 1881. The association wanted to provide standardized rules for scoring and equipment and sponsor a national championship. Delegates of the USNLTA decided that Rhode Island's newly constructed Newport Casino would serve as the championship site, and August 31, 1881, marked the first national lawn tennis championship. (Today, the Newport Casino Tennis Club hosts the International Tennis Hall of Fame and an annual men's tournament.) The early competitors in American tennis hailed from families of elite social and economic standing, and initially only men took part in the tournaments. Richard D. Sears recalled (in the 1930s) the inaugural years of tennis (in the 1880s) in the United States:

> A large number of the players wore Knickerbockers, with blazers, belts, cravats, and woolen stockings in their club colors. Their shoes were rubber-soled and generally of white canvas and buckskin. None of their sleeves were cut off, . . . while the large majority rolled them up. . . .
>
> The second year the championship found all of the players serving overhand with more or less speed, mostly less, with everyone coming in to volley as soon as any good opening presented itself; but as both Dwight and I had taken up lobbing, a stroke, which, to be effective, requires a good deal of practice, a certain amount of discouragement appeared, and when these players also tried this stroke they generally lobbed much too short, giving us an easy kill. (qtd. in Gillmeister 212)

Depictions of new sport forms spread interest and fostered a more national and uniform sporting culture.

Image courtesy of Library of Congress, LC-USZC4-1180

Tennis grew increasingly popular among elite white men at country clubs and private tennis courts, and more tournaments were staged. As with earlier boat races (as discussed in chapter 4), the playing of lawn tennis in the United States led to international competitions. In fact, according to tennis historian Heiner Gillmeister, "the greatest achievement of American tennis is the creation of the Davis Cup," in which competitors from various countries play singles and doubles matches for their national teams. A precursor to the first Davis Cup took place in 1883, when a team from England, then a world tennis power, defeated the American team (Gillmeister 213). In 1899, Dwight Davis commissioned the Davis Cup trophy, and in 1900 the first Davis Cup match was played, with the American team defeating the British Isles 3-0 in Boston. Members of the victorious team were Malcolm Whitman, Dwight Davis, and Holcombe Ward (Gillmeister 218), all of whom played for Harvard. Holcombe Ward was also an intercollegiate and national doubles champion that year.

Though competitive matches for women were only in their infancy at this time, tennis did gain popularity in the 1880s among white middle-class women who played at country clubs (especially those women with a father or brothers who held club membership), both as a social function and for healthy exercise. At one well-known club, the Germantown Cricket Club in Philadelphia, women played tennis and pursued some competitive opportunities. In 1887 and 1888, the club offered a women's tournament, which gained prominence and became the United States Tennis Championships for women in 1889.

Collegiate Activities

The white women of the upper and middle classes achieved greater freedom with the establishment of women's colleges. When his daughters were refused admission to existing colleges, Matthew Vassar opened his own namesake school for women's higher education in 1861. The institution included a gym for physical training, a horse stable, and opportunities for archery, croquet, and shuttlecock (badminton), and students also adopted ball games, boating, and gymnastics as healthful pursuits. By 1875, Vassar women fielded three baseball teams. Smith College followed suit in 1878, and Mount Holyoke organized a women's baseball team in 1884 (Guttmann, *Sports* [2004] 132–133).

The University of Wisconsin admitted women in 1873 and provided a gymnasium for their use. A year later, Henry Fowle Durant and Pauline Fowle Durant founded Wellesley College, with facilities including a gym and with students required to exercise. Students boated on the adjacent lake, where they skated during the winter; in warmer weather, they also practiced tennis. Wellesley women began adopting specific attire as sportswear in the 1880s. Under the direction of Lucille Eaton Hill, who became director of physical training at the school, the women engaged in intramural but serious rowing competitions. The competitors learned from the men's crews at Harvard and Yale and even employed rowing machines for training purposes. By 1891, the best rowers composed an all-college crew. The next year, the women purchased modern shells with sliding seats for greater efficiency, and trousers soon replaced skirts (Warner, *When* 182–192). At the Boston school later known as Radcliffe College, women imported Dr. Dudley Sargent from Harvard to teach gymnastics in 1881.

Even noncollege women increasingly engaged in physical activities. In addition to croquet, women gained a greater measure of exercise by ice skating; and the roller skating craze that swept the country during the 1870s provided evidence that females sought greater freedom in their lives.

During this post–Civil War period, active women of the Gilded Age continued their campaign for suffrage, divorce rights, temperance, and access to higher education. Such politically and physically active women upset the dominant patriarchal system, as they sought greater control over their lives and questioned the traditional expectations of the ideology of domesticity. As these women worked toward increasing their individual agency in American society, they used various recreational activities, such as croquet, skating, and later cycling, to enjoy a measure of new freedom unencumbered by Victorian prescriptions for feminine behavior.

Regulation of Sport: Amateurism Versus Professionalism

Class issues restricted freedom considerably for many male and female athletes during the latter nineteenth century. The upper classes deemed those who played sport for money or other forms of remuneration to be undignified, unworthy, and highly questionable in their honor and motives. The elite assumed that their social inferiors could be bought by gamblers, and their concept of amateurism rested upon the English aristocratic ideal of a man who engaged in sport for play or recreation rather than for compensation. The close association of professional boxers, pedestrians, and baseball players with gamblers and saloons of the bachelor subculture only reinforced such speculation and stereotyping.

The elite concept of amateurism conflicted, however, with perceived primary attributes of the American character—competitiveness and the need to win—and in the 1870s even elite Northeastern college students hired professional coaches to train them for regatta competitions. The regatta at the 1876 Centennial Exhibition in Philadelphia included both amateur and professional events, and by 1882 Harvard employed a professional coach for its track-and-field athletes. Yet men such as Albert Spalding and Henry Chadwick continued to extol the character-building qualities of sport and its promise as a means of social control for wayward youth. Thus Americans wrestled with competing perceptions of the values of sport, and a plethora of sport-related governing bodies tried, with increasing difficulty, to regulate distinctions between amateurs and professionals. Among the first, the American Association of Amateur Oarsmen was organized in 1872, and the Intercollegiate Association of Amateur Athletes of America (IC4A) addressed similar issues for track-and-field competitions in 1876. Noncollegiate athletic clubs banded together in 1879 as the National Association of Amateur Athletics of America (N4A), offering national championships that were open to those it deemed nonprofessional.

Some athletes posed a dilemma for the governing body, and in the minds of status-seeking clubs the desire to win superseded class and eligibility issues. Lawrence "Lon" Myers represented such a problem for the Manhattan Athletic Club (MAC). As a slight and sickly youth, Myers took up baseball and track as a remedy. Though less than 5 feet 8 inches tall and a mere 115 pounds, he became the world's greatest runner, with records from 50 yards (46 meters) to a mile (1.6 kilometers). The MAC, desirous of his services, willingly overlooked his Jewish ancestry and provided him with paid employment at the club. Like other "amateurs" of the era, Myers quickly pawned the medals and trophies he won for ready cash. In 1885, the MAC even organized a fundraiser that provided $4,000 to their champion. Myers accumulated such riches as an amateur for eight years before publicly declaring his professionalism in an 1886 stakes race with British champion Walter George. The runners split the gate receipts for the commercialized event that drew six thousand spectators for the first race in a best-of-three series at varying distances. Myers won easily at 1,000 yards (about 914 meters) and again at three-quarters of a mile (1.2 kilometers) to pocket the $2,000 prize money, still representing the MAC. In 1888, fifteen prominent athletic clubs, upset with the N4A's reluctance to confront the sham, joined together in the Amateur Athletic Union (AAU), an organization that managed to supersede all others as the primary governing body and regulator of amateur sport in the United States. Notions of amateurism would be increasingly challenged with the growth of intercollegiate and interscholastic sports, particularly as larger numbers of working-class youth entered the educational institutions in the twentieth century.

The vast flow of immigrants to America after 1880 presented issues well beyond amateurism; yet sport held great value in addressing the myriad concerns. At the dawn of the Progressive Era, social reformers developed a particular ideology of socialization, education, assimilation, and acculturation associated with the practice of sport. They attempted to bring greater cohesion and homogeneity to American society based on a clearer identification of what it meant to be an American.

Summary

This chapter has examined the forces, conditions, and issues which promoted and affected sport in the latter nineteenth century. The increasing urbanization of American society, the ongoing immigration of largely European ethnic groups, and the presence of divisions based on race, ethnicity, and social class all played major roles in the organization of American society and the practice of sport. Class differences were registered in the composition of athletic clubs, the governance of sport, and debate over amateurism and professionalism. Sports entrepreneurs adopted business practices to both commercialize and professionalize athletic contests.

Sporting practices also played a major part in gender relations and the definition of gender roles. Power sports, in particular, along with the bachelor subculture that followed their practice, marked one's masculinity, while women increasingly challenged their prescribed domestic roles and restrictive clothing through their participation in sporting activities. The Gilded Age thus proved to be a transitional era in the growth and meaning of sport in American culture.

DISCUSSION QUESTIONS

1. In what ways did sport unite Americans during the Gilded Age?
2. In what ways did sport cause divisions within the society?
3. How did gender play a role in sport in the Gilded Age?
4. How did the town of Pullman serve as a social experiment? Was it successful?
5. How did sport assume an expanded commercial role?
6. How did entrepreneurs shape a sporting culture?
7. What role did sporting practices play in perceptions of social mobility?
8. How and why did professional teams emerge?

American Sport and Social Change During the Progressive Era

1890–1920

CHAPTER OBJECTIVES

After reading this chapter, you will have learned about the following:

- The Progressive reformers' vision of American society and the reactions of alternative groups

- The changes wrought in American culture by industrialization and the need for urban and suburban recreational spaces

- The role of sport in the acculturation process

- The Social Darwinist belief system that subordinated and segregated non-whites

- The role of sport in the imperial process

- The function of sport as a symbol of social class, race, ethnicity, and gender

- The transformation of the modern Olympic Games from a peace movement to a nationalistic enterprise

The intense rivalries that emerged in association with big-time intercollegiate football programs during the Progressive Era reflected changes occurring in American society as a whole. The use of paid professional coaches marked a greater emphasis on winning, which became a characteristic trait of American culture, as corporations and college teams alike sought to dominate their rivals. Noted Harvard football coach Bill Reid became immersed in the heated rivalry between Harvard and Yale. He wrote in his diary about the quest for victory, his prioritizing of winning above his players' other activities, and his expectation that players would attend practice even at the expense of academic work:

> Some of the men were a little late getting down to the field this afternoon and I got after them. Brill it seems came down fifteen minutes late having been attending a lecture which he said he was afraid to cut. Knowing as I do that the marks for November hour examinations will not be in until after the Yale game, I knew that he could not be put on probation and so I told him to cut whenever it was necessary in order to be on time for practice. I don't care how much of a student a fellow cares to be at other times—[but] four days before the Yale game . . . I don't see how a man can help feeling that hardly anything is more important than to beat Yale. (qtd. in Smith, *Big-Time* 291, 300–301)

In sport, as in the larger American society, such attitudes about winning and gaining wealth, as well as corruption and other perceived problems in the excesses of the Gilded Age—together with the rapid transition from a rural agricultural economy to an urban industrial one—caused many to question the nature of the evolving American culture. Social critics known as Progressive reformers urged a variety of changes to address the problems, curb the excesses of the Gilded Age, and improve the lives of the burgeoning urban population. They often targeted the growing number of immigrant newcomers to America, and they often employed sport in a variety of programs to educate and assimilate immigrants and address perceived social ills.

This chapter examines how immigration, industrialization, urbanization, imperialism, and the assimilation of disparate groups changed the face of America.

Social Reformers of the Progressive Era

The Progressives, consisting of loosely organized or independent white, Anglo-Saxon, Protestant (WASP) men and women, led the way as social reformers. They proposed a wide variety of goals, remedies, and middle-class values to confront social ills such as corrupt government, unbridled wealth, exploitation of the masses, and unequal rights in a supposedly democratic republic. Their analyses and solutions derived from a distinct Protestant moral code known as the Social Gospel. Moral crusaders campaigned against pornography and prostitution and in favor of temperance. In 1919, the success of the latter effort resulted in the passage of the Eighteenth Amendment (commonly known as Prohibition), which prohibited the manufacture, sale, and transport of nonmedicinal alcohol and prohibited beer and liquor consumption, thus curtailing the favored leisure activity of many Americans, especially among ethnic minorities (Powers, *Faces* 82–83). Therefore the measure imposed a particular morality based on ethnic, religious, and class differences.

Reformers also sought to enable fair competition within the capitalist economic system, as workers organized themselves into labor unions to achieve better wages and conditions. Most workers labored at least 10 hours a day, 6 days a week, for $9 per week (Blum et al. 467). Some labor leaders, such as Eugene Debs, advocated socialism; others favored anarchism, or, in the case of the Industrial Workers of the World (IWW), more radical or even violent means to achieve their ends of a more equitable society. In this environment, a series of conflicts between employers and their workers questioned the nature of American liberty, democracy, and opportunity. A national railroad strike in July 1877, for example, crippled the transportation network, and Chicago, the center of the anarchist movement, witnessed the Haymarket Massacre on May 4, 1886, when an altercation between workers and police killed eight and wounded sixty. The police responded with indiscriminate gunfire that felled many more. Over the next eight years, Chicago suffered 528 strikes, at a cost of $9 million (Gems, *For Pride* 3–4).

Workers confronted employers throughout the 1890s, and an army of unemployed citizens even marched on Washington in 1892. By the early twentieth century, the federal government had incorporated some Progressive measures and moved to bust the large corporate trusts, dissolve commercial monopolies, and impose an income tax on the more affluent to address the exploitation of human and commercial resources. At the local level, workers in settlement houses (social agencies located within immigrant neighborhoods) and park supervisors worked to assimilate children and used sport as a means to distract them from the radical sympathies of their parents.

Investigative journalists known as "muckrakers" exposed the corrupt practices of politicians and employers that fostered poverty among the multitudes that immigrated to America in search of betterment. During the 1870s, 2.5 million people arrived in the United States, followed by another 5 million in the 1880s; from 1865 to 1915, the number of immigrants reached 25 million. By 1890, 80 percent of New Yorkers were foreigners or children of immigrants (Garraty 444, 473, 477).

Urban ghettos housed millions of people, often in overcrowded tenements marked by abysmal conditions that spawned disease and crime, and city services neglected hygiene or even basic amenities for those who were impoverished. In 1882, 50 percent of the children in Chicago died before age five (Pierce, *A History* [Vol.3] 55). Social work, a new vocation, emerged as an antidote, and many of the social workers were educated women who found in the new occupation a parallel to the caretaking roles previously assigned to them in the domestic sphere. Strong women also challenged social inequality in gender-based crusades such as campaigning for suffrage, birth control, and general respect.

Progressive reformers devised a three-tiered procedure designed to assimilate the various ethnic and working-class groups residing within the national borders, and sporting activities factored into this process. The first step rested partly upon humanitarian concerns. Children worked long hours in factories, and due to fatigue they often fell victim to injury or even death. Horses trampled others who played or worked in the streets. Progressives campaigned for child labor laws that restricted full-time employment, but such measures met with opposition from parents. With no minimum wage requirements in effect and no retirement plans for workers, immigrant families relied on a full complement of household laborers to make ends meet and to care for the sick, the unemployed, and the elderly.

Unemployed children simply roamed the streets, joining gangs or engaging in petty crimes or mischief. Progressives then passed mandatory education laws (the second step) that required children to go to school. By 1918, every state had enacted such legislation (Clement and Reiner 476). Truancy officers enforced mandatory attendance, but a captive audience did not assure either learning or Americanization, as many ethnic-minority children did not speak English. In this regard, physical education proved a boon, and soon became a requirement (the third step) in many public schools. Trained physical educators taught children to play competitive American sports such as baseball, football, and basketball, and these forms of competition ingrained the basic tenets of the capitalistic economic system; team sports also taught the rudiments of the cooperation and leadership necessary to a democracy. Moreover, supervised games taught deference to authority in the form of a coach, referee, or umpire—a lesson cherished by capitalistic employers facing radical or stridently unhappy workers. Employers' ardent belief in the transformative powers of sport prompted them to provide funding, which, along with state resources, could be used to support the increasing number of public schools charged with achieving the acculturation goals.

1891

> James Naismith invents basketball

1892

- Senda Berenson becomes director of physical education at Smith College, Massachusetts

- Pudge Heffelfinger becomes the first pro football player

- Corbett defeats Sullivan in first gloved bout for heavyweight championship

- First women's basketball game played at Smith College

1893

- Economic depression occurs

- First Stanley Cup awarded

1894

- Pullman Strike staged

- Coxey's Army marches on Washington

- United States Golf Association (USGA) formed

- Temple Cup Series begins in baseball

Overcrowded tenements led to conditions ripe for propagation of measles, typhoid fever, diphtheria, tuberculosis, and other contagious diseases.

Image courtesy of Library of Congress, LC-USZ62-8836.

Play and Games in American Ideology

The overcrowding of cities called for a restructuring of urban landscapes and the creation of open space. At the 1893 World's Columbian Exposition in the host city of Chicago, historian Frederick Jackson Turner announced the closing of the American frontier and claimed that the frontier experience was integral in shaping the American character: Without lands or American Indian tribes to conquer, and with the massive influx of European immigrant groups, the aggressive, militaristic, independent character of the American WASP culture faced decline, if not extinction. Psychologist G. Stanley Hall offered some hope for WASPs in his recapitulation theory, which asserted that societies, like individual human beings, passed through evolutionary stages evident in their styles of play. In this view, simple running and throwing activities reflected primitive stages that gave way to games of chase or tag resembling hunting experiences. Eventually, children learned more complex and cooperative games that required leadership, strategy, and the characteristics of civilized societies.

Hall's beliefs merged with the pragmatic educational philosophy of John Dewey, one of his former students, to provide a firm foundation for the play movement. In Dewey's scheme, one learned by experience—by participation in activities that might encompass leadership, teamwork, and self-sacrifice for the good of the whole. For example, baseball, the primary vehicle at the time for instilling such values in ethnic-minority youth, might mesh the seemingly incongruous values of ethnic communalism and American individualism, since all players worked together as a defensive team but gained individual honors with the bat. Through the ideas of Hall and Dewey, then, sport gained legitimacy, and by the end of the Progressive Era historian Frederic Paxson declared sport to be the new frontier, in which Americans or immigrants might seek the social mobility no longer available in the West, as well as psychological release from urban stress.

Within this context, playing sport and games assumed an essential role in the physical training and moral education of youth. Under the guidance of coaches and trained physical educators, it was hoped, boys in particular might learn to become loyal, disciplined, ethical, and patriotic Americans—rather than degenerate hoodlums—by engaging in games and physical activities, especially team sports such as baseball, football, and basketball that elicited the desired outcomes of cooperation and respect for authority. Authorities hoped that by learning to follow a leader and play together, students would learn the practical application of democratic principles. Accepting the judgment of referees or umpires instilled obedience, while the competitive nature of sport reinforced the basis of a capitalistic economy. Moreover, football promoted the martial qualities deemed necessary to keep the nation strong and defend the tenets of capitalism, democracy, and individual rights. Theodore Roosevelt claimed that

> in any republic, courage is a prime necessity for the average citizen if he is to be a good citizen; and he needs physical courage no less than moral courage, the courage that endures, the courage that will fight valiantly alike against the foe of the soul and the foes of the body. Athletics are good, especially in their rougher form, because they tend to develop such courage. (qtd. in Gems, *For Pride* 77)

Despite the death of one of his own players in 1909, University of Virginia president Edwin Alderman refused to ban football, stating that "in dealing with this game you are dealing with our national characteristics" (Gems, *For Pride* 83).

Boys had long initiated their own interscholastic contests in baseball and football. They scheduled games with a variety of opponents, arranged travel to playing sites, and covered their own expenses, resisting any attempts by school authorities to regulate their extracurricular activities. Thus while educators and administrators debated the values of the gymnastic curriculum, male students continued the pursuit of competitive sport forms throughout the late nineteenth century.

Physical Education of Youth

At the college level, American educators adopted European gymnastic systems to improve the fitness levels of both male and female students. In 1885, Oberlin College in Ohio began training physical educators. The German Turners offered their own courses in Milwaukee and Boston, and graduates of the Turner system introduced German gymnastics to public high schools in Kansas City in 1885 and throughout the Midwest thereafter. In 1889, Mary Hemenway, a wealthy Bostonian, founded the Boston Normal School of Gymnastics, which favored the Swedish system that emphasized flexibility rather than strength. At Harvard, Dr. Dudley Sargent introduced weight-training machines and anthropometric measurements. The YMCA opened its own teacher-training center in Springfield, Massachusetts. These various competing philosophies and training methods became known as the Battle of the Systems, as colleges and public high schools deliberated on the best procedure for training students.

In the cities, the transition to rationalized, commodified sport continued. In 1888, students in Boston high schools formed a football league, and similar organizations soon appeared throughout the Midwest. In Chicago, the high school football league charged dues, which covered the cost of a championship banner. The second-place team received the remaining cash in the league treasury. Trophies, rewards, and media attention promoted school spirit, communal pride, and an intense desire to win. High school newspapers lionized school athletes, local merchants honored them, and students feted their warriors with banquets and adulation as well as financial support. Intense rivalries triggered the use of "ringers"—exceptional athletes who were only part-time students or who had no affiliation with the school at all.

•1895

- William Morgan invents volleyball

- American Bowling Congress formed

- Big Ten Conference formed

- USGA holds men's and women's national amateur golf championships

- First American auto race held

- *Plessy v. Ferguson* Supreme Court decision allows segregation

•1896

❯ First modern Olympics held (Athens, Greece); American Robert Garrett wins the gold in the discus

•1897

- First Boston Marathon held

- Cheyenne Frontier Days launched

•1898

- Hawaii annexed

- Spanish-American War fought

•1898–1900

- African American Major Taylor reigns as cycling champion

Lax eligibility regulations plagued contests at both the interscholastic and intercollegiate levels, and even faculty members played in some competitions. In 1891, the Manual Training High School in the Chicago league protested that it was the only league member actually using its own students. Such practices openly violated the amateur standards of the governing bodies and upset reformers who adhered to a belief in sport as a character-building mechanism.

In June 1893, the University of Illinois invited high schools to participate in its athletic meet, an event that drew more than two hundred athletes for track-and-field events, cycling races, a football kick, and a baseball throw. The University of Chicago, founded with John D. Rockefeller's money, opened in 1892 and began offering interscholastic tournaments in track and basketball. Its coach and athletic director, Amos Alonzo Stagg, played in the first-ever basketball game, a sport invented by James Naismith at the YMCA School in Springfield, Massachusetts, in 1891. On March 10, 1892, Stagg wrote the following letter to his sister, Pauline Stagg:

> There is a great furor among the boys in the school over a new game which Naismith our center rusher invented, called basket foot ball. It is played indoors in the gymnasium or some good sized room. Any number of persons on a side. A basket with large enough opening to take the ball easily is hung at each end about eight feet from the floor. The object is for the ball to be thrown or pitched into these baskets. The ball cannot be run with, although no limitations are placed on any one when not having the ball. This of course places a premium on passing the ball to others and so work it down the field. Fouls are declared for running with the ball and for kicking it. Any one has a right to the ball at all times if he can get it. I think the game could be easily adapted to girls – the main point being to get a basket as big as a house. The faculty of the school play best team composed of the Secretarial men tomorrow. We expect a great time. (Gems, *Sports* 143)

The game was intended to provide a winter activity that would occupy energetic young men during the interim period between football and baseball seasons, and it further allowed physical educators to gain greater control over unruly males throughout the entire year. The early rules, however, permitted a high number of players and the use of rough tactics akin to those of a wrestling match. A few months later, Senda Berenson, an instructor at Smith College in Massachusetts, devised alternative rules for women's play, and the game soon became a favorite of high school girls as well. Berenson organized the first women's game, in 1892, after reading about the new game of basketball at Springfield College. She modified the men's rules to make the game less rough, divided the basketball court into three zones, and thereby restricted strenuous play. Girls could not cross over the zones, which necessitated a cooperative strategy to score points. No physical contact between players was allowed, so that they could not "snatch" the ball or block players as in the men's game (Hult, *Century* 24–25). Basketball quickly became a popular sport for women and girls of diverse ethnic backgrounds at various social organizations and settlement houses. Josephine Wilkin, in a letter to her mother on March 6, 1892, related the first game played at Smith College:

> Friday afternoon at the Gym, we played a game, instead of going through the ordinary performances. Two waste-paper baskets were hung, one on either side of the Gym about three feet above our heads. Two of the girls choose sides, + those on our side were distinguished from the other by handkerchiefs tied on their arms. Three girls from each side were sent over to the other and the game began. We had a football which was to be touched only with the hands, + the object was to get it into your opponent's basket + keep it out of your own. When it was sent over to our side, the girls on that side who had been sent from the other tried to get it and throw it into the basket while the rest tried to catch it + throw it back to their helpers on the other side. See? It was great fun, + very exciting, especially when we got knocked down, as frequently happened. The side I was on had the misfortune to be beaten, but we had the ball in their basket several times, including the first time. (qtd. in Gems, *Sports* 147–148)

Some women, like their male counterparts, participated in sports for physical health and competition, but they did so in a disputed context, as physicians, psychologists, and educators debated the appropriateness of sport for women. Some of these authorities worried about the stress of competition, while others feared damage to reproductive capacities or the accumulation of aggressive male characteristics. Nevertheless, women found a variety of sporting opportunities at schools, settlement houses, and in industrial recreation programs.

In 1895, William Morgan, a graduate of the YMCA Training School, invented volleyball, another indoor sport, at nearby Holyoke, as adults increasingly sought to assume greater control over students' extracurricular activities. Thereafter, YMCA missionaries carried both games throughout the world, as sport provided one means of attracting young men in the quest for converts. As the new century approached, then, sport presented a battleground contested by various groups, as immigrants struggled with assimilation, youth rebuffed adult control in schools and play spaces, and professional athletes challenged the amateur ideal.

In 1898, faculty members at the Chicago high schools formed the Board of Control to govern student athletics. They standardized rules, established eligibility requirements, addressed unsporting behavior, and prohibited money prizes. The Board of Control scheduled contests only at approved sites, such as school gyms, YMCAs, or settlement houses, where adults might oversee students' activities. The Board even enacted competitive divisions based on size and weight to equalize competition. Students, however, protested the loss of their freedom and the curtailment of their own initiatives. They even revolted, attempting to establish their own league outside the jurisdiction of school authorities. The venture failed when the superintendent of schools expelled the revolutionary students (Pruter, "Chicago High").

1900
- Davis Cup tennis competition begins

1901
- American League (baseball) debuts

1902
- First Rose Bowl football game played
- Young Women's Hebrew Association formed in New York City

1903
- Chicago Hebrew Institute organized
- Wright Brothers achieve flight
- Public Schools Athletic League established in New York City by Dr. Luther Gulick
- First World Series played

1904
- National Ski Association formed

1905
- Radical labor organization Industrial Workers of the World (IWW) founded

Senda Berenson initiated women's basketball at Smith College in 1892.

Image courtesy of Sophia Smith Collection, Smith College.

School rivalries extended well beyond the local scene. By the turn of the twentieth century, high school teams traveled throughout the country for regional and national competitions. Debates over contrasting styles of play resulted in a national football showdown. Eastern schools favored the plodding, mass plays (i.e., players closely bunched to produce mass force), and brute strength exhibited by the New England college teams, while Midwesterners favored speed, end runs, and reverses, sometimes running in excess of one hundred plays during a game (no huddles). For some time, challenges between the Eastern and Midwestern college powers went unheeded, but in 1902 Brooklyn's Polytechnic High School met Chicago's Hyde Park High School in a postseason confrontation in Chicago. The Midwestern style of play overwhelmed the New Yorkers, and Chicago won by a score of 105-0. Brooklyn claimed that Poly did not represent its best team, and Charles Ebbets, owner of its professional baseball team, guaranteed funding for a rematch in New York the next year. In the event, darkness forced a cessation, with Chicago's North Division High School in a commanding 75-0 lead over Brooklyn Boys' High.

New York fared better than other localities in its regulation and administration of local high school sports. Dr. Luther Gulick became director of physical training in the New York school system in 1903 and instituted a comprehensive athletic program that offered competition in baseball, basketball, soccer, swimming, tennis, track and field, crew, cross country, lacrosse, and riflery. Boys could earn distinctive badges for successful completion of physical fitness tests, and classes might win honors by surpassing average scores of other classes. School teams competed for district and city championships symbolized by trophies that were proudly displayed at schools. In 1907, a crowd of fifteen thousand witnessed the championship baseball game held at the Polo Grounds.

The organization of the Public Schools Athletic League (PSAL) in New York included even the elementary schools. In 1905, a girls division was created to offer folk dancing, but it limited athletic competition in other activities to intramural events. Numerous other cities adopted the New York model, as adults increasingly controlled students' leisure pursuits. As child labor laws directed considerable numbers of ethnic-minority and immigrant youths into the school system, adult educators employed sport in efforts to Americanize them. For others, who remained outside the jurisdiction of school authorities, Progressive reformers employed similar strategies for supervised play instruction at parks, playgrounds, and settlement houses across America. When successful, such programs served as an effective social control device, curtailing juvenile delinquency and increasing adult guidance.

Emergence of Football

Football gained dominant status as the preeminent sport on college campuses during the Progressive Era. Thanksgiving championship games became urban spectacles by the 1880s, as fans paraded to games and alumni feted their warriors in sumptuous banquets held after the games, in which teams strove for regional prestige and national recognition. The parade before the 1893 Yale–Princeton game started four hours before kickoff. Richard Harding Davis described the lively scene in *Harper's Weekly*: "The city surrenders herself to the students and their game as she never welcomes any other event, except a Presidential election. . . . [E]very other young woman you meet, and every little boy, and elderly men even, begin to parade Broadway with bows of blue stuck on their persons, or long strips of orange and black ribbon . . . which proclaim their allegiance and their hopes" (qtd. in Riess, *Major* 117). Forty thousand fans attended and paid as much as $150 each for box seats. Some came from as far as Oregon and Texas, and a hotel bartender was entrusted with $50,000 in wagers from complete strangers.

The cult of the athletic hero was reinforced when football pioneer Walter Camp and sportswriter Caspar Whitney began naming an All-American team in 1889 to signify individual and specialized excellence. Between 1865 (when the Civil War was ended) and 1898 (when the Spanish-American War was fought), young men had found no war in which to prove their courage and masculinity, and football sufficed as a worthy alternative, given the injuries and deaths produced by its mass play and brutal tactics. Nearly one hundred colleges were fielding teams by 1892, and football assumed distinct military purposes. As Senator Henry Cabot Lodge put it, "the injuries incurred . . . are part of the price which the English speaking race has paid for being world conquerors. [V]ictories . . . are the manifestation and evidence of a spirit, which is all important. [T]his great democracy is moving onward to its great destiny. Woe to the men or nations that bar its imperial march" (qtd. in Gems, *For Pride* 26). Helmets were not required until 1939, so players wore their hair long for padding, but this minimal protection offered little safeguard, as 18 deaths and 159 serious injuries occurred in 1905 alone. In 1909, the death toll was 33, and the rising casualty lists fostered a backlash.

College officials from 68 institutions met in 1905 to organize a governing body. The Intercollegiate Athletic Association of the United States soon became the National Collegiate Athletic Association (NCAA). New rules, such as allowance of forward passes, were instituted to open up the game and decrease the mass plays. Few teams adopted the new strategy, however, because defenders tended to attack pass receivers and because, by rule, incomplete passes resulted in a turnover until further changes were made. Notre Dame, a small Catholic college in Indiana, did much to popularize the new technique by employing the strategy in a stunning 35-13 upset of a powerful Army team in 1913.

Football became big business by the dawn of the twentieth century. John D. Rockefeller, benefactor of the University of Chicago, offered a $3 million donation for a win over Wisconsin in 1895, and the team responded with a 22-12 come-from-behind victory. By the 1890s, Yale raised $100,000 through its football program, and in 1904 Harvard had a $50,000 surplus in its football budget; in fact, only tuition produced greater revenue for the institution. In 1903, Harvard built a concrete stadium with forty thousand seats to accommodate the multitudes who paid to watch its team perform. Other schools followed Harvard's lead in stadium construction. In 1906, the $42,000 excess in the University of Chicago's football receipts funded all other sports in its athletic program.

1906
- National Collegiate Athletic Association founded
- Playground Association of America founded

1908
- Production begins on Model T Ford cars

- African American Jack Johnson defeats Tommy Burns to gain the heavyweight championship

1909
- National Association for the Advancement of Colored People (NAACP) founded

1910
- Mann Act passed; prohibits interstate transport of women for immoral activities
- Jack Johnson–Jim Jeffries (the "Great White Hope") heavyweight championship fight occurs

Independent promoters capitalized on the commercialization of football as well. James Wagner, president of the Rose Parade committee in Pasadena, offered the University of Michigan a $3,500 guarantee to meet Stanford in the first Rose Bowl game in 1902. Meant to bolster a burgeoning California tourist industry, the game proved a mismatch. Michigan had scored 501 points that season while holding its opponents scoreless. Its coach, Fielding Yost, had been dismissed from Stanford and took revenge in a 49-0 rout of the Californians. Stanford's players suffered so many injuries that the game could not continue, and the Rose Parade committee discontinued the spectacle for 14 years.

Yost's star player, Willie Heston, had followed him to Michigan from California, and such moves by "tramp athletes," as well as recruitment of star players by coaches and alumni, had been underway for at least two decades by that time. Yale proved particularly effective at recruiting, with nouveau-riche alumni throughout the country funneling information to football managers. Under Walter Camp, the football program achieved a machinelike precision in a bureaucratic, businesslike organization that produced efficient and effective results. Between 1886 and 1895, Yale won 124 games, losing only 3 and tying 3. Its 1888 contingent scored 698 points, while holding opponents scoreless. Other schools sought former Yale players as coaches and introduced the Yale system. William Rainey Harper, a former Yale professor and the newly appointed president of the University of Chicago, hired Amos Alonzo Stagg, a Yale All-American, as the school's first football coach. Harper gave Stagg tenured faculty status and a salary that exceeded that of most professors, providing college coaches with immediate credibility and prestige. Over the previous decade, students had hired temporary professional trainers, who would prepare the team (only during the season) to enhance its chances against intercollegiate rivals.

Stagg's teams soon challenged even his alma mater for national honors. As with Yale, Stagg's recruiting network secured top athletes with substantial inducements, as the coach manipulated an $80,000 scholarship fund for ostensibly needy students. One of Stagg's recruits, who later won All-American honors, warned Midwestern rivals, "You fellows can't get me at Northwestern, and they can't get me at Wisconsin, you haven't got the money. I am going to Chicago" (Jordan 19–20, 23 [qtd. passage from Jordan cited in Gems, *For Pride* 94]). In 1901, Yale recruited 27-year-old James Hogan, who, as team captain in 1904, got free tuition, room, and board; a Caribbean vacation; a share of profits from the sale of baseball programs; and commission on all packages of cigarettes sold in the city of New Haven.

The combination of such incentives with community pride, increased emphasis on winning, and associated gambling led to the overt professionalization of football. Walter "Pudge" Heffelfinger, a Yale All-American and the most acclaimed player of his day, began accepting "expenses" to play for a Chicago athletic club team in 1892. Later that season, the Allegheny Athletic Association paid him $500 for one heavily wagered game against its archrival in Pittsburgh. Professionalism quickly spread throughout western Pennsylvania and eastern Ohio, as communities imported players for big games. In 1897, even Butte, Montana, bought players for its games against West Coast teams. With money on the line, teams sought any player who might make the winning difference, and even racism was sometimes diminished, as Ohio teams signed African American stars such as Charles Follis and Charles "Doc" Baker to contracts. Football thus offered more opportunities at the highest levels than baseball or the nascent sport of basketball for African American and working-class athletes.

Many professional teams started as company organizations. Among them, the Columbus (Ohio) Panhandles represented the Pennsylvania Railroad starting in 1901. The six Nesser brothers, the sons of German immigrants who worked as boilermakers for the railway company, formed the backbone of the unit and terrorized opponents into the 1920s. The roughness of football meshed naturally with the hard lives of working-class participants and fans. Unlike middle-class adherents, who needed the game to prove their masculinity due to their increasingly sedentary lives, working-class players admired toughness and athletic prowess as a reflection of their own value systems. For the latter, roughness was an inherent part of life.

Football drew mixed reactions from women. Some idolized football heroes, while others agreed with men like President Teddy Roosevelt, who saw football as a necessary antidote to the increasing feminization of culture. As middle-class boys spent more time with their mothers and with female schoolteachers, male leaders feared the potential loss of virility, aggressiveness, and martial spirit that characterized American competitiveness. The Georgia legislature moved to ban the sport when one of its players died in an 1897 game with Virginia—until the player's mother protested the proposal. But when four players died in separate incidents on the same day in 1909, mothers railed against the collegiate emphasis on football, the anti-intellectualism associated with the game, and the ongoing drive for victories and commercial profits, as well as the brutality. In 1907, a millionaire heiress, Anna Jeanes, died and left her estate worth millions in coal and mineral rights to Swarthmore College on the condition that it abolish its athletic program. The gift marked the most prominent effort by a woman to transform the commercialized patriarchal ideology of sport that had become fixated among boards of trustees and alumni. The Swarthmore president suspended play for a year but finally declined the gift rather than forgo competition. The sanctity of the game as a male bastion—and the projection of its aggressive, militaristic virtues as American cultural characteristics—overrode concerns about brutality and commercialization.

Recreational Spaces

Reformers sought to alleviate the urban ills of pollution, overcrowding, and disease by restructuring the teeming cities and bringing a measure of aid and relief to their inhabitants. Children, who were most at risk, elicited particular concern and were the focus of Progressive assimilation efforts. Whereas children commonly played on their own in streets, alleys, and vacant lots, Progressive plans called for playgrounds, parks, and ball fields with adult supervision. The initiative started modestly when Bostonians provided a sand garden at the Parmenter Street Chapel in 1885. Within two years, the city was offering 11 sandlots to meet the needs of small children, and Philadelphia and New York soon expanded upon the concept to construct small parks. While some immigrant parents welcomed such safe play spaces in the neighborhood, others opposed the interventions of well-meaning Progressive reformers. Play spaces such as settlement houses, parks, and playgrounds were controlled and supervised by Anglo-American men and women whose influence over children might undermine parental authority. In fact, a number of intended beneficiaries—Americans Indians, immigrant ethnic groups, women from diverse backgrounds, and members of the working class—did not readily or entirely accept the dominant WASP vision, which generated social tensions and political debate.

Settlement Houses

Settlement house workers, often allied with and supported by socialites and commercial interests, attempted to shape cities in accord with their particular visions of order, efficiency, and morality. As part of the Americanization process, reformers founded settlement houses in the urban immigrant neighborhoods of New York, Boston, Chicago, Detroit, Philadelphia, and other cities. They believed that they might fashion a more homogeneous society and bridge the class and social divisions created by the capitalistic industrial process. Reformers situated settlement houses squarely in teeming ethnic neighborhoods to engage residents in their assimilation programs. The settlements provided educational classes and an orientation to American society, and programs included sport and physical training—promoted as alternatives to the immoral and unhealthy amusements available in city life—along with English instruction, civics classes, vocational education, stenography for women, clubs, and other activities that reformers deemed wholesome and appropriate.

1911–1914

1911

> First Indianapolis 500 auto race held; Ray Harroun wins the inaugural race

1912

- Jim Thorpe wins Olympic gold; is named world's greatest athlete
- Theodore Roosevelt founds the Progressive Party
- Woodrow Wilson elected president

1913

- Sixteenth Amendment ratified (power to levy income tax)

> Amateur Francis Ouimet wins U.S. Open golf tournament

1914–1918

- World War I fought (United States enters in 1917)

1914

- Panama Canal opened
- Federal League (third major baseball league) organized

Hull House in Chicago is one example of a settlement house aimed at assisting families in an immigrant ghetto. It was founded by Jane Addams, one of the first generation of college-educated women, and she eschewed the traditional roles for women. After touring Europe and observing the social work being done in the slums of London, Addams returned to Chicago in 1889 and, along with Ellen Gates Starr, her college friend, she opened Hull House that year to provide assistance and education to myriad indigent European Americans. Typical of most settlement settings, the Hull House area housed seventy thousand residents representing 18 nationalities. The average family of five members lived in three (or fewer) rooms and subsisted on a weekly income of $5 (Ely 17–21). Addams used her considerable social contacts to provide funding for her charitable and social programs in an attempt to acculturate members of diverse ethnic minorities, despite opposition by Irish American politicians who controlled the ethnic vote. Her initial attempts to introduce high culture through art classes drew few participants, but the kindergarten provided much-needed childcare. With the support of wealthy patrons who questioned the excesses of the capitalist system or exhibited charitable motives, Hull House expanded its programs and facilities, attracting youth to its play spaces and sponsoring athletic teams for boys and girls.

To escape the steamy Chicago summers, Addams and her staff also took immigrant children and adults on excursions to experience outdoor sports. Bowen Park in Waukegan, Illinois, became the summer retreat for children and adults of Jane Addams' Hull House

PEOPLE & PLACES

Chicago Hebrew Institute

One example of a prominent Jewish settlement house was the Chicago Hebrew Institute, organized in November 1903 to promote the moral, physical, religious, and civic welfare of Jewish immigrants in America. It served as a key institution in the Americanization of Eastern European immigrants, offering a comprehensive range of classes in citizenship, English, commerce, domestic science, Jewish culture, literature, art, physical culture, drama, and music; it also featured one of the best athletic departments of the early 1900s. Harry Berkman, athletic director from 1908 to 1923, explained the institute's approach in a 1913 newspaper article: "Developing the body as well as the mind is a religion with us. . . . We train the boys and girls to be self-reliant, independent, and on the square in everything" ("Good, Clean Sport'" n. pag.).

The sports programs proved to be one of the primary means for gaining respect and a measure of acceptance in American society, and the Institute produced Jewish champions in several sports. Its extensive athletic fields and splendid facilities attracted males and females of all ages, with more than 113,000 program participants in 1913 alone (Chicago Hebrew Institute Observer). Journalist Bertha A. Loeb, writing in the American Jewish paper The Sentinel in 1914, asserted that the "undersized, anaemic 'Jewish weakling' will soon be a recollection of by-gone days" (qtd. in Borish, "Athletic Activities" 253). The Chicago Hebrew Institute's wrestling team won the Amateur Athletic Federation championship in 1911 by defeating other athletic clubs and the YMCA. Benjamin Reuben, a five-time Amateur Athletic Union (AAU) wrestling champion, represented the United States, along with a Chicago Hebrew Institute teammate, in the 1920 Olympic Games in Antwerp, Belgium (Gems, "The Rise of Sport" 152–153). Jewish women also excelled at sport. In 1921, the girls' basketball team went 26-0 and won the Central AAU Girls' Basketball Championship. That same year, the girls' swimming team, coached by a Danish Olympian, won the open city swimming championship of Chicago.

Association, organized in 1895. In this natural setting away from the density of Chicago, Hull House residents found a wholesome retreat where they engaged in sports and outdoor recreation activities such as tennis, swimming, walking, basketball, and baseball.

Churches, other religious organizations, and social agencies soon copied the Hull House model, founding 68 settlement houses in Chicago alone by 1917. Other municipalities in densely populated urban areas embarked on similar quests that emphasized sport as a means of assimilation and acculturation. As in Chicago, New York social workers such as Stanton Coit, Lillian Wald, and Mary Simkhovitch ran settlement houses in blighted areas. Operating much like Jane Addams, Wald founded the popular Henry Street settlement in 1895 with the aid of philanthropists. Reformers in other cities soon initiated similar ventures, and by 1910 nearly four hundred settlements cared for needy residents in American communities (Fass 762).

Despite their charity, settlement houses displayed a distinctly middle-class, WASP-oriented value system that was not always intelligible to—and was often at odds with—the religious and working-class cultures of ethnic immigrant groups. As a result, Catholics and Jews countered with their own programs. Wealthy German Jews who had assimilated into the American capitalist system but wished to maintain their religious faith endeavored to integrate their more orthodox Eastern European brethren into modern American society by founding their own settlement houses in New York, Milwaukee, Boston, Pittsburgh, and Chicago (Borish, "Women").

Playgrounds

Settlement house directors such as Jane Addams and Lillian Wald joined their concerns about health issues with those of physicians Luther Gulick and Henry Curtis in a Washington, D.C., conference that produced the Playground Association of America (PAA) in 1906. The PAA directed national efforts to incorporate supervised play and sport as wholesome ways to achieve the moral and civic education of youth. Curtis (a former student of G. Stanley Hall) and Gulick (who taught at the YMCA training school and organized New York's Public Schools Athletic League) adhered to the psychological theory of play as a scientific rationale for their use of sport and their call for appropriate play spaces. Jane Addams fostered the concept of pragmatic experimentation, invoking John Dewey's belief in learning by doing. Dewey, a philosophy professor at the University of Chicago, became a Hull House trustee in 1897, and support from such an eminent personage provided a great impetus to the playground movement. By 1917, reformers counted 3,940 playgrounds in the United States (Gorn and Goldstein 177), and 504 American cities offered recreational programs, most of them modeled on the Chicago plan (Riess, *Sport* 142).

The Chicago plan included trained park directors and a watchful police officer or assistant to insure proper play and lessons in Americanization. Women offered summertime kindergarten and craft classes for girls, while a professional coach instructed the boys in sports skills. In 1905, the Chicago Parks Commission optimistically reported that "this feature of the playground work has saved many a young man, by drawing him away from bad companions and the vicious atmosphere of saloons and dance halls" (*A Plea for Playgrounds* 17.) The city took further steps to attract boys and girls by constructing field houses in the parks, and by 1904 these large buildings served as community centers, with meeting and craft rooms, separate gyms for boys and girls, playgrounds, and even swimming pools in some cases. The field house concept provided for year-round usage, especially during the winter months, when staff members had previously had fewer opportunities to inculcate Progressive values in the neighborhood children. Many municipalities then copied the Chicago model of year-round usage of facilities under trained adult supervisors.

In New York City, Mayor Abram Hewitt campaigned in 1887 for parks and public baths to serve the needs of poor residents. Although he managed a $1 million subsidy from the state government, real park development began with the administration of Mayor William Strong in 1896. Strong also built recreational piers along the waterfront,

1916
- Professional Golf Association (PGA) founded
- American Tennis Association (for black players) organized

1917
- National Hockey League established
- Women's Swimming Association founded (New York City)

1919
- Red Scare occurs
- Eighteenth Amendment ratified (Prohibition)
- Black Sox baseball scandal erupts

1920
- Nineteenth Amendment ratified, granting women's suffrage
- Negro National League founded

1920

➤ U.S. women swimmers compete in the Olympic Games; Ethelda Bleibtrey and others compete
- American Professional Football Association formed (later renamed the NFL)

Dvorak Park, located on the Lower West Side of Chicago and named after Czech composer Antonin Dvorak (1841-1904), was one of several Chicago playgrounds.

Courtesy of John Graf.

and the Board of Education required that its schools have playgrounds (some of which were constructed on the schools' fenced rooftops). By 1905, New York schools were home to more than 100 playgrounds, and the city operated 15 municipal baths, but even this proved inadequate (Riess, *City* 136). The playgrounds accommodated less than 10 percent of the children, and youth gangs had their own agenda, using the parks as headquarters for gambling, fighting, and criminal activities, thus thwarting reformers' efforts to socially control recalcitrant youth (Riess, *Sport* 142).

Still, Clarence Rainwater, director of Chicago's playgrounds, believed that such spaces gave the authorities "the opportunity to gain control of 80 percent of the population during the 64 hours per week when even laborers are at leisure" (Hogan 70). E.B. DeGroot, athletic director of the city's South Park District, instructed his staff to "bring about order and esprit de corps, to teach obedience to authority and instant execution of orders" (Halsey 32). In 1908, sociologist Allen T. Burns concluded that the Chicago system had reduced delinquency by more than 28 percent but admitted that prevention did not constitute reformation (Halsey 34). The desire for tight control of unruly juveniles also led Chicago to establish the first juvenile court in the United States in 1900 as a way to address delinquent behavior. The strict supervision of playgrounds and athletic fields by urban playground workers and social workers was meant to prevent youth from getting into trouble or skipping school by instilling WASP-oriented, middle-class standards, but youngsters continued to challenge the tight control of city spaces.

Parks

The adoption of the Chicago model throughout the United States brought some resolution to a contentious debate that had persisted throughout the latter half of the nineteenth century over the proper usage of parks. Early park advocates agreed on the need for open spaces and fresh air in the congested urban environments, but class interests collided in determining the nature and design of recreational spaces. Wealthy park patrons proposed and sponsored amenities and facilities in the parks—such as museums, zoos, libraries, and art galleries—that reflected their own interests in education and high culture. In such environments, in order to maintain the aesthetic ambience and the sense of order and respect, authorities forbade even walking on the grass. The laborers of the working class, on the other hand, wanted to make more active use of park acreage.

By the 1870s, Sunday picnic crowds numbered as high as thirty thousand in Chicago's massive Lincoln Park, and ball players, cyclists, horse racers, and tennis players all defied orders to "Keep Off the Grass." In 1904, the Chicago Parks Commission

Members of the upper classes wanted aesthetic parks suitable for repose and reflection. In its heyday, Ellis Park, one of the oldest parks in Chicago, contained fountains, large trees, well-manicured lawns, and pathways for strolling (Graf 59).

Courtesy of John Graf.

recorded more than a million users of the city's playgrounds, but not all were deemed desirable, and some failed to learn the prescribed lessons of the playground supervisors (*A Plea for Playgrounds* 17). For example, football games had to be discontinued due to the rough tactics employed by older boys. Some middle-class interests gained greater favor, however, and they claimed space for their games. In 1885, Central Park in New York City featured 30 tennis courts, and by 1915 Chicago had 300 just in its South Parks system, one of three separate park administrations in that city. Van Cortland Park in New York opened a public golf site in 1895, and public golf courses arrived in Boston's Franklin Park in 1898. By 1910, only 24 public links existed in the United States. These public golf courses enabled affordable play for middle-class participants and began to diminish the elite status of the game (Riess, *City* 62). As urban parks increasingly accommodated the interests of the middle and working classes, the wealthy sought more exclusive environs for their recreational practices.

Racetracks

Before the advent of country clubs, elites enjoyed their leisure time at opulent racetracks. In Chicago, the horse-racing center of the Midwest, the lavish Washington Park Jockey Club was opened in 1884 with General Philip Sheridan as its president. By 1892, 96 of Chicago's 278 millionaires held membership in the organization, and entry required a unanimous vote of the executive council. Its 500 members were acknowledged to be worth $300 million, and they built a $50,000 clubhouse reserved for the upper echelon of society and a $40,000 grandstand. The private clubhouse included a café, a dozen dining rooms, a wine room, a billiard parlor, sleeping rooms, and servants' quarters in the attic. An expansive veranda and balcony decorated the exterior, and two rooftop observatories afforded sweeping vistas. The club's American Derby proved to be the highlight of the social season, as women displayed their finery and men basked in their ownership of thoroughbreds. Such grand spectacles permitted the wealthy to demonstrate their power, privilege, and status to fellow citizens and to one another. Sociologist Thorstein Veblen labeled such demeanor "conspicuous consumption"—a means to construct social-class lines in a supposedly classless democracy. Members of the sport's plebeian following gawked at the elites in their finery, thus reinforcing the class distinctions.

At the elite tracks, expensive thoroughbreds competed for stakes as high as $50,000. Railway lines, trolley cars, and wide boulevards permitted even the lower classes to attend, and, more important, wager on the races. The incessant gambling led to corruption at many tracks, and track owners formed a Board of Control in 1891 to address such abuses. In 1894, the sport's leaders formed the Jockey Club to further regulate conduct by codifying rules, licensing jockeys, registering horses, and appointing proper officials. The following year, the New York legislature initiated a racing commission to augment state control. Despite such supervision, problems persisted, and states enacted periodic bans on horse racing throughout the remainder of the Progressive Era. The restrictions, however, merely inconvenienced the wealthy, who transferred their betting interests to golf, tennis, cards, and other activities at their private country clubs.

In the West, horse racing assumed different forms and carried different class connotations. Since wealthy owners lived in the East, near top racing sites, a lack of thoroughbreds in the West forced a reliance on work animals, requiring shorter competitive distances. Quarter horses specialized in short sprints or raced in quarter- or half-mile (0.4- or 0.8-kilometer) events. As early as 1883, cowboys tested their work skills in competitive rodeos in Pecos, Texas, and early contests offered money prizes and accepted wagers on horse races, calf roping, bronco riding, and even dancing. Such work-related skills tested the physicality of participants—a very different approach than that employed by the wealthy thoroughbred owners of the East. By 1888, the rodeo concept appeared as far west as Prescott, Arizona, and 1897 saw the first edition of the annual Cheyenne Frontier Days festival, which by 1900 offered separate competitive horse races for men, women, and American Indians. The Native American participants displayed their lost ferocity in a war dance, and the white settlers enjoyed an evening with an orchestra at a grand ball. Other exhibitions of technology and civilization at the festival included a baseball game and a parachutist who jumped from a hot air balloon. Conducted in conjunction with the local newspaper and the Union Pacific Railway, the celebration drew competitors and spectators (in the thousands) from throughout the West by creating a commercialized civic spectacle that merged work skills with recreation and promoted particular Western sport forms and regional identity.

Country Clubs

In the more congested cities of the East and Midwest, upper-class Americans seeking a place to maintain their elite status also reorganized metropolitan spaces by developing country clubs in outlying areas, making them inaccessible to all but the elites by virtue of both location and steep membership fees, thus further establishing the social stature of participants. As a social and sporting haven for the rich, country clubs upheld their exclusive membership by excluding all but white, Anglo-Saxon, Protestant applicants. Golf and tennis, in particular, appealed to those wishing to maintain elite status.

Because golf required expensive equipment and a large parcel of land, it carried distinct class connotations. Although played in Scotland for centuries, the sport arrived in the United States relatively late. Scotsmen introduced the game in the 1880s and, led by John Reid, founded the St. Andrew's Golf Club in 1888 with a primitive course. Three years later, wealthy New Yorkers built a nine-hole course at Shinnecock Hills on Coney Island. Charles Macdonald, a second-generation Scotsman and an organizer of the Chicago Golf Club in 1893, established himself as a course architect. His Chicago club built the first 18-hole course in the United States. Other Scots served as teaching professionals and equipment manufacturers. Socialites formed country clubs with restrictive membership covenants where boys toted their bags as caddies.

National tournaments appeared in 1894, and five clubs formed the United States Golf Association in 1895 as a governing body. The first U.S. Open was held at the Newport Country Club in October of that year, and a women's tournament followed only a month later at the Meadowbrook Club on Long Island. Since it was an open tournament, amateurs and professionals alike could compete, and among the golfers in the second U.S. Open at Shinnecock Hills were John Shippen, an African American who had learned the game as a caddie, and Oscar Bunn, a Shinnecock Indian, whose tribe had helped build the course. When the white players protested and threatened a walkout, club president Theodore Havemeyer courageously upheld the right of Shippen and Bunn to compete—a bold move that contrasted starkly with the typical social conditions for minorities at that time. The Intercollegiate Golf Association was formed in 1897, and by the end of the century there were enough clubs on the

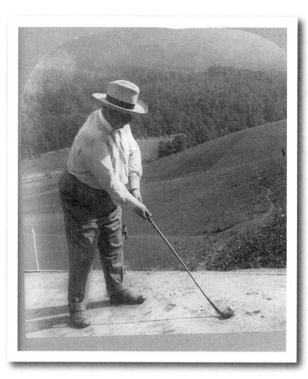

Golf soon became the sport of choice for American presidents, such as avid golfer William Howard Taft, who wished to portray a vigorous image.

Image courtesy of Library of Congress, LC-USZ62-41721.

West Coast to form the Southern California Golf Association. Golf course development in the warmer Southeastern states allowed the wealthy to pursue their pastime on a year-round basis.

Like golf, tennis required an expanse of land on which to build a court or courts. Adopted from the British, it too provided an aristocratic pretense, and it soon became a favorite pastime of upper-class men, and then women, who played on the lawns of country clubs. At the Seabright Lawn Tennis and Cricket Club, organized in Rumson, New Jersey, in 1877, tennis became a major focal point of the sporting scene. One of the earliest clubs in the United States, it hosted well-known American and international tennis players in the Seabright Invitational Tournament starting in 1884 (women's competition was added in 1920). The site consisted of a cricket crease from England and three tennis courts in 1886, and substantial additions brought the total to 22 tennis courts by 1910.

Back-to-Nature Movement

City dwellers' concerns about moral and physical well-being fostered an outdoor recreation movement during the latter nineteenth century. Many perceived the overcrowded cities as dirty slums teeming with infection and overridden by vice and corruption. Moreover, the increasing number of white-collar, middle-class occupations seemed to produce increased stress, as well as the confounding condition known as neurasthenia (nervous breakdown) that affected sedentary workers. The West and outlying areas seemed more attractive and healthier to urban residents beset by grime and pollution in the industrial cities, and those who could afford it built palatial homes in areas away from the city, while others sought relief in the back-to-nature movement that encouraged outdoor pursuits and wilderness excursions. The confrontation with nature and the elements, it was thought, required hardiness and sometimes courage, and thus might restore one's vigor and manhood.

Riflery originally served a utilitarian function for sustenance, but it had little use other than sport in the crowded cities, where what were once outdoor recreations soon became competitive events. The National Rifle Club was organized as early as

The Hiking Movement—a Youth Initiative

In the wake of industrialization and the social changes taking place in Western countries, new occupations developed and work changed fundamentally. This led to higher demands on the skills of employees, which made a prolongation of education necessary. Thus a new age group—youth—emerged, a cohort of young adults with specific wishes, needs, and behavior patterns. Among the responses to the growing significance of childhood and youth were organizations and initiatives aimed at supervision and education. One of these initiatives was the Scout Movement, which spread to the United States from its origin in England. With the help of outdoor skills, especially camping and hiking, the movement's aim was to train boy and girl scouts to become good citizens. Scout leaders were invariably adults.

In Europe, by contrast, a youth movement arose with the motto "Youth leads youth," which in Germany grew into a mass movement. The restrictive climate of the German Reich led to generational conflicts, especially in paternalistic and authoritarian middle-class families, and young people reacted with opposition. With a back-to-nature outlook on life, they sought to escape the pressures of bourgeois society, the confines of the cities, and what they perceived as menacing processes of modernization. Hiking, with its promise of freedom and adventure, seemed to offer a way out of a civilization they experienced as oppressive. The hiking movement began in Berlin, the capital of the Reich, at the turn of the century. The hiking craze swiftly spread among the city's bourgeois youth, and in 1901 they formed an association, naming themselves *Wandervögel* (migrating birds). A similar movement emerged in France with a focus in Normandy and Brittany.

In Germany, the Berlin group was the nucleus of a large movement that included a huge number of groups, some more strictly organized and others less so. Nonetheless, the many thousands of *Wandervögel* were bound together by a sense of belonging and pursued similar practices and forms of organization. The leaders were young adults whom the others were willing to follow on account of their personal authority. Their main activity was hiking together in a group for days or even weeks on end, an activity which became a self-defined way of life. It was a frugal way of living; they slept in the open or in barns and cooked on campfires. Instead of stiff shirt-fronts and collars, the *Wandervögel* wore open shirts, and instead of polished boots they wore sandals. They had a longing for a glorified past, which they tried to re-create with their songs and folk dances. Although the majority of the *Wandervögel* were young men, some clubs accepted girls and women or even consisted entirely of girls, who set off into the wilds with a young woman as their leader.

In 1913, shortly before the First World War, three thousand *Wandervögel* took part in a festival along with other reform-oriented youth groups on a hill called the Hoher Meissner in Hesse. With the prospect of war looming, they felt moved to protest against national chauvinism, and their standpoint was summed up in the declaration: "Free German youth wishes to shape its future in self-determination, bearing its own responsibility and faithful to an inner truth." After the German defeat, the youth movement turned into an assemblage of numerous youth groups, some of which were well organized and harbored nationalist sentiments. In 1933, the youth organization of the National Socialists (Nazis), named the Hitler Youth, pressed their claim to be the sole representatives of all young people. All other groups were prohibited.

Information from Laqueur, Walter. *Young Germany: A History of the German Youth Movement.* New York: Basic Books, 1962.

1858, and many immigrant and labor groups formed their own militias for drill and marksmanship practice. Target matches for men and women were being held by the 1870s, and in 1888 George Ligowsky invented the first practical clay pigeon, allowing for trapshooting championships. Such competitive simulations of hunting merged modern technology with premodern pastimes to ease the ills of the urbanization process. Others distanced themselves from the cities by hiking, fishing, camping, or attempting to conquer natural impediments through mountaineering.

European immigrants brought their winter pastimes with them to America, but informal ice-skating contests took on greater regulation and standardization with the formation of the American Skating Congress in 1868. Scottish immigrants introduced speedskating contests to the United States, and the first national championship for men was staged in 1889. The International Skating Union, organized in 1892, offered the first world championship that winter in Amsterdam. Competition for women speedskaters did not develop until the twentieth century. The National Amateur Skating Union, which had been organized in 1886, merged with the International Skating Union in 1907 as the governing body for both speed- and figure skating.

Snowshoeing and skiing served a practical function during the winter months and allowed particular ethnic groups to retain their traditional sports. Scandinavians brought skiing techniques to America as a recreational activity, but during the mid-century California Gold Rush, skiers delivered the winter mail to mining camps. Downhill skiing competitions for both men and women ensued, and the immigrants who settled in the northern areas of the Midwest began to hold organized competitions by the 1890s. The first tournament of the United States Ski Club took place at Ishpeming, Michigan, in 1891. The next year, the Aurora Club of Red Wing, Minnesota, used the Ishpeming site for a ski jumping exhibition that promoted Scandinavian culture.

The winter sports introduced to the United States by Nordic immigrants produced a reverse cultural flow as they were adopted by Americans in the northern states.

Image courtesy of Library of Congress, LC-USZ62-135333.

Meanwhile, adapting rules from rugby and lacrosse, Canadians had produced a version of ice hockey by the 1870s. Played outdoors on frozen waterways when weather permitted, it became a Canadian favorite. In the United States, Yale and Johns Hopkins universities adopted the game by 1893, and New York teams formed an amateur league in 1896. A Baltimore league appeared a year later, followed by creation of the Intercollegiate Hockey League in 1898 and a professional league in 1903, but the organization of such winter sports further removed them from their rural connotations and favored urban and middle-class standards of practice. By the 1890s, indoor ice rinks in New York City fostered a transition from the rural pastime to an urban game (Kirsch, Harris, and Nolte 231), and the ongoing organization of hockey by governing bodies created regulations and rules that coincided with and promoted sportification (the competitive organization of previously recreational activities).

Other outdoor sports, such as camping, fishing, boating, and hiking, attracted numerous practitioners to remote areas. For them, fresh air meant health and peaceful solace. Perhaps the most famous of such groups, the Boone and Crockett Club, numbered one hundred members, including Theodore Roosevelt, who engaged in big game hunting and wilderness adventures. Such excursions required adequate leisure time and expendable income, limiting these sport forms to wealthy participants. As president, Roosevelt designated millions of acres as federal reserves and created 18 national monuments to preserve historic sites, natural resources, and areas of particular beauty intended for future generations and all classes. In 1916, President Woodrow Wilson authorized the National Park Service to manage the public lands, but private entrepreneurs and railroad companies had already begun operating tours and hotels in many of the most scenic locations. The lack of sufficient travel funds or vacation time denied such opportunities to most workers, however, restricting the growing tourism industry to middle- and upper-class prospects.

Cities, however, began efforts to conserve nearby natural areas that were somewhat more accessible to laborers. Famed architect Daniel Burnham developed city plans for Washington, D.C., Cleveland, San Francisco, Chicago, and even Manila and Baguio, the capital and summer haven, respectively, of Americans in the (at that time) U.S. colony of the Philippines. In Chicago, Burnham provided an integrated design for parks and playgrounds, with the lakefront safeguarded as public space. Forest preserves ringed the perimeter of the city, and wide boulevards strategically connected its parts via public transport systems. Still, the outer reaches remained inaccessible for most of the urban poor.

Sport and Colonialism

Progressive reformers even invoked sport to inculcate American WASP values in overseas colonies. Under the guise of the "white man's burden," European powers colonized the globe, rationalizing their occupation of foreign lands as bettering the populations by bringing Christianity and white civilization to them. The British, foremost of the imperial powers in the nineteenth century, counted their worldwide dominions and bragged that the sun never set upon the British Empire. Foreign colonies provided natural resources, cheap labor, and markets for surplus goods in the expanding industrial economies. The United States lagged behind the Europeans in such acquisitions until 1898, but after its victory in the brief Spanish-American War the young country claimed the previous Spanish colonies of Cuba, Puerto Rico, Guam, and the Philippines. That same year, it annexed Hawaii in the wake of a coup orchestrated by American businessmen who had wrested control of the islands from the Hawaiian monarch in 1893. A quote from Albert J. Beveridge's speech to the U.S. Senate in 1900 highlights part of the reasoning behind such acquisitions:

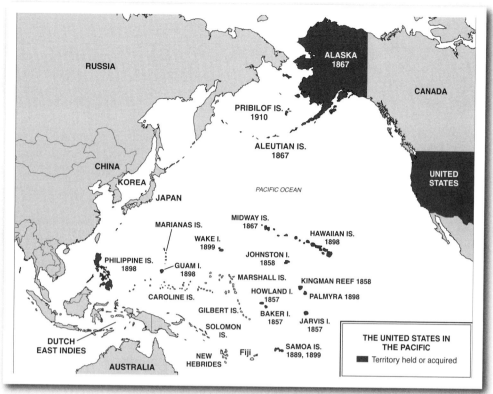

Map of American imperialism in the Pacific following its victory in the Spanish-American War.

Map p.546 from THE AMERICAN NATION: A HISTORY OF THE UNITED STATES, 5th ed. By John A. Garraty. Copyright © 1983 by John A. Garraty. Reprinted by permission of Pearson Education, Inc.

God has not been preparing the English-speaking and Teutonic peoples for a thousand years for nothing but vain and idle self-admiration. No. He made us master organizers of the world to establish system where chaos reigned. He has given us the spirit of progress to overwhelm the forces of reaction throughout the earth. He has made us adept in government that we may administer government among savage and senile peoples. Were it not for such a force as this the world would relapse into barbarism and night. And of all our race He has marked the American people as His chosen nation to finally lead in the redemption of the world. (qtd. in Blum et al. 536)

American missionaries had been active in the islands long before that time. Arriving in 1820, they won favor by ingratiating themselves with the monarchy over the next generation and imposed their own values by banning the Hawaiian sports of surfing, canoe racing, and boxing, as well as gambling and the erotic hula dances. The missionaries introduced residential boarding schools to inculcate their religious beliefs in native children, and their efforts to Americanize Hawaiians also included the introduction of baseball. When Alexander Cartwright, formerly the secretary of the New York Knickerbockers baseball club, moved to Hawaii in 1849, he was surprised to see the game already being played in the islands. By the 1870s, Honolulu featured a four-team league that drew thousands of spectators. In the following decade, polo, tennis, and track-and-field competition were pursued, but the cultural transition remained incomplete and contested. Native Hawaiians resurrected canoe racing in 1875, and hula dancers entertained the nationalistic King Kalakaua at his birthday party in 1886. The rising sense of Hawaiian nationalism led to a clash with the American minority, and white businessmen imposed a new constitution on the king in 1887, stripping him of his powers. When his successor, Queen Liliuokalani, proved just as fierce in her independence, the whites, aided by an American diplomat and a contingent of U.S. Marines, imprisoned her and elected one of their own, plantation owner Sanford Dole, as president until the U.S. government heeded their request for annexation.

Duke Kahanamoku bridged cultures as an athlete and racial pioneer.
Image courtesy of Library of Congress, LC-DIG-ggbain-10653.

Like their mainland counterparts, the plantation owners used sport as a means of social control, organizing baseball leagues for their polyglot labor force of Filipino, Japanese, Chinese, and Portuguese workers. A Chinese Hawaiian baseball team traveled to the mainland in 1910 and won a majority of its games. By 1913, they had won 54 of 59 games played against American college teams. The Asahi team of Japanese Hawaiians, formed in 1905, won the Hawaiian championship 15 times and traveled to Japan, the Philippines, and the United States on successful baseball tours. As with mainland immigrants, the second generation of Japanese and Chinese immigrants to Hawaii adopted and even excelled in mainstream sport forms, but their successes also reinforced the racial pride denied them in other spheres of life, such as the workplace.

The aquatic sports of the Hawaiians even reversed the cultural flow, as Hawaiian swimmers formed the backbone of the U.S. Olympic team from 1912 through the 1920s. Its most famous member, Duke Kahanamoku, won six Olympic medals from 1912 through 1932 and served as a cultural ambassador for sport, popularizing Hawaiian surfing around the world. His native land served as a cultural crossroads in the Pacific, hosting both American and Japanese teams. Kahanamoku's travels, his fame, and his perceived exoticism generated interest in and tourism to the islands.

Even before the United States began its imperial march, American traders had sought foreign ports. American expatriates brought baseball to China as early as 1863, and teachers, missionaries, and the YMCA promoted American games throughout Asia. Baseball became a favorite of the Japanese, and their elite Ichiko prep school defeated several American teams during the 1890s. In the early twentieth century, baseball became a form of surrogate warfare, as Japan and the United Sates contended for leadership in the Pacific. Japanese university teams barnstormed to Hawaii and the United States, and the universities of Washington and Wisconsin lost to Japanese schools in 1908 and 1909, respectively, on tours characterized as "invasions" of the Asian nation. The University of Chicago redeemed American pride by going undefeated against the Japanese in 1910, then declaring its team the "champions of the Orient."

A similar spirit arose in the Philippines when Waseda University of Japan played a Filipino team from Cebu in 1905. The Japanese viewed the Filipinos, then under American rule, as lackeys, and the game was described as a bitter rivalry played for blood. When Cebu triumphed 3-1, its players became national heroes. The United States took control of the Philippines after the 1898 war with Spain, but guerrilla warfare and a strong nationalist movement thwarted full domination, and the Filipinos finally gained their independence in 1946. During the time of U.S. control, however, American administrators enacted a program of social reform in the archipelago even more comprehensive than those in the United States. As with efforts to transform stateside ethnic groups, sport proved a primary means of Americanization activity in

Colonial administrators used baseball in efforts to Americanize subject peoples.

Dean Worcester/National Geographic Image Collection.

the Philippines. American soldiers introduced baseball and boxing to Filipinos shortly after arriving in 1898, and General James Franklin Bell, commander of U.S. forces in Manila, claimed that "baseball had done more to 'civilize' Filipinos than anything else" (Seymour 324–325). W. Cameron Forbes, a former Harvard football coach and heir to the Bell Telephone Company with political connections, served as governor-general of the islands. He constructed a polo field and a golf course at the summer capital in Baguio and promoted widespread emphasis on physical education in the schools; boys and girls competed for interscholastic, district, and provincial honors. Schools added sports facilities, including tennis courts and tracks, to instill competitive spirit, discipline, a strong work ethic, and community pride.

Forbes further extended the use of sport in conjunction with the YMCA. Under YMCA direction, the Manila Carnival, initially a commercial fair, became an athletic spectacle that spurred town and tribal rivalries, offering national championships in men's and boys' baseball, basketball, volleyball, and track and field, as well as girls' basketball, along with open competition in swimming, tennis, track, golf, polo, soccer, football, and bowling. The baseball tournament included a team from Japan, and under the leadership of Elwood Brown of the YMCA, the Manila Carnival invited other Asian nations and became known as the Far Eastern Olympics.

By the end of Forbes' administration, more than 1,500 uniformed baseball teams competed for trophies and prizes, and 95 percent of public school students participated in sport and games (Beran 74). The YMCA prepared the official recreation manual, trained playground directors, and spread its own games of basketball and volleyball. The Filipinos adopted basketball as their national sport, and Filipino boxers became world champions, as sport became one of the more subtle means of acculturation. Thus the Americans quelled Filipino discontent and rebellion with a brutal military occupation, then transferred indigenous nationalism into athletic rivalries with Japan, a country perceived as a common rival in the Pacific.

In Caribbean nations, baseball preceded American occupation, as several Cuban students learned the game while studying in the Unites States and taught it to other islanders upon their return in 1864. Games with American teams began in 1866, and the Cuban professional league started play in 1873. Cubans introduced baseball

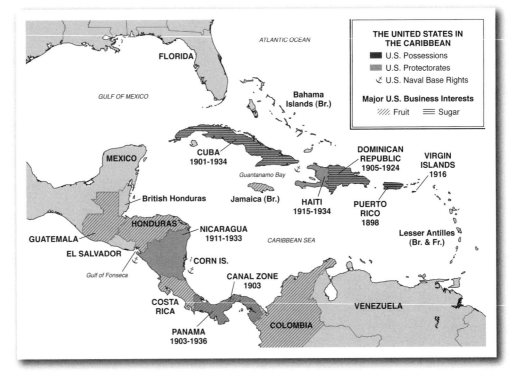

By the early twentieth century, the U.S. had quickly expanded its dominion and influence to the Atlantic and Pacific regions.

Map p.556 from THE AMERICAN NATION: A HISTORY OF THE UNITED STATES, 5th ed. By John A. Garraty. Copyright © 1983 by John A. Garraty. Reprinted by permission of Pearson Education, Inc.

to Puerto Ricans and Dominicans even before American troops arrived to garrison their new possessions after the Spanish-American War. The arrival of the Americans, however, greatly promoted the sport, and company and school teams were engaging in tournaments by 1900.

Even as American administrators and evangelical missionaries brought sports to the islands, they attempted to eliminate some activities. They banned bullfights, cockfights, and gambling, and the Woman's Christian Temperance Union tried to prohibit alcohol. Protestant missionaries carved up the islands in denominational jurisdictions, trying to convert the already Christian Catholics, and English was made the required language in the reorganized schools. The YMCA opened operations in Cuba in 1904 and in Puerto Rico a few years later, and it introduced a particular WASP brand of morality. Along with racially segregated facilities, the Y invoked Sabbatarian restrictions, refusing to allow play on Sundays. Cultural differences became apparent in 1906, when a Y director explained to a Cuban athlete that Sunday was the day to think about God. The Cuban replied that he did so 6 days a week, but Sunday was his only opportunity for fun (Gems, *Athletic* 89).

Cuba endured a brief series of occupations by American troops for a decade after the Spanish-American War, but as an independent nation it soon reverted to its Spanish language and Latin culture. Americans developed a perception of Caribbean life as exotic, and Cuba became a favorite destination as a vacation playground for wealthy Americans in search of gambling and illicit pleasures not readily available on the more inhibited mainland. Professional American baseball teams found the Caribbean climate particularly salubrious and many made annual winter barnstorming trips to the island. Cuban teams often beat the Americans, and the best of the light-skinned Cuban players signed contracts with American major league clubs.

Puerto Ricans fared less well, as the United States maintained an ongoing presence that eventually resulted in commonwealth status. The YMCA introduced basketball and volleyball, and U.S. government administrators tried to Americanize the islanders through sport and games on playgrounds and at settlement houses. Baseball prospered, but Puerto Ricans clung to their Spanish language and Catholic religion despite the ongoing efforts of the YMCA. The Y even permitted boxing as a means to attract members, but with little success. Boxing did, however, produce the first national sport hero in Puerto Rico, when Sixto Escobar won the world bantamweight championship in the 1930s. Puerto Ricans chose a limited assimilation, adopting American sport forms but employing national teams and their own flag in athletic competitions to emphasize their independent cultural identity. Americans soon reflected upon their growing international importance:

> The West Indies drift toward us, the Republic of Mexico hardly longer has an independent life, and the city of Mexico is an American town. With the completion of the Panama Canal all Central America will become part of your system. We have expanded into Asia, we have attracted the fragments of the Spanish dominions, and reaching out into China we have checked the advance of Russia and Germany. . . . We are penetrating into Europe, and Great Britain especially is gradually assuming the position of a dependency. . . . The United States will outweigh any single empire, if not all empires combined. The whole world will pay her tribute. Commerce will flow to her from both east and west, and the order which has existed from the dawn of time will be reversed. (qtd. in Blum et al. 537)

Resistance to Social Reform

While subordinate groups adopted mainstream American sport forms in the schools, parks, and playgrounds of the American cities and colonies, these activities did not guarantee their acceptance of middle-class WASP values. Just as island residents retained their languages and customs, alternative values persisted in the States as well. Catholic and Jewish groups formed their own settlement houses to attract youth, and the Knights of Columbus, a Catholic fraternal organization, promoted competitive athletic events to counter the Protestant influences of the YMCA. Such groups allowed middle-class and aspiring Americans outside the WASP realm to seek accommodation with the mainstream culture without sacrificing their religious beliefs. The YMCA also found little success in its attempts to convert and instill middle-class morality in either ethnic-minority youths of the working class or the bachelor subculture tied to saloons and pool halls.

For example, Ed Morris, a professional baseball player for the Pittsburgh team, did join the YMCA in 1887. However, he took out a newspaper ad to assure his friends in the sporting fraternity that he had not gotten religious. He joined the YMCA, he maintained, only to have access to the gymnasium. Physicality and the retention of his physical prowess enabled him to retain his identity and status among his blue-collar supporters.

In urban parks and playgrounds, reformers often faced a difficult task. Ethnic and racial rivalries arose over the use of these public spaces—as did transgressions into contrary ethnic neighborhoods—which prompted combat as groups sought to protect their own spaces from outside intrusion. Specific ethnic groups claimed particular locations as their own and drove off rivals in violent confrontations. While Jim Crow laws enforced racial segregation in the South, the Northern cities marked boundaries by control of the parks, thus establishing de facto segregation as oppositional groups vied for contested spaces. In a study of Chicago gangs, one researcher noted that "about one-fourth of the membership of the WWW's [a Jewish gang] is composed of professional prize fighters, and more than once this gang has struck terror into the hearts of overaggressive Polish groups" (Thrasher 150). Reformers involved with settlement houses wanted to sublimate such Old World animosities into less sanguinary athletic competitions.

Such problems were exacerbated by the fact that neighborhood gangs adopted sports but used them as a vehicle for gambling. Politicians organized and sponsored some gang activities and even provided headquarters for neighborhood clubs with the expectation of their loyalty—and often their heavy-handed support on election day. Some gangs even took over parks and playgrounds as their center of activity. One of most notorious gangs in Chicago originated as the Morgan Athletic Club. It changed its name to the Ragen's Colts in 1908, when Frank Ragen, a future county commissioner, became club president. With more than two thousand members, the Colts ruled the Sherman Park area, often terrorizing residents. From 1900 to 1913, Chicago newspaper publishers engaged in circulation wars and employed the Colts as intimidators; during that time, 27 newspaper vendors were killed. The Colts also proved largely responsible for the 1919 race riot that rocked Chicago and resulted in 38 deaths. Such political athletic clubs contributed significant support to urban political machines, and several members of such "social athletic clubs" (some of which were just gangs and used the letters S.A.C. after their name to provide the perception of greater legitimacy) eventually became mayors of Chicago.

In the 1880s, rowdy laborers in Worcester, Massachusetts, used its parks for drinking parties. Working-class voters in Worcester and other American cities mobilized in a successful effort to gain more active usage of park space, resulting in the construction of ball fields, though Sabbatarian blue laws forbade Sunday games in some locations (Boston, for example, banned Sunday baseball games until 1920).

As schools made efforts to educate and control children, most boys and young men lingered in the workforce in an effort to resist compliance with schooling laws. In 1902, the YMCA organized an industrial recreation branch, and businesses sponsored enough bowling and baseball teams in cities to organize their own industrial leagues. Company teams proved attractive not only to athletes but to their co-workers as well. Despite employers' intentions of providing wholesome recreation for employees, workers realized that they might increase their meager wages by gambling on games. A procession of vehicles often followed company teams to away games. In 1914, a crowd of 115,000 witnessed a baseball game in Cleveland between the White Auto Company and the Luxus team of Omaha. Some of the earliest pro football teams developed from early industrial programs. The Columbus Panhandles, made up of blue-collar railroad workers, traveled the Midwest football circuit on weekends, while the Acme Packers represented the small town of Green Bay, Wisconsin. The Staley Starch Company team of Decatur, Illinois, eventually moved to Chicago, where it became the Bears. With players supplementing their paychecks by earning money on the field, fellow workers often attempted to do so by betting, yielding mixed results for employers, as employees simultaneously wagered their earnings (which contradicted the middle-class values that the employers hoped to instill) and developed a loyalty to the company as it competed with commercial rivals. For such workers, then, leisure pursuits revolved around the physicality of the working-class lifestyle, and they adapted employer offerings to fit their own needs.

Even though Progressive Era social reformers didn't always meet their goals, many immigrants and other working-class groups did achieve a greater measure of acceptance in the culture of the United States through sport.

Sport, Ethnicity, and the Quest for Social Mobility

The perception of sport as a meritocracy, where one might gain a measure of wealth and social mobility based on the cherished physicality of the working class, helped to defray the discontent of lower-rank citizens. Immigrant parents, often steadfast in their adherence to a strong work ethic and their European cultures, acquiesced to sport as sons brought home additional income derived from semipro or neighborhood contests. Nonplayers such as the famous gambler Arnold Rothstein might earn even more than the players by organizing athletic competitions.

At the 1893 World's Fair in Chicago, German Turners staged a mass display of their gymnastic prowess intended to convince the American mainstream of its benefits. The skill of ethnic-minority athletic clubs attracted the notice of amateur governing bodies who sought their inclusion. Membership solicitations fostered ethnic pride but also gradually diminished the isolation of such groups by bringing them closer to the mainstream culture. By 1897, the Amateur Athletic Union governed the national championship competitions.

Ethnic minorities managed to retain a measure of their alternative sporting culture in soccer leagues. In the Illinois leagues, Swedes, Danes, Germans, Norwegians, Hungarians, Czechs, Scots, Englishmen, Jews, and Yugoslavs transferred their rivalries to the field. By 1917, the Czechs had enough teams to form their own league, where the Sparta team proudly adopted the Czech national colors. In the Czech contests, even religious differences transferred to the athletic field, as the reds (atheists) battled the blues (Catholics). Such sporting practices enabled ethnic communities to retain a measure of their European traditions and lifestyles, which by World War I was causing some nativists to question their loyalty.

Boxing

For the boys and young men engaged in tough urban street life, boxing proved a popular attraction and even a necessity. Irish Americans held most of the boxing titles through the 1890s, but by the turn of the century other ethnic groups adored their own idols, though some adopted Irish names in order to win favor with the dominant powers in the boxing world. Among Jewish boxers, Harry Harris won the bantamweight title in 1900, and Abe Attell conquered the featherweights from 1901 to 1912. Attell won the crown at age 17 by defeating the popular black champion, George Dixon. Attell's use of cocaine and his gambling on his own fights diminished his appeal, but Jews took great pride in lightweight champion Benny Leonard. Born Benjamin Leiner to parents who were Russian Jews, he grew up fighting Irish and Italian youths in a tough New York neighborhood. His Orthodox parents disapproved of fighting, so he changed his name as a professional boxer. As a symbol of his Jewish pride, Leonard wore the Star of David on his boxing trunks, and he won the lightweight title in 1917. In one of his many memorable bouts, he pounded "Irish" Eddie Finnegan until Finnegan clinched and whispered in Leonard's ear in Yiddish to take it easy because he was really Seymour Rosenbaum. The prominence of Jewish ring champions did much to overcome stereotypes of cowardice and debility (Riess, "Tough Jews" 75–76).

The greatest Polish athletic star of the Progressive Era emerged in the boxing ring. Stanislaw Kiecal, known as the "Michigan Assassin," Americanized his name to Stanley Ketchel as a professional boxer. He won the middleweight championship in 1908 after being orphaned as a youth and living a hard life in Western mining camps and lumberyards. A savage fighter, Ketchel courageously battled the much larger Jack Johnson for the heavyweight crown in 1909 and managed to knock down the titleholder before succumbing. Despite the loss and a relatively short career, many considered Ketchel the best middleweight of all time. In 1910, the husband of his lover killed him with a rifle shot in the back, cutting short his flamboyant life at the age of 24. For such athletes, sport proved a temporary respite in a hard life. Few achieved more than local fame, yet working-class youth idolized the athletes' displays of physical prowess. In tough urban neighborhoods, one gained social capital with fists more often than with money.

Italians followed in the parade of champions. Pete Herman, whose real surname was Gulotta, learned to box in his hometown of New Orleans, and in 1916, at the age of 20, he fought a draw for the bantamweight championship. He earned the crown a year later. Though he suffered only one knockout during his boxing career, the accumulation of blows to his head caused blindness. Such tragedies failed to deter athletic aspirants, who had little hope of reaching greater socioeconomic status without money or an education.

Baseball

As with boxing, baseball provided a measure of social mobility and served as a marker of assimilation. Immigrant youth might aspire to the professional ranks, but even some lesser players earned substantial incomes on neighborhood semipro contingents or on company teams in the industrial leagues.

Italian Ping Bodie, whose real name was Francisco Stefano Pezzole, fared well as a professional baseball player, enjoying a career that lasted from 1911 through 1921 with the Chicago White Sox and the New York Yankees. Bodie emerged as one of the early players of Southern or Eastern European extraction. Before that time, Irish and German players had dominated the ranks of baseball rosters. Honus Wagner, the best of the Germans, won eight batting championships. Considered the greatest of shortstops, he hit over .300 for 17 straight years in a long career (1897–1917). Polish athlete Oscar Bielaski played professional baseball as early as 1872 and appeared on the Chicago White Stockings team that won the National League championship in 1876. Ed Delahanty, one of numerous Irish stars, began his long pro career in 1887 at the age of 20. During the 1890s, he batted over .400 three times, and finished with a lifetime average of .345. "Wee Willie" Keeler matched Delahanty's career average in 18 seasons from 1892 through 1910. Though less than 5 feet 5 inches (1.7 meters) and only 140 pounds (64 kilograms), Keeler starred at bat, hitting .432 in 1897 and going more than a hundred games without striking out in 1906. Such performances, along with the comparatively large salaries paid to athletes, endeared them to ethnic-minority and working-class youth and created heroes in urban neighborhoods.

The growth of baseball, particularly the professional and semiprofessional varieties, provided opportunities for the best players (or those with business acumen) to achieve social mobility. Ban Johnson, president of the Western League, renamed it the American League and promoted it as a moral alternative to the gambling and beer-drinking environments of the senior circuit (i.e., the National League) in 1901. When the National League proved unable to run the fledgling organization out of business, it consented to the National Agreement of 1903, which bound both leagues to recognize player contracts and established a three-man commission to govern the sport. The initial World Series between the two league champions was played that year.

Ban Johnson, president of the American League.

Image courtesy of Library of Congress, LC-USZ62-105623.

By 1914, a third major league aspired to share the profits of the national game. The entry of the new Federal League forced National and American league owners to offer substantial salaries to obtain or retain their star players. With Ty Cobb earning $20,000 for the 1915 season, young boys on sandlot teams aspired to reach fame and fortune in America by developing their physical skills. Cobb's salary dwarfed that of a teacher ($578), and skilled craftsmen earned less than one-tenth ($1,591) of his baseball income. The expansion of the minor leagues from 13 leagues in 1901 to 46 in 1912 provided more opportunities for the realization of such dreams.

While baseball began attracting many second-generation ethnic-minority youth, the Irish still predominated in the ranks of both players and managers. Charles Comiskey progressed from player-manager of the St.

Louis Browns in the American Association to owner of the Chicago White Sox in the American League. John McGraw started as a player for the Baltimore Orioles in 1891 but won lasting fame as manager of the New York Giants, leading them to 10 pennants in a managerial career that lasted from 1899 to 1932. In 1915, 11 of the 16 big-league managers were Irish (Riess, *City* 104). Connie Mack (Cornelius McGillicuddy) held the greatest longevity. After starting as a catcher in 1886, he advanced to player-manager in 1894. In the new American League of 1901, as one of the cofounders of the league, he was granted the Philadelphia Athletics franchise, a team which he owned and managed in sartorial splendor until 1950.

For such men, sport provided economic mobility. In 1910, baseball salaries averaged $3,000, well above the annual wages of blue-collar workers (Riess, *City* 87). Even college-educated players increasingly signed professional contracts after 1900. Christy Mathewson, educated at Bucknell, starred as a pitcher for the New York Giants from 1900 through 1916. He won 30 games in three different seasons and amassed 20 or more wins in twelve others. Portrayed as an idealistic gentleman, a true Muscular Christian, he brought greater middle-class respectability to the game. Mathewson then managed Cincinnati for two years before joining the American military effort in World War I, and his exposure to a poison gas in Europe would lead to his early death in 1925.

By the turn of the century, even the German, Czech, and Polish gymnastic clubs and Jewish associations fielded baseball teams to retain their young male members. The following accounts (derived from the *Chicago Tribune*, July 7, 1889, p. 12; *Svornost*, June 2, 1890; and the *Dziennik Chicagoski*, August 10, 1896, respectively) show how baseball symbolized assimilation and a degree of inclusion in American society:

THE LITERARY LEAGUE

Six of the Jewish literary societies of Chicago have organized what is known as the Library Base-Ball League. The rivalry existing between the societies has run into the channel of base-ball and the boys are having it out every Sunday morning on the diamond. The societies are B'nai Abraham, Cremieax Haking, Emerson, Voltaire, Laskav, and Fidelity. The clubs are pretty evenly matched and some good games are witnessed. The standing of the league is as follows:

	Won	Lost	Percent
B'nai Abrahams.............................	2	0	100
Cremieax Hakings.........................	2	0	100
Emersons......................................	1	1	50
Voltaires.......................................	1	1	50
Laskava..	0	2	50
Fidelitys.......................................	0	2	50

The following games will be played today B'nai Abrahams vs. Cremieax Hakings at Athletic Park. Voltaires vs. Emersons at South Side Ball League grounds, and Fidelity vs. Laskavs at South West City League grounds. Games called at 9:00 p.m.

BOHEMIAN BASEBALL GAME

Yesterday morning the "Pilsen Sokols" team played the "Klatovsky Sokols," a game of baseball in the field at 20th and Fisk St. The score ended 28 to 8 in favor of the "Pilsen" team. The "Pilsen" battery was pitcher Kostal, Catcher Turek; for "Klatovsky," pitcher Benes, catcher Kalus.

POLISH SOCIETIES PLAY A BASEBALL GAME

Two Polish Societies from the St. Stanislaus Kostka parish, the St. Casimir's Young Men's Society and the St. Cecilia Society played a baseball game yesterday in Avondale.

The St. Cecilia Society team was captained by its president, Mr. John Czekala, and the St. Casimir Society by its president, Mr. John Nering. On Mr. Czekala's team were the following: M. Schultz, P. Marks, J. Marks, J. Kondziorski, J. Petlak, J. Marks, S. Politowsky, Mroz, and F. Arendt. On Mr. Nering's team were F. Budzban, S.C.P. Myks, J. Budzban, M. Budzban, J. Kanabas, Kimlitz, and J. Bogucki.

The game began at three o'clock in the afternoon on a field near the St. Hyacinth church in Avondale, and was very lively, because both teams were in excellent condition. The heat finally forced the players to quit, after three hours of playing. The Cecilia team won by a score of thirteen to seven. (qtd. in Gems, *Sports* 118–119)

As they became more engaged in American sport forms within the mainstream culture, such organizations increasingly turned away from their radical labor activities, although German Turners helped to elect a socialist mayor in Milwaukee. The Germans had even greater influence, however, in the promotion of bowling, a sport closely tied to the saloon culture.

Bowling, Pool, and Saloon Culture

The urban working-class saloon provided the most convenient form of leisure for young men. There, patrons found camaraderie in a club atmosphere that served a free lunch with a 5-cent beer and might even provide showers for bathing. Gambling and sport offered an additional lure. Card games, bookies, and billiards coincided with drinking rituals and customary toasts to friends, acquaintances, and athletic heroes. Some saloons included bowling alleys or adjacent poolhalls, and (in the East) even handball courts.

By the 1890s, bowling had become fashionable among middle-class urbanites. The Brunswick Company helped to organize the American Bowling Congress in 1895, standardizing rules and equipment, and Germans served as governing officers for many years. By the turn of the century, commercial and industrial bowling leagues proliferated in cities, especially in New York and Chicago. In the latter, merchants, jewelers, bankers, clothiers, and mechanics all had their own leagues, where Anglo-Americans and citizens from various ethnic-minority groups mixed with each other; wagering fixed attention on commercial rivals and enhanced company pride. Some companies formed touring male all-star teams, and bowling tournaments offered significant cash prizes. Women were competing in their own tournaments by 1907, and the Woman's International Bowling Association (later the Women's International Bowling Congress) was founded in 1916. In 1920, it offered more than $2,000 in prize money at a national tournament.

By 1909, half of Chicago's taverns featured billiard tables. New York had four thousand poolhalls in the 1920s. Detroit's Recreation Room held 142 pool tables, making it the largest establishment of its kind in the United States (Riess, *City* 73–74). Pool games, like beers, cost a nickel, and the Brunswick Company offered both, initially manufacturing the billiard tables and equipment and then branching out to construct bars and bowling alleys.

The best pool players could earn a living as professionals or local hustlers; the latter feigned incompetence, then won wagers against unwily opponents. Professionals competed in tournaments for prize money or engaged in challenge matches for additional wagers in large amphitheaters in front of hundreds of betting fans. Promoters organized pari-mutuel betting operations similar to those at horse-racing tracks, where winners split the proceeds and sponsors drew a commission. In small Western mining towns, competitors played for stakes of $500. In cities, the best players earned enough to open their own businesses.

The largest saloons offered a variety of entertainment, including concerts, vaudeville, and boxing matches. Pictures of boxers and other athletes adorned saloon walls, and many former athletes became owners or proprietors when their playing days had expired, but prizefighters held particular appeal for the laboring classes who earned their pay through physical toil. Boxers were renowned for their power, strength, courage, and endurance. In 1893, Andy Bowen of New Orleans and Jack Burke of Texas fought for 109 rounds in a bout that lasted nearly seven and one-half hours with no clear winner. A year later, Bowen died in the ring, the victim of a knockout but no less a hero to his fans.

Assimilation of Disparate Groups in American Society

As the multitude of largely urban, European ethnic groups wrestled with the assimilation efforts of Progressive reformers, other immigrants faced a variety of responses based on prevailing racial and racist sentiments. Asians, particularly those of Chinese or Japanese origin, faced exclusion by law, as their migration to the United States was forbidden. African Americans were largely ignored or, after the Supreme Court ruling in the *Plessy v. Ferguson* case of 1896, legally segregated from white society in the South. Some politicians even advocated the relocation of blacks to Africa. Native Americans, who were conquered but could not be deported, faced forced assimilation in residential boarding schools under white administration.

Native American Acculturation

As with urban ethnic-minority groups, reformers used sport and education in attempts to foster assimilation of Native American tribes. The process of formal acculturation began in 1879, with the opening of the Carlisle Indian School at an abandoned Army barracks in Pennsylvania. Carlisle was the first of many schools across the country designed to convert Native Americans to white notions of civilization. It housed American Indians

A gymnastics class at the Carlisle Indian School.

Image courtesy of Library of Congress, LC-USZ62-120987.

PEOPLE & PLACES

James M. Toy

Sioux Indian James M. Toy assimilated successfully, at least temporarily, by masquerading as a white baseball player. (His death certificate lists him as white.) The first Native American to reach the major league level, Toy appeared as a catcher and infielder for Cleveland in 1887 and for Brooklyn in 1890 before an injury ended his career. Louis Sockalexis, a Penobscot tribe member from Maine, left a more lasting impression as a Cleveland outfielder from 1897 to 1899. Sockalexis endured a barrage of racial taunts by other players and fans before injury and alcoholism chased him from the game. Even Hall of Fame pitcher Charles Bender endured the seemingly inevitable sobriquet "Chief" during his long career. Bender responded by calling white antagonists "foreigners." A product of the Carlisle Indian School, Bender pitched in five World Series for the Philadelphia Athletics between 1903 and 1914 in a career that lasted until 1927. John Tortes Meyers, of the California Cahuilla tribe, caught for the New York Giants from 1909 to 1915, and in his 14 years as a professional he resisted racist taunts and jeers but still felt treated as an outcast (Powers-Beck 77).

from 70 different tribes and imposed on them the English language, vocational skills, and WASP values. Forced to cut their hair, don clothing typically worn by whites, and assume WASP standards of decorum, American Indian youth struggled to maintain their own cultural identities.

While Native Americans adapted well to baseball, the Carlisle football team constituted the most visible success in the forced assimilation process. The team began play in 1890 and within five years embarked on a national schedule. In 1898, its quarterback, Frank Hudson, became the first of many Native American players to win recognition as an All-American.

With no home field, the Carlisle football team traveled across the country, and in 1912 even played in Canada, where it defeated Toronto University 49-1 in a combined game of rugby and football. Carlisle matched its wit and brawn against the best of the collegiate teams, nearly defeating Harvard and Yale in 1896, and beating Penn in 1899. It ranked among the best teams in the country from 1900 to 1914. The 1912 team featured members of 10 tribal groups, including the famed Jim Thorpe. They led the nation in scoring with 504 points, and Jim Thorpe accounted for 25 of the team's 66 touchdowns (Gems, *For Pride* 119).

The Carlisle team became a major attraction in the commercialized world of intercollegiate football, drawing huge crowds in urban stadiums. The University of Michigan provided a $2,000 guarantee for a 1901 game in Detroit, and the University of Chicago

This cartoon, from an 1896 edition of the *World*, is like many newspapers that caricatured and stereotyped Native Americans as savages undergoing the processes of civilization.

Image from *World*, Nov. 20, 1896.

THE EVOLUTION OF THE INDIAN.

PEOPLE & PLACES

Jim Thorpe

Photo courtesy of National Baseball Hall of Fame Library.

Selected for the 1912 United States Olympic team, Jim Thorpe captured the gold medal in both the pentathlon and the decathlon. A year later, he ran afoul of the AAU's definition of amateurism when it was discovered that he had played minor league baseball in the summer of 1909 for pay. Forced to return his medals and stripped of his Olympic victory, Thorpe turned to the professional ranks to make a living. He played major league baseball but had a bigger influence as the premier attraction on the nascent pro football circuit, where physical prowess counted more than race or social status. By 1915, town teams paid him as much as $250 per game for his services. In 1920, the fledgling pro league named him its first president in order to capitalize on his national celebrity, and in 1922 and 1923, as player-manager, he guided the Oorang Indians team, composed entirely of Native Americans from 12 different tribes, in the National Football League.

paid $1,700 for a 1907 contest. Their success might have provided a rehabilitated image of Native Americans, but they were often portrayed as noble savages, and their coach, Glenn "Pop" Warner, got most of the credit for their trick plays and innovative formations (for example, Carlisle nearly beat Harvard by hiding the ball under a player's jersey in 1903). The attribution of this success to Warner's genius only reinforced the Social Darwinist belief in the need for white leadership, and Warner reinforced stereotypes by refusing to number the players' jerseys in the belief that since all American Indians looked alike the identical jerseys would deceive opponents. Of the deceptive plays, he asserted that "[t]he public expects the Indians to employ trickery and we try to oblige" (Beale 147).

White sportswriters characterized the Carlisle team as tricksters who won by deceit or by "massacres" if they scored a lot of points. Such media descriptions were meant to reinforce a perception of whites as morally superior, yet American Indians often displayed better sporting behavior than their white opponents. For them, football offered an opportunity to exhibit racial pride and exact a measure of revenge. Their ancestors had suffered at the hands of the American military in its quest for Indian lands, and they took particular joy in defeating the West Point team. The team's historian stated that in confronting Army, the "Redskins play football as if they were possessed" (Steckbeck 95). In the 1912 game, when Jim Thorpe's touchdown run was called back for an alleged infraction, he responded by scoring another on the very next play in a 27-6 victory. For the tribes, such games represented a continuation of the frontier wars.

Football also allowed Native Americans to challenge the Social Darwinists' racial stereotypes by outsmarting their supposedly superior opponents. The 1906 rule changes allowed for forward passes, stipulating only that the ball had to be caught within the boundaries of the playing field. In a 1907 win against the elite University of Chicago team, the Carlisle receiver ran around the opponents' bench and returned to the field to catch a touchdown pass. In 1911, Carlisle defeated mighty Harvard 18-15 when Thorpe scored four field goals and a touchdown. After the game, his teammates mimicked the Bostonians' accents in a parody of their elitist attitudes.

After beating Penn, a Carlisle player determined that the white men might be better with cannons and guns, but the Native Americans displayed equal intelligence on the football field (Warner 46).

At least one adaptation exhibited cross-cultural flow between Native Americans and people of Anglo descent, as both Canadians and Americans adopted the traditional American Indian game of lacrosse by the nineteenth century. By the Progressive Era, American Indians were mixing traditional loincloths and moccasins with Anglo team jerseys and athletic shoes. The game became more regulated when a national lacrosse league adopted Canadian rules and held a championship at Newport, Rhode Island, in 1879. An intercollegiate lacrosse association was formed in 1882, and teams from New York and Boston engaged Canadian rivals. All-star teams began making barnstorming trips to England and Ireland by 1888. The Amateur Athletic Union (AAU) assumed governance of the sport in 1890 and promoted regional tournaments, but the game retained its greatest popularity among whites in New England and the Atlantic Coast areas thereafter. Native Americans who remained on reservations resisted the sportification process imposed on those who lived at boarding schools, retaining their traditional game of lacrosse with its inherent symbols, rituals, and meanings. By the 1890s, whites deemed them to be professionals and excluded them from mixed competition. White clergy also protested lacrosse play among American Indians because they often chose the game over church attendance (Vennum 277).

Plight of African Americans

Like the newly arrived immigrants, African Americans continued to try to find their place in the mainstream culture of the predominantly white, Protestant United States. The years following the Civil War saw temporary gains by blacks in politics, but that progress ended when Southern Democrats regained control of the region in exchange for delivering the 1876 presidential election to Republican Rutherford Hayes, who lost the popular vote but garnered a one-vote victory in the electoral college (Blum et al. 925). The change meant that freedmen reverted to virtual slavery as sharecroppers under the yoke of white supremacy. By the 1890s, rural Southern blacks had begun their prolonged exodus to Northern cities in search of a better life, and between 1914 and 1919 five hundred thousand blacks traveled to the North in a movement known as the Great Migration (Garraty 606). This shift provided opportunities for black entrepreneurs, as well as chances (albeit limited) for involvement in sport.

Rube Foster, pioneer of black baseball and founder of the Negro National League.

Image courtesy of Chicago Historical Society.

Rise of African American Baseball

The growing African American presence in the North supported a number of black baseball teams in the larger cities. In 1895, the all-black Page Fence Company team of Adrian, Michigan, sported a 118-36-2 record. By 1900, Chicago supported two black teams, and the Leland Giants, formed in 1905, competed in the Chicago City League against topflight white competition. In 1906, the Chicago Cubs and Chicago White Sox won their respective league pennants and met in the World Series, but a City League team, the Logan Squares, had beaten both of them that year, an indication of the quality of play. In 1909, Frank Leland's Giants won the City League championship and played the Cubs in a series of postseason games.

The brutality of the Chicago Race Riot in 1919 left 38 people dead.

Image courtesy of Chicago Historical Society.

The next year, the Giants' star pitcher and manager, Andrew "Rube" Foster, split with the owner and joined John Schorling, a white tavern keeper, in forming the Chicago American Giants in 1911, but a harsh racial climate, exemplified by a resurgent Ku Klux Klan, boded ill for blacks, especially in the South. The increasing number of black migrants that flooded Northern industrial centers in search of employment also faced racism and ostracism as scab laborers who served employers as strikebreakers. Southerners lynched more than 70 African Americans in 1919, and race riots ensued in Washington, D.C., East St. Louis (Illinois), Chicago, and Tulsa, thus negating the best intentions of the Progressive reformers (Blum et al. 616). In 1920, Rube Foster led the formation of the Negro National League, which included teams in Chicago, Detroit, Dayton, Indianapolis, Kansas City, and St. Louis, thus forming a parallel sporting structure that employed, catered to, and depended on African Americans.

Horse Racing

While black baseball players struggled to gain acceptance, African American jockeys met with greater success, at least on the turf, where they could compete with white opponents. Isaac Murphy won three Kentucky Derbys (in 1884, 1890, and 1891) and commanded a large salary. Yet his fame and talent could not win a full welcome in the white world, and he died of alcoholism in 1896 at the age of 35. Willie Sims replaced Murphy as the top jockey, winning the Kentucky Derby in 1896 and 1898, as well as numerous other stakes races. By the time Simms retired in 1901, he had totaled $300,000 in earnings, surpassing even Murphy. Jimmy Winkfield won consecutive Kentucky Derbys in 1901 and 1902, but retaliation by white jockeys forced him to take up residence in Europe, where he enjoyed a long and successful career.

Cycling

African Americans also claimed the best cyclist in the world at the turn of the century in the person of Marshall "Major" Taylor of Indianapolis, who began his professional career in 1896. In 1898, he set a new mark in the 1-mile (1.6-kilometer) event, and a year later he won the world championship. Taylor held seven world records between 1898 and 1900, despite the actions of jealous white opponents who tried to thwart his efforts by means of blocking and obstruction tactics. Taylor chose to race in Europe and Australia after 1901, winning as much as $10,000 annually.

Tour de France

The Tour de France is the most famous cycling race and the ultimate endurance event in sport. It lasts three weeks, during which the cyclists travel at an average speed of 42 kph for four or five hours each day. They traverse the Alps and Pyrenees, covering heights equivalent to climbing Mount Everest three times. The cyclists, called "giants of the road," frequently exceed their physical capacities, often supported by drugs, and a few of them paid for the chance of gaining immortal fame with their lives.

The Tour de France was held for the first time in 1903 at the instigation of Henri Desgrange, the publisher of the newspaper *L'Auto*. Eighty-five years previously, in 1818, Baron von Drais' "riding machine" had been introduced to a wider public in the Parc de Luxembourg, but these heavy and clumsy *draisiennes* did not catch on. It was not until technological advances were made in wheel-making during the 1860s and the invention of the chain-driven "safety bicycle" with two equal-sized wheels in the early 1880s that cycling became truly popular. All over Europe, the years that followed saw a surge of bicycle-related culture. Manufacturing companies were established, clubs and associations were founded, race tracks were built, records were set, and races were organized.

In the 1890s the bicycle became a symbol of progress, rationalism, technology, and dynamism—a hallmark of the new era and its striving for innovation. It held the promise of prestige as well as the experience of new dimensions and physical sensations. It was during this time that the Tour de France was invented, promising a further heightening of excitement and drama because it pushed the limits of what the human body could endure and kept both participants and spectators in suspense for days on end. The Tour de France was clearly staged with an eye on its marketing potential, and this is true for the organizers, the cyclists, and the media alike. All in all, the prize money today amounts to roughly four million dollars.

The Tour de France is a stage race, in which each daily stage is held as a separate race and the times recorded for each cyclist are accumulated. In addition, there are special prizes for victories in such contests as time trials, sprints, and mountain climbs.

In 1903 the Tour consisted of 6 stages covering 2,428 km. As early as 1911, the cyclists had to complete 5,343 km in 15 stages. The greatest challenges of the race are the mountains, especially the Col de Tourmalet, which has a constant uphill gradient of 10 percent.

The Tour de France also has a history of problems and scandals ranging from financial difficulties to fraud and deception, although these did nothing to hinder the growing popularity of the contest. The history of the Tour is also a history of doping, which in the early years was not prohibited. Substances such as alcohol, strychnine, ether, cocaine, and caffeine were used initially to alleviate pain but also to increase performance. In the years that followed, however, the list of performance-enhancing drugs grew longer and longer, with amphetamines, anabolic steroids, glucosteroids, and EPO either replacing or complementing one another. Up to the present day, the antidoping strategies of international sports federations have been unable to take any effective action against doping in professional cycle racing.

The uniqueness of the Tour de France is due both to its backdrop (i.e., the route, which takes the riders around the whole of France) and to its staging, which puts roughly 18 million spectators and viewers under its spell. The extreme demands on the riders, the dangerous downhill stretches, the great distance covered, the few days of rest, the heat, the rain, the cobblestones—all of these contribute to the drama of the race and provide the yarn which the sports media weaves into an epic narrative of masculine heroism. In times of national self-doubt the Tour de France has always provided the French people with the opportunity to become acquainted with France in its geographic entirety and its history as well as the opportunity to identify with the "grande nation."

Information from <www.hickoksports.com/history/tourdefrance.shtml>; Fife, Graeme. *Tour De France—The History, the Legend, the Riders*. Edinburgh: Mainstream Publishing Co., 1999.

This kind of success achieved by African American athletes cast doubt on whites' perceptions of their own racial superiority, particularly in individual sports featuring head-to-head competition. Whites rationalized defeats by African Americans in scientific analyses claiming that blacks' primitive natures, akin to animals, gave them innate anatomical advantages. Even in the more liberal atmosphere of France, French scientists X-rayed and measured Taylor's body in search of racial explanations for his victories.

Boxing

Unlike Taylor, black boxers enjoyed the luxury of fighting back. Peter Jackson, a black heavyweight from Australia, fought a 61-round draw with James J. Corbett in 1891, but white champion John L. Sullivan refused to fight Jackson (or any other black boxer), and when Corbett took the crown from Sullivan a year later he upheld the color ban. Similarly, other great black fighters such as Sam Langford, Sam McVey, Joe Jeannette, and Harry Wills never got title fights. Most often they were forced to fight each other, and Langford fought 14 bouts against Jeannette, 15 against McVey, and 23 against Wills (Roberts 45). Canadian-born George Dixon became the first black world champion when he won the bantamweight title in 1890, and a year later he added the featherweight crown. Joe Gans garnered the lightweight championship in 1912 and held it for six years, but the elusive heavyweight prize symbolized the Social Darwinist triumph, allowing whites to claim physical superiority.

When Jim Jeffries retired as the undefeated heavyweight champ in 1905, the title fell to Canadian Tommy Burns, and Jack Johnson, the flamboyant African American champ, chased Burns around the globe until he secured a title fight in Australia in 1908. Johnson toyed with and pummeled the undersized Burns en route to becoming the first black heavyweight champion. Johnson's victory engendered an immediate and ongoing search for the "Great White Hope" who might restore Anglo-Americans' pride and confidence in their racial superiority. When none could defeat the brash Johnson, whites prevailed upon the never-vanquished Jim Jeffries to come out of retirement. The historic confrontation took place in Reno, Nevada, on July 4, 1910, for a purse exceeding $100,000 and including movie rights. Twenty thousand spectators trekked to the blistering desert to witness the affair, and journalists came from as far away as Europe and Australia. Promoter Tex Rickard served as referee to insure a fair decision for the enormous wagers, with bettors favoring Jeffries. Rickard had little to fear, as Johnson won decisively, knocking the seemingly invincible white through the ropes and thoroughly crushing the Social Darwinist belief in black inferiority.

White hopes were crushed with Jack Johnson's historic defeat of the previously unbeaten Jim Jeffries.

Photo courtesy of Nevada Historical Society.

African Americans celebrated the victory, and whites retaliated with beatings and lynchings. Race riots killed 11 people across the country, as reported by the *Chicago Daily Tribune:*

RACES CLASH AFTER PRIZE FIGHT.

	Dead	Injured
Uvaldia, Ga	3	5
Mounds, Ill	2	0
Little Rock	2	1
Shreveport	2	1
Houston, Tex	1	3
Keystone, W. Va	1	0
New Orleans	0	2
Wilmington, Del	0	12
New York	0	5
Baltimore	0	3
Cincinnati	0	3
St. Joseph	0	1
Roanoke	0	6
Pueblo	0	27
Los Angeles	0	3
Chattanooga	0	2

At least eleven killed and scores of others wounded in race clashes last night in various parts of the United States marked one result of the Jeffries-Johnson fight.

There were battles in the streets of practically every large city in the country. Negroes formed the greater number of those who were victims of the outbreaks. They were set upon by whites and killed or wounded because of cheers for Johnson's victory. ("Eleven Killed in Many Race Riots")

After his loss to Jess Willard, Jack Johnson claimed that he was not knocked out but merely shielding his eyes from the sun.

Image courtesy of Library of Congress, LC-USZ62-33753.

Johnson further infuriated his critics by consorting with and marrying white women (three). The federal government indicted him on Mann Act charges, which forbade the transport of women across state lines for "immoral purposes." Forced to flee the country, Johnson escaped to Europe in 1913. When World War I erupted a year later, he had few opportunities to earn a living. He agreed to a 1915 bout in Havana, Cuba, against the giant Jess Willard, a raw Kansas cowboy. Johnson suffered a mysterious knockout in the twenty-sixth round. He later claimed that he had a secret deal with the government to return to America after he lost the fight, an unsubstantiated and never-effected agreement. He continued to wander until submitting to a one-year prison sentence upon his return to the United States in 1920. He never got another championship match.

Football

The direct racial confrontations of the boxing ring were somewhat masked on the gridiron, since it was teamwork that brought success in football, but individual black players did win acclaim and some measure of respect in the North and Midwest. George Jewett starred as a running back for the University of Michigan in 1890 but had to endure taunts and threats from opponents and rival fans. In the East, William Tecumseh Sherman Jackson played halfback for Amherst, and William Henry Lewis won All-American honors as a center for Harvard in 1892 and 1893. He later coached the Harvard squad and also distinguished himself beyond the football field, winning election to the city council in Cambridge, Massachusetts, and serving in the state legislature before his appointment as assistant U.S. attorney general for Boston. He served in the national attorney general's office during the administration of President William Howard Taft. Thus football provided Lewis with fame, and education enabled him to achieve prominence and social mobility as he obtained a measure of social whiteness in the traditionally more liberal environment of New England. W.E.B. DuBois, an African American leader and a Harvard PhD, subsequently asserted that educated blacks could compete with whites on a level playing field.

Black colleges initiated their own intercollegiate rivalries that paralleled those of the elite New England schools. The Lincoln–Howard game became a Thanksgiving spectacle in Washington, D.C., starting in 1894. Tuskegee and Atlanta followed in 1897, and in 1912 Lincoln University of Pennsylvania joined three Southern schools to form the Colored Intercollegiate Athletic Conference. The precedent of the U.S. Supreme Court ruling in the 1896 *Plessy v. Ferguson* case, which legalized segregation, insured that such associations would remain separate from their white counterparts, and black teams, unable to compete with whites, had to contend for mythical black championships well into the twentieth century.

Nevertheless, after the turn of the century, individual African American football stars became increasingly prominent on high school and college teams. At the University of Minnesota, Bob Marshall gained election to the All-American team in both 1905 and 1906 before mounting a long career as a professional player. Edward Gray was an Amherst All-American in 1906, and Archie Alexander won all-conference honors for Iowa in 1910 despite the refusal of Missouri opponents to play against him. In 1912, Ray Young even fulfilled a leadership role, one of the few accorded to African Americans, as line coach at Northwestern University. By World War I, two outstanding black athletes garnered national media attention. Fritz Pollard, an All-American at Brown in 1916, led his team to the Rose Bowl, then joined the professional circuit, where he became the first black quarterback and first black head coach in the National Football League. Paul Robeson, an All-American end for Rutgers in 1917 and 1918, joined Pollard in the professional ranks before achieving international renown as an actor, singer, and social critic. The successes of these black athletes belied the racial conditions in the United States, as blacks generally faced mounting prejudice, bias, and discrimination in both the South and the North.

Challenging Gender Boundaries

As with the activities of other subordinate groups, women's increasing involvement in sporting culture over the last two decades of the nineteenth century forged new roles, challenged stereotypes, and frequently exasperated white men. Some women's groups began to bring their feminist perspective to bear more forcefully in agitating for more than suffrage or temperance. Suffrage, first proposed at the Seneca Falls Women's Rights Convention in New York in 1848, remained an arduous battle for women demanding a measure of citizenship equal to that of men. Between 1870 and 1910, suffrage referenda appeared on 17 occasions, and by 1917 more than two million members had joined the National American Woman Suffrage Association, but women had to wait until 1920 before they could vote in national elections (Coben 94). Women also agitated for jobs, and as more women entered the workforce they gained greater independence—that is, they were less tied to reliance on men.

Activists such as Charlotte Perkins Gilman, Margaret Sanger, and Emma Goldman also called for women to take more control over their lives and bodies. Gilman argued against the exploitation of women and favored socialism. Goldman promoted anarchism, atheism, free speech, and free love, claiming that marriage forced dependency and objectified women as merely sexual beings, and both she and Sanger preached birth control as a means of bettering women's lives.

Women sought greater freedom in their leisure lives as well, and, as they moved from passive to more active leisure practices, sport proved to be a highly visible symbol of cultural change. Gilman promoted athletics for women and helped form a club for that purpose in Providence, Rhode Island. Female practitioners had been accorded usage of some facilities at male clubs when they were not in use by men, and by the 1880s in some New York clubs women could bowl, play billiards or tennis, swim, and row boats at designated times. By 1901, wealthy women were forming their own clubs and uniting in the Federation of Women's Athletic Clubs. The Chicago Women's Athletic Club featured a gymnasium, a bowling alley, a billiard room, a swimming pool, and facilities for basketball and gymnastics.

Artist Charles Dana Gibson began portraying slim, athletic women in his 1890s illustrations. The "Gibson Girl" symbolized activity, independence, vivaciousness, and a distinct break from the sedate, domestic, and restricted ideal woman of the Victorian Era. These

PEOPLE & PLACES

Annie Smith Peck

Image courtesy of Library of Congress, LC-USZ62-11827.

A Smith College scholar and a suffragist, Annie Smith Peck (1850–1935) was also a mountain climber who, when she started mountaineering, was told by a man to "go home where you belong." Instead, she set mountain-climbing records, making most of her ascents without the aid of oxygen. Peck used the sport of mountaineering to further the cause of women, seeking equality in a man's world. A committed campaigner for a constitutional amendment that would grant American women the right to vote, Peck hoped to prove that men and women could achieve equality in all fields, and she decided to set a woman's record for altitude. Peck climbed Mount Coropuna in Peru (21,079 feet, or 6,425 meters) and, upon reaching the peak, hung a banner that read, "Vote for Women."

"new women" dismantled many gendered stereotypes and shunned the domesticity of Victorian culture. They represented a new physical vitality and independence. As the Progressive Era moved to a close, women—working-class women in particular—rapidly joined the mass, popular, and public culture that included amusement parks, vaudeville, movies, dance halls, night clubs, and sports.

Educational and Sporting Opportunities for Women

The new women's colleges provided opportunities for recreational play and instruction. Vassar College fielded women's baseball teams as

Thirty Years of "Progress"!

Sport helped to transform the image and roles of women within one generation.
Image from *Life Magazine*, 1926.

early as 1866, and the women of Mills College in Oakland, California, were playing the game by 1872. Three years later, two women's teams in Springfield, Illinois, competed in a baseball game before paying spectators. Such activities challenged the traditional feminine passivity assigned to women and generated widespread debate that would persist through the next century regarding the propriety of sporting activity by women.

> Danville, Ill, June 9—The "Ladies" base ball club, composed of women from Chicago and Cincinnati, defeated the Danville Browns by a score of 23 to 12 to an attendance of 2,000. Last evening state's attorney Blackburn swore out a warrant for their arrest for unlawfully disturbing the peace and good order of society. Officer Patterson arrested them as they were leaving town in carriages for Covington, Indiana. (*Ottumwa [Iowa] Daily Democrat*, June 11, 1890)

Mary Taylor Bissell, a female physician wrote:

> …so long as baseball and football and the boat race stand for the national expression of athletics, the experience of girls in any similar department will seem like comparing moonlight unto sunlight, and water unto wine…. The spirit for physical recreation has invaded the atmosphere of the girl's life as well as that of the boy, and demands consideration from her standpoint. (qtd. in Gems, *Sports in North America* 9)

Educators and physicians fulminated over the advantages and disadvantages of sport and education for women. A writer for *Popular Science Monthly* stated that, since "the average brain weight of women is about five ounces (142 grams) less than that of men . . . we should . . . expect a marked inferiority of intellectual power in the former" (qtd. in Marks 103). A Harvard medical professor claimed that intense study caused women to suffer from neurasthenia (nervous breakdown). G. Stanley Hall, the eminent psychologist, declared that "it was a pity to spoil a good mother to make a grammarian" (qtd. in Townsend 207), and motherhood became a prominent issue in considerations of female participation in sport, as the WASP birthrate declined at the end of the nineteenth century and, as some whites saw it, hordes of immigrants overran the country. Thus it was felt that cultural supremacy was at stake, as doctors worried about possible damage to reproductive organs caused by overexertion, even as others extolled the need for strong bodies to produce healthy WASP children. With the onset of the cycling fad of the 1880s, moralists raised further concerns, with some suggesting that the activity diminished sexual impulses, while others believed that it induced masturbation.

Dudley Sargent, a medical doctor and Harvard professor, began offering physical culture (an early term for physical education) classes to women and opened his own school in 1881, using numerous weight-lifting machines and training teachers. Mary Hemenway's Boston Normal School of Gymnastics (BNSG), opened in 1889 and directed by Amy Morris Homans, also trained a multitude of women as teachers. In 1909, BNSG became a branch of Wellesley College for Women. Many graduates of Sargent's and Homan's programs assumed leadership roles in the women's sports movement over the next half century, including Senda Berenson, who adapted basketball rules for women's play, and Dr. Delphine Hanna, who initiated a physical education program for women and men at Oberlin College in Ohio.

The female graduates of such programs enjoyed a friendship and camaraderie that greatly influenced their sporting ideology. They eschewed the highly competitive and commercialized male model in favor of a less competitive ideal of sport for fun and health; thus women began to define their own sporting culture. Many became leaders in the Association for the Advancement of Physical Education, established in 1885, and they advocated a nurturing, protective relationship between and among women.

Bryn Mawr, a college for women, was founded in 1885 and offered its students basketball, field hockey, and track-and-field activities by 1901. Indeed, most college women engaged in intramural contests or interscholastic play days, in which two schools merged teams for recreational play to deter rabid spectators, institutional rivalry, and personal enmity. Pre- or postgame festivities might include sharing tea or a picnic, and these sportswomen often claimed that they played for social rather than competitive reasons. However, not all women adhered to the idea of sport as a social rather than a competitive outlet. In 1895, Chicago high school girls started interscholastic basketball competition, and working-class girls enjoyed the sport on settlement house teams. In 1896, California lost to Stanford, 2-1, in the first basketball game between women's colleges.

Sport as a Challenge to Traditional Domesticity

Some women further challenged the feminine stereotypes of domesticity and debility. In 1885, Annie Oakley (Phoebe Ann Mozee) became a celebrity as a trick-shot artist with a rifle in Buffalo Bill Cody's Wild West Show. Her astounding feats included hitting a dime tossed into the air, shooting a cigarette from her husband's lips, and hitting a moving target while perched on a galloping horse. By 1899, women were racing horses in the Wyoming rodeo known as Cheyenne Frontier Days, and they soon took up steer roping and bronco busting as well.

Women challenged the male domain in their demonstration of both physical skills and endurance. Female cyclists engaged in a 6-day race in Madison Square Garden in 1896. Women also competed in endurance cycling races in New York. Numerous other women completed century runs of 100 miles (161 kilometers) by bicycle, and throughout 1899 a number of female cyclists pushed the endurance tests to 1,000 miles (about 1,610 kilometers) over a 5-day period. Elizabeth Cochran Seaman, operating under the pseudonym of Nellie Bly as a reporter for a New York newspaper, traveled around the globe in 72 days. In 1890, Fay Fuller donned bloomers and boys' boots and rode astride a horse like a man rather than in the customary sidesaddle position, as she conquered the 14,410-foot (4,392-meter) peak of Mount Rainier in Washington. Three years later, Helga Estby, wearing a short skirt and accompanied by her daughter Clara, walked the length of the continent from Spokane,

The image of the Western frontier elicited exhilaration and a sense of freedom in many white men and women.

Image courtesy of Library of Congress, LC-USZC4-2351.

Washington, to New York City in a quest for an announced prize of $10,000 to support her family (Hunt). However, the sponsor was unwilling to pay up due to a technicality: she had stopped temporarily due to her daughter's illness.

Women in the New England colleges continued to play baseball, and a few women's teams—notably, the Chicago Stars, the Boston Bloomer Girls, and the St. Louis Stars—barnstormed around the country playing against men's teams after the turn of the century. A number of other barnstorming women's baseball teams gave such enterprises a negative connotation when it was discovered that they were no more than brothels advertising their wares. Several women, however, earned a respectable living as baseball players. Lizzie Arlington, whose real name was Lizzie Stroud, played in a minor league for the Reading, Pennsylvania, men's team during the 1890s. She earned as much as $100 weekly as a pitcher. Alta Weiss earned enough money pitching for an Ohio semipro team from 1907 to 1910 to go to medical

PEOPLE & PLACES

Eleanora Sears

The wealthy Bostonian Eleanora Sears defied convention in her fashion, lifestyle, and romances. If not for her social standing, she would have been roundly criticized for her behavior. Sears wore pants and challenged men in athletic competitions. She swam and played baseball, golf, and field hockey, but the field in which she excelled was that of racket sports. She won the national doubles title in tennis four times (and the mixed doubles twice) between 1911 and 1917. She rode astride horses as men did, rather than in the customary sidesaddle position expected of women, and in 1912 she became the first woman to play polo. That same year, she walked 108 miles (174 kilometers) in less than 20 hours. Not content with the constricted life ascribed to women, she also raced in cars and airplanes. In 1928, Eleanora Sears won the national squash championship at the age of 44.

The movement of women into the male sphere of athletics fostered great anxieties in some men.

Image from *National Police Gazette*, June 22, 1895.

school and become a doctor. She continued playing until 1922, and Amanda Clement even umpired men's games throughout the Midwest from 1905 to 1911. Such individual accomplishments signaled a change in women's self-perceptions, indicating a growing sense of independence, confidence, and assertiveness.

Though they maintained their domestic images, both Alice Camp and Stella Stagg served vital functions in assisting their husbands in their football coaching responsibilities. While Walter Camp worked throughout the day at his job at the New Haven Clock Company, it was his wife Alice who attended football practices, carefully taking notes for his evening meetings with team captains, and Mrs. Stagg even charted the plays from the press box at the stadium.

Sport, Fashion, and Liberation

The advent of women's golf and tennis played at country clubs—along with the cycling fad of the latter decades of the nineteenth century—led to a revolution in dress. Bustle skirts, which inhibited movement on the court, links, and cycle paths, eventually gave way to shorter skirts, bloomers, and pants. Women cyclists adopted such attire because skirts got caught in the spokes of wheels, causing accidents. The transition to bloomers or pants did not sit well with men, who felt threatened by women's donning of "masculine" clothing and their involvement in sports that evoked speed or power. Some municipalities banned the wearing of bloomers, while ministers charged that female cyclists were possessed by the devil. Doctors warned that women who cycled faced physical deformities and heart problems. Some even speculated that women's widespread interest in the sport had sexual motivations as the women sought gratification from friction with the bicycle seat (Vertinsky, *Eternally*).

As female tennis players became more competitive, they too shed their restrictive clothing, which had included long skirts, long-sleeved blouses, corsets, and hats. Californian May Sutton adopted short-sleeved tops and short skirts, and she used powerful strokes resembling men's play to win the American singles championship in 1904. In the following year, she became the first American woman to win the Wimbledon title. Women initially played tennis in doubles matches that limited the necessity for running or agility, but in 1887 they participated in a national singles championship at the Philadelphia Cricket Club, and a mixed doubles championship was held in 1891.

Women also took up golf but were relegated to using the country clubs when men were not on the links. The Meadowbrook Golf Course on Long Island sponsored the first national championship for women in 1895, and Chicagoan Margaret

Abbott became the first American female Olympic champion when she scored a 47 at the 1900 Paris Olympics in the nine-hole golf competition for women. Abbott, who adopted more suitable clothing, bested competitors who showed up in high heels.

Body Culture

The transition in gender norms affected both men and women as they departed from Victorian standards of decorum and strict morality. The body became a source of pleasure and eroticism. Just as feats of prowess glorified the physical, classical Greek sculpture was hailed as exemplifying male morphological ideals. Scientists viewed the body as a machine that might be made more efficient and effective, and sport performance was used to measure human capabilities. Sport—in schools, parks, playgrounds, settlement houses, and even colonial territories—served the purposes of Americanization, leadership training, and character development. As some sought the perfection of the body, others sought the reparation of sickly ones, or simply good health in specialized treatment centers.

Blouses and dresses became shorter and less restrictive as women became more competitive, as shown by May Sutton.
© Hulton Archive/Getty Images

The Perfect Body

Eugen Sandow, born Friederich Wilhelm Mueller, in Prussia, symbolized the international ideological transition. He began his career as a circus performer and acrobat before graduating to weight-lifting stunts and exhibitions in vaudeville shows and theatrical tours. Sandow portrayed his physique as a work of art, carefully marketed as the new standard of health and vitality. His chiseled body had an erotic appeal, and he posed nearly nude, wearing only loincloths or simple fig leafs to cover his genitals. At the Chicago World's Fair of 1893, he became an American sensation, and one wealthy socialite paid $300 to feel his muscles in a private exhibition. Sandow made global tours thereafter. He organized the first bodybuilding competition in London in 1901 and opened a chain of physical culture studios to train men in pursuit of the new ideal in body composition. Sandow expanded his enterprise to include selling health products and exercise devices, and his books promised fitness, vitality, and muscular development through strength training.

Sandow's counterpart in the United States, Bernarr Macfadden, insisted that "weakness was a crime." He advocated physical fitness through exercise, the consumption of natural rather than processed foods, and a lifestyle that included bodybuilding and outdoor activities. The flamboyant Macfadden railed against prudery, and he organized national contests to determine the most perfectly developed man and woman. These activities brought arrests on obscenity charges, but Macfadden persisted. By 1903, his *Physical Culture* magazine was selling more than one hundred thousand copies per month. The publication endured for more than 50 years, and Macfadden created a publishing empire of books, magazines, and films that made him a millionaire (Ernst). Macfadden's emphasis on natural beauty led him to oppose corsets, makeup, high-heeled shoes, and constrictive clothing for women. Contestants in his beauty contests posed in formfitting tights, and their photos in his publications undoubtedly titillated viewers. Macfadden established a health resort in New Jersey;

Eugen Sandow: the idealized male body.
Image courtesy of Library of Congress, LC-USZ62-95729.

schools to train teachers, coaches, and therapists; and a sanitarium in Battle Creek, Michigan.

Battle Creek Sanitarium

The most important health retreat in Battle Creek, however, gained its fame from its founder, Dr. John Harvey Kellogg. The Battle Creek Sanitarium, built in 1903, was designed as a comprehensive facility for health, exercise, and medicine. It provided a healthy diet to treat dyspepsia (digestive trouble) and offered some sports to help patients improve their bodily health. Thus health became not only a medical issue but a business concern as well.

The Battle Creek Sanitarium gained worldwide recognition, attracting famous patients and visitors who included athletes, politicians, and other public figures. It housed a swimming pool, gymnasium, and solarium. Kellogg developed a program of "biologic living" and promoted new types of treatment and new foods to improve the health of patients and visitors. He advocated a vegetarian diet and urged patients to abstain from alcohol, tobacco, and fad medicines, preferring instead to help them through healthy diet, physical exercise, outdoor excursions, water therapy, physical therapy, and exposure to proper air, heat, and light. In the kitchen, Kellogg invented the first corn flakes in 1894, launching the cereal industry in Battle Creek. In 1902, a huge fire destroyed most of the sanitarium's structures, and the new, larger sanitarium building, five stories high, was constructed in 1903. In this new facility, treatment rooms provided places for men and women to receive therapy, and guests also used indoor gymnasium facilities. The grounds of the Sanitarium included a lovely garden and a lakefront area for outdoor exercise.

President William H. Taft became the hundred-thousandth person to register as a guest in 1911. Other famous people who visited the Sanitarium and used the health and sport facilities in the first decades of the twentieth century included John D. Rockefeller, George Bernard Shaw, Henry Ford, J.C. Penney, Clara Barton, Eleanor Roosevelt, Eddie Cantor, Booker T. Washington, Montgomery Ward, Johnny Weissmuller, Admiral Richard E. Byrd, and William Jennings Bryan. Visitors could participate in indoor or outdoor gymnastics, swimming, biking, boating, horseback riding, hiking, and other athletic activities to achieve vigorous health, and thousands of health-seeking persons came to the institute yearly (Butler).

Sport and Technology

The Progressive Era, with its quest for human and societal improvement, spawned new technologies that affected sporting practices, and this was the beginning of an increasingly close relationship between sport and technology. The Dunlop pneumatic tire, patented in 1881, changed cycling and harness racing. The development of the safety bicycle in 1888 replaced the more dangerous high-wheeler and enabled the setting of numerous speed records. In 1899, Charles Murphy covered a mile (1.6 kilometers) in less than a minute by drafting behind a train. The new bicycle sulkies, with ball-bearing axles, enabled Star Pointer, a pacer, to break the 2-minute barrier for the mile in 1897.

The growing media also served as a primary spur to the growth of sport. Newspapers were increasing in number, circulation, and coverage of sporting events. In addition to the prominence given to boxing in the *National Police Gazette,* the *Spirit of the Times* provided extensive coverage of horse racing and track-and-field competitions. A mechanical typesetting machine became available in 1886, greatly increasing production, and the *Sporting News,* the bible of baseball, appeared that same year. Such publications proved especially popular with the bachelor subculture and gamblers. By the 1890s, the *New York World* newspaper featured a special page devoted to sports, and other papers soon followed suit. By that time, middle-class magazines such as *Harper's Weekly, Outing, Popular Science, Cosmopolitan,* and the *Atlantic Monthly* were among the many that devoted space to sports coverage as sporting practices assumed greater emphasis among the middle class. Ethnic newspapers also reported on baseball games played by German, Czech, Polish, and Jewish teams. Illustrations and photographs enhanced the stories, helping athletes make improvement in technique and performance.

Thomas Edison invented the kinetoscope in 1889, and motion pictures soon followed. Boxing films appeared by 1894 and held great interest for both men and women. Theater owners scheduled matinees to accommodate the large numbers of women attracted to the erotic sight of barely clad young men displaying their physical prowess. The gradual acknowledgement of women's carnal passions, which had long been accepted in and expected of men, moved the mainstream middle-class culture further from Victorian inhibitions of the past.

Thomas Edison's invention of the electric light in 1879 made it possible to provide artificial lighting in sports arenas, and experimentation with night baseball games started as early as 1883. The Chicago World's Fair of 1893 featured electric lighting for evening strolls, and football fans witnessed five night games, all enabled by the new technology. The Olympic Club of New Orleans opened the first modern boxing venue in 1890, and the extensive network of railroads provided for transport from across the country.

In the 1880s, German engineers developed internal combustion engines, which soon led to horseless carriages in the form of automobiles and motorcycles. Frank and Charles Duryea of Springfield, Massachusetts, built the first American model in 1893. In

Photography, such as this Muybridge motion photo sequence, greatly enhanced imagery of and research into sport performance.

Image courtesy of Library of Congress, LC-USZ62-103032.

June 1894, the first auto race took place in France (from Paris to Rouen), sponsored by the *Le Petit Journal* newspaper, which offered a $1,000 prize. Larger races from Paris to Bordeaux followed a year later, and the *Chicago Times-Herald* promoted the first American race, with $5,000 in prize money, on November 2, 1895. Only one vehicle (built and driven by the Duryea brothers) finished the 53-mile (85-kilometer) course.

Motorcycle racing began during the same year, and local promoters built enclosed racecourses in cities such as Atlanta, Daytona Beach, and Indianapolis. Eighty thousand spectators attended the first Indianapolis 500 car race, held in 1911 (Riess, *Sport* 41). Commercial production of cars allowed for a more mobile society and greatly changed the nature of American culture, as the assembly-line production of Henry Ford's Model T and other affordable models made ownership possible for an increasing number of people. A one-cylinder auto producing three horsepower built by Ransom Olds (and called the Oldsmobile) sold for $650. In 1904, Olds sold more than 5,000 vehicles (Foner and Garraty 64–65). Within the decade, human flight was achieved, and air races soon followed.

Modern Olympic Games

Progressive Era idealists tackled substantial issues ranging from body culture to feminism to health reform, but some attempted even grander schemes. In France, a minor nobleman, Pierre de Coubertin, envisioned a more peaceful world and saw athletics as a means to achieve his goal. Affected by the French loss in the Franco-Prussian War of 1870, he sought a mechanism to restore French vigor and to teach friendship and harmony. He toured both Great Britain and the United States and determined that they derived their strength from their educational systems in general, and their pursuit of athletics in particular. He felt that fair competition brought good health, strong values, and improved morality. In 1894, he organized an international athletic conference in Paris and called for a resurrection of the ancient Olympic Games in order to bring individual athletes together in a festival of fellowship and camaraderie.

De Coubertin realized his dream in the first modern Olympics, held at Athens, Greece, in 1896. A chauvinist, he and the Greek organizers refused to let women compete in the scheduled events. Males competed as individuals rather than as rep-

As had been the case with horses, the new horseless carriages were tested on racetracks against competitors.

Image courtesy of Library of Congress, LC-USZ62-100197.

resentatives of a country, but nationalistic reporters soon began to tally medal counts based on citizenship or political affiliation. Thirteen American athletes answered the initial call, including one swimmer, two marksmen, and ten track-and-field athletes, one of whom quit Harvard in order to make the trip when his request for a leave was denied. This defector, James B. Connolly, won the first event, the triple jump, and the other Americans, from Princeton and the Boston Athletic Association, nearly monopolized the track-and-field events, but a Greek shepherd, Spiridon Louis, won the marathon. Fellow Greeks showered him with gifts, including free meals, clothes, and haircuts for the rest of his life.

The 1900 Olympics, enveloped within the Paris World's Fair, lost the grandeur and cohesion established in Athens. Many competitors were unaware that they had even participated in anything more than an adjunct to the exposition, which in addition to competitions for men also provided competition for women in tennis, golf, yachting, croquet, hot air ballooning, and equestrian events.

INTERNATIONAL PERSPECTIVE

Hidden From History—Female Marathon Runners at the Olympic Games in 1896

Baron Pierre de Coubertin, founder of the modern Olympic Games, held the opinion that women should not "sully the Olympic arena with their sweat." The Olympic Games, he thought, should be a men's preserve, a celebration of masculinity. Accordingly, only male athletes were allowed to participate in the first Olympic Games, held in Athens in 1896—at least officially.

Unofficially, two women did participate in the Games, and perpetrated further sacrilege by running the marathon, an event especially contrived for the 1896 event. The marathon race was intended to glorify Greek antiquity and enact Greek heroism at a time when Greece had become a small and poor country, still partly occupied by the Turks. It did not matter in the slightest that the "marathon story"—that is, the story of a Greek soldier running from Marathon to Athens in order to proclaim the Greek victory over the Persian army, and of his subsequent death due to exhaustion—was a legend based on no historical evidence. For the Greeks, the marathon race was a "place of remembrance," and the victory of native son Spiridon Louis was unquestionably the highlight of the Games.

Whereas Louis became a celebrity, the first female marathon runners remained hidden from history. A young woman who called herself Melpomene wanted to register for the race but was not accepted by the organizing committee. She refused to give up, however, and ran the 26 miles (42 kilometers) from Marathon to Athens in 4 1/2 hours before the official start of the Games. Another woman, Stamatia Rovithi, was so excited about Spiridon Louis' achievement that she decided to follow his example. According to sources, this 35-year-old mother of seven children completed the distance in 5 1/2 hours. She confessed that she could have been faster if she had not done some window shopping along the way. Official textbooks do not mention the two female runners because they participated in the Games without approval. Thus they do not appear in the official sources and have not become part of the accepted history. Although both runners had proven that women were capable of completing the marathon distance, it took almost 90 years for women to be allowed to participate officially in the event.

Information from Tamini, Noel. "Women Always in the Race." *Olympic Review* (1993): 204–208, 221. <http://www.la84foundation.org/OlympicInformationCenter/OlympicReview/1993/ore308/ORE308a.pdf>.

Some of the best American male athletes were excluded from the 1900 event finals because they refused to compete on Sundays. Similarly, the 1904 Games ran in conjunction with the St. Louis World's Fair, and in the end they amounted to a national competition, as few beyond the American shores made the inland journey. One notable feature of the fair was its Anthropology Days, featuring competitions between various racial and ethnic groups on exhibit in tribal villages. The events included races, pole climbing, a tug-of-war, and even a mud fight. Western sport forms, unknown to most of the contestants, resulted in hapless, even ludicrous, outcomes that served to reinforce white beliefs in their own racial superiority (Dyreson, *Making*). George Poage challenged such beliefs, however, as the first African American medal winner by taking third place in the 200- and 400-meter hurdles. At the same world fair, in the unofficial women's basketball championship, the Native American girls from the Fort Shaw Indian School in Montana overwhelmed all competition, further undercutting the assertion of Anglo-American supremacy.

With Olympic spirit waning, de Coubertin accepted the Greek offer to stage an interim competition in Athens in 1906. This time, President Theodore Roosevelt served as honorary chairman of an Olympic committee that chose an official American team. They did not disappoint, winning 11 of the 19 track-and-field events. France won the overall competition, which included shooting contests, fencing, cycling, rowing, wrestling, tennis, gymnastics, soccer, weight lifting, rowing, and archery. Sport was given increasing nationalistic significance as countries measured themselves against others in international competition.

The quest for athletic and national supremacy reached an acrimonious peak in 1908, when London served as host. The British, with an empire that spanned the globe, considered themselves the preeminent world power, but the Americans, whose economic output had already surpassed that of the British, held notions of republican superiority. In addition, the United States team included many Irish Americans who resented the British occupation of their ancestral homeland. One of them, flag bearer Ralph Rose, refused to lower the Stars and Stripes to honor the British king in the opening parade. Rose's teammate Martin Sheridan replied to the outraged English that "this flag dips to no earthly king." Thus despite de Coubertin's intentions, the Olympic Games had become politicized.

Several international quarrels ensued, but the heated rivalry between the United States and Great Britain engendered the greatest fury. The host nation supplied the officials, and the Americans charged conspiracy when the English judges

The Anthropology Days competition proved to be an exercise in racism and an aberration of the Olympic ideal.

Image courtesy of St. Louis Public Library

disqualified both American runners who had apparently beaten the British competitor in the 400-meter run. The Americans refused to rerun the race, and the judges awarded the victory to their countryman by default. The American tug-of-war team also withdrew in protest when the British team was allowed to wear steel-rimmed boots, which provided greater traction, for their match. The marathon, too, produced animosity, when the Italian runner Dorando Pietri (aka Pietri Dorando) reached the stadium in first place but then collapsed on the track before finishing the race. With Irish American Johnny Hayes running a close second, British officials lifted Pietri and assisted him to the finish line. The marathon proved yet another debacle, but the officials eventually returned the victory to Hayes. The United States claimed the track-and-field championship, but Great Britain boasted of the overall victory in myriad other contests that had few if any American entrants. The resulting backlash by both antagonists caused the International Olympic Committee to appoint neutral judges for future competitions.

In a welcome reversal, the 1912 Olympics, held in Stockholm, proved a resounding success. With teams representing 26 countries from Europe, North America, South America, Asia, Africa, and Australia, the well-organized and efficiently staged events received ample media coverage, including headlines in U.S. newspapers. Jim Thorpe, the Native American winner of both the pentathlon and decathlon, won acclaim as the greatest athlete in the world, though a year later it was discovered that he had played summer baseball for money, and this violation of Olympic amateur rules resulted in the forfeiture of his Olympic medals. The 1912 Games were the first for female swimmers, as the Swedish organizers included women's aquatic competition without approval from the Olympic committee. The games also included the first use of electric timing devices for track events, indicating a greater reliance and emphasis on the Progressive values of science, technology, quantification, and rationality.

Throughout the staging of these early Games, women fought to achieve inclusion and gradually made progress toward that goal. At the St. Louis Games in 1904, only six American women (who were archers) represented their country. It was not until 1908, when the Olympic Games were held in England, the birthplace of modern sport, that women's sports achieved a modest upswing, with competition in four disciplines—tennis, sailing, ice skating, and archery—all carrying high social prestige. In

British officials assist the fallen Dorando Pietri to a disputed marathon victory, which was later reversed.

1908 and in 1912, women's gymnastic teams from Denmark, Norway, Sweden, Great Britain (1908), and Finland (1912) demonstrated their physical skills and capabilities. In 1908, according to the *London Telegraph*, "the ladies who took part lent to the exhibition a grace and charm all their own" (qtd. in Daniels and Tedder 43). In 1912, the "feminist" Swedes (the term used in the minutes of the IOC assembly in 1911) allowed women to compete in swimming events (Mitchell 212). The inclusion of such a popular sport in the women's program contributed considerably to the participation of women athletes from other countries, and 11 nations sent female athletes to Stockholm. More than 50 women, representing 2.2 percent of all competitors, took part in these Olympic Games.

More generally, while de Coubertin's idealistic plan for the modern Olympic movement sought to achieve international peace through athletic competition, the nationalistic recriminations of the 1908 Games had exposed the obstacles to achieving such a vision, and the eruption of World War I in 1914 rocked the globe and signaled the failure of Progressive reformers' attempts to achieve world peace. The conflict forced the cancellation of the 1916 Olympics scheduled for Berlin.

Sport During World War I

In the United States, sport became a means to train combatants and produce camaraderie, nationalism, and patriotic spirit. In 1914, General Leonard Wood produced a manual for the physical training of soldiers. Dr. Joseph Raycraft, director of athletics at Princeton, assumed leadership of the Army sports program, and Walter Camp, famed football coach at Yale, did the same for the Navy. Camp compiled a "daily dozen," a series of exercises to produce fitness in sailors, but competitive sport fostered the greatest interest, and baseball, football, basketball, volleyball, and tug-of-war activities were used to encourage aggressiveness and courage. Professional boxers became instructors for bayonet training, where parrying, slashing, and defense reflected the intimate conflicts that occurred in the ring.

Such athletic training was intended to produce pugnacious warriors for trench warfare and furious assaults, but it also addressed moral concerns. Sport was thought to serve the purpose of social control in Europe by keeping soldiers away from prostitutes and alcohol in their leisure hours. Venereal disease felled many American soldiers in France, and the Army eventually organized a baseball league that included more than two million players (Pope, *Patriotic* 148). Bible classes and YMCA activities were held to further deter the doughboys from indulging in illicit pleasures.

In the United States, the Boy Scouts adopted Camp's training regimen, and mayors in major American cities advocated physical education for fitness. More than 80 percent of Army applicants in 1915 and 1916 were rejected due to various deficiencies, and one-third of draftees were deemed unfit, sparking a national concern. After the war, 22 states adopted mandatory physical education laws, and West Point, under the direction of General Douglas MacArthur, initiated a comprehensive athletic program for all trainees (Pope, *Patriotic* 128, 129, 197).

During the war, the armed services produced some of the best football teams in the nation. The 1918 Rose Bowl featured the Mare Island Marines from Vallejo, California, against the Camp Lewis Army team from Tacoma, Washington. The Marines won 19-7, and proceeds from the contest benefited the Red Cross. Sport taught self-sacrifice for the good of the whole, and nearly half of the 32 players in the game eventually made the ultimate sacrifice, losing their lives while in military service. The following year, with the war over, Mare Island faced the Great Lakes Naval Training Station team from Illinois. Great Lakes emerged victorious, 17-0, and 10 players in the contest earned recognition as professional football players during the 1920s, including George Halas, founder of the Chicago Bears franchise (Hibner 42, 58).

The Armistice of November 11, 1918, effectively ended hostilities, but many American servicemen awaited ships to carry them home, while others were stationed in the occupied European territories. Sport served as a more wholesome and enjoyable means of training than military drill, and from June 22 to July 6 the joint administrators organized the Inter-Allied Games, similar to the Olympics. Soldiers built Pershing Stadium in Paris, and 16 of the 29 allied countries entered teams in events that included grenade throwing and various athletic competitions. Charles Paddock set a world record in the 200-meter dash (and later won an Olympic championship at 100 meters in the 1920 games at Antwerp, Belgium). French scholar Thierry Terret has ascertained that the Inter-Allied Games were a demonstration of American power and ascendance in Europe.

The Inter-Allied Games, a postwar military Olympics, signaled American ascendance.
Image courtesy of Library of Congress, 262-135332, Lot 7711.

American involvement in World War I greatly changed the nation's relationship with the rest of the world, establishing for it a new role as global leader—one which it was unwilling to fully accept. The war and its aftermath caused Americans to examine their own values, their democratic institutions, and what it meant to be an American. Those deemed to be disloyal were arrested, imprisoned, or deported, and immigration was curtailed. The 1920s would bring a homogenization of culture and a solidification of cultural identity, greatly prompted by a flourishing popular culture that revolved around movies, radio, and sport, with the media enthralling the populace with stories of celebrities, who became the new American heroes and heroines.

Summary

This chapter has described the Progressive reformers' vision of society and their attempts to restructure cities, alleviate social inequalities, and Americanize diverse immigrant groups based on their own white, Anglo-Saxon, Protestant, middle-class value systems. Sport was given a primary role in the acculturation process. The chapter has also examined the varying reactions to these programs by women seeking greater freedom and by numerous racial, ethnic, religious, and social groups. Some attempted to retain their own sporting cultures, while others both adopted and adapted American games to meet their own needs. The practice of sport proved to be a liberating experience for some, as in the case of white women, and an often-segregating factor for African Americans. For others, such as Native Americans and European ethnic minorities, sport ultimately fostered a more homogeneous culture, as youths were assimilated in the schools, parks, playgrounds, and settlement houses. Baseball prospered as the national sport, while football gained precedence on college campuses as a commercialized business enterprise focused intently on victory.

The modern Olympic Games were originated in order to extend brotherhood and fraternity to an international audience as Western sport forms migrated to colonized peoples, but the dreams of both the Olympics and the Progressive movement were shattered in the flames of World War I, which produced a new homogenized American culture and changed the meaning of being an American, as immigrants selectively adopted and adapted mainstream social values.

DISCUSSION QUESTIONS

1. Explain the process by which various immigrant ethnic groups were acculturated.

2. What role did settlement houses play in the lives of women and ethnic immigrants?

3. How did interscholastic athletic programs become rationalized as part of the educational curriculum?

4. In what ways did sport liberate women?

5. How did African American athletes dispel the theory of Social Darwinism?

6. Was the Progressive Movement successful? Why or why not?

7

Sport, Heroic Athletes, and Popular Culture

1920–1950

CHAPTER OBJECTIVES

After reading this chapter, you will have learned about the following:

- Why the United States took an isolationist stance after World War I
- How racial, ethnic, and religious distinctions affected American culture
- Why American society needed heroes in the aftermath of World War I and the Great Depression
- How the Great Depression affected sporting culture, and how entrepreneurs responded
- The media's role in constructing a popular culture
- The government's role in the developing popular sporting culture
- Social ramifications of the desegregation of baseball

Outlined against a blue-gray October sky, the Four Horsemen rode again. In dramatic lore they are known as Famine, Pestilence, Destruction, and Death. These are only aliases. Their real names are Stuhldreher, Miller, Crowley, and Layden. They formed the crest of the South Bend cyclone before which another fighting Army football team was swept over the precipice at the Polo Grounds yesterday afternoon as 55,000 spectators peered down on the bewildering panorama spread over the green plain below.

A cyclone can't be snared. It may be surrounded, but somewhere it breaks through to keep on going. When the cyclone starts from South Bend, where the candle lights still gleam through the Indiana sycamores, those in the way must take to storm cellars at top speed. Yesterday the cyclone struck again, as Notre Dame beat the Army, 13 to 7, with a set of backfield stars that ripped and crashed through a strong Army defense with more speed and power than the warring cadets could meet. (Rice 177)

Thus did Grantland Rice describe the Notre Dame juggernaut that won the national football championship after the 1924 season. With such florid prose, Rice and other sportswriters created a bevy of athletic heroes throughout the decade as sport and media transformed American culture. Another prominent sportswriter, Paul Gallico, described athletic stars as "the Golden People," noting that in the years following World War I sport had "its first million-dollar prizefights[,] and the adulation of sports heroes [rose] to the point almost of national hysteria" (13).

As World War I came to a close, however, the "Golden People" were anything but. The horrible devastation of the war and its terrible new weapons had shattered the idealistic notions of the Progressive reformers. And shortly thereafter, the limits of the Progressive moral agenda were again exposed in a sport scandal that shocked the nation, as even the national game of baseball, which had been used to assimilate millions of immigrants, proved corruptible. Gambling had long been a part of baseball, and widespread betting pools served as a poor man's lottery, where bettors might gamble on games, hits, runs, and so on over the course of a week, with newspapers reporting the box scores. Wealthier gamblers staked their bets instead with big bookies, but all relied on the honesty of the game and of its players' performances. As in the nineteenth century, however, sport continued to serve as both a means of community formation and a site of conflict, and the Black Sox scandal of 1919 registered the conflicting pressures and the anomalies in sport.

The Chicago White Sox had defeated the New York Giants in the 1917 World Series, but World War I service had depleted the team roster during the next year. In 1919, however, the Sox fielded one of the best teams in baseball history. Star pitcher Eddie Cicotte won 29 games, and outfielder "Shoeless" Joe Jackson hit .351 (though five points below his lifetime percentage of .356). Despite their sterling performances, Cicotte was denied a bonus, and Jackson had played six

When Grantland Rice wrote the account of the Four Horsemen, he penned some of the most famous lines in sportswriting history in lyrical but overstated prose. An astute publicist photographed the stars on horseback, sealing an indelible image.

Associated Press

years without a raise in his $6,000 salary. In contrast, the best hitter on the Cincinnati team, their 1919 World Series opponents, made $11,000 per season (Frommer 86). Thus the White Sox players felt underpaid and underappreciated by club owner Charles Comiskey, and, at the behest of a tangled web of gamblers, some of them colluded to throw the series to the underdog Cincinnati team. The gamblers ultimately crossed each other and the players, paying them only a fraction of the promised bribes. Nevertheless, the White Sox dropped the nine-game series. Although suspicions about their faulty play lingered for a year, the 1920 season produced record attendance that stood for more than a quarter century (it was surpassed in 1946). That year, despite featuring four 20-game winners on the pitching staff and taking a 3-1/2-game lead late in the season, the White Sox finished third. By September of the 1920 season, a Chicago grand jury investigated alleged widespread gambling fraud in baseball, eventually indicting eight of the White Sox players for fixing the 1919 World Series.

The jury trial, held in Chicago, produced evidence that seven of the eight players had received between $5,000 and $10,000 for their participation in the conspiracy. Third baseman George "Buck" Weaver claimed that he had had knowledge of the scheme but had not participated in it. Despite their admissions of guilt, and signed confessions by some, which mysteriously disappeared during the trial, the Chicago jury exonerated the players. The illiterate Joe Jackson's confession resurfaced when he later sued Comiskey for back pay. Despite the players' acquittal, baseball authorities quickly enacted the National Agreement of 1921, which produced a commissioner of baseball. Judge Kenesaw Mountain Landis, a flamboyant and controversial federal magistrate, assumed the role in dictatorial fashion. He immediately banned all eight Chicago players from the game and purged it of any gambling influences. Buck Weaver spent the remainder of his life trying to clear his name of the charges. Weaver's reluctance to implicate his teammates had exemplified ongoing class differences within America. Weaver had sought to maintain his personal and working-class honor by not snitching and by playing his best (he hit .324 and made no errors) during the World Series. Despite the fact that he accepted no bribe money, however, the commissioner judged him to be equally guilty. The differences in perception reflected social-class distinctions that continued to haunt American society, but journalists soon attempted to rectify the divisions by portraying sport as a meritocracy and resurrecting the promise of opportunity and mobility in the United States.

The decade of the 1920s was termed the "Golden Age of Sports," and the media's creation of sports heroes during this time provided a stabilizing influence in a rapidly changing American culture. Sports stars were lionized as All-American types who exemplified American cultural values. The Four Horsemen of Notre Dame represented the American ideology of spirit, teamwork, and assimilation of diverse groups within society. Babe Ruth, the most famous of all the athletic heroes, symbolized the American dream, the land of opportunity and meritocracy, where one could succeed despite humble origins. The depiction of such heroes presented a more homogeneous culture and solidified an American cultural identity, but it also masked social tensions inherent in the United States in the aftermath of World War I and during the Great Depression and World War II.

War, Depression, and the Shaping of America

After World War I, the United States declined to join the League of Nations despite the efforts of President Woodrow Wilson in launching the organization intended to achieve world peace. Thus isolated from international affairs, the United States focused on domestic issues. The 1920 census indicated that, for the first time, most Americans lived in cities, and this increasing urbanization brought cultural transitions that produced tensions and conflict. Employment issues and worker discontent resulted in labor unions that continued to question the capitalist economy, with thousands of workers participating in strikes to protest their miserable wages and working conditions (Dawley 234). Socialists,

•1920

• Warren Harding elected president

• First commercial radio broadcast begins

•1920s–1930

> Helen Wills wins U.S. tennis championships

•1920s–1930s

• Bill Tilden dominates men's tennis championships

•1921

• Dempsey–Carpentier fight staged

•1922

• U.S. Field Hockey Association founded

• Glenna Collett wins U.S. Women's Amateur Golf Championship for the first time

•1923

• Teapot Dome oil scandal exposed

• President Warren Harding dies, and Calvin Coolidge serves as president communists, and anarchists challenged the government, and, after Bolsheviks toppled the Russian tsar, capitalists feared a similar revolt in the United States, thus prompting the Red Scare. The Department of Justice arrested thousands of suspected radicals on a single night in 1920, deporting many as undesirable aliens. Anti-immigrant paranoia ensued, and for many European immigrants the promises of America went unrealized. Nativists, those persons wanting to uphold the values and power of white, native-born, United States citizens, reacted to perceived threats to the dominant WASP culture by enacting restrictive immigration laws in 1924 that established quotas for Southern and Eastern Europeans and curtailed Asian immigration in an attempt to safeguard the republic for Anglo-Americans. In 1920, the Nineteenth Amendment granted women the right to vote, further threatening some aspects of male hegemony and the traditional gender order.

Throughout the 1920s, blacks, Jews, and members of other ethnic groups asserted their own forms of expression in popular culture. Blues and jazz evolved out of African American experiences in the South, and during the Great Migration the music moved to the North, where it combined with urban experiences to produce new genres. In the movies, ethnic-minority (especially Jewish) producers drew upon their immigrant pasts in featuring working-class heroes and heroines, and film became a primary means of entertainment and recreation during the decade. Young urban women also challenged dominant middle-class norms by engaging in the risqué "flapper" lifestyle. Eschewing the religious strictures of the past, they smoked cigarettes, frequented speakeasies (where they freely drank prohibited alcohol), and danced to the new music. The dance fads of the era were considered lascivious by traditionalists, and the sexual escapades of celebrities and common flappers shocked even the liberal elements of society.

The Stock Market Crash of 1929, however, created a worldwide economic depression and abruptly halted the sports boom of the 1920s. Unemployment skyrocketed, and American workers increasingly questioned the capitalist system. By 1932, the unemployed numbered eleven million. In Chicago alone, seven hundred thousand people (accounting for 40 percent of the workforce) were unemployed, and in Boston more than forty thousand families sought relief funds. With the failure of more than 4,300 banks between 1929 and 1931, there was little to be had (Blum et al. 656).

Cities weren't the only areas affected by the depression. Poor people in rural areas also lived in dilapidated conditions.

Image courtesy of Library of Congress, LC-USF-3301-31322

Protests ensued, and hunger marches made clear the desperate state of poor people. Millions of homeless people wandered the country in search of work or begged on urban streets. The state of the economy proved especially dire for African Americans. Sixty-nine percent of the black population in Pittsburgh was unemployed, and in Detroit the figure reached 75 percent (Ashby 240.)

President Franklin Delano Roosevelt's economic recovery plan, known as the New Deal, entailed a massive recreational program that allotted $1.5 billion to labor and construction costs in a wide variety of federal agencies. The Civilian Conservation Corps (CCC), started in 1933, employed five hundred thousand people within two years in conservation projects and environmental programs in rural areas, improvement of national and state parks, and construction of hiking trails throughout the country. The Civilian Works Administration (1933), the Federal Emergency Relief Administration (1934), the National Youth Administration (1935), and the Works Progress Administration (1935) all employed multitudes in the construction of stadiums, swimming pools, sports fields, playgrounds, parks, gymnasiums, and winter sports facilities. Such programs created jobs, and the fruits of this labor addressed the forced leisure needs of unemployed citizens throughout the 1930s (Foner and Garraty 177, 1168).

The entry of the United States into World War II alleviated any economic concerns. Production boomed in order to supply materials for the war effort, and men were needed to fill the military ranks. Football coaches extolled the values of their game as preparation for battle, and President Franklin Roosevelt maintained that baseball was necessary for the national morale. Previously disparate groups united to confront the fascist threat to democracy, as class consciousness diminished, nationalism triumphed, and capitalists prospered.

Social Change and the Spread of Sport

The United States' concerted efforts against the fascist powers in World War II unified the members of the nation's previously disparate cultures. Second-generation immigrants sought to prove their loyalty and their American identity.

Sport and the Accommodation of Religious Groups

The Protestantism of mainstream America had long held alternative faiths, such as Catholicism or Judaism, at bay. The entry of different religious groups into the sporting culture brought them closer to the mainstream, reduced ignorance about their contrasting beliefs, and fostered a somewhat greater degree of acceptance, though nativists such as the Ku Klux Klan continued to oppose their citizenship.

Notre Dame and the Acceptance of Catholics

Under famed coach Knute Rockne, Notre Dame, a small Catholic college in South Bend, Indiana, fashioned a national football powerhouse. Rockne eschewed individualism when his tragic but flawed All-American George Gipp (a non-Catholic) died after the 1920 season. A nonconformist who eschewed practice and academic classes, Gipp nevertheless possessed brilliant athletic abilities that brought Notre Dame to national prominence. After his death, however, Rockne opted for an emphasis on team play, and to this day Notre Dame football players do not have their names on the backs of their jerseys. The return to a team-centered approach better suited traditional Catholic communalism, and Rockne's 1924 squad, featuring quickness and teamwork, went undefeated and beat Stanford 27-10 in the Rose Bowl to claim the national championship. Rockne created national rivalries by scheduling contests throughout the country, thus unifying the Catholic constituency. He gained the support of ethnic-minority communities by stocking his polyglot team with Irish, Italians, Poles, Germans, assorted Eastern Europeans, and even Protestants and Jews, thus fashioning a team that more

• 1924
- Intercollegiate football features Red Grange and the Four Horsemen

  › First Winter Olympics held; Sonja Henie and Gilles Grafstrom compete in ice skating
- Immigration Quota Law passed by Congress

• 1925
- Scopes Trial conducted

• 1926
- Gertrude Ederle swims the English Channel

• 1927
- Sacco and Vanzetti Trial conducted
- Babe Ruth hits 60 home runs
- Charles Lindbergh makes first solo, nonstop transatlantic flight
- First talking movie appears (*The Jazz Singer*)
- Dempsey–Tunney rematch held (the long-count fight)
- Harlem Globetrotters begin barnstorming tours

closely resembled the makeup of American society. Even here, however, blacks were excluded. Still, Rockne exemplified the American dream of the hard-working immigrant who gained wealth, status, and celebrity by virtue of his abilities.

Notre Dame's football success did much to foster Catholic pride when Catholics felt besieged by the likes of the Ku Klux Klan. The KKK had marched on South Bend before the 1924 season. Notre Dame students repulsed the KKK, but racists managed to gain control of the state government. Notre Dame stood as a bulwark against such WASP fanaticism. In 1928, Al Smith, the Catholic presidential candidate, was swamped in the national election as the KKK campaigned ardently against him, further indicating a lack of full acceptance of Catholics. Football, however, provided Catholics with a semblance of religious respect, as Notre Dame demolished its foes. In the process, it helped incorporate an ethnically diverse and largely working-class constituency into American mainstream culture, and other Catholic colleges and high schools copied the Rockne system to release social tensions on the gridiron.

Notre Dame established a similar dynasty in the 1940s, when it won four national championships. Under coach Frank Leahy, a Rockne protégé, the Catholic juggernaut built a record of 107-13-9, going undefeated from 1946 through 1949. During World War II, Leahy took a coaching respite to join the U.S. Navy, and he urged his players to enlist in the Marines. Football held a close ideological relationship to warfare, not only in its strategy but also in its inculcation of martial spirit, toughness, courage, and leadership ability, and Leahy's admonitions further tied previously marginalized Catholics to a militaristic and nationalistic Americanism during the war. Shortly after the U.S. entry into the war, one-third of the NFL players enlisted, and 638 pros eventually served in the armed forces. By 1950, 80 Navy admirals and 98 Army generals had been football players (Gems, *For Pride* 99–100).

The West Point team proved the biggest challenge for Notre Dame during the war. Featuring Felix "Doc" Blanchard, a bruising fullback, and fleet-footed halfback Glenn Davis, Army rolled over its opponents in 1944 and 1945, averaging more than 50 points per game. Army beat Notre Dame 59-0 and 48-0 in those years,

The Ku Klux Klan arose from nativist sentiments.

Image courtesy of Library of Congress, LC-USZ62-8655.

while Leahy and his charges lent their brains and brawn to the military. The Navy cadets at Annapolis fielded the number two team until Leahy returned to restore Notre Dame to the top. Army and Notre Dame played to a scoreless tie in 1946, but the latter notched a 27-7 victory over Army in 1947. Forty-two of the players from that squad went on to the professional football ranks (Littlewood 135). For many Catholics, Notre Dame, like Seabiscuit, the famed thoroughbred of the late Depression era, represented the underdog, the independent, the outsider who forged a path to success despite the odds.

The Catholic Youth Organization (CYO)

The perception of boxing as a sporting meritocracy, coupled with the hardships of working-class lives, attracted many young men to the sport. World War I demonstrated the need for combative skills, and 23 states authorized boxing by 1917. New York lifted its ban in 1920, and Illinois did so in 1926. By 1928, the *Chicago Tribune* and the *New York Daily News* sponsored regional tournaments designated as the Golden Gloves competition, with winners fighting for the national championship. The Chicago tournament, under the direction of Irish Catholic sports editor Arch Ward, had close ties to the Catholic Youth Organization (CYO), which supplied him with a steady stream of seasoned fighters. By 1933, Golden Gloves champions were competing against international teams, channeling working-class and ethnic skepticism into mainstream American nationalism and patriotism.

That transition proved especially true for Catholics of various ethnic backgrounds who had maintained their traditional lifestyles in communal parishes often directed by Old World priests, who resisted the assimilation efforts of the Irish American hierarchy. In 1930, Bishop Bernard Sheil of Chicago organized the CYO to combat delinquency through sport. The CYO's programs included the largest basketball league in the world, with 120 teams in 1931, and it offered a host of other activities as well, but boxing remained at the root of its popularity and success. Sheil accepted all races and creeds in his boxing tournaments but required a pledge of allegiance to God and country. CYO team members received free medical care, a full suit of clothes, jobs or college scholarships, and all-expenses-paid international trips. Three CYO boxers represented the United States on the 1936 Olympic team, and many others pursued professional careers in the ring. CYO managers assured watchful care, as criminal elements increasingly operated in the pugilistic arena. Though a Catholic enterprise, the CYO followed Sheil's guidelines, which fit nicely with the WASP prescriptions of the Progressive Era, as contesting religious groups found some common ground in sport.

By the end of the decade, Sheil's program had reached nationwide proportions, and he assumed national prominence as a social and labor activist, opposing anti-Semitism and racial discrimination, and as an advisor to the president, his influence extended all the way to the White House. His use of sport to bring about the assimilation of disparate Catholic ethnic groups within mainstream American culture further thwarted working-class radical sentiments, as religious faith triumphed over class consciousness under his guidance. By 1948, the partnership of Bishop Sheil and Arch Ward produced a Golden Gloves tournament that featured 120 bouts, with fights conducted simultaneously in three rings and featuring participants from 31 states (Littlewood 80). The fusion of Catholicism with nationalistic patriotism in the sporting culture pushed a previously ostracized group into mainstream acceptance.

Boxing and Jewish Americans

As with Catholics, sport provided an entrée into mainstream popular culture for Jewish Americans. Despite anti-Semitic sentiments, Jews reached the pinnacle of boxing success during the 1920s and 1930s. Eighteen Jewish champions rose to prominence during that period, most notably Benny Leonard (aka Benjamin Leiner),

1928
> Amelia Earhart becomes first woman to fly across the Atlantic
- Herbert Hoover elected president

1929
- Stock Market Crash signals the Great Depression
- Carnegie Report on intercollegiate athletics issued

1930
- Bobby Jones wins Grand Slam in golf
- Catholic Youth Organization founded

1932
- Franklin D. Roosevelt elected president for his first term
- Olympic Games held in Los Angeles; Babe Didrikson, Lillian Copeland, Eleanor Holm, and other U.S. women triumph

1933
- Twenty-First Amendment ratified (repealing Prohibition)
- Civilian Conservation Corps established
- First MLB All-Star Game played

the lightweight titleholder. Jackie Fields (Jacob Finkelstein) won a gold medal as a featherweight in the 1924 Olympics at the age of 16, and five years later he won the professional welterweight championship. Barney Ross (Barnet Rosofsky) wore the Star of David on his trunks en route to winning three world titles in the 1920s. Such boxers changed their names to hide their pugilistic activities from Orthodox parents who disdained fighting. As youths, these fighters had learned their trade on demand in encounters with other ethnic-minority opponents in rough urban ghettos, and Jewish settlement houses even provided boxing lessons. The best became professionals, and their successes, often against other ethnic-minority boxers, helped dispel stereotypes of Jewish frailty and weakness.

Jewish athletes also starred as basketball players. The South Philadelphia Hebrew All-Stars gained a national reputation, and Irish and Polish barnstormers and numerous semipro contingents offered competition in Midwestern cities. So many Jews starred on the basketball court that observers considered it to be "a Jewish sport," for which Jews had a particular affinity and aptitude.

Ascendancy of a Black Sporting Culture

During and after World War I, more than a million blacks left the South for Northern cities in a mass exodus. In the Northern urban centers, a vibrant African American culture revolved around churches, music, sport, and the arts. Black nationalists such as Marcus Garvey and W.E.B. DuBois preached black pride, self-esteem, and economic independence. The black pride movement, centered in the Harlem area of New York City, became known as the Harlem Renaissance. In 1922, Robert Douglas founded the Harlem Renaissance basketball team (aka the Harlem Rens), composed entirely of African Americans. During the 1925–1926 season, the Rens split a 6-game series with the white New York Celtics before winning 88 straight games. Among the top basketball clubs of the era, the Celtics established themselves by barnstorming throughout the country, and in 1923 they won 204 of the 211 games they played (Riess, *City* 108). Thus the Rens' series with the Celtics proved that they could compete with the best white teams. In 1939, the Rens won the first national professional championship tournament. At that time, the marginal status of professional basketball followed the developmental pattern of pro baseball and football, with teams accepting black players in order to reach a level of acceptability and greater profit, then dismissing them as unworthy.

While New York remained the primary center of the black pride movement, Chicago developed a similar hub of activity. More than 100,000 blacks had flocked to Chicago by 1920, and a decade later the city counted nearly 234,000 African American residents. They established a thriving community within the city known as Bronzeville, and basketball games accompanied the dances at the Savoy Ballroom. The local team, known as the Savoy 5, found it increasingly difficult to find fair play when facing white teams, but with the aid of manager (and then owner) Abe Saperstein, a Jewish agent, they persevered to become one of the most famous basketball teams in the world. In 1927, they began barnstorming, and they thrilled crowds with the swift play, crisp passing, and flair that had distinguished black teams for at least a decade. They adopted a new sobriquet, the Harlem Globetrotters, as a measure of their racial pride and aspirations. Initially operating throughout the Midwestern heartland, the Globetrotters purposely kept games close against town teams in order to insure return engagements. They lost to the Rens in the first pro tournament but captured the national championship a year later, proving their abilities against the best teams in the United States. International tours and the clowning that characterized Globetrotters' games intensified after the National Basketball Association began signing black players at mid-century, which deprived Saperstein of his near monopoly on black talent. For African Americans, basketball became an economic and expressive outlet, and it assumed a growing importance in black urban culture.

Rube Foster, the baseball magnate, also followed Marcus Garvey's lead and founded the Negro National League in 1920 after the race riots of the previous year. Forced to live in urban ghettos and banned from participation in major league baseball—the national pastime—African Americans felt particularly excluded from the mainstream culture. Under Foster's leadership, the Negro National League served as a parallel and an alternative to the white major league system. Independence allowed blacks greater control over their own destiny, but factionalism soon led to a second professional black circuit, known as the Eastern Colored League (ECL). In 1923, one of the ECL teams, Hilldale of Philadelphia, defeated white major league teams in six of seven contests. Such victories by black athletes upset whites' belief in their racial superiority, and baseball commissioner Kenesaw Mountain Landis banned unauthorized interracial play (Mangan and Ritchie 106).

Dark-skinned Latin American players suffered the same indignities as black athletes. Denied the chance to perform in the major league system, Cuban stars joined the Negro National League in 1935. The Cuban stars team was operated by influential New York racketeer Alex Pompez; their polyglot roster included African American, Hispanic, and West Indian players. Pompez constructed a $60,000 stadium, complete with lights for night games, in Manhattan. When the stadium was not in use for baseball, he featured Cuban boxers and an African American football team known as the Brown Bombers, in deference to heavyweight boxing champion Joe Louis. In such ways, nonwhite athletes, promoters, and fans fashioned a parallel, commercialized sporting culture of their own (Burgos).

In Pittsburgh, the underground economy merged with sport, as Gus Greenlee, a local African American rackets boss, also owned the dominant black baseball team, the Pittsburgh Crawfords. Greenlee organized the second Negro National League after the death of Rube Foster, and served as its first president. Under his leadership, the league held its first all-star game at Chicago's Comiskey Park in 1933; the nation's largest black newspapers, the *Chicago Defender* and the *Pittsburgh Courier,* promoted the spectacle. The Crawfords, however, played in their own stadium, rather than renting a white facility, marking their success as a black enterprise, created by and for African Americans (Wiggins, *African* 129; Lester, "Black").

As football rivalries heated up, the search for top athletes provided more opportunities for exceptional African American stars at Northern schools. Fritz Pollard and Paul Robeson had won All-American honors at Brown and Rutgers, respectively, but much was expected of such stars by their white critics and black fans. They had to succeed not only for themselves but also for those who would follow. Jack Trice, the first black athlete to attend Iowa State, wrote himself a note before the 1923 game with Minnesota: "[T]he honor of my race, family and self is at stake. Everyone is expecting me to do big things. I will . . . " (Gems, *For Pride* 117). He played despite a serious injury and died two days later. Such athletes carried the burden of hope and respectability for generations of African Americans. Fred "Duke" Slater proved a standout lineman for Iowa in the early 1920s, earning All-American recognition and playing professionally for the Chicago Cardinals before pursuing a legal career that won him a judgeship. Six different professional teams hired more than a dozen total African American players, until owners banned black players after the 1933 season.

Similarly, Northern college teams routinely left their African American players at home, rather than offend Southern sensibilities, when traveling to the South for interregional contests. Such "gentleman's agreements" between coaches and institutions continued for decades. In one well-known case in 1937, Syracuse left its star player, Wilmeth Sidat-Singh (an African American who had been adopted by a Hindu doctor), behind when it traveled to Maryland, which won the contest 14-0. The following year, in a rematch played at Syracuse, Sidat-Singh took part and led his team to a 51-0 rout.

1934
- First college all-star football game played
- First Masters Tournament (golf) held

1935
- National Youth Administration established
- Works Progress Administration established
- Social Security Act signed
- Congress of Industrial Organizations (CIO) formed
- MLB begins playing night games
- First Heisman Trophy awarded (to Jay Berwanger)

1936
- Avery Brundage, president of U.S. Olympic Committee, elected to International Olympic Committee
- Berlin Olympics ("Nazi Olympics") held: Jesse Owens triumphs, some Jewish athletes boycott

In the boxing arena, top black challengers such as Sam Langford and Harry Wills were denied the opportunity to fight for the heavyweight title; as a result, Langford and Wills fought each other 22 times (Wiggins, *African* 408). The problem lay in the fact that after Jess Willard finally wrested the crown from Jack Johnson, he imposed a color ban, which was maintained by successive white champions. African Americans would wait another generation before Joe Louis got his chance.

Social Significance of Baseball

Baseball's wide popularity clearly established it as the national game, a favorite of the Progressive reformers until the Black Sox scandal. The game quickly redeemed itself during the following decade. The heavy drinking and rowdy baseball players and the brewers who owned several teams threatened the stature of the sport with a negative image, resulting in the formation of the rival American League as a "moral alternative" in 1901. Thereafter baseball adopted a more patriotic and nationalistic stance. During World War I, professional baseball players, who largely avoided the military draft by getting jobs in war-related industries such as shipbuilding, had faced accusations of being unpatriotic slackers. To counter such charges, baseball team owners began playing the "Star-Spangled Banner" at the 1918 World Series games (though it did not become the official national anthem until 1931).

Baseball authorities also took concerted steps to generate more interest in the game (which would, in turn, help create the Golden Age of Sports during the 1920s) by banning the pitch known as the "spitball" (which deceived batters with its unpredictable trajectory) and by using more lively balls. The result was an offensive barrage, particularly an upsurge in home runs, which prompted a strategic shift from the tactical ("scientific") baseball of the past to a new power-oriented game. Whereas only 384 home runs had been hit in 1915, sluggers produced 1,565 in 1930 (Rader, *American Sports* [1983] 203), and the most prodigious power hitter, George "Babe" Ruth, was crucial in ushering in American sport's Golden Age. Even as a pitcher, Ruth had set a new home

Joe Jackson, a central figure in the Black Sox scandal.

Image courtesy of Library of Congress, LC-USZ62-78070.

run record of 29 in 1919, and when the New York Yankees bought him in 1920 for $125,000, he became an everyday position player and hit 54 home runs that year, more than any other *team*, earning a $52,000 salary. The media attention given to Ruth's prodigious blasts helped assuage the injury of the breaking Black Sox scandal and soon produced a cult of celebrity as newspapers assigned reporters to cover Ruth's daily activities.

Despite the tribulations of baseball in the beginning of the decade, the media continually portrayed sport and athletes in an idealistic manner. They espoused sport as a common good, a prime element in the democratic process that fostered a unified, homogenous culture while building character in individual participants. Babe Ruth served as a typical example. Portrayed as an orphan (which was untrue) and raised by Catholic clergy who taught him to play baseball, he soon demonstrated his great potential to reach the pinnacle of success. Despite his humble origins, Ruth was by the end of the decade requesting a higher annual salary than the president of the United States, and sportswriters regaled readers with accounts of his generosity and concern for sick children. In reality, Ruth had been placed in the St. Mary's Industrial School for Boys near his Baltimore home for theft and incorrigibility. Sportswriters also overlooked his gluttony, drinking, womanizing, and generally rough behavior in order to lionize his physical feats in the construction of an American hero. Fans identified with his flaws and human appetites as they cheered his prodigious baseball feats. Indeed, Ruth brought greater cohesion to baseball fans, as middle-class executives might value his productivity, while members of the working class could identify with his physical prowess. Thus baseball, as the national game, represented the values of divergent groups within the society.

Baseball also remained a national measuring stick for race relations. For years, African Americans, along with a few liberal white sportswriters and the communist press, had clamored for the integration of baseball as a symbolic gesture of true freedom and democracy within the United States. World War II, supposedly a struggle for freedom against fascism, seemed an exercise in hypocrisy to African Americans. During the war, at the request of President Franklin Roosevelt, major league baseball was continued as a morale builder for Americans, but, even though team rosters were depleted by military service, owners still refused to hire black players. In 1945, the Washington Senators even employed Bert Shepard, a one-legged veteran of the war, as a pitcher, and the St. Louis Browns featured one-armed Pete Gray in the outfield. In this context, Branch Rickey, general manager of the Brooklyn Dodgers, devised a plan to desegregate the game.

A devout Methodist who was sympathetic to the plight of African Americans, Rickey also proved a shrewd businessman. In order to integrate baseball, he needed a particular player and a viable scheme. To this end, he organized the United States Baseball League, purportedly another major league for black teams. The league soon ceased operations, but a New York law required that military veterans retain their jobs. Rickey had signed Jackie Robinson to a contract, and Robinson, a four-sport letterman at UCLA, had been an Army lieutenant during World War II. His older brother, Mack, though a 1936 Olympic medalist, found work only as a menial laborer upon his return. Jackie demonstrated leadership qualities and confronted racism when he was court-martialed (but exonerated) for refusing to obey segregationist norms during the war. Rickey admired Robinson's courage and fortitude. After his military discharge, Robinson played baseball for the black Kansas City Monarchs before signing with Rickey's black franchise. When the sham league was abandoned, Rickey assigned Robinson to a minor league affiliate in Montreal, a cosmopolitan Canadian city in the International League, to ease his transition to the white circuit. Robinson led the league in batting average, and the next year Rickey brought him to the parent organization. There he endured segregated spring training, racial taunts, threats of violence, and lurking strikes by teammates and opponents. Despite the overwhelming prohibitions and obstacles, he persevered, with the weight of all African Americans to bear. If Rickey's "Great Experiment," as it was termed, failed, it could have ramifications for race relations and blacks' social mobility for years to come.

Record crowds overflowed baseball stadiums when the Dodgers came to town. African Americans traveled hundreds of miles to cheer their hero, who not only conducted himself with the utmost honor but also won the Rookie of the Year award. In 1949, Robinson won the National League's Most Valuable Player award, and he played with the Dodgers until 1956, leading them to six National League championships and a World Series title. Moreover, his dignified demeanor and performance paved the way for other African Americans, and, in 1948, Bill Veeck, the flamboyant owner of the Cleveland Indians, hired Larry Doby, the first black player in the American League. In 1959, the Boston Red Sox became the last team to integrate, and by that time black ball players had won 9 of the 13 Most Valuable Player awards in the National League

1938
- National Invitational Tournament (basketball) launched
- Joe Louis–Max Schmeling boxing rematch staged

1939
- First televised baseball game is shown
- National Collegiate Athletic Association basketball tournament is launched
- New York Rens (all-black team) reign as pro basketball champions
- Little League Baseball founded

1941–1945
- U.S. involved in World War II

1943–1954
- All-American Girls Baseball League operates

1945
- United Nations founded

Jackie Robinson: More than an athlete, a racial pioneer.

AP Photo/John Rooney

since 1947 (Gorn and Goldstein 217). Many of the black stars played for the Brooklyn Dodgers, emphasizing the visionary acumen of Branch Rickey and the pioneering fortitude of Jackie Robinson.

Robinson's entry to the ranks of major league baseball came six years before the crucial *Brown v. Board of Education* case, in which the Supreme Court struck down segregation. In that sense, Robinson, Rickey, and Brooklyn served as catalysts to social change in the United States. Robinson's exciting play, along with his dignified demeanor, as well as the thousands of African Americans who turned out to witness his games, indicated that a significant transition had already occurred in race relationships.

Attraction of Sport for the Working Class

Inner-city sports attracted large numbers of participants and spectators during the enforced leisure of the Depression. For the best athletes, sports even provided a way to earn a living. Both men and women played softball, which required little equipment and less space than baseball. The American Softball Association offered championships for men and women in 1933, and by 1940 it claimed three million players. Chicago, the birthplace of the game, fielded hundreds of teams in nightly games.

Neighborhood teams played for pride and money. Even boys' teams earned $10 to $20 for their victories, as gamblers and taverns operated local leagues. By 1933, teams could earn $1,500 in prize money per tournament, the equivalent of the annual family income that year. Mario Bruno, one of many Italian players in the city, won $1,650 in one game at a time when the local bank would not offer $100 for a paid-up home. Another legendary Italian player, Rocco "Lewa" Yacilla, pitched for more than 50 years, as softball provided workers with a measure of autonomy and economic mobility. This sport-based black market economy available to the working class during the Depression upheld the faith in capitalism, thus negating the efforts of the radical workers' sport movements, and, unlike developments in Europe, socialist sport movements dissipated in the United States after the Depression.

The Windy City Softball League started play in 1934, and the tournament of the *Chicago Evening American* newspaper consisted of 4,800 games witnessed by more than a million spectators. Women's games proved particularly attractive to many fans, as some teams featured players in satin shorts. During the summer months, the women's games drew a greater following than the Chicago White Sox did at their professional baseball games (Gems, *Windy* 190–191).

For many unemployed young men, billiard halls also proved to be a strong attraction during the Depression. With the repeal of Prohibition in 1933, taverns reopened and catered to the bachelor subculture with cheap, coin-operated pool tables. Some taverns also provided alleys for bowling, a sport that surpassed even

INTERNATIONAL PERSPECTIVE

The Workers' Sport Movement

At the end of the nineteenth century, workers' gymnastic and sport movements began to develop in various European countries. They were founded by men who could not identify with the conservative political leanings of the existing gymnastic and sport organizations. Moreover, the fact that the bourgeois gymnastic and sport associations had increasingly begun to dissociate themselves from the proletariat played a considerable role in this development. The rise of workers' sport was also due, finally, to improved living and working conditions, such as the regulation of working hours. The workers' gymnastic and sport movement was primarily a political movement, whose members were predominantly skilled workers and whose leaders were not infrequently intellectuals.

The largest association in the international workers' sport movement was the Workers' Gymnastic Federation (later the Workers' Gymnastics and Sports Federation, or ATSB), founded in Germany in 1893, which, in spite of fierce opposition on the part of the traditional associations, already had 350,000 members by the First World War and boasted 1.2 million members by 1929. After the turn of the century, workers' sport associations also developed in Belgium, France, England, Italy, and Austria, and after the war they appeared in many other countries of Europe, including Finland, Denmark, Norway, Czechoslovakia, and Switzerland. The workers' sport clubs and associations were closely linked with the workers' movement, and their members were more or less radical supporters of socialism and international solidarity.

In 1913, Belgian, Italian, German, English, and French workers formed the first International Federation in Ghent, Belgium, which was revived in 1920 as the Lucerne Sport International, later known as the Socialist Worker Sport International (SASI). The line between social democracy and communism was drawn by international workers' sport federations in 1921, when the Red Sports International (RSI) was founded under the control of the Communist International as a countermovement to SASI. In Germany, however, the social democracy–oriented ATSB did not separate from its communist clubs until 1928, with the latter subsequently joining the so-called "Red Sports" movement. Both nationally and internationally, relations between the socialist and communist sport organizations were entirely hostile, not least because of their quite different aims and objectives.

The workers' sport movement aimed, among other things, to make the daily lives of workers less burdensome, to provide opportunities for pleasure and relaxation, to create solidarity, and to improve the workers' health—not only in preparation for the next day's work but also for the coming class struggle. While socialists favored changing the system by democratic means, the communist workers' sport movement was bracing itself for an armed struggle with its middle- and upper-class foes. From the very beginning, the workers' sport movement regarded itself as a more humanely inspiring alternative to bourgeois sports, which reproduced the pressures of the working day in their orientation toward competition and record setting. The workers' sport movement, in contrast, wanted to provide sport for everyone and attached little importance—at least in theory—to comparing performance and success. However, such was the fascination for strong sporting performance and the setting and breaking of records that attempts to organize sports without judging performance—playing mere "friendly matches" in football (soccer), for example, instead of forming leagues—was simply not feasible.

Thus, despite the enmity between the workers' and the middle-class sport movements on the political front, there were no significant differences in their sporting activities, with the spectrum of sports played in both movements ranging from German *Turnen* (gymnastics) and swimming to soccer and track and field. Unlike the middle-class sport associations, the workers' sport movement publicly advocated equal rights for men and women, at least on paper. In actual fact, however, women faced enormous prejudice and opposition even in workers' sport.

>> continued

•1947

• Jackie Robinson reintegrates baseball

•1949

• National Basketball League (NBL) and Basketball Association of America (BAA) merge to form National Basketball Association (NBA)

• Ladies Professional Golf Association (LPGA) founded

>> *continued*

Highlights in workers' sport included national and international festivals, such as those held in Germany in 1921 and 1929, in which more than a hundred thousand athletes took part. A distinctive feature of the workers' sport movement was its international orientation, and even national sport festivals attracted numerous athletes from abroad (for example, those held in Austria in 1926, in Belgium in 1930, and in Latvia in 1932 and 1936).

Workers' sport festivals and Olympiads were intended as a countermovement to the Olympic Games, with their nationalist tendencies and their fixation on records. The first workers' sport Olympiad, for instance, organized by the SASI and held at Frankfurt am Main, Germany, in 1925, had as its motto, "No more war." All 150,000 partici-pants were required to take part in mass outdoor exercises. In 1931, at the second workers' sport Olympiad in Vienna, one hundred thousand working-class athletes from 26 countries marched through the festively decorated streets of the Austrian capital.

The RSI held its own sport festivals, the *spartakiades*, named after the Roman rebel slave Spartacus. They took place in Moscow in 1928 and in Berlin in 1931. The last workers' sport Olympiad took place in Antwerp, Belgium, in 1937. Organized by the two Internationals, it was intended as both a sporting and a political response to the 1936 Olympic Games in National Socialist (Nazi) Berlin. The Olympiad in Antwerp was a successful demonstration of worker solidarity, even if the German and Austrian workers' sport organizations had already been crushed by that time.

Although workers' sport organizations survived the Second World War in several countries, such as Finland and Israel, workers' sport as an international movement fell victim not only to the Cold War but also to changes in living conditions. Indeed, numerous answers might be offered to the question of why workers' sport—even in its heyday in the 1920s—was never able to develop into the leading sport movement. Reasons range from the workers' own lack of financial resources, insufficient support from their political parties, and political quarrels within the movement to the general fascination surrounding competitive sport and the breaking of records. Even in Germany, the country with the largest workers' sport movement, the overwhelming majority of workers belonged to bourgeois sport clubs.

Information from Steinberg, David A., "The Workers' Sport Internationals 1902–28," and Wheeler, Robert, "Organized Sport and Organized Labour: The Workers' Sport Movement"; Krüger, Arnd and James Riordan, eds. *The Story of Worker Sport.* Champaign, IL: Human Kinetics, 1996.

softball during the 1930s, gaining particular prominence in Midwestern cities such as Detroit, St. Louis, and Chicago. The latter counted nearly five hundred thousand bowlers in more than nine hundred leagues by the end of the decade. Bowling was the most popular sport for women, and during the 1930s in Chicago alone more than fifteen thousand held membership in the Women's International Bowling Congress (WIBC). The 1935 national tournament, held in Chicago, provided more than $15,000 in prizes (Gems, *Windy* 191), and more than ten thousand women registered for one local tournament (Riess, *City* 78). Poles displayed a particular affinity for the game, and Polish champions became heroes in their ethnic neighborhoods. Some earned enough to forgo working-class occupations in favor of buying their own businesses, while others were elected to political offices. Many working-class youth continued to view sport as a meritocracy where one might gain social mobility based on physical prowess rather than on wealth, lofty social status, or education.

Alternative political parties made feeble attempts to gain greater visibility and resurrect class consciousness among workers. The Communist Party organized a Workers' Olympics in Chicago during the summer of 1932 as a cultural alternative to the IOC events held in Los Angeles, as sport assumed greater political connotations. Another workers' athletic meet took place in New York in 1936 but found little success. The communists urged sport for all instead of emphasizing elite athletic stars. They

Bowling offered both male and female working-class patrons the opportunity for social mobility.

Image courtesy of Library of Congress, LC-USZ62-122873.

especially championed the cause of African American athletes, but their efforts made little difference at the polls. For most Americans, sport had become an integral part of the capitalist system, providing an opiate for the disenchanted masses. While those stricken by poverty might question the failed economy, they still maintained hope in sport as a meritocracy that valued their cherished physicality. In the 1932 presidential election, the socialist candidate garnered only nine hundred thousand votes, while the communist entrant gained just one hundred thousand (Pope, *The New* 293).

Sport as a Political Tool

The federal government became increasingly involved in sport after World War I, with the United States Supreme Court ruling in 1922 that baseball was exempt from antitrust laws. Baltimore, one of the defunct teams in the Federal League, a third major circuit that lasted from 1913 to 1915, had sued major league baseball in an antitrust suit, but the court reasoned that baseball was not a business and thus could not be held to the same commercial statutes that affected other businesses engaged in interstate commerce. This exemption allowed baseball team owners to operate with impunity in regard to labor relations for most of the twentieth century.

Throughout the 1930s, sport was given more overt political significance, as fascists gained control of government in Italy, Germany, Spain, and Japan. Hitler's doctrine of Aryan supremacy could be challenged within the athletic sphere, particularly in sports that required individual competition, and a Jewish American boxer, "Slapsie" Maxie Rosenbloom, upheld Jewish dignity by defeating the German light heavy-weight champ, Adolph Heuser, in 1933. Thereafter, Hitler refused to allow competition between Germans and Jews. Other sporting events highlighted the ideological differences between democracy and Nazi fascism throughout the remainder of the decade, as illustrated by two boxing bouts between Joe Louis and German heavy-weight Max Schmeling.

Louis and Schmeling first battled on June 19, 1936. Though not a Nazi, Schmeling represented the Nazi regime of Adolf Hitler in the eyes of Americans. Hitler had already embarked upon his program of anti-Semitic oppression and European aggression, and by that time the United States had assumed a position of leadership in the world community of democratic, nontotalitarian governments. Thus the fight represented more than just a boxing match, as conflicting ideologies clashed in the pugilistic arena. Schmeling shocked America and delighted Hitler with a 12th-round knockout of the seemingly invincible Louis.

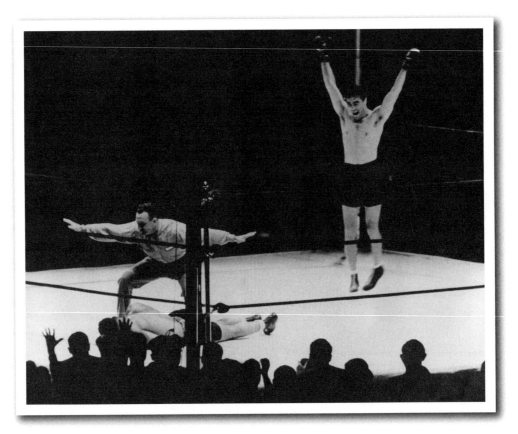

Despite Schmeling's stunning victory, Hitler's belief in the construction of an Aryan super race suffered a severe setback in August 1936. Germany hosted the Olympic Games that year, and Hitler and German sport officials used the occasion to glorify the Nazi Reich and its fascist ideology in its efficient organization, neoclassical architectural monuments, and introduction of rituals and symbols in grand spectacles and lavish displays. Nazi administrators ensured that no "pure" Jews represented the German Olympic team, so as not to compromise Hitler's racist doctrine. The Nazi persecution of both Jews and Roma ("Gypsies") raised international concerns. The treatment of the former even prompted an Olympic boycott movement, but Avery Brundage, head of the American Olympic Committee, declined to participate in the protest.

At the competition, African American athletes severely damaged the doctrine of Aryan supremacy by defeating German male athletes in the most prominent track-and-field events. Jesse Owens, the collegiate champion from Ohio State University, won four gold medals, a record that lasted nearly 50 years. The last, in the 400-meter relay, elicited great controversy in the United States, when Coach Lawson Robertson substituted Owens and another African American, Ralph Metcalfe, for Sam Stoller and Marty Glickman, both of whom were Jewish. In the 1600-meter relay, however, the coach failed to use his black stars, one of whom, Archie Williams, was the Olympic champion, and the United States finished second to Great Britain. Both decisions saved Hitler from further international embarrassment as events weren't won by those he deemed inferior to Aryans.

Despite Owens' heroics at the Olympics, he returned to a largely racist America. Stripped of his amateur status by the AAU for refusing to participate in a post-Olympic tour of Europe (he wanted to return home), he had few prospects in the United States. At a New York reception in his honor, he could not even enter through the front door of the prestigious Waldorf-Astoria Hotel. In addition, the AAU denied him the Sullivan Award, honoring the best amateur athlete, and thereafter Owens earned income by racing against dogs and horses in deplorable exhibitions. Thus his heroic stature proved tenuous as an African American—and temporary once his usefulness had been expended.

In 1937, Joe Louis knocked out Jim Braddock to become the heavyweight champion, and on June 22, 1938, he met Schmeling in a rematch at Yankee Stadium. Louis avenged his earlier loss with a first-round knockout, as an estimated 67 percent of Americans listened by radio (Rader, *American Sports* [1983] 326). Louis held the title for 12 years, but shortly after the attack on Pearl Harbor he entered the Army. Throughout the war, he lifted morale with patriotic speeches, and he donated the proceeds of exhibition matches to the Navy and Army relief funds that benefited war orphans. And, though the military still practiced segregation, he promoted treasury bonds in the black community. After the war, eroded skills caused Louis to retire temporarily, but, despite his loyalty and generosity to the government, he was sued by the Internal Revenue Service for back taxes, leaving him bankrupt. Ezzard Charles, another African American, beat him in a 1950 title fight, and Louis spent his later years as a doorman in Las Vegas (Max Schmeling paid for his funeral), a sad ending symbolic of the treatment of African American heroes whose past exploits were too often forgotten.

Sporting confrontations between the United States and Germany continued for several years before open conflict erupted in World War II. Don Budge, an American who learned to play tennis on public courts in California, lost a Wimbledon match to the German baron, Gottfried von Cramm, in 1935. In their rematch on July 20, 1937, as part of international team play in the Davis Cup tournament, Budge won one of the greatest tennis matches ever played, and he led the Americans to victory over England, providing their first Davis Cup title since 1926. In 1938, Budge won the Australian, French, British, and U.S. open championships, becoming the first to achieve the Grand Slam in tennis. Still, Budge failed to gain the attention accorded to other sport stars, as Europe moved closer to another devastating war.

As American athletes confronted fascism abroad, other Americans struggled in their quest for acceptance within the American polity. Asian Americans and African Americans still labored in segregated schools and unequal social conditions, and with the outbreak of the war Japanese Americans on the West Coast were sequestered in internment camps, suspected of treachery and collusion with the enemy due merely to their ancestry. In such camps, the Nisei, second-generation Japanese Americans, practiced American sport forms as one means of demonstrating their loyalty and patriotism. At the Gila River Relocation Camp in Arizona, three baseball leagues featured 28 teams, and four to five thousand spectators showed up for the big games (Elias, *Baseball* 127). Nisei men petitioned the government to let them fight for their country, and eventually the Army's 442nd Regimental Combat Team, composed of Nisei soldiers, embarked for Europe, where they became the most decorated unit in the entire Army, dispelling any notions of conflicted national allegiance.

During the war, some African Americans also served (and devotedly), in segregated units, and they became increasingly dissatisfied with their lot. They

Jesse Owens, star of the 1936 American Olympic track team.
Associated Press

campaigned for jobs, an end to segregation, and fair housing practices, and they staged sit-ins and protest marches. In 1943, the volatile situation erupted in reactionary race riots, with attacks by whites against Mexican Americans in Los Angeles and against blacks in New York and Detroit. Riots in Detroit resulted in two days of fighting over recreational space in a public park.

Problems of Intercollegiate Sport

After World War II, the GI Bill allowed military veterans to attend college via government subsidy. By 1946, more than two million American veterans enrolled in higher education classes (Spears and Swanson 303). Their introduction to campus life provided a boon to intercollegiate athletics, as the veterans strengthened college teams that played before immense crowds of cheering fans. The high expectations of success intensified recruiting efforts by coaches and boosters, and widespread cheating, dubious inducements, and unethical recruiting practices led the National Collegiate Athletics Association (NCAA) to issue its Sanity Code in 1948 in order to reinforce amateurism, provide limited financial aid to athletes, spur adherence to academic standards, and enable greater institutional control over growing athletic enterprises. In the absence of strong enforcement efforts, however, the athletic wars and transgressions continued, most noticeably in basketball and football.

Basketball, in particular, grew in popularity, and in some rural states, such as Indiana, Kentucky, and parts of the South, basketball became entrenched in the local culture, as local or state teams symbolized civic or state pride. Oklahoma A&M featured a nearly 7-foot-tall (2.13-meter-tall) center, Bob Kurland, whose defensive goaltending forced the NCAA to adopt a new rule making it illegal to swat shots from the basket. Offensively, however, no rule prevented Kurland's dunk shot, and Oklahoma A&M won national championships in 1945 and 1946. In the latter year, Kurland led the nation in scoring.

The popular image of sport suffered a severe shock in 1950, when the United States Military Academy expelled almost the entire varsity football team for cheating on exams. A year later, a bigger scandal erupted when the New York district attorney charged more than 30 college basketball players with point-shaving. Gangsters, gamblers, and racketeers had long been associated with professional boxing, billiards, horse racing, and even baseball, but collegiate sport had enjoyed a relatively pristine image in that regard. Investigations revealed, however, that the point-shaving practice had been in effect since 1945. Under the scheme, oddsmakers bribed players with cash to keep scores within their predicted totals in order to assure their winning bets. By 1951,

INTERNATIONAL PERSPECTIVE

Gretel Bergmann—Jewish Athlete at the 1936 Olympic Games

When the National Socialists (Nazis) took power in 1933, the 1936 Olympic Games (which had already been assigned to Berlin in 1931) were at risk for a number of reasons. For one thing, the internationalism of the Olympic Games and their orientation toward records and competition were not in keeping with the political ideology of the new leaders, who valued men's physical exercise as a means of bringing forth men fit and able to fight for their fatherland. However, Adolf Hitler was soon persuaded by the benefits that the publicity of the Games would bring. He intended that they would demonstrate the superiority, and also the purportedly peaceful intentions, of the Third Reich. As a result, the National Socialists organized and staged a sport festival that diffused national socialist ideology through rituals and symbols.

But the Games were also jeopardized by the National Socialists' racial ideology and policies, such as their delusions of superiority. The race politics of the Nazis led to the marginalization of, and finally the attempt to eradicate, races deemed inferior, especially the Jews but also the Roma ("Gypsies"). In many countries, including the United States, some called for a boycott of the Games, but these efforts were unsuccessful, due in part to racist attitudes in many Western countries. Nevertheless, the National Socialists had to accept the participation of Jewish athletes from other countries. At the same time, they made every effort to keep the German team "free of Jews" without arousing the attention of the rest of the world as to their intentions. One victim of their policy was Gretel Bergmann.

Margarethe Bergmann was born in 1914. An enthusiastic athlete from her childhood, she was active in many types of sport, including running, swimming, tennis, and skiing. From the age of 10, she competed successfully in various track-and-field competitions, and in 1933 her jump of 4 feet 9 1/2 inches (1.51 meters) placed her among the best high jumpers in Germany.

With the Nazi ascent to power, Jewish life in Germany underwent rapid and radical change. Among other discriminations, Jews like Gretel Bergmann were excluded from "German" sport organizations. They were allowed, for a time, to become members of Jewish sport groups, which were at first tolerated but then abolished after the Olympic Games in 1936. The Bergmanns soon realized that there was no future for Jews in Germany, and, during a business trip to London. Edwin Bergmann registered his daughter at the London Polytechnic, where she was immediately accepted by the college's sports teams. In June 1934, Gretel Bergmann became the British champion with a high jump of 5 feet (1.55 meters).

In 1934, Bergmann returned to Germany to participate in preparations for the 1936 Olympic Games, since refusing to do so might have had negative results for her family and for Jewish sport organizations. The Third Reich's sports leaders wanted Jewish champions to participate in training for the Olympics in order to counter international charges of racism. In the meantime, however, Germany had begun intense preparations for the Olympics, and while "Aryan" athletes of both sexes received enormous support, Jews had to train in poor conditions. Gretel Bergmann was the only Jew permitted to attend a training camp with other "German" athletes, doing so in the autumn of 1934 and the spring of 1936.

At the Württemberg Championships in 1936, Gretel Bergmann high-jumped 5 feet 2 1/2 inches (1.6 meters), equaling the German record set by Elfriede Kaun. Since this would normally have won her a place on the Olympic team, she was surprised to learn on July 16, 1936—about two weeks before the opening ceremony—that she would not be part of the German team. Only two athletes were nominated for the women's high jump, and she was not one of them. The National Socialists thus gave up a good chance of winning a medal simply to avoid having a Jew on their team.

Since the American team was already en route for the Games at the time of Bergmann's exclusion, no major protest on their part was to be expected. Her German teammates were told that an injury prevented her from participating. In the end, only "half-Jews" were included in the German team: Rudi Ball, one of the most popular of German ice hockey players, and Helene Mayer, a fencer, who was teaching at an American college at the time.

With no hope of any future in Germany, Gretel Bergmann left her home country in May 1937 to settle in the United States, determined never to set foot in Germany again. She married a former Jewish athlete and physician and had two children, and she did visit Germany in 1999, when sport facilities in Berlin and her native city were named in her honor.

Information from Bergmann, Gretel. *Ich war die große jüdische Hoffnung.* Ed. Haus der Geschichte Baden-Württemberg. Karlsruhe: 2003; Teichler, Hans Joachim. "Zum Ausschluss der deutschen Juden von den Olympischen Spielen 1936 (on the exclusion of German Jews from the Olympic Games 1936)." *Makkabi Deutschland 1965-1995.* Ed. Makkabi Deutschland. München: Makkabi 1995, 47–62.

players at seven different colleges in New York and the Midwest faced conspiracy indictments for fixing games over the previous two seasons. The NBA banned all charged players for life, the NCAA suspended the University of Kentucky for a year, and Long Island University suspended its own basketball program for six years. Critics assailed the crime nexus in New York City, which effectively diminished the previous attraction of games in Madison Square Garden. Consequently, the NCAA basketball tournament assumed greater prominence than the NIT (National Invitational Tournament). As football recruiting scandals and overt subsidization of athletes came to light, the NCAA forfeited its Sanity Code regulations in favor of acknowledged athletic scholarships but enhanced its enforcement capabilities with a corps of investigators.

Fan loyalty and boosterism also generated numerous problems. The over-emphasis on winning pushed coaches' salaries beyond those of college presidents, and even average coaches made more money than full professors. Teams vied for the best players to improve their records and status, and schools and municipalities built ever-larger stadiums to hold increasing numbers of fans as commercialization engulfed collegiate football. Notre Dame even left its campus for the biggest "home" games, opting to play at Chicago's mammoth Soldier Field. In 1929, the Carnegie Foundation published a three-year study of intercollegiate sports that confirmed the existence of serious ethical improprieties. Students and other loyal fans bet thousands of dollars on games, and Ohio State University supporters considered their team victories a "financial investment." In addition to the rampant commercialization and materialism associated with college sports, coaches and alumni, as well as interested "boosters," went to great lengths to insure winning teams, including widespread recruitment and subsidization of star athletes. While the Carnegie Report raised a red warning flag, it had little influence and no power to effect change, and conflict persisted between the ideal of amateurism, on one hand, and commercialization and emphasis on winning, on the other. Only the University of Chicago eventually discontinued its athletic program (in 1939).

Sport and the Maintenance of Class Status

Although sport brought ethnic-minority, racial, and working-class groups into the mainstream culture, it still allowed for the retention of social differences based on wealth. The expense of some sports largely excluded those who could not afford equipment, lessons, or club membership fees. Moreover, the aristocratic concept of amateurism still held sway among the upper classes.

The Interwar Era saw an increase in the popularity of golf, as illustrated, for example, by the creation of the Walker Cup—a trophy donated in 1922 by George Walker, former president of the United States Golf Association (USGA)—to foster nationalism, as amateur teams from Great Britain and the United States competed for the prize. Five years later, Samuel Ryder, a British businessman, offered a similar award for professional teams. Americans began to take notice when Francis Ouimet, a working-class caddy and amateur player, defeated British professionals in the U.S. Open tournament in 1913. Walter Hagen, an American pro, dominated the game thereafter and spurred reforms of elitist covenants that had restricted clubhouse usage to the wealthy. As the star player, clubs had to relax their standards against professionals to allow Hagen to use their facilities. Gate receipts and prize money spawned professional tours, with Hagen accumulating most of the winnings and product endorsements. His extravagant lifestyle captured public attention and gained him celebrity status.

Only Bobby Jones, one of the last amateur gentlemen, rivaled Walter Hagen in prominence. A lawyer who retained his amateur status throughout his competitive career, Jones won 13 of the 21 tournaments that he entered from 1923 through 1930. His most amazing feat occurred in 1930, when he won the American and British amateur titles, as well as the open championships in both countries, which at that time constituted golf's Grand Slam. Jones then retired from active competition at the age of 28 and devoted time to designing the Augusta National golf course in Georgia, which began hosting the Masters Golf Tournament in 1934.

On the men's professional circuit, Sam Snead and Ben Hogan became household names. Both started their careers in the 1930s, but Snead played over six decades. Snead's graceful swing and his development of the innovative straddle technique for putting resulted in 81 victories on the Professional Golfers' Association (PGA) tour. Both Snead and Hogan derived from working-class roots, and both learned to play the game by working as caddies. The intense Hogan rivaled Snead for golfing laurels. He turned professional at the tender age of 17 in 1929 but didn't win a tournament until 1940. Though small in stature at 5 feet 8 inches (1.7 meters) and 135 pounds (61 kilograms), he won 62 more tournaments thereafter. His greatest triumph, however, occurred after a horrific auto accident in 1949. Playing in pain and still in bandages, Hogan persevered to win the 1950 U.S. Open in a playoff. In 1953, he founded a golf equipment manufacturing company that made him a millionaire. At his death in 1997, his estate held a value of $100 million. For many, Hogan represented the American dream. He literally fought his way out of poverty, beating other boys in battles over newspaper sales and caddying opportunities, and a strong work ethic, along with fierce pride and courageous will, allowed him to overcome the odds and achieve great success. Despite such rags to riches stories, however, the cost of golf greatly limited working-class participation.

Tennis, too, maintained a sense of elitism, with access to the sport at country clubs and tennis clubs reserved largely for upper-class white men and women. The 1920s star "Big Bill" Tilden dominated the tennis world. A tall, thin, graceful athlete, Tilden overpowered his opponents, winning six consecutive U.S. championships starting in 1920. Sports journalist Paul Gallico described Tilden this way:

> Of all the colorful champions of that era, this man was far and away the oddest fish. As a player he dominated the decade at a period when there were more stars, national or international, to challenge him than ever before or since. As a box office attraction both amateur and professional, he lifted the gate from peanuts into the million-dollar class. As a person he was as strange, independent, and controversial a figure as ever strutted across the sports scene. . . . He was a colossus! He was a tremendous athlete of unparalleled skill and inexhaustible endurance. (Gallico 120)

Bobby Jones became the darling of golf fans. The working class could identify with his temper and competitive zeal, and the upper classes admired his etiquette, sense of fair play, and adherence to the amateur code. He even penalized himself for an infraction.

Image courtesy of Library of Congress, LC-USZ62-98076

Tilden was the first American to win the Wimbledon singles crown (doing so in 1920 and repeating the feat in 1921 and 1930), and he dominated American tennis throughout the decade. He authored books and plays thereafter but lost favor due to his homosexuality and even served prison time for pedophilia in the 1940s (Leab 429–431). In the eyes of the working class, tennis retained an effete image well into the twentieth century (Gems, *Windy* 158).

Women's Fight for Inclusion

While female athletes did not gain the media coverage or accolades accorded to men, they did make substantial gains in sport during the 1920s as part of the larger sweep of social change and of women's activism in pursuit of public roles. One of the major goals of the women's movement in the United States was achieved in 1920, when women won the right to vote. Music, theater, and movies all presented more liberated images of women, and young urban women in particular sought new ways to express themselves. Prominent female members of the American Physical Education Association favored physical activity and gender-specific sports such as basketball as beneficial to women's health; however, they opposed competition in public spectacles as damaging to women's physiology and deemed such competition unhealthy and morally corrupting for women, who they feared might succumb to the problems that marked men's sports. Despite such obstacles, U.S. women persevered, and many working-class women competed on athletic club and company teams. American women also took note of changes in sport and society beyond American shores, as in France, where Alice Milliat forcefully advocated greater female participation in track-and-field competition.

While women made gradual progress in American life throughout the 1920s, many onlookers still questioned their abilities, as well as the propriety of female participation in the sporting culture. Women were still expected by many to be passive supporters of male athletes, and even cheerleading roles had remained the province of men because it was assumed that fans would not follow or take orders from a female leader. Women did enter the ranks of cheerleaders during the 1920s, however, and throughout the following decade they continued to challenge the traditional roles assigned to them.

In spite of the myth of being a weaker sex, women entered various sporting contests that were looked upon as male domains. Female pilots, for example, proved that they had abilities equal to those of men. In 1932, Amelia Earhart flew solo across the Atlantic Ocean, matching the historic adventure of Charles Lindbergh in 1927. Jacqueline Cochran received her pilot's license in 1932, and by the time she retired she had surpassed all pilots, male or female, in flight records for speed, altitude, and distance. Though less prominent than those women who conquered natural obstacles, Jackie Mitchell drew national attention as a baseball player. In a 1931 exhibition game, the 17-year-old phenom pitched for the Chattanooga Lookouts in a contest with the New York Yankees and, to the amazement of all, struck out both Babe Ruth and Lou Gehrig. Baseball commissioner Kenesaw Mountain Landis responded by voiding her contract on the dubious grounds that the game was too strenuous for women.

Baseball

In 1943, with many professional baseball players serving in the military, Cubs owner Philip Wrigley initiated the All-American Girls Baseball League (AAGBL) as a Midwestern alternative. It was originally designed as a softball organization, but the women soon graduated to baseball rules and enjoyed immense popularity. They drew nearly a million patrons in 1948, and the league lasted until 1954. While such initiatives provided opportunities for women, the players had to adhere to middle-class norms of respectability, which required proper etiquette, makeup, and a skirted uniform. The all-white league also further marginalized long-suffering African American athletes.

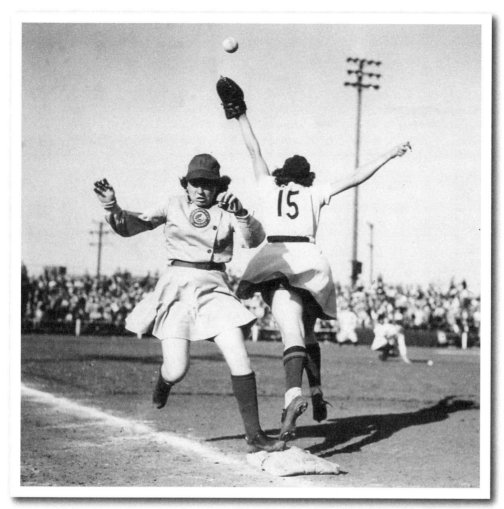

Marie Mahoney of the South Bend Blue Sox is safe at first as Margaret Danhauser reaches for a high throw during an AAGBL game in 1947.

Photo by Mark Rucker/ Transcendental Graphics, Getty Images

Track and Field

Throughout the 1920s, many women were exposed to track-and-field competition in the industrial recreation programs of large employers, but Lillian Copeland attended the University of Southern California and became an outstanding athlete, winning nine national titles and setting world records in javelin and discus. In the United States, the Amateur Athletic Union (AAU) offered its first track-and-field championship for women in 1924. At the 1932 Los Angeles Olympic Games, Copeland won the gold medal in the discus throw, setting another world record. Her teammate Mildred "Babe" Didrikson had initially gained fame as an All-American basketball star for the Employers Casualty Insurance Company of Dallas, and the company entered her in the national track championship of 1932, where she single-handedly captured the team title by winning six events, setting four world records (Guttmann, *Sports: The First Five Millenia* 127). At the 1932 Olympics, she won gold medals in the javelin and hurdles and won a controversial silver in the high jump despite a world record (judged a faulty jump).

Tidye Pickett, an African American woman, fared considerably worse as a basketball and track star. Both Pickett and Louise Stokes, another African American, qualified for the 1932 Olympic track team, only to be belittled by teammates and snubbed. Neither was chosen to compete, though Pickett did run for the 1936 Olympic team, where, though favored in the hurdles race, she broke her foot in a preliminary and could not compete. Unlike Fritz Pollard, whose son won a bronze medal at the 1936 Games, Pickett faded into obscurity. Women received little fanfare compared with the coverage of men, and in Pickett's case only the African American newspapers cared at all.

Milliat and the Push for Female Track and Field

Alice Milliat of France was the driving force behind the international women's sport movement, which fought for women's access to and their acknowledgment in various sports (including soccer), with a focus on the premier Olympic sport of track and field. In 1921, she was elected president of the French Association of Women's Sport (founded in 1917). In the same year she initiated an international women's meeting in soccer and track and field and organized a conference where the International Federation for Women's Sport (FSFI) was founded. Under Milliat's presidency, the FSFI organized four very successful "Olympic" Games for women: in Paris in 1922, Gothenburg in 1926, Prague in 1930, and London in 1934. Held in 1922, the first Women's Olympics offered a day-long international track-and-field meet in Pershing Stadium in Paris, where competitors set 18 new records. The record setters included two American schoolgirls: Camille Sabie, who set the mark in the 100-yard hurdles race, and Lucile Godbold, who won the shot put (www.colacoll.edu/edenslibrary/jane/Teammates.htm). Twenty thousand spectators watched the women's efforts, and the festival's success fostered a larger competition at the second women's World Games in Gothenburg, Sweden.

The controversial finish of this race curtailed Olympic endurance events for women, and the 800-meter event was not restored until 1960.

Photo by Central Press/Hulton Archive/Getty Images

Concerned over the women's appropriation of the Olympic name, and faced with losing control over a growing sphere of athletics, the IOC and the International Amateur Athletic Federation (IAAF) negotiated with the FSFI. One of the most controversial issues was the number of events. The FSFI demanded 10 track and field events for women at the 1928 Olympic Games in Amsterdam, but the IOC and the IAAF ultimately offered only five: high jump, discus throw, 100-meter dash, 4 × 100 meter relay, and 800-meter run. After long debates, the FSFI accepted this offer, and women participated for the first time in Olympic track events. A 16-year-old Chicagoan, Elizabeth Robinson, won the 100-meter race. Nine athletes participated in the 800-meter event, which was won by the German runner Lina Radke-Batschauer in the world-record time of 2:16.8, but the race proved controversial.

After the competition, several runners sat on the ground, exhausted and disappointed. This allegedly unfeminine behavior and unaesthetic sight caused indignation among the officials and journalists who reported on the collapse of fainting and delirious women, sweating and panting with open mouths and distorted faces. John Tunis wrote of "eleven wretched women, five of whom dropped out before the finish, while five collapsed after reaching the tape," and critics protested any inclusion of women in future Olympic events (Guttmann, *Sports: The First Five Millenia* 265). This fatigue struck critics as the ultimate proof that women were not equal to the demands of the middle distances. But Tunis had taken considerable journalistic license. There were only nine competitors, and all finished the race (Guttmann, *Sports: The First Five Millenia* 265). Several officials and physicians pointed out that the female athletes had not been overexerted and that they showed no more signs of fatigue than male athletes after such a run. Two of the allegedly exhausted athletes were Jean Thompson, world-record holder for 800 meters, and Bobbie Rosenfeld, the silver medal winner of the 100-meter run. It made no impression on the IOC or the public when Rosenfeld noted that she was a 100-meter specialist and had not trained for the 800-meter distance—or that none of the runners had experienced health problems. The 800-meter run was removed from the Olympic program for women until 1960.

Alice Coachman, another African American, replaced Didrikson as the reigning star of the sport. Coachman competed for Tuskegee Institute as a sprinter and high jumper, winning the national championship 10 times in the latter event, and the Tuskegee women's track team won the national AAU championship 11 times between 1937 and 1948 (Cahn, "Cinderellas" 216). African American women from segregated black schools in the South became the backbone of the American Olympic team thereafter. Coachman captured the Olympic high-jump title in 1948, but the white media still took little notice of accomplishments by black women.

Swimming

The physical freedom that women experienced in swimming coincided with the political freedom of suffrage, as in the case of Charlotte Epstein and her reform-minded National Women's Life Saving League teammates. Epstein promoted both bathing suit reform and political progress in her leadership of swimming organizations, and her endorsement of suffrage visibly linked women's swimming and physical mobility with political power. At an outdoor swimming contest in 1915 at New York's Manhattan Beach, 50 women competed in races to highlight the Women's Life Saving League's advocacy of suffrage. The women were both good swimmers and suffragettes. Epstein was also one of the swimmers on the National Women's Life Saving League team that competed in intercity swimming races in Philadelphia, in turn spurring additional competitions (Borish, "The Cradle"). Others, such as Lucy Freeman, excelled at distance swimming, thus challenging the perception that women could not muster the stamina needed for such grueling events.

To advance women's competitive swimming, Charlotte Epstein founded the Women's Swimming Association (WSA) in New York in 1917. Through her own initiative, she rented a hotel pool and secured use of the Young Women's Hebrew Association pool; she also arranged for famed coach Louis deB. Handley to volunteer in teaching swimmers the trudgeon-crawl stroke, a trademark of the famous WSA swimmers. Epstein espoused distance swimming for health benefits and publicized its value for women's physical fitness in order to challenge gender barriers. She challenged male Olympic officials to include female swimmers in the 1920 Olympic Games, and she served as U.S. Olympic Women's Swim Team manager as the Americans captured the championship in Antwerp, Belgium. Epstein fulfilled that role for the 1924 Olympics in Paris and the 1932 Olympics in Los Angeles. Stars of the 1920 Games included Ethelda Bleibtrey, who won two events and added a third gold medal as part of a relay team, and 14-year-old Aileen Riggin, who secured the diving title. American women dominated Olympic swimming and diving contests over the next 12 years, producing 51 world records under Epstein's guidance. American and Olympic swimming heroines such as Alice

PEOPLE & PLACES

Sybil Bauer

After learning to swim at age 15, Sybil Bauer became the first woman athlete to beat a man's world record in swimming. In 1922, at a meet in Bermuda, Bauer lowered the world record time in the 440-yard (402-meter) backstroke by four seconds to beat Stubby Kruger's (male) record. She earned acclaim as an outstanding backstroker, winning the National Amateur Athletic Union (AAU) 100-yard (91-meter) championships consecutively from 1921 through 1926, as well as the national championships for the 100-meter (109-yard), 150-yard (137-meter) and 220-yard (201-meter) backstroke (events in the United States and the United Kingdom are measured in yards, while events in Europe are measured in meters). She was also part of a team that set a world record and won a national championship in the freestyle relay. At age 22, Sybil Bauer held all 23 existing world records for women in the backstroke.

Lord, Helen Wainwright, Helen Meany, Gertrude Ederle, Eleanor Holm, and Doris O'Mara popularized competitive swimming for women in American culture (Borish, "The Cradle").

In addition to Epstein's efforts, other athletic clubs for women offered facilities and training for competition. Bertha Severin founded the Illinois Women's Athletic Club in 1918, recruiting working-class girls and allowing them to train for free as long as they retained amateur standing and displayed ladylike behavior. Chicagoan Sybil Bauer set nine records by 1922 and surpassed even the men's record in the backstroke. The *New York Times* speculated that she would swim against men in the Olympics, but the IOC would not consider such a confrontation (Gems, *Windy* 145). Bauer easily won the women's 100-meter backstroke event in the 1924 Olympics, and she remained undefeated at her untimely death from cancer in 1926.

U.S. women swimmers again found success at the 1924 Olympics, where one of the most famous woman athletes of the twentieth century, Gertrude Ederle, earned gold and bronze medals. Ederle, a German American, recalled that she had learned to swim at Epstein's swimming club, where she had been taught the American crawl stroke. Ederle set 29 American and world records between 1921 and 1925. Perhaps even more impressive, on August 6, 1926, at the age of 19, Ederle became the first woman to swim the English Channel, establishing a new record to boot by covering the arduous 21-mile (34-kilometer) stretch of rough water in 14 hours and 31 minutes, thus smashing the men's record by more than 2 hours. Hailed as "Queen of Swimmers" and "America's Best Girl," Ederle attracted national acclaim. New York City provided an immense ticker-tape parade, with the public cheering her amazing athletic feat. Sports journalist Paul Gallico described the huge outpouring: "Spectators usually lined the sidewalks to watch the procession go by, but for Ederle, the largest crowd ever turned out, spilling from the curbs and jamming the thoroughfares" (Gallico 52). Ederle spent the next two years touring the United States and Europe in swimming exhibitions and vaudeville shows, hailed by the media, but the intense pressure of the limelight caused a nervous breakdown and a consequent lapse into anonymity.

Tennis

While not as popular as Olympians Ederle and Holm, female tennis stars also won a measure of fame in American life. Suzanne Lenglen won her native French championship at the age of 14 and took the Wimbledon crown after World War I in 1919. She nearly monopolized the latter, racking up six victories by 1926. She cavorted around the courts sporting risqué attire and a surly demeanor, challenging conventional norms and attracting great media attention and a multitude of fans. In 1926, Lenglen met her American rival Helen Wills Moody—winner of six American and eight British titles, as well as singles and doubles titles at the 1924 Olympics—before an overflow crowd at Cannes, France. Lenglen emerged with a narrow victory, then joined the professional ranks, while Wills went on to rule the amateurs, winning every set between

1927 and 1933. *New York Times* reporter Allison Danzig wrote about Wills winning the U.S. national tennis title in 1928: "The most devastating power ever applied to a tennis ball by a woman, the power described as revolutionizing at Wimbledon, carried Miss Helen Wills, twenty-three-year-old Berkeley (Cal) girl to her fifth national championship yesterday, bringing to a close the campaign that has seen her win the premiere laurels of tennis at Auteuil, Wimbledon and Forest Hills without the loss of a set in three months of play" (18).

Tennis also reached the African American community, where, unable to play against whites, blacks formed their own governing organization. In 1924, Ora Washington won the American Tennis Association singles title, and she held the championship for 12 years. Sports such as tennis and golf upheld middle-class standards of respectability regardless of racial segregation.

Golf

Women golfers appeared on American links by the 1880s, but it was Glenna Collett (in a career lasting from 1922 to 1935) who achieved golf-star status among women, winning six national amateur championships and earning renown for her 200-yard (183-meter) drives off the tee. Collett authored a book on golf in 1928 and participated in the first Curtis Cup match (a women's team competition between the United States and Great Britain) in 1932. Another star was Elaine Rosenthal, a Jewish golfer from the Chicago area, who was runner-up in the U.S. Women's National Amateur Championship in 1914 and won a major victory on March 29, 1917, at the Women's North and South Amateur Championship at Pinehurst (North Carolina) Country Club. In 1915, Rosenthal won the first of her three Western Women's Golf Association championships (Borish, "Women" 84).

Women's golf gained greater media attention in the 1940s with the appearance of Olympic great Babe Didrikson on the women's tour, where her working-class demeanor challenged upper-class standards of the game. In addition to Didrikson's accomplishments on the women's professional circuit, women's golf benefited from the staging of an intercollegiate tournament for women at Ohio State University in 1941. Organized by Gladys Palmer, the women's competition departed from the play-day concept still favored by many educators. It marked a long and gradual return to intercollegiate athletics for women over the remainder of the century.

Basketball

Throughout the states, basketball gained great popularity among women as it spread quickly from New England to the Midwest, the South, and the West Coast. Many female physical educators at the time disliked competition, but athletic clubs, YWCAs, Young Women's Hebrew Associations, commercial businesses, and some schools fielded teams. The AAU initiated its first national basketball championship for women's teams in 1924, and within two years the

Glenna Collett dominated women's golf during her long career.

women's tournament adopted men's rules. Iowa's high schools, however, adhered to their distinctive three-court game as (in their view) more suitable for females. The Iowa version of the game preceded the women's national tournament, as its state association sponsored the first state championship tournament, featuring 24 teams, in 1920. By 1926, Iowa high schools sponsored 159 girls' teams. In 1921, Kentucky offered its first state basketball tournament for girls, but it eventually bowed to pressure from female educators in 1932. Kentucky colleges fielded women's teams throughout the 1920s (Hult and Trekell 167–180).

The nature of female sport remained contested, as female educators battled male administrators and governing bodies over competition (many female leaders felt that aggressive competition was masculine and damaging to women's psyches and bodies), rules, and playing conditions. Many schools where female educators exerted more influence opted for less competitive play days. Concern over females' sporting practices continued well into the twentieth century, as administrators, educators, and other parties of differing class interests disagreed over the nature of women's physicality. While some adhered to notions of female debility, others opposed the male emphasis on competition and winning.

Although opportunities dwindled into intramural contests for many girls in high schools and colleges, older and working-class women found options on club teams and company-sponsored squads. In California, the Pasadena Athletic Club hosted the women's national AAU basketball championship in 1926, with the club's own team emerging as the winner, and the California women's leagues adopted men's rules in 1928. Many companies found women's sports teams to be a popular means of advertising their products, and by 1930 newspapers in Dallas, Texas, covered 48 women's teams in that city alone. The Sunoco Oil Company team from Dallas went undefeated from 1927 through 1929 and won the national AAU championship each year from 1928 through 1930. Their main rivals, the Employers Casualty Insurance Company of Dallas, featured numerous All-American athletes on its basketball and track teams, including the most celebrated of all, Babe Didrikson. Employers and private athletic clubs began recruiting female as well as male athletes to bring greater prominence and publicity to their establishments.

In the more conservative South, both black and white women formed basketball teams, suggesting various perceptions of femininity based on class, race, and gender. White women of the working class and black women who participated in sports were assumed to be and stereotyped as more physical and sexual. The women of Bennett College dominated black intercollegiate play in North Carolina during the 1930s but lost a three-game series in 1934 to the *Philadelphia Tribune* team that featured Ora Washington, the national black women's tennis champion. By 1942, however, intercollegiate contests gave way to the play-day concept favored by mainstream educators (Liberti). The All-American Red Heads, a white team organized in 1936 in Missouri, barnstormed throughout the country playing against male teams. Playing by men's rules, the Red Heads won more than 80 percent of their games over a 50-year span. In 1949, Hazel Walker, a former Red Head, formed a similar venture, the Arkansas Travelers, who won more than 85 percent of their games played against men. The Travelers endured for 16 seasons, as Didrikson's influence left a lasting legacy for women's sports in general.

Church leagues offered yet another venue for female basketball players, particularly African Americans. In Chicago, black social clubs played each other in women's games as early as 1911, and Olivet Baptist Church, reputedly the country's largest with eleven thousand members, was sponsoring both men's and women's teams by 1919. As with teams sponsored by businesses, these squads attracted a large following and even promoted church attendance. The Chicago Roamers, rivals to the Olivet church team, began play in 1921. Managed by Sol Butler, a former Olympic track star, they featured Isadore Channels, the national African American women's tennis champion. The Roamers played against other women and against boys' teams. The latter competitions pushed the established gender boundaries without invading the traditional demarcation of adult male space.

During this time, Chicago accommodated numerous women's basketball teams in city and church leagues, as well as on industrial and independent teams. In a 1926 interracial match, Olivet lost to the white Taylor Trunks, who had claimed the national women's championship. Such teams proved quite democratic, as domestic workers, meat packers, clerks, schoolteachers, and students joined to form egalitarian teams where ability counted more than social rank. During the early 1930s, the Club Store Co-Eds dominated opponents with a center who stood 6 feet 7 1/2 inches (2 meters) tall and Olympic track team member Tidye Pickett. Still, the Spencer Coal Company overcame the wealth of local talent to emerge as national women's champs. Such games attracted thousands of spectators and drew coverage in local magazines, and this kind of media attention to women's athletic exploits and abilities further dismantled stereotypes of feminine frailty.

Jewish women also played basketball, against both Jewish and non-Jewish teams. Across the country—at such locales as the Nashville (Tennessee) YWHA, the New York City YWHA, settlement houses such as the Jewish Educational Alliance of Atlanta, and the Jewish Community Center in Washington, D.C.—basketball was a very popular game for young Jewish women and girls during the first decades of the twentieth century.

Heroes in the Golden Age

Technological advances produced new sport forms and new heroes in the twentieth century. Chicago hosted the first auto race in the United States in 1895. In Indianapolis, a series of automobile races with bigger cars and more powerful engines took place in 1909, and in 1911 the famed 500-mile (805-kilometer) contest in Indianapolis drew fans to the speedway, which was enlarged over the course of the century to accommodate more than 250,000 spectators around its 2.5-mile (4-kilometer) oval. In 1923, the date of the race became fixed on Memorial Day, a holiday commemorating war fatalities, and nearly 150,000 people participated in a festival that increasingly tied sport to nationalism. The introduction of aircraft produced similar events, with air shows, and races for speed and endurance for both men and women. The transatlantic feats of Charles Lindbergh and Amelia Earhart were hailed as nationalistic triumphs. But while technological advances held general interest, cars and planes remained out of the reach of many Americans. Other sport forms provided more immediate benefits.

Baseball Heroes

For Americans outside the mainstream, baseball offered a quicker road to cultural assimilation. Second-generation immigrant youth who had learned the game on public playgrounds or in schools emerged as stars in the Interwar Era, perhaps most notably the German Americans Babe Ruth and Lou Gehrig. Jews took great pride in the accomplishments of Hank Greenberg, the son of immigrants. Greenberg refused to play on Yom Kippur, one of the Jewish High Holy Days, during the playoffs, and some opponents taunted him with anti-Semitic slurs. Even so, "Hammerin' Hank," as his fans called him, amassed outstanding statistics as a slugging first baseman for the Detroit Tigers. He hit 58 home runs in 1938 and led the American League four times in home runs and in RBIs (runs batted in). He made the all-star team each year from 1937 through 1940 and earned Most Valuable Player honors in 1935 and 1940, before military service in World War II interrupted his baseball career.

Joe DiMaggio, one of three Italian American brothers to make it to the major leagues, emerged as a star with the New York Yankees. He displayed excellence in all areas of the game—as a hitter, fielder, and dashing runner—in a career that lasted from 1936 until 1951. For Italian American Catholics, DiMaggio sparked a sense of pride, esteem, and long-sought acceptance in American society. He began patrolling center-field for the New York Yankees during his rookie season, and in his 13 seasons with

Mildred "Babe" Didrikson

The multitalented Babe Didrikson (right in this photo from the 1932 Olympics) challenged gender boundaries in several sports.

Associated Press

The distinction of best all-around athlete during this period clearly belonged to a woman: Mildred "Babe" Didrikson. Born into a Norwegian working-class family in Beaumont, Texas, Babe gained her nickname for her baseball hitting abilities, but she won fame as a brash, multitalented athlete. Her prowess as a high school basketball player earned her a nominal job with the Employers Casualty Company in Dallas, where she was employed as a stenographer; her real value to the company, however, lay in her stellar play for the company basketball team, where she gained All-American recognition from 1930 through 1932 and led the team to the national AAU championship in 1931. In 1932, competing as an individual, she won the national track team championship single-handedly by winning six events. At the 1932 Olympics in Los Angeles, she was limited to three events and won gold medals in the 80-meter hurdles and the javelin throw with world-record performances. A *Los Angeles Times* journalist described her performance: "Mildred (Babe) Didrikson, 128 pounds [58 kilograms] of feminine dynamite, came through yesterday when all competitors of the so-called stronger sex failed in the world record-wrecking attempts. . . . More than 50,000 spectators joined in a wild cheer as the doughty Didrikson dame rifled the javelin 143 ft. 4 in. [43.7 meters] on her very first effort, a mighty heave which erased the former world mark of 133 ft. [41 meters]" (Dyer, "Babe" 9). She would have won the high jump as well, but officials claimed her diving style to be an illegal jump and awarded her the silver rather than the gold medal.

Although Didrikson had a bowling average of 170 and could reputedly punt a football 75 yards (68.6 meters) and swim at record pace, she made a living as a barnstorming baseball player and professional basketball player after the Olympics. She then turned to golf and won the West Texas Open in 1935, but the social set did not appreciate her working-class roots or crude manners. A braggart, supremely confident in her abilities, she once asked in the ladies' locker room, "All you girls showed up just to see who would come in second?"

In 1938, she married ex-wrestler George Zaharias, mitigating her "tomboy" image but not curtailing her self-promotion. Her social skills gained some refinement with age, but she never became the darling of the golfing community. Nevertheless, Didrikson's startling success drew attention to the women's golf tour. She won 34 tournaments, including 17 in a row at one point (1946–1947). In 1948, she became one of the pioneers who organized the Ladies Professional Golf Association (LPGA). Despite suffering colon cancer at the relatively young age of 41, she returned to golf, winning Comeback Player of the Year in 1953 as awarded by sportswriters. She died in 1956, leaving an incredible athletic legacy. The Associated Press honored her as Female Athlete of the Year six times and named her the top female athlete of the half-century in 1950. The example set by Didrikson inspired numerous women to challenge prescribed gender and social roles, and her performances brought considerable media attention not only to women's growing participation in sport but to their considerable abilities as well.

the team they won 10 league championships and 9 World Series. DiMaggio gained his greatest acclaim in 1941, when he shattered the major league record for consecutive games with a hit. For 56 straight games that summer, baseball fans briefly forgot the European war as they were mesmerized by the feats of the Yankee Clipper.

Though the incredible streak ended on July 17, the 1941 season still held great interest, as Ted Williams, an outfielder for the Boston Red Sox, attempted to become the first player since 1930 to achieve a .400 batting average. On the last day of the season, Williams' average rested at .39955, a figure which would have been rounded off to an even .400, but he chose to play in a doubleheader, thus jeopardizing the amazing achievement. In the course of the two games, he batted eight times, getting six hits and finishing at .406. No one has achieved the .400 mark since, and few have even come close.

The attack on Pearl Harbor on December 7, 1941, shattered the jubilation of the baseball season. Both Williams and DiMaggio entered the military after the 1942 season, forfeiting three seasons of their careers. Williams also served as a marine combat pilot during the Korean War, then continued a Hall of Fame baseball career until his retirement in 1960. (He still hit .388 in 1958.) DiMaggio retired after the 1951 World Series, and in 1954 he married movie star and sex symbol Marilyn Monroe. Though the marriage lasted only briefly, it symbolized the acceptance of immigrant Italians into mainstream American society. Athletes such as DiMaggio could take much credit for the transition in the Italian image from that of gangsters to one of wholesome American citizens, a distinction that proved particularly important as Italy, under the fascist dictator Benito Mussolini, joined the Axis powers aligned against the Allies in World War II. In choosing to join the military service, DiMaggio put to rest any concerns about Italian American loyalty.

Stan Musial became a hero of Polish Americans. He started his long career with the St. Louis Cardinals in 1938 but rose to prominence as the top hitter in the National League in 1943. He continued to play for another 20 years, amassing numerous records.

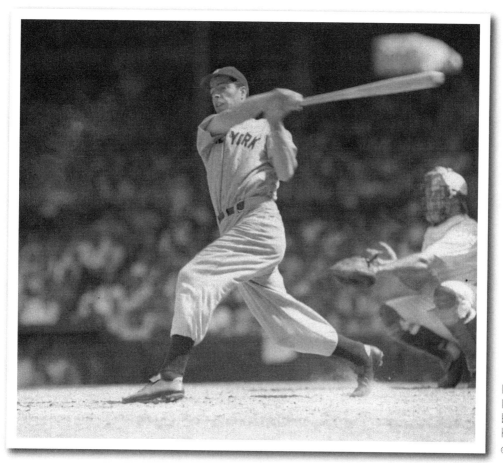

In Joe DiMaggio, an Italian American hero became an American hero.
© Associated Press

He won the batting championship 7 times, the Most Valuable Player award 3 times, and election to the All-Star team 24 times. As ethnic-minority players such as Musial achieved respectability in the national pastime, their transplanted countrymen gained acceptance, "whiteness," and greater social capital in the mainstream culture.

Though overshadowed by Babe Ruth, teammate and fellow German American Lou Gehrig quietly but distinctively forged a remarkable career with the New York Yankees from 1923 to 1939. Known as the "Iron Horse," Gehrig set a record for consecutive games played at 2,130 and established another mark with 23 grand-slam home runs. He also earned the Most Valuable Player award four times, before affliction with amyotrophic lateral sclerosis, now known as Lou Gehrig's disease, ended his career and his life.

Italians proudly claimed Tony Lazzeri, yet another New York Yankee (1926 to 1937). Lazzeri finished his major league career elsewhere in 1939, but as the Yankees' second baseman he overcame epilepsy to establish league records, including two grand-slam home runs in a single game and eleven runs batted in during one contest. The composition of the Yankee team mirrored the polyglot population of New York, and its successes indicated the possibilities of multiethnic cooperation in a democracy. Sport thus fostered the inclusion of various ethnic and religious groups within mainstream American culture.

The 1930s produced numerous athletic heroes, some of them memorialized in baseball's Hall of Fame, which opened in Cooperstown, New York, in 1939. Little League Baseball, which began play that same year, provided a chance for young boys, who emulated their baseball idols, to pursue their own dreams of greatness.

Boxing Heroes

As World War I placed a new emphasis on combative sport, and boxing gained a new respectability, the working class found a new hero in heavyweight champion Jack Dempsey. The United States government, however, considered Dempsey a "slacker." Born poor in the small mining town of Manassa, Colorado, Dempsey grew up tough but failed to join the war effort. A brawling slugger known as the "Manassa Mauler," Dempsey knocked down then-champion Jess Willard, who had beaten Jack Johnson, five times in the first round en route to winning the title in 1919. Thereafter, Dempsey's manager, Doc Kearns, and sports promoter Tex Rickard skillfully built Dempsey into a boxing sensation.

Rickard arranged a 1921 battle against Georges Carpentier, the European light heavyweight champion. The bout assumed nationalistic and social-class dimensions when Rickard touted the Frenchman as a sophisticated war hero in a struggle against the rugged and raw American. Rickard built a stadium in Jersey City, and more than eighty thousand fans paid a total of nearly $2 million to see the fight, which Dempsey won easily. In 1923, Rickard reaped another windfall by publicizing a giant, awkward Argentinean, Luis Firpo, as "the Wild Bull of the Pampas." Dempsey met Firpo at the New York Polo Grounds in one of the wildest fights in boxing history. It lasted only two rounds but produced plenty of excitement for the onlookers. After being dropped to the canvas at the start of the fight, Dempsey floored Firpo seven times in the first round before the Argentinean knocked the champion through the ropes and out of the ring. The ringside patrons pushed Dempsey back into the slugfest, and he felled Firpo three more times in round two before the South American challenger succumbed to a knockout (Rader, *American Sports* [1983] 190).

Rickard followed that brawl with a 1926 match pitting Dempsey against Gene Tunney, billed as an erudite Marine war hero and favorite of the social set (i.e., the "upper crust"). More than 120,000 attended, and millions listened by radio to the Philadelphia bout, which, surprisingly, Tunney won by a decision. He used his "scientific" style to score points while avoiding the punitive charges of the less refined Dempsey. The outcome begged for a rematch, and more than 104,000 fans filled Chicago's Soldier

Field in 1927, paying a record $2,658,660. Among them, a host of celebrities, the richest Americans, and over a hundred politicians contributed to the proceeds. Seventy-three radio stations affiliated with NBC broadcast the controversial encounter to an estimated 50 million listeners, including 75 percent of all American men (Rader, *American Sports* [1983] 192; Evensen 100, 110, 117, 118). In the seventh round, Dempsey seemingly knocked out Tunney, but new rules required him to await the count in a neutral corner. As the referee directed Dempsey to the proper location, Tunney gained valuable time and recovered at the count of nine over what was actually a 14-second interval. Tunney finished the fight with a victory by decision, resulting in a massive but unsuccessful petition by Dempsey fans to overturn the verdict. The ruling seemed to symbolize the fate of working-class Americans, who felt overwhelmed and cheated by the corporate interests that dominated urban life. Sport here symbolized the class and cultural tensions within the evolving American society (Gorn, "The Manassa" 27–47).

Jews, Italians, and African Americans also found heroes in the ring. Barney Ross (aka Barnet Rosofsky), a former employee of Al Capone, wore the Star of David on his trunks to proclaim his Judaism. His loyal followers marched to his bouts and thrilled at his successes. Ross won the amateur Golden Gloves featherweight title in 1929, and as a professional he garnered the lightweight, junior welterweight, and welterweight titles. He earned $500,000 in the ring and donated much of it to Jewish charities. With the eruption of World War II, Ross joined the Marine Corps and proved heroic in the Battle of Guadalcanal. His wounds led to morphine addiction, yet another opponent that he eventually conquered. Hollywood producers made two biographical movies about his life, which, along with his autobiography, reinforced the idealistic notion of assimilation and progress through sport.

Joe Louis (Barrow), the eighth child of black Alabama sharecroppers, also got his boxing start in Golden Gloves bouts. His family had moved to Detroit when he was 12, though his father, a patient at an insane asylum, had stayed behind. When his mother remarried, his stepfather brought another eight children to the family. Louis had to go to work in an auto plant for $5 a day but found a refuge from his bleak life in boxing. He lost only two bouts as an amateur, but in the professional ranks white heavyweights refused to offer championship matches to black fighters after the provocative reign of African American Jack Johnson a generation earlier. Louis' manager and trainer insisted on a carefully crafted plan to assure white America that he was not another Jack Johnson. He was never to be photographed with a white woman nor gloat over a fallen white opponent, and he had to appear modest and deferential in his demeanor. The strategy won favor with fans and promoters, and by 1936 Louis emerged as a top heavyweight, as well as a role model for youth in his life as a devoted son, outstanding athlete, and patriotic American. The paragon of African American heroes during his boxing career, his later life was mired in neglect and disregard.

Henry Armstrong (Henry Jackson), another African American boxer, took Barney Ross' welterweight title in 1938 despite a 14-pound (6.4-kilogram) weight disadvantage. Armstrong had already won the featherweight championship against Pete Sarron in 1937, a year in which Armstrong had knocked out 22 opponents with a relentless attacking style. Between the Sarron and Ross bouts, Armstrong amassed another 14 wins. He then beat Lou Ambers for the lightweight crown in August 1938, thus holding all three championships. In 1940, Armstrong fought Filipino Ceferino Garcia for the middleweight laurels, but that fight ended in a draw.

Sugar Ray Robinson (Walker Smith) won Golden Gloves titles in 1937 and 1940 before entering the professional ranks. His pro career lasted 24 years and 200 bouts. A quintessential boxer, he recorded knockout victories in most of them by mixing speed, power, agility, grace, and showmanship. He held the welterweight championship between 1946 and 1951 and won the middleweight crown five times from 1951 to 1960 en route to becoming an international celebrity. His flamboyant style in the ring was matched by his public life, with European tours accompanied by a large retinue

PEOPLE & PLACES

George "Tex" Rickard

Image courtesy of Library of Congress, LC-B2- 5461-13

Tex Rickard led an adventurous life as a cowboy, sheriff, Alaskan gold miner, and gambler, but he gained fame as a boxing promoter, invoking nationalist spirit in staging Jack Dempsey's fight against French and Argentinean challengers. In 1920, Rickard assumed a 10-year lease on Madison Square Garden in New York City and turned it into the main indoor sports venue in America. He not only staged lucrative prizefights but also turned his attention to ice hockey, and the Boston Bruins joined the National Hockey League as the first major United States entry in 1924. Chicago, Detroit, and New York entered the league in 1926, and Rickard drew upon his past (raised in Texas) to promote the New York contingent as Tex's Rangers. He changed the names of the Canadian players on the team to reflect New York's ethnic composition. Jews and Italians came to the games expecting to see their countrymen perform and built a fan base for the new sport. Rickard then brought horse and dog racing to Florida, before succumbing to appendicitis in 1929. Fifteen thousand viewed his casket in Madison Square Garden, and nine thousand attended his funeral, confirming his own celebrity status (Rader, *American Sports* [1983] 187–193).

that included a valet, a barber, a trainer, and a Little Person who served as a mascot. In the United States he traveled in a pink Cadillac, and his boxing earnings enabled him to engage in several entrepreneurial ventures, including a Harlem nightclub, at a time when economic opportunities for African Americans were generally rather limited.

The sporting successes and business ventures of black athletes served to stimulate African American aspirations, and the larger black population called into question the continuing socioeconomic inequalities in American society, leading the NAACP to challenge segregation policies in the *Brown v. Board of Education* case. Thurgood Marshall won the case and later became the first African American to serve on the U.S. Supreme Court.

As African Americans slowly moved toward fuller acceptance, Italian Americans also gained greater recognition through sport. In addition to Joe DiMaggio in baseball, Italian boxers reached the pinnacle of success. Jake LaMotta, a brawler known as the "Raging Bull," defeated Sugar Ray Robinson in 1943, the only man to do so between 1939 and 1951. Robinson prevailed in five rematches, but LaMotta won the middleweight crown in 1949. He lost it to Robinson two years later. Unlike some other athletes, boxers like LaMotta retained their working-class lifestyle even after securing sizable incomes, and his (and others') adherence to class habits encouraged fans to form a continuing identification with their heroes.

Rocky Graziano (Thomas Rocco Barbella), a contemporary of LaMotta, displayed a similar style in the middleweight ranks. In 1945, he won Boxer of the Year honors from sportswriters. In three brutal championship bouts with Tony Zale (Zaleski), Graziano displayed the indomitable courage that made him a fan favorite. The 1948 bout, held at Chicago Stadium, close to Zale's Polish base of support, drew a record crowd. In 1952, Graziano lost to Sugar Ray Robinson in another title fight, but in contrast with LaMotta his post-boxing career included pursuits as an artist, actor, and writer. His life, like LaMotta's, became the subject of a popular movie, but the two exemplified the pitfalls and promises, respectively, of athletic glory. LaMotta went through six marriages and endured a stint in prison, while Graziano's marriage lasted 47 years as his fame translated into roles in the burgeoning entertainment industry (Hauser and Brunt 107, 135).

The greatest of the Italian champions and the undefeated king of the heavy-weights, Rocky Marciano (Marchegiano), had hoped to become a baseball player. A high school dropout, he learned to box as a soldier in World War II and won the heavyweight title by knocking out Jersey Joe Walcott in 1952. Though only 5 feet 11 inches (1.8 meters) and 185 pounds (84 kilograms), Marciano was a devastating puncher who knocked out 43 of his 49 opponents before he retired in 1955. He died a premature death in a 1969 plane crash, still idolized by boxing fans, many of whom considered him to be the greatest boxer in modern history.

Emergence of Black Stars

Joe Louis proved to be the greatest of African American athletic heroes during the era, but he certainly was not the only one. Eddie Tolan and Ralph Metcalfe earned fame as sprinters at the 1932 Olympics, and Negro League baseball enjoyed a heyday. Josh Gibson, known as the "black Babe Ruth," surpassed even the legendary feats of his white counterpart. As a catcher for the Homestead Grays and the Pittsburgh Crawfords from 1931 through 1934, he hit more than 60 home runs each season. In another season, he hit as many as 89 (the statistics are a bit sketchy as the records are incomplete). He batted over .400 several times, including one season of hitting .464 and another of hitting .457, yet after a stellar 18-year career he died at age 35 from alcoholism and brain hemorrhage without an invitation to the white major leagues.

Some of Gibson's teammates on the Pittsburgh teams of the 1930s and 1940s displayed similar outstanding abilities. James "Cool Papa" Bell played the outfield for several contingents. A switch-hitting speedster, Bell had already established his credentials as the fastest man in baseball during the 1920s. He had circled the bases in 13.1 seconds on a wet field and reputedly covered the distance in 12 seconds on a dry one.

One of the Negro Leaguers who eventually did make a belated entry into major league baseball, Leroy "Satchel" Paige, enjoyed international repute as the greatest pitcher of all time. His career included playing appearances in five different decades (from the 1920s to the 1960s) as an active player, and he thrilled crowds with his phenomenal abilities, humor, and flamboyance. Though records of his achievements are incomplete, Paige reportedly pitched 55 no-hit games, as well as hurling 29 games in a single month and recording over 100 wins in a single season (MacCambridge 121). Paige made his major league debut with the Cleveland Indians in 1948, and more than 78,000 fans showed up to watch the 42-year-old (at least) pitcher perform. In 1952, at the age of 46, he still made the American League All-Star Team, and at the age of 59 in 1965 he made yet another appearance, for the Kansas City Athletics.

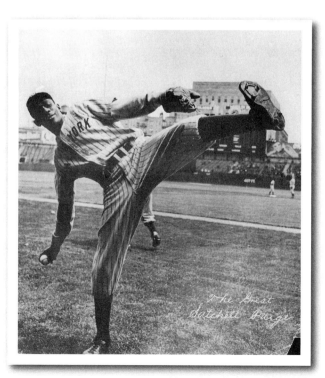

Satchel Paige mixed speed with guile and tricksterism as perhaps the greatest pitcher of all time.

Image courtesy of National Baseball Hall of Fame Library.

Other groups besides African Americans also found heroes in sports. Johnny Weissmuller, the son of an Austrian immigrant, became a swimming sensation during the 1920s, capturing all the freestyle world records from 100 yards (91.4 meters) to a half-mile (0.8 kilometer). Weissmuller was the first to swim 100 meters in less than a minute, and he won five total gold medals in the 1924 and 1928 Olympic Games. In the former, he added a bronze medal as a member of the water polo team. After touring Europe and Japan in swimming exhibitions, Weissmuller starred in Hollywood movies over the next two decades, showing his athletic physique as Tarzan.

Horse Racing

Not all heroes or champions were human. Seabiscuit, a small western horse—not part of the elite racing circle—captivated millions of Americans in an improbable run to glory in 1938. In a remarkable upset, underdog Seabiscuit defeated the 1937 Triple Crown winner, War Admiral, in a match race and went on to become the all-time champion in terms of prize money. He seemed a fitting symbol for hard-pressed Americans emerging from the poverty of the Depression.

Eddie Arcaro, the son of a fruit peddler, had a long career as one of the world's greatest jockeys. Arcaro won the first of his five Kentucky Derby victories in 1938. He also triumphed in the Belmont Stakes five times and the Preakness six times, and he emerged as the leading money winner in six different racing seasons. During the 1940s, he won the Triple Crown twice—in 1941 with Whirlaway, and in 1948 aboard Citation. The latter horse won 19 out of 20 races entered that year en route to Horse of the Year honors. Arcaro ended a 30-year career in 1962, then founded the Jockeys' Guild, a benevolent organization that provided benefits to his colleagues. The 1940s proved an exciting decade for horse-racing fans. In addition to Arcaro's feats, Count Fleet also won the Triple Crown in 1943, as did Assault in 1946.

Fleeting and Limited Fame

Bowling enjoyed considerable popularity in the 1940s, especially in the Midwest, and the best bowlers earned substantial sums. For most, however, success proved more modest. The American Bowling Congress memorialized its stars by opening its Hall of Fame in 1941, and the National Hockey League promoted its best players in its first All-Star game in 1947. Neither of these sports offered the rewards enjoyed by the top baseball players or boxers, and overall most professional athletes still worked in off-season occupations. Even the vast majority of those who did reach the pinnacle enjoyed only temporary acclaim, as professional sporting careers were generally short-lived. Education still proved to be the best route to social mobility and financial reward for most Americans.

Media and the Commercialization of Sport

The new communication medium of radio became commonplace in the 1920s and contributed to the publicizing of athletic heroes, as announcers dramatized and sensationalized sports events for remote audiences. While radio broadcasts catered to a wide variety of popular and ethnically specific tastes in drama and music, sports programming focused on American games, and broadcasts of events such as baseball games, the Kentucky Derby, the Indy 500, and the Rose Bowl tied listeners to American traditions. At first, sports team owners feared radio as a threat to live attendance, but commercial stations bought rights to game broadcasts by selling advertising time. During the 1920s, seven different radio stations broadcast the Chicago Cubs' baseball games, yet the team drew more than 14 million spectators during the decade (Noverr and Ziewacz 76). In 1926, the National Broadcasting Company (NBC) launched a network of stations, and the Columbia Broadcasting System (CBS) followed a year later. These consolidated networks, often owned by newspapers, created media conglomerates that focused power in the hands of a few.

College football broadcasts rivaled baseball coverage with transmission of the Texas–Texas A&M game on Thanksgiving Day in 1920. The *Chicago Tribune* newspaper forged a media corporation with its WGN (short for "World's Greatest Newspaper") radio station. Its broadcast of the 1924 Illinois–Michigan contest solidified the popularity of Harold "Red" Grange, already a famous football player. Before more than 67,000 fans in the stadium, along with countless radio listeners, Grange returned the opening kickoff 95 yards (87 meters) for a touchdown. He followed that with touchdown runs of 67 yards, 56 yards, and 44 yards in the first 12 minutes of the game. He then rested until the second half, when he scored on an 11-yard run, then passed for an 18-yard touchdown, thus accounting for more than 400 yards (366 meters) of offense during the game.

Sportswriters extolled Grange's shy modesty and plebian background. His mother died five years after his birth, and his father, a policeman, returned to his hometown of Wheaton, Illinois, a Chicago suburb, with four children. There, as a teenager, Red earned money doing farm chores and hauling blocks of ice, earning the sobriquet "the Wheaton Iceman." Writers fashioned an image of a rural innocent who succeeded by virtue of a strong work ethic and abstemious habits. They later dubbed him "the Galloping Ghost" for his on-field exploits and elusive running style, and when Grange left college after the 1925 season to join the professional Chicago Bears team, he was the most acclaimed football player in America (Carroll).

Some of the male sportswriters who made athletes famous became celebrities in their own right. Journalists such as Paul Gallico, Grantland Rice, Damon Runyon, Allison Danzig, Arch Ward, Westbrook Pegler, Ring Lardner, and Heywood Brown popularized and idealized athletes as heroes and role models for youth. Grantland Rice, considered the dean of the sportswriters, dramatized athletic contests rather liberally, enhancing accounts to the point of exaggeration to create interest among readers.

Another, Nat Fleischer, began his career in sports journalism in 1912 and served as sports editor for several New York newspapers. In 1922, he cofounded *The Ring*, a magazine considered the bible of boxing, and he remained an influential voice in the promotion of boxing for more than 50 years. He wrote numerous books on the sport and its practitioners, served as a referee for championship bouts, provided boxer rankings in each weight class, and conferred championship belts. As a reformer, he campaigned for medical examinations of fighters and the creation of state boxing commissions to regulate the sport (Kirsch et al. 158). Indeed, his scrutiny of the sport made him the most reliable commentator on boxing during the twentieth century.

Among the many others who helped popularize sport, Graham McNamee emerged as a famous radio announcer. Colleges began broadcasts of their football games in 1920, and professional baseball teams and boxing promoters followed suit in 1921. Quickly assuaging owners' fears about radio broadcasts, McNamee used his dramatic style, emotional involvement, and insightful commentary to generate even greater interest, and he became the preferred announcer for major sporting events of the 1920s. His rendition of the 1925 World Series elicited fifty thousand letters from baseball fans (Rader, *American Sports* [1983] 198).

Marketing of Athletes and Coaches

Professional baseball and college football players were held in such high esteem that manufacturers paid them hefty sums to advertise their products. Babe Ruth endorsed not only sports equipment but also men's clothing, candy, cigarettes, cars, milk, appliances, gum, cereal, and a host of other goods; he also appeared in movies and published ghostwritten newspaper articles. His myriad ventures eventually required the services of a sports agent, Christy Walsh, who served as a business manager (Creamer 271–276). Though many products advertised by athletes had little or no relationship to sport, advertisers linked them to more abstract concepts such as quality, luxury,

Red Grange's nickname—the "Galloping Ghost"—was one of the colorful monikers that endeared athletes to fans in the 1920s.

Image courtesy of Library of Congress, LC-USZ62-49414.

or performance that promised material and physical comforts as part of the American dream that was supposed to be attainable by means of a strong work ethic. Red Grange, the football sensation of the 1920s, hired an agent, Charles C. "Cash and Carry" Pyle, during the fall of his senior year in 1925. Pyle negotiated Grange's contract with the Chicago Bears and arranged endorsements for clothing, dolls, candy, and soft drinks, as well as a movie contract.

In 1916, Fritz Pollard became the first African American running back selected for the All-American football team and the first black to play in the Rose Bowl. He then achieved stardom as the first black quarterback and the first African American head coach in the National Football League. Though paid handsomely for his skills, Pollard faced racist taunts, physical violence, and social ostracism during his athletic career, and, rather than enjoying the sweeping financial rewards that came to white stars such as Grange, he found his numerous business ventures largely limited to the African American community. In addition to his athletic occupations as player and coach, he became a sports promoter, banker, real estate agent, newspaper publisher, theatrical and musical booking agent, movie producer, and tax consultant. Thus, though he was denied the endorsement deals of his white counterparts, Pollard's athletic exploits did gain him social contacts that benefited his varied entrepreneurial enterprises and established him as a hero within the African American community (Carroll 186–206, 224–226).

Some coaches also assumed star status. Knute Rockne of Notre Dame joined Christy Walsh's publishing agency, profited from coaching schools and summer camps, guided tourists on sports-related trips, gave paid lectures, and endorsed products ranging from sporting goods to shaving cream to automobiles. The Studebaker Auto Company even named one of its models (the Rockne) after Rockne, and by 1929 his annual earnings approximated $75,000. He turned down a $50,000 offer for a vaudeville tour in 1930 but agreed to a $30,000 radio contract to cover football games (Sperber 238–239). Rockne's humor and motivational skill also made him a highly sought speaker for corporate groups and social gatherings.

Forging a Commercialized Sporting Culture

The Tunney–Dempsey fights had been fought in the civic stadiums of Philadelphia and Chicago, both capable of accommodating crowds in excess of 100,000, and such spectacles attested to the popularity of sport and its potential as a vehicle for both cultural cohesion and commercial exploitation. The widespread and growing interest in sports, ardently promoted by the media, combined with the economic boom of the 1920s to produce a flurry of stadium construction. Colleges built concrete structures to accommodate larger crowds and reap bigger profits. Ohio State University opened its football stadium in 1922 at a cost of $1.3 million, but even its 66,000 seats proved insufficient for the 71,138 fans who showed up for the rivalry game with Michigan. In turn, Michigan inaugurated a 72,000-seat stadium in 1927 and later enlarged it to accommodate more than 100,000. In 1923 in New York, after renting the Polo Grounds from 1913 through 1922, the New York Yankees opened Yankee Stadium, which was quickly dubbed "The House That Ruth Built" because of the patronage drawn by the New York slugger. The Yankee owners paid $600,000 for the Bronx lot in 1921 and spent $2.5 million to construct the edifice which seated 63,000. That same year, New York's West Side Tennis Club built a 14,000-seat facility to host the U.S. Open (Creamer 276; Riess, *City* 221). The Rose Bowl, in Pasadena, California, had been built a year earlier at a cost of only $325,000, with a seating capacity of more than 52,000, and it was later enlarged to hold 100,000.

Other grandiose municipal stadiums soon followed, and World War I spawned a number of memorial stadiums to commemorate the war dead. Los Angeles Memorial Coliseum was opened in 1923, and its seating capacity was increased to 105,000 to host the 1932 Olympics. Baltimore's Municipal Stadium was opened in 1924, with accommodations for 88,000, at a cost of $500,000, and Cleveland's Municipal Stadium held 78,000 upon its 1931 debut. The largest of the municipal and memorial stadiums was Soldier Field, opened in Chicago in 1924. At its completion in 1929, it held more than 120,000, hosting some of the biggest athletic events of the decade. More than 100,000 saw the 1926 national championship football game between Army and Navy that ended in a 21-21 tie, and in 1927 more than 100,000 fans watched the championship rematch between boxers Jack Dempsey and Gene Tunney. That same year, approximately 117,000 showed up for the Notre Dame football game against the University of Southern California, and a decade later the Chicago high school football championship game drew more than 120,000—at that time the most fans ever to witness a game in U.S. history (Riess, *City* 144, 239). The size, cost, and commemorative value of such edifices displayed not only technological advancement but also the emergence of certain American cultural values in the boom times preceding the Stock Market Crash, as lavish amounts of money and vast spaces were devoted to sites for athletic and commercial spectacles that occurred only infrequently.

The spectacular growth of sport during the Golden Age of the 1920s made it a big business. Baseball's World Series, which had drawn 150,000 fans and earned $326,000 in 1913, attracted 500,000 spectators and generated $1.8 million in

Red Grange was the first professional athlete to have his own candy bar.

Wheaton College Archives and Special Considerations.

Babe Ruth, the biggest celebrity in the Golden Age of Sports, helped foster the commercialization of sport.

© AP Photo/National Baseball Library, Cooperstown, N.Y.

1928. Similarly, whereas the 1921 Dempsey–Carpentier boxing match brought in $1.8 million and 80,000 fans, the 1926 Dempsey–Tunney fight took in $2 million and drew 120,000 spectators, and the 1927 rematch was even bigger, pulling in more than $2.6 million and drawing an estimated 50 million listeners by radio. In 1922, the U.S. Golf Association registered 522 golfing clubs, but by 1930 that figure had risen to 1,195. Indianapolis 500 crowds surged from 110,000 in 1920 to 160,000 a decade later, and in horse racing the number of races and horses, as well as the amount of prize money, nearly doubled over the decade. Man-o-War, the premier horse in 1920, won 20 of 21 races and earned $8,000 for a victory in the Belmont Stakes. Total prize money amounted to $7.8 million that year, whereas in 1930 purses totaled $13.7 million, and Gallant Fox, the 1930 Belmont winner, earned $66,000. The nascent National Hockey League grew to 10 teams in two divisions by 1927, and the National Football League expanded to 22 franchises in 1926. Between 1921 and 1932, the NFL awarded 36 different memberships before gaining some stability in the 1930s. Previously, the NFL had enjoyed little status, and one commentator had referred to it as "a dirty little business run by rogues and bargain-basement entrepreneurs" (Carroll 102).

When the Depression hit, it left most Americans with little or no expendable income, which of course took a toll on commercial sport. Sporting goods sales, which had reached $88 million in 1929, fell to $38 million by 1933. Similarly, game attendance and profits both dwindled. In 1933, the St. Louis Browns baseball team of the American League averaged only 1,159 fans per game (MacCambridge 126). Professional team owners limited their rosters and offered lower salaries to those they did employ, and sports promoters developed innovative strategies to regain lost patronage during the Depression. Major league teams began offering doubleheaders, giving fans two games for the price of one. In Cincinnati, general manager Larry MacPhail introduced night baseball on May 24, 1935, in order to attract men who were still employed (his Reds beat the Philadelphia Phillies 2-1). In the seven night games that year, the Reds averaged 17,713 spectators, compared with only 4,699 for day games. By 1938, the Dodgers were drawing 30,000 for their evening contests (Spirou and Bennett 112–113). Innovative black teams had played night baseball games years earlier with portable lights, thus giving a lesson to white proprietors. Arch Ward, a *Chicago Tribune* sportswriter, employed a novel strategy that allowed fans to see their favorites all at the same time. He assembled the best players from both leagues for an "all-star" game at Chicago's Comiskey Park in July 1933. Comiskey Park quickly sold out for the affair, with fans coming from 46 states to witness the grand gathering of baseball talent. Fittingly, Babe Ruth hit a home run that provided the American League with a 4-2 victory, and an annual midsummer tradition had begun (Littlewood 66–76).

On August 31, 1934, Ward initiated the College All-Star Football Game, a preseason exhibition that pitted the top college players against the defending NFL champs, the Chicago Bears, at Soldier Field. Fans and sportswriters had speculated for years about the quality of play at the two levels, and though the game resolved no arguments (ending in a 0-0 tie) it drew nearly eighty thousand spectators. By the end of the decade, interest in pro games was generating average crowds of twenty thousand (Rader, *American Sports* [1983] 253). The NFL had already adopted new rules to increase scoring and created two divisions, as well as a postseason playoff, in 1933; in 1936, it conducted its first "draft" of college players, a strategy that gave weaker teams the first choices in the interest of promoting a measure of parity. It also saved team owners money by preventing bidding wars for the best talent.

The Rose Bowl game had long drawn attention to Southern California, and during the 1930s sports promoters in other areas began to use football as a means to pursue civic recognition, tourism, and profit in their own areas. In 1933, Miami hosted the first Palm Bowl, which was renamed the Orange Bowl on New Year's Day of 1935, the same day that New Orleans initiated its Sugar Bowl. Dallas followed in 1937 with the Cotton Bowl. Such festivals mixed sport with entertainment and expressions of civic or regional pride that drew tourists to the host cities.

The first Heisman Trophy, awarded by the New York Athletic Club to the best college football player, went to Jay Berwanger of the University of Chicago in 1936. That same year, the Associated Press developed its weekly poll to determine college football rankings, generating interest and angst among loyal followers and alumni across the country. Such awards, along with a mythical but conferred national championship, sparked fans' interests and speculations throughout the season, and these promotional strategies increased newspaper and magazine sales and attracted radio listeners.

Basketball, too, revised its rules and initiated new tournaments to build fans' interest in the game. The 3-second rule appeared in 1935 to keep offensive players from monopolizing the free-throw lane around the basket, and two years later the center jump after each basket was eliminated in order to speed up the game. In 1938, the National Invitational Tournament (NIT), staged in New York City, served as the national championship, and it greatly overshadowed the NCAA tournament that started in 1939. The NIT continued as the premier collegiate basketball event until the 1950s.

Growth of Professional Franchises

Organizers made headway in this regard after the war, as indicated by the organization in 1946 of a second professional football league, known as the All-America Football Conference (AAFC)—yet another entrepreneurial venture by sportswriter Arch Ward. The new league expanded to the South (Miami) and, enabled by the availability of airline service, to the West. Meanwhile, the NFL's Cleveland franchise moved to Los Angeles, and another was formed in San Francisco. The AAFC's Browns replaced the departed team in Cleveland and featured two outstanding African American players, guard Bill Willis and fullback Marion Motley. Two other black players—Kenny Washington and Woody Strode, who starred for UCLA in 1939 and on semipro teams thereafter—signed with the Los Angeles Rams team. The pro football rivalry lasted for four years, until the best AAFC franchises (Baltimore, Cleveland, and San Francisco) merged with the NFL in 1949.

College basketball was still centered in New York City, but professional circuits expanded in the Midwest, and the best of the Eastern and Midwestern pro teams formed the Basketball Association of America (BAA) in 1946. The BAA competed with the American Basketball League operating in the East since 1934, and the National Basketball League (NBL), founded in 1937 and based in the Midwest, featured industrial and small-town teams. In 1949, the BAA and the NBL merged to form the National Basketball Association (NBA). With profits tied to gate receipts at larger arenas, most small towns could not compete with large cities, forcing their teams to drop out of the league or move to bigger urban areas. The merger had produced a 17-team league with three divisions, but by 1954 only eight franchises remained. Big cities and big men began to dominate play, as epitomized by the Minneapolis Lakers and their 6-foot-10-inch (2.1-meter) center, George Mikan. As in the loosely organized days of early professional baseball and football, pro basketball teams sought skilled players regardless of race, and the desegregation of pro football in 1946 and of major league baseball in 1947 proved propitious for the new league. The NBA began drafting African American players in 1950, a move that eventually forced the Harlem Globetrotters to seek new sources of profit by extending their barnstorming tours beyond American borders.

Transition to Televised Sport

Technological advancements provided photo-finish equipment at the Olympic Games during the 1930s, and the Berlin host site also featured some of the earliest television. Leni Riefenstahl's coverage of the 1936 Games in the film *Olympia* even featured slow motion and underwater photography, and the new technology also proved a boon to coaches and athletes questing for improved performance. Telecasts of baseball and football games in the United States began in 1939, but few owned the primitive sets that cost as much as $600 (Gems, *For Pride* 188), and even a decade later fewer than a million families owned televisions; by 1955, however, the cost was affordable for even the working class, and 67 percent of American families began to change their recreational habits by owning a TV (Gorn and Goldstein 238).

Summary

With the end of the Progressive Era and the conclusion of World War I, the United States turned inward, taking an isolationist stance toward world affairs and focusing instead on national issues. Intent on homogenizing American culture, Congress enacted immigration quotas, activists used vast and comprehensive sports programs in an effort to acculturate immigrant youth, and idealistic sportswriters portrayed ethnic-minority and working-class sports heroes as role models. The booming 1920s brought increasing commercialization of sporting culture in the form of huge stadiums, sports agents, and the intensifying promotion of athletes as celebrities, but the Great Depression of the 1930s forced entrepreneurs to find innovative means to attract spectators. As fascist regimes assumed power in Europe and Asia, sporting contests were given greater political significance, and when that surrogate warfare erupted into real carnage, sports provided a morale boost in the United States.

The atomic bombs that effectively ended combat cast the world into the nuclear age and the ensuing Cold War, as political alliances were forged along sharp ideological lines. Capitalist and communist forces stood locked in rivalry for the remainder of the century, and sport became a political tool in a global battle. Indeed, capitalism subsumed the American culture, directing work as well as leisure behavior. Within the United States, commercialized sport practices dictated the nature of sport organizations, governance, strategies, and even styles of play. In 1945, the New York Yankees franchise was sold for $2.8 million, even though the federal government did not consider baseball to be a business. Two years later, major league baseball televised the World Series, and sponsors paid $65,000 for advertising rights (MacCambridge 150).

Despite such successes in the economy, American society still faced social turmoil. The war for democracy was marked by hypocrisy in U.S. sports until Jackie Robinson achieved the successful desegregation of major league baseball. In the process Robinson joined a host of sport stars that achieved the celebrity status fostered by the broadcast media since the 1920s. The advent of televised sporting events soon spurred a second Golden Age of Sports in the United States. Television exerted an undue influence on sport and society thereafter, shaping economics, power relationships, and perceptions.

DISCUSSION QUESTIONS

1. Why did the United States need heroes during the 1920s?

2. Why was the Black Sox scandal so devastating to the American psyche?

3. How has sports journalism changed since the 1920s?

4. How did government agencies address the forced leisure of the Depression era?

5. How did sports entrepreneurs address the conditions imposed by the Depression?

6. Why did the 1936 Olympics have great political significance?

7. In what ways did World War II affect the practice of sport?

8. What is the social significance of Jackie Robinson's entry into National League baseball?

8

Sport as TV Spectacle, Big Business, and Political Site

1950–1980

CHAPTER OBJECTIVES

After reading this chapter, you will have learned about the following:

- The role of sport in Cold War politics
- The economic impact of televised sport
- The symbiotic relationship between sport and television
- The ascent of pro football as the national pastime
- The role of sport in the Civil Rights Movement
- The social impact of Muhammad Ali (Cassius Clay)
- The influence of women in challenging gender roles and promoting Title IX and feminism in sport and society

A boxer—subject to so many manly ravages—was unlikely to serve as an Eternal Child, but Clay/Ali fit the bill. He was undeniably playful. Even sitting atop a pile of cash for a *Sports Illustrated* cover, he seemed unfettered by material—or adult—concerns. In his early years his skin was smooth and pretty, his verses elementary and comical. Even after his body had begun to go slack, his demeanor remained boyishly mercurial. As trickster supreme, he was impossible to pin down. He wore at one time or another each of the masks that various historians have identified as those that blacks donned to survive slavery: the deferential "Jack," the submissive "Sambo," the ferocious and threatening "Nat." In scheduling his fights from Manila in the Philippines to the African jungles of Zaire, his restless globetrotting made the world his home.

The myth of the Eternal Child also holds that the trickster in that child represents a "[p]owerfully anarchic, anti-authoritarian impulse, a drive to revolt, to disrupt or overturn the existing order." In an age that featured a rejection of old authority and a search for new, Ali was most vivid as a figure who recognized little authority other than his own. (Zang 299)

Muhammad Ali symbolized the "Baby Boomer" generation that transformed American society in the years following World War II. They questioned authority, pursued the social ideals expounded by youthful leaders like John F. Kennedy and Martin Luther King Jr., and carried out their own varied crusades focused on diversity, individualism, civil and equal rights, feminism, gay rights, and environmentalism. Their efforts generated a culture war that challenged nationalism, patriotism, sexism, and materialism and produced a more liberal and multicultural America (Steinhorn).

In the years immediately following the war, American society presented a facade of homogeneity, stability, and prosperity that masked underlying tensions and anxieties. Youthful questioning of the supposed stability emerged in the mid-1950s, as the exuberance and sensuality of rock 'n' roll music provided a release for the young and challenged mainstream norms and values. Sport, too, became a contentious entity in the culture wars that developed over the course of the next generation.

For many, the 1950s represented a second Golden Age of Sports in the United States. New technology, developed during World War II, enabled superior performance; for example, aluminum, steel, and fiberglass changed the nature of pole vaulting, and aluminum club shafts and vinyl golf balls improved scores on the links. New sports, such as hang gliding, racquetball, and skateboarding, arose to fit into new lifestyles, often symbolizing youth and freedom. The National Hot Rod Association was formed in 1951 to regulate drag racing, as speed fascinated an exploding population. Jet planes reduced air travel times, and rockets even penetrated outer space. It seemed that humans were on the verge of conquering the natural world.

In 1957, the Soviet Union heightened American fears of its power by launching Sputnik, the first space satellite.

AP photo/TASS

As in the 1920s, the media promoted athletes as heroes and role models for youth, and—much like the scientific advancements of the era—prodigious athletic performances seemed to suggest almost boundless potential. In 1953, New Zealander Edmund Hillary and Tenzing Norgay of Nepal, his Sherpa guide, conquered Mount Everest. In 1954, Roger Bannister, a British medical student, ran the seemingly impossible 4-minute mile (1.6 kilometers) when he finished in 3:59.4 at Oxford, England, and once this physical and psychological barrier had been broken other runners soon followed suit. Australian John Landy lowered the mark to 3:57.9 only a month later, and, in 1958, Herb Elliott, another Australian, ran a mile in 3:54.5. In the 1960s, American high schooler Jim Ryun beat the four-minute mark, and by the end of the century Moroccan Hicham El Guerrouj had lowered the record to 3:43.13.

The successes of sport symbolized the social progress of some citizens in the United States, as ethnic sport stars mirrored the social mobility of some groups, but masked the unequal situation of many nonwhites. Following World War II, the GI Bill enabled many to attend college, and increased socioeconomic mobility (greater than their parents had enjoyed) allowed many second-generation members of ethnic-minority groups to move to the suburbs, achieving their American dream of home ownership away from the bustle and pollution of the big city. While suburbanization denoted a visible sign of progress for families of Southern and Eastern European descent, the "white flight" from inner cities eventually left Northern manufacturing centers in a state of despair and destitution, resulting in ghettoization over the next generation. The deterioration of urban society and the desperation of inner-city life, combined with constraints on opportunities available to minorities and women, produced campaigns for civil rights and sometimes violent clashes with authorities. The local and national crusades to change American culture coincided with the international threat of expanding communism, and these internal and external tensions besetting the United States in the post–World War II era were played out in sport, which became a highly visible means of protest and cultural transformation as various groups sought their fair share of the American Dream. The perceived threat of the Soviet Union and its growing Communist bloc, however, overrode domestic issues, as the urgency and danger of nuclear war left all else pale in comparison.

Sport in the Cold War

While the happy days of the 1950s offered the American Dream for some, the era was fraught with the international tension known as the Cold War. The Communist Soviet Union, though allied with the United States against the fascist powers in World War II, emerged from that struggle as an international power espousing a competing political, philosophical, and economic ideology. China and Eastern European nations adopted the communist stance, and capitalist countries battled communism in the Korean War from 1950 to 1953. The Soviet Union achieved nuclear capability by 1951, negating the American atomic advantage that had ended World War II, and the threat of a nuclear holocaust loomed thereafter as the political rivals jockeyed for world domination. In the United States, in a move similar to the Red Scare after World War I, Senator Joe McCarthy led a federal investigation that alleged widespread spying throughout the nation. The Korean War ended in stalemate, with the division of the country into communist and capitalist opponents separated at the 38th parallel, and though McCarthy's witch hunt ended in discredited ignominy, the Red Scare in general persisted.

In 1953, the Kraus-Weber physical fitness tests conducted in Europe and the United States indicated that 60 percent of American youngsters failed, while only 9 percent of Europeans did so. This lack of fitness, an essential factor in any war, disturbed U.S. government officials and physical educators. The nation was apparently becoming one of spectators rather than practitioners, which undercut the tough image

1950 1956

• 1950–1953
  • Korean War fought

• 1951
  • Major college basketball scandal erupts

• 1951–1954
  • McCarthyism exerted

• 1954
  • Brown v. Board of Education decision by U.S. Supreme Court begins desegregation of public schools

• 1954–1960s
  • African American Civil Rights Movement challenges segregation

• 1955
  • AFL–CIO merger takes place
  • Disneyland opens in Anaheim, California

• 1956

› Althea Gibson becomes first African American woman to win Wimbledon tennis title that politicians wanted to portray, and, in 1955, President Dwight D. Eisenhower established a presidential physical fitness commission. By 1954, Soviet weight lifters began using steroids to induce better performances, and their U.S. rivals soon followed the practice in their attempts to prove individual and national superiority. The United States seemed to be losing both its physical and its scientific prowess, thus jeopardizing its role as a world leader. If war erupted, the nation might not be able to win, and the American sense of confidence and self-assurance was greatly shaken.

In this context, athletes thrilled the masses throughout the 1960s, providing a psychological escape from the ongoing stress of the Cold War and the intensification of the Civil Rights Movement. When the Soviet Union placed ballistic missiles in Cuba, President John F. Kennedy issued an ultimatum that brought the two superpowers to the brink of nuclear war in 1962. The Soviets relented, but a year later JFK was assassinated in Dallas. Only two days later, with the nation deep in mourning, the NFL continued with its regularly scheduled games, as the business of sport had come to supersede even a national tragedy.

When the Soviet Union joined the Olympic movement in 1952, the ideological confrontation of the Cold War extended to sport. Nationalism abounded at the Games in Helsinki, Finland, as Americans took pride in the election of Avery Brundage as president of the International Olympic Committee but the competition itself revealed the Soviets to be a formidable foe. The communist women clearly outclassed their American counterparts, whereas U.S. men still prevailed in track and field, and both sides claimed overall victory. The Olympics would serve as a surrogate form of warfare thereafter. The Soviet Union demonstrated its might by capturing the overall Olympic championship in 1956. While a stellar U.S. track-and-field squad captured most of the gold medals, the communist aggregation outscored the Americans in many other areas.

American nationalism again confronted Soviet athletes at the 1960 Olympics, when the United States hosted the Winter Games at Squaw Valley, California, largely thanks to the promotional efforts of Alexander Cushing, a stakeholder in the small ski resort. Few spectators traveled to the remote location, as most opted to watch on television, and the games resulted in a financial and psychological loss. Although Americans David Jenkins and Carol Heiss garnered the figure-skating laurels, the Soviet Union clearly outclassed all other nations in the overall standings, overcoming any supposed home-field advantage for the Americans and making clear how quickly the Communists had achieved world-class sporting status.

At the summer games, held in Rome, the Soviets again fielded a well-rounded team, while the Americans concentrated on swimming and track and field. A trio of African American stars captured the attention of their fellow citizens, and one of them, Wilma Rudolph, a tall sprinter from Tennessee A&I University who had been crippled as a child, surprised the Russian women by winning three gold medals. The Soviets, however, had concentrated heavily on preparing their female athletes, and despite Rudolph's heroics the Communists prevailed in overall competition.

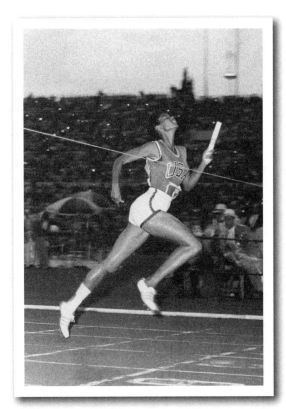

Wilma Rudolph was one of several African American stars who proved equal to Soviet athletes at the 1960 Summer Olympics.
Associated Press

INTERNATIONAL PERSPECTIVE

Diplomats in Tracksuits: Athletes and Sport in East Germany

In the confrontation between the political systems of the East and West, sport played a major role from the 1950s onward. Sport was an instrument of politics, a weapon deployed in the Cold War with huge success, especially by the former German Democratic Republic (East Germany), which, until reunification with West Germany in 1989, was a socialist country and a close ally of the former Soviet Union. The GDR was the most successful sporting country in the world, gaining by far the most Olympic medals in relation to its seventeen million inhabitants (winning 514 medals between 1968 and 1988).

From the very beginning, East German officials had aimed not only to undermine West Germany's claim to be the sole representative of the entire German nation but also to end the GDR's isolation and gain diplomatic recognition both inside and beyond the world of sport. In other words, they used sport as a tool in an attempt to demonstrate the superiority of the socialist system and to bombard the Western world with socialist propaganda. Athletes should not only gain medals but also act as "diplomats in tracksuits." Back at home in the GDR, it was hoped that sporting victories would also help to strengthen people's identification with the system.

As in other rigid socialist countries, sport was shaped by the policies of the state political party, which in East Germany was the SED (the Socialist Unity Party of Germany). The key figures, institutions, and organizations of sport, along with all sport-related practices, were oriented toward the state's political objectives and subordinated to the political will of the SED. Responsibility and control lay in the hands of SED committees and the state apparatus, as well as the umbrella organization of East German sport, the German Gymnastics and Sports Federation. The objectives of competitive sport were laid down by the politburo of the SED's Central Committee. At the administrative level, the body responsible both for sport and for sport science was the State Secretariat for Physical Culture and Sport. Scientific research was harnessed and systematically oriented to the enhancement of performance, and the centralized supervision and management of sport and sport sciences made a substantial contribution to the GDR's success of top-level sport. Other important factors in the GDR's sporting success were the system of identifying and selecting talent, the systematic and generous backing given to young generations of athletes, and the arrangements made to efficiently combine sport with education or work.

The most effective instruments of selection from 1965 onward were the *Spartakiaden* competitions, in which thousands upon thousands of children competed in many kinds of sport at the school, county, and regional levels, with the very best athletes going on to compete against each other nationally. From 1973 onward, a series of tests was carried out annually in the first and third school years, and twenty-five to thirty thousand children were selected to undergo a course in various sports at a training center over a period of (usually) three years. The most talented of these children, about ten thousand altogether, were sent to attend the children's and youth sport schools, which guaranteed that a sporting career was reconcilable with school education. The highest level of athletic preparation took place in training centers stocked with excellent resources funded and controlled by the state. Of key importance in the training were "planning and control" procedures, that is, precise plans concerning athletes' expected performance (aimed at Olympic success).

Scholars also attribute the GDR's "sports miracle" (*Andreas Michaelis* Die DDR und Olympia http://www.dhm.de/~jarmer/olympiaheft/olympi10.htm) to the enormous resources of both human power and money that were invested, the system of material and nonmaterial incentives (privileges mostly unattainable for average citizens, e.g., excellent career prospects, travel abroad, use of cars and telephones, and awards), and the systematic use of doping.

Information from Pfister, Gertrud. "Cold War Diplomats in Tracksuits: The Fraueinwunder of East German Sport." *European Sports History Review* 5 (2003): 223–252.

1959 - 1964

1959
- American Football League founded; play begins in 1960

1960
- African American Wilma Rudolph wins three gold medals at Rome Olympics

1960s–1970s
- Modern women's rights movement seeks equality in educational institutions, increased sport participation, and equality in overall society

1961
- Peace Corps established

> Alan Shepard becomes first American in space

1963
- Betty Friedan publishes *The Feminine Mystique*, sparks debate about women's rights in the U.S.
- President John F. Kennedy assassinated

1964
- Muhammad Ali becomes heavyweight boxing champion

In boxing, the light heavyweight crown went to the fast and flashy (and, at that time, apolitical) Cassius Marcellus Clay, destined of course to become more famous as Muhammad Ali. In the decathlon, African American Rafer Johnson battled his UCLA teammate, Asian American C.K. Yang, who competed for his homeland of Formosa (Taiwan). The two-day affair lasted 26 hours, and, after both had broken the existing record, Johnson emerged as champion by a mere 58 points. Beyond the competition itself, Yang's participation itself caused a stir, as the Communist government of China, known as the People's Republic of China, protested the inclusion of noncommunist Formosa in the Games and boycotted the competition (and all others thereafter until 1984). Thus international sporting contests had come to provide a stage for the engagement of political issues (Guttmann, *Sports: the First Five Millennia* 209–210).

The Olympics spawned countervailing forces and interests. Whereas governments used the games as political vehicles to fight surrogate wars and promote nationalism, individual athletes formed the friendships that Olympics founder Pierre de Coubertin had originally intended. In this sense, sport offered a temporary conciliation during the Cold War and exemplified its potential for amicable competition between otherwise ideologically opposed rivals. In 1962, as the United States and the Soviet Union were courting a potential holocaust over the Cuban missile crisis, Payton Jordan, the Stanford track coach, invited the Soviet track-and-field team to compete in California, thus extending a series of meets that had begun a few years before. The largest non-Olympic crowd (153,500) ever to watch a sporting event in America turned out for the 2-day affair in Palo Alto and cheered world-record performances by both sides. The rival athletes bonded on a personal level and concluded the meet with a joint march around the track, arm in arm, as 81,000 rose in acknowledgement. The "magical moment of camaraderie" even produced some lifelong friendships (Cavalli 7).

The quest for athletic supremacy amidst larger ideological struggles exacerbated ongoing tensions between the AAU and the NCAA over the control, jurisdiction, and regulation of amateur athletics in the United States. In 1960, the NCAA canceled its agreements with the AAU and stopped recognizing its decisions on athletic eligibility and sanctions. The U.S. government interceded in the dispute in order to field a team for the 1964 Olympics, and in 1968 the American Olympic team produced phenomenal records despite great controversy (discussed later in this chapter).

Throughout the fearful Cold War, then, sport provided a diversion, a psychological escape from the sense of impending doom, and the perception of a strong national spirit. Sport assumed characteristics of ideological warfare; yet that assuaged the ongoing potential for real bloodshed. It also provided cheap programming for television networks in search of an ever-growing fan base.

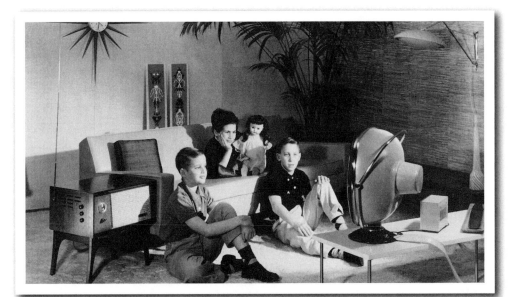

Television began to change American leisure habits in the 1950s.

Evolution of the Sport–Media Relationship

In September 1946, *Sport* magazine published its inaugural issue with the intent "not so much to glorify the athlete but to reveal him in all his dimensions" (Silverman 4). Such an approach, if implemented, would indeed be a distinct departure from the hagiographic sportswriting provided by sports journalists in the first Golden Age of Sports during the 1920s. In a weekly format, *Sport* employed some of the best-known sportswriters of the time, including Grantland Rice, who had been perhaps the most effusive of writers during the earlier golden age. Others, such as Red Smith, occasionally cast a critical eye, but in 1961 *Sport* began producing a series of biographies that celebrated the then-current stars of baseball, football, basketball, and boxing.

A rival, *Sports Illustrated*, appeared in 1954 to challenge *Sport* with a different approach. Published weekly by Time Inc., it aimed for an upscale audience with slick photography and crisp writing. Early issues featured yachting and polo, but the focus was soon expanded to appeal to a wider audience. The magazine's initial swimsuit issue, published in 1964, achieved legendary status and became an annual feature, spawning an eponymous calendar, as well as videos and its own television show. The magazine itself would eventually grow to more than three million subscriptions, with an estimated twenty-three million readers weekly ("Sports Illustrated Facts"). The popularity of such magazines reflected the booming interest in sport and complimented the instant gratification of television coverage with a more reflective and analytical approach that appealed to middle-class, and especially male, consumers.

Television as a Social Phenomenon

The televising of sporting events began in the United States in 1939 with coverage of a Columbia–Princeton baseball game (televised sport had appeared in Germany in 1936). The broadcast used relatively primitive apparatus—two cameras, two tables, and a water cooler, which served as the transmitter. By 1948, approximately seven thousand Americans owned television sets, and that figure exploded to four million by 1950, but technological limitations initially restricted coverage to sports with a narrow visual focus, such as boxing, wrestling, and roller derby (Davies 230). In short order, however, college and professional games were being televised on a regular basis, creating instant celebrities and, at least to some degree, assuaging political tensions. Viewers lived vicariously through athletes' exploits, and young boys in particular dreamed of athletic careers. Contests increasingly focused on civic and regional rivalries, and sport became a social opiate, as fans religiously followed their athletic heroes.

Baseball

The first national telecast of baseball games was made in 1951, when the American Telephone and Telegraph Company (AT&T) assembled a cable system. The 1951 World Series was scheduled to be the first live event to be broadcast across the entire country, but when an unexpected three-game playoff series became necessary to break a regular-season tie between the National League's Brooklyn Dodgers and New York Giants, the Columbia Broadcasting System (CBS) decided to broadcast the series. The Chesterfield cigarette company sponsored the national transmission of the last two games from the Polo Grounds, the Giants' home field. Chesterfield served as the broadcast sponsor and reaped big dividends, indicating that sports-related advertising had the potential to reach large audiences, and thus setting a pattern for the future. Taverns, too, found that televisions drew patrons. Department stores put televisions in their store windows, and hotels placed them in their lobbies, as crowds gathered in fascination. The teams split the first two games, and in the final contest the Dodgers led 4-1 going into the bottom of the ninth inning. The Giants scored a run to make it 4-2 and had two men on base with one out when Bobby Thomson came to bat. A double play would end the game and give the Dodgers a trip to the World Series. Instead, Thomson delivered a home run (sportswriters called it the "shot heard 'round the world") to give the Giants a dramatic victory. Television delivered instant results, and an estimated seventy million watched the ensuing World Series games (Elias, *Baseball* 178–179). Twenty

• 1965

› Malcolm X murdered

• Houston Astrodome opened

• 1965–1973
  • Vietnam War fought

• 1966
  • National Organization for Women (NOW) founded
  • Major League Baseball Players Union formed

• 1967
  • First Super Bowl played
  • American Basketball Association begins play

• 1968
  • Martin Luther King Jr. and Robert F. Kennedy assassinated
  • Two U.S. athletes stage Black Power protest on the medal stand at Mexico City Olympics
  • North American Soccer League formed

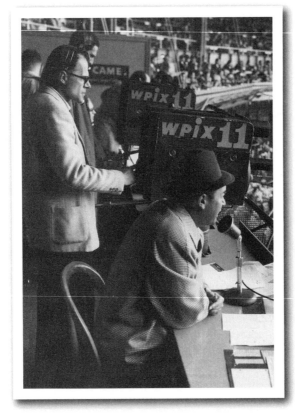

New York Yankees announcer Mel Allen, seated, reports the game between the Yankees and Detroit Tigers from the television box behind home plate at Yankee Stadium on May 11, 1956.

Associated Press

million American households had purchased televisions by 1953, and nearly 90 percent owned one by the end of the decade (Gorn and Goldstein 238).

The lure of the new medium proved irresistible for Americans but worried professional team owners, who feared a decline in paying spectators at their games and thus a reduction in profit. They retaliated by refusing to televise local games, a practice known as "blacking out" games, but, in a series of judicial cases in 1953, courts ruled that blackouts constituted an illegal restraint of free trade. With blackouts halted and no territorial rights standing in their way, television companies began to saturate local markets, and game attendance dropped dramatically, from a total of about 40 million fans in 1949 to only 15 million in 1957 (Rader, *American Sports* [1983] 286).

Many minor league baseball teams went out of business, unable to compete with televised coverage of major league action, and the 51 minor leagues of 1949 shrank to 36 by 1954 (Rader, *American Sports* [1983] 286). Even major league franchises sought new markets in cities where there were no other teams and thus no competition for paying spectators and television viewers. As air travel made transportation easier, some team owners moved clubs westward or into the South. In 1953, after televising their games and seeing attendance drop from almost one and a half million spectators in 1948 to less than three hundred thousand in 1952, the Boston Braves moved to Milwaukee (Rader, *American Sports* [1983] 286–287). The next year, the St. Louis Browns moved east and became the Baltimore Orioles, and, in 1955, the Philadelphia Athletics transferred to Kansas City. By 1958, even the nation's largest city could not support multiple teams, and the New York Giants and Brooklyn Dodgers both left for California. The new host cities, eager to attract professional sport franchises, provided favorable conditions, including publicly financed stadiums, as an inducement.

A host of star players also drew fans to the game, if not to the ballpark. Television allowed for greater intimacy, as fans could now put faces to the imaginary figures of the radio. Young stars such as Mickey Mantle of the Yankees, Willie Mays of the Giants, and Hank Aaron of the Braves excelled in all facets of the sport. Cleveland pitcher Bob Feller proved, by means of comparison with a speeding motorcycle, that he could throw a ball 90 miles (145 kilometers) per hour. In Boston, Ted Williams continued his torrid batting after military service in the Korean War, and Polish fans claimed Stan Musial of the St. Louis Cardinals as a hero. In terms of team play, the New York Yankees dominated professional baseball, winning six World Series during the 1950s, but the greatest individual performance was given by Yankee pitcher Don Larsen, who threw a perfect game in the 1956 championship series against the Brooklyn Dodgers, retiring 27 batters in a row. Television viewers experienced such thrills not only instantaneously, as with radio, but also visually, and therefore more personally.

College Football

Televised games between local or regional rivals generated passionate followings and brought esteem to previously undistinguished populations. In 1946, the president of the University of Oklahoma decided to emphasize the school's football team to counter the image of his state as a "dust bowl" (Ashby 284). The team overpowered its opponents in the 1950s, winning three national championships and building a 47-game winning streak before a 10-7 upset loss to Notre Dame in 1957.

College football had always enjoyed widespread popularity but had lacked strict regulation and organization until the NCAA assumed greater power under the leadership of a new executive director, Walter Byers. Hired in 1951, Byers organized NCAA members in a fashion similar to the economic cartel used by the NFL, used investigative officers and actually enforced rules in order to enhance uniform compliance with regulations, and pursued negotiations with television networks for both football and basketball broadcasting rights that brought a financial bonanza to the NCAA. His long tenure (lasting until 1988) assured the growth and ever-increasing power and wealth of the NCAA.

Pro Football

Under the astute guidance of NFL commissioner Bert Bell, pro football proved to be well-suited to the new medium of television. Whereas baseball owners often acted in their own best interests, football owners united behind Bell (former owner and coach of the Philadelphia Eagles) upon his selection to the commissioner's office in 1946, forming an economic cartel, with Bell negotiating television contracts as part of a package that protected each team from territorial incursions. By sharing the television revenue equally among the teams there was no need to compete against each other for broadcast rights. Revenue sharing allowed teams in smaller cities, such as Green Bay, to survive.

Pro football at this time also benefited from exciting developments on the field. A free substitution rule promoted greater specialization and fan interest. Whereas players previously had to play both offense and defense as well as kickers and special teams players, the new rules expanded team personnel and allowed for improved performances. In addition, the 1958 NFL Championship Game ended in a gripping sudden-death overtime, with forty million watching by television as Johnny Unitas quarterbacked the Baltimore Colts to a stunning victory. The popularity of professional football grew enormously, and over the next decade football began to surpass baseball as America's national game.

The tremendous financial potential of sport produced rivalries that altered the bureaucratic structures of sport organizations. In 1959, when two Texas millionaires, Lamar Hunt and Bud Adams, were denied franchises in the NFL, they decided to form their own league, and the American Football League began play in 1960, with teams in Boston, Buffalo, Houston, Dallas, New York, Denver, Oakland, and San Diego. In 1963, the Dallas Texans franchise of the AFL moved to Kansas City and became the Chiefs. The NFL, under new commissioner Pete Rozelle, also put teams in Dallas and Minneapolis, and this expansion of pro franchises to the South and West brought greater integration of those areas into the national sporting culture.

The rivalry between the two leagues led to bidding wars and escalating salaries for the best players, and the AFL nearly went bankrupt in the process, losing about $3 million during its first year of operation. The AFL recouped some of its losses by selling television rights to all league games to the American Broadcasting Company (ABC). The NFL packaged all of its games for CBS in 1961. These arrangements were pursued by the leagues, operating as cartels, and the teams shared in the revenue. Such negotiations had been legalized when Congress passed the Sports Broadcasting Act of 1961 (cartels had previously been considered monopolies and restraints of free trade). The resultant television contracts pushed league and team incomes to unimagined levels. CBS paid $4.5 million to the NFL for the right to broadcast its games in 1962 and just two years later had to pay

1969
- United States makes moon landing

1970
- Women tennis players protest against the USTA for more prize money
- Gladys Heldman founds Virginia Slims Tour (women's professional tennis tour) with Billie Jean King and other women players
- *Monday Night Football* launched

1971
- Association for Intercollegiate Athletics for Women (AIAW) founded

1972
- Title IX of the Education Amendments Act ratified

➤ Swimmer Mark Spitz wins seven Olympic gold medals in Munich

- Israeli athletes killed by Palestinians at Munich Olympic Games
- Curt Flood unsuccessfully takes case for baseball free agency to the U.S. Supreme Court

$14 million to outbid its rivals (NBC and ABC). Each of the NFL teams received a million dollars. NBC then outbid ABC for the rights to broadcast AFL games, but it had to pay $42 million over five years to do so, and each AFL team received $850,000. Players' salaries escalated accordingly, and owners in both leagues sought African American players at lower wages (Rader, *American Sports* [1983] 257).

The two leagues ended their rivalry by merging in 1966, eventually forming two separate conferences within the same league—the National Football League (NFL)—with the new championship game, known as the Super Bowl, beginning in 1967. Such an action again constituted a monopoly, but Louisiana congressmen (Senator Russell Long and Congressman Hale Boggs) promoted successful legislation (the Football Merger Act of 1966) that exempted football owners from such charges, and Louisiana was rewarded with a franchise of its own in New Orleans. The conference arrangement ensued in 1970 with some rearrangement of franchises to equalize the television markets (Rader, *American Sports* [1983] 258).

The growing popularity of professional football became evident on November 17, 1968, when two bitter rivals, the New York Jets and the Oakland Raiders, met in Oakland. The exciting game was broadcast by NBC and featured five lead changes. With 1:05 left to play, the game was going down to the wire, with the Jets leading 32-29, but NBC had scheduled a movie, *Heidi*, to begin promptly at 7 p.m. When the game ran beyond its allotted time, NBC went to a commercial, then switched to the movie. Oakland then scored two touchdowns within seconds, and irate fans who missed the ending placed so many calls that the telephone switchboard broke down. NBC was forced to issue a public apology, and the *New York Times* provided front-page treatment the next day. Consequently, future television schedules and NFL contracts required that all games be broadcast in their entirety regardless of the score.

Basketball

Basketball faced similar growing pains. Pro basketball, still in its infancy as a national endeavor, laid the foundation for growth and popular appeal in the 1950s, and two of the key developments were the entry of African American players into the league and the stardom of a white player, the Boston Celtics' Bob Cousy. At the start of the decade, Nat "Sweetwater" Clifton, a star for the black team known as the Harlem Globetrotters, joined the New York Knicks, and the Boston Celtics drafted another African American player, Chuck Cooper. As with baseball, the entry of black players enhanced the fan base as the racial comparisons and speculations that had gone on for years were now realized at the highest levels of play.

The National Basketball Association (NBA) established an all-star game in 1951, and Bob Cousy, a white guard for the Celtics, dazzled fans with a black style of play, exhibiting a style of showmanship that had been evident in black players since the 1920s. Cousy dribbled and passed behind his back, intuitively threw "blind" passes, and scored with both hands. He led the league in assists eight times and once made 28 in a single game.

Under pressure from the NBC television network, the NBA also initiated a new rule in 1954 to increase scoring and eliminate intentional stalling of the game (Rader, *American Sports* [1983] 296). The change was deemed desirable as a way to spice up low-scoring games such as one in 1950, when, much to the chagrin of fans, the Fort Wayne Pistons had beaten the Minneapolis Lakers by the measly score of 19-18. Under the new rule, each team had to shoot within 24 seconds or lose possession of the ball, thus assuring more aggressive offensive efforts, which were highly appreciated by audiences. Thus television networks began to influence the nature of the game. Professional basketball's stature, however, grew slowly, due partly to its provincial nature. Many early teams represented small cities, and basketball also had to contend with the established popularity of football and baseball; as a result, basketball owners did not garner large television contracts during this period. NBC decided not to broadcast basketball games in 1962, and ABC offered the relatively small sum of $650,000 for rights to broadcast NBA games on Sundays in 1964.

By 1959, 10 years after its creation by the merger of the NBL and the BAA, the resultant NBA had moved most of it franchises to larger urban centers. The eight teams drew more than two million fans to games in 1959, but such popularity spawned the rival American Basketball League in 1961. It lasted only until 1963, but rivalry rose anew with the organization of the American Basketball Association in 1967. The new league distinguished itself with a red, white, and blue ball, a 30-second shot clock, and a long-range three-point shot—rules which made the game more aggressive and attractive to many fans. As with league rivalry in football, the competition for players increased salaries dramatically until the two competitors merged in 1976.

Boxing

One of the first sports tied to television, boxing fared less well after an initial surge in popularity. The Gillette Razor Company began sponsoring weekly televised bouts as early as 1944, and their popularity led other commercial sponsors to follow suit, but the widespread telecasts proved a bane rather than a boon. Sponsors wanted to assure viewership by promoting only winning boxers and exciting slugfests; as a result, as had happened with minor league baseball, the independent fight clubs lost patrons who opted for the televised bouts. Even more detrimental to the sport, more gangsters assumed management of boxers, inflating their records against weak opponents, fixing fights, and exploiting athletes for their own gain. Bribery, extortion, and violence permeated the sport even outside of the ring, as the International Boxing Club (IBC) controlled 80 percent of championship fights from 1949 to 1953 (Riess, *City* 180). In the latter year, the U.S. government initiated antitrust legal action against the IBC as a monopoly, and Congress conducted investigative hearings that exposed widespread corruption, leading to the termination of the IBC. Boxing virtually disappeared from television screens in the early 1960s.

Glorification of Athletic Heroes

As major sporting organizations came to recognize their historical importance, they began to fete their heroes and preserve associated artifacts in halls of fame. The Baseball Hall of Fame had opened in 1939, but others emerged in the 1960s: the Pro Football Hall of Fame (1963), the International Swimming Hall of Fame (1965), and the Basketball Hall of Fame and the United States Hockey Hall of Fame (both in 1968). This trend went hand in hand with the media's glorification of star players in order to promote greater interest among observers and convert some into outright fans.

In hockey, for example, Canadians like Maurice "Rocket" Richard had drawn American fans to the winter sport, and by the 1960s two other players had firmly established the game in U.S. cities. Gordie Howe led the Detroit Red Wings to four Stanley Cup victories during the 1950s and won the MVP trophy six times. He led the NHL in scoring during six seasons and made the all-star team 21 times before a temporary retirement in 1971. In 1961, Bobby Hull, destined to succeed Howe as a fan favorite, led the Chicago Blackhawks to the only Stanley Cup win of the decade by an American team. Known as the "Golden Jet" for his blond locks and blazing speed, Hull—or, rather, his treatment by the media—illustrated how sportswriters in the 1960s repeated the strategies of colorful nicknaming and dazzling statistical quantification that had been used in the 1920s to promote particular sports and their top stars. Hull possessed a blinding slap shot that traveled well in excess of 100 miles (161 kilometers) per hour, and he led the NHL in scoring during seven seasons. In the 1965–1966 campaign, he registered 54 goals in 65 games, surpassing the record of 50 set by Maurice Richard, a feat equivalent to Roger Maris breaking Babe Ruth's single-season home-run record. He became the first NHL player to earn a salary of $100,000 for a single season. In 1972, he opted for the new World Hockey Association, where the Winnipeg Jets offered him in excess of $1.3 million per year.

1972–1980

- **1972**
  - The Equal Rights Amendment passes the U.S. Senate and the House of Representatives and is sent to the states for ratification

- **1973**
  - Billie Jean King beats Bobby Riggs in "Battle of the Sexes" tennis match

- **1974**
  - President Richard Nixon resigns due to Watergate scandal

- **1976**
  - Women's basketball becomes Olympic sport at the Montreal Summer Games (U.S. team wins the gold)

- **1977**
  - Janet Guthrie becomes first female Indy 500 driver

- **1979**
  - ESPN launched

- **1980**
  - U.S. men's hockey team wins Olympic gold in the "Miracle on Ice"

  - United States boycotts Summer Olympics in Moscow

In the much more genteel environment of the country club, two golfers had surpassed the $100,000 mark by 1962. The phenomenal success of Arnold Palmer and Jack Nicklaus spurred television coverage, fan interest, and larger purses. The Associated Press chose Palmer as its Athlete of the Decade, and his numerous endorsements made him a multimillionaire. Palmer began his string of victories as national amateur champ in 1954 and as winner of the Masters professional tournament four years later, and he made an indelible mark by coming from seven strokes back to win the 1960 U.S. Open. Such comeback "charges" became characteristic of Palmer's success, and the relentless, chain-smoking, often disheveled Palmer—perceived as a working-class hero—drew a legion of fans, known collectively as Arnie's Army, who followed him around the course. Palmer's brand of popularity thus countered the notion of golf as an elitist sport, as blue-collar participants began to frequent public courses and golf tournaments became a mainstay of television programming.

Palmer's biggest rival, Jack Nicklaus, eventually won 20 major tournaments (two as an amateur) in his long career. His first big victory over Palmer came in a playoff at the 1962 U.S. Open. Not as charismatic as Palmer, but more consistent, Nicklaus hit long, towering drives that forced golf course developers to restructure their courses. Sportswriters dubbed him the Babe Ruth of golf, and after the most successful career in golf history Nicklaus turned to designing world-famous courses. The media-generated rivalry between the disparate personalities of Nicklaus and Palmer only strengthened public interest in their confrontations.

ABC and the Transformation of Televised Sport

As the youngest of the television networks during the 1950s, ABC seemed excluded from the broadcasting boom, and, as one strategy for winning a larger audience, its corporate executives decided to increase its sports programming. Under the leadership of Roone Arledge, the network sports division created an extensive schedule of offerings, technological innovations, and controversial coverage that sold sport as entertainment. Producers expanded upon the natural drama of sporting events to create spectacles, using multiple cameras and conducting interviews with competitors in order to provide viewers with new insights. (In 1963, CBS developed instant replay.) Cameramen sought out comely spectators and cheerleaders for "T and A" ("tits and ass") shots to titillate a presumably male audience; in turn, coverage of the fans encouraged attention-getting behaviors, and the crowd became a more active part of the televised scene (Roberts and Olson 270–272).

Howard Cosell ignited ABC's television ratings as the most controversial sports announcer and journalist of the era.

Associated Press

In 1961, Arledge initiated the Emmy Award–winning *Wide World of Sports*, a weekly program that traveled the globe to cover sometimes-esoteric events. The Gillette Razor Company paid $8.5 million to sponsor the immensely successful program. By the mid-1960s, the show included interviews featuring controversial athletes and the equally controversial announcer Howard Cosell, who became a national celebrity as commentator for *Monday Night Football*, which appeared in 1970. The weeknight scheduling of ABC's football coverage assured the network of a captive audience of football fans (no other games were played on Mondays) and changed the nocturnal and recreational habits of millions of Americans.

This packaging of sport as entertainment drew viewers and revenue to the networks, and some of the programming not only sensationalized but also trivialized the nature of sport. Evil Knievel, a daredevil motorcyclist, became a household name by performing incredible stunts. Jumping over increasingly imposing obstacles and distances, he courted possible death and suffered numerous injuries as astonished viewers tuned in to watch his escapades.

ABC also improved its share of the television market by winning the NCAA college football contract in 1964 at a cost of $3 million per year. That price doubled by the end of the decade, but financial expenditures for football coverage enabled television networks to win concessions from the college and professional administrators, and both schedules and rule modifications were made to suit the needs of the networks. High schools played on Friday nights, college games took place on Saturday, and professionals competed on Sunday. Prime-time schedules assured the maximum audience, and even some churches eventually changed the times of their Sabbath services, lest they lose members to football coverage. Television producers dictated rule changes that promoted more offense and scoring to maintain viewers' interest, and, in order to allow their sponsors more space for advertisements, they instituted otherwise unnecessary "TV time-outs," as well as football's "two-minute warning" as a game neared its end. Such innovations changed the structure, rhythm, and flow of games but proved to be a wise business decision. ABC moved from last place to first place in overall viewership during the next decade.

Marriage of Television and Sport

Football team owners flourished thanks to the television contracts negotiated by the league's commissioner. In 1970, the year the NFL–AFL merger took effect, the NFL signed contracts with the three major networks worth $142 million. CBS got rights to the National Football Conference's Sunday games, NBC got the American Football Conference's Sunday contests, and ABC initiated *Monday Night Football,* which involved airing 13 games featuring teams from both conferences. The arrangement offered value to the NFL and the possibility of marketing the sport, while forcing the networks to compete with each other. All three networks used play-by-play announcers and analysts to provide viewers with insights, and ABC spruced up *Monday Night Football* telecasts by adding innovative halftime highlights of the Sunday games, whereas the other stations featured marching bands. *Monday Night Football* enjoyed phenomenal success and made celebrities of its broadcasting team of Howard Cosell, Don Meredith, and Frank Gifford. Cosell, in particular, displayed an erudite, combative personality that attracted fans devoted to extremes of adoration or hatred. Cosell freely criticized the sports establishment, while championing the cause of Muhammad Ali and other black athletes. His ruminations found a welcome reception in liberal areas but generated indignation in the heartland. One Indiana bar procured an old television each week, then raffled off a brick with which the winner could shatter Cosell's image at halftime. Regardless of the game, however, Cosell entertained viewers, and ABC's ratings soared. A Nielsen survey showed that nearly one-third of Americans tuned into the show, and Tuesdays topped Mondays in the rate of absent workers in some businesses (Pope, *New American* 377). In cities scheduled for Monday night games, the event assumed the qualities of a festival, with fans becoming participants in the production by dressing in outlandish garb and performing attention-getting stunts in order to be featured on the telecast, as sport moved even closer to pure entertainment.

The success of *Monday Night Football* spawned a whole series of pseudosport telecasts that became known as "trashsport." On the program *Superstars,* for example, athletes competed against each other in disparate sports other than their own (e.g., weight lifting or running an obstacle course). Networks then followed the same format in pitting actors, actresses, and other nonathletic celebrities against one another for the amusement of viewers. Such programming eventually lost its appeal (only to be resurrected more recently in the form of "reality" shows).

In 1974, the NFL's package with the three main networks accounted for $200 million in revenue, and CBS began adding pregame and postgame shows to its coverage. The next year, CBS added Phyllis George, a former Miss America, to its coverage team. In 1978, the networks offered the NFL a billion dollars to televise games. For their largesse, the NFL agreed to add two games to the regular-season schedule (increasing the total from 14 to 16) and to allow another (wild-card) team into the postseason, thus creating an extra playoff game. While CBS and NBC split the conference coverage, ABC retained Sunday and Monday night games and added a contest on Thursday evening. Throughout the decade, the NFL enacted new rules to produce more scoring, as desired by many television viewers. Hash marks were moved closer to the center of the field, and goalposts were narrowed, in order to discourage field goals and encourage more tries for touchdowns. Other changes designed to increase offensive production included moving the kickoff position to the 35-yard line from the 40-yard line, which promoted more returns, and reducing penalties for holding. In order to promote greater emphasis on passing, rules were also instituted by the end of the decade to safeguard quarterbacks and reduce the freedom of defensive backs to interfere with receivers trying to catch a pass. Scoring did increase, games lasted longer, and television networks had more time to sell commercial products.

The riches pouring into the coffers of professional teams flowed into the collegiate ranks as well, and while critics questioned the inherent violence of the game and its link to militaristic and corporate structures, President Richard Nixon, one of football's biggest fans, presented trophies to the top college teams. In 1973, the NCAA reorganized itself into three divisions for intercollegiate sports competition. The Division I football powers garnered the vast bulk of the television revenue, spurring escalating recruitment wars for the best high school athletes. ABC had paid $3 million for broadcast rights to college football games in 1969; the cost rose to $29 million a decade later, and in 1981 ABC and CBS split the collegiate offerings at a rate of a combined $65.7 million per year (Rader, *American Sports* [1983] 271).

Many more colleges played Division I basketball than football, due to the smaller team size, lower costs, and greater possibilities for national recognition (whereas multiple top athletes were necessary for a good football team, just one might vault a basketball quintet to nationwide exposure). The intensity of recruitment may have surpassed even that of football, and the NCAA sanctioned several schools for recruiting violations, but the guilty coaches simply left for another school anxious to become a basketball powerhouse, and the vast amounts of money involved led to widespread abuses and recruiting violations.

Chasing the Television Market

Television profits also fueled an expansion of major league baseball, as new franchises emerged and old ones relocated in search of greater market share. Following the initial moves of the 1950s, other franchises followed suit. In 1961, the Washington Senators left the nation's capital to become the Minnesota Twins. The American League quickly replaced the enterprise in Washington, D.C., and added another in Los Angeles. In 1962, the National League established the Mets in New York. In 1966, the Braves abandoned Milwaukee for a lucrative television deal in Atlanta, where there was no competition for viewers in the Southeast. A year later, the Athletics deserted Kansas City for Oakland, California. Seattle got an American League franchise in 1968; a year later, San Diego joined the National League, and a team known as the Brewers returned to Milwaukee in 1970. Within 15 years, major league baseball had expanded from 16 teams to 24 franchises.

Expansion, of course, required a concomitant increase in the player pool, and critics argued that such growth caused a dilution in talent. From 1962 through 1968, the New York Mets lost more than 100 games in five of their six seasons, and in 1963 the loveable losers were a civic phenomenon, as a million fans attended their games to witness their hapless antics. The Mets then startled the baseball world in 1969 by wining the World Series, but the large metropolitan areas inevitably enjoyed an economic advantage; big-market teams had big money. Unlike NFL owners, baseball proprietors refused to share their revenues equally, so teams in the biggest cities or with the best television contracts enjoyed the greatest profits, enabling them to buy the best players.

The New York Yankees used their wealth to buy Roger Maris' services from the Kansas City Athletics, and Maris hit 61 home runs in 1961, breaking the record long held by Babe Ruth. Purists decried the feat, however, because Maris achieved the mark in 162 games, whereas Ruth did so in only 154. The extra eight games had been added to provide greater profit for networks and team owners, but Maris was the one saddled with the role of villain, rather than hero, for his displacement (albeit qualified) of a national icon. Thus sports was producing story lines not unlike the popular soap operas, with their idols, rogues, and rascals.

Incorporation of Alternative Heroes

Sport drew adherents from all sides of the social struggle. It provided a highly visible symbol of racial integration in all major sports by 1950, yet traditionalists continued to esteem the conservative values promoted by coaches and the white power structure. The nature of sport, however, changed greatly during the decade, due largely to the impact of television. Interest in sport expanded exponentially with intensified media coverage, rises in players' salaries, and the increasingly stellar play of athletes. In a period of racial and ethnic tension, athletes symbolized social mobility within the mainstream WASP culture, and various groups found heroes in the athletic world. The marketing of ethnic- or racial-minority heroes fueled greater interest in sport among diverse groups and larger profits for team owners and television networks.

In baseball, Jewish pitcher Sandy Koufax dominated the National League for the Dodgers before injury forced him to retire at the age of 30. A left-hander with a searing fastball and a devastating curve, Koufax struck out more batters than any other pitcher in four different seasons. In 1965, he set a single-season record by striking out 382 batters, and he averaged more than 300 strikeouts per year. He pitched four no-hitters in four years, including a perfect game in 1965, and he won the Cy Young Award, given to the best pitcher in the major leagues, three times. In 1963, he even won the Most Valuable Player trophy (more often awarded to a daily position player), and twice he led the Dodgers to World Series wins over the Yankees. His religion, however, took priority, and, due to his Yom Kippur observance, he did not pitch the opening game of the 1965 World Series, but he returned to shut out the Yankees in two other games, winning the series Most Valuable Player award for the second time. The Baseball Hall of Fame inducted him at the young age of 36. Acknowledgment of his Jewish faith in the media increased awareness and knowledge of a religion that was still seen by many as somewhat alien. Thus Koufax won not only ball games but also greater acceptance of Judaism in America, and that wholesale approval could not have been obtained, particularly in televised fashion, had he been an accountant or a shoemaker.

Upon Koufax's retirement, Bob Gibson, a right-handed African American pitcher for the St. Louis Cardinals, assumed dominance. He competed with a fixation on winning, and his icy glare and blazing fastball made him a fearsome presence. He became only the second pitcher to record 3,000 career strikeouts, and in 1968 he posted an earned run average of only 1.12 for the season. The next year, MLB lowered the height of the pitcher's mound to give hitters a better chance. Gibson led the Cardinals to World Series wins in 1964 and 1967 and earned two Cy Young Awards. Gibson excelled at a position not usually accorded to blacks; as a pitcher, he held a place of leadership and trust, slowly dismantling yet another stereotype.

Sandy Koufax, a dominant pitcher, led the Dodgers to the World Series while adhering to his Jewish faith.

Associated Press

In Pittsburgh, the Pirates enjoyed the services of Puerto Rican outfielder Robert Clemente. Although he was the best all-around player in the game, Clemente rarely received accolades from sportswriters, who lacked an understanding of Latin culture and the Caribbean notion of "beisbol romantico" (the Latin flair for exciting play and love of the game). They often characterized him as sullen and vain, belying his true love for the game and his quest for respect. No one, however, could deny Clemente's impact. He amassed exactly 3,000 hits and batted over .300 in 13 seasons. He won the Most Valuable Player award in 1966, led the league in batting average four times, and made the National League All-Star Team twelve times. He secured the World Series MVP award in 1971 against the Orioles after hitting .414 with 12 hits. On the last day of December in 1972, he traveled to bring food and supplies to earthquake victims in Nicaragua, but his plane crashed, killing him. Only months later, baseball writers finally acknowledged his greatness by voting him into the Hall of Fame. Clemente's death confronted stunned readers and viewers with the humanity of athletes, who, of course, had lives beyond the ball field. Many Latin players revered him as a god—the Jackie Robinson of the Caribbean.

Football also produced a bevy of Hall of Famers during the decade, but the one who most symbolized the machismo of the game hailed from Chicago. Dick Butkus, the son of Lithuanian parents with a working-class background, roamed the field as a linebacker for the Bears. Butkus covered the playing area with reckless abandon, relentlessly pursuing ball carriers and anyone else in the way. Fast and fearsome, he terrorized opponents by snarling, allegedly biting, and generally acting nasty. His 245 pounds (111 kilograms) crashed into blockers, runners, and receivers with stunning force. Despite playing on a losing team for most of his nine NFL seasons (1965–1973), he won election to the all-league team seven times. Coaches and opponents considered him to be the prototype of a football player. For many working-class fans, his sheer physicality, prowess, and heedless approach to the game reflected images of their own lives, as they faced the obstacles of life directly and relentlessly. In a time when professional sport reached for a greater bourgeois image, players such as Butkus kept working-class fans captivated by the game of football.

Professional Sport and Labor Relations

Despite the glorification of athletic heroes and immense profits to be had in the sporting world, employers and employees did not share equally in the rewards, and professional athletes and team owners continued to quarrel over salaries, pensions, and rights to free agency. In 1970, the NFL players launched a strike, and Oscar Robertson led NBA team members in a lawsuit against their employers. Although Curt Flood proved unsuccessful in his baseball case, the NBA players won greater freedom from their previously binding contracts, and, in 1972, Baltimore Colts player John Mackey, president of the football players' union, successfully sued the NFL and negated the famed "Rozelle Rule," which allowed commissioner Pete Rozelle to set the compensation if any player left his assigned team for another. Since the commissioner inevitably sided with team owners, the rule effectively denied players the chance to test their value on an open market. Despite the favorable ruling, NFL team owners showed little interest in free agents, and the average player's salary reached only $69,000 by 1980 (Rader, *American Sports* [1983] 353).

Baseball players had greater success in their pursuit of free agency. Under the guidance of Marvin Miller, executive director of the players' union, pitchers Dave McNally of the Montreal Expos and Andy Messersmith of the Los Angeles Dodgers implemented a different strategy. Having completed the terms of their contracts, they played the 1974 season without signing an agreement with the team owner. Without a contract, they argued that they were free agents, able to negotiate with any club for their services. An arbitration panel and federal appeals courts agreed, essentially breaking the reserve rule that for nearly a century had bound players to one team. Players' salaries nearly tripled over the next five years, as owners outbid each other to stock their teams with the best players (Rader, *American Sports* [1983] 352).

In professional basketball, the bidding wars between the NBA and the rival ABA also resulted in higher salaries for players. When the owners of the two leagues attempted a merger in 1970, the players blocked it with a lawsuit. The ABA ceased operations in 1976, when its Indiana Pacers, Denver Nuggets, San Antonio Spurs, and New York Nets franchises joined the NBA. Lucrative television contracts provided $880,000 to each NBA team in 1980 (Rader, *American Sports* [1983] 298).

Sport and the Civil Rights Movement

Adding to political leaders' social concerns, youth of the 1950s began to assume a questioning and rebellious attitude, noticeable in their dress, their hairstyles, and especially their musical tastes. African American singers adapted the laments of the blues to a new genre known as rock 'n' roll, which carried sexual connotations, and Fats Domino, Chuck Berry, and Little Richard attracted fans across racial lines. When the white singer Elvis Presley assumed the black style, rock 'n' roll acquired the status of a national social phenomenon.

Native Americans

While some Americans prospered in such transitions, others had less faith in the system. Many Native Americans, among the poorest of U.S citizens, languished on desolate reservations or in urban ghettos. In the post–World War II era, American Indians invoked their traditional lifestyles to maintain some semblance of cultural cohesion, but some also used sport as a means to greater recognition and supplemental income by means of participation in rodeos. Both men and women assumed prominent roles in rodeo associations and generated alliances that served political ends, such as protest movements in the 1960s and 1970s. Native American pride was also given a boost with the 1964 Olympic victory of Billy Mills, an orphaned Oglala Sioux. Mills won the 10,000-meter race in record time, becoming the first American ever to win that event at the Olympic Games. After his running career, Mills devoted himself to activism, instilling pride in and bringing hope to Native American youth.

African Americans

Nearly a century after their emancipation, African Americans still faced widespread inequalities. In 1954, they moved to address such disadvantages in the courts by challenging segregated school systems. In the case of *Brown v. Board of Education,* the Supreme Court banned the practice of segregation in all areas—not just education—thus igniting the Civil Rights Movement. But social discrimination cannot be eliminated by law alone, and it continued in many areas, including the labor market, as well as sport.

In 1963, Martin Luther King Jr., the acknowledged leader of the nonviolent Civil Rights Movement of African Americans, led a march in Washington, D.C., which, because of its symbolic meanings (located at the Lincoln Memorial [emancipation] and in Washington, D.C. [the location of federal responsibility and the seat of the national government]), drew enormous attention to the cause.

> When we let freedom ring, when we let it ring from every village and every hamlet, from every state and every city, we will be able to speed up that day when all of God's children, black men and white men, Jews and Gentiles, Protestants and Catholics, will be able to join hands and sing in the words of the old Negro spiritual, "Free at last! Free at last! Thank God Almighty, we are free at last." (Martin Luther King speech, August 28, 1963)

At the same time, athletes began increasingly to question the accepted idealism of sport and its function as an integrative force in American society. Congress passed a civil rights bill in 1964, but escalation of the Vietnam War, a military draft (conscription), and widespread poverty led to urban riots and mass protests throughout the decade.

In the world of sports, African American Althea Gibson appeared as an early harbinger of change and generated much-needed interest in tennis. American tennis had languished, as top amateur players joined the professional ranks, and the United States managed only three Davis Cup victories between 1950 and 1967. Still, in 1950, Gibson proved a bright spot as the first African American allowed to participate in the United States Lawn Tennis Association's national championship. Aided by the former white champion Alice Marble, Gibson fulfilled an integrative role similar to that of Jackie Robinson in baseball. She won the French Open in 1956, as well as the Wimbledon singles and doubles titles, and she won the U.S. championship the following year. The Associated Press named her its female Athlete of the Year in 1957, a first for a black woman, and she earned the honor again the next year. She entered the professional ranks in 1959 and turned to professional golf as a member of the LPGA in 1964.

Gibson's success paved the way for her male counterpart, Arthur Ashe Jr. Gibson's discoverer, Dr. Robert Walter Johnson, a black physician, also took an interest in Ashe and provided him with instruction. In 1968, Ashe won both the U.S. amateur championship and the U.S. Open before leading the American team to a Davis Cup win. The next year, he became the first African American on the men's pro tour, and in 1970 he won the Australian Open. In 1973, he became the first black player in a major South African tournament. Because of his success in a "white sport," and because of his political activities, Ashe helped to break the bonds of racial segregation in the United States and abroad.

In 1975, he became the first African American to triumph in the men's singles at Wimbledon, and he recaptured the Australian Open in 1977. His life took a decisive turn in 1979, when, after he suffered the first of a series of heart attacks, requiring surgery, he contracted AIDS from a contaminated blood transfusion. Despite his ensuing illness, he founded tennis programs for poor urban youth, became a social activist, and wrote a history of African American athletes. He died in 1993.

Other African American athletes prospered in football and basketball. Jim Brown starred in four sports at Syracuse University before joining the Cleveland Browns football team in 1957. He won the Rookie of the Year award, then dominated the league over the next eight years with a combination of speed and power. During that time, Brown led the league in rushing eight times, averaging more than 5 yards (4.6 meters) per carry and more than 100 yards (91 meters) per game. In 1965, he won the Most Valuable Player award for the second time and scored 21 of his 126 career touchdowns. He retired at the height of his fame, at only age 30, became an actor, and launched a new movie genre featuring black action heroes. Thus the way was paved for what would eventually become a stream of athletes making the transition from sport to the entertainment industry. For minorities, however, the road to success had always been littered with more obstacles, and pioneers carried an extra burden. If a black athlete, carrying the hopes of black citizens, failed, it could mean untold years of waiting for another prospect, one acceptable to the establishment, to come along.

Tennis player Arthur Ashe was an activist, entrepreneur, author, and race-relations pioneer.

Associated Press

Sports events provided other highly visible images of social change in America. In 1966, the NCAA's championship basketball game featured Texas Western College (now the University of Texas at El Paso) against favored Kentucky, a perennial collegiate power. Kentucky's starting lineup, consisting of five white players, faced five African American starters for Texas Western, which won 72-65, thus marking a transition in team composition and race relations in America.

African Americans had long been allowed to entertain white audiences as musicians and athletes, and the best could accumulate a measure of wealth and fame, so long as they did not disrupt the prescribed social order of white dominance. By the late 1950s and early 1960s, however, black athletes began to emerge as stars in all major team sports except hockey. In basketball, from 1957 through 1969, the Boston Celtics dominated pro basketball, winning 11 NBA championships, largely through the efforts of Bill Russell, the team's African American center and, later, player-coach. Russell had led his University of San Francisco team to national collegiate titles in 1955 and 1956 before joining Boston in the pro ranks. He played unselfishly, tenaciously grabbing rebounds, blocking shots, and intimidating opponents on defense. With Red Auerbach, the Celtics' cigar-chomping Jewish coach, the team won 9 titles. Off the court, Russell refused to accept the role of the acquiescent African American. He spoke out against racism and social inequalities, and, although Boston was one of the most segregated cities in America, the Celtics elected Russell their captain and leader. In 1967, the front office went further and named him head coach, making him the first African American to fulfill that role in the NBA. He consequently directed the team to two more NBA championships, countering the stereotype of blacks' inferior intellectual and leadership abilities.

Other black basketball stars also addressed American racism, though not as forcefully as Russell. On the court, however, their play stood out. Elgin Baylor captivated fans with a combination of power, fluid agility, and leaping ability that would later be characterized as "black style." As a 6-foot-5-inch-tall (2-meter-tall) guard for the Minneapolis Lakers in 1960, he scored 71 points in a game, and he averaged more than 27 points per game over his 14-year career in the NBA. His white Laker teammate, Jerry West, a consummate shooter, also averaged 27 points a game over 14 years. When Baylor's playing career ended in 1971, he overcame another racial stereotype by becoming a coach and executive in the NBA (Raffety 61–62).

Oscar Robertson, another African American, led the nation in scoring for three straight years as a collegian at the University of Cincinnati. Standing 6 feet 5 inches (2 meters) as a guard, he was drafted by the NBA's Cincinnati Royals in 1960 and played offense and defense equally well for them. During the 1961–1962 season, he amazingly averaged a triple-double (i.e., double figures [ten or more] in scoring, rebounds, and assists) for the entire season. Such superlative play forced even the white media to take notice of his accomplishments.

The biggest and tallest challenge to Bill Russell was 7-foot-1-inch-tall (2.2-meter-tall) Wilt Chamberlain, the center for the Philadelphia 76ers. After playing at the University of Kansas, then for one year with the Harlem Globetrotters, Chamberlain joined the NBA in 1959. In his rookie year, he averaged more than 37 points per game, and two years later he averaged a phenomenal 50.4 points per game. Chamberlain also averaged more than 24 rebounds per game in three different seasons, and he set the records of 55 in one game, 27.2 as a per-game average for a season, and 22.9 per game for his career average. In 1962, he scored 100 points in a single game (a feat yet to be matched). Another year, he led the league in assists. His rivalry with Bill Russell produced classic confrontations between the unstoppable offensive force and the immovable defensive bulwark. In the end, teamwork prevailed over individualism, as Chamberlain's 76ers won only one title (in 1967) during Russell's amazing title run with the Celtics. Together, however, the two giants signaled a transition in basketball from a game dominated by white players to a black game rooted on city playgrounds.

On the collegiate level, UCLA, with legendary coach John Wooden at the helm and star centers Lew Alcindor and Bill Walton, dominated the NCAA basketball world, winning 10 titles between 1964 and 1975, including 7 in a row from 1967 through 1973. Alcindor reflected the growing African American discontent of the era by refusing to play for the 1968 Olympic basketball team. He later adopted the Muslim religion as Kareem Abdul Jabbar; his religious change was symbolic of his discontent with the white establishment.

Football as the Harbinger of Social Change in the South

College football coaches developed new high-scoring offensive systems that pleased their rabid fans. Both the United Press International (UPI) coaches poll and the Associated Press (AP) sportswriters poll rated the football teams each week, enhancing fans' interest and enjoyment even as they increased the pressure on coaches and players to win more games—and to do so in decisive fashion. At the University of Alabama, Coach Paul "Bear" Bryant produced three national championships during the 1960s, but his success represented an adherence to traditional Southern values. Since the early part of the century, Southern football teams had employed the sport as a means to uphold the "Lost Cause" of the Confederacy, extolling regionalism and using only white players. Southern schools even refused to let opposing players who were black participate at games on their fields. When Southern teams played Northern teams, football games constituted a sort of surrogate reenactment of the Civil War, as bands played "Dixie" and fans waved the Confederate flag. Seven years after the historic *Brown v. Board of Education* court decision, Alabama and Mississippi still had not integrated their public schools.

Bryant had coached at Maryland, Kentucky, and Texas A&M, all Southern schools, before returning to his alma mater in 1958. An autocratic coach, he used brutal practices to instill discipline, toughness, and undying determination in his charges. As Birmingham police attacked civil rights marchers with dogs and fire hoses, Alabama's football team remained emblematic of the South's self-righteous racial attitudes. Its violent play on the field mirrored the treatment meted out to civil rights activists within the region. For his fans, Bryant and his team stood for Southern honor, defiant against the lack of respect with which the rest of the country viewed the region (Doyle).

To maintain its football prestige Alabama accepted invitations to postseason bowl games, where, by the mid-1960s, it encountered black athletes. Not an avowed racist, Bryant responded in pragmatic fashion, placating white boosters until the need for recruiting of black talent became obvious to all. He then kept a low profile on racial matters in order to maintain the benefits of the booster clubs. The turning point was a bowl game pitting Alabama against the University of Southern California (USC) in 1970. USC won 42-21, with Sam Cunningham, its black running back, accounting for four touchdowns. Bryant began recruiting black athletes, and other Southern coaches followed. With integrated teams, Bryant and the University of Alabama won three more national titles in the 1970s, and Bryant counted more victories than any major college coach in history until he was surpassed by Eddie Robinson, the African American coach at historically black Grambling State University.

Athletic Revolution

Vince Lombardi, famed coach of the Green Bay Packers, joined that team in 1959. He led them to five NFL championships (including the first two Super Bowls) by insisting on discipline, decorum, and precision. He believed in the traditional patriarchal hierarchy and assumed the roles of field general and paternal critic in his relationships with players. Revered as a hero in Green Bay, he became a national icon of traditionalists, with his small-town team serving as the David who slew the Goliaths of the staid NFL. In stark contrast, Joe Namath, a white player, represented brash, rebellious, urban youth as quarterback of the New York Jets in the colorful, rambunctious AFL. An untamed, long-haired bachelor, Namath led a fast and hedonistic life that challenged traditional norms. Known as "Broadway Joe," he wore a full-length fur coat, sported a Fu Manchu moustache, and even donned women's panty hose for a television commercial. After the NFL won the first two Super Bowls, he publicly guaranteed that his AFL Jets would win the third, and, like Muhammad Ali, he delivered on his bold promise in a stunning 16-7 upset of the Baltimore Colts in 1969. On display in New York, the media capital of the world, his independence, affluence, and influence reverberated throughout the nation as a counterculture figure.

Black discontent magnified itself in the person of Muhammad Ali. Both loved and reviled, Ali transcended sport and became a focal point of many tensions of the era. With Ali, sport became a stage for the cultural warfare taking place in America, as rebels battled traditionalists in a struggle to define the nature of sport and the larger society. Traditionalists adhered to an idealistic belief in sport as character building, and Avery Brundage, president of the IOC, steadfastly held to the principle of amateurism despite the many circumventions of the practice. UCLA basketball coach John Wooden maintained his belief in the old-fashioned values of work ethic and respect for authority, and a host of football coaches, most notably Bear Bryant at Alabama, Woody Hayes at Ohio State, and George Allen and Vince Lombardi in the professional ranks, preached discipline and conservative values. Coaches often dictated dress codes, haircut styles, and dating choices for athletes, with interracial matches as a distinct taboo. Their challengers—including both black and white athletes, who were characterized by coaches and much of the media as unwholesome rebels or outlaws—opposed such directives as oppressive, exploitative, and patriarchal. They tested authority with new styles and innovations and provoked radical change in the norms, standards, and mores of mainstream American society. This movement, termed the "Athletic Revolution," found its leader in Muhammad Ali.

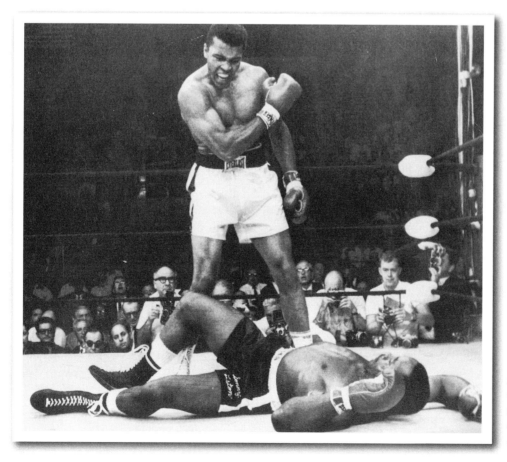

Perhaps the most significant athlete of the twentieth century, Muhammad Ali forced America to confront itself.

Associated Press

After his Olympic victory as Cassius Clay, Ali embarked on a professional career as a heavyweight. He danced, shuffled, and clowned in the ring, entertaining fans while distracting and frustrating opponents. Exceedingly fast for a heavyweight, Clay ducked opponents' punches and threw flurries of his own. He claimed that he could "float like a butterfly and sting like a bee," and he promoted himself and his prowess in poetry, braggadocio, and ranting interviews. Unlike black champions Joe Louis or Floyd Patterson, he extolled his blackness and demanded respect from white fans and the white-controlled media, who generally found his antics somewhat amusing but hard to accept. Despite his quick ascendance, Ali faced another black boxer, heavyweight champion Sonny Liston, as a 7-1 underdog in 1964. Liston, a sullen, scowling, fearsome brute of a man, an ex-convict, and a pawn of underworld gangsters, seemed invincible in the ring. Still, Clay stopped Liston, then announced his name change and conversion to the militant, separatist Black Muslim faith, which many whites viewed as a mysterious, anti-American threat to themselves and the established order.

Ali declared himself "the greatest" and became more vocal in his criticism of U.S. society. With the heavyweight throne as his pulpit, he became more defiant and more influential. He defeated a string of challengers, including former champion Floyd Patterson, who had promised to return the title to Christian America. Ali punished him severely in the ring for his insolence. To many, he seemed the devil incarnate, and for others he represented black retribution (Miller and Wiggins 293). Ali even predicted the specific rounds of his knockout victories, but though he remained undefeated in the ring the federal government stopped the verbose champ by indicting him for evading the military draft in 1967. Ali refused to join the Army and fight in Vietnam, saying that he had no quarrel with the Viet Cong, and he sought conscientious objector status based on his religious beliefs. The government not only denied his request but also levied a five-year prison sentence and a $10,000 fine. Ali appealed his case to the U.S. Supreme Court, but as he awaited the verdict state boxing associations banned him from the sport. Stripped of his title and unable to pursue his livelihood, he assumed the role of a principled martyr who placed his values above lucre, fame, and glory. His enforced absence only made him more celebrated as the antiwar movement escalated.

Popular lyrics of protest songs exemplified discontent with the Vietnam War and its reliance on poor and working-class soldiers, with blacks providing an inordinate number of draftees. A popular rock song exemplified the sense of working-class fatalism:

> And it's one, two, three, what are we fighting for? Don't ask me, I don't give a damn. Next stop, VIETNAM! And it's five, six, seven, open up the pearly gates. Ah, there ain't no time to wonder why. Whoopee! We're all goin' to die! (Country Joe and the Fish)

Forced to relinquish his crown by judicial fiat, but undeterred in his mission, Muhammad Ali staged perhaps the most dramatic and prolonged comeback in sports history. Ali engaged deeply in the most serious issues of the nation, including race, religion, and patriotism, but he pursued his fistic encounters with a malevolent sense of play, both clowning and teasing opponents. After wresting the title from Sonny Liston in 1964, he defeated nine straight challengers. Three years later, his conviction on the charge of dodging the draft precluded more fights either at home or abroad, as the State Department revoked his passport. Thus Ali spent the best physical years of his life in professional limbo.

In 1971, however, the U.S. Supreme Court overturned the 1967 ruling. Meanwhile, Ali had found a way to begin an epic quest to regain his title in 1970 by fighting in Georgia, a state without a boxing commission. After knocking out two white opponents that year, he met then-champion Joe Frazier in Madison Square Garden for the heavyweight crown. Their contrasting styles made for some of the greatest bouts in boxing history. Ali's long absence had diminished his speed and his ability to slip punches, thus forcing him to use more guile. Frazier, a relentless brawler with a devastating left hook and slurred speech, presented a distinct divergence from the loquacious Ali. Frazier emerged victorious in a hard-fought 15-round decision, but Ali earned a 12-round judgment in a return match in 1974. Later that year, Ali met George Foreman in Kinshasa, Zaire, for the heavyweight championship. The younger, bigger, stronger Foreman, a lumbering slugger and patriotic hero of the 1968 Olympics, presented a formidable foe. Ali employed his "rope-a-dope" strategy, letting Foreman hit him with punishing blows as he covered up along the ropes. By the eighth round, Foreman had dissipated his strength and succumbed to a knockout by Ali. In 1975, Ali and Frazier faced each other a third time, in the Philippines, in an epic fight known as the "Thrilla in Manila." Each man took turns battering the other until both could barely stand, yet they continued to answer the bell. Both demonstrated remarkable courage and a steadfast resolve not to admit defeat. The referee awarded Ali a technical knockout (TKO) in the 14th round, but both fighters exhibited qualities of greatness.

Ali continued to fight well past his prime, but even in retirement he remained a worldwide icon. In 1980, he became a government envoy to Africa, and a decade later he traveled to Iraq to help free 15 American hostages. Later silenced by Parkinson's disease, he continued to demonstrate an unwavering spirit. In 1996, he lit the Olympic torch to open the Atlanta Games. As an athlete, rebel, and social protagonist, he remained a symbol of a defiant generation and of the evolution he helped to spur in American society.

The black athletic revolt coincided with Ali's plight. In 1965, African American players organized a boycott of the AFL All-Star Game and maintained numerous grievances throughout the decade, including lower salaries than their white colleagues, the lack of black coaches, and the practice of "stacking," which assigned African Americans to roles that required athleticism but not leadership or the utmost intelligence, as coaches presumed whites were superior in such areas. Black baseball players, for example, were usually assigned to the outfield, and black football players might be receivers or cornerbacks but never the center or quarterback.

Black discontent occasionally exploded in violence. Malcolm X, the charismatic spokesman of the Nation of Islam, was assassinated by rivals in 1965. That same year Watts, a black neighborhood in Los Angeles, erupted in a riot that resulted in 35 deaths and $40 million in damage. Two years later, riots ravaged Cleveland, Newark, and Detroit, as Black Power advocates called for social, political, and economic potency. Others, such as Stokely Carmichael and H. Rap Brown, leaders of the Student Non-Violent Coordinating Committee (SNCC), extolled racial pride and self-reliance, but extremists like the Nation of Islam favored a separate black nation, and the militant Black Panther Party engaged in violent confrontations with the white power structure.

After Ali's sentencing, Harry Edwards, a black sociology professor at San José State College, organized the Olympic Project for Human Rights (OPHR), an attempt to have black athletes boycott the 1968 Olympic Games. The OPHR listed several demands: restoring Ali to his heavyweight championship; removing the conservative and seemingly racist International Olympic Committee (IOC) president Avery Brundage; excluding countries that practiced segregation from Olympic competition; appointing black coaches to the United States Olympic Committee; and integrating African American athletes into the powerful, all-white New York Athletic Club (NYAC). Black athletes boycotted the NYAC indoor track meet in February 1968, and the IOC did exclude South Africa, an apartheid state, from the Olympics that spring. At the same time, it seemed that American society had been rent asunder, with the assassinations of Martin Luther King and Robert Kennedy. College students and antiwar protesters, battered by Chicago policemen at the Democratic National Convention, mocked the political and judicial system. At least 37 colleges faced athletic boycotts, as well as student demands for black student centers and more black coaches of athletic teams, and the NBA players' association decided to strike.

Edwards' movement lost its cohesion when the student-athletes went on summer break, but athletes maintained their attitudes and their defiance at the Olympic Games, which produced some amazing performances. The most stunning image of the festival appeared after the 200-meter final, in which African American Tommie Smith won the gold medal in world-record time and fellow African American John Carlos took the bronze. On the victory stand, they stood in black socks and raised clenched fists in black gloves to form the Black Power salute as the national anthem played. Thus a worldwide audience bore witness to America's troubled race relations. The USOC suspended both from the American team and sent them home the next day.

Challenge to Athletic Serfdom

In 1969, the United States took great pride in the *Apollo 11* moon landing, but that success did not allay racial issues in sport, as athletes in general, and African American athletes in particular, sought greater control over their lives. In basketball, the NBA–ABA league rivalry led the Denver Nuggets of the ABA to sign Spencer Haywood, a 20-year-old sophomore from the University of Detroit who had played on the 1968 Olympic team. Haywood had a phenomenal year in the ABA, leading the league in scoring and rebounding and earning recognition not only as Rookie of the Year but also as Most Valuable Player. The next year, he opted for the Seattle SuperSonics of the NBA, but NBA draft rules stated that no player could be signed to a contract until his college class had graduated, a rule intended to keep athletes from leaving school early to join the professional ranks. A federal court decided the issue in Haywood's favor, stating that he constituted a hardship case because he provided necessary financial support for his family. The ruling eventually altered the NBA draft system, forcing the league to allow players to enter its draft regardless of their age.

In pro basketball, Julius "Doctor J" Erving created even more excitement for fans. He left the University of Massachusetts after two years to join the Virginia Squires of the ABA in 1971 before playing in the NBA, first for the New York Nets and then for the Philadelphia 76ers. His style of play was electrifying, as his phenomenal jumping ability, combined with expressive flair that later became known as "black style," enabled him to take over a game, shifting the offensive focus from the big center under the basket to the brilliant individualist who was extremely mobile with the ball. Erving ended his career in 1987 as the only noncenter to record thirty thousand points. Such accomplishments raised African Americans to the pinnacle of the sports world and thoroughly demolished any lingering Social Darwinist doubt about the abilities of nonwhites.

In baseball, Curt Flood challenged the reserve clause (standard in players' contracts), which tied them to one team. An all-star centerfielder for the St. Louis Cardinals, he refused to accept a trade to the Philadelphia Phillies in 1969 because he detested being treated like a piece of property. He sat out the 1970 season, then returned to play with a different team, the Washington Senators. The Supreme Court narrowly ruled 5-3 against him (with one justice abstaining), invoking the 1922 trial concept that baseball did not constitute a business and therefore could not be sued as a monopoly. The baseball players' union, established in 1953, assumed real power with the hiring of Marvin Miller as its executive director in 1966. Under Miller, players continually challenged the reserve clause and the owners' ability to bind them to one team and hold down their salaries. In 1969, they boycotted spring training, and three years later they went on strike, forcing the owners to grant better pension plans.

With the changes wrought by the Civil Rights Movement and an increasing acceptance of diversity, African American athletes attained greater exposure in the media, and their athletic presence fostered societal changes. In 1974, Frank Robinson became the first black manager in Major League Baseball when he was named to lead the Cleveland

Indians. That year also saw Hank Aaron hit his 715th home run, thus surpassing the seemingly insurmountable record set decades earlier by Babe Ruth—and doing so amidst death threats by racists who still subscribed to a false belief in white supremacy. He finished his career with a total of 755 home runs and a .305 batting average and held the career records for most extra base hits, most total bases, and most runs batted in. In track and field, Edwin Moses won the 400-meter hurdles race at the Montreal Olympics in 1976, and a year later he started a 122-race winning streak that lasted nearly 10 years.

NFL players had formed a labor union in 1956, but it lacked impetus until the NFL–AFL merger in 1966. Thereafter, the players demanded batter salaries and pension plans, as well as the right to counsel during contract negotiations. Players went on strike before the 1968 season and won some concessions from owners, who raised the minimum salary from $7,000 to $12,000 (Rader, *American Sports* [1983] 350). The owners retaliated, however, by trading or demoting the player representatives who had led the strike.

While salary, retirement benefits, and respect formed the focus of most professional athletes' concerns, racism fostered other activism in the professional and college ranks. In 1965, African American players refused to play in the AFL All-Star Game in New Orleans after being refused service there, and league officials were forced to move the contest to Houston. The 1969 season brought several player rebellions to collegiate campuses. At Oregon State University, 47 players quit the football team, and player revolts elsewhere protesting harsh treatment of players (e.g., prohibitions on interracial dating, lack of black coaches, and the stacking of athletes) led to the firing of coaches at the universities of Maryland, Wyoming, and Washington (Wiggins, *Glory Bound*).

Sport and Feminism

Adding to the clamor for change, the National Organization for Women fostered a feminist voice in 1966, and female physical educators began advocating for girls and women to have sports opportunities equal to those available to boys and men. Thus the athletic rebellion spread to women's sport as well.

In 1968, Billie Jean King, a top female tennis star, exposed the hypocrisy of the famous Wimbledon tournament, which billed itself as an amateur affair. King boycotted the competition, refusing to play unless she was accorded her true value in the clandestine payments made to male players. Consequently, Wimbledon officials dropped the hypocrisy and declared the matches an open event, admitting professional players, and King went on to win the women's championship.

Women made great gains in securing their own opportunities during the 1970s, and Billie Jean King led the way. In 1970, she and seven other female pros refused to play in a Los Angeles tennis tournament that offered the women only a fraction of the men's purse. Instead, they enrolled in the newly founded Virginia Slims Tour, sponsored by a cigarette company that marketed itself to women, and in 1971 King earned $100,000 by playing tennis, becoming the first female athlete to reach that figure.

Billie Jean King was a champion of women's rights both on and off the court.

AP Photo/Harry Harris

PEOPLE & PLACES

Gladys Medalie Heldman

Gladys Medalie Heldman started playing tennis only after her two daughters were born, but her contributions were profound. Heldman founded *World Tennis* magazine in 1953, serving as publisher and editor in chief, and she championed the founding of the women's professional tennis tour to provide more equity in prize money for women. In 1970, she spearheaded the movement of the best women's players like Billie Jean King, Rosie Casals, and Nancy Richie to form their own professional tour. Heldman signed these women to $1 contracts with *World Tennis* to play in a pro event in Houston. The Virginia Slims Circuit became the women's professional tour, and this women's professional tour gained popularity, eventually merging with the United States Tennis Association (USTA). Heldman is an inductee of the International Tennis Hall of Fame and the International Jewish Sports Hall of Fame.

She gained much greater fame and social significance, however, for her 1973 match against Bobby Riggs, a former tennis champion, a self-promoter, and an acknowledged chauvinist, then 55 years old, who claimed that he could still defeat any woman. He emphasized his point by easily beating Margaret Court, one of the top women, 6-2, 6-1, on Mother's Day in 1973. The loss seemingly checked the growth of women's tennis and to some extent the feminist movement, until Billie Jean King accepted Riggs' challenge. Offered $100,000 to play and double that if she won, King showed up at the Houston Astrodome before more than thirty thousand spectators, the largest crowd to ever witness a tennis match. Satellite television delivered the contest to thirty-six countries throughout the world. In a lavish, exaggerated spectacle promoted as the "Battle of the Sexes," King destroyed Riggs, 6-4, 6-3, 6-3, to make an emphatic statement about the rightful place of women in sport (Rader, *American Sports* [1983] 344). The win also established King as a leader in the feminist movement, and she used her television appearances as an outspoken advocate for the women's rights movement.

Title IX

In 1971, women formed the Association for Intercollegiate Athletics for Women (AIAW) in order to promote more sports opportunities for female college students. Lobbying efforts by female activists in Congress produced a federal law, known as Title IX of the Education Amendments of 1972, which required equal opportunities for both genders in any high school, college, or university that received federal aid. Title IX states:

> No person in the United States shall, on the basis of sex, be excluded from participation in, be denied the benefits of, or be subjected to discrimination under any education program or activity receiving Federal financial assistance. (qtd. in Carpenter and Acosta 3)

The law was very often applied to gain equal opportunities in sport, and, though it was challenged by the NCAA, schools, coaches, and individuals, the courts consistently upheld it, thus prompting wholesale changes in the funding and selection of teams in all public school programs (Ware). Girls even won the right to play on Little League baseball teams. Interscholastic girls' teams proliferated, and participants jumped from only 294,000 at the beginning of the decade to almost 2 million at its end (Rader, *American Sports* [1983] 341). At the college level, the AIAW initiated separate championships for women in various sports.

Because female administrators initially intended to forgo the commercialized, overly competitive model of the men's programs, they did not want to offer incentives to the athletes like scholarships. However, a 1973 court case initiated by a female athlete required athletic scholarships for women similar to those granted to men, and women's basketball, the most popular of female sports, soon had its own version of the recruiting wars that marked men's programs.

The rising popularity of women's sports led the NCAA to offer its own intercollegiate championships for women in 1981 in direct competition with the AIAW. Unable to compete with the overflowing NCAA treasury, which controlled television contracts, the AIAW suffered. Moreover, athletic directors at coed schools were almost universally male, and they tended to opt for membership in the NCAA rather than the AIAW. By 1983, the AIAW had ceased operations and sued the NCAA as a monopoly, a case that it lost due to the existence of the National Association of Intercollegiate Athletics (NAIA), an alternative governing body which provides its own intercollegiate championships. Despite the promise of Title IX, the demise of the AIAW severely retarded the growth of leadership opportunities for women, as well as any sense of power within the intercollegiate bureaucracy. Male athletic directors tended to hire male coaches, even for women's teams. In 1972, more than 90 percent of women's teams had been led by female coaches, but that number would dwindle to 44 percent by 2004. Similarly, more than 90 percent of women's intercollegiate programs had a female athletic director in 1972, but that figure fell to only 18 percent by 2004 (Acosta and Carpenter, "A Longitudinal Study" 2–3).

Despite such dire trends, women and girls achieved great success in some areas. In 1970, Diane Crump became the first female jockey to ride in the Kentucky Derby, and in 1974 at least 60 women earned their living as jockeys. That same year, Billie Jean King organized World Team Tennis, a new format that provided more opportunities for female professional players. The Ladies Professional Golf Association (LPGA) also continued to grow, providing 33 tournaments and $3 million in prize money for female golfers by 1977. Women also entered the male world of auto racing. Janet Guthrie joined the NASCAR ranks in 1977, and she also competed in the Indy 500. Shirley Muldowney, a drag racer beginning in 1972, garnered three national championships. Such household names established auto racing beyond its rural roots, eventually attracting middle-class Northern suburbanites, both male and female, to its fan base.

While such firsts presented evidence of women's interests, abilities, and accomplishments, one popular female sporting event continued to attract players and fans. The Iowa girls' high school basketball championship surpassed that of the boys in interest. The first state tournament was held in 1920, when six contestants per team played on a divided court that limited players' exertions (the game began a gradual shift to the more conventional full-court game, with five players per team, in 1985). Partly because of their distinctive, traditional style of play, the girls' teams had developed a loyal following, and the girls' tournaments received television coverage as early as 1951. Tournament games were played in the state capital, and tickets and hotel rooms had to be booked months in advance. Tournament week even became a long holiday for some schools, and the festival atmosphere and accompanying rituals of honor bestowed respect upon the players and indicated the value placed on girls' physicality in Iowa. As with boys' sports in other states, winning teams promoted civic pride and local traditions. By the end of the 1970s, a national survey found that Iowa had the nation's highest percentage of female high school athletes (Hult and Trekell 200). Thus the case of Iowa showed not only that girls could play basketball but also that there were sizable audiences for girls' sport.

Sport, Narcissism, and the Existential Search for Self

The expansion of sport coincided with an ongoing transition in American culture. The Vietnam War dragged on into the 1970s, escalating tensions between protestors and authorities, and in May 1970 the National Guard fired upon protestors at Kent State University in Ohio,

Soccer in Europe: From a Men's Sport to a Women's Game

While soccer was played at women's colleges in the United States as a recreational activity from the early 1900s onward, women's soccer met with considerable opposition in Europe, where it was viewed as one of those sports completely unsuited to a woman's nature and therefore properly left entirely to men. In the United States, soccer seems to be viewed as feminine and as a women's game, while in the rest of the world soccer is seen as a male domain that arouses the connotation of masculinity.

Despite all reservations, however, a women's soccer movement began to develop in a number of European countries at the end of the nineteenth century, especially in England and France. In 1894, the British Ladies' Football Club was inaugurated, and only a year later various women's teams competed against each other, cheered on by thousands of spectators of both sexes. Women's soccer reached a peak of popularity at a time of great national fervor during World War I, when soccer games between women's teams were held in order to raise money for the care of wounded soldiers. After the war, however, the Football Association (FA; the governing body of football in England) called upon its clubs to withdraw their support from women's soccer matches, which it regarded as unworthy of the "fair sex." This development constituted a severe setback to, but not the end of, women's soccer in England.

During the First World War, women's soccer teams were also founded in France, where the first women's soccer championship occurred in 1917, and two cup tournaments were introduced in 1922. During the 1920s, numerous matches were played, not only between French teams but also against women's teams from other European countries. However, even though women's sport in France had its own federation, the Fédération des Sociétés Féminines Sportives de France (FSFSF), women's soccer met with increasing resistance, since it allegedly resulted in women players becoming too masculine. In the 1930s, news about women's soccer in France became increasingly scarce. The development of women's soccer in England and France can be explained by specific conditions. In England the purpose of the games for charity compensated for the transgression of femininity by the players. In France, a strong women's sport movement supported the expansion of women's football.

In contrast to the situation in England and France and in some other countries in Europe, there was never any question in Germany that a soccer pitch was no place for women. (On women's soccer in other countries, see, for example, page 18 of issue number 9 of *Sport und Gesundheit* [Sport and Health] from 1938.) Thus, the attempt of a number of women to found a women's soccer club in Frankfurt was doomed to failure.

After the Second World War, interest in soccer was revived among women in various European countries, but soccer associations reacted with either indifference or outright rejection. In 1955, for example, the German soccer association prohibited its clubs from opening women's sections or even making grounds available for women's teams. As evidence to support this stance, the federation cited doctors who warned about the risks to women's health. In several countries, including Denmark and England, women players founded their own associations, but these groups mustered few clubs. In other countries, such as Italy, professional women's teams were formed with the help of private sponsors, but women's soccer continued to play only a marginal role. It was not until the late 1960s that individual initiatives were bundled, pressure on associations was increased, and the ban on women's soccer was lifted in many countries. Women's soccer was then integrated into men's soccer associations, not least because soccer officials did not wish to lose control over the women's soccer movement. In all European countries, cup competitions and leagues were introduced along the lines of those already established in men's soccer.

The growing popularity of women's soccer is also due to the international matches played since 1969. In that year, for example, the privately financed Federation of Independent European Soccer, based in Italy, organized an official tournament called the Europe Cup with teams from France, Denmark, England and Italy, and one year later an unofficial world championship was organized which enthralled fifty thousand spectators. However, it was not until 20 years later, in 1991, that the first official world championships were held, in China.

In 1996, when the Olympic Games were held in Atlanta, women's soccer was added to the list of Olympic sports, and today women's soccer is popular all over the world. According to statistics from the Fédération Internationale de Football Association (FIFA), around 26 million girls and women play soccer, with 4.1 million of them registered for competitions.

Nevertheless, prejudices and difficulties still abound, ranging from the image of women players (who are widely thought to be too "mannish") to the lack of financial resources and the insufficient attention they receive from the media. However, whereas the media made fun of the spectacle of soccer-playing viragos right up to the 1980s, women's soccer is a recognized sport today, albeit one with a limited audience (Pfister).

In a certain respect, women's soccer is ensnared in a vicious circle. The media's lack of interest, and as a result the lack of public interest, leads to a lack of interest among sponsors, which in turn hinders professionalization and lowers the status of women's soccer.

Information from Hong, Fan, and J. A. Mangan, eds. *Soccer, Women, Sexual Liberation: Kicking Off a New Era.* London: Cass, 2003; Pfister, Gertrud. "The future of football is female!? On the past and present of women's football in Germany." Tomlinson, A. and Young, C. *German Football. History, Culture, Society.* London/New York: Routledge, 2006: 93–126

killing four students. This overreaction raised questions about the limits of free speech and the authoritarian responses of a police state. The United States suffered additional turmoil in the Watergate scandal of 1972, when reporters for the *Washington Post* revealed that President Richard Nixon had authorized a burglary of the offices of the Democratic Party's national committee. Nixon's lies in attempting to cover up the fiasco led to his impeachment, and to even greater concern for the moral and ethical state of the nation.

Because aggressive, martial games were thought to produce or encourage warlike behavior, and because the Cold War brought fears of nuclear annihilation, educators began questioning American cultural values during the 1960s, and some physical educators proposed a New Games Movement consisting of noncompetitive activities, such as Frisbee. Many Americans turned inward, developing an interest in the self, the one thing they might control. Some focused on their appearance or on developing new abilities, while others turned to psychoanalysis to reveal new truths. Many sought refuge or pleasure in new lifestyles, experimenting with Asian religions or unconventional sexual practices. In such a state of inquiry, many people also sought relief in myriad therapies, some of which included experimentation with drugs, especially marijuana. Drugs became commonplace among athletes as well.

Athletes' Fall From Grace

Despite athletic successes—both at the individual level and in the general growth of certain sports—sport lost much of its idealistic connotations. Sportswriters and, in some cases, athletes themselves wrote critical exposés of sport that examined drug use, alcohol abuse, sexual escapades, "wife swapping," and exploitation of players. Jim Bouton's *Ball Four* (1970) became a best seller, and Peter Gent's novel *North Dallas Forty* (1973) further examined the corruption of professional sport and American society. Indeed, the ideology of sport had been transformed by the 1970s. The media no longer uniformly idolized athletes, as investigative reporters delved into their private lives with sensationalized coverage, revealing their all-too-human frailties and failures. In addition, athletes became entertainers and were thus subject to the same stew of adulation, exposure, and criticism that other stars faced. And as their salaries increased, distancing them from the working classes, commoners increasingly lost a sense of identification with their former heroes.

Sport and Physical Activity as an Elixir for Health

The tarnished image of athletes, along with the increasing media portrayal of sport as entertainment, diminished some of its idealistic notions, but physical activity for personal enjoyment or betterment, such as improving one's health, assumed greater importance. While many young people turned to the bright lights and pulsating sounds of disco dancing to relieve their tensions, others found sport. Doctors, philosophers, and psychologists began to extol the virtues of running for health and happiness. Dr. Kenneth Cooper, NASA scientist and later personal physician to President Ronald Reagan, promoted a national campaign for aerobic exercise, which developed into a major activity for women and exerted a large influence on many women's lives. Cardiologist George Sheehan wrote a best-selling book on the existential benefits of running, and theologian Michael Novak equated sport (especially running) with a mystical, religious experience. Approximately 20 million Americans, including President Jimmy Carter, began jogging during the 1970s (Rader, *American Sports* [1983] 359). *The Complete Book of Running*, written by Jim Fixx (who, ironically, died of a heart attack while jogging), sold more than a million copies, and a fitness craze was under way, as many Americans sought health and fulfillment in a narcissistic pursuit of human perfection (Plymire).

The exploits of American running stars such as Steve Prefontaine, Frank Shorter, and Mary Decker (Slaney) thrilled onlookers and set many on a path to fitness. Shorter won the Olympic marathon in Munich in 1972, as well as several national championships in distance races. Decker ran a marathon at age 12, and in 1973, at age 14, she defeated Russian women in a dual meet in the 800 meters. A year later, she owned three world records, and she remained America's best throughout the ongoing Cold War, setting numerous records during the 1980s and inspiring many women and young girls to run.

INTERNATIONAL PERSPECTIVE

Sport for All: A European Sport Concept

In many societies there are physical cultures that have always been oriented toward encouraging the participation of a wide section of the populace. In the nineteenth century, Swedish gymnastics and the *Turner* movement in Germany, for example, aimed to provide a comprehensive system of physical exercise for the population (albeit males only). Modern sport, on the other hand, was based on the principles of competition and performance, engaged only a small sporting elite. In the United States, for example, sport is generally organized around staging competition for the best athletes rather than encouraging sport for all.

In recent decades, however, European sport has undergone a huge process of differentiation. An increasing number of sporting activities, from aerobics to roller skating, that are oriented toward neither competition nor performance, have become popular. This process of "de-sportification" has motivated new target groups—women, senior citizens, and disabled persons, among others—to take up sport; and sport is transforming into an activity that attracts and includes large sections of the population.

In the 1970s, various European countries sponsored advertising devoted to the idea of "sport for all" (i.e., recreational sporting activities as well as basic-level competitive sports). The German Sports Federation, for example, propagated the "sport for all" movement with slogans like "Trimm Dich durch Sport" [Fit through Sport].

The aim of convincing as many people as possible, if not everyone, of the benefits of sport was strongest in those European countries in which the main providers of sport were sports clubs. A representative survey of participation in sports and physical activities in the countries of the European Union (Eurobarometer 2003) showed that the percentage of the population that had taken part in either some or a lot of sports and physical activities during the past seven-day period was more than 50 percent in Sweden, Finland, Germany, and the Netherlands (among other countries), whereas in Greece and Romania the corresponding figure was 19 percent.

Sports clubs are nonprofit organizations with charitable status and democratically elected executive boards. They are responsible for sports training and the organizing of competitions as well as for providing recreational sporting activities. Small clubs that offer only one sport exist side by side with huge sports associations that have several thousand members. Members not only take part in the numerous sports provided by their clubs but also make use of the clubs' fitness rooms, swimming baths, restaurants, and other facilities. Germany (around 80 million inhabitants) has 90,000 sports clubs while Denmark (5 million inhabitants) has 14,000, and Netherlands (16.5 million inhabitants) has 29,000.

In countries such as the Netherlands, Belgium, Germany, and the Scandinavian countries, more than 30% of the population are members of a sports club. Sports clubs attract more men than women (who make up around 38% of membership), more young people than older people, and scarcely any immigrants.

Clubs are partly financed by membership fees and entrance fees for events and other activities; this income is supplemented by money from sponsors and public funding in particular. In addition, clubs benefit from the free use of sport facilities, mostly schools' facilities, which they are allowed to use in the evenings and on weekends. In this way clubs can provide a comprehensive and inexpensive range of sports.

Clubs form the base of a pyramid, with regional associations at the next level and national federations at the apex. National federations (like the football or swimming federation) are responsible for a specific sport; they form an umbrella organization which coordinates and oversees sport and physical activities in a country and represents sport in its dealings with the state and the public.

Sports organizations from the club level to the national federation level are based on the principles of democracy and autonomy as well as those of volunteering and reciprocity. The leaders of sports organizations are volunteers, and many of the coaches and instructors are only reimbursed for their expenses or paid a small amount of money in recognition for their work. The principle of reciprocity signifies that the work put in by volunteers is compensated for by the work of others. A club's public relations official, for example, may write reports for the press without getting paid, but he or she is also able to take advantage of the work done free of charge by others (for instance, the trainers).

In most European countries, the state provides the legal as well as the material basis of sports organizations and supports their activities. Funding for sports frequently comes from national lotteries, and grants are given because sports organizations claim to provide work of great value to the society as a whole. The relationship between state and organized sport is characterized by partnership and cooperation.

Information from European Commission. *Eurobarometer—Physical Activity.* 2003 <http://www.eufic.org/upl/1/default/doc/ebs_183_6_en.pdf>; Heinemann, Klaus. Ed. *Sport Clubs in Various European Countries.* Hofmann Verlag Schorndorf, 1999.

Women Dispel Notions of Physical Debility

Although the modern marathon had been invented for the Olympic Games in 1896, it was only after World War II that new and more realistic opinions about women's endurance capacities began to take hold. Female athletes were allowed to compete in the 800-meter run in the 1960 Olympics and the 1500-meter distance in the 1972

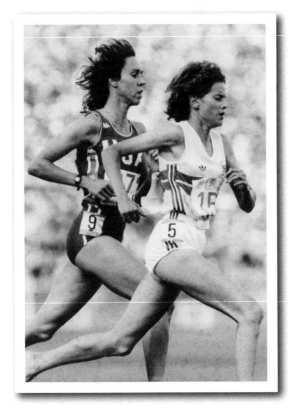

Mary Decker Slaney (in back), America's best runner, never realized her dream of Olympic gold but gave world-record performances in other competitions.
© Bettmann/CORBIS

Games. Women's participation in the marathon, however, was still considered unthinkable by those who held the power in the running world, and attempts by women to run in legendary races such as the Boston Marathon were looked upon as sacrilege.

Nonetheless, in 1966, Roberta Gibb participated without registering. She mixed into the pack shortly after the start and reached the finish line in about 3 1/2 hours without being detected. In 1967, Kathrine Switzer registered as "K.V. Switzer" and got a start number. Soon after the race began, however, she was discovered as a woman, and, though supported by other runners and cheered by the media, she was physically attacked by one of the race's codirectors, who tried to pull her out of the race. Her 235-pound (107-kilogram) boyfriend intervened, hitting the attacker with a cross-body block, and Switzer continued on to finish the race. Not until 1972 could women participate "officially" and without disguise in the Boston Marathon. One year earlier, a female runner had fulfilled the dream of every long-distance runner by participating in the legendary New York City Marathon. In the 1980s, women's long-distance running experienced its breakthrough. The first women's marathon world championship took place in 1983 in Helsinki, and in 1984, for the first time, women could compete for Olympic laurels in the marathon. That year, American Joan Benoit, a former collegiate runner, won the gold medal.

PEOPLE & PLACES

Steve Prefontaine

© Associated Press

Upon his early death in a 1975 car accident at age 24, runner Steve Prefontaine (pictured at the front of the pack) held 14 American distance records and had attracted a legion of loyal followers. Brash, outspoken, and confident, like Muhammad Ali, the white Prefontaine expressed a singular devotion to his sport that assumed the characteristics of religious zeal. Prefontaine campaigned against what he considered to be outdated amateur ideals and attacked the bureaucracy for failing to support and develop athletes. His public and verbal war against the AAU attracted disenfranchised youth, who saw him as a hero willing to confront the establishment. Among the first to wear Nike running shoes, Prefontaine provided a major boost to the fledgling company that his University of Oregon coach, Bill Bowerman, had cofounded with Phil Knight, one of Bowerman's former runners. Ironically, Prefontaine's rebellious image was transformed into a corporate icon after his death.

Scientific Advancements and the Growth of Sport

While football surpassed baseball as American's most popular game in the 1960s, other sports also rose in prominence, as scientific advancements allowed both for the expansion of sport to new locations and for the birth of new kinds of sport.

In 1966, thanks to the building of indoor ice arenas, the National Hockey League expanded its traditional winter sport into the South (Atlanta) and to the West Coast (San Francisco and Los Angeles) in hopes of reaping television profits from such large markets. In 1965, Houston built the Astrodome at a cost of $45 million, launching an era in which such facilities changed the nature of sport, allowing for year-round play, eliminating the effects of weather, and (due to artificial turf) increasing the velocity of players and balls in baseball and football, thus placing greater emphasis on speed-based strategies. Leagues staged more night games in order to accommodate daytime workers and to draw additional television viewers during prime-time programming. Technology also changed the nature of coaching, as the Dallas Cowboys began using computers to aid analysis and planning in preparing for specific opponents and drafting prospective players.

The effect of new technology was particularly marked in auto racing, as better-designed cars and more powerful engines (along with outstanding drivers) attracted more fans. Popular drivers included A. J. Foyt, who won three Indy 500 races during the 1960s, added a fourth in 1977, and also raced on the United States Auto Club (USAC) circuit, earning five championships, and in the European Grand Prix at Le Mans in 1967. His rival, Italian immigrant Mario Andretti, proved equally popular, winning the 1965 USAC championship, the 1967 Daytona 500 (a NASCAR event), the 1969 Indianapolis 500, and the 1977 European Grand Prix in a sleek Formula One racer. Meanwhile, Richard Petty dominated the NASCAR (stock-car) racing circuit, established in 1949 and centered in the South by the 1960s. A North Carolinian, Petty became a superstar by winning 200 races, seven championships, and seven Daytona 500s. His racing team, composed of family members, developed technological innovations to aid their driver, including a safety roll bar, two-way radios to communicate with the pit crew, and a cooling helmet.

Bowling was also affected. In 1956, the Brunswick Company, a bowling equipment manufacturer, began installing automatic pinspotters in bowling alleys, thus turning a tedious manual job (previously reserved for "pinboys") over to machines that performed the task cheaply, effectively, and efficiently. Bowling alleys began to expand in size, and matinee bowling leagues became a popular attraction for women (Rader, *American Sports* [1983] 337) The Brunswick Company's sales figures rose from $33 million in 1954 to $422 million in 1961, and Brunswick sponsored a championship bowling series on television. Large bowling emporiums appeared in cities and suburbs, with the Edison, New Jersey, establishment featuring 112 lanes (Kogan 172–173). As with boxing, however, bowling's initial popularity would eventually recede, until bowlers assumed the role of entertainers by amusing spectators not only with their skills but also with antics and emotional displays.

In addition, the confluence of sport and the still-developing modern medium of television continued to pay great dividends for both sides, as regional and previously minor sports became mainstream, providing programming for networks and greater exposure for athletes. Corporate sponsors flocked to support athletic contests, enriching the networks, college teams, professional team owners, and athletes in a symbiotic relationship.

Summary

This chapter has detailed the impact of television on sport, including the innovative broadcasting strategies that generated great popularity, the increased revenue produced by the broadcasting of sporting events, and the labor relations issues created by such wealth. The continual growth of professional football within this process allowed it to surpass baseball as the national sport.

During the Cold War, sport also became a political tool, with the Olympics being used for nationalistic purposes and highlighting ideological differences between capitalism and communism. Within the United States, minorities and women used sport to address and attack social inequalities and achieve a greater measure of civil rights and women's rights.

While various sports moved closer to pure entertainment, and the behavior of some athletes caused them to lose their luster, physical activity assumed greater personal importance. The fitness boom fostered a running fad as part of a larger pursuit of health and self-enhancement strategies. The Baby Boomer generation (the one following World War II) produced enormous social change in American society, and sport proved to be an integral part of that process.

DISCUSSION QUESTIONS

1. What parallels can be drawn between the 1920s and the 1950s in sport?

2. How did sports journalism change from the 1920s to the 1980s?

3. How did television affect sporting culture?

4. How did the economics of sport change after the introduction of television?

5. In what ways did sport serve a political function during the Cold War?

6. How did the social movements of the 1960s affect sport?

7. Explain the importance of the "Battle of the Sexes" in tennis with regard to challenging gender roles in sport and society.

8. Discuss the various roles of Muhammad Ali as an agent of change in American society.

9. How did Title IX influence the relationships among sport, gender, and American culture?

9

Globalized Sport
1980–2007

CHAPTER OBJECTIVES

After reading this chapter, you will have learned about the following:

- The growth of media conglomerates and their relationship to sport
- The role of stadiums in achieving urban status
- The effects of sport on tourism
- Labor negotiations that have structured sport finance
- The ascendance of Michael Jordan as a global icon
- The globalization of sport
- The growing participation of girls and women in sport
- The issues that have marred the images of athletes and sport
- The appearance of new sport forms

The world of sport is expanding and changing rapidly. Some might trace the transformation to 1984, the year Michael Jordan entered the National Basketball Association (NBA):

> Jordan has been called "the new DiMaggio," and "Elvis in high-tops," indications of the Herculean cultural heroism he has come to embody. There is even a religious element to the near worship of Jordan as a cultural icon of invincibility, as he has been called a "savior of sorts," "basketball's high priest," and "more popular than Jesus," except with "better endorsement deals." (Dyson 259)

Regarding a 1997 trip by Jordan to Paris, the French media proclaimed, "Michael Jordan is in Paris…. That's better than the Pope. It's God in person" (qtd. in Halberstam 4).

When Jordan joined the Chicago Bulls, the franchise was in dire straits, valued at only $18.7 million, with few fans or television viewers. Ten years later, its value had surpassed $190 million (LaFeber 49). Concomitant with the rise and rivalry of Larry Bird and Earvin "Magic" Johnson, the NBA enjoyed a resurgence of interest. By 1996, NBA games were broadcast in 40 languages to more than 175 countries (LaFeber 135). Two years later, *Fortune* magazine credited Jordan with generating $10 billion for the U.S. economy (LaFeber 137). Within a decade of his entry into the NBA, the merger of Jordan, his numerous corporate sponsors, and the media complex dominated the athletic world and achieved prominence in the global communications industry. Jordan's international luster fostered an economic battle by multinational corporations for ever-larger markets, and the NBA, Major League Baseball (MLB), the National Hockey League (NHL), and even the National Football League (NFL) began importing non-American athletes who might embellish their rosters and, more importantly, attract new viewers inside and outside of the United States.

Yao Ming represents a new phase in American sport—globalization. Here, Yao battles with Zydrunas Ilgauskas of Lithuania during an NBA game in Houston, Texas, in 2008. Globalized sport indeed.

AP Photo/David J. Phillip

Thus American sporting culture became a global enterprise, a fact perhaps best seen recently in Yao Ming, the 7-foot-5-inch (2.3-meter) Chinese import, who has had the greatest economic impact of any NBA rookie since Michael Jordan. Home attendance for his team, the Houston Rockets, rose 17 percent, and for the first time in years the Rockets were also a draw on the road. The NBA is now aired on six Chinese TV networks ("New World Order").

Now comes Yao Ming—and all the ill-conceived clichés about those strange Chinese have been shattered like a glass backboard after a monstrous slam dunk. There is no living Chinese in the world today who is as famous as the lantern-jawed National Basketball Association rookie sensation. . . . Ratings for NBA games broadcast on Chinese TV [sic] have never been higher than this year as the nation keeps track of its new favorite team, Yao's Houston Rockets. . . .

Across North America, Yao's clean-cut, tattooless visage sells everything from Visa cards . . . [to] Apple computers. . . . Doubtless, marketers see Yao as their entry into the prized Chinese market, but who knew that an oversized hoopster with fragmented English would become the next It Boy for Madison Avenue? (Beech)

Yao represents the growing interest in, opportunity for, and expansion of American professional sport organizations in areas outside the United States. Such developments mark a departure from the ethnocentric and insular bias that had previously restricted teams and players to North American locales.

The intercontinental transport of sport forms and players accelerated after 1980, driven by the capitalist search for profitable markets and the growing competition between big media conglomerates. Such expansion had repercussions, however, as American popular culture permeated the world, bringing greater cultural homogeneity at the cost of diversity. In addition to American sports, movies, music, and clothing fashions, the English language also spread inexorably, and American corporations, with their aggressively competitive business practices, intruded upon local cultures. While some embraced aspects of change, such incursions sometimes prompted volatile responses, as some groups felt threatened with loss of their identity and traditional culture. They feared the overt commercialization, greed, plutocracy, violence, and drug abuse that they associated with the worst of American culture. More traditional patriarchal cultures feared the changing gender roles and youth culture that they perceived in the United States as a potential source of breakdown in their prescribed social divisions. As the Cold War persisted, both communist governments and some theocracies alike questioned American values, economic practices, and leadership.

In 1979, Iranians seized the United States Embassy in Tehran and held Americans hostage for more than a year. President Jimmy Carter's inability to win their release, along with high inflation and his unpopular boycott of the 1980 Olympics in Moscow, limited his presidency to one term. In the wake of the Iran hostage crisis, the United States elected Ronald Reagan, the California governor and former Hollywood actor, to the presidency. Reagan proved to be the most conservative chief executive in two generations, and his attacks on welfare and social programs hampered the livelihoods of the poverty stricken, who were further endangered by an economic recession in 1982. Moreover, memories of the Vietnam War still racked America with pangs of defeat and guilt. The unveiling of the Vietnam War Memorial in 1982 in Washington, D.C., was intended to soothe tensions, but its controversial and nontraditional design only heightened anxieties and sparked debate on the proper nature of honor, the construction of national memorials, the definition of heroes, and even the nobility of war itself.

Apprehension increased a year later, when the United States invaded the Caribbean nation of Grenada after a military coup installed a Marxist government. With Cuba ensconced in communism, the American government firmly opposed the spread of beliefs antithetical to its ideology. Reagan won a second term and conducted a clandestine war on another Marxist government, this one in Nicaragua. Meanwhile, as financial wizards amassed fortunes on Wall Street, the number of homeless Americans increased, more people became addicted to drugs (particularly crack cocaine), and AIDS began to devastate the population. Americans were riding a social roller coaster, and the nation as a whole mourned when the U.S. space shuttle *Challenger* exploded shortly after takeoff in 1986, killing all seven astronauts. The disaster called into question Americans' faith in their social, economic, and technological superiority even as the Soviet Union began to crumble.

Amidst the thriving of corporate culture and corporate values during the Reagan administration, common sport forms and practices were extended, sometimes regulated by unilateral sport governing bodies that increased their reach and influence. Thus the governing associations of the sporting culture assumed even greater significance.

1984
- Eastern Bloc nations boycott Summer Olympics in Los Angeles

› Joan Benoit wins first women's Olympic marathon

1986
- *Challenger* space shuttle explodes shortly after takeoff

1990
- Hubble Space Telescope launched

1990s
- Michael Jordan becomes global icon

1991
- Willy T. Ribbs becomes first African American Indy 500 driver
- U.S. women's soccer team wins the World Cup

1995
- World League of American Football (later NFL Europe) launched

Corporate Sporting Culture

Cable television, satellite dishes, and eventually the Internet produced a global explosion of sport in the last two decades of the twentieth century, as promoters fostered particular sport forms and processes of expansion linked to multinational corporate culture. In many cases, this process spread a more homogeneous Western sporting culture throughout the world, though indigenous pastimes and residual sport forms on the national, regional, and local levels resisted the globalization process.

American sports programming, such as ABC's *Wide World of Sports,* occasionally featured sports such as Afghan Buzkashi (an equestrian event with a goat head as the focus) or Japanese sumo wrestling as anomalous or exotic events. The Western sporting process, however, emphasized commercialized, quantified, and male-dominated sport forms, marketed and commodified to sell products, bodies, and ideas within a capitalist market economy. Western European sport associations especially fostered the growth of soccer, and the leaders of North American sports including football, baseball, basketball, and (to a lesser degree) ice hockey, sought larger economic markets on a global scale.

The marketing of American popular culture, athletes, and leagues themselves greatly expanded under the shrewd guidance of corporate-minded commissioners. Players, too, hired agents and managers to polish their images, win endorsements, and negotiate even larger salaries laden with incentive clauses in the major team sports. In individual sports, athletes increasingly filled roles as entertainers as well as competitors. Endorsement contracts often depended on visibility, appearance, and lifestyle as much as (or more than) on performance. Free agents continually sought larger markets, larger salaries, and greater endorsement opportunities.

As athletes sought and received more endorsement contracts, agencies were formed to help them manage these new dimensions of their careers. One of the first to cater to athletes in this capacity was Mark McCormack, a Cleveland lawyer who served as manager for the golfer Arnold Palmer. He expanded his company in the 1960s, and the resultant International Management Group (IMG) eventually employed more than 2,200 workers in 70 offices in 30 countries, becoming a major player in international sporting enterprises by the end of the century. Its success generated its own television division that produced sports programming for global distribution, spreading the influence of American sports and personalities around the world. As the economy transitioned from its industrial basis to one based on personal consumption in the latter twentieth century, companies relied increasingly on the marketing of goods to convince consumers of their value. The IMG enterprise branched out to include famous entertainers and models as well as athletes among its clients. Similar agencies arose to manage, market, and promote celebrities and their products both on and off the field.

Media Conglomerates

The establishment of the Entertainment and Sports Programming Network (ESPN) gave fans ever-increasing opportunity to saturate their lives with sport. The idea for a sports network originated in 1979 with Bill Rasmussen (public relations director for the New England Whalers), his son Scott, and entrepreneur Ed Eagan. Their modest objectives involved local markets in Bristol, Connecticut, but the enterprise soon exploded into 24-hour-a-day sports programming that met the wishes of "sports junkies" and provided greater exposure to sports previously considered marginal. To fill its schedule, ESPN offered women's basketball, field hockey, soccer, tennis, and golf, as well as men's intercollegiate ice hockey, basketball, tennis, skiing, and motor sports. Even the NFL draft found a host of viewers in a prime-time slot.

Sport Interest and Media Coverage in Various Countries

Interest in sport and sport consumption (in person or via the media) is not self-evident and natural but learned in and enforced through socialization processes. In numerous accounts or recollections, fans talk about their first encounters with "their" sport, which in most cases occurred in the family. Children develop a liking for sport, and a knowledge of certain sports, not only by playing them but also by watching television with their families or friends. Spectators identify with athletes and teams, thus "getting involved" in the action and developing a close commitment to the sporting activities which are popular in their respective cultures. Thus sport audiences differ, in their tastes as well as their practices, depending on their society's sporting traditions.

This phenomenon can be seen by analyzing the characteristics of those sports that are in the public gaze. What, for example, makes soccer in Europe so much more popular than artistic gymnastics or fencing? Attempts to answer this question with arguments referring to the "nature" of the different sports—their rules or the skills required to play them—soon lead to a dead end, not least since the same sport can be regarded as exciting and attractive in one country but tame and boring in another. In the United States, for example, baseball is a popular spectator sport, with huge crowds filling stadiums and mass audiences watching via television. In Germany and in many other European countries, however, baseball is virtually nonexistent. Thus it is not the sport but the inclination of the audience which determines the attraction of a sport or game, and this sense of taste is determined not only by individual preference but also by cultural and subcultural codes and scripts.

The differing interests of different audiences are mirrored in sports coverage, which varies to a high degree from country to country. In 2005, the International Sports Press Survey, conducted by the Danish newspaper *Mandag Morgen* (Monday Morning) in cooperation with universities in 10 different countries, revealed the following priorities in Australian sports coverage: Australian football (28 percent), rugby (22 percent), soccer (9 percent), equestrian sport (8 percent), and cricket (7 percent). In contrast, sports coverage in Europe showed an overwhelming focus on soccer (51 percent), with all other sports receiving only marginal coverage—for example, cycling (6 percent), tennis (6 percent), Formula One car racing (3 percent), and golf (3 percent). More than 50 Olympic sports, from rowing to track and field, are not visible in the media at all, either in Europe or in the United States. Coverage does, however, differ from country to country. Ski sports get more attention in Norway than in all other countries of the world, as does cricket in England and team handball in Denmark. Despite such differences, sports coverage in Australia, Europe, and the United States shares some general qualities, specifically the focus on top-level sport, on results, and on current events, with an emphasis on men's sport. Only 6 percent of the 10,007 articles included in the survey were dedicated to female athletes or teams, whereas 86 percent focused on men (the remaining 8 percent of the articles focused either on both males and females or on general issues). Important issues—such as sport politics, doping, and sport for all (physical activity in the general population)—are highly marginalized and often simply ignored. The media's choice of coverage affects a country's tastes and interests, and vice versa.

Information from Schultz Jørgensen, Søren. "The International Sports Press: The World's Best Advertising Agency." <http://www.playthegame.org/Knowledge%20Bank/Articles/International%20_Sports_Press_Survey_2005.aspx>.

1996
-
2008

1996
• U.S. women's soccer team wins Olympic gold

1997
• Women's National Basketball Association (WNBA) founded

1998
• U.S. women's ice hockey team wins Olympic gold

1999
• U.S. women's soccer team wins World Cup

2004
• U.S. women's soccer team wins Olympic gold

2006
• Japan wins the World Baseball Classic

2008
› Summer Olympics held in Beijing, China (first Asian host country)

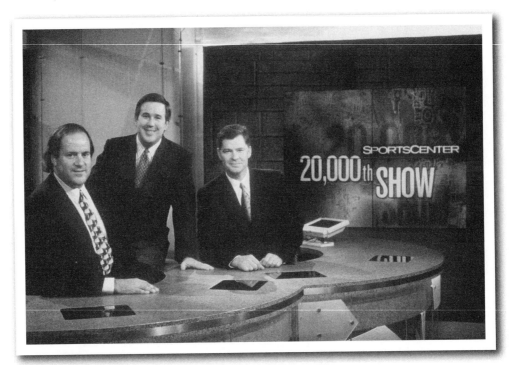

ESPN attracted the young male demographic, appealing to its members with a fraternity house atmosphere of raucous sportscasters and commentators. They presented highlights of previous games with voiceovers by loud, brash, irreverent reporters and analysts who became celebrities in their own right. Eventually, female reporters began to patrol the sidelines of events, sometimes exposing the ignorance or crudeness of some athletes in telling interviews. For example, an obviously drunken and slobbering Joe Namath asked one such reporter for a kiss during a nationally televised football game. A few women earned roles in the studio or even as football broadcasters. ESPN interviews and analyses might make or break athletic heroes. In the process, ESPN changed the way that Americans viewed and interpreted sports.

The phenomenal success of ESPN led to greater sports coverage on the major television networks, the creation of local sports channels, and innumerable sports-talk radio shows in imitation. ESPN itself became a media conglomerate, producing numerous spin-offs, such as ESPN HD (i.e., using high-definition broadcasting technology), ESPN2, ESPN2 HD, ESPN Classic, ESPNEWS, ESPN Sports PPV (pay-per-view), ESPN Deportes (Spanish-language), ESPNU (aimed at college students), ESPN360.com (video content player), ESPN Mobile TV, ESPN.com, ESPN Radio, *ESPN The Magazine*, ESPN Zone restaurants, EXPN, and ESPN International, which was broadcast to 180 countries in 21 languages by the turn of the twentieth-first century. By that time, the network was valued at $15 billion and had been bought by Disney. With its incorporation into the mainstream media, ESPN lost some if its edge but gained even greater global influence (Freeman). The power of the media to effect cultural change has become evident in the way in which ESPN and its imitators have affected gambling odds with miniscule bits of information or overwhelming analyses of contests. By 2006, ESPN, always questing for more markets and new viewers, promoted competitions such as poker and paintball as televised sports events with great success. The mass opiate of sports proved highly addictive.

This seemingly overwhelming interest in sports caused an avalanche of ESPN imitators. Professional leagues initiated their own television companies, such as the NFL Network, NBA TV, and NBA Preview to gain a larger segment of the viewing market. Collegiate athletic conferences followed suit. Other operations focused on particular activities; examples include the Golf Channel, the Outdoor Channel, and the Fox Soccer

Channel. The Comcast SportsNet offered local and regional programming, as well as an HDTV option, and Nickelodeon Games and Sports focused on the children's market, grooming them for later viewing as adults. For those still unsatiated by the cornucopia of athletic offerings, numerous other companies provided pay-per-view programming for selected events, and even those networks whose primary fare was not sports programming increased their sports coverage. Ted Turner, owner of the Turner Broadcasting System (TBS) and the Atlanta Braves, sold its baseball programs to cable stations throughout the United States, and WGN, owned by the *Chicago Tribune* newspaper, which also owned the Chicago Cubs, did likewise. Both teams thus created a national fan base while generating additional profits for the parent company. The NBC network controlled Europe's Super Channel, which served 60 million viewers, and, with nearly 80 percent of European programming originating in the United States, the focus on American offerings produced cultural backlashes in some locations (Maguire, *Global* 150–154).

In 1997, Australian media mogul Rupert Murdoch bought the Los Angeles Dodgers for $311 million. Already owner of Fox Sports Net and 20th Century Fox, as well as worldwide newspapers and cable television units such as Fox College Sports, Murdoch also bought the broadcast rights to Yankees games in New York, then purchased national rights from MLB for $565 million (Elias, *Baseball* 210). As owner of British, Asian, and Japanese satellite systems, Murdoch wielded the power and influence to further Americanize the world.

Such financial arrangements proliferated, as the Disney Company owned ABC, ESPN, and portions of European sports channels, as well MLB's Anaheim Angels and the NHL's Anaheim Ducks. The clear benefits led media conglomerate Time Warner Inc. to purchase TBS and the Braves. Such ownership across business genres raised numerous issues, as corporate and large-market teams superseded the ability of small-market or privately owned teams to procure top players. Salaries escalated, as did ticket prices for spectators. The media giants even had the power to manipulate scheduling times to insure maximum exposure for their teams, resulting in more night games. These interlocking corporations also posed dilemmas for the media wings of the parent companies, as journalistic integrity became suspect when reporting upon one's own corporate "family."

Maximizing Profits From Sport

Television networks, league executives, and team officials all worked toward innovations that would increase success both on the field and in terms of attracting fans. Television producers used technological innovations to enhance viewers' interest in broadcasts. In 1986, the widespread use of instant replay (first introduced by CBS in 1963) allowed viewers to become, in a sense, their own referees and thus further enhanced their involvement in the game. Major League Baseball began scheduling more games at night in order to maximize the television audience and added the League Championship Series, a seven-game playoff, as a semifinal round prior to the World Series (Gorn and Goldstein 239–240).

The NFL introduced its own innovations, as one of its teams, the San Francisco 49ers, directed by cerebral head coach Bill Walsh, attracted new fans with a ball-control passing strategy known as the West Coast offense. Under the guidance of unflappable quarterback Joe Montana, the 49ers won four Super Bowl titles in the 1980s, and other teams adopted the innovative offense.

The lucrative growth of sport also initiated challenges to established organizations. The United States Football League (USFL), for example, started play in 1983, scheduling its games in the spring to avoid direct competition with the NFL. It lasted three years before switching to the more traditional fall season and suing the NFL as a monopoly that prohibited it from securing a network television contract. The USFL won the case, but the New York jury awarded it only $1 in damages, rather than the nearly $2 billion it had sought. The jury reasoned that most of the USFL's problems resulted from its own mismanagement, and their decision effectively put it out of business.

Despite a strike-shortened season of 1981, baseball produced a national phenomenon known as Fernandomania, focused on Fernando Valenzuela, a rotund, 19-year-old, Spanish-speaking Mexican pitcher who arrived in the National League at the end of the 1980 season. Appearing in 10 games as a relief pitcher for the Los Angeles Dodgers, he compiled a flawless 0.00 earned run average and struck out 16 batters in 17 innings. In 1981, manager Tommy Lasorda made Valenzuela the Dodgers' top starting pitcher, much to the pleasure of the large Mexican and Mexican American population of Southern California. Valenzuela did not disappoint, providing timely hitting as well as stellar pitching for the resurgent Dodgers. Record crowds turned out to witness Valenzuela's heroics and inimitable style, and he led National League pitchers in strikeouts and won both the Rookie of the Year Award and the Cy Young Award (for best pitcher). The Dodgers won the World Series, their first since 1965, and the excitement generated by Fernandomania produced a Hispanic hero that boosted ethnic-minority pride and created a shared interest among mainstream Americans, established Chicanos, and thousands of immigrants and migrant workers.

The latter endured poor working conditions, flimsy housing, and meager wages in servile positions. The burgeoning Chicano nationalism of previous decades had been met with suppression. When Alianza (Alliance), led by Reies López Tijerina, had tried to reclaim the New Mexico lands lost to whites, the U.S. Army had responded and the leader had been imprisoned. Similarly, boxer turned politician, Rodolfo "Corky" Gonzalez, directed the Crusade for Justice movement in search of betterment, but it was Cesar Chavez who had the most success, organizing migrant laborers into the United Farm Workers Union and initiating a national boycott of grapes. Thus the Hispanic population of the Southwest, previously perceived as docile, began to assert itself. In that context, baseball assuaged some social wounds and unified differing factions in a nonviolent, communal attraction by providing some psychological escape when the parties were not immersed in their own economic problems.

Stadium Construction as a Civic Subsidy

Baseball owners, who did not share their revenue equally (though they did share the $130 million paid by the Arizona Diamondbacks as a new-franchise entry fee in 1995), sought new ways to maximize profits. Small-market teams, in particular, faced distinct disadvantages. Without the broadcasting profits of large-market teams, they had less to offer in acquiring new players. Professional team owners in all sports sought to maximize their income and began to put increasing pressure on municipalities to fund or subsidize construction of revenue-generating venues for sporting events. They held cities hostage as they threatened removal to more advantageous locations. Seven NFL franchises did relocate between 1982 and 1997, and thirty-one professional teams got new stadiums at public expense between 1989 and 1997 (Guttmann, *Sports: The First Five Millennia* 139; also see the table on pages 313-314). Thus new ball parks became a primary means by which owners hoped to attract new customers.

Corporate skyboxes, personal seat licenses, and exclusive rights to parking fees, subsidies, and sales of food, drink, and clothing swelled owners' coffers. Teams also sold naming rights to corporate donors and displayed commercial advertising to increase revenue. For example, in 2000, Pacific Bell paid $54 million to the San Francisco Giants for stadium naming rights lasting 24 years (the company had agreed to the contract even before construction), and Bank One bought naming rights to the Arizona Diamondbacks' ball park at a cost of $66 million for 30 years (Elias, *Baseball* 209). Between 1992 and 2001, NFL teams renovated or constructed 15 stadiums, and, following the great success of the Baltimore Orioles' new venue, baseball teams opened 13 new ball parks between 1995 and 2000 (Spirou and Bennett 188). As stadiums took on the appearance of theme parks, some, like PETCO Park in San Diego, even featured a playground for young children, and mascots, not unlike Disney characters, entertained spectators. Politicians rationalized the expenditures as urban development—the redevelopment of downtrodden areas into entertainment districts to attract tourist dollars.

Stadium Construction and Renovation, 1990-2010

Year	Team and stadium	Cost (in millions) to build or renovate
Baseball stadiums		
1991	Chicago White Sox/U.S. Cellular Field	$150
1992	Baltimore Orioles/Oriole Park at Camden Yards	$235
1994	Cleveland Indians/Progressive Field Texas Rangers/Rangers Ballpark in Arlington	$173 $191
1995	Colorado Rockies/Coors Field	$215
1996	Oakland A's/Network Associates Coliseum (shared with Raiders NFL team)	$225 (renovation)
1997	Atlanta Braves/Turner Field San Diego Padres/Petco Park (shared with Chargers NFL team)	$235 $78 (renovation)
1998	Arizona Diamondbacks/Chase Field Anaheim (Los Angeles) Angels/Edison International Field (later renamed Angel Stadium of Anaheim) Tampa Bay Devil Rays/Tropicana Field	$355 $117 (renovation); $85 (when opened in 1990); $65 (renovation in 1998) $115
1999	Seattle Mariners/Safeco Field	$517
2000	Detroit Tigers/Comerica Park Houston Astros/Minute Maid Park San Francisco Giants/AT&T Park	$290 $266 $306
2001	Milwaukee Brewers/Miller Park Pittsburgh Pirates/PNC Park	$414 $233
2003	Cincinnati Reds/Great American Ball Park	$361
2004	Philadelphia Phillies/Citizens Bank Park San Diego Padres/PETCO Park	$458 $456
2006	St. Louis Cardinals/Busch Stadium	$365
2008	Washington Nationals/Nationals Ballpark	$611
2009	New York Mets/Citi Field New York Yankees/Yankee Stadium II (working name)	$600 $800
2010	Minnesota Twins/Twins Ballpark (working name)	$480
2009-2012 (projected)	Oakland A's/Cisco Field	$400-500
undecided	Florida Marlins/Marlins Ballpark	$420
Football stadiums		
1992	Atlanta Falcons/Georgia Dome	$214
1995	Jacksonville Jaguars/Alltel Stadium St. Louis Rams/Edward Jones Dome	$135 (renovation) $300
1996	Carolina Panthers/Bank of America Stadium Oakland Raiders/Network Associates Coliseum (shared with A's MLB team)	$298 $225 (renovation)

>> continued

>> continued

Year	Team and stadium	Cost (in millions) to build or renovate
Football stadiums		
1997	San Diego Chargers/Qualcomm Stadium (shared with Padres MLB team) Washington Redskins/FedEx Field	$78 (renovation) $251
1998	Baltimore Ravens/M&T Bank Stadium Tampa Bay Buccaneers/Raymond James Stadium	$229 $190
1999	Tennessee Titans/The Coliseum Buffalo Bills/Ralph Wilson Stadium Cleveland Browns/Cleveland Browns Stadium	$292 $63 (renovation) $309
2000	Cincinnati Bengals/Paul Brown Stadium	$452
2001	Denver Broncos/Invesco Field at Mile High Pittsburgh Steelers/Heinz Field	$360 $244
2002	New England Patriots/Gillette Stadium Detroit Lions/Ford Field Houston Texans/Reliant Stadium Seattle Seahawks/Qwest Stadium	$395 $300 $402 $430
2003	Green Bay Packers/Lambeau Field Chicago Bears/Soldier Field Philadelphia Eagles/Lincoln Financial Field	$295 (renovation) $632 (renovation) $520
2006	Phoenix Cardinals/University of Phoenix Stadium	$455
2008	Indianapolis Colts/Lucas Oil Stadium	$675
2009	Dallas Cowboys/Cowboys Stadium	$1 billion
2009	Miami Dolphins/Dolphins Stadium	Amount not yet available
2010	New York Giants, New York Jets (shared)/New York Stadium (working name)	$1.3 billion
2012 (planned)	Minnesota Vikings	$1 billion

Data from Slezak, Carol. "What's in a name?" *Chicago Sun-Times*, 2 March 2008: 56A; <www.ballparks.com>, <www.ballparksofbaseball.com>, <www.leagueoffans.org/mlbstadiums1990.html>, <www.stadiumsofnfl.com>, <www.indystar.com/apps/pbcs.dll/section?Category=sports0305-47k->, and <www.proplayerstadium.com/content/architecture.aspx>.

Sport as Tourism

The Chicago White Sox built a new Comiskey Park (later renamed U.S. Cellular Field) in 1991, and in 1992 Baltimore opened the Camden Yards ball park as the new home of the Orioles; nearby locations are home to a separate facility for the NFL's Baltimore Ravens and the Babe Ruth Birthplace Museum. The complex was intended to revitalize the inner-city area by creating or reconstructing historical memories. Babe Ruth's birthplace serves as a general historical link to the city's modern team, which now plays in a new park but one designed with retrospective features to provide the illusion of (and elicit nostalgia for) the stadiums of the past; meanwhile, genuine older venues such as Fenway Park in Boston and Wrigley Field in Chicago continued to attract crowds regardless of their team's fortunes on the field. The smaller playing dimensions of the new parks also allowed for more home runs, always a fan favorite, and the stadiums in Baltimore were linked to the nearby inner harbor area that features restaurants, shops, and other forms of entertainment. Thus sport, and sport complexes, became tourist attractions, subsidized by cities and thus requiring somewhat limited team expenditures. The cities often paid for maintenance of the structure, traffic control, and safety measures, and even insured prescribed attendance levels with subsidies.

Part of that civic restoration involved the organization of sports halls of fame to attract fans. Historians Eric Hobsbawm and Terence Ranger have termed such institutions or events "invented traditions," meant to create significance and identification over time. Some municipalities erected structures to commemorate local history, while others claimed national or even international status as places of remembrance and nostalgia. Such shrines glorified athletic heroes—mostly white, male professionals—in a particular exhibition of masculinity that bordered on a civic religion, and fans made pilgrimages to view the sacred objects of revered stars from baseball, football, basketball, hockey, tennis, golf, boxing, horse racing, soccer, motor sports, swimming, and track and field at various locations throughout the country.

In this vein, the entire city of Indianapolis bills itself as the "Amateur Sports Capital of the World" and has practically become a shrine to sport. *ESPN The Magazine* named it the top professional sports city in 2003, and the city has built its economy largely around sport—and sport tourism. In addition to the historic Indy 500 auto race, it also hosts the Allstate 400 at the Brickyard and a Formula One event. Besides the professional Colts (football) and Pacers (basketball), the city is home to the headquarters of the National Collegiate Athletic Association (NCAA), USA Gymnastics, USA Track and Field, U.S. Diving, U.S. Synchronized Swimming, the American College of Sports Medicine, the Indy Racing League, the Black Coaches Association, the National Federation of State High School Associations, and a host of other organizations. After politicians generated a successful move to a new county governance structure, business interests secured corporate control of the city and outlying areas (Schimmel, Ingham, and Howell 234–237). Between 1977 and 1991, sports-related purchases enriched the local economy by more than $2 billion ("Amateur Sports Capital of the World"). Little of that income trickled down to the poor families displaced by the widespread construction of athletic facilities.

Labor Relations and the Sharing of Profit

Although professional sports produced excitement for fans, their enthusiasm was often tempered by labor issues. In 1981, Major League Baseball players went on strike in midseason over free agency issues. They returned, 50 days later, only after owners agreed to recognize the players' rights to negotiate their contracts and salaries. In return, the owners got compensation for departing free agents through draft choices, cash, or the trading of other players.

In 1994, fans were outraged when players went on strike again, forcing cancellation of the World Series for the first time in 90 years. At the time, a Canadian franchise, the Montreal Expos, led the National League; Tony Gwynn of the San Diego Padres was batting nearly .400, a mark no one had (or has) reached since Ted Williams hit .406 in 1941; and Matt Williams of the San Francisco Giants had already hit 43 home runs, giving him a chance to surpass the record of 61, set by Roger Maris in 1961. Moreover, MLB had set an attendance record during the preceding season. Faced with the strike, however, many thoroughly disappointed fans vowed never to return. They blamed both players and owners as greedy. The latter demanded a salary cap, and the former refused. The strike lasted 234 days before a federal judge sided with the players. The 1995 season began under the existing contract, and neither side managed to change the collective bargaining agreement substantially. Before the strike, MLB had been averaging 31,256 attendees per game; a decade later, teams had yet to recover to that level—the 2004 average was 30,290 (*Chicago Sun Times*).

Despite the sharp drop in baseball attendance in 1995, even disgruntled fans took interest in the endurance feat achieved by Cal Ripken Jr., who was amassing a huge streak of consecutive games played. Indeed, for five years during the 1980s, he had not missed even a single inning of play, and on September 6, 1995, the Baltimore Orioles' iron man surpassed Lou Gehrig's record by playing in his 2,131st consecutive game. More than 5 million American households tuned in to the nationally televised game. Ripken's longevity, work ethic, and humility, similar to qualities that had been admired in Gehrig, sparked a nostalgic and idealized outpouring of national empathy. Amidst ongoing labor strife and political discord, Ripken represented what Americans wanted to see in themselves—a quiet leader who set the right example. He not only did his job, playing through injuries without complaint, but performed at an all-star level as a power-hitting shortstop, and even his private life, apparently beyond reproach, seemed to symbolize a more traditional and innocent era.

Commissioner Bud Selig had introduced another baseball innovation in 1994 by implementing the wild-card system, which allowed one additional team to enter the season-ending playoffs based on compiling the best won-loss record of all the teams that did not win their respective divisions during the regular season. Though rendered moot by the strike in 1994, the change took effect in 1995, and two years later the wild-card Florida Marlins, a 1992 expansion franchise, captured the World Series. Selig initiated yet another change in 1997 by scheduling regular-season interleague play (i.e., games played between teams from MLB's two different leagues), something that previously had been seen only in the World Series; this shift also allowed MLB to match intercity rivals from the different leagues in large markets including New York, Chicago, Los Angeles, and the San Francisco Bay area. The strategy sustained local interest throughout the season.

The 1998 season provided the greatest impetus to the resurgence of baseball, when the Chicago Cubs' Dominican slugger Sammy Sosa battled the St. Louis Cardinals' Mark McGwire for the home-run championship. Both chased Roger Maris' single-season record of 61, and McGwire broke the record against the Cubs on September 8, only to see Sosa exceed him by hitting 66 home runs. McGwire, however, swatted five homers in his last eleven at-bats to finish at 70. While fans reveled in their heroic feats, others wondered about the use of a more tightly wrapped (and thus livelier) ball, as well as the possibility that one or both players had used performance-enhancing steroids. McGwire admitted to using androstenedione, a purported ergogenic muscle-building substance. Although the NCAA, the NFL, and the IOC banned the product as a steroid, MLB failed to address the issue, and in 2001, under a similar cloud of suspicion, Barry Bonds broke McGwire's record with 73 blasts. Frenzied fans filled the seats and fought over Bonds' home-run balls despite the looming ethical issues. Bonds' consequent breaking of Hank Aaron's career home-run mark of 755 faced even greater scrutiny, and the significance of such a feat was further questioned when he was indicted for lying about his use of performance-enhancing substances.

It was clear that home runs attracted fans, and Sosa (who, like Bonds, appeared noticeably heavier and thicker than in earlier years) represented a growing market for MLB players and audiences in the Caribbean. The friendly rivalry between Sosa and McGwire had portrayed racial amity and joint happiness in a shared love of the game—a perception that MLB hoped would heal several wounds of the players, owners, and fans. During the home-run barrage, Chicagoans flew Dominican flags alongside American banners, as baseball seemed to transcend both race and nationalism in a unified (if possibly tainted) quest for excellence.

For owners, Latin American players represented a cheaper means of stocking their rosters, and by the turn of the twenty-first century Dominicans accounted for nearly 10 percent of MLB players, while Latin Americans constituted 26 percent. Sosa had been signed by Texas in 1985 for only $3,500, and the Dodgers had initially gotten Pedro Martinez, who became a dominating pitcher, for a mere $8,000 in 1988. American baseball academies housed, fed, and tutored young players who were signed to contracts. MLB finally enacted a rule requiring signers to be at least 16 years of age, but independent agents continued to exploit the talents of promising boys as young as 12 (Knisely; Le Batard).

Major league baseball also experienced growing pains when its Montreal Expos franchise failed to attract enough fans in French-speaking Quebec. During the 2003 and 2004 seasons, the team played some of its "home" games in Puerto Rico, and before the 2005 season it moved to Washington, D.C., and became the Washington Nationals. By that time, the internationalization of the game had come far enough that foreign athletes made up 28 percent of MLB rosters and nearly $100 million in international revenue, an 800 percent increase in revenue from 1989 (Jozsa 8, 17).

Franchise value increased exponentially during the 1990s, as a globalized labor force helped owners keep costs down even as it promoted larger consumer markets. Before 1980, no MLB team rated $20 million, but during the 1990s teams were sold for more than $100 million,

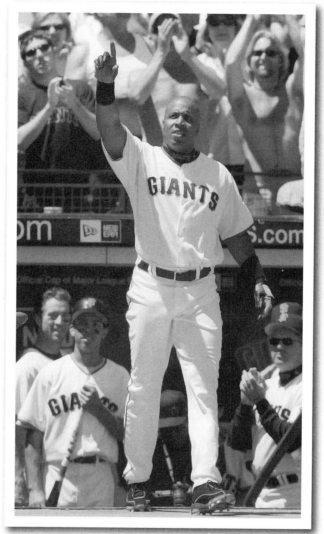

With his 715th career home run on May 28, 2006, Barry Bonds surpassed Babe Ruth in the all-time home-run record.
AP Photo/Eric Risberg

and the New York Yankees franchise was valued at $900 million (Guttmann, *Sports: The First Five Millennia* 363); by 2006, it became the first pro sports team valued at a billion dollars. Team owners began importing top Japanese stars, as well. Bringing the best athletes might be expensive, but owners incurred little development cost in training these proven stars. Ichiro Suzuki provided virtually guaranteed value for the Seattle Mariners, and indeed he set the major league record for hits in a season with 262 in 2004. As early as 2001, Seattle had established a foothold in Asia by broadcasting its games to Japan. In 2006, the Boston Red Sox paid more than $51 million just for the rights to negotiate with Japanese pitcher Daisuke Matsuzaka, then signed him to a six-year contract worth much more (Browne).

Such costs might be offset by merchandising in foreign markets. By 2003, MLB was selling products in 109 countries and broadcasting its games to 215. PepsiCo sponsored an Australian baseball league, as American popular culture and American products expanded around the world (Miller, Lawrence, McKay, and Rowe 14–17). In 2007, an MLB promotional delegation traveled to Africa; Ghana had fielded its first national baseball team in 1999, and MLB delegates judged it to be a potentially rich source of baseball talent. Young Ghanaian players might someday even replace the declining number of African American players in the league (9 percent of MLB in 2005) and present yet another market for the game (Rogers 6-7).

In 2006, Major League Baseball spent $50 million to organize the World Baseball Classic, inviting 16 countries from 5 continents to participate in the first edition of what is expected to be a quadrennial event. Much to the dismay of American fans, Japan and Cuba advanced to the title match, with Japan emerging victorious. (Japan had clamored for a true world series with the United States as early as the 1930s.) The competition, intended to develop new markets and new sources of profit (Rojas), was staged as a spectacle not unlike the Summer Olympic Games. Such programming and scheduling heightens interest, raises expectations, increases nationalistic fervor, and builds an international audience and market for subsequent products (an invented tradition).

NFL players followed their MLB counterparts' lead in going on strike shortly after the opening of the 1982 season. They returned 57 days later after negotiations had increased the minimum salary and postseason pay and accorded players new rights that included severance allowances. The owners, however, retained control of television revenues and player transfers. During the 1990s, the NFL quelled labor wars within its ranks under new commissioner Paul Tagliabue, but owners proved less than accommodating in their search for greater profits, and teams left Houston, Cleveland, and Los Angeles. Tagliabue secured new teams for Houston and Cleveland and granted expansion franchises to Charlotte and Jacksonville in 1993. The lack of a team in Los Angeles, however, left a gaping hole in the nation's second-largest market. Despite that shortcoming and its lackluster internationalization efforts, the NFL signed the most lucrative television contract of all professional leagues in 1998. The pact provided more than $17 billion over eight years and guaranteed each team about $75 million per year. Commercial television ads for the 2003 Super Bowl cost sponsors $2 million for a 30-second spot (Guttmann, *Sports: The First Five Millennia* 154). By 2007, the value of NFL franchises had skyrocketed to the point where even the least valuable (the Minnesota Vikings) was worth $720 million, while the Washington, D.C., Redskins franchise was assessed at just over $1.4 billion. The year before, the NFL had received nearly $5.5 billion in television revenue, with 59.5 percent of that earmarked for players' salaries (Bergen). Even the lowest-paid NFL head coach made $1.45 million, and some earned as much as $8 million ("Where's the Love?" 86A).

While both baseball and football prospered, basketball fared even better, enjoying explosive growth during the 1980s under the guidance of new commissioner David Stern, who assumed the commissioner's role in 1984. Stern's astute business sense and the presence of superstars Kareem Abdul Jabbar, Earvin "Magic" Johnson, Larry Bird, and new arrival Michael Jordan did much to popularize the sport. The new focus on individualism within the team concept further marked athletes as entertainers. Johnson, a 6-foot-9-inch (2.1-meter) point guard and a magician with the ball, could play any position and often accomplished the "triple-double," a designation of all-around excellence achieved when a player garners at least 10 points, 10 rebounds and 10 assists during a game. Johnson, along with the 7-foot-2-inch (2.2-meter) Jabbar, also one of the all-time greats, led the Los Angeles Lakers to five NBA titles during the decade. Johnson's rival, Larry Bird, who also stood 6 feet 9 inches, led the Boston Celtics to three championships during the same period. Portrayed as a bumpkin from small-town Indiana, Bird possessed great fundamental basketball skills, particularly as a passer and shooter, and he won the NBA's Most Valuable Player award three times. Sportswriters' portrayal of his whiteness in contrast to Johnson's blackness focused not only on their styles of play but also on geographical and social distinctions in American society. Sport had room for both, and the NBA thrived on the rivalry, promoting its inclusiveness while enjoying contrasts, not unlike the antithetical caricatures portrayed in professional wrestling.

Much of the league's prosperity rested upon Stern's considerable business acumen. He brokered the labor agreement between players and owners that gave players 53 percent of gross revenues but gave the latter a salary cap that held down escalating costs. Stern also marketed the league and its players to the youthful demographic, creating presumably lifelong fans by projecting a cooler, more exuberant image that appealed to young consumers, in contrast to the more traditional image of baseball. The NBA All-Star game expanded to include a slam-dunk contest and a three-point-shooting competition that highlighted individual abilities, and during the ascendancy of Michael Jordan the NBA marketed individual stars and personalities covering the spectrum from corporate values to hip-hop culture, thus attracting a following that ranged from business executives to childhood emulators.

As baseball, basketball, and football expanded their domain the NHL followed with its own strategies for growth. In 1997, it played a game in Japan, and with the fall of the Iron Curtain it began importing more European and Russian players to its ranks. The NHL expanded to 30 teams, 24 of them located in the United States. The Canadian winter sport migrated southward to such unlikely places as Georgia, Florida, Texas, California, and Arizona, but support proved only lukewarm in some locations. In the 1999–2000 seasons, the NHL initiated a new four-on-four overtime format to boost fan interest, but owners locked out the players in a labor dispute before the start of the 2004 campaign, relegating the NHL to the status of baseball a decade earlier. When the players' union and the owners could not agree on a salary cap they forfeited the entire 2004–2005 season. Hockey, like baseball, tried to recapture fans by generating more offense. In 2005, it placed greater restrictions on goalies and initiated shootouts to settle overtime deadlocks (Podell 93A).

Michael Jordan and the Globalization of American Sport

Jordan seemed to define the 1990s as an intensely competitive artist who painted memorable images on the basketball court—a one-man highlight film who reaped the pecuniary benefits of his dazzling artistry. His legend began as a college freshman when he hit the winning shot to give the University of North Carolina the 1982 NCAA title. Two years later, he was deemed the top college player of the year and won the first of two Olympic gold medals as he led the Olympic team in scoring.

He eschewed his senior year in favor of the NBA, where he led the Chicago Bulls to the playoffs. In recognition of his individual accomplishments, he earned an NBA All-Star team berth and Rookie of the Year honors. Despite a broken foot, Jordan displayed his forceful determination by returning to play at the end of the 1985–1986 season, pouring in 49 and 63 points in playoff contests. By that time, his spectacular dunks attracted a legion of fans and commercial sponsors. In 1985, Nike produced the first of its Air Jordan basketball shoes, which brought the company and the player worldwide exposure. The savvy marketing of the NBA and Jordan made basketball a global phenomenon encroaching on the international popularity of soccer.

Michael Jordan's fame and that of the NBA reached global proportions.
AP Photo/John Swart

Jordan's further exploits only fueled the growth of the game as youth around the world attempted to "Be like Mike," one of the advertising slogans attached to Jordan's lucrative endorsement deals. During the 1986–1987 season, Jordan led the league in scoring, and in the following year he won the MVP award and was named Defensive Player of the Year. He topped off that season, and the next, by winning the NBA's televised slam-dunk contest, and in 1987–1988 he added the All-Star game's MVP laurels to his growing list of accomplishments. Despite his individual displays of glory, however, his team failed to win any championships. That shortcoming began to change with the development of teammate Scottie Pippen (who would eventually be voted an all-time top-50 NBA player himself) and the arrival of now-legendary head coach Phil Jackson. In 1991, the Bulls beat the Los Angeles Lakers for their first NBA championship, and Jordan led the league in scoring, capturing MVP honors for both the regular season and the playoffs. He repeated in all three categories the next year, as the Bulls won 67 regular-season games before dismantling the Portland Trail Blazers in the championship.

In the summer of 1992, Jordan led the United States "Dream Team," composed for the first time of professional players, to an easy gold medal at the Barcelona Olympic Games. Jordan was accompanied by Pippen, Johnson, Bird, Charles Barkley, Karl Malone, Clyde Drexler, and collegian Christian Laettner, and this group of the NBA's best overwhelmed their opponents by an average of 44 points per game. Their triumphal tour of Europe produced enormous crowds and swelled the popularity of the sport.

The following season, the Bulls won their third consecutive title, besting the Phoenix Suns, as Jordan averaged 41 points per game in gaining the MVP award once again. Off the court, Nike and Jordan experienced unprecedented success. He appeared omnipresent in ads, and his bald pate became a fashion statement, copied by millions of men. Jordan's exuberance suffered a tragic blow when his father was murdered during the summer of 1993, and for the first time he appeared human, less than invincible, even vulnerable. Criticism of his gambling habits questioned his carefully crafted image, and he decided to retire before the 1993 season. After a two-year hiatus and an unsuccessful flirtation as a minor-league baseball player, Jordan returned to the hardwood at the end of the 1995 season. Though he scored 55 points in a playoff game, the Bulls failed to reach the championship.

With Jordan playing a complete season in 1995–1996, however, and the acquisition of the eccentric rebounder and defender Dennis Rodman, Chicago won a record 72 regular-season games and another NBA title. They followed that banner year with consecutive championships in 1997 and 1998, with Jordan leading the NBA in scoring each season. He announced his second retirement in 1999 after winning ten scoring titles, six league championships, and five NBA MVP awards. ESPN named him the greatest American athlete of the century.

In Jordan's absence, the NBA's television ratings dropped 14 percent in 1999, but the retirement proved brief (Hughes 176). Jordan became part owner of the Washington Wizards franchise in 2000, but his competitive fires still burned, and he renounced his ownership stake in an attempt to rescue his inept team by returning to play through the 2002–2003 season. Jordan still averaged an impressive 20 points per game, but his longevity paled in comparison to his legacy as a cultural phenomenon that globalized the sport of basketball, as well as American consumer goods—and himself, as a paragon of capitalism.

Jordan had earned a salary of more than $33 million for the 1997–1998 season, and much more in endorsement contracts (MacCambridge 284). He became a global icon, deified as the "black Jesus." His 1999 retirement announcement made headlines from Beijing to Bosnia, despite the ongoing war in the latter (Miller and Wiggins 305–306). He had become the most popular person in the world, and the most recognizable since Muhammad Ali. Many African American youth virtually equated Jordan with God as their most admired entities (Miller and Wiggins 312).

The NBA capitalized on such popularity by expanding to Canada with franchises in Toronto and Vancouver in 1995 (the latter returned to the United States, specifically Memphis, in 2001). Between 1988 and 2004, seven new franchises joined the league, and the market value of teams increased significantly. Despite being a small-market team, the Vancouver Grizzlies sold for $160 million in 2000; the Boston Celtics brought $360 million, and the Phoenix Suns commanded $401 million ("Great American" 71). The NBA enjoyed $500 million in revenue through international sales of its products in 1996 but still sought a larger market (Spirou and Bennett 18), and it pursued a greater female audience by initiating and subsidizing the Women's National Basketball Association (WNBA) in 1996. By 2005, the WNBA featured at least 30 players from abroad and televised its games in 193 countries and 31 different languages (Friedman). In the process of commodification, Jordan transcended boundaries of race, social class, and nationality in promoting both basketball and the capitalist value system. By 2000, the NBA was broadcasting its games in 42 languages to more than 750 million people in 205 countries (Miller and Wiggins 308).

Internationalizing American Sport Forms

Baseball and football also worked to capture a greater share of the international market. To that end, Major League Baseball created an international business division in 1989, and the NFL followed suit in 1996, opening regional offices in Mexico, Canada, and Japan and planning games in China. The NFL had played games in Canada as early as the 1950s and had traveled to Tokyo and Mexico City for exhibitions in the 1970s. An international football league was planned in the 1970s, but the U.S. government, fearing an increase in terrorist activities by radical European groups (e.g., the Red Brigade in Italy, Baader-Meinhof in Germany) that had already staged kidnappings due to nationalist and political tensions, intervened and thwarted the scheme. The following decade featured the American Bowl in London, which drew 86,000 spectators in 1986 (Ford and Foglio; Jozsa 70). Similar games followed in Sweden, Canada, Japan, Germany, Ireland, Spain, and Australia. A ten-team venture known as the World League of American Football initiated play in 1991 but lasted only briefly. In conjunction with the Fox television network, the NFL then established a European league of six teams in 1995, but the American version of football has failed to supplant the entrenched attraction of soccer. Even Budweiser, the league patron, has not been able to supplant the European beers and had to forsake its name when advertising in Austria, because an Austrian brewery had claimed that name since the seventeenth century. In Mexico, Japan, and the Pacific, American football has had greater success. More than a million children are engaged in flag football programs outside of the United States, and Samoans often graduate to American colleges and even to the NFL, while more than 200 Japanese colleges field American-style football teams. The international marketing ventures of the NFL amounted to nearly $100 million in 2002, with $16 million of NFL goods sold in Mexico alone. In Russia, the Super Bowl has attracted 10 million viewers (Jozsa 76–98).

PEOPLE & PLACES

Karl "Tuffy" Rhodes

From 1990 to 1995, Tuffy Rhodes played for several MLB teams, with a career batting average of .224 and 13 home runs, but he found success in Japan. In 1996, he signed with the Kintetsu Buffaloes in the Pacific League of Nippon Professional Baseball, and through 2007 he had played with two other teams as well. During that time he hit 402 home runs, the most of any foreign player in Japanese baseball history, and he tied the single-season record for any player with 55 in 2001. By 2007, he had surpassed the 3,000-hit mark and recorded 1,089 runs batted in ("Tuffy Rhodes").

Like baseball, the NBA experienced labor strife, including a strike in 1998, and it, too, turned to international players to partially alleviate costs. The value of such athletes became clear in 2002, as Team USA lost to Yugoslavia, Spain, and Argentina in the world championships, finishing thoroughly embarrassed in sixth place. Two years later, the United States finished in third place at the Athens Olympic Games. NBA clinics throughout the world helped promote the game, as did NBA exhibitions in places such as the Dominican Republic, Puerto Rico, Mexico, Spain, France, Italy, Greece, and Japan. Such locations might provide owners with future players at lower cost, not to mention current income from sales of NBA merchandise, such as caps, jerseys, and jackets. In 2002, the NBA broadcast its regular-season games to 212 countries (Jozsa 110) and drafted 17 foreign players, among them 7-foot-5-inch (2.3-meter) Yao Ming of China. The next year, an estimated 10 million Chinese families tuned in to NBA broadcasts, opening the world's biggest market to NBA products (Jozsa 17). The nature of Yao Ming's contract, a large part of which devolved to the Chinese government, meant that sports skills had become an exportable commodity in that nation's communist economy.

Another communist country, Cuba, which had been hindered by an American economic embargo, sold the expertise of its coaches to other developing nations. In fact, Cuba used sport not only as an economic export but also as a political tool, defeating the United States at its own game, first by winning the Olympic gold medal in baseball in 1992 and 1996, and then by challenging the professional Baltimore Orioles and splitting a two-game series in 1999. Cuba regained the Olympic title in 2004, again using sport as a surrogate form of political conflict. The political significance of sport was on display yet again when the U.S. government threatened to bar Cuba from competing in the 2006 world championship held in the United States.

Symbiotic Relationship of Television and Intercollegiate Sport

The NCAA had steadfastly adhered to the amateur ideal, refusing any compensation other than the tuition, room, and board provided by athletic scholarships for college athletes. Many players, however, contended that they were employees of the universities, and, indeed, an NCAA survey in 1988 found that college athletes spent more time in practice than in academic pursuits, averaging 26 hours per week on scholastic matters but 30 hours on sports (Gorn and Goldstein 233). Such protests questioned the entrenched ideology of amateurism and institutional control. Despite the athletes' contentions, the NCAA adhered to its regulations, but in many cases boosters' clandestine efforts continued to lure and subsidize football and basketball stars in particular.

Colleges and universities derived national media exposure from successful athletic teams, and competition for the top players increased. A series of scandals called into question not only the amateur ideal but also the ethical practices of the coaches and alumni found guilty of committing various wrongs—illegal recruiting tactics, grade tampering, under-the-table financial inducements, eligibility violations, transcript fakery, and phantom courses—in order to attract and retain athletes. When coaches guilty of such infractions left or were fired from their posts, they often found new employment quickly with other would-be contenders. The institutions, however, faced probationary penalties from the NCAA. In 1980, for example, five members of the prestigious Pac-10 Conference were placed on probation for such transgressions, making half of the league ineligible for the football championship.

The following year, the NCAA enacted legislation to address the abuses, requiring at least minimal course goals, academic progress, substantial coursework, acceptable grade point averages, and substantiation of eligibility by school administrators. Even so, abuses continued, even as television payouts escalated. NBC paid $7 million for the broadcast rights to the 1983 Rose Bowl football game (Pope, *The New* 376), and the NCAA netted $75 million overall that year (Gorn and Goldstein 235). Major college football programs joined together in the College Football Association (CFA) to challenge the NCAA over the television profits. The big (Division I) schools asserted that because their games produced the most interest and the greatest profits from the television networks, they should receive greater remuneration. The smaller (Division II and III) institutions opposed the CFA, since they wanted to continue sharing in the NCAA distribution of funds from the television packages. The universities of Georgia and Oklahoma, both traditional football powers, sued the NCAA over the matter and won their case, and by 1985 the athletic conferences (and even individual schools) had the right to negotiate their own television contracts.

With such competition for the lucrative payoffs, abuses continued despite new NCAA rules. In 1987, Southern Methodist University, already on probation for numerous NCAA violations, received the "death penalty" for providing illegal payments to its football players. Banned from football competition for the 1987 season and limited to seven away games (and no home games) the following year, and with its team depleted of players who transferred or graduated, the school decided to abandon the sport. The dismissal proved temporary, as school officials submitted to pressure from alumni and boosters and resurrected the football team in 1989.

The top college football conferences began to increase their revenue by entering into their own agreements with the television networks. In 1992, the previously independent bowl selection committees formed an alliance (known as the Bowl Coalition) with the major football conferences in an effort to match top teams in a championship game. The Big Ten and Pac-10 conferences, however, remained contractually obliged to send top teams to the Rose Bowl. In 1995, the Bowl Alliance emerged, wherein the Fiesta, Sugar, and Orange bowls agreed on a rotating schedule in which each would get the best teams regardless of regional affiliations. Thus regional teams no longer had guarantees of bowl games, but the Rose Bowl remained committed to its two traditional conferences; as a result, if either the Big Ten or Pac-10 produced a team ranked as number one or number two, the Bowl Alliance could not claim a national championship game. In 1997, the Rose

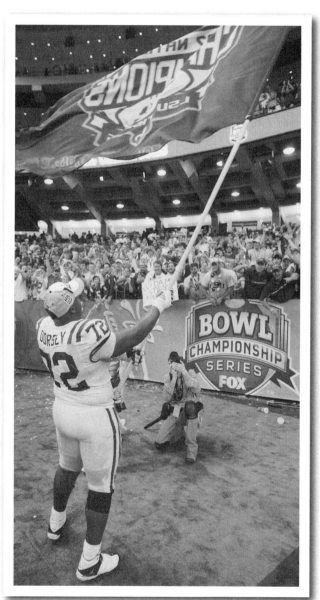

BCS bowl games approximate a national football championship for Division I football teams.
AP Photo/Rob Carr

Bowl joined the others after Michigan, a Big Ten team, had to settle for a share of the national title with Nebraska (the teams had each beaten worthy bowl opponents but had not played each other). In this fashion, the sportswriters' rankings and the coaches' rankings sometimes conflicted, creating never-ending and unwinnable arguments between fans as to which team merited the national title.

Even when all the bowls united in the Bowl Championship Series (BCS), a national title game was still not assured if the two polls lacked agreement, and the issue could be exacerbated if several teams managed to go undefeated throughout the season. The BCS arrived at a computerized mathematical formula to establish a supposedly neutral and objective polling system, but the rankings failed to quell complaints by partisan fans.

The squabbling over collegiate football superiority continued into the twenty-first century, as college presidents and the NCAA refused to agree to a national playoff system for Division I institutions (such systems were already in place for the smaller schools found in Division II and Division III). Administrators maintained that the continuation of the long football season only detracted from student-athletes' academic responsibilities, and an examination of graduation rates for schools involved in bowl games after the 2004 season confirmed this concern. The NCAA allowed students on athletic scholarships six years to complete the normal four-year course of study. Among all Division I institutions, only 54 percent of players managed to complete their curriculum during that time frame. Among those engaged in bowl games, the rates were considerably worse. While Boston College, Syracuse, and Notre Dame graduated more than 75 percent of their players within the specified time, most institutions fell below the average, and several graduated fewer than a third of their players (Wieberg and Carey 5B).

While a handful of top football teams garnered the biggest profits from television, the NCAA devised another prosperous scheme by expanding its basketball tournament from 48 to 64 teams in 1985, thus providing greater regional interest in the quest to find a national champion, and the Final Four semifinal round assumed the stature of a national athletic festival. The next year, the NCAA added the 3-point shot, bringing a new dimension to the game, and in one 1992 game Troy State attempted 109 3-pointers (making 51) in a game against DeVry Institute. Other teams also favored the "run-and-gun" style of offense, often a fan favorite, with little pretense of defense. In 1989, the team from U.S. International (in California) scored 150 points against Loyola Marymount and still lost, as the winners tallied 181 points in a game that resembled a track meet. Troy State surpassed even that total, scoring a record 123 points in the first half of the record-breaking game against DeVry. They immediately beat that mark by scoring 135 in the second half en route to a 258-141 win. Such prolific scoring glorified the capitalist emphasis on production, gained national prominence for smaller schools, and intensified fan interest.

Commercialization of the Olympics

American athletes thrilled their nationalistic supporters with stunning victories in the 1980 Winter Olympics at Lake Placid, New York. Speedskater Eric Heiden won five gold medals, setting Olympic records in each event he entered from 500 to 10,000 meters. Even more startling, the U.S. hockey team, composed of little-known collegiate players, defeated the mighty Soviet team, regarded as the best in the world. The Americans had lost an exhibition game to the Russians only 13 days earlier by a score of 10-3. After winning their improbable semifinal match by a 4-3 margin amidst pandemonium on their home ice, the young Americans then triumphed over Finland, 4-2, by scoring three third-period goals in the gold-medal game. This unlikely march to the top was seen as marking a triumph for capitalism in its ongoing economic war with the forces of communism. The *New York Times* called the American success "one of the most startling and dramatic upsets in Olympic history" (Eskanazi 1). Immediately after the game with the Soviets, President Jimmy Carter telephoned the team in the dressing room to offer his congratulations, and when a performance at New York's Radio City Music Hall was interrupted to announce the gold-medal triumph theatergoers paused to sing the American national anthem.

The American celebration temporarily relieved national tension as the new revolutionary Islamic government of Iran held 66 Americans hostage after the overthrow of the Shah. However, the USSR had invaded Afghanistan in December 1979, and U.S. President Jimmy Carter had retaliated by threatening to boycott the Summer Olympics to be hosted in Moscow. The threat became reality when the United States led 36 countries in spurning the competition. Once again, the Olympics had become a pawn in global power struggles.

In the midst of this turmoil, Juan Antonio Samaranch, a Spanish aristocrat, replaced Lord Killanin at the helm of the IOC, but he could not prevent the USSR's retaliation, as 13 nations from the Eastern Bloc refused to participate at the 1984 Summer Games in Los Angeles. In spite of their absence, the American Olympics proved a financial bonanza under the leadership of Peter Ueberroth, who commercialized the Olympics through licensing, merchandising, and marketing. The television contract with ABC guaranteed $225 million, and the festival concluded with a surplus of more than $200 million, an astounding improvement over the 1976 Games, which cost Montreal $1.5 billion (Rader, *American Sports* [1983] 310). The successful transformation of the Olympics into a capitalist venture, rather than a drain on the civic treasury, engendered a wholesale competition for future sites and greatly enriched the coffers of the IOC, which ultimately controlled the selection. Thereafter, the IOC imposed its Western values and standards on all solicitors in regulating the Olympic movement.

The 1984 Games saw Carl Lewis begin his long string of Olympic successes by taking four gold medals in track-and-field events. In fact, Lewis and other African American men accounted for 40 of the 49 golds won by the U.S. in track and field, and 10 of 11 medals won by American boxers (Verney 91). Off the track, Carl Lewis and Juan Antonio Samaranch emerged as two key figures in the gradual decline of Olympic amateurism as it had been treasured by Olympics founder Pierre de Coubertin. Some countries partially or fully subsidized their top-level athletes. Athletes of the USSR and other Eastern European countries were employed by public expense, often as members of the military. In the capitalist countries numerous successful athletes could make money via clandestine endorsements, such as being paid to wear a certain logo or a particular brand of shoes. As early as 1974, the IOC allowed such payments to go to national sports governing bodies, which paid the athletes a salary. Swimmer Mark Spitz, winner of seven gold medals at the 1972 Games, and decathlete Bruce Jenner, the 1976 champion, soon became spokesmen for a host of products (Rader, *American Sports* [1983] 312–313). Carl Lewis and others later managed to maintain their amateur status by placing endorsement revenues in personal financial trusts that disbursed only living expenses. Journalists dubbed such practices "shamateurism," and Samaranch, desirous of seeing the best athletes at the Olympics, gradually conceded. In 1985, the IOC and national sport federations voted to allow professional competitors in tennis, hockey, and soccer; other sports soon followed.

Women and Sport

Since the enactment of Title IX legislation in 1972, girls and women have gained access to virtually all sports, from Little League baseball to collegiate wrestling. Indeed, the feats of female athletes have been among the most impressive achievements in the generation since the enactment of Title IX. Girls' participation in interscholastic sports has risen continually. In 1971, a total of 294,015 girls played high school sports, but by 2004 that figure had grown to 2.7 million (Summers), and a 2001 survey found that 48 percent of all girls between the ages of 6 and 17 played on an organized team

(Eitzen and Sage 318). At the college level, women accounted for only 15 percent of athletes in 1971 but 42 percent in 2000 (Eitzen and Sage 322). In 2006, nearly three million female athletes (the most ever) played on school teams—half a million in basketball alone ("High School Sports Participation Increases" 4). Girls now have role models of their own.

Despite such remarkable growth, Title IX has proved a mixed blessing. Whereas more than 90 percent of women's collegiate teams were coached by females in 1972, that number dwindled to 44 percent by 2004. Similarly, female administrators directed 90 percent of women's intercollegiate athletic programs in 1972 but only 18.5 percent by 2004. Male athletic directors retained their power when programs merged, and they tended to hire other men as head coaches (Acosta and Carpenter 64). During the 1980–81 academic year, the Association for Intercollegiate Athletics for Women (AIAW), a sports governing body organized by and for women, offered 39 championships, but the NCAA, the predominantly male organization, began direct competition with the AIAW in 1981, effectively running it out of business. Under the NCAA, 80 percent of American universities still had not reached compliance with gender equity standards in 2004, more than 30 years after Title IX became law. And while women accounted for 56 percent of all college students in 2003, they received only 36 percent of athletic budget funding and only 32 percent of the money allocated for athletic scholarships (Priest 29; Yiamouyiannis 53). In 2003, men continued to hold the vast majority of NCAA leadership roles, including that of president, 15 of the 20 positions on the executive committee, and all of the conference commissioners' offices at the Division I-A level (Lapchick; Pfister, "Female").

However, despite the entrenched male power structure in sports governing bodies—and the reluctance to grant equal opportunities to women—female athletes continued to destroy myths of physical frailty by setting new standards and overcoming perceived obstacles. Indeed, women registered unprecedented successes, many of them at the Olympic Games. Anita DeFrantz, captain of the women's U.S. Olympic Rowing Team in 1976, won appointment to the IOC in 1986, becoming both the first American woman and the first African American to gain such stature. DeFrantz became an IOC vice president in 1997. Other Olympics successes included Mary Lou Retton, who became a national hero as winner of the women's all-around gymnastics championship at the 1984 Summer Games. Meanwhile, the women's competition grew to include rhythmic gymnastics, as well as synchronized swimming. Connie Carpenter-Phinney, an American cyclist, captured the gold medal in the women's road race, and Joan Benoit won the first Olympic women's marathon despite recent knee surgery. Figure skater Debi Thomas, who won national figure skating titles in 1986 and 1988, went on to win Olympic bronze in 1988, becoming the first African American athlete to win a medal at the Winter Games.

In track and field, the flamboyant Florence Griffith-Joyner, known as "Flo Jo" to fans, dominated the 1988 Summer Olympics in Seoul, Korea, by winning four medals (three gold, one silver). Overcoming unproven allegations of steroid use, Flo Jo set an

Louisiana Tech women's basketball coach Sonja Hogg is carried off the floor following the Lady Techsters' 79-59 win over Tennessee in the AIAW National Basketball Championship on March 29, 1981.

AP Photo/Harley Soltes

Olympic record at 100 meters and a world record at 200 meters and added another gold as part of the 400-meter relay team. The versatile Griffith-Joyner even ran a leg of the 1600-meter relay for her silver medal. The United States, France, and the Soviet Union all acknowledged her as Athlete of the Year. Her talents reached well beyond the track, as she popularized avant-garde track attire, designed new uniforms for the NBA's Indiana Pacers, and appeared on-screen in a movie, in television shows, and as a sports commentator. She also wrote children's books and became a spokeswoman for several charities. In 1993, she became the first female to cochair the President's Council on Physical Fitness and Sports. The next year, she established a philanthropic foundation for poor children. Her glamorous life ended in 1998 when she fell victim to an epileptic seizure at the age of 38.

Griffith-Joyner's sister-in-law, Jackie Joyner-Kersee, proved equally versatile, if not as ostentatious. Born to poverty in East St. Louis, Illinois, in 1962, Jackie Joyner earned a basketball scholarship to UCLA, where she became an All-American. There she also met and eventually married track coach Bob Kersee. (Her brother, Al Joyner, Florence Griffith's husband, took the Olympic gold medal in the 1984 triple jump.) Joyner-Kersee won the seven-event heptathlon and the long jump at Seoul in 1988 despite suffering from asthma. In the process, she broke her own heptathlon world record and set a new Olympic mark in the long jump. In 1992, she repeated her heptathlon triumph at the Barcelona Olympics. Throughout her career, Joyner-Kersee won numerous honors as athlete of the year, and in 2000 *Sports Illustrated for Women* named her the top female athlete of the century. In retirement, she founded a youth center in her hometown.

Bonnie Blair, a speedskating sensation, won five Olympic gold medals and one bronze between 1988 and 1994. No other American woman has accomplished such a feat, and Blair added the Sullivan Award as the top amateur athlete in the United States in 1992. The U.S. Olympic Committee named her as Sportswoman of the Year in 1992 and 1994, and in the latter year the Associated Press selected her as Female Athlete of the Year.

Also on the ice, Kristi Yamaguchi won the 1991 Olympic gold medal in figure skating, becoming the first Asian American woman to win a gold medal. Another Asian American figure skater, Michelle Kwan, retired in 2006 after winning nine national championships, five world championships, and two Olympic medals. On the slopes, Picabo Street won a silver medal at the 1994 Winter Olympics and then, in 1995, became the first American woman to win the World Cup downhill skiing competition. In 1998, the U.S. women's ice hockey team won the Olympic gold medal.

Women during this period also performed several striking endurance feats. Throughout the 1970s, Diana Nyad surpassed men's records for endurance swimming by circling Manhattan Island, as well as covering more than 100 miles (161 kilometers) in the Atlantic Ocean (from the Bahamas to Florida), and covering the distance from Cuba to the United States. In 1983, women organized an all-female triathlon in California that drew more than 600 entrants. Two years later, Libby Riddles won the Iditarod sled-dog race across Alaska against male competitors, and Susan Butcher beat the men in that event four times between 1986 and 1990. In 1987, Lynne Cox swam from Alaska to the Soviet Union across the Bering Strait, a feat that no man had ever accomplished. A year later, Stacy Allison climbed Mt. Everest, and in 1989 Ann Trason won the Western States 100, an ultra-endurance race that lasted more than 18 hours.

The popularity of basketball extended to female athletes, who also emerged as stars. The Women's Basketball League (WBL), a professional circuit, initiated play in 1980 but went out of business in 1981. It was succeeded by the Women's American Basketball Association (WABA) which lasted only one season (1984). In each venture, Nancy Lieberman (later Lieberman-Cline) proved to be the top attraction. Raised

Nancy Lieberman (shown here with the basketball) exemplified the best of early pro basketball for women.

AP Photo/Michael O'Brien

in a broken home, Lieberman had sought solace and recognition in sports (Berlage 41). While still a high school student, she played on U.S. national basketball teams at the Pan American Games and the World Championships in 1975. The following year, she won a gold medal at the Montreal Olympics. She led Old Dominion University (ODU) of Norfolk, Virginia, to two national AIAW titles, and ODU home games drew ten thousand spectators. In 1981, Lieberman played in a men's semipro league until the Dallas Diamonds of the WBL offered her a $100,000 contract. The WABA Dallas franchise then paid her $250,000, and she led them to the league championship. With the demise of the WABA, she then joined a men's pro league, appearing in the United States Basketball League with the Springfield (Massachusetts) Fame. During the 1987–88 season, she joined the Harlem Globetrotters. She returned to pro basketball with the Phoenix Mercury of the Women's National Basketball Association (WNBA) in 1997 (Berlage 42). Her income far outstripped that of most women but still pointed to ongoing gender inequalities insofar as it was hardly comparable to the money earned by male basketball stars in the NBA.

Like Billie Jean King, Lieberman pioneered opportunities for female athletes. When her playing days ended, she became a television analyst for men's and women's games, authored books, directed basketball camps for girls, and served as president of the Women's Sports Foundation. She assumed administrative duties as head coach and general manager of the Detroit Shock of the WNBA in 1998 and as coach of the Dallas Fury in 2004 in the National Women's Basketball League (NWBL). She had already been inducted into the Basketball Hall of Fame in 1996.

Women also made great strides in soccer during this period. In 1991, the U.S women's soccer team defeated Norway in the championship match of the World Cup, and Mia Hamm, a prolific scorer, became the role model for aspiring young girls throughout the country. The increasing success of women's sports became most noticeable in 1999, when nearly 79,000 fans at the Meadowlands in New Jersey watched the United States women's soccer team win a World Cup match against Denmark. The team then captured the world championship in an overtime shootout with China. Exhilaration soon shifted to debate after Brandi Chastain, who scored the winning goal, ripped off her shirt in celebration, leaving her upper body clothed only in a sports bra. Although male soccer players had cavorted in similar fashion for years, Chastain's action prompted discussion of morality, sexuality, and gender.

In professional golf, too, female players made great strides. Nancy Lopez earned nearly $4 million on the women's pro golf circuit by 1994, and more than 260 women were competing on the LPGA tour by 2002 (Jones 247; Eitzen and Sage 329). They included an international coterie of entrants from Europe and Asia, as well as the United States. Michelle Wie, from Hawaii, qualified for her first LPGA event at the age of 12 in 2002. A year later, she played in a men's PGA tournament. While women's sports organizations expanded and viewers became more accepting of women on the golf tour, the top female players earned only a fraction of the men's purses, and female golfers deemed pretty, "domestic," or fashionable garnered a greater share of the limited endorsement money than those considered less feminine.

Brandi Chastain's impromptu celebration and resultant criticism indicated ongoing differences between gender expectations.
AP Photo/The San Francisco Examiner, Lacy Atkins

Women also found opportunities in bowling, where they had greater control over matters through the Women's International Bowling Congress (WIBC). The 1988 WIBC tournament attracted a record 77,735 competitors. When the women's professional bowling tour went out of business in 2003, Liz Johnson, a native of Buffalo, New York, qualified for the men's Professional Bowling Association (PBA) the next year. Johnson had won the national amateur bowling championships in 1993 and 1994. In 1996, she had earned Rookie of the Year honors as a professional, and she won 11 tournaments on the women's tour before becoming the first woman to compete on the men's circuit. Despite her success, however, she aroused little interest among advertising executives, as female athletes continued to struggle to reach equitable levels of exposure and compensation in a male-dominated sports world.

Nonetheless, inspired by female professional athletes in various sports—even racing, as Lyn St. James won 1991 Rookie of the Year honors as the first woman on the Indy car circuit—American girls and women during this period continually increased their rates of sports participation. By 1998, more than a thousand girls' teams played in the national ice hockey association, and nearly two thousand girls joined their high school wrestling teams (though male competitors often forfeited matches rather than face a girl). Thus, throughout the generation that followed the enactment of Title IX, courageous female athletes fought the restrictions of patriarchy to attain excellence, and their efforts brought great social change to the American cultural landscape.

Athletes' lifestyles came under increased, and often intensive, media scrutiny after the Athletic Revolution of the 1960s, and for women, who were displaying more and more athletic prowess—and sometimes sheer power—this scrutiny often involved consideration of gender and sexuality. A case in point was Martina Navratilova, who defected from Communist Czechoslovakia in 1975. A teenage tennis phenom, she proved inconsistent in the United States until she hired basketball great Nancy Lieberman as

PEOPLE & PLACES

Mia Hamm

Born in 1972, the same year that Title IX became law, Mariel Margaret "Mia" Hamm would come to symbolize the growing possibilities for female athletes. The daughter of an Air Force colonel and a former ballerina, Hamm grew up in a large family, including two adopted brothers. She began playing soccer in youth leagues, and at age 14 she joined the Olympic Development Team. A year later, she became the youngest member of the women's national soccer team.

Hamm entered the University of North Carolina in 1989 and led its women's soccer team to four NCAA championships before graduating with a political science degree in 1994. She was named to the All-American team three times, and she led the national team to World Cup victories in 1991 and 1999, as well as Olympic gold medals in 1996 and 2004. During that time, Hamm scored more goals than any other female player in the world, and her stardom and celebrity led to an unprecedented interest in soccer among young girls. Nike signed her to an endorsement contract, and FIFA named her the top player in the world in 2001 and 2002.

Mia Hamm starred as a player for the Washington Freedom team in the short-lived women's professional soccer league (shut down in 2003). She retired in 2004 and was elected to the National Soccer Hall of Fame in 2007. In 1999, she launched the Mia Hamm Foundation to inspire young women through sport and to provide funding for bone marrow research to solve the disease that claimed one of her brothers' lives (Dyer, "Hamm").

her trainer in 1981. Proper nutrition and weight training turned her into a power hitter who revolutionized the women's game. She dominated the prestigious Wimbledon tournament from 1982 through 1987, winning a record total of nine singles championship there, and she held the top ranking in the world for seven years. She also received abundant media coverage for her acknowledged lesbianism. In contrast, her consummate rival, Chris Evert, won fame not only for her play but also for her femininity. Her glamour, stylish couture, and style of play differed from that of Navratilova, and the contrast only heightened the interest in women's tennis. Evert won 90 percent of her matches during a long career (1971–1989), but Navratilova enjoyed a 43-37 edge in their 80 head-to-head matches. More lasting than her tennis victories, however, Navratilova's openness about her sexuality forced promoters, sponsors, opponents, and fans to confront their own values and biases.

As early as the 1890s, doctors and social critics had denigrated sports as having a masculinizing effect on women. By 1980, however, Olympian Florence Griffith Joyner was projecting an image of both physical power and alluring femininity that was at odds with the stereotype of the masculine tomboy. She showed that female athletes could be both strong and beautiful, successfully marketing herself as an erotic attraction and paving the way for the current modeling careers of athletic women such as the statuesque volleyball star Gabriella Reece and the Olympic softball sensation Jenny Finch. This eroticization of the female athletic body has split feminists and fostered controversy over the past two decades, as promoters of women's sports have used aesthetic and sometimes sensual appeal to publicize their events and attract viewers. The LPGA used Jan Stephenson, an attractive pro golfer, in featured photos in *Sports Illustrated* to publicize the women's tour, and some female tennis stars have attracted more media coverage for their appearance than for their play on the court. Anna Kournikova reached star status based on her glamorous appeal, although she had never won a major tournament, whereas Venus and Serena Williams combined top-level talent with beauty in their rise to the top echelon, and their combination of power and sexuality heightened interest in women's tennis. By 2002, the number of professional women tennis players had more than tripled from 1977, and the best players earned prize money equivalent to that of some of their male counterparts (Eitzen and Sage 328). Despite the recriminations of some feminists, then, sex became a primary attraction on the women's tennis circuit.

The Women's Sports Foundation, an ardent supporter and promoter of female athletic endeavors and equality, has objected to the use of sexual displays as a marketing device. The Olympics Games, however, have harbored no such qualms, even requiring beach volleyball players to wear skimpy and revealing bikinis to attract television viewers. Similarly, swimmer Jenny Thompson, winner of seven Olympic gold medals, posed wearing only shorts for *Sports Illustrated* magazine, and the U.S. Olympic women's swimming team shunned its suits altogether as they draped an American flag around their naked bodies for a publicity shot. Eros thus became a more overt factor in sports marketing despite the concerns of both moralists and feminists.

Sport and Cynicism in America

Throughout the latter quarter of the twentieth century, an increasing emphasis on individualism transformed team sports. Athletes sought, and the media provided, individual attention. Incentive-laden contracts and free agency produced astronomical salaries for professional athletes, greatly diminishing any sense of popular identification with heroes, and frequent player trades and departures weakened the former sense of loyalty and communal identity associated with team sport. And, like players who leave their adoring fans, team owners have regularly deserted cities in search of bigger markets and greater profits.

Styles of play changed to emphasize individual brilliance rather than team cohesion, and this transition, most noticeable in basketball, sometimes produced negative results. In the 1988 Olympics, U.S. collegians, usually dominant in the sport, finished a disappointing third. The ascendance of Michael Jordan rectified that aberration in the short term but only exacerbated the rise of individualism. Jordan personified the globalization of American commercial and popular culture at its best and worst. His competitive drive, work ethic, ambition, and success portrayed the possibilities of American life, but criticism of his selfish and domineering control of the team, his promotion of Nike products despite exploitative labor conditions in overseas sweatshops (Coakley 404–405), and his reluctance to use his celebrity to address social conditions indicated the price to be paid in attaining and maintaining his glorified stature.

The quest for national championships and the consequent abuses that often accompanied the unbridled pursuit of victory even infected the high school ranks. Television stations lobbied for additional sports programming, and media outlets such as ESPN touted interscholastic rankings and teenage phenoms. LeBron James, a high school basketball sensation, became a national celebrity even before his entry into the NBA, reportedly amassing more than $100 million in endorsements before his first pro game (Guttmann, *Sports: The First Five Millennia* 321). Some high school football teams boasted million-dollar budgets and private planes, and ESPN featured high school football and basketball teams in nationally televised games, touting their abilities in mythical national rankings.

Drug Abuse

Many athletes engaged in the blind pursuit of winning at any costs, with some using drugs or abusing alcohol to ease stress and tension and others turning to performance-enhancing drugs that promised greater potential rewards. Endurance athletes, particularly cyclists, had used strychnine to ward off fatigue in the late nineteenth century. By 1935, German scientists had succeeded in isolating the male hormone testosterone, which produced greater muscle mass and strength. During the 1950s, weight lifters injected synthetic forms of testosterone into their bodies to improve their performances. The practice soon spread to track-and-field athletes, swimmers, and American football players. Athletic governing bodies finally banned steroid usage in 1975 and began testing athletes, which led, however, only to various nuanced means of avoiding the tests or masking the results.

Allegations of substance abuse clouded athletic hero worship throughout the 1980s and continue to persist. The day after the Boston Celtics drafted Len Bias, an All-American at the University of Maryland, he died of a cocaine overdose. The attempted cover-up cost the coach, Lefty Dreisell, his job and besmirched the university. Eight days later, Don Rogers of the Cleveland Browns died at his own bachelor party, another victim of cocaine. Others stars, including baseball greats Dwight Gooden and Darryl Strawberry, simply lost their jobs and control of their own lives. New York Giants linebacker Lawrence Taylor, who used great strength, blazing speed, and a violent attitude to wreak havoc on opposing quarterbacks during his Hall of Fame career, saw his accomplishments tainted by his drug use. His addiction to cocaine resulted in arrests, suspensions, and, finally, his 1993 retirement, thus damaging his reputation as one of football's greatest players.

In baseball, Donnie Moore, a pitcher for the California Angels, gave up a home run in a 1986 League Championship Game that cost his team the pennant. Beleaguered by fans and the media, and tormented by his own self-doubts and depression over the incident, Moore committed suicide three years later. Steve Howe joined the Los Angeles Dodgers as a pitcher in 1980, and his cocaine addiction resulted in seven suspensions from major league baseball. Despite this repeated abuse, Howe found employment with three other teams eager for his services until Commissioner Fay Vincent finally imposed a lifetime ban on the unrepentant hurler in 1992. Even that measure failed, as Howe won a court case that claimed he needed cocaine for attention deficit disorder. The Yankees did not give up on Howe until his fastball finally deserted him in 1996, but, as a result of such struggles, professional sports teams began investigating players' lifestyles in an attempt to avoid drafting and investing millions of dollars in compromised employees.

Substance abuse reached a crisis stage at the 1988 Olympics in Seoul, Korea, when Canadian Ben Johnson set a new world record in the 100-meter race, easily defeating the prohibitive favorite, Carl Lewis. Dismay turned to disbelief when Johnson tested positive for a performance-enhancing substance (the anabolic steroid stanozolol). He then asserted such use was widespread among track stars. Worse, the drugs had been supplied by his doctor and encouraged by his coach as a necessary step toward winning. That belief persisted, and drug usage spread to winter sports competitors, baseball players, and even American high school youth desirous of athletic success or just a better body image.

In an attempt to deter steroid usage, the NCAA instituted mandatory drug testing for athletes involved in football bowl games and championship contests. This attempt at redressing the blemished image of sport and of athletes failed miserably, however, as collegiate players successfully sued, charging that such measures constituted invasions of their privacy. In the quest for wins and self-imposed pressures to succeed, then, some athletes sought any means, even illegal ones, to enhance their performances, and many coaches and administrators looked away when they did not actually condone such usage.

In 2004, Jason Giambi, a power hitter for the New York Yankees, admitted to steroid use and implicated Barry Bonds and others associated with the Bay Area Lab Cooperative (BALCO). Victor Conte, the lab owner, claimed that he had supplied the drugs to top football players and world-class track stars as well. Marion Jones finally admitted her guilt in 2007 after years of denial. Public and journalistic outcries, along with a government inquiry, finally forced baseball authorities to address the issue, but Commissioner Bud Selig responded with a weak testing and enforcement policy until a congressional investigation forced more stringent measures including a 50-game suspension for first-time offenders.

Despite the best efforts of the World Anti-Doping Association (WADA) and the United States Anti-Doping Agency (USADA), athletes persisted in trying to outwit detection by the governing bodies, and performance-enhancing drugs seemed particularly rampant on the European cycling tour. In 1986, Greg LeMond became the first American to win the prestigious Tour De France, succeeding despite a hunting accident that nearly claimed his life, and he repeated his victory in 1989 and 1990. Next up was Lance Armstrong, who succeeded LeMond as America's greatest cyclist and, despite repeated but unproven allegations of performance-enhancing drug use, overcame a bout of testicular cancer to claim seven consecutive Tour de France wins from 1999 through 2005. Thirteen riders were banned from the 2006 cycling circuit for blood doping, but Americans paid little attention until Floyd Landis, winner of the Tour de France, failed drug tests for testosterone usage and forfeited his crown (*Mercury Sport* 24).

Damaged Bodies

For female steroid users, very noticeable improvement in performance was accompanied by the growth of masculine physical characteristics, such as wider shoulders, greater muscle mass, facial hair, and a deeper voice. Girls and young women faced alternative conceptions of beauty that changed from the voluptuous figure of Marilyn Monroe in the 1960s to the waiflike image of Twiggy and the slender supermodels of the 1990s. The media emphasis on thin bodies pushed many to fad diets, weight-loss pills, and even anorexia and bulimia.

Among other detrimental side effects of steroid usage, violent temper (sometimes termed *'roid rage*) caused particular concern. Sociologists and psychologists have debated whether the practice of sport alleviates or enhances aggressive tendencies. Noncontact sports (e.g., swimming, gymnastics) seem to be inconsequential in this regard, whereas contact sports (e.g., football, hockey, soccer) can exacerbate animosity (Coakley 173–201), and athletes using steroids may be more prone to such outbursts.

Violence in Sport

Such issues only increased existing concern over the aggressive nature of some sports, and psychologists disagreed over the value of sport as a means of dissipating violent tendencies. More recent sociological studies, however, showed increased hostility in postgame football viewers, regardless of the outcome. Another study discovered that domestic assaults against women increased after the Super Bowl. Other aggressive sports, such hockey and wrestling, prompted similar escalations in hostility, whereas no such change was noted in viewers of swimming or gymnastics events (Eitzen and Sage 133). In certain sports, such as hockey, boxing, or football, intensive aggressiveness is even necessary for success. Boxing rules, of course, allow the violent actions required for winning, and hockey violence also serves a sanctioned ritualistic function in the demonstration of masculinity. Hockey teams even employ "goons" as enforcers to safeguard their star players and intimidate opponents. Uncontrolled aggression, however, has sometimes turned to outright violence.

Hockey has a long history of violent acts, often considered endemic to the game and part of its promotion of tough masculinity. In 1933, Boston Bruins defenseman Eddie Shore slammed the Maple Leaf's Ace Bailey into the ice, fracturing his skull and ending his career. In 1955, Maurice Richard hit an opponent over the head with his stick, then punched a game official. When NHL president Clarence Campbell suspended Richard, Montreal fans rioted, causing $500,000 in damage. In a 1969 preseason game which did not even count in the championship race, Wayne Maki of St. Louis and Ted Green of Boston engaged in a brawl that ended with Maki clouting Green with his stick. Green's fractured skull left him near death, requiring three operations and a year of recovery.

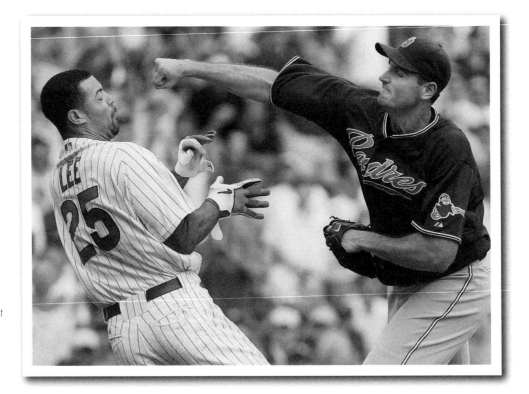

Athletic violence has cast doubt on the character-building qualities of sport.

AP Photo/Nam Y. Huh, file

Violence still riddled the game at the turn of the twenty-first century. Bryan Marchment, an NHL player, equated the violence to a display of masculinity: "Hey, it's a man's game. If you can't play, get out and play tennis" (Coakley 181). The reinforcement of one's masculinity, especially in the presence of other males, is a big factor in winning group acceptance, and that sense of identity has long been an essential socially constructed desire for boys and young men. Professional hockey finally faced forceful restraint in 2000, when Marty McSorley of Boston slashed Donald Brashear of Vancouver across the head. The resulting concussion ended up in a civil lawsuit that restricted McSorley's play, effectively causing his retirement.

Such assaults seemed commonplace in hockey, and youth began to emulate their professional idols. In youth sports, even some parents attacked coaches and game officials. In a Chicago hockey game, one player, at the urging of his coach, attacked an opponent after the game as he left the ice, resulting in a spinal cord injury and paralysis (Felsenthal). In Massachusetts, a brawl between hockey parents resulted in a death during the 2000 season; a game was not even at stake as a father beat the coach into unconsciousness over the nature of a practice session. The offender faced manslaughter charges.

Reports of such violence involving athletes permeated newspapers throughout the latter part of the twentieth century and the start of the twenty-first. In a particularly infamous case, the Oakland Raiders' Jack Tatum, known as "The Assassin," paralyzed the Patriots' Darryl Stingley in an especially brutal hit in 1978. Other incidents included one in which Woody Hayes, famed football coach at Ohio State University, punched a Clemson player in the 1978 Gator Bowl, which cost him his job. College football players faced numerous charges of rape and assault during the 1990s, and NFL player Rae Carruth, found guilty of conspiracy charges in the murder of a pregnant woman who carried their child, received a long prison sentence. Carruth's conviction followed in the wake of the O.J. Simpson debacle, as the NFL was trying to improve its image amid allegations of tolerating or even encouraging violent behavior.

Simpson had enjoyed fame, fortune, and celebrity as a superstar running back for the Buffalo Bills, breaking Jim Brown's single-season rushing record, and upon retirement his celebrity status won him a role on the *Monday Night Football* broadcast team, as well as movie parts and roles in corporate ads on national television, making him the first African American to gain that distinction. After the murders of his white wife and her male friend, however, Simpson led police on a long, televised car chase, and though he was acquitted of murder charges in 1995 after a highly controversial, racially charged criminal trial, he was found liable in a civil suit two years later.

Shortly after Simpson's indictment, star quarterback Warren Moon went to trial on domestic abuse charges, as did Jim Brown in 1999. A year later, Ray Lewis, a popular linebacker for the Baltimore Ravens, faced murder charges. Though convicted only of obstruction of justice for his role in the cover-up, the case did little to repair the NFL's soiled image or to soften the association between football and violence.

While hockey and football engaged in damage control, boxing could claim crisis as a perpetual state, particularly after the arrival of Mike Tyson. In 1986, he gained the World Boxing Council (WBC) heavyweight championship at the age of 20, and he added the World Boxing Association (WBA) crown four months later. A devastating puncher, he amazed fans by knocking out virtually all opponents in amassing a 37-0 record by 1990. In 1992, however, a jury convicted Tyson of raping Desiree Washington, a contestant in an Indianapolis beauty contest. After three years in prison, Tyson returned to the ring and fought a pair of matches against another champion, Evander Holyfield. In their 1997 fight, a frustrated Tyson bit off part of Holyfield's ear. A year earlier, Tyson had earned $75 million in prize money but not a cent in endorsements (MacCambridge 284). He had transgressed even the sanctioned violence of the boxing arena.

Other sports were also tarred with images of aggression or outright violence. Even the pristine sport of figure skating experienced a scandal when Tonya Harding conspired with thugs to injure and thus eliminate her rival, Nancy Kerrigan, from the 1994 national championships. In baseball, Roberto Alomar spit in the face of umpire John Hirschbeck near the end of the 1996 season. The American League issued a mild suspension, then withdrew it when Alomar's team entered the playoffs. Apparently, winning and television ratings meant more than respect. In 2000, Dodger players fought with Cub fans at Wrigley Field, and in 2002 White Sox fans left the stands at Comiskey Park to attack an opposing coach. A year later, another Sox fan attacked an umpire. In 2004, Rangers pitcher Frank Tanana threw a chair at hecklers, breaking a woman's nose.

Basketball also struggled with ongoing issues involving violent behavior. In 1977, Kermit Washington of the Los Angeles Lakers earned a 60-day suspension for punching Rudy Tomjanovich of Houston, leaving him unconscious in a pool of blood with a fractured skull. In 1994, Coach John Chaney of Temple University issued a death threat to his opponent, John Calipari of Massachusetts. Eleven years later, the controversial Chaney earned a suspension after directing one of his players to "send a message" to opponents, resulting in a foul that produced a broken arm. During the 1996 NBA season, Dennis Rodman and Nick Van

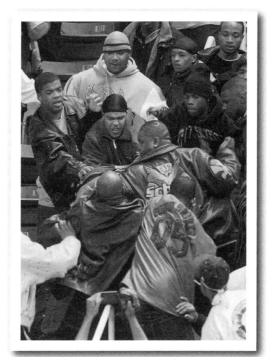

Violence among fans has become commonplace, too, even at the high school level.

AP Photo/The Oakland Press, Jose Juarez

Exel both accosted referees during a game, and in 1997 Latrell Sprewell attacked his coach, P. J. Carlesimo, with a choke hold. The NBA suspended him for a year, but the players' union filed a grievance on his behalf that reduced the penalty to seven months. Jayson Williams of the New Jersey Nets faced manslaughter charges when his shotgun killed his chauffeur in 2002. Though acquitted of that crime, he suffered conviction on four counts in attempting to hide the tragedy by portraying it as a suicide. And one of the game's biggest stars, Kobe Bryant of the Los Angeles Lakers, nearly lost his career after a young woman filed rape charges in 2003. Though the case was dropped, Bryant admitted to adultery and wrongdoing, then settled the civil case out of court, sullying his clean image and hindering the rehabilitation efforts of the NBA. The dust from that affair had hardly settled when, early in the 2004 season, three Indiana Pacers players attacked Detroit fans, resulting in a year's suspension for Ron Artest.

Gambling

Aggressiveness made Pete Rose a star on the baseball field but also led to the biggest baseball scandal since the Black Sox of 1919. A working-class overachiever, intensely competitive, and driven to succeed, Rose spent 24 years (1963–1986) in the National League with the Cincinnati Reds, Philadelphia Phillies, and Montreal Expos. Known as "Charlie Hustle," he slid headfirst into bases and even ran to first base after receiving a walk. Rose led his teams to six World Series appearances and often led the league in hitting. In 1978, he had a 44-game hitting streak, and in 1985 he surpassed Ty Cobb's seemingly insurmountable record for career hits. Rose finished with a total of 4,256 hits, appearing as a player-manager for Cincinnati after 1984. He continued to manage the Reds until 1988 but as an inveterate gambler he even wagered on his own team. When confronted with the allegations, Rose persistently denied his actions, resulting in a lifetime ban from baseball and ineligibility for the Hall of Fame. His troubles continued in 1990, when the government charged him with tax evasion and imposed a five-month jail sentence. Once again, gambling had stained the reputation of baseball, and critics questioned the value of sport and its relationship to the unsavory behavior that seemed so prevalent during the era.

Homophobia

Similar to Chris Evert, diver Greg Louganis enjoyed polished movie-star looks and consummate athletic skill. He won six world championships and four gold medals at the Olympic Games (in 1984 and 1988). Of Samoan heritage and a dyslexic, Louganis also exemplified success for those two groups. After a dramatic double win (springboard and platform diving) at the Seoul Olympics, in which he recovered from a head wound caused by hitting the diving board, Louganis acknowledged not only being gay but also that he had contracted AIDS. In 1994, he competed in the Gay Games, overcoming new social barriers to "coming out" in the process, and he declared, "Being gay and being in sports isn't supposed to mix. I think I proved that wrong" (MacCambridge 258). Thus gay athletes such as Louganis, Billie Jean King, and Martina Navratilova used sport as a means to challenge dominant notions of gender and sexuality. They won greater, if grudging, acceptance for their achievements, regardless of their sexual preferences. In some sports, at least, ability counted more than lifestyle. In the sports of baseball, football, basketball, and hockey, however, the dominant sense of the requisite machismo pressured male athletes to publicly conform to traditional roles and characteristics throughout the twentieth century. When David Kopay admitted his homosexuality in his 1977 autobiography, five years after his retirement from the NFL, he faced ostracism by former teammates. When John Amaeche, a former NBA player, acknowledged in 2007 (well after retirement) that he was gay, some NBA players ardently disassociated themselves from him and even publicly proclaimed their disgust.

Promiscuity

Professional athletes are never at a loss for willing sex partners; Wilt Chamberlain claimed to have bedded 20,000 women. Such promiscuity, however, can have dire results. In 1991, Earvin "Magic" Johnson, a heterosexual NBA star, acknowledged that he had been infected with the HIV virus due to his promiscuous lifestyle. The announcement shocked the NBA, spread fear among teammates and opponents, and led to Johnson's retirement. The revelation triggered widespread concern over the lifestyles of athletes, many of whom fathered illegitimate children without supporting them. Despite Charles Barkley's contention that, as a professional basketball star, he was not a role model, children and youth perceived him and other athletes as such. The ongoing issue of whether athletes are role models called into question athletes' responsibilities to society, as youth quickly copied the fashions, mannerisms, and playing styles of their athletic idols.

Seeking a Better Body

The quest for the perfect body, known as the Adonis complex, sought the mesomorphic ideal and well-defined musculature of Greek sculptures. That particular image of masculinity was reinforced in popular beach movies, muscle magazines, and bodybuilding contests. Teenage boys and young men fell prey to the psychological addiction, turning to steroid usage and extreme bouts of weight lifting, as well as dangerous dehydration that lowered their body fat. High school and college wrestlers, too, sought to "cut" weight in order to gain an advantage over opponents by competing in a lower weight class. Such a practice became so widespread that the NCAA mandated that collegiate wrestlers maintain an acceptable level of body fat and hydration in order to compete.

The denial of nutrients to one's body causes considerable harm, but athletes, particularly males, are programmed to play with pain. Such stoicism earns social capital among one's peers, teammates, and fans, though at great cost to one's body. NFL players have a decidedly shorter life span than others; still, most relish their playing days. Jim Otto, a Hall of Fame center for the Oakland Raiders, has undergone twenty-three surgeries, including installation of five artificial knees. In 1993, a study by the NFL Players Association revealed that more than 40 percent of players left the game due to injuries, and more than 60 percent suffered permanent injuries. Still, Dan Hampton, a Hall of Fame defensive end for the Chicago Bears, asserted that, "The true players don't worry about injuries or any of that crap. . . . You can take MRIs, X-rays and all that, and you can stuff it. . . . People accept hazards in all kinds of jobs. My God. Football players ought to be willing to take their panties off, get out there and hit somebody" (Hewitt, 17B).

Girls and young women, too, have been greatly affected by the body images portrayed in the media. Cross country runners, in particular, seem susceptible to anorexia or bulimia in attempts to keep their weight at low levels. A high percentage of female runners also suffer from amenorrhea, the absence of menstruation, due to a lack of body fat. While the latter seems a temporary condition, the former can be life threatening. Such maladies also have been particularly widespread in gymnastics, where performance standards favor smaller bodies.

Racism

Nearly a half century after Jackie Robinson's "Great Experiment," the stain of racism endured in American sport. Marge Schott, the bigoted owner of the Cincinnati Reds, further defamed the sport with a series of racist pronouncements. In 1992, she greatly offended Jews by her admiration of Adolph Hitler and her possession of a Nazi armband. That same year, she referred to some of her players as "million-dollar niggers." The league imposed a $25,000 fine and a one-year suspension from team involvement, but when her demeanor failed to improve, a two-year ban followed in 1996, leading to her sale of the team in 1999.

Schott's remarks reflected a lingering racism within the sports world, in spite of advancements made by African American and Hispanic players. Major League Baseball teams increasingly signed Latin American athletes throughout the decade, African American players filled the NBA, and the NFL selected Johnny Grier as its first black referee in 1988. Still, few minorities gained positions as head coaches, team administrators, or owners. On the playing field, the practice of stacking (i.e., assigning white players to the "cerebral" positions such as quarterback and relegating blacks to positions where physical abilities superseded mental qualifications) remained problematic in the midst of a painfully gradual progression toward proper recognition of nonwhites' intellectual capabilities. Scientists, anthropologists, and sociologists theorized about black dominance in some sports, and the comments of Jimmy "The Greek" Snyder, a football analyst for CBS, created a national controversy in 1988. Snyder professed that black success resulted from breeding practices during slavery, suggesting biological determinism as an explanation. He even claimed running advantages due to larger thighs in African Americans. CBS fired Snyder the next day, but the heated debate continued. Scientists discovered no genetic superiority for blacks, but sociologists suggested cultural reasons as well as practical opportunities (Pope, *The New* 312–338). The number of African Americans in major league baseball has declined considerably (to only 9 percent), due, in some degree, to the lack of urban playing spaces

Eldrick "Tiger" Woods, the successor to Michael Jordan as ubiquitous spokesman for Nike and a host of other commercial products, won the 1997 Masters Golf Tournament at the age of 21, not only setting a new record at 18 strokes under par but also dominating his opponents, the nearest of whom finished 12 strokes behind. The son of a father who was African American, Native American, and Chinese, and a mother who is Thai, Chinese, and European, Woods described himself as a Cablinasian. In any case, he has transcended racial lines and brought new constituencies to the previously white-dominated golf circuit. In 2000, Woods won more than $9 million in prize money and much more in endorsements. His high profile in the white world of golf, along with his replacement of Michael Jordan as a primary spokesman for American commerce, suggests a significant decline in the level of racism that had previously marked American society.

The greater acceptance and visibility of people of color in American sport did not extend to all minorities. In 1983, Native Americans formed the Iroquois Nationals lacrosse team, which, like Puerto Rico, competed in international contests as an independent nation with its own national anthem and a distinct flag. Sport provided the most visible avenue to public recognition for the Indian confederacy. One step in amelioration with Native Americans was taken when the NCAA required its member schools to banish all Indian mascots for sports events or face the penalty of ostracism by being barred from hosting championship events.

Tiger Woods is one of the most popular athletes in American sport. His success on the golf course has not only earned him millions of dollars in prize money and endorsement deals, it has also helped to further break down walls of racism.

AP Photo/Matt York

Enduring Icons of Sport

Despite ongoing negative images generated by some athletes, others upheld the idealistic beliefs treasured by sports fans, strengthening faith in the potentially regenerative quality of athletics. As discussed earlier in the chapter, the various sports halls of fame portrayed such idealistic virtues as the norm, though this was clearly not always the case.

The Edmonton Oilers won four NHL championships during the middle and latter 1980s, and their success rested largely on the efforts of Wayne Gretzky, who began playing professional hockey in the WHA at the age of 17. Despite a lack of great size or skating speed, Gretzky overshadowed all other players, winning the Hart Trophy, given to the league's MVP, 9 times. He led the NHL in scoring 10 times and topped all others in assists for 13 consecutive seasons. In 1988, the Oilers traded him to the Los Angeles Kings, an act considered a sacrilege and a national tragedy in Canada, where Gretzky was idolized as a national hero of virtuous character.

The immense popularity of Gretzky transferred to the United States, allowing hockey to claim status as a major sport, and the NHL expanded to include franchises on the West Coast and in the South, thus introducing a winter sport to warm climates. Gretzky continued his stellar play throughout the 1990s for the St. Louis Blues and the New York Rangers, and upon his retirement after the 1999 season he had set the record for points scored with 2,857. The NHL quickly retired his jersey in deference to his achievements. In 2005, the Phoenix Coyotes made him their head coach, hoping that his magic could help resurrect the struggling league.

As Gretzky excited hockey fans, Walter Payton stunned opponents of the Chicago Bears, endearing himself to fans in that city and earning the respect of all others. At only 5 feet 10 inches (1.8 meters) and 205 pounds (93 kilograms), he seemed small for an NFL player when the Bears drafted him from a small college, Jackson State, in 1975. He was, however, possessed of rare athletic gifts, frenetic energy, and a playful spirit, and he transformed a weak team into a Super Bowl champion. A versatile player who excelled in all phases of the game, Payton retired after 13 seasons as the all-time leading rusher in NFL history, having amassed 16,726 yards (15,294 meters). He ran for more than 1,000 yards (914 meters) in a season 10 times, and he won the NFL MVP award twice. Playing for a mediocre team through most of his career, Payton became a Chicago icon before Michael Jordan joined the Bulls. His cheerful attitude in spite of adversity, his indomitable work ethic, his infectious enthusiasm for the game, and the physical way in which he played it led blue-collar fans of the former industrial center to identify with their star player. His charitable works only deepened his bonds of attachment with the inhabitants of Chicago. In 1985, the Bears assembled a compelling cast of characters under head coach "Iron" Mike Ditka, producing a 15-1 record that culminated in a 46-10 demolition of the New England Patriots in the Super Bowl. Their song and music video, the "Super Bowl Shuffle," clearly exposed the juncture of sport and entertainment as a pop-culture commodity. Payton retired after the 1987 season to engage in entrepreneurial ventures and auto racing, and he owned a CART (Championship Auto Racing Team) car in the Road America series. In 1999, however, he fell victim to a rare liver disease, and, as with the premature demise of baseball great Lou Gehrig, the city and the league mourned his death. In both cases, fans empathized and identified with tragic athletic heroes in whom they saw pieces of themselves or fragments of who they wanted to be. Such idealizations served functionalist theories (sport as good, beneficial to all, and a character-building endeavor) of the role of sport in society and its need for heroes. Payton assumed near-martyr status in Chicago, his relics housed in his own suburban hall of fame.

Other athletes fulfilled identification roles for other constituencies, though not with the grace and approbation of Gehrig, Gretzky, or Payton. The intimidating Bo Jackson became a media sensation and a pitchman as a multisport athlete, starring in both professional baseball and football. After a hip injury forced Jackson's early retirement, the loquacious "Neon Deion" Sanders assumed the role of self-congratulatory, glamorous, dual-sport superstar. Sanders arrived (by limousine) at his last college game dressed in a top hat and tails. He backed up his flamboyance, arrogance, and boastful swagger by being the only athlete to appear in both the World Series and the Super Bowl. In the era of free agency, he took his talents to a succession of highest bidders, but by 1998 he had renounced his profligate ways and become a born-again Christian, thus reconstructing his image in the manner of celebrities in the movie and music industries.

With the departure of Muhammad Ali from the boxing scene, another fighter, almost as colorful and charismatic, emerged as the consummate showman. Sugar Ray Leonard sported 145 wins in 150 amateur fights before taking the light welterweight gold medal at the 1976 Olympics. He turned professional under the tutelage of Angelo Dundee, the former trainer of Muhammad Ali, and in 1979 he defeated Wilfred Benitez for the WBC welterweight crown. Throughout the 1980s, the flashy, garrulous Leonard became a fan favorite and a media darling as he fought in a series of bouts against other Hall of Fame boxers of the era, including Roberto Duran, Tommy Hearns, and Marvin Hagler. Each of the memorable battles was among the best in ring history. A detached retina in 1982 required surgery and forced Leonard's retirement, though he soon defied medical authorities to return to the ring. From 1984 to 1989, he battled a cocaine habit but managed to accumulate five world titles in five different weight classes before a final retirement in 1997. Such success stories continued to fuel adolescent dreams, nurture the promise of sport, and deny the deleterious aspects of the sporting culture.

Alternative Sports

While women challenged social barriers, young men and women (some still boys and girls) also pushed the boundaries of sport. Individual sports such as rollerblading, mountain biking, windsurfing, cycling, motocross, auto racing, skydiving, kayaking, and skateboarding grew in appeal. In such endeavors as extreme skiing, rock climbing, and mountain climbing, individuals challenged themselves, sometimes surpassing their limitations to the point of death. The quest for self-fulfillment and rebellious identification, the search for peak experiences (i.e., adrenaline rush) such as bungee jumping, and adventurous treks in isolated or natural settings served as a distinct reaction to urban routines of the era. Such pastimes resonated with restless spirits, renegade mentalities, and outlaw images that served as alternatives to the major corporatized sports and drew youthful, disaffected participants.

Clothing manufacturers capitalized on such symbolism to produce styles and gear that fostered nonmainstream images. The pervasiveness of such reproductions only drew such practices closer to prevailing norms, hastened by attempts to televise the practices as conventional fare. Corporate-sponsored triathlons and adventure races for prize money, along with snowboarding contests and skateboarding competitions, were soon integrated within standard commercialized programming. Snowboarding, freestyle skiing, canoeing, taekwondo, and triathlon were all integrated into the Olympic program, securing their absorption into the corporate mainstream.

As some pursued adventure sports, such as skydiving, surfing, windsurfing, mountain biking, kayaking, whitewater rafting, adventure racing, rock climbing, snowboarding, and extreme skiing, other activities such as in-line skating, skateboarding, and BMX (motocross) bicycling became so prevalent that many communities built half-pipe ramps to accommodate practitioners in their attempts to perform tricks and flips.

The inherent risk, the rebellious image, and the opportunity for self-expression attracted multitudes to such new sport forms in a counterculture set apart from the competitive capitalist model (Beal). Snowboarding grew from 1.6 million participants in 1992 to 3.6 million in 1999, and skateboarders numbered more than 11.5 million by the turn of the century (Barcett; Dean). By 2005, females composed at least

Adventure Races

Adventure races (ARs) are mass-media productions which gratify people's craving for heroes, sensation, and intimate glimpses into the lives and suffering of others. Like other dangerous sports, these races give expression to a postmodern outlook on life that drives participants to their limits, to self-discovery and self-reassurance, and even as far as playing with their own lives. The yearning for untamed nature and wilderness, the exaggerated and idealized belief in team spirit, and the sense of belonging to an elite group may be other motives for participants, who, to a large extent, are made up of former long-distance runners and triathletes. A large percentage of participants are management-level corporate agents, and roughly 10 percent are AR professionals.

The origins of adventure races are a matter of debate, but multisport events have been organized since as early as the 1960s. By 1980, the Alpine Ironman race in New Zealand required running, paddling, and skiing. The Alaskan Mountain Wilderness competition in 1982 took six days to complete, and the Raid Gauloises, sponsored by the Gauloises cigarette company and held in New Zealand in 1989, covered more than 400 miles (644 kilometers). The Raid Gauloises inspired TV producer Mark Burnett, who also developed the idea of the *Survivor* reality show, to create the show *Eco-Challenge*, staged for the first time in Utah in 1995. This was the beginning of a symbiotic relationship between AR and TV companies, which own the races and sell them as reality TV shows, thus turning AR into a multimillion-dollar business. *Eco-Challenge* wooed audiences not only with adventure but also with being environmentally friendly—which did not, however, save it from protests by environmentalists, who declared all interference in environmentally sensitive areas to be irresponsible.

ARs are multiday expeditions in remote, often exotic, wilderness areas in which only the starting point, certain checkpoints, and the finish point are fixed. These races belong to the category of extreme sports, which in addition to extreme endurance capacities require a variety of skills in order to master disciplines such as orienteering, rappelling, mountain biking, rafting, paddling or kayaking, swimming, spelunking, climbing, and traversing.

AR is a team sport. In some races, teams are accompanied by a support crew, and in others the members have only themselves to rely on. They have to carry equipment, provisions, and water and decide on routes and breaks among themselves. Teams are often made up of four or five members; in many ARs there must be at least one female member, and all team members must finish the race for the team to be included in the scoring. Dropout rates are high. Bad weather, difficult terrain, and, above all, sleep deprivation are frequent causes of injury and illness. Teams are often sponsored by corporations who benefit from the media exposure and the imagery of performance under extreme conditions.

Shorter variations of ARs may last only hours instead of days. Other events accommodate urban teams that combine orienteering skills with the facing of city challenges such as running to the top of skyscrapers, navigating waterways or byways by various means of locomotion, and overcoming diverse obstacles. One of the better-known urban adventure races is the City Chase, created in Canada in 2004 and conducted in nine Canadian cities; it was immediately given enormous media coverage. In the City Chase, teams of two run through a city and have to fulfill numerous physical and mental tasks. The first world championship took place in Chicago in 2006. Adventure races and city chases are clear illustrations of a current trend in which sports and sporting events no longer undergo a slow and lengthy process of development and adaptation at the hands of the players themselves but are, rather, the product of invention and marketing in the hands of the mass media.

Information from Kay, Joanne, and Suzanne Laberge. "The 'New' Corporate Habitus in Adventure Racing." *International Review for the Sociology of Sport* 37.1 (2002): 17–36; and <www.citychase.com>.

Shaun White is one of many athletes helping to popularize "alternative" sports.

AP Photo/Reed Saxon

one-third of the snowboarders and surfers and more than one-quarter of the skateboarders (Thorpe 219). By the last decade of the twentieth century, however, sport promoters and clothing designers had succeeded in co-opting the activities and fashions for mainstream structures. Surfing, snowboarding, and skateboarding accounted for $9.9 billion dollars a year by 2006, with nearly 80 percent of the expenditure on clothing, shoes, and accessories (Thorpe 219). ESPN featured the X Games competition beginning in 1999, and even the Olympics adopted snowboarding in 1998. Within a few years, skateboarder Tony Hawk and motocross rider Jeremy McGrath ranked among the most recognized athletes among American youth. Marketed and managed by sports agencies, Hawk and surfing champ Kelly Slater became multimillionaires, and even lower-level competitors earned $250,000 per year, equivalent to the minimum salaries of NFL rookies. The incorporation of such rebel sports into the corporate media complex became clear by 2006, when Kevin Monahan, vice president of NBC Sports, announced that the lack of paying spectators at live events was inconsequential. "The tour's about providing programming for the network and Universal, USA, NBC wireless, Internet broadband, Universal DVD, and Telemundo. All those channels can replay parts of the tour, edit highlight shows, or sell DVDs of the gnarliest [best] tricks" (qtd. in Dean 55).

The previously regional activity of stock car racing produced national heroes as it mushroomed from its Southern origins to become the fastest-growing sport. By 2000, only football drew a larger percentage of television viewers than NASCAR (*Sports Illustrated* 121), whose events typically drew nine million television viewers by 2003, and the sport claimed thirty-five million fans a year later (Cobb, *Away* 324). Departing from its rural and male roots, stock car racing attracted urbanites, and nearly half of its fan base consisted of women. Shawna Robinson, a female driver, became one of the attractions when she entered the Winston Cup series of races in 2001.

NASCAR achieved explosive growth by merging technology, corporate sponsorship, and a nostalgic sense of rugged individualism attributed to those who push the limits. In 1998, racing fans purchased $950 million in NASCAR paraphernalia (MacCambridge 284). In 1999, television rights to Winston Cup races sold for $6 billion over six years. Dale Earnhardt's aggressive driving style earned him the nickname "The Intimidator" and the love of hard-core fans. Drivers accumulated points based on their order of finish in a series of races, and Earnhardt dominated the standings during the 1990s, earning more than $3 million a year and eventually capturing the elusive Daytona 500 in 1998. By 2001, he had reached $41 million in prize money before dying in a fiery crash on the last lap of the Daytona 500. NASCAR fans mourned the loss of the auto racing dignitary for years afterward but transferred their loyalty to his son and successor, Dale Earnhardt Jr.

Both NASCAR drivers and the drag racers of the National Hot Rod Association (NHRA) belied the lower-class images of their initial years as the costs of participation increased. Many teams on the former circuit required corporate sponsors, and even NHRA participants had to sustain the maintenance and replacement of parts for cars that exceeded 250 miles (400 kilometers) per hour. For drag racers, a $1,000 set of tires lasted about 10 trials, and a crankshaft could cost $2,500. Cars themselves cost as much as $150,000. Competitive racing at higher levels was no longer a poor man's sport. Nor was it exclusively male, as an increasing number of females piloted the four-wheeled missiles. One female competitor at the 2003 Darlington Nationals in Hartsville, South Carolina, stated, "I like going fast, but I like winning more than anything. . . . [Y]ou earn a lot of respect by winning" (Warren 116). By 2005, the diminutive Danica Patrick had emerged as a rising star on the Indy Racing League circuit. Sport served such women as a vehicle for dismantling traditional gender roles.

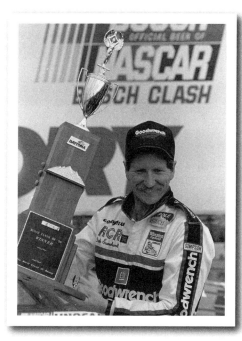

Dale Earnhardt was a major factor in the increase of NASCAR's popularity in the late 1980s and its continued popularity through the 2000s.

AP Photo/Kathy Willens

Such courage continued to reinforce the heroic qualities of sport for some, while it held different meanings for diverse ethnic, racial, religious, gender, social, political, economic, and age groups; sport is not heroic for all but rather a means to a livelihood, leisure, identity, and so on. The elderly continually push physical boundaries in masters competition. The ever-increasing salaries offered to professional athletes enticed several prodigies, like Michelle Wie in golf, to embark on early sports careers. Freddy Adu entered the ranks of Major League Soccer with DC United as a 14-year-old in 2004. Venus and Serena Williams joined the professional tennis tour at the same age. In 1998, Kevin Garnett entered the NBA as a 19-year-old, and during the 2003–2004 season 18-year-old basketball phenom LeBron James won Rookie of the Year honors with the Cleveland Cavaliers. Such success fueled unrealistic dreams for millions of other young Americans.

Summary

This chapter has explained how the corporate mentality and structure came to pervade sports. Private owners of sports teams pressured municipalities into subsidizing public stadiums with threats of franchise relocation. Politicians promoted such ventures as entertainment zones featuring restaurants, theaters, halls of fame, and assorted amusements to draw tourists to the urban areas. The marketing of sport as entertainment and of athletes as celebrities further transformed the ways in which sport was perceived by viewers and social critics.

The globalization of American sport forms and American business practices escalated with the ascendance of a global superstar in the person of Michael Jordan. American cultural values were transmitted to the world, often to the detriment of local cultures. Even the Olympic Games became a commercialized spectacle under the management of Americans in 1984, changing its espoused values thereafter.

The vast amounts of revenue produced by the confluence of sport and various competing television networks led to labor issues between owners and players over the division of the spoils, producing strikes, lockouts, and arbitration. Owners turned to a global labor force to reduce their costs and maximize their profits.

Greater commercialization also affected intercollegiate and interscholastic sports programs, fostering even more abuses in the quest for victories and bigger profits. Cynics decried the greed, violence, homophobia, and lingering racism that seemed all too present in the sporting culture, even as certain athletic heroes and heroines upheld the purported idealistic values of sport. Women, in particular, made great strides in athletic participation after the passage of Title IX in 1972.

Young people ill at ease with the commercialized competitions of the mainstream sporting culture initiated a host of alternative sports, only to be coerced, co-opted, and enticed into the mainstream by television networks and marketing companies. As youth continue to question the values of corporate sport, such alternative sport forms may reappear, but one thing is certain: With 41 million children involved in sports programs in the United States (Carney 21), sport will remain a major component of American culture.

DISCUSSION QUESTIONS

1. How has ESPN revolutionized sport?

2. How does globalization affect sporting practices?

3. Compare the social and economic influences of Muhammad Ali and Michael Jordan.

4. How has commercialization changed the Olympic Games? Intercollegiate sport? Interscholastic sport?

5. Are subsidized stadiums for professional teams good or bad? Why?

6. How do sports halls of fame create and perpetuate particular value systems?

7. How has women's sport changed since the passage of Title IX in 1972?

Afterword

The role of sport in American society today demonstrates the ongoing influence of the earlier trends in sport that occurred during the various time periods presented in *Sports in American History*. The increasing numbers of participants and spectators at all levels of sport suggest that the importance of sport in America remains consistent. Yet some of the major elements in the sporting culture, such as the values attributed to sport by early advocates in the nineteenth century—good health, character-building, preparation for men's and women's gender roles, the Americanization of immigrants—may not follow the traditions and patterns of the past. New technologies, the use of different types of performance-enhancing substances, conflicts and debates about professionalism and amateurism, and issues of fair play are just a few of the factors that could affect the role of sport. The meanings of sport change as people's experiences and events in American culture change. However, the influence that sport has on diverse groups of people across the United States certainly persists, and sport will continue to be a major force in American society.

After the Progressive Era, American sporting culture experienced cycles of creation, incorporation, and resistance to a uniform, hegemonic structure. Throughout U.S. history, ethnic minorities had used sport as a means both to assimilate into the mainstream culture and to retain traditional leisure forms. For racial groups, often excluded from mainstream sporting activities, sport had often been marked by creation of parallel organizations, struggles for recognition and acceptance, and development of culturally expressive styles of play.

Religious factions have, at various times, both condemned sport as immoral and condoned it as a tool for achieving physical and spiritual health. For institutions like the Young Men's Christian Association and the Young Women's Christian Association, sport became a means of Protestant proselytism and a vehicle to teach appropriate behaviors. For Catholics and Jews, it brought greater unity between divisive internal factions, as ethnic Catholic parishes gradually accepted the leadership of an Irish American hierarchy. In the growth of reform Judaism in the later decades of the nineteenth century, reformed middle- and upper-class German Jews strived to acculturate the more orthodox and lower-class Eastern European Jews journeying to America by organizing sport and physical health programs for men and women in settlement houses.

Women have confronted sex discrimination in their struggle for sporting opportunities and for the choices to participate actively—and, for some, professionally—in sport. In sport and society American women have agitated for a change in culturally prescribed gender roles. Other groups of people have also been underrepresented in sport, such as gay, lesbian, bisexual, and transsexual athletes, who remain largely ostracized. Title IX, 36 years after its passage, continues to be implemented unevenly at various institutions. Compliance with Title IX remains a challenge; some athletic programs, because of their emphasis on major collegiate sports for men, resist the growth of gender equity in sports. A consequence of Title IX in coming years might be to improve the condition of collegiate athletics: "Because the financial resources of modern educational institutions are increasingly stretched, some believe Title IX has the potential to reform and reshape collegiate athletics by causing a halt to the 'arms race' that has caused athletic budgets to escalate in a unending quest for national prominence" (Ware 26). The impact of Title IX on the non–revenue-producing sports, or "minor sports," in collegiate athletics still garners the scrutiny of athletic and college administrators trying to determine what seems fair for male and female student athletes on campus. Gains in women's sports from Title IX, often linked to the success of women athletes in the Olympics at the end of the twentieth century, will be scrutinized as some women's sports are cut from Olympic competition; in the coming years, men and women in collegiate sport programs will need to explore how this will affect women's sport in the United States. Supporters who want to preserve Title IX within the male-dominated culture of collegiate sport find that the battle continues in governmental and educational institutions.

Despite a bulk of evidence to the contrary, sport retains associations with social mobility for the American underclass. Interscholastic athletes adhere to faith in an American meritocracy, a strong work ethic, and character development, though heroic role models have become rare. The lessons of sport sometimes contradict the professed values of American society, as schools teach individuality, inquiry, and freedom of expression as a basic right, yet athletes are expected to follow the dictates of coaches and officials unquestioningly.

Sport has served political groups in a variety of ways. In different historical eras many people have viewed sport as a vehicle for propaganda, for promotion of nationalism, and for socialization and Americanization; it has also been used as a means of retaliation and protest and as a cultural expression of varied political agendas. The Olympics have become as much a political event as they are a global athletic spectacle.

Economic ties to sport are equally extensive, and this relationship is likely to continue. The competitive impulses and values of organized sport reinforce a capitalist economy that dominates world trade. On the national level, public subsidization of teams and stadiums even affects nonfans. The considerable costs and expenditures of training national teams and elite athletes might be more wisely spent on sport-for-all programs that address national health concerns of importance to the general public. The business of professional sport has far-reaching global dimensions and employs an international labor force. Bodies are for sale, as African runners sell their abilities to richer Olympic teams, and Latin Americans and Asians leave their homelands for employment on American baseball teams. In a reversal of the international labor flow, American basketball players stock European teams.

While sports may bring nations together in common pursuits for peaceful purposes, they are also used to promote national or commercial interests. Multinational business firms have transcended the controls of individual governments, promoting their particular ideologies, images, and symbols around the world. Such companies promote the capitalist model of competition, individualism, commodification, and consumption to a global audience. Reacting to such globalization, local cultures try to retain their separate identities through resistance and persistence in their traditional pastimes.

In some cases, non-Western nations have risen to prominence in sport, as with Kenya's long-distance runners or the spread of Asian martial arts to the global arena. Other groups have organized festivals, such as the Gay Games and the Paralympic Games, to meet their own needs, allowing participants of these groups to show their athletic capabilities. But the ongoing spread of a monolithic sport system endangers local, regional, and national communities. Cultural imperialism—in the form of the English language, global trade, political and economic power relationships (e.g., World Bank policies, multinational corporations' employment practices), and uniform capitalistic sporting practices—has dire consequences at local levels, disrupting economies and causing unemployment as companies cut costs and seek greater profits. With enforced idleness, recreation and leisure practices assume even greater importance.

The recreational patterns and choices of the U.S population differ by age and interest. Youth sport programs permeate the country, serving as surrogate parenting for some. Despite such proliferation, the emphasis on elite or professional sport tends to relegate most Americans to the role of spectators. As heart disease and obesity climb toward epidemic proportions, health and fitness programs take on greater importance, and older adults search for lifelong activities. Americans spent nearly $24 billion on sports equipment in 2005, most of it on golf, hunting, fishing, and camping gear ("The Health Fact: Spending on Sports" 6A). At the same time, the aerobic activities of the health-conscious have been incorporated within the dominant capitalist business structure in the form of fitness studios, health clubs, and personal trainers. Even jogging for health reasons has been eclipsed by the media emphasis on long-distance spectacles such as marathons, triathlons, and iron-man contests.

Technology has greatly improved sports equipment, facilities, and skill development, but it has also generated new sedentary pastimes in the form of video games. Sedentary "athletes" no longer need to leave the couch in order to compete; instead, they can take part in fantasy games and simulated experiences. Should this trend continue, the history of American sport may take a dramatic turn away from the social interactions that have characterized it in past centuries, perhaps in the process greatly changing the nature of American culture. The desire to play sport, evident in the lives of Americans in the past and present, might shape new forms of sport and meaningful experiences for future Americans.

Bibliography

Entries marked with an asterisk are primary sources.

Acosta, R. Vivian, and Linda Jean Carpenter. "Women in Intercollegiate Sport." *Women in Sport and Physical Activity Journal* 13.1 (Spring 2004): 62–89.

Acosta, R. Vivian, and Linda Jean Carpenter. "Women in Intercollegiate Sport: A Longitudinal, National Study." <http://webpages.charter.net/womeninsport/2008%20Summary%20Final.pdf >.

Adams, David Wallace. *Education for Extinction: American Indians and the Boarding School Experience, 1875–1928.* Lawrence: University Press of Kansas, 1995.

*Adams, John. Letter from John Adams to Abigail Adams, Philadelphia, July 3, 1776. *Constructing the American Past: A Source Book of a People's History.* Vol. 1. 3rd ed. Eds. Elliot J. Gorn, Randy Roberts, and Terry D. Bilhartz. New York: Addison-Wesley Longman, 1999. 115.

Adelman, Melvin L. "The First Modern Sport in America: Harness Racing in New York City, 1825–1870." *Journal of Sport History* 8.1 (Spring 1981): 5–32.

Adelman, Melvin L. *A Sporting Time: New York City and the Rise of Modern Athletics.* Champaign: University of Illinois Press, 1986.

"Al Reach." Baseball Library.com. <http://www.baseballlibrary.com/ballplayers/player.php?name=Al_Reach_1840>.

Altherr, Thomas L., ed. *Sports in North America: A Documentary History, Volume I, Part I: Sports in the Colonial Era, 1618–1783.* Gulf Stream, FL: Academic International Press, 1997.

Altherr, Thomas L., ed. *Sports in North America: A Documentary History, Volume I, Part II: Sports in the New Republic, 1784–1820.* Gulf Stream, FL: Academic International Press, 1997.

"Amateur Sports Capital of the World." Greater Indianapolis Chamber of Commerce Web site. <http://www.indychamber.com/sportsRec.asp>.

"A. Molyneaux Hewlett, director of the Harvard College gymnasium, ca. 1860." Photographer unknown. A Directory to Photographs at Harvard, Weissman Preservation Center, Harvard University Library. <http://preserve.harvard.edu/photographs/directory_entries.html?a=410&>.

Andrews, David L., ed. *Michael Jordan, Inc.: Corporate Sport, Media Culture, and Late Modern America.* Albany: State University of New York Press, 2001.

Arnesen, Eric. "Whiteness and the Historian's Imagination." *International Labor and Working Class History* 60 (Fall 2001): 3–32.

Ashby, LeRoy. *With Amusement for All: A History of Popular Culture Since 1830.* Lexington: University Press of Kentucky, 2006.

Avrich, Paul. *Sacco and Vanzetti: The Anarchist Background.* Princeton, NJ: Princeton University Press, 1991.

Baker, William J. *Sports in the Western World.* Rev. ed. Urbana and Chicago: University of Illinois Press, 1988.

Barcett, Bruce. "American Flyers." *Outside* (February 2006): 58–69.

Barney, Robert Knight. "Knights of Cause and Exercise: German Forty-Eighters and Turnvereine in the United States During the Antebellum Period." *Canadian Journal of History and Sport* 13 (1982): 62–79.

*"Base Ball." *Wilke's Spirit of the Times* 25 August 1860: 389.

*"Base-Ball Match for the Championship." *Frank Leslie's Illustrated Newspaper* 26 August 1865: 356.

Beal, Becky, and Lisa Weidman. "Authenticity in the Skateboarding World." *To the Extreme: Alternative Sports, Inisde and Out.* Eds. Robert E. Rinehart and Synthia Sydnor. Albany: State University of New York Press, 2003. 337-352.

Beale, Morris A. *A History of Football at Harvard, 1874–1948.* Washington, DC: Columbia, 1948.

Beech, Hannah. "Asian Heroes: Yao Ming." *Time* 24 April 2003. <www.time.com/time/asia/magazine/article/0,13673,501030428-446202,00.html>.

*Beecher, Catharine E. *Calisthenic Exercises for Schools, Families, and Health Establishments.* New York: Harper & Brothers, 1856.

*Beecher, Catharine E. "Health of Teachers and Pupils." *[Barnard's] American Journal of Education* 2 (1856): 399–408.

*Beecher, Catharine E. *Letters to the People on Health and Happiness.* New York: Harper & Brothers, 1855. Rpt. New York: Arno Press, 1972.

*Beecher, Catharine E. *Physiology and Calisthenics for Schools and Families.* New York: Harper & Brothers, 1856.

Ben-Porat, Guy, and Amir Ben-Porat. "Unbounded Soccer: Globalization and Localization of the Games in Israel." *International Review of Sport Sociology* 39.4 (Dec. 2004): 421–436.

Beran, Janice A. "Americans in the Philippines: Imperialism or Progress Through Sports?" *International Journal of the History of Sport* 6 (May 1989): 62–87.

Bergen, Kathy. "Bears Winning Off the Field." *Chicago Tribune* 4 February 2007: 1,4.

Bergmann, Gretel. *"Ich war die große jüdische Hoffnung."* [I was the great Jewish hope.] Karlsruhe: Haus der Geschichte Baden-Württemberg, 2003.

Berlage, Gai Ingham. "Lieberman-Kline, Nancy." *Scribner Encyclopedia of American Lives.* Ed. Arnold Markoe. Vol. 2. New York: Charles Scribner's Sons, 2002: 41–43.

Berryman, Jack W. "The Tenuous Attempt of Americans to 'Catch-Up With John Bull': Specialty Magazines and Sporting Journalism, 1800–1835." *Canadian Journal of History of Sport and Physical Education* 10 (1979): 43–61.

Berryman, Jack W., and Joann Brislin. "The Ladies' Department of the *American Farmer,* 1825-1830: A Locus for the Advocacy of Family Health and Exercise." *Her Story in Sport: A Historical Anthology of Women in Sports.* Ed. Reet Howell. West Point, NY: Leisure Press, 1982. 57–69.

Betts, John Rickards. "Public Recreation, Public Parks, and Public Health Before the Civil War." *History of Physical Education and Sport.* Ed. Bruce L. Bennett. Chicago: Athletic Institute, 1972. 33–52.

*Bissell, Mary Taylor. "Athletics for City Girls." *Popular Science Monthly* December, 1894: 145–153.

Block, David. *Baseball Before We Knew It: A Search for the Roots of the Game.* Lincoln: University of Nebraska Press, 2005.

Blum, John M., Edmund S. Morgan, Willie Lee Rose, Arthur M. Schlesinger, Jr., Kenneth M. Stampp, and C. Vann Woodward. *The National Experience: A History of the United States.* New York: Harcourt Brace Jovanovich, 1981.

Borish, Linda J. "'Athletic Activities of Various Kinds': Physical Health and Sport Programs for Jewish American Women." *Journal of Sport History* 26 (Summer 1999): 240–270.

Borish, Linda J. "Benevolent America: Rural Women, Physical Recreation, Sport, and Health Reform in Antebellum New England." *The International Journal of the History of Sport* 22 (November 2005): 946–973.

Borish, Linda J. "'The Cradle of American Champions, Women Champions…Swim Champions': Charlotte Epstein, Gender and Jewish Identity, and the Physical Emancipation of Women in Aquatic Sports." *The International Journal of the History of Sport* 21 (March 2004): 197–235.

Borish, Linda J. "'A Fair, Without *the* Fair, Is No Fair at All' Brulia, Tim. "A Chronology of Pro Football on Television." *Coffin Corner* 26.4 (2004): 18–20.

Building Character for 75 Years: Published on the Occasion of the 75th Anniversary of the Young Men's & Young Women's Hebrew Association. New York: 1969.

Burgos, Adrian Jr. *Playing America's Game(s): Baseball, Race, and Latinos.* Berkeley: University of California Press, 2007.

Bushman, Richard L. *The Refinement of America: Persons, Houses, Cities.* New York: Vintage Books, 1993.

Butler, Mary. *The Battle Creek Idea: Dr. John Harvey Kellogg and the Battle Creek Sanitarium.* Battle Creek, MI: Heritage, 1994.

Butterfield, Kenyon L. "Farmers' Social Organizations." *Cyclopedia of American Agriculture, Volume 4: Farm and Community.* Ed. Liberty Bailey. New York: MacMillan, 1909. 289–297.

Cahn, Susan. "Cinderellas of Sport: Black Women in Track and Field." *Sport and the Color Line.* Eds. Patrick B. Miller and David K. Wiggins. New York: Routledge, 2004. 211–232.

Cahn, Susan. *Coming on Strong: Gender and Sexuality in Twentieth Century Women's Sport.* New York: Free Press, 1994.

Carney, Steve. "Youth Sports Participation." *UpdatePlus* (September/October 2006): 21.

Carpenter, Linda Jean, and R. Vivian Acosta. *Title IX.* Champaign, IL: Human Kinetics, 2005.

Carroll, John M. *Red Grange and the Rise of Modern Football.* Urbana and Chicago: University of Illinois Press, 2004.

Carson, Jane. *Colonial Virginians at Play.* Williamsburg, VA: Colonial Williamsburg, 1965. Rpt. Charlottesville: University of Virginia Press, 1989.

Carson, Mina. *Settlement Folk: Social Thought and the American Settlement Movement, 1885–1930.* Chicago: University of Chicago Press, 1990.

*Catlin, George. "George Catlin Describes a Choctaw Lacrosse Match, c. 1830s." *Major Problems in American Sport History: Documents and Essays.* Ed. Steven A. Riess. Boston: Houghton Mifflin, 1997. 27–31.

*"Cattle Shows." *New England Farmer* (New Series) 9 (January 1857): 14–15.

Cavalli, Gary. "Cold War: Warm Welcome." *Stanford Magazine* (May/June 2005): 7. <http://www.stanfordalumni.org/news/magazine/2005/mayjun/features/track.html>.

Cavallo, Dominick. *Muscles and Morals: Organized Playgrounds and Urban Reform, 1880–1920.* Philadelphia: University of Pennsylvania Press, 1981.

Cayleff, Susan E. *Wash and Be Healed: The Water-Cure Movement and Women's Health.* Philadelphia: Temple University Press, 1987.

*Chicago Hebrew Institute Observer December 1913.

Chicago Sun-Times 1 August 2004: 84A.

*Chicago Tribune 16 March 1887: 9.

Chisholm, Ann. "Incarnations and Practices of Feminine Rectitude: Nineteenth-Century Gymnastics for U.S. Women." *Journal of Social History* 38.3 (Spring 2005): 737–763.

Clement, Priscilla Ferguson, and Jacqueline S. Reiner, eds. *Boyhood in America.* Santa Barbara, CA: ABC-CLIO, 2001.

**Clift, William. "The Tim Bunker Papers, or Yankee Farming." 1868. Rpt. Freeport, NY: Books for Libraries Press, 1970.

Coakley, Jay. *Sports in Society: Issues and Controversies.* New York: McGraw-Hill, 2001.

Cobb, James C. *Away Down South: A History of Southern Identity.* New York: Oxford University Press, 2005.

**Cobb, Sylvanus, Jr. "An Unexpected Race." *Provincial Freeman* 26 May 1855.

Coben, Stanley. *Rebellion Against Victorianism: The Impetus for Cultural Change in 1920s America.* New York: Oxford University Press, 1990.

Collier, Brian S. "Running." *Native Americans in Sport.* Ed. C. Richard King. Armonk, N.Y: Sharpe, 2004. 262–266.

Costa, D. Margaret, and Sharon R. Guthrie, eds. *Women and Sport: Interdisciplinary Perspectives.* Champaign, IL: Human Kinetics, 1994.

Country Joe and the Fish. "I Feel Like I'm Fixin' to Die Rag." 1968.

**"Country Sport." *Hampden Federalist* 23 January 1817: 3.

Creamer, Robert W. *Babe: The Legend Comes to Life.* New York: Simon & Schuster, 1974.

Crepeau, Richard. "There Seems to Be No End in Sight." *Journal of Sport History* 27.3 (Fall 2000): 525–527.

**"A Croquet Problem." *Harper's Weekly* 14 September 1867: 583.

**Crowther, Samuel, Jr., and Arthur Ruhl. *Rowing and Track Athletics.* New York: Macmillan, 1905.

**"Cruelty to Animals." *New England Weekly Journal* 25 September 1732: 1.

**"Cruelty to Animals—'Which Are the Brutes?'" Illustration. *Harper's Weekly* 23 February 1867: 121.

Crunden, Robert M. *Ministers of Reform: The Progressive Achievement in American Civilization, 1889–1920.* New York: Basic Books, 1982.

Daniels, Bruce C. *Puritans at Play: Leisure and Recreation in Colonial America.* New York: St. Martin's Griffin, 1995.

Daniels, Roger. *Coming to America: A History of Immigration and Ethnicity in American Life.* New York: Harper & Row Perennial Library, 1991.

Daniels, Stephanie, and Anita Tedder. *'A Proper Spectacle': Women Olympians 1900–1936.* Bedfordshire, Australia: Walla Walla Press in conjunction with ZeNaNa Press and the Centre for Olympic Studies, 2000.

**Danzig, Allison. "National Tennis Title Won by Miss Wills." *New York Times* 28 August 1928: 18.

Davies, Richard O. *Sport in American Life: A History.* Malden, MA: Blackwell, 2007.

Dawley, Alan. *Struggles for Justice: Social Responsibility and the Liberal State.* Cambridge, MA: Belknap Press, 1991.

Dawson, Kevin. "Enslaved Swimmers and Divers in the Atlantic World." *Journal of American History* 92.4 (March 2006): 1327–1355.

Dean, Josh. "Cool Millions." *Outside* (February 2006): 51–55.

Demaree, Albert Lowther. *The American Agricultural Press, 1819–1860.* 1941. Rpt. Philadelphia: Porcupine Press, 1974.

Dewey, Edward H. "Football and the American Indians," *New England Quarterly* 3.4 (Oct. 1930): 736–740.

Diner, Hasia R. *A Time for Gathering: The Second Migration, 1820-1880,* Vol. II. *The Jewish people in America* series. Baltimore, MD: Johns Hopkins University Press, 1992.

Doyle, Andrew. "Bear Bryant: Symbol for an Embattled South." *Colby Quarterly* 32.1 (March 1996): 72–86.

Dublin, Thomas, ed. *Farm to Factory: Women's Letters, 1830-1860.* 2nd ed. New York: Columbia University Press, 1993.

Du Bois, W.E.B. *The Souls of Black Folk.* New York: Penguin Books, 1989.

Duis, Perry R. *The Saloon: Public Drinking in Chicago and Boston, 1880–1920.* Champaign: University of Illinois Press, 1983.

Dulles, Foster Rhea. *A History of Recreation: America Learns to Play.* New York: Appleton-Century-Crofts, 1965.

**Du Ru, Father Paul. "Journal of Paul du Ru [February 1 to May 8, 1700] Missionary Priest to Louisiana," in Ruth Lapham Butler, trans. 1700. *Sports in North America: A Documentary History, Volume I, Part I: Sports in the Colonial Era, 1618–1783.* Ed. Thomas L. Altherr. Gulf Stream, FL: Academic International Press, 1997. 455.

*Dyer, Braven. "Babe Didrikson Cracks World Javelin Record." *Los Angeles Times* 1 August 1932: 9.

Dyer, Leigh. "Hamm, Mariel Margaret ("Mia"). *Scribner's Encyclopedia of American Lives*. Ed. Arnold Markoe. New York: Scribner's, 2002. 384–385.

Dyreson, Jodella K. "Sporting Activities in the American-Mexican Colonies of Texas, 1821–1835." *Journal of Sport History* 24.3 (Fall 1997): 269–284.

Dyreson, Mark. *Making the American Team: Sport, Culture, and the Olympic Experience*. Urbana and Chicago: University of Illinois Press, 1998.

Dyreson, Mark. "Media Nationalism and the 'War' Over Olympic Pictures in Sport's 'Golden Age.'" *The International Journal of the History of Sport* 22 (November 2005): 938–989.

Dyson, Michael Eric. "Be Like Mike? Michael Jordan and the Pedagogy of Desire." *Michael Jordan, Inc.* Ed. David L. Andrews. Albany: State University of New York Press, 2001. 259–268.

Dyson, Rick. "Hoop and Pole." *Native Americans in Sport*. Ed. C. Richard King. Armonk, NY: Sharpe, 2004. 148–149.

Eisen, George. "Early European Attitudes Toward Native American Sports and Pastimes." *Ethnicity and Sport in North American History and Culture*. Eds. George Eisen and David K. Wiggins. Westport, CT: Praeger, 1994. 1–18.

Eisen, George, ed. "One Hundred Years of 'Muscular Judaism': Sport in Jewish History and Culture. Special Issue." *Journal of Sport History* 26.2 (Summer 1999).

Eisen, George, and David K. Wiggins, eds. *Ethnicity and Sport in North American History and Culture*. Westport, CT: Praeger, 1994.

Eitzen, D. Stanley, and George H. Sage. *Sociology of North American Sport*. New York: McGraw-Hill, 2003.

*"Eleven Killed in Many Race Riots." *Chicago Daily Tribune* 5 July 1910.

Elias, Norbert. *The Civilizing Process: The History of Manners*. Trans. from German by Edmund Jephcott. Vol. 1. New York: Urizen Books, 1978.

Elias, Norbert. *The Civilizing Process: Power and Civility*. Trans. from German by Edmund Jephcott. Vol. 2. New York: Pantheon Books, 1982.

Elias, Norbert. "The Genesis of Sport as a Sociological Problem." *The Sociology of Sport: A Selection of Readings*. Ed. Eric Dunning. London: Cass, 1971. 88–115.

Elias, Norbert, and Eric Dunning: *Quest for Excitement: Sport and Leisure in the Civilizing Process*. Oxford: Blackwell, 1986.

Elias, Robert, ed. *Baseball and the American Dream*. Armonk, NY: Sharpe, 2001.

*Ely, Richard T., ed. *Hull House Maps and Papers*. Boston: Crowell, 1895. Rpt. New York: Arno Press, 1970.

*E. M. C. "Farmers' Wives." *American Agriculturist* 4 (September 1845): 287–288.

*Epstein, Charlotte. "Swimming." *Amateur Athlete* (July 1934): 7, 9.

Ernst, Robert. *Weakness Is a Crime: The Life of Bernarr Macfadden*. Syracuse: Syracuse University Press, 1991.

Eskanazi, Gerald. "U.S. Defeats Soviet Squad in Olympic Hockey by 4-3." *New York Times* 23 February 1980: 1.

Evensen, Bruce J. *When Dempsey Fought Tunney: Heroes, Hokum, and Storytelling in the Jazz Age*. Knoxville: University of Tennessee Press, 1996.

Fagan, Major Louis Estell. "Samuel Nicholas: First Officer of American Marines." *The Marine Corps Gazette* 18.3 (November 1933): 1–20. <www.ussnicholas.org/first_officer.html>.

*"The Farmer's Daughter." *Massachusetts Ploughman* 27 (February 15, 1868): n. pag.

Fass, Paula S. *Encyclopedia of Children and Childhood in History and Society*. New York: Macmillan, 2004.

Felsenthal, Carol. "Shattered." *Chicago* 49.5 (May 2000): 94–97, 137–145.

*"Female Jockeys." *The Homestead* 1 15 November 1855: 142.

Fielding, Lawrence W. "War and Trifles: Sport in the Shadows of Civil War Army Life." *Journal of Sport History* 4 (1977): 151–168.

Folsom, Franklin. *Impatient Armies of the Poor: The Story of Collective Action of the Unemployed, 1808–1942*. Niwot: University Press of Colorado, 1991.

Foner, Eric, and John A Garraty, eds. *The Reader's Companion to American History*. Boston: Houghton Mifflin, 1991.

Ford, Mark L., and Massimo Foglio. "The First 'NFL Europe.'" *Coffin Corner* 27.6 (2005): 3–7.

*"Fortieth Anniversary of American Independence." *New Hampshire Patriot* 16 July 1816: 2.

*Franklin, Benjamin. *The Autobiography and Other Writings, 1779*. Ed. Kenneth Silverman. New York: Penguin Books, 1986.

Freeman, Michael. *ESPN: The Uncensored History*. Dallas: Taylor, 2000.

Friedman, Michael Jay. "President Bush Praises U.S. Athletes." <http://usinfo.state.gov/scv/Archive/2006/May/17-645638.html>.

Frommer, Harvey. *Shoeless Joe and Ragtime Baseball*. Dallas: Taylor Publishing, 1992.

*Gallico, Paul. *The Golden People*. Garden City, NY: Doubleday, 1965.

Garraty, John A. *The American Nation: A History of the United States.* New York: Harper & Row, 1983.

Gems, Gerald R. *The Athletic Crusade: Sport and American Cultural Imperialism.* Lincoln: University of Nebraska Press, 2006.

Gems, Gerald R. *For Pride, Profit, and Patriarchy: Football and the Incorporation of American Cultural Values.* Lanham, MD: Scarecrow Press, 2000.

Gems, Gerald R. "The Rise of Sport at a Jewish Settlement House: The Chicago Hebrew Institute, 1908-1921." *Sports and the American Jew.* Ed. Steven A. Riess. Syracuse: Syracuse University Press, 1998. 146–159.

Gems, Gerald R. *Sports in North America: A Documentary History, Volume 5: Sports Organized, 1880–1900.* Gulf Breeze, FL: Academic International Press, 1996.

Gems, Gerald R. *Windy City Wars: Labor, Leisure, and Sport in the Making of Chicago.* Lanham, MD: Scarecrow Press, 1997.

Gems, Gerald R., and Linda J. Borish. "Sports, Colonial Era to 1920." *Boyhood in America.* Vol. 2. Eds. Priscilla Ferguson Clement and Jacqueline S. Reinier. Santa Barbara, CA: ABC-CLIO, 2001. 637–643.

Gems, Gerald R., and Linda J. Borish. "Sports, 1921 to Present." *Boyhood in America.* Vol. 2. Eds. Priscilla Ferguson Clement and Jacqueline S. Reinier. Santa Barbara, CA: ABC-CLIO, 2001. 643–647.

Gilfoyle, Timothy. *A Pickpocket's Tale: The Underworld of Nineteenth-Century New York.* New York: Norton, 2006.

Gillmeister, Heiner. *Tennis: A Cultural History.* New York: New York University Press, 1998.

*"'Good, Clean Sport,' Motto of C.H.I." Philip L. Seman Collection, Scrapbook, Vol. I, 1910–1916, The Jacob Rader Marcus Center of the American Jewish Archives, Cincinnati, OH.

Goodman, Cary. *Choosing Sides: Playground and Street Life on the Lower East Side.* New York: Schocken Books, 1979.

Goodyear, Frank H., III. "'Nature's Most Beautiful Models': George Catlin's Choctaw Ball-Playing Paintings and the Politics of Indian Removal." *The International Journal of the History of Sport* 23 (March 2006): 138–153.

Gorn, Elliott J. "'Gouge and Bite, Pull Hair and Scratch': The Social Significance of Gouging in the Southern Backcountry." *Sport in America: From Wicked Amusements to National Obsession.* Ed. David K. Wiggins. Champaign, IL: Human Kinetics, 1995. 35–50.

Gorn, Elliott J. "The Manassa Mauler and the Fighting Marine: An Interpretation of the Dempsey-Tunney Fights." *Journal of American Studies* 19 (1985): 27–47.

Gorn, Elliott. *The Manly Art: Bare-Knuckle Prize Fighting in America.* Ithaca, NY: Cornell University Press, 1986.

Gorn, Elliott J., and Warren Goldstein. *A Brief History of American Sports.* New York: Hill and Wang, 1993.

Gould, Stephen Jay. *The Mismeasure of Man.* New York: Norton, 1996.

Graf, John C. *Chicago's Parks: A Photographic History.* Chicago: Arcadia Publishing, 2000.

"The Great American Sports Atlas." Year-End Double Issue. *Sports Illustrated* 27 December 2004–3 January 2005.

Green, Harvey. *Fit for America: Health, Fitness, Sport, and American Society.* Rochester, NY: Margaret Woodbury Strong Museum, 1986.

Guarneri, Carl. *America in the World: United States History in Global Context.* New York: McGraw-Hill, 2007.

Guterl, Matthew Pratt. *The Color of Race in America, 1900–1940.* Cambridge: Harvard University Press, 2001.

GutsMuths, Johann Christoph Friedrich. *Gymnastik für die Jugend.* Schnepfenthal, 1793.

Guttmann, Allen. *Sports: The First Five Millennia.* Amherst: University of Massachusetts Press, 2004.

Guttmann, Allen. *From Ritual to Record: The Nature of Modern Sports.* New York: Columbia University Press, 1978.

Guttmann, Allen. *Games and Empires.* New York: Columbia University Press, 1994.

Guttmann, Allen. *Sports Spectators.* New York: Columbia University Press, 1986.

Guttmann, Allen. *Women's Sports: A History.* New York: Columbia University Press, 1991.

"Gymnastics 5. 19th-Century European Gymnastics." <www.hickoksports.com/history/gymnastics05.shtml>.

Halberstam, David. *Playing for Keeps: Michael Jordan and the World He Made.* New York: Random House, 1999.

Halsey, Elizabeth. *The Development of Public Recreation in Metropolitan Chicago.* Chicago: Recreation Commission, 1940.

Hardy, Stephen. "Adopted by All the Leading Clubs: Sporting Goods and the Shaping of Leisure." *Sport in America: From Wicked Amusements to National Obsession.* Ed. David K. Wiggins. Champaign, IL: Human Kinetics, 1995. 133–150.

Hardy, Stephen. *How Boston Played: Sport, Recreation, and Community, 1865–1915.* Boston: Northeastern University Press, 1982.

*Hartwell, Edward M. "President's Address—The Condition and Prospects of Physical Education in the United States." *Proceedings of the American Association for the Advancement of Physical Education, at the Seventh Annual Meeting Held in Philadelphia, PA, 1892.* Springfield, MA: Press of Springfield Print and Binding, 1893. 13–40.

*Harvard Advocate 24.5 (November 16, 1877): 49.

*Harvard Graduates Magazine 5.17 (September, 1896): 66–68.

Hauser, Thomas, and Stephen Brunt. The Italian Stallions: Heroes of Boxing's Glory Days. Toronto: Sport Media Publishing, 2003.

"The Health Fact: Spending on Sports." Chicago Sun-Times 13 August 2006: 6A.

Hewitt, Brian. "A Game of Pain." Chicago Sun-Times 19 September 1993: 17B–19B.

Hibner, Charles. The Rose Bowl, 1902–1929. Jefferson, NC: McFarland, 1993.

*Higginson, Thomas W. "A Letter to a Dyspeptic." Atlantic Monthly 3 (April 1859): 465–474.

*Higginson, Thomas W. "The Murder of the Innocents. A Second Epistle to Dolorosus." Atlantic Monthly 4 (September 1859): 345–356.

*Higginson, Thomas W. "Saints, and Their Bodies." Atlantic Monthly 1 (March 1858): 583–590.

"High School Sports Participation Increases." Journal of Physical Education Recreation, and Dance 78.1 (January 2007): 4.

*A History of the Schuylkill Fishing Company of the State in Schuylkill, 1732–1888. Philadelphia: Members of the State in Schuylkill (Schuylkill Fishing Company), 1889.

Hofmann, Annette R. "Lady Turners in the United States: German American Identity, Gender Concerns, and Turnerism." Journal of Sport History 27 (Fall 2000): 389–390.

Hogan, David J. Class and Reform: School and Society in Chicago, 1880–1930. Philadelphia: University of Pennsylvania Press, 1985.

Holland, Barbara. Gentlemen's Blood: A History of Dueling from Swords at Dawn to Pistols at Dusk. New York: Bloomsbury, 2003.

Hong, Fan, and J. A. Mangan, eds. Soccer, Women, Sexual Liberation: Kicking Off a New Era. London: Cass, 2003.

"The Horse: A Silent Hero of Our History." The Ground Beneath Our Feet. A Documentary Film Series and Website About Virginia's History After the Civil War. <www.vahistory.org/horse_film/index.html>.

Horsman, Reginald. Race and Manifest Destiny: The Origins of American Racial Anglo-Saxonism. Cambridge: Harvard University Press, 1981.

"Sports Illustrated Facts." <http://sportsillustrated.cnn.com/thenetwork/tour/sifacts/>.

Hoxie, Frederick E. A Final Promise: The Campaign to Assimilate the Indians, 1880–1920. New York: Cambridge University Press, 1989.

Hughes, Glyn. "Managing Black Guys: Representation, Corporate Culture, and the NBA." Sociology of Sport Journal 21.2 (2004): 163–184.

Hult, Joan, and Marianna Trekell, eds. A Century of Women's Basketball: From Frailty to Final Four.

Reston, VA: American Alliance for Health, Physical Education, Recreation and Dance, 1991.

Hunt, Linda Lawrence. Bold Spirit: Helga Estby's Forgotten Walk Across Victorian America. New York: Anchor Books, 2006.

Ignatiev, Noel. How the Irish Became White. New York: Routledge, 1995.

Isaac, Rhys. The Transformation of Virginia, 1740–1790. Chapel Hill: University of North Carolina Press, 1982.

Isenberg, Michael T. John L. Sullivan and His America. Champaign: University of Illinois Press, 1988.

Jable, J. Thomas. "Pennsylvania's Blue Laws: A Quaker Experiment in the Suppression of Sport and Amusements." Journal of Sport History 1 (1974): 107–121.

Jable, J. Thomas. "Social Class and the Sport of Cricket in Philadelphia, 1850–1880." Journal of Sport History 18.2 (Summer 1991): 205–223.

Jacobson, Matthew Frye. Barbarian Virtues: The United States Encounters Foreign Peoples at Home and Abroad, 1876–1917. New York: Hill and Wang, 2000.

Jacobson, Matthew Frye. Whiteness of a Different Color: European Immigrants and the Alchemy of Race. Cambridge: Harvard University Press, 1998.

Jennings, Peter, and Todd Brewster. The Century. New York: Doubleday, 1998.

Johns, Maxine James, and Jane Farrell-Beck. "'Cut Out the Sleeves': Nineteenth-Century U.S. Women Swimmers and Their Attire." Dress 28 (2001): 53–63.

Johnson, Elmer L. The History of YMCA Physical Education. Chicago: Association Press, 1979.

Johnson, Janis A. "Equestrian Competitions." Native Americans in Sport. Ed. C. Richard King. Armonk, N.Y: Sharpe, 2004. 105–107.

*Johnson, Laurence, J. "Half Century of American Swimming." Amateur Athlete (December 1938): pp. 9, 51, 55.

Jones, Constance. 1001 Things Everyone Should Know About Women's History. New York: Broadway Books, 2003.

*Jordan, Edward S. "Buying Football Victories." Collier's 11 November 1905: 19–20, 23.

*"Joshua Ward. The Champion Sculler of America." Frank Leslie's Illustrated Newspaper 8 August 1863: 315.

Jozsa, Frank P., Jr. Sports Capitalism: The Foreign Business of American Professional Leagues. Burlington, VT: Ashgate, 2004.

Kay, Joanne, and Suzanne Laberge. "The 'New' Corporate Habitus in Adventure Racing." International Review for the Sociology of Sport 37.1 (2002): 17–36.

Keith, Susan. "Double Ball." Native Americans in Sport. Ed. C. Richard King. Armonk, NY: Sharpe, 2004. 101–102.

Kennedy, John H. *A Course of Their Own: A History of African American Golfers.* Lincoln: University of Nebraska Press, 2000.

Kerber, Linda K. *No Constitutional Right to Be Ladies: Women and the Obligations of Citizenship.* New York: Hill and Wang, 1998.

King, Richard C., ed. *Native Americans in Sport.* Armonk, NY: Sharpe, 2004.

Kingsdale, Jon M. "The Poor Man's Club: Social Functions of the Urban Working Class Saloon." *American Quarterly* 25 (October 1973): 472–489.

Kirsch, George B. *Baseball and Cricket: The Creation of American Team Sports, 1832-72.* Urbana and Chicago: University of Illinois Press, 1989.

Kirsch, George B. "Baseball Spectators, 1855–1870." *Major Problems in American Sport History: Documents and Essays.* Ed. Steven A. Riess. Boston: Houghton Mifflin, 1997. 103–110.

*Kirsch, George B., ed. *Sports in North America: A Documentary History, Volume 3: The Rise of Modern Sports, 1840–1860.* Gulf Stream, FL: Academic International Press, 1992.

*Kirsch, George B., ed. *Sports in North America: A Documentary History, Volume 4: Sports in War, Revival and Expansion, 1860–1880.* Gulf Stream, FL: Academic International Press, 1995.

Kirsch, George B. "Young Men's Hebrew Association." *Encyclopedia of Ethnicity and Sports in the United States.* Eds. George B. Kirsch, Othello Harris, and Claire E. Nolte. Westport, CT: Greenwood Press, 2000. 501–502.

Kirsch, George B., Othello Harris, and Claire E. Nolte, eds. *Encyclopedia of Ethnicity and Sports in the United States.* Westport, CT: Greenwood Press, 2000.

Knisely, Michael. "Everybody Has the Dream—Baseball Scouting and Players' Hopes of Success in Dominican Republic." *Sporting News* 19 February 2001. <http://findarticles.com/p/articles/mi_m1208/is_8_225/ai_70926950>.

Kogan, Rick. *Brunswick: The Story of an American Company from 1845 to 1985.* Skokie, IL: Brunswick Corp., 1985.

Koppedrayer, Kay. "Archery." *Native Americans in Sport.* Ed. C. Richard King. Armonk, NY: Sharpe, 2004. 19–23.

Kreitzer, Matthew E. "Diamonds, Ovals, and Rings: Northwestern Shoshone Sports at the Washakie Colony of Northern Utah, 1903–1929." *The International Journal of the History of Sport* 23.2 (March 2006): 232–246.

LaFeber, Walter. *Michael Jordan and the New Global Capitalism.* New York: Norton 1999.

Lapchick, Richard. "Lack of Diversity Among Campus, Conference Leaders at Division IA Schools May Contribute to Lack of Diversity in Head Football Coaching Positions." *The Buck Stops Here: Assessing Diversity among Campus and Conference Leaders for Division IA Schools.* November 17, 2004. Orlando, FL: The Institute for Diversity and Ethics in Sport at the University of Central Florida. <http://64.233.169.104/search?q=cache:BZ3mExo_Co4J:www.ncaasports.org/articles.htm+%22richard+lapchick%22+%22diversity+in+head+football+coaching+positions%22&hl=en&ct=clnk&cd=1&gl=us>.

Larkin, Jack. *The Reshaping of Everyday Life in America, 1790–1840.* New York: Harper & Row, 1988.

Laqueur, Walter. *Young Germany: A History of the German Youth Movement.* New York: Basic Books, 1962.

*"A Law, Relative to the Park, Battery and Bowling Green." *New York Courier* 27 March 1816: 3.

Leab, Daniel J. "Tilden, William Tatem, Jr. ("Bill")." *Scribner Encyclopedia of American Lives.* Ed. Arnold Markoe. Vol. 2. New York: Charles Scribner's Sons, 2002. 429–431.

Le Batard, Dan. "Next Detour." *ESPN The Magazine* 24 December 2001: 105–111.

Ledbetter, Bonnie S. "Sports and Games of the American Revolution." *Journal of Sport History* 6 (1979): 29–40.

Lester, Larry. "Black Baseball's National Showcase: The East–West Classic," paper presented at the 8th Annual Jerry Malloy Negro League Conference, Chicago, IL, 2005.

Lester, Robin. *Stagg's University: The Rise, Decline, and Fall of Big-Time Football at Chicago.* Champaign: University of Illinois Press, 1995.

Levine, Peter. *A. G. Spalding and the Rise of Baseball: The Promise of American Sport.* New York: Oxford University Press, 1985.

*Levine, Peter. *American Sport: A Documentary History.* Englewood Cliffs, NJ: Prentice Hall, 1989.

Levine, Peter. *Ellis Island to Ebbets Field: Sport and the American Jewish Experience.* New York: Oxford University Press, 1992.

*Lewis, Dioclesian. *New Gymnastics for Men, Women, and Children.* Boston: Ticknor and Fields, 1862.

Lewis, R.M. "American Croquet in the 1860s: Playing the Game and Winning." *Journal of Sport History* 18.3 (Winter 1991): 365–386.

Liberti, Rita. "'We Were Ladies, We Just Played Like Boys': African-American Womanhood and Competitive Basketball at Bennett College, 1928–1942." *Sport and the Color Line: Black Athletes and Race Relations in Twentieth-Century America.* Eds. Patrick B. Miller and David K. Wiggins. New York: Routledge, 2004. 83–99.

Lieser, Ethen. "Time for APAs to Embrace Yao Ming." *AsianWeek* (July 19–July 25, 2002). <http://asianweek.com/2002_07_19/sports_yao.html>.

Littlewood, Thomas B. *Arch: A Promoter, Not a Poet.* Ames: Iowa State University Press, 1990.

Lucas, John A. "A Prelude to the Rise of Sport: Ante-Bellum America, 1850–1860." *Quest* 11 (December 1968): 50–57.

Lucas, John A., and Ronald A. Smith. *Saga of American Sport.* Philadelphia: Lee & Febiger, 1978.

*Lyde, Byfield. *Boston Weekly Newsletter* 5 August 1736: 2.

MacCambridge, Michael, ed. *ESPN: Sports Century.* New York: Hyperion, 1999.

MacGregor, Alan Leander. "Tammany: The Indian as Rhetorical Surrogate." *American Quarterly* 35.4 (Autumn 1983): 391–407.

Maguire, Joseph. "Body Cultures: Diversity, Sustainability, Globalisation." *Games of the Past—Sports for the Future?* Ed. Gertrud Pfister. Sankt Augustin, Germany: Academia Verlag, 2004.

Maguire, Joseph. *Global Sport: Identities, Societies, Civilizations.* Cambridge: Polity Press, 1999.

Majumdar, Boria, and Sean Brown. "Why Baseball, Why Cricket? Differing Nationalisms, Differing Challenges." *The International Journal of the History of Sport* 24.2 (February 2007): 139–156.

Mangan, J.A. *Athleticism in the Victorian and Edwardian Public School: The Emergence and Consolidation of an Educational Ideology.* New York: Cambridge University Press, 1981.

Mangan, James A., and Roberta J. Parks, eds. *From "Fair Sex" to Feminism: Sport and the Socialization of Women in the Industrial and Post-Industrial Eras.* London: Cass, 1987.

Mangan, James A., and Andrew Ritchie, eds. *Ethnicity, Sport, Identity: Struggles for Status.* London: Cass, 2004.

Markoe, Arnold, ed. *The Scribner Encyclopedia of American Lives: Sports Figures.* New York: Scribner's, 2002.

Marks, Patricia. *Bicycles, Bangs, and Bloomers: The New Woman in the Popular Press.* Lexington: University Press of Kentucky, 1990.

McAleer, Kevin. *Dueling: The Cult of Honor in Fin-de-Siècle Germany.* Princeton, NJ: Princeton University Press, 1994.

*McClymer, John, ed. *This High and Holy Moment: The First National Woman's Rights Convention,* *Worcester, 1850.* San Diego: Harcourt College Publishers, 1999.

McMurry, Sally. "Who Read the Agricultural Journals? Evidence from Chenango County, New York, 1839–1865." *Agricultural History* 63.4 (Fall 1989): 1–18.

Meneses, Diana. "Shuttlecock." *Native Americans in Sport.* Ed. C. Richard King. Armonk, NY: Sharpe, 2004. 280–281.

Meneses, Diana. "Kick Stick." *Native Americans in Sport.* Ed. C. Richard King. Armonk, NY: Sharpe, 2004. 168.

*Menna, Larry K., ed. *Sports in North America: A Documentary History, Volume 2: Origins of Modern Sports, 1820–1840.* Gulf Stream, FL: Academic International Press, 1995.

Mercury Sport. 28 July 2006: 24.

Meyerowitz, Joanne J. *Women Adrift: Independent Wage Earners in Chicago, 1880–1930.* Chicago: University of Chicago Press, 1988.

"Mia Hamm." Answers.com. <http://www.answers.com/topic/mia-hamm>.

"Mia Hamm." Spiritus-Temporis.com. <http://www.spiritus-temporis.com/mia-hamm/>.

*Miller, Elizabeth Smith. "The Bloomer." *This High and Holy Moment: The First National Woman's Rights Convention, Worcester, 1850.* Ed. John F. McClymer. San Diego: Harcourt Brace College Publishers, 1999. 46–47.

Miller, Patrick B., and David K. Wiggins, eds. *Sport and the Color Line: Black Athletes and Race Relations in Twentieth-Century America.* New York: Routledge, 2004.

Miller, Toby, Geoffrey Lawrence, Jim McKay, and David Rowe. *Globalization and Sport: Playing the World.* London: Sage, 2001.

Mitchell, Sheila. "Women's Participation in the Olympic Games 1900–1926." *Journal of Sport History* 4 (1977): 208–228.

Mrozek, Donald J. *Sport and American Mentality, 1880–1910.* Knoxville: University of Tennessee Press, 1983.

*Naismith, James. *Basketball: Its Origin and Development.* Lincoln: University of Nebraska Press, 1996.

Narragansett Boat Club. "History of NBC." <http://www.rownbc.org/history.php>.

Nash, Gary B., Julie Roy Jeffrey, John R. Howe, Peter J. Frederick, Allen F. Davis, and Allan M. Winkler. *The American People: Creating a Nation and a Society.* Brief 3rd ed., Single Volume Edition. New York: Addison-Wesley Longman, 2000.

Nash, Gary B., Julie Roy Jeffrey, John R. Howe, Peter J. Frederick, Allen F. Davis, and Allan M. Winkler. *The American People: Creating a Nation and a Society.* Vol. 1: To 1877. Brief 5th ed. New York: Longman, 2006

*Nast, Thomas. "Central Park in Winter." Illustration of winter scenes. *Harper's Weekly* 30 January 1864: 72.

Nathan, Daniel A. "Sometimes, ESPN Seems Ubiquitous." *Journal of Sport History* 27.3 (Fall 2000): 528–531.

National Museum of American History, Smithsonian Institution, *Communities in a Changing Nation: The Promise of 19th-Century America.* Exhibition opened in Washington, D.C., 1999.

Neely, Wayne Caldwell. *The Agricultural Fair.* 1935. Rpt. New York: AMS Press, 1967.

Nelson, David M. *Anatomy of a Game: Football, the Rules, and the Men Who Made the Game.* Newark, DE: University of Delaware Press, 1994.

"New World Order." *Sports Illustrated* 5 May 2003. <http://sportsillustrated.cnn.com/si_online/2003/new_world_order/1_20/>.

*"The New York Times Reports on an International Match: The Harvard-Oxford Boat Race, 1869." *Major Problems in American Sport History, Documents and Essays.* Ed. Steven A. Riess. Boston: Houghton Mifflin, 1997. 113–114.

Noverr, Douglas A., and Lawrence E. Ziewacz. *The Games They Played.* Chicago: Nelson-Hall, 1983.

O'Fearghail, Caoimhin. "Ball Race." *Native Americans in Sport.* Ed. C. Richard King. Armonk, NY: Sharpe, 2004. 29–30.

*"O'Leary's Tournament." *Chicago Tribune* 1 Sept 1880: 3.

Oxendine, Joseph B. *American Indian Sports Heritage.* Lincoln: University of Nebraska Press, 1988.

Park, Roberta J. "'Embodied Selves': The Rise and Development of Concern for Physical Education, Active Games and Recreation for American Women, 1776–1865." *Sport in America: From Wicked Amusements to National Obsession.* Ed. David K. Wiggins. Champaign, IL: Human Kinetics, 1995. 69–93.

Park, Roberta J. "Physiologists, Physicians, and Physical Educators: Nineteenth-Century Biology and Exercise, Hygienic and Educative." *Journal of Sport History* 14 (1987): 28–61.

Park, Roberta J. "Physiology and Anatomy Are Destiny! Brains, Bodies, and Exercise in Nineteenth-Century American Thought." *Journal of Sport History* 18.1 (Spring 1991): 31–63.

Park, Roberta J. "Sports and Recreation Among Chinese American Communities of the Pacific Coast From Time of Arrival to the 'Quiet Decade'

of the 1950s." *Journal of Sport History* 27.3 (Fall 2000): 445–480.

Pearson, Daniel M. *Baseball in 1889: Players vs. Owners.* Bowling Green, OH: Bowling Green University Press, 1993.

Pfister, Gertrud. "Cold War Diplomats in Tracksuits: The Fräuleinwunder of East German Sport." *European Sports History Review* 5 (2003): 223–252

Pfister, Gertrud. "Cultural Confrontations: German Turnen, Swedish Gymnastics and English Sport—European Diversity in Physical Activities From a Historical Perspective." *Culture, Sport, Society* 6 (2003): 61–91.

Pfister, Gertrud. "Female Leaders in Sports Organizations—Worldwide Trends." *Hat Fuhrung ein Geschlecht? Genderarrangements in Entscheidungsgremien des Deutschen Sports.* Eds. Gudrun Doll-Tepper and Gertrud Pfister. Cologne: Strauss, 2004. 49–63.

Pfister, Gertrud, and Annette R. Hofmann. "Turnen—a Forgotten Movement Culture: Its Beginnings in Germany and Diffusion in the United States." *Turnen and Sport: Transatlantic Transfers.* Ed. Annette R. Hofmann (Hrsg.). Münster: Waxmann, 2004. 11–24.

*"Philadelphia, 13 May." *Federal Gazette* 13 May 1789.

*"Physical Recreation." *New England Farmer* 4 (October 1852): 483–484.

Pierce, Bessie Louise. *A History of Chicago.* Vol. 2. New York: Knopf, 1940.

Pierce, Bessie L. *A History of Chicago: The Rise of a Modern City, 1871–1893.* Vol. 3. New York: Knopf, 1957.

A Plea for Playgrounds. Special Report by the Chicago Parks Commission, 1905.

Plymire, Darcy C. "Positive Addiction: Running and Human Potential in the 1970s." *Journal of Sport History* 31.3 (Fall 2004): 297–315.

Podell, Ira. "New-look NHL Set to Drop Puck on Return Season." *Chicago Sun-Times* 2 October 2005: 93A.

Pope, Steven W., ed. *The New American Sport History: Recent Approaches and Perspectives.* Urbana and Chicago: University of Illinois Press, 1997.

Pope, Steven W. *Patriotic Games: Sporting Traditions in the American Imagination, 1876–1926.* New York: Oxford University Press, 1997.

Powers, Madelon. *Faces Along the Bar: Lore and Order in the Workingman's Saloon, 1879–1920.* Chicago: University of Chicago Press, 1998.

Powers-Beck, Jeffrey. *The American Indian Integration of Baseball.* Lincoln: University of Nebraska Press, 2004.

Priest, Laurie. "The Whole IX Yards: The Impact of Title IX: The Good, the Bad, and the Ugly."

Women in Sport and Physical Activity Journal 12.2 (Fall 2003): 27–43.

Proctor, John Clagget. "Potomac Boat Club Won National Fame." *Sunday Star* 6 April 1930: 8–9.

Pruter, Robert. "Chicago High School Football Struggles, the Fight for Faculty Control, and the War Against Secret Societies, 1898–1908." *Journal of Sport History* 30.1 (Spring 2003): 47–72.

Pruter, Robert. "Chicago Lights Up Football World." *College Football Historical Society* 18.2 (Feb. 2005): 7–9.

"Queen of the Green." MSNBC Sports. <http://www.msnbc.msn.com/id/5454494/>.

Rader, Benjamin G. *American Sports: From the Age of Folk Games to the Age of Spectators.* Englewood Cliffs, NJ: Prentice Hall, 1983.

Rader, Benjamin G. *American Sports: From the Age of Folk Games to the Age of Televised Sports.* Englewood Cliffs, NJ: Prentice Hall, 2004.

Rader, Benjamin G. *American Ways: A History of American Cultures, 1500–1865.* Vol. 1. 2nd ed. Belmont, CA: Thompson Wadsworth, 2006.

Rader, Benjamin G. "The Quest for Subcommunities and the Rise of American Sport." *American Quarterly* 29 (1977): 355–369.

Raffety, Matthew Taylor. "Elgin Baylor." *Scribner Encyclopedia of American Lives.* Ed. Arnold Markoe. Vol. 1. New York: Charles Scribner's Sons, 2002. 61–63.

*Ray, Bob. "Eleanor Holm Wins Swim Crown." *Los Angeles Times* 12 August 1932: 9.

*Ray, Bob. "Field Day Held by Swim Stars." *Los Angeles Times* 10 August 1932: 11.

"Record May Prove Man's Stature as First Native American Player in Baseball History." *Bangor Daily News* 26 January 2006. <http://hnn.us/roundup/entries/21008.html>.

Redmond, Gerald. *The Caledonian Games in Nineteenth-Century America.* Cranbury, NJ: Associated University Presses, 1971.

Reel, Guy. *The National Police Gazette and the Making of the Modern American Man, 1879–1906.* New York: Palgrave Macmillan, 2006.

*Rice, Grantland. *The Tumult and the Shouting: My Life in Sport.* New York: Barnes, 1954.

Riess, Steven A. *City Games: The Evolution of American Urban Society and the Rise of Sports.* Urbana and Chicago: University of Illinois Press, 1991.

Riess, Steven A., ed. *Major Problems in American Sport History: Documents and Essays.* Boston: Houghton Mifflin, 1997.

Riess, Steven A. *Sport in Industrial America, 1850–1920.* Wheeling, IL: Harlan Davidson, 1995.

Riess, Steven A., ed. *Sports and the American Jew.* Syracuse: Syracuse University Press, 1998.

Riess, Steven A. "Tough Jews: The Jewish American Boxing Experience, 1890-1950." *Sports and the American Jew.* Ed. Steven A. Riess. Syracuse: Syracuse University Press, 1998. 60–104.

Rinehart, Robert E., and Synthia Sydnor, eds. *To the Extreme: Alternative Sports, Inside and Out.* Albany: State University of New York Press, 2003.

Roberts, Randy. *Papa Jack: Jack Johnson and the Era of White Hopes.* New York: Free Press, 1983.

Roberts, Randy, and James Olson. "The Roone Revolution." *Sport in America: From Wicked Amusements to National Obsession.* Ed. David K. Wiggins. Champaign, IL: Human Kinetics, 1995. 269–283.

Roediger, David R., ed. *Black on White: Black Writers on What It Means to Be White.* New York: Schocken Books, 1998.

Roediger, David R. *The Wages of Whiteness: Race and the Making of the American Working Class.* London: Verso, 1999.

Rogers, Phil. "Path to the States?" *Chicago Tribune* 11 February 2007, section 3: 6–7.

Rojas, Enrique. "Organizers Have Spent $50 Million on Classic." ESPN.com 16 March 2006. <http://sports.espn.go.com/mlb/worldclassic2006/news/story?id=2371119>.

Rorabaugh, W.J. *The Alcoholic Republic: An American Tradition.* New York: Oxford University Press, 1979.

Rosengarten, Theodore, and Dale Rosengarten, eds. *A Portion of the People: Three Hundred Years of Southern Jewish Life.* Columbia: University of Southern Carolina Press, 2002.

Rosenzweig, Roy. *Eight Hours for What We Will: Workers and Leisure in an Industrial City.* New York: Cambridge University Press, 1983.

Rosenzweig, Roy, and Elizabeth Blackmar. *The Park and the People: A History of Central Park.* Ithaca, NY: Cornell University Press, 1992.

Rotundo, E. Anthony. *American Manhood: Transformations in Masculinity from the Revolution to the Modern Era.* New York: Basic Books, 1994.

Sage, George H. *Power and Ideology in American Sport: A Critical Perspective.* Champaign, IL: Human Kinetics, 1990.

*Sahagún, Fray Bernardino de. "The Florentine Codex: General History of the Things of New Spain, Book 8." Spanish missionary commenting on the Aztec game of tlachtli ca. 1550–1569. *Sports in North America: A Documentary History, Volume I, Part I: Sports in the Colonial Era, 1618–1783.* Ed. Thomas Altherr. Gulf Stream, FL: Academic International Press, 1997. 449–450.

Scharff, Virginia. *Taking the Wheel: Women and the Coming of the Motor Age.* New York: Free Press, 1991.

Schimmel, Kimberly S., Alan G. Ingham, and Jeremy W. Howell. *Professional Team Sport and the American City: Urban Politics and Franchise Relocation.* Champaign, IL: Human Kinetics, 1993.

Seymour, Harold. *Baseball: The People's Game.* New York: Oxford University Press, 1990.

Shaulis, Dahn. "Pedestriennes: Newsworthy but Controversial Women in Sporting Entertainment." *Journal of Sport History* 26.1 (Spring 1999): 29-50.

Silverman, Al, ed. *Best from Sport.* New York: Bartholomew House, 1961.

*"Skating." Article and image. *Harper's Weekly* 12 February 1859: 100–101.

*"Skating on the Ladies' Skating Pond." *Harper's Weekly* 28 January 1860: 56–57.

Sklar, Kathryn Kish. *Catharine Beecher: A Study in American Domesticity.* New York: Norton, 1973.

*Smith, Ronald A., ed. *Big-Time Football at Harvard, 1905—The Diary of Coach Bill Reid.* Champaign: University of Illinois Press, 1994.

Smith, Ronald A. *Sports and Freedom: The Rise of Big-Time College Athletics.* New York: Oxford University Press, 1988.

*Smith, Wilfred. "Thousands See 900 Race in Tribune Swim—Claudia Eckert Wins Senior Girls' Crown." *Chicago Tribune* 28 July 1930, section 2: 21, 23.

*Smith, Wilfred. "J.P.I. Enters 53 in Tribune Swim Events." *Chicago Tribune* 11 July 1930, section 2: 2.

Spears, Betty, and Richard Swanson. *History of Sport and Physical Education in the United States.* Dubuque, IA: Brown, 1988.

Sperber, Murray. *Shake Down the Thunder: The Creation of Notre Dame Football.* New York: Holt, 1993.

Spirou, Costas, and Larry Bennett. *It's Hardly Sportin': Stadiums, Neighborhoods, and the New Chicago.* DeKalb, IL: Northern Illinois University Press, 2003.

Sports Illustrated 27 December 2004-3 January 2005: 121.

"Sports Illustrated Facts." <http://sportsillustrated.cnn.com/thenetwork/tour/sifacts/>.

*"Sports of the Turf." Advertisement. *City Gazette* 26 February 1816.

*Stagg, Amos Alonzo. Letter to his sister Pauline Stagg, March 10, 1892. *Sports in North America: A Documentary History, Volume 5.* Gerald R. Gems. Gulf Breeze, FL: Academic International Press, 1996. 143.

Stanard, William G. "Racing in Colonial Virginia." *Virginia Magazine of History and Biography* 2 (1894–1895): 296–301.

Steckbeck, John S. *Fabulous Redmen: The Carlisle Indians and Their Famous Football Teams.* Harrisburg, PA: McFarland, 1951.

Steinberg, David A. "The Workers' Sport Internationals 1920–28." *Journal of Contemporary History* 13.2 (Apr. 1978): 233–251. <http://links.jstor.org/sici?sici=0022-0094(197804)13%3A2%3C233%3ATWSI1%3E2.0.CO%3B2-Q>.

Steinhorn, Leonard. "How Baby Boomers Made America Better." *Chicago Sun-Times* 15 January 2006: 1B, 4B.

*Stempfel, Theodore. *Festschrift, Celebrating the Completion of Das Deutsche Haus in Indianapolis.* 1898. Rpt. German/English Edition. Ed. Giles R. Hoyt, Claudia Grossmann, Elfrieda Lang, and Eberhard Reichmann. Indianapolis: German-American Center and Indiana German Heritage Society, 1991.

Stepp, John Richard. "Interactions Between the Mississippi Choctaw and European Americans Through the Sport of Toli." *The International Journal of the History of Sport* 23.2 (March 2006): 285–293.

Sterngass, Jon. "Cheating, Gender Roles, and the Nineteenth-Century Croquet Craze." *Journal of Sport History* 25.3 (Fall 1998): 398–418.

Story, Ronald. "The Country of the Young: The Meaning of Baseball in Early American Culture." *Sport in America: From Wicked Amusements to National Obsession.* Ed. David K. Wiggins. Champaign, IL: Human Kinetics, 1995. 121–132.

Struna, Nancy L. "'Good Wives and Gardeners, Spinners and Fearless Riders': Middle- and Upper-Rank Women in the Early American Sporting Culture." *From 'Fair Sex' to Feminism: Sport and the Socialization of Women in the Industrial and Post-Industrial Eras.* Ed. J.A. Mangan and Roberta J. Park. London: Cass, 1987. 235–255.

Struna, Nancy L. *People of Prowess: Sport, Leisure, and Labor in Early Anglo-America.* Urbana and Chicago: University of Illinois Press, 1996.

Struna, Nancy L. "The Sporting Life in Puritan America." *Major Problems in American Sport History: Documents and Essays.* Ed. Steven A. Riess. Boston: Houghton Mifflin, 1997. 39–48.

Summers, Nick. "It's Too Soon to Tell if Title IX Is Done Yet." *Columbia Spectator.* 21 February 2003. <http://www.columbiaspectator.com/?q=node/11616>.

Tamini, Noel. "Women Always in the Race." *Olympic Review* (1993): 204–208, 221. <http://www.la84foundation.org/OlympicInformationCenter/OlympicReview/1993/ore308/ORE308a.pdf>.

Terret, Thierry. "The Military 'Olympics' of 1919: Sport, Diplomacy and Sport Politics in the Aftermath of World War One." *Journal of Olympic History* 14.2 (August 2006): 22–31.

*Thomas, Robert B. "Farmer's Calendar." *The Old Farmer's Almanac.* May 1851. Boston: Jenks, Palmer, 1850.

Thorpe, Holly. "Betties, Babes, and Bad-Asses: A History of Female Surf, Skate and Snow Boarders." Unpublished graduate student essay, University of Waikato, 2005.

*Thrasher, Frederic. *The Gang: A Study of 1,313 Gangs in Chicago.* 1927. Rpt. Chicago: University of Chicago Press, 1963.

"Time-Line of Rowing: 1850–1899." Friends of Rowing History. <www.rowinghistory.net>.

*Title IX of the Education Amendments of 1972, P.L. 92-318,20 U.S.C.S. Section 1681 et seq.

Todd, Jan. "The Classical Ideal and Its Impact on the Search for Suitable Exercise: 1774–1830." *Iron Game History* 2.4: 6–16.

*"To Our Friends and the Friends of Improved Farming." *The Homestead* 1 (September 4, 1856): 787.

Townsend, Kim. *Manhood at Harvard: William James and Others.* New York: Norton, 1996.

"Tuffy Rhodes." Baseball-Reference.com. <http://www.baseball-reference.com/bullpen/Tuffy_Rhodes>.

Twombly, Wells. *200 Years of Sport in America: A Pageant of a Nation at Play.* New York: McGraw-Hill, 1976.

Vennum, Thomas, Jr. *American Indian Lacrosse: Little Brother of War.* Washington, DC: Smithsonian Institution Press, 1994.

Verbrugge, Martha H. *Able-Bodied Womanhood: Personal Health and Social Change in Nineteenth-Century Boston.* New York: Oxford University Press, 1988.

Verney, Kevern. *African Americans and US Popular Culture.* New York: Routledge, 2003.

Vertinsky, Patricia. *The Eternally Wounded Woman: Women, Exercise, and Doctors in the Late Nineteenth Century.* Manchester: Manchester University Press, 1990.

Vertinsky, Patricia. "A Militant Madonna: Charlotte Perkins Gilman, Feminism and Physical Culture." *International Journal of the History of Sport* 18 (2001): 68.

Wakefield, Wanda Ellen. *Playing to Win: Sports and the American Military, 1898–1945.* Albany: State University of New York Press, 1997.

Walters, Ronald G. *American Reformers, 1815–1860.* New York: Hill and Wang, 1978.

Ware, Susan. *Title IX: A Brief History with Documents.* Boston: Bedford/St. Martin's, 2007.

*Warner, Glenn S. "Heap Big Run—Most-Fast." *Collier's* 24 October 1931: 19, 46.

Warner, Patricia Campbell. *When the Girls Came Out to Play: The Birth of American Sportswear.* Boston: University of Massachusetts Press, 2006.

Warren, Lynne. "Zoom Town." *National Geographic* 206.6 (December 2004): 114–120.

* Watson, Elkanah. "Elkanah Watson's Misgivings on Cockfighting, 1787." *Major Problems in American Sport History: Documents and Essays.* Ed. Steven A. Riess. Boston: Houghton Mifflin, 1997. 27.

*Watson, John F. *Annals of Philadelphia and Pennsylvania, in the Olden Time.* 1830. Rpt. Ed. Willis P. Hazard. Vol. 1. Philadelphia: Edwin S. Stuart, 1884.

*"The Weather and the Park—Glorious News for the Boys!" *Harper's Weekly* 28 January 1860: 64.

*The Wheel. *Sporting Life,* 28 November 1882: 6.

Wheeler, Robert F. "Organized Sport and Organized Labour: The Workers' Sports Movement." *Journal of Contemporary History* 13.2 (April 1978): 191–210. <http://links.jstor.org/sici?sici=0022-0094(1978 04)13%3A2%3C191%3AOSAOLT%3E2.0.CO %3B2-S>.

*"Where are the *Grahamites*?" *Yankee Farmer* 3 (January 14, 1837): 11.

"Where's the Love?" *Chicago Sun-Times* 25 February 2007: 86A.

*Wilkin, Josephine. Letter to her mother, March 6, 1892. *Sports in North America: A Documentary History, Volume 5.* Gerald R. Gems. Gulf Breeze, FL: Academic International Press, 1996. 147-148.

The White House Historical Association. *White House Horses: Presidents at the Races.* <http://www.whitehousehistory.org/02/subs_horses/04.html>.

Whorton, James C. *Crusaders for Fitness.* Princeton, NJ: Princeton University Press, 1982.

Wieberg, Steve, and Jack Carey. "Bowl participants' graduation rates mostly below average." *USA Today* 8 December 2004: 5B.

Wiggins, David K., ed. *African Americans in Sports.* Armonk, NY: Sharpe, 2004.

Wiggins, David K. *Glory Bound: Black Athletes in a White America.* Syracuse: Syracuse University Press, 1997.

Wiggins, David K. "Good Times on the Old Plantation: Popular Recreations of the Black Slave in Antebellum South, 1810–1860." *Journal of Sport History* 4 (1977): 260–284.

Wiggins, David K. "Sport and Popular Pastimes: Shadow of the Slavequarter." *Canadian Journal of History of Sport* 11 (May 1980): 61–88.

Wiggins, David K., ed. *Sport in America: From Wicked Amusements to National Obsession.* Champaign, IL: Human Kinetics, 1995.

*Wood, William. *The Law of Athletics, Showing How to Preserve and Improve Health and Beauty, and to Correct Personal Defects Caused by Want of Physical Exercise.* New York: Dick & Fitzgerald, 1880.

*Wood, William. *Manual of Physical Exercises, Comprising Gymnastics, Calisthenics, Rowing, Sailing, Skating, Swimming, Fencing, Sparring, Cricket, Base Ball, Together With Rules for Training and Sanitary Suggestions.* Vols. 1 and 2. New York: Harper & Brothers, 1867.

*Wood, William. "New Englands Prospect, A True, Lively and Experimental Defcription of that Part of America, Commonly Called Nevv England." 1634. *Sports in North America: A Documentary History, Volume I, Part I: Sports in the Colonial Era, 1618–1783.*

Ed. Thomas L. Altherr. Gulf Stream, FL: Academic International Press, 1997. 160–161.

Yiamouyiannis, Athena. "The Future of Title IX: Ensuring Success Through Proactive Approaches." *Women in Sport and Physical Activity Journal* 12.2 (Fall 2003): 45–54.

Zang, David W. "The Greatest: Muhammad Ali's Confounding Character." *Sport and the Color Line: Black Athletes and Race Relations in Twentieth-Century America.* Eds. Patrick B. Miller and David K. Wiggins. New York: Routledge, 2004. 283–303.

Index

About the Authors

Gerald R. Gems, PhD, is an international scholar and the author and editor of 8 books and more than 125 publications. He currently is a professor in health and physical education at North Central College in Naperville, Illinois. Gems serves on the Executive Council and Scientific Committee of the International Society for History of Physical Education and Sport and is a past president of the North American Society for Sport History. He has been the book review editor of the *Journal of Sport History* since 1996.

Dr. Gems was honored as a Fulbright Senior Specialist for 2007 to 2012 and was an Illinois Road Scholar in history from 1999 to 2003. He earned his PhD in sport history at the University of Maryland.

Linda J. Borish, PhD, an associate professor of history at Western Michigan University, has focused her research on American women's sport history. She was selected in 2001-2002 as the International Ambassador for the North American Society for Sport History and also served on its Executive Council and Publications Board. She is executive producer and historian of the documentary film *Jewish Women in American Sport: Settlement Houses to the Olympics* and has received numerous research grants related to American women and sport history in rural and urban contexts. Borish was the book review coeditor of the *Journal of Sport History* from 1996 to 2000.

Dr. Borish earned her PhD in American studies from the University of Maryland. In addition to her role at Western Michigan, Borish is a research associate at the Hadassah-Brandeis Institute, Brandeis University.

Gertrud Pfister, PhD, is a professor at the University of Copenhagen in Denmark. She was president of the International Sport Sociology Society from 2001 to 2007. Pfister was also president of the International Society for the History of Sport and Physical Education from 1993 to 2000 and won the association's award for lifelong achievements in the area of sport history in 2005.

Dr. Pfister earned an honorary doctorate from Semmelweis University in Budapest. She is a fellow of the American Academy for Kinesiology and Physical Education and the European College for Sport Science. She earned a PhD in history from the University of Regensburg and in sociology from Ruhr-University Bochum.

A Man Walks On To a Pitch

A Man Walks On To a Pitch

STORIES FROM A LIFE IN FOOTBALL

HARRY REDKNAPP

EBURY
PRESS

3 5 7 9 10 8 6 4

Published in 2014 by Ebury Press, an imprint of Ebury Publishing
A Random House Group company

Copyright © Harry Redknapp 2014

The Random House Group Limited Reg. No. 954009

Addresses for companies within the Random House Group can be found at
www.randomhouse.co.uk

A CIP catalogue record for this book is available from the British Library

The Random House Group Limited supports the Forest Stewardship
Council® (FSC®), the leading international forest-certification organisation.
Our books carrying the FSC label are printed on FSC®-certified paper. FSC
is the only forest-certification scheme supported by the leading environmental
organisations, including Greenpeace. Our paper procurement policy can be
found at www.randomhouse.co.uk/environment

Designed and set by seagulls.net

Printed and bound in Great Britain by Clays Ltd, St Ives PLC

HB ISBN 9780091955526
TPB ISBN 9780091957568

To buy books by your favourite authors and register for offers visit
www.randomhouse.co.uk

For everyone I have ever worked with, played with or enjoyed watching in my life in football

PROLOGUE

I was sitting in the changing-room at Wembley after our play-off final. The wild celebrations were going on all around – champagne, cheering, singing, bouncing, the usual. Queens Park Rangers were going up. We hadn't deserved it, I knew that. Derby County had been the better side, but we had won the game, in the last minute and with 10 men. That's what happens sometimes. My telephone rang. It was Harry Gregg, the old Manchester United legend – one of the Busby Babes. He had been watching the game. He knew the mixed emotions I would have been feeling. 'Harry, I want you to hear a quick story,' he said. And he told me about the time Northern Ireland beat England 3–2 at Wembley in 1957. Harry was in goal that day, against an England team that included his Manchester United team-mates Duncan Edwards, Tommy Taylor and Roger Byrne, plus Billy Wright as captain and Johnny Haynes at inside-forward. Some great players there. After the game, Walter Winterbottom, England's manager, said he thought Northern Ireland had been lucky. This was put to their captain, Danny Blanchflower. 'Ah yes,' he said, with a smile, 'but sometimes it's better to be lucky than good.' And I believe that. I can hear Danny, a clever man, saying it now. Every manager will know what he means. We have all had good days that have not been lucky, and lucky days when we've not been good – and I know what days I prefer. It was a good story to hear just then.

I don't know why I was feeling so ambivalent about the way we'd won against Derby. Maybe, in my head, when Gary O'Neil got sent off I was mentally preparing myself for my last game in football. I would have retired had we lost, I'm pretty sure of that. I don't even know if the owners would have wanted me to stay on; it's quite likely they would have desired a change, too, and I understand that. Yet in my heart I knew I couldn't go another season in the Championship with the limitations to our squad. I knew the calibre of players we could buy would drop considerably and there was enough dead wood around as it was. I had done my best in my first full season there and it hadn't been good enough. It would have been time to let someone else have a go, to see if a fresh eye on the place could bring it back to life. I'm not saying this was going through my mind as I stood on the Wembley touchline – I was completely focused and absorbed by the game – but it was something I had considered in previous weeks. I knew the likely consequence of failure would be that I was managing my last match in professional football.

When we went down to 10 men, I couldn't really see any way out of it, to be honest. I'd be a liar if I said I still thought we could win in open play. My hope was that we would survive and get to penalties. And even that was going to be difficult. We played with two strikers, which, looking back, was a mistake. There wasn't a lot in the game but they had more possession and that comes from having an extra man in midfield. Once O'Neil went off it was just backs to the wall. I thought we might struggle through 90 minutes, but I wasn't confident about the additional 30 minutes' extra time, with everyone exhausted. We weren't a young team and a few looked like they were running on empty already. I had my best striker Charlie Austin playing on the left wing, where he looked as if he didn't have a clue, but my only option was to play two banks of four with Bobby Zamora up on his own. I couldn't have asked Bobby to do Charlie's defensive shift. It was a mess.

And then, suddenly, it was a miracle. With seconds on the clock, the ball dropped to Bobby, and he stuck it right in the corner. It was too late for Derby to do anything about it. They knew they were done.

It was a strange feeling after the game, really. Sandra had come up with our grandchildren, so she had to go home to the South coast, Jamie was away at the Champions League final and I felt too emotionally drained to do much celebrating. I knew they would all be back at Loftus Road getting drunk, but I didn't fancy that at all. I had to stay in London because we had a parade at the ground the following morning, so I planned a quiet night. I showed my face at the party, then sneaked out the back door and went back to the Grosvenor House hotel for a late dinner and the Champions League final. Club sandwich, plate of chips, cup of tea, lovely. And then, watching the football, I got a phone call from Don Shanks, the old Rangers player. He's a good lad, Don, and I'd got him a ticket for the game. He was with a friend of his and they were about to arrive at Aspinall's club in Curzon Street for a glass of wine. So I watched extra time and joined them. I'm not sure I was great company. The reality of it all was beginning to dawn on me.

I woke up in the hotel the following morning still feeling a bit guilty about our win. I felt for Steve McClaren, Derby's manager, I felt for their players and the people at the club. I was still uncomfortable about the way we had made it back to the Premier League. But then another thought hit me. Two years ago I had flown to Munich to watch Chelsea play in the Champions League final. I was manager of Tottenham Hotspur and we had finished fourth, qualifying for the Champions League. Chelsea had come sixth. And like the sixth best team in the Premier League, they got completely outplayed by Bayern Munich on the night, just as they were by Barcelona in the semi-final. Yet somehow they won. Bayern smashed them to pieces, Chelsea equalised with two minutes to go; Bayern missed a penalty in extra time, Chelsea won the shoot-out. And because they did, they took our Champions League place. Twenty-five days later, I was sacked by Tottenham. Had we reached the Champions League that wouldn't have happened. And at that moment I thought – and pardon the language – fuck it. What am I beating myself up for? It's football. Stuff happens. So we didn't deserve to win? What about the times when we merited victory and didn't get it? What about me getting the sack because Chelsea by some miracle ended up with our Champions League place? I walked down to breakfast, feeling better at last, and who should be standing there but Roberto Di Matteo, the Chelsea manager in Munich. He looked happy enough. Why was I agonising over a football match we had won? Yes, it was rough on Derby – but there are a lot of good people at Rangers, too. Let them be happy for a change, I thought. And I never looked back.

Yet looking back is what this book is about. It's a look back on my 60 or so years in and around the British game, from the earliest memories of going to Millwall and Arsenal with my dad, to my thoughts on thankfully not having to face up to Luis Suárez again as a Premier League manager this season. For each decade, I've picked a best XI, too, and told as many stories as I can remember about the characters involved. I hope you enjoy it. And, don't forget: if you can't be good, be lucky.

CHAPTER ONE

. . . .

THE FIFTIES

We used to go to Arsenal a lot, me and my dad, but football wasn't as tribal then as it is now, so Highbury wasn't our only destination. Millwall's ground, The Den, was another haunt, and coming from East London we would wait at the entrance of the Rotherhithe Tunnel for a lift across the river. A lot of Millwall punters did the same. Eventually a car would stop and in we'd jump. It didn't take too long. I bet you would wait there for hours now, but in those days people were friendlier and more trusting. They were going to football, we were going to football, so we all went together. My dad might give them two bob for the petrol and we'd set off.

It was all part of the tradition of watching Millwall. They were the dockers' club really, and a lot of the men on our estate worked on the docks. I would have been about seven when I first started going there – it was certainly before I went to Arsenal – with my dad and his brother George. Arsenal was my dad's club, but football was cheaper then and fans didn't think twice about going to watch another team play. Millwall were in the

Third Division (South) but it was always a tasty atmosphere. On Saturdays they used to come out of the docks, go into the pub, and out of the pub and into The Den. Football hooliganism was unheard of, but once I began travelling around, even as a kid I knew Millwall felt different. Then there was the time my dad got his jaw broken.

I don't know what happened exactly, I wasn't there, but he went over to Millwall with his mate Johnny Wood, who was a bit of a rogue and spent most of his life in prison. Johnny lived in Poplar when he wasn't inside and was known for being a bit cheeky. My mum blamed him every time there was trouble. Well, he must have picked on the wrong bloke that day, because someone took offence and my old man ended up getting a clump. It was just before Christmas and he ended up with his jaw wired all over the holiday; he couldn't even eat his turkey dinner.

He didn't have much luck with Christmas dinner, my dad. Another year, he knocked off on Christmas Eve and went straight to the pub, as the dockers always did. He had one job that day – to pick up the capon chicken for tomorrow's dinner from Coppins butchers. Unfortunately, he got a bit side-tracked. By night time, with all the shops closed, he still hadn't come home. I was sitting indoors with my mum and I could tell that she'd gone a bit quiet. Suddenly, she sprung out of her chair. 'Right,' she said, 'we're going out to find your father.' And off we went, around every pub in Poplar looking for him. Mum was lifting me up at the windows and I was looking in. At the Earl of Ellesmere pub in Ellesmere Road, we found him. The Far Famed Cake Company was in Rifle Street nearby, and all the girls from the factory were having a Christmas knees-up, too. Dad was there, with Johnny Wood and a crowd of his mates, all dancing with the girls and having a right laugh. 'There he is, Mum,' I said. 'I can see him.' 'Right,' she said, 'call him out, get him out here.' So I went to the door and got his attention. 'Hello, Harry,' he said, all merry from the party. 'Here's my Harry boy. What do you want, Ha –' and, bosh, she'd got him. Claimed hold of his collar and kicked his backside all the way home to our flats. Every 10 paces she'd kick him again. 'Where's our chicken?' Wallop. 'What do you mean you ain't got no chicken?' Boot. 'How can you forget the chicken?' Bash. Crack of dawn the next morning Dad and I were down Petticoat Lane, around the old Jewish stallholders, who were the only ones that traded on Christmas Day, trying to buy a chicken. My dad didn't even know what he was looking for, really. He didn't have a clue what was good or bad. He came home with a boiling chicken, not the lovely big roaster that mum had ordered from Coppins. It was the chicken they use to make stews and soups. So he got hit round the head with that and all. It ate like string. Tough as anything.

He didn't have a clue about the niceties, my dad. All he cared about was football. Most of my earliest memories of watching games in the fifties involve my dad. On the odd occasion I'd go with a mate. I had a friend called Johnnie Jennings whose dad was a big West Ham fan and occasionally I'd go over to Upton Park with them – but even though we lived in the East End it wasn't all Hammers fans on our estate.

By the time I was 11, I was being scouted by professional clubs, so we used to get offered a lot of tickets. Then we could take our pick of matches: Arsenal, Tottenham Hotspur, West Ham United, even Chelsea, which was a bit far afield for us on public transport. We would go if one of our favourites was playing, though. My dad had a few players he really liked, but top of the pile was probably Tom Finney. If Finney was in town with Preston North End he would always want to go. I remember one night at Arsenal when Tommy Docherty played centre-half and Finney was the striker. You could tell The Doc was in awe of Finney because he barely kicked him. Usually he took no prisoners as a defender, but on this day he let Finney walk all over him. Preston won 3–0.

It was a real thrill seeing the big players in those days, it was something you looked forward to and talked about at school all week long. The only match that was on television was the FA Cup final, and that was so special the streets would be deserted when the game was on. Everybody would find somebody they knew with a television and watch the game – and then afterwards all the doors would be flung open and the kids would come roaring out to play football and pretend to be their heroes.

Few people wore colours in those days. I remember my mum knitted me a red and white scarf for when I went to Arsenal, but there were no replica shirts or club merchandise. We had a wooden rattle, like everybody else, but that was about it. These days the police would confiscate it at the turnstile, they would think you were going to club somebody over the head with it – but crowds then were not even segregated. You see old film of the fans in their caps sharing cups of tea – my dad even used to put a collar and tie on to go to some games. That was just the way people dressed.

Everyone went by bus, including the players. Peter Sillett was the captain of Chelsea – Stanley Matthews rated him as his most difficult opponent at full-back – and he used to tell a story about going out to the bus stop to get home after one game. Chelsea had lost and there were still a few fans hanging about. Players weren't recognisable figures in those days – we didn't see them being interviewed on television every week – so they didn't know that they had a Chelsea player standing beside them. The fans were going through the team, slaughtering them all one by one, and finally it was Peter's turn. As they tore him to shreds, Peter says he sunk deeper and deeper into his overcoat in case they spotted him. 'Finally,' he said, 'just to be on the safe side, I joined in.'

I was lucky growing up in London because there was so much good football on my doorstep. We could afford to be picky. There was always a game a bus ride away – we rarely needed to get the train. Fulham, too far. Wembley, too far. We didn't go to the England games. The only ground I can remember visiting by train was Tottenham, once they were interested in signing me. They would send two tickets to every home game for us, and they had some great players in that era, like Danny Blanchflower, who were worth the trip. That meant a 106 bus to Stoke Newington, a train to Seven Sisters, and then a bloody long walk.

The most memorable games of the time involved foreign teams – clubs from Moscow coming over to play Arsenal, or Honved of Hungary against Wolverhampton Wanderers. Even the programmes felt different for those games, glossier and thicker as if to say: this is important. We didn't see foreign teams or foreign footballers in those days: with one exception. I'm going to start my team of the 1950s with this individual, because his story really is quite remarkable.

BERT TRAUTMANN
(MANCHESTER CITY)

Bert was the first foreign star in English football, and a really strange one because he came here as a German prisoner of war, and stayed. I'm not sure that could happen now, with all the media attention and the way supporters are. I think it would be too horrible for him. Trautmann was a typical German. As kids, he was what we all imagined Germans to be – blond hair, blue eyes, tall, imposing. He'd been a member of the Hitler youth, a Luftwaffe paratrooper, and had fought on the Eastern front in Russia. It seems amazing to me even now just thinking about it. He was captured and sent to a prisoner-of-war camp in Lancashire, and when the war was over he ended up playing for St Helens Town, who were an amateur team in the Lancashire Combination league. Frank Swift, who was Manchester City's goalkeeper, contracted TB and they went in for Trautmann. There were huge protests at first, particularly among the Jewish community, but the chief rabbi of Manchester came out in his defence and it calmed down.

Back then you went to matches just to watch certain individuals, and Trautmann definitely came into that category. He was exotic, he was different. The media wasn't as sensationalist back then, but we all knew his background, all knew whose side he was on in the war. I suppose it is testament to what he was like as a player and a person that he won the crowds over. He would smile and applaud them if they were nice to him and, in the end, he became one of us. Incredible, really, when you think what people had gone through with the bombing and losing loved ones – for him to be accepted like that, it shows how good we can be as a country when we put our minds to it.

Back then, people just got on with life. They loved their football, they loved their team, but they didn't have the hatred you see now. It sounds sentimental and nostalgic but I won't make apologies for that; fans were different towards each other, and it was better without that nastiness towards the opposition at games. A player who went back to his old club would be applauded. Nowadays they spit at him in the street. It would be the same for Trautmann. Now, he would be targeted, slagged off the whole game. Back then, it didn't happen. We saw him for what he was: a goalkeeper who had endured a unique set of circumstances. There was no question of verbal abuse the times I saw him. Fans weren't segregated then, anyway. Over at Arsenal, you could find yourself next to some Manchester City fans and you'd end up having a cup of tea together. So you couldn't then start calling their goalkeeper every name under the sun. It must still have been very, very difficult for Trautmann, though, because of his background, and that's why he makes my team ahead of, say, Ted Ditchburn at Tottenham Hotspur or Sam Bartram of Charlton Athletic. I just look at where he came from and think, 'If we all ended up liking a bloke who had fought for the Nazis, he must have been good.' And in 1956 he was the first foreign player to win the Footballer of the Year Award – it was the year he also won the FA Cup, playing with a broken neck.

I remember watching that game, too. Manchester City beat Birmingham City 3–1 and Don Revie was brilliant playing as a deep centre-forward, quite a radical position for the time. He was the man of the match, but what everyone remembers now is that Trautmann broke his neck and played on, although we didn't have a clue he was so badly injured at the time. There were about 15 minutes to go and Peter Murphy was chasing the ball into the penalty area. Trautmann came out, as brave as anything, and dived head first at his feet. Murphy's knee hit his neck and broke it, although that only showed up in the X-ray later. I can guarantee one thing: the trainer wouldn't have had any idea. In my imagination, I can hear him now. 'Come on, Bert, give it a twist, lad, you'll be all right.' Drop of water down his jumper with a sponge and off he'd go again – there were no substitutes then, so all the trainer was interested in was keeping 11 on the field. 'That's better, Bert. You'll be fine now, son.' It seemed every FA Cup final some poor soul broke something. There was no sports science in those days, no proper physiotherapy or qualified medical staff.

The money aside, in many ways it was a great time to be a footballer. Trautmann was a draw and very famous, but there was no media swirl around him as there would be now. I remember watching Mesut Ozil miss a penalty for Arsenal last season, and the next morning everyone was on at him for being German and missing a penalty. Germans don't miss penalties, you see. Now you think of the baggage that Trautmann had with him so soon after the war ended, but he was allowed to be what he was. If anything, it may even have worked in his favour, because to me as a kid he seemed more imposing, bigger and athletic because of his background.

The English goalkeepers? Bartram at Charlton was a local hero. He kept goal for the club either side of the war. London used to have thick smogs and one day he was playing for Charlton at Chelsea when the fog came in and the game was stopped. It cleared a little and the match restarted with Charlton now on top. Then the fog got worse than ever. Sam noticed the crowd had got quieter but thought it was because they couldn't see and Charlton were playing so well. Then a figure appeared out of the gloom before him. Sam got ready to dash out and make a save. It turned out to be a copper. 'What are you doing out here?' he said. 'They all went inside 10 minutes ago.' As I say, different days.

Sam went on to be a journalist for the *Sunday People*. He used to pay me for tips when I was a player at West Ham United, so when I went to Bournemouth I thought I'd have a bit of fun. The night before my debut in 1972, I phoned Mel Machin, one of the other players. I put on a Northern accent and said I was Sam Bartram and was looking for inside information on Bournemouth. I said I'd pay £50 upfront, with a £25 weekly retainer. Mel was right up for it. He said he was in the same card school as our manager, John Bond, so always heard the latest gossip. He said Bobby Kellard at Portsmouth was a current target. 'That's lovely, Mel,' I told him. 'The cheque's in the post and I'll call next week.'

The following day Mel rocked up in a new suit. He was sitting next to Ted MacDougall, telling him all about this great deal he had. I couldn't contain myself. I leaned into the conversation. 'Hello, Mel,' I said, in my best Sam Bartram voice. 'Er, hello, Harry,' Mel replied, a little unsure of what was going on. I carried it on for a little while. 'What are you talking like that for?' he said. 'I'm Sam,' I told him, 'Sam Bartram.' Mel went spare, but John Bond loved it. 'Harry's going to run rings around you lot,' he predicted. Then in the afternoon we lost 3–2 to Watford.

Later when he was going through all the players individually he turned on me. 'And if you think you can come down here taking the piss out of everybody ...'

As a goalkeeper Sam was more the traditional type, whereas Trautmann seemed to have more flair; he was almost acrobatic, and we hadn't seen that before. He still had to look after himself, mind you, because every goalkeeper took a physical battering. That never seemed to bother him, though. I suppose when you've thought you were about to be taken off by the Russians and shot, it wouldn't.

ALF RAMSEY
(TOTTENHAM HOTSPUR)

We all know what Alf is remembered for, but at first he was the right-back in the great Tottenham Hotspur team of the 1950s, the 'push and run' team. It is hard to explain their significance to a younger generation, but I would compare them to the modern Barcelona, the way their game was all about short passing and movement. It wasn't quite as sophisticated, obviously, but when Tottenham started playing that way they won the Second Division title and the next season won the league by four points (the equivalent of six today). That 1950–51 team was special, with Arthur Rowe coaching and Eddie Baily pulling the strings at inside-forward. Eddie went on to be Bill Nicholson's assistant at Tottenham in the 1960s and a scout at Chelsea and West Ham. He was a brilliant footballer, a fantastic, intelligent quick passer, but as a scout nothing much impressed Eddie. 'Players? Fucking players?' he'd say. 'They get you the fucking sack.' He's not wrong, by the way.

What they called push and run back then is now known as the one-two and every team does it. But at the time it was revolutionary. A player would find his team-mate with a short pass and then carry on his run to receive another short pass in return. Newcastle United came fourth and won the FA Cup in 1950–51, but Tottenham beat them 7–0 playing push and run that season. And Ramsey was a master at it. He had come to prominence playing for his army division during the war, and went to Portsmouth and then Southampton, before Tottenham got him.

He wasn't fast, so there is no way he could play right-back now, but Alf excelled at the intricate passing that made Rowe's Tottenham tick. He was good on the ball, very cultured for the time, and an outstanding penalty taker. They used to call him 'The General' at Tottenham because he was always in charge, so it is no surprise that he went on to be such a successful manager.

Alf's use of the ball was always first class. And I think people forget how hard it was to play good football with the equipment they had in those days. Look at the boots with the big hard toe-caps. How could you have had any feel for a football with a set of those on? Clearing out the garage the other day, I found a pair of my dad's old boots. Forget push and run, it's a wonder they could run at all. Metal toecaps, studs banged in the bottom with the nails coming through the sole. And the ball was so heavy that when it got wet it as good as filled with water. Modern players really feel the ball; they have light boots and moulded soles. Even the ball is lightweight. Those boys didn't even have rubber studs – by late in the season when it had dried out, or in the middle of winter when it was frozen, the only thing harder than the studs was the pitch. Apart from August and September

15

there were two kinds of surface, rock hard or mud heap. So it was unbelievable, really, to show the skill that the Tottenham team demonstrated in that gear. I'd love to organise a game one day, get 22 top players together, the stars of the Premier League, put them in the old equipment and see how they coped. Now that would be interesting.

I remember Bryan Robson telling me that when Juninho first came over to Middlesbrough in the 1995–6 season, he couldn't believe the quality of our pitches. In the FA Cup that year they played against Notts County, who were a third-tier team, and Juninho thought Bryan was lying to him about the division they were in. He looked at the neat little stadium and the nice pitch, and decided they were in a higher division than Bryan was saying. A team at that level in Brazil would have been playing on dirt, he said. Notts County were too posh. That is how far we have come, but in Alf's day they just had to overcome those disadvantages.

I never got to know Alf as a manager, which was a shame. He came from that pre-war generation, very old school, very aloof. He was born in Dagenham in East London, but had elocution lessons, which was strange for the time. Maybe he thought it would help him keep his distance from the players. I know Terry Venables came from the same area and when he got called into the England team, his dad thought it might help him with the manager to mention some old names from the past. He knew this bloke that was friends with Ramsey, so he told Terry to say that Charlie – or whoever – sent his regards. After the first training sessions, Terry thought it would be the right moment. Catching up with him as they left the field he seized his chance. 'Mr Ramsey, my dad told me to say hello to you from Charlie, in Dagenham.' Ramsey looked at him very coldly. He had done everything to cover his old accent and now pronounced Argentina with an H. The last thing he wanted was to be reminded of his past. Finally, he spoke in the most cultured accent he could muster. 'Fuck off, son,' he said. I think Terry only played for him twice.

When you think how much Ramsey and Bobby Moore achieved together for England, it's surprising how seldom Alf's name comes up in conversation. I think he was a quiet man, not given to great shows of emotion. And in those days managers were still distant figures, who took their lead from the managers that they had worked with as players. Tommy Lawton played in the same era as Ramsey, certainly throughout the early 1950s, and I remember watching a fascinating interview with him about his time at Everton before the war. He went in to see the committee – Everton was run by a committee in those days – because his contract was up. Players only signed for a year back then. Tommy said he knocked on the door and walked in, and the head of the committee, Theo Kelly, looked up as he entered. 'Lawton,' he said, 'go outside the door, knock again and when I say enter, come in and stand over there by the door. When I say come over, you can come over to my desk and when I say sit down, you can sit down at my desk.' So Tommy said he went outside and did the whole thing exactly as Kelly said. He was the leading goalscorer in England that year, but by the time he left Kelly's office he felt he would be lucky to get a game at Tranmere Rovers. No surprise that it was Kelly who failed to persuade Lawton to stay at Everton after the war.

Yet that was the football culture that Alf Ramsey came from, so it is any wonder he stayed aloof from his players?

BILLY WRIGHT
(WOLVERHAMPTON WANDERERS)

Looking at the photographs of that great Wolves team, the first thing that strikes you about Billy Wright is his size. These days, the centre-halves are giants, but Billy actually looks slightly smaller than many of his team-mates. There really was nothing of him. '10 stones in weight, but 10 tons in the tackle' was one phrase I heard about him, and he was only 5 ft 8 in. The best central defenders of that time didn't have to be tall. Joe Shaw at Sheffield United was another one. He might have been even smaller than Billy.

If you look at what he achieved, it seems impossible. He played 70 consecutive games for England, captained them 90 times and won 105 caps – the first player to reach the century in world football. And this was a time when England did not have a huge amount of games, and Billy lost seven seasons to the Second World War. Imagine the records he could have set.

He got his break at Wolves because they were advertising for trialists in the local newspaper. With modern scouting networks, that would never happen now. Wolves thought he was too small at first, but Major Frank Buckley, the manager, relented and took him on as an apprentice for eight months. He was a centre-forward, then a wing-half and eventually a centre-half.

One of the things those of us who grew up in the fifties most remember about the game at that time was the first matches under lights against international opposition. Wolves installed floodlights at Molineux in 1953 and played a succession of matches against foreign teams: Racing Club of Buenos Aires, Moscow Dynamo, Spartak Moscow, and in 1954 they played Honved, the Champions of Hungary. It was a year after Hungary had beaten England 6–3 at Wembley, and then 7–1 in Budapest, and Wright was the captain of that humiliated England team. I cannot emphasise enough what an effect those matches had on us, because these players were our heroes and to see them taken apart like that – well, we couldn't believe it.

Billy Wright, in particular, was as much a celebrity as a footballer. He didn't live life like David Beckham, or George Best, and I don't think he had that personal charisma, but he was good looking with really blond hair, and had married one of the Beverley Sisters. Everyone knew him, as kids we all looked up to him, and suddenly we were seeing him getting pulled all over the Wembley pitch by Ferenc Puskás. Destroyed, really. So why is he still in this team? He was the best of his generation in Britain. There was no shame in getting beaten by the Hungarians. They were the best of their generation in Europe.

Hungary were the first to play a deep-lying centre-forward, and their wingers would withdraw to midfield to help with defence. Puskás called them the first total-football team, because everybody attacked and everybody fell back. I suppose the formation would be 2–3–3–2, although that is hard to picture for anyone brought up on the modern game. Wright ended up following Puskás as he dropped nearer to midfield and was left completely exposed when Hungary broke. It wasn't his fault. We had never seen anything like it. There were 105,000 at Wembley for the first game and

Hungary were a goal up in a minute and 4–1 up after 27 minutes. We thought we would get revenge in Budapest, but they put seven past us, which was just stunning.

Hungary should have won the 1954 World Cup but suffered a series of brutal matches on the way to the final, meaning they lost to West Germany, although they'd beaten them 8–3 in the group stage. That was one of only two games they lost between 1949 and the Hungarian Uprising in 1956, and in that time they revolutionised football. The system and ideas of their coach Gusztáv Sebes, evolved into 3–2–3–2, then 4–2–4 with high wingers and eventually the 4–4–2 pressing game. He started the policy of picking a team, rather than just the best players, thinking that if he selected from a handful of clubs rather than just a wide collection of individuals, there would be more unity. Finally, his idea that any player should be capable of playing anywhere pre-dated Holland and total football.

So this was the background when Honved came to Wolves in 1954, with Billy up against five of the Hungarian players that had won 7–1. It was more than a friendly. It really felt as if the future of English football was at stake. The game was so big that it was shown on television, with Wolves wearing special old-gold shirts made out of satin, and when Honved went 2–0 up after 14 minutes we all feared the worst. Yet Wolves fought back to win 3–2 and Billy was fantastic in the rest of that game. Wolves were a great team at the time and Billy was a real footballing centre-half, so much more than a tackler. Even at 2–0 down, and with all that had happened before, he was a great competitor, and you can see why he was England's captain for so long. You would have to be a special player to get through that, and he did.

ROGER BYRNE
(MANCHESTER UNITED)

A few years back I watched a television drama called *United* about the Busby Babes and the Munich air disaster. According to the programme, the team's captain was Mark Jones, the big centre-half. I was horrified and still cannot understand why nobody corrected that mistake when the script was being looked over. Left-back Roger Byrne was the captain of the Babes. He wasn't the greatest footballer in that team by any means, but he was a magnificent leader and one of the finest full-backs of his time, a huge part of Manchester United history.

Byrne broke into the United team in 1951 and was captain by 1953, through to his death at Munich less than five years later. In that time he also made 33 England appearances and once he got into the team was never out of it, an achievement that remains a record. He wasn't the greatest tackler, nor the best header of the ball, and he had no left foot despite playing on the left, but Byrne played full-back like a sweeper with tremendous intelligence and reading of the game. And when he had the chance he went on great forward runs, which was unusual in fifties football, when the full-back positions were often given to the least athletic members of the team. He was ahead of his time, and those who saw him regularly tell me that, among the wingers, only Peter Harris at Portsmouth was faster.

When you look back on those days, with two full-backs and one centre-half, I always wonder what would have happened if teams had started playing two up, because every club set up the same way at the back. The full-backs could not have covered because they had the wingers to deal with – but tactics weren't as big a part of the game. Byrne was ahead of his time the way he played, because of his attacking instincts. The special qualities of the lesser known members of the Babes are lost now because we tend to focus on Duncan Edwards and some of the other individuals. Players like Byrne get forgotten – but they were an extraordinary team, a magical team, and going to see them always felt like an event.

Byrne was 28 when he died, so he was more experienced than many of the boys around him, and it is a tribute to his ability, his tenacity and the way he could inspire by example that Sir Matt Busby trusted him with the leadership of the group. He was their father figure, a player with a lot of class and charisma that outweighed his technical shortcomings. I suppose only in retrospect, with the knowledge that this was one of the greatest club teams in history, do we realise how good Byrne was. At the time, of course, people weren't going to see Manchester United for the performance of the solid left-back. They wanted to watch Duncan. It seems a shame Byrne is still getting pushed into the background even now. He really deserves more credit.

DUNCAN EDWARDS
(MANCHESTER UNITED)

People always ask whether Duncan Edwards was as good as everybody says. Absolutely, he was. Bobby Charlton was a fantastic player, but he said watching Duncan made him feel inadequate. The day he died the *Daily Mirror* headline read, 'A boy who played like a man', and I think that's right. He was so young, but you would never have known it because he was the driving force of that great Manchester United team. He had it all: left foot, right foot, phenomenal balance and poise; he could dribble, he could tackle; there was 14 stone of him, strong as an ox. When he got on a run he couldn't be stopped.

He had a saying before games, apparently: 'We haven't come here for nothing.' Bobby said to me that if United were ever in trouble, the players would be thinking, 'Come on, Duncan, get us out of this.' And he'd go up and smash one in from 30 yards, straight in the corner. We'll never know what he might have achieved had he lived; he could have been England's captain in 1966, instead of Bobby Moore. He would only have been 29 then, and it is hard to see him not being in that England team.

I saw the last game the Busby Babes played in this country, a 5–4 win at Arsenal on 1 February 1958, and that would have stuck in my mind even without Munich. It was a fantastic game, such incredible quality, and the next I heard was a radio bulletin saying Manchester United's plane had crashed on the way back from Belgrade. It wasn't like today with 24-hour news stations; you had to wait until the morning paper or until it was time for the news on the radio to find out what was going on. I would have been a 10-year-old schoolboy, listening to the radio in our flat on the estate with my mum and dad. Mum always had the radio on: *The Billy Cotton Band Show*, *The Archers* and the news, and that's where I heard about Manchester United and Duncan Edwards. I remember going into school and we said prayers for them all. Everyone was very, very upset, even the teachers, and as kids it really affected us. I think we were in shock, particularly when he died, because for so long the bulletins had been positive.

Matt Busby and Duncan Edwards were recovering, they said. I kept a scrapbook and I'm sure there is a picture from a newspaper in it of Duncan sitting up in his hospital bed: he was going to be all right. Sadly, his condition worsened due to severe kidney damage, and he died. I was devastated. He was my idol.

Those early European games were an ordeal for English clubs. I have spoken to a number of players who were involved in them and they have said it could get really scary, particularly behind the Iron Curtain. The plane would be joined by MiG jets, which would escort them, often keeping them deliberately low so the flight would be skirting the top of the clouds and really bumpy. Obviously, that wasn't what caused the Munich disaster, but flying was a pretty unnerving experience in those days.

So what made Duncan special? In modern terms he was probably a defensive midfield player, but he had so much more to his game. His shot was tremendous, so much power. I remember reading that in youth tournaments for United he was so exceptional, so much better than any player on the pitch, he'd start up front, get a couple of goals and then move back to centre-half and defend the lead. He was only 18 when he made his debut for England against Scotland, yet even with so many great players around him he didn't look out of place. England won 7–2 and the age of his team-mates shows how exceptional Edwards was. Stanley Matthews played at the age of 40, Bert Williams the goalkeeper was 35, Billy Wright the captain was 31, Nat Lofthouse was 29. And there was Duncan Edwards – 18 years, 183 days, and probably better than any of them.

And it was all natural ability. Not coaching. Natural ability. Like all the best players of that time in England, Edwards worked off his instincts. There wasn't teaching as we know it now. Maybe you would get some advice from your dad or you'd go to watch your favourite players and see how they did it, but we all learnt our football the same way, on the streets, and Duncan Edwards would have been no different. There was nothing else to do but play outside, nothing for kids on TV even if you had one, so we lived our whole life playing football, and that was where you developed your skills. It was better than sitting indoors watching the potter's wheel or test card, waiting for the next programme to come on.

There was no special gear, no special boots. The young Duncan would have got home and put his slippers on – plimsolls, like you wore for gym – and gone out and played until it was time for dinner, or bed. I would say until it got dark, but even that didn't matter some days. In the winter we just ran around in the dark for as long as we could. So there was no one to tell you to play on the half-turn or how to kill a ball in mid-air. You just worked it out. My Sunday football team was taken by a couple of lovely old dockers. They wouldn't have thought to coach us or known how, really. We just played.

Even when you went to a professional club it was no different. At West Ham we trained on the forecourt, where the main entrance was. Tuesday and Thursday nights, with a few old floodlights. You never saw a pitch. If we couldn't get outside we'd go into the little gym they had under the main stand. There was just enough room to do some short passing or have a small game. And every player would be wearing slippers, just the same. It was not greatly different at Tottenham, except they had a proper big gymnasium, so had a tiny advantage over the other clubs. But the most sophisticated training we did was playing three against four; there still wasn't room for much else. Seven or eight of you would have a little game, then make way for the next group. That was it. No proper technical work. Nobody taught you how to play a position or where to run. What Duncan Edwards did would have been all his own instinct or reasoning.

Take dribbling. Running with the ball was a big part of Edwards's game, but he would have had to learn that control without coaching. No different to George Best in the 1960s, no different to all the other wingers, including me. You learnt on the streets. There might be 14 on each team, so you didn't see much of the ball. When it arrived you wanted a few touches, so you tried to keep it as long as you could by learning to run with it and beat people. Scotland had a great tradition of producing players like that – Jimmy Johnstone and Willie Henderson had a famous rivalry in the 1960s with Celtic and Rangers – and I still think nothing beats seeing a winger going on a run, just surging past people. There is a Scottish phrase – the tanner-ball player – and people now think it was a compliment, but that isn't true. The Scots used to refer to tanner-ball players because rubber balls cost a tanner and there were thousands of kids who could do anything with them. When it came to the big pitch, and a big game, with a real ball and the need for tackling, heading and intelligent positional play, they couldn't convert those skills. That's all they were – tanner-ball players. Johnstone and Henderson were a lot more than that. But every kid knew how to dribble. These days it is all passing – that's what makes players like Lionel Messi and Cristiano Ronaldo stand out – but great dribblers were 10 a penny in Duncan

Edwards's day. The ones who made it had something more. They were clever, like Duncan.

The greatest players have all got that innate, natural feel for the game. Even Messi. Yes, he came through the academy at Barcelona, but when they brought him over he was already a fantastic little dribbler who had learnt in street football in Argentina. They took one look at him, and offered him a contract written on a napkin because they had no paper to hand; but he wouldn't have been able to get a trial had he not been extra special, and that initial talent was all natural. Diego Maradona was the same. See some of the early video footage and the pitches he's playing on are horrendous, but then this little figure comes into view, playing with the ball, juggling the ball – he's tiny but the stuff he is doing is incredible. The player that I remember as a manager was Joe Cole. At the age of 11 he was like that too. He could do everything with the ball. His dad, George, had no interest, never kicked a ball in his life, never played football. So that was all Joe.

In the fifties, though, all the clubs did was assess those kids. They would organise a few sessions, a bit of passing, back and forward, side-foot, nothing too difficult, then put on a game to see who was best. Duncan Edwards took his skills to Manchester United, really – he gave them more than they gave him. I'm not saying Sir Matt Busby did not coach, but Duncan wouldn't have anywhere near the work going into him that went into Messi at La Masia. Imagine a young Edwards at Barcelona today. His talent would have been amazing. In those days, even the professional clubs had very unsophisticated regimes. A few times around the cinder track, or up and down the steps of the terraces for fitness.

I remember jogging down the Epping New Road with the West Ham team along a path with no pavement and giant lorries thundering past. If you slipped, you were dead. You'd have great players like Eddie Baily advertising cigarettes. I saw an old copy of *Charlie Buchan's Football Monthly* that said Leyton Orient had introduced a great new fitness regime involving cross-country running, and first prize for coming top at the end of the week was a set of golf balls. I've known players who would give up a £20,000 fine to get out of a hard running session.

What we know now and what we knew then, it's like two different worlds. Imagine the players now if they were sent running through the forest. Muddy and wet, slipping down hills, tripping over the roots of trees. How people didn't injure themselves, I don't know. But we all just ploughed on. Now, in a typical week you might play on Sunday because of a television commitment, so on Monday the players have a little stretch and a rub down, and the fitness coach advises you to keep it light on Tuesday because you are still getting over the game. Wednesday is a day off, so you train properly on Thursday and do fuck all again on Friday, because it's the day before you play again on Saturday. So that's one day training all week. The boys from Duncan Edwards's era wouldn't believe it. They used to play on Saturday, day off Sunday, and the manager would run the bollocks off them on Monday because he would know half of them had been out on the beer all weekend. They ran those boys like there was no tomorrow. You couldn't do that now. Players ask: 'Why are we running? What good is this going to do?' They think they are such perfect specimens. Yet none of them could live with Duncan Edwards.

DANNY BLANCHFLOWER
(TOTTENHAM HOTSPUR)

Intelligence – that's what stands out about Danny. He wasn't just a phenomenal footballer, he was a phenomenal brain. A great reader of the game, a great leader, he was the mind behind the best teams Tottenham have produced, as well as being such a clever midfield player and passer. Danny's Tottenham team did the double at the start of the 1960s, but it was being built throughout the 1950s, when he was the supreme wing-half of his generation, following the tragic demise of Duncan Edwards. Danny's brother Jackie was among the Manchester United players involved in the Munich air crash, and was so badly injured he could not resume his career.

Danny went to Tottenham from Aston Villa in 1954 and was at the peak of his powers from about 1957 onwards. He was more wiry than powerful, but could dictate the tempo of a game and was clever at finding space. He'd burst into unguarded areas and set up the centre-forward with a perfect pass, all in an instant. The best teams strike fast, and Blanchflower's speed of thought made Tottenham the fastest counter-attacking team of all. He arrived under Arthur Rowe, who retired in 1955 due to ill health, and it wasn't until Bill Nicholson came that he began to thrive. At first, they clashed and Danny was dropped; but Nicholson was an astute man and when Danny came back into the side he did so as captain and the club never looked back.

He must have been infuriating to manage at times – rearranging tactics on the field without consultation if he thought they were not working, which he did in the 1956 FA Cup semi-final, only for Tottenham to then lose 1–0 to Manchester City – but I don't think British football has ever produced a better thinker. For example, he invented the wall. You know, the wall that every team in the world now puts in front of a free-kick taker to block his shot? Danny Blanchflower thought of it first.

It was a World Cup qualifier, Northern Ireland against Italy in Rome, on 24 April 1957. Italy had a brilliant free-kick and penalty taker called Sergio Cervato, who played for Fiorentina. In those days, players just marked up from free-kicks, but Danny knew that was pointless because this guy always took a direct shot. So before the game he suggested to the manager that they put a line of players, a wall, between Cervato and the goal. The manager, Peter Doherty, didn't know what he was talking about. He thought Danny was mad. But the players listened, and did it. Italy got a free-kick after three minutes and the players all lined up in a wall. Danny told me that Italy seemed perplexed by the tactic, and so was the referee. So when Cervato picked up the ball, moved it five yards wide of the wall, turned round and shot it into the net, he gave a goal. Italy won 1–0, but Northern Ireland ended up winning the group and went to the 1958 World Cup. Danny got Footballer of the Year that season – he could have got it for that idea alone.

I was lucky enough to play against Danny for West Ham when I was a teenager. I would have been about 16, playing in the A team against Tottenham at our training ground in Chadwell Heath, and he was coming back from injury. He seemed a lovely guy, not at all aloof like the managers of the day, very approachable and down to earth. I remembered him from my time as a schoolboy, training with Tottenham in the summer and watching all the first-team players doing their tricks and showing off for us during the lunch break. We were all in awe of him. We'd go to watch the midweek European games as well, and Danny was always the star. I remember him exactly as he was against West Ham's A team that day, spraying the ball about with long passes, keeping it tight with intricate short passes; his team knew if they fed him the ball he wouldn't give it away. He had that control – the game revolved around him. His finger was on the pulse; he knew when to slow it down, when to launch a quick attack. He was just a tremendous brain; a true football intellectual.

Jimmy Greaves told me that there were occasions when Tottenham were losing and Danny would just take over at half-time. Bill Nicholson was a great manager, but he was a quiet man, whereas Danny was so confident, whatever the situation. If Bill was stuck, he would let him speak. As a manager, there are times when it just feels right to let a senior player have his say. If he's a good guy, and you know he has good ideas, there is no harm in it at all. Not every time, and not so it becomes a free-for-all; but I imagine Bill trusted Danny, and trusted him to make a positive impact. Jimmy said Blanchflower dictated the culture of the dressing-room at Tottenham and it was never vicious or negative.

Danny is responsible for one of the greatest quotes about football. 'The great fallacy is that the game is first and last about winning,' he said. 'It's nothing of the kind. The game is about glory. It is about doing things in style, with a flourish, about going out and beating the other lot, not waiting for them to die of boredom.' But there is another of his that should be equally famous. 'Winning isn't everything,' he said. 'Wanting to win is.' Nothing in the modern game makes either of those sayings less true.

We miss people like Danny because in recent years the teams have become a lot quieter. I don't believe players think about the game today the way they once did; they are not as interested in the tactics or the philosophy. That is what makes some of the pundits they have on Sky so special, the guys who work alongside my son Jamie, like Gary Neville and Jamie Carragher. They want to talk about every element of football, which so few players do – and that is why they stand out. Very few players have an awful lot to say now. I think in Danny's day a lot of the lads had more to say, a bit of personality. When I hear about the strength of character in Danny's Tottenham team, I am slightly jealous because my Tottenham team certainly wasn't like that. The dressing-room became very quiet if we were losing and no one had much to say at all. I'd never stop players making a contribution, so I don't think it was a lack of encouragement from the management – they just weren't interested.

There are exceptions in the modern game, obviously; Tony Adams, John Terry. I watched the game last season in which Chelsea won at Manchester City, and during the warm-up Terry must have held court with the rest of the players for about 10 minutes. They were going through their stretches in a big circle and he was pointing at this one and that one, really laying down the law. You could see straight away why, no matter how many times Chelsea have changed managers, he has been the captain. I imagine Adams would have been the same. And when Chelsea came out that night, they absolutely bossed City and you could see Terry's influence all over the field, in the way they went about their work. Yet there is a world of difference between carrying that message as a player and inspiring players to think about the game, or through the sheer intelligence of your words – which is what Blanchflower did. When he stopped playing he carried that conviction into his newspaper column. It isn't easy being that guy when you haven't got the ball at your feet, but Danny never stopped thinking, never stopped stating his case, even after he had retired.

BOBBY COLLINS
(EVERTON)

Right, I'm going to cheat here a little bit. Bobby Collins spans two decades as an inside-forward. He made his debut for Celtic in 1949, joined Everton in 1958 and moved to Leeds United in 1962, where he is credited with being the driving force behind the creation of Don Revie's great team. Yet that 1960s team is hard enough to pick as it is, so I'm going to find room for Bobby a decade earlier, not just for his great performances with Everton, but for what he was going to do later in his career – and also because my friend Joe Jordan would kill me if I didn't select him. Joe idolises Bobby. There was nothing of him, he was the smallest player on the pitch, but with the biggest heart and the fiercest tackle. Leeds had a production line of them under Revie – Billy Bremner and Johnny Giles were cast from the same mould. Yet Bobby was arguably the best of them all.

Most memories of Bobby focus on his fearsome physical approach. He could be brutal, and would take on players who were head and shoulders bigger than him, but there was more to

his game than just a vicious streak. He played for close to a quarter
of the century, only retiring in 1973, and no one can sustain that
career on nothing more than brute force. Yes, he was a terror, but
he was also a master of passing, shooting and ball control, the full
midfielder's repertoire. He could curl a ball from distance as well
as anyone in the game, and he was another thinker, a fine tactician
and motivator, with limitless energy and desire.

Roy Vernon, a team-mate with Everton, called Collins 'the
complete inside-forward', and there were times when his approach
seemed to teeter on the brink of madness, tearing around the
pitch as if his life depended on it. Opponents never had time on
the ball when Collins was around, yet once possession was won
he could slow the game down and dictate the play from there.
I think it sums up his ability that when Harry Catterick decided
Bobby had run his course at Everton at the age of 31, two of the
greatest managers of any era, Bill Shankly at Liverpool and Revie
at Leeds, wanted him to sign. Revie won out and Bobby helped
transform the club. Leeds were known as a team that could look
after themselves, and it was Bobby who started that.

Jack Charlton told me that the day before the FA Cup final
against Liverpool in 1965, Leeds were playing a little five-a-side
game just to warm up and Norman Hunter hit a ball which
smacked Collins in the face, making his nose bleed. It was a
complete accident, but when the game restarted, Collins flew
at Norman, caught him two-footed halfway up his leg, knocked
him over and then knelt over him throwing punches, and Jack
had to drag him off. 'Come on, Bobby,' he was shouting, 'we've
got the Cup Final tomorrow.' But that's how he was. The Leeds
players all said he could go off like a madman in an instant, yet

they respected him completely. Maybe he did rule by fear but, by God, it was effective. Few players have changed a club around the way Bobby did Leeds.

I know Sir Alex Ferguson thinks Eric Cantona was a transforming influence on Manchester United because of his standards and attitude, and I feel that about Paolo Di Canio at West Ham. One player can make a difference. Even at Bournemouth, we were never the same after Luther Blissett arrived – he had been to Italy and just introduced a new level of professionalism. That is what Collins did at Elland Road. Jack says Bobby would kill his own mum for a win – and that rubbed off on the rest of the players. Joe says he was a massive influence on all the players, particularly the young ones who became that next generation. He was just the governor. He would teach all the kids how to look after themselves on the football field, how to sort an opponent out if he was getting too cocky. Maybe that is what comes from being brought up on those Old Firm derbies. I know Bobby was a friend of Tommy Docherty, but the first time they played each other, The Doc put him in the stand. He said he knew from that moment how he would have to play to survive – and that is the knowledge he passed on. He wasn't dirty – he just taught them both sides of the game.

JOHNNY HAYNES
(FULHAM)

Johnny Haynes was the golden boy of his generation. The great inside-forward. He had this marvellous reverse pass – he'd look one way and switch the ball in the other direction, across field, out to the opposite wing. Tommy Trinder, the Fulham chairman, said he was so good he'd pay him £100 a week if he could. The maximum wage was £20 at that time. Then they got rid of it, so Johnny asked for his hundred quid. He got it, too. He was the highest paid footballer in the land – deservedly – although he could have made that twice over with AC Milan.

I would have been a baby when Johnny became a television star, playing for England Schoolboys against Scotland at the age of 15. Few people had televisions in those days, so they watched whatever was on and saw this kid in an England shirt dominating the game from the inside-left position with a range of extraordinary passing. Johnny's name was made that day. He was born in Tottenham territory, Edmonton, and supported Arsenal – but he was persuaded to join Fulham and played for them from 1952 to 1970.

It was different then and players tended to stay with the team they joined as a boy, unless the club got rid of them or took a transfer fee. You didn't think about leaving unless the manager wanted you out. Nobody thought, 'I'll sign a contract here, and then move on in three years.' There were no agents or people taking their cut to sell you. It just wasn't part of the game. I don't think many players even left to better themselves – not between clubs in the same division, anyway. It was preferable, really – because a club like Fulham could have the best inside-forward in Britain, and keep him for close to 20 years. Imagine if Wayne Rooney had come through at Fulham 10 years ago – how long would he have lasted? They couldn't even keep him at Everton. Yet, in the 1950s, Preston North End had Tom Finney, Fulham had Haynes – it made the game more interesting. I suppose the one exception in the modern era was Matt Le Tissier at Southampton. He could have left the club on a number of occasions, but had no real ambition. He just wanted to be a great footballer and play for his club. He could have gone to Tottenham, many times, and Matthew Harding, the wealthy director at Chelsea who died in a helicopter crash, used to keep a picture of him in his wallet. Signing Matt was his dream. Yet he wasn't interested. He's a bright lad and he knew exactly what he wanted; he was happy where he was.

So loyal club men were more common in Johnny's day, but Fulham knew they had to pay top wages to keep Johnny. Every club in the country would have taken him in his prime – sometimes offering promotion too, with Fulham often outside Division One – and it was just a pity that he suffered a terrible knee injury in a car crash in Blackpool in 1962 or he would surely have made Sir Alf Ramsey's World Cup-winning team in 1966. He fought his way back to play another eight seasons in the league, but never got back into the England set-up after that accident. I don't think Alf ever picked him.

Johnny wasn't one for dribbling past opponents. He beat them the modern way – with his passing. He scored plenty, too, but the goals he created were the best – for Jimmy Hill at club level and Jimmy Greaves with England. Jimmy Greaves said he was his favourite team-mate, putting him even above Sir Bobby Charlton. I know Jimmy thought Johnny was the more ambitious passer – he would pick out eye-of-the-needle through passes all the time, and goalscorers love those because it sets them up one on one against the goalkeeper – whereas Bobby would sometimes switch the play too much. Jimmy would make his run, get into the kind of position where Johnny might have tried to find him, only to see the ball from Bobby sailing over to the opposite flank. So he'd have to check his run, go out and come in again – and Jimmy didn't like running at the best of times. So he loved Johnny, always splitting the defence, finding the gap and the clever angle. Johnny could hit those long balls, too – but he was at his best finding the spaces that others didn't see, often making his best passes blind, as if telepathic. In the 1960–61 season, Johnny orchestrated a run of six England victories that accrued 40 goals. They didn't keep lists of assists in those days – but I'd guarantee his name would have been on the majority of them.

Bobby Collins was my other inside-forward and I think they would be a good blend: chalk and cheese. Bobby was a good player, but he'd sort a few out as well. Johnny wasn't like that. He didn't go around kicking people; he was just class. I've seen very few midfield players with his awareness; he seemed to know where everybody was before the ball had even arrived. He was like a quarter-back in American football. It was as if the whole game was unfolding in front of him and he was just looking to put that ball on a sixpence; except it all seemed to happen in an instant around Johnny. If you look at how a player like Toni Kroos operates for Bayern Munich, that was Johnny. He would have fitted straight into any team run by Pep Guardiola. He was like a Barcelona player, really; he would have loved tiki-taka. Nobody could get it off him when he was on his game; he would turn, play the right pass, keep it simple, get it back, go on – and then hit the killer pass that opened up the team.

People often have the debate about whether players from Haynes's era could have survived modern football, but I've no doubt about it. Johnny Haynes could have lived with anyone, in any era. I'm not so sure about the modern players surviving in his time, though. I see a lot of good athletes about today, but not so many with great ability, natural ability. Technically, I'm not sure they would have been able to deliver.

I met Johnny later on in his career, through Bobby Moore, who was a mutual friend. He used to come and have a drink with us at the Baker's Arms and was a normal fella, just one of the chaps. My dad was always excited when I said I'd been with Johnny because he absolutely loved him as a player. I played in a couple of charity games with him and saw, first-hand, how perfectly he passed the ball. He really was a different class. The clubs don't allow it now, but we seemed to play quite a lot of games for charity in those days and they could get quite competitive.

I remember one down at Margate in the sixties, and I think Johnny might have been there. We played the Lord Mayor's XI versus the Jimmy Tarbuck XI and about seven of us went down, just from West Ham. It was the day after the season ended but, even so, can you imagine that now, the manager letting seven of his team risk injury to play in some poxy charity game? It was at Hartsdown Park, where Margate play, and it was a sell-out. The Lord Mayor had all the local stars, good non-league players from Margate and Ramsgate, around that area, Jimmy had himself, a few celebrities and us. It was a fairly even game, sensible, not too competitive, but the professionals just see it as a bit of fun anyway. Even the non-league players know the score. They're up for it, but not in a silly way. Nobody was going to get injured. It's the celebrities you have to watch, though. They're always the first ones to lose it.

Sure enough, with five minutes to go, we got a penalty when Tommy Steele, the musical actor, was brought down. He picked the ball up and prepared to take it. With that, Tarbuck took the ball off him, put it on the spot and got ready to shoot. Then they started having a furious row. Tommy thought he should take the penalty because he earned it, but Jimmy got the last word. 'Tom, have a look at the programme,' he said, deadly serious. 'It says Jimmy Tarbuck XI – that's me.' And he took the ball and scored. At the end of the match, Tommy stormed into the dressing-room, snatched his clothes off the peg and took off with the raging hump. 'Don't ever ask me to play again,' he said as he left. I'm told he didn't speak to Tarbuck for ages. They fell out like you wouldn't believe. All over a silly penalty in a charity match. Mind you, it could have been worse. Driving back from Margate after a good night out, Bobby Moore's car ended up on the top of a roundabout. He missed the junction completely. I must have still had my wits about me, though. I knew something was wrong when one minute I was following his rear lights, and the next his headlights were facing me.

STANLEY MATTHEWS
(BLACKPOOL)

When Matthews came to town, you'd want to go. Simple as that. He could fill a stadium, almost on his own, even at the age of 50. To play at that age is incredible, particularly on the wing, but I think it says most about the way the game has changed. Ryan Giggs has played for Manchester United into his forties, which is an amazing achievement, but he has had to move into central midfield. The game was so much easier for wingers then because the tactics and athleticism were not so advanced. If you watch the old footage, the ball comes out to Stan on the wing and he would start taking it forward, almost jogging with it, as if there was an obstacle in the distance ahead. Suddenly, after about five seconds, into the picture comes the left-back to meet him. Now he'd jockey, just jockey, concede ground, go backwards and Stan would run the ball up to him. Now the left-back has to take a gamble, he'd lunge at the ball with a slide tackle and Stan would just flick it over his foot and go past him. And that was him gone, out of the game, while Stan was on his way to the byline to pick out a cross – it was always the same. And don't get me wrong, he was brilliant at it. If Stan had to adapt to modern football, I'm sure he would – yet these days he'd be confronted with a left-back who is faster than any winger and as soon as the wide player came near him – bosh! In the 1950s, full-backs played like sweepers and had to cover a swing of 50 yards. So Matthews, Finney and the rest had all the time in the world. Full-backs could even be slow. It's incredible to think of it now, but if you didn't have a lot of pace, they would stick you at full-back. That is probably the biggest change in modern football. The pace at the back.

I think Matthews in the modern era would have had to change his game. Wingers cannot simply stay wide these days because every coach has worked that one out. A player as important as Stan would be confronted with specific defensive tactics. He'd be marked. Not by the full-back, by an extra player. As soon as he got the ball, that player would have been on him. I saw it happen to Gareth Bale at Tottenham; when clubs see an individual is so important, they double up. That is why we had to move him inside or switch flanks. I'm sure it was happening to Stan by the end. He played with Stoke City until 1965, so I am certain by then he was not being allowed to carry the ball into space without pressure. He was 50, too, and I think they used to water the pitches quite heavily at the Victoria Ground to slow the game down for him. As a winger of the time, I might be biased, but I think that period in the sixties was the hardest for the wide men. The game was changing, with quicker full-backs, but you got little protection from the fiercest tackles. So Liverpool had Tommy Smith, who was fast, but was also allowed to kick you without the referee being greatly interested. I would have lost a lot of money to a friend of mine who said Smith only got sent off once in his career. I put it at eight or nine, but when we looked it up he was right: just the once. The tactics had changed, although they weren't particularly complicated. See that quick bastard with the ball – as he goes past, kick him. If they had thought of it sooner, maybe Stan wouldn't still have been turning out so late in life.

Yet, despite the limitations of defensive play in that era, the bottom line remains: if Stan came to your town, you would pay to see him play. Always. My team was Arsenal and I reckon Stanley Matthews in a Blackpool shirt used to put 10,000 on the gate at Highbury – he often drew the biggest crowd of the season. We're spoiled now. We see the best players every week, on television. In those days, to coin a phrase used by American sports writers – if you don't go, you don't know. It's one of those feelings of excitement that football has lost in the all-seater era. Now, you have your ticket, row P seat 47, and if you haven't booked it weeks in advance for a big match you'll be lucky to get one. Back then, you might play for the school team on Saturday morning and then you and a few lads would get together and decide which game to go to. You didn't need an advance ticket, there wasn't segregation. If Matthews was playing at Tottenham, or Tom Finney at Arsenal, that made your mind up.

I was too young to remember the 1953 FA Cup final – the Matthews final as it was called – but I think we had just got a television set in our flat. It had a tiny 9-inch screen with a magnifying glass hooked on with a couple of big army belt straps to make it into a 12-inch. We'd sit there looking at nothing most days, and there was about 30 minutes between each programme, but the FA Cup final was always the highlight. One match a year wasn't much to keep you entertained, though, so if you wanted to see Stan it had to be at the game, in the flesh.

And everyone wanted to see Stan. He was such a big star he even had his own brand of football boots – made by the Co-op in a factory in Heckmondwike, West Yorkshire. Very few players did endorsements in those days – one was Johnny Haynes, who was the frontman for Brylcreem – but to advertise kit was something unique. The Co-op made one million pairs of Stanley Matthews boots between 1948 and 1964. Sportswear wasn't really a commodity in the fifties. There were no replica shirts and when they did come out in the late sixties, it was only a plain shirt that you sewed a badge on, so Nottingham Forest, Liverpool and Manchester United all had one shirt and the difference was the club emblem, which came separately. Even the players bought their boots and shin pads from local sports shops – in West Ham's case it was A. E. Sedgwick's in Forest

Road, Walthamstow. The club had an account and the players used that. You had one pair of boots, which came with a packet of studs – maybe two pairs once rubber and moulded studs came in – and if you didn't like the boots the club provided you had to pay the difference. It didn't matter who you were. If Bobby Moore's boots amounted to a quid more than the allowance, it came out of his pocket. If you lost your boots, you had to buy a new pair, and no excuses. You couldn't just go in and say your kit had been stolen – you still got the cost deducted from your salary at the end of that week. And nobody swapped shirts. They'd have killed you. Your kit was your kit and you would try to hang on to it, tie-ups and all.

I don't think players now realise what it was like in those days. It didn't matter who you were – even Stanley Matthews would have had to pitch in and help with the skip containing the team's kit. When West Ham played away, we'd all dump our stuff in the skip and get on a minibus from Upton Park, driven to one of the big stations by Stan, the assistant manager. It was an old vehicle, not some long, luxurious air-conditioned coach, and often there would be two basket skips – one for boots, one for kit. Now, there is container after container full of gear wherever you go because every player travels with five pairs of boots. It's like moving an army – quite incredible. In those days all the players would be squeezed around the two skips in the bus, and whenever Stan stopped sharp the bloody things would fall on your head or your foot. At the station all the players helped with the skips, pushing them along the platform, and then you'd have to give a hand loading it on and off the train. Some clubs would leave the shifting to the reserves – particularly in the days before substitutes. You travelled with extra players in case of unforeseen injuries, meaning the directors had to pay any win bonus to everybody in the 13-man squad. They didn't like that, so for your two quid – the win bonus, which you might not get – you were given the job of carrying the skip. Even if Stanley Matthews was coming back from injury and wasn't in the team that day it would have been no different. In the days of maximum wages, nobody would have complained. That extra money would come in handy – even for a player who could put 10,000 on the gate.

TOM FINNEY
(PRESTON NORTH END)

Every era throws up its greats, from Lionel Messi and Cristiano Ronaldo to Tom Finney and Stanley Matthews. I'll lean on my old man here, and say Finney for me. Dad was Finney mad. If he was in town he went to see him play and I was lucky enough to see him at his peak playing centre-forward for Preston against Arsenal one night. What a player. I think it was his versatility that shades it over Stan. Matthews was a right-sided winger, and one of the best, but his left foot was weak and his heading ordinary – Finney could do the lot. He could play wide on either flank or through the middle. Tommy Docherty still says he's the best he's ever seen, and Bill Shankly said he would have been great, even playing in an overcoat. I know some who watched football in that era compare him to Messi, and that's good enough for me. These days players are defined by what they win – they have to be with a Champions League team, have to have a cupboard full of medals, yet Finney never won a single trophy with Preston and is still regarded as an all-time great. We set different standards for success then. He played in a team that couldn't win anything, but that never counted against him. He was still the best – and everybody acknowledged that. He was in the England team, he was revered – we seem to have lost touch with such qualities as a measure of success. Now it's all medals, medals, medals. Adam Lallana and Luke Shaw have a good year for Southampton and suddenly people are saying, 'When are they going to leave for a proper club?' – just as they used to about Matt Le Tissier. As if no club is proper unless it's up the top. Preston had one of the finest, most versatile, footballers in the world – but that couldn't happen today.

Finney learnt to play by dribbling around lamp-posts while doing his newspaper round. He used to go to Preston's ground as a schoolboy for coaching and free milk. His hero was Alex James, a Scottish inside-forward who spent four years with Preston before leaving for Arsenal. I think kids now try to imitate something they see Ronaldo or Messi do, but it was different for us because everything happened in real time. We didn't have TV and slow-motion replays; we couldn't watch every detail of a drag-back or a trick. You were there, Finney got the ball and he was away – you'd have to have great eyes and fantastic memory to see how he pulled it off. The exception was the FA Cup final, but even then you wouldn't imitate the players – just the teams. As soon as the game ended, all the kids would be out and we'd be pretending to be Manchester United, say, or Aston Villa. That day was the highlight of the year – but Finney only got to one FA Cup final, in 1954, and

Preston lost 3–2 to West Bromwich Albion. I was only seven so I can't really say I remember it, but I know that Finney didn't play well. He spent the night before the game receiving the award for Footballer of the Year in London before travelling back to Preston's base in Weybridge, so maybe that explains it. That ceremony is more sensibly held on the Thursday before the FA Cup final now – and these days if the winner is playing on the Sunday, his manager will make sure he collects his prize and goes home. Players were not protected the same way in those days. On the back of a week of interviews and photographic sessions – and no doubt a few hundred calls from old friends wanting tickets – the last thing Finney would have needed is a late night and more glad-handing. No wonder he played as if exhausted; being Preston's most famous son would have weighed heavily on him that week.

Finney was another that could add numbers to the gate, but when you were walking to the ground you had no idea where he was going to be playing, so there was always extra excitement. I think the most incredible thing about that time was that England lost to the United States in the 1950 World Cup. When you look at the players in the team that day: Finney, Stan Mortensen, Billy Wright, Jimmy Dickinson, Wilf Mannion … it is quite incredible. They left Matthews out, and he couldn't get on because there were no substitutes. Can you imagine the outcry about that result now? They would be saying that England should never pick those players again.

Yet Finney remained loved. What made him special? I think, basically, he had such elegance, such poise and grace – and his personality reflected the way he played the game. It wasn't just that he never got booked – nobody did in those days; you had to almost kill someone for the referee to take your name. What set Finney apart is that few can remember him even being spoken to by a referee. He was never in trouble, always the gentleman. Amazingly, he didn't even begin his professional career until he was 24 because the Second World War intervened, but the impact he made kept Preston as a First Division club through much of his career. They were relegated after he retired and have never played in the top division without him.

Even Matthews idolised Finney. In his autobiography he placed him beside four others: Pelé, Diego Maradona, George Best and Alfredo Di Stefano. In one game he played for England, the Portuguese captain Alvaro Cardaso walked off the field and demanded to be replaced because he was so tired of being given the runaround by Tom. England won 10–0. Not only could he play wide or up front, Finney also converted to the deep lying centre-forward position in some games, once England had seen the Hungarians playing it. He was voted Footballer of the Year for his performances there in 1957 – the first person to win the award twice. He scored 27 goals from that position in one season, and 26 the following year. And he was brave. Bill Shankly described him as a player that would go through a mountain; and for all the reports of his fanciness on the wing, his opponents say he tackled as hard as any defender. It says everything that the moment he retired, Preston began falling through the league, never to return. It would be no insult to call him a one-man team – and he would have been that at a lot of clubs bigger than Preston, too.

JOHN CHARLES
(LEEDS UNITED)

King John, they called him. I've got him ahead of Stan Mortensen in my team. Mortensen was a wonderful striker, still the only player to score a hat-trick in an FA Cup final, for Blackpool against Bolton Wanderers in 1953. Yet John's versatility sets him apart. He could play centre-forward, he could play centre-half. He was a hero in the English game, then he became a legend in Italy with Juventus. Mortensen was one of the great goalscorers in the English game – but Charles was that, and more. He may have been the best all-round footballer to have come out of Britain.

What people most remember about John is his strength in the air. He was a classic gentle giant – that was what they called him in Italy, 'Il Buon Gigante' – a lovely man away from the football pitch, but a monster on it, fearless and strong, a real powerhouse. He was always the best in the penalty area, and at either end. There wasn't a better player in the team to defend a corner, and not a better player to attack one either. Yet he went to Italy, where the game was more technical and tactical, and fitted straight in; he had a very high level of skill for a player his size. He started off in defence at Leeds United, but they moved him to the front line in the 1952–3 season. They spotted there was more to his game than just heading and physicality. He had a lovely first touch that was wasted playing at the back in those days. So they changed him and he scored 26 goals in his first season as a striker. The next year he was the Football League's top scorer.

He was a prolific goalscorer for Leeds, but it was after seeing him play for Wales against Northern Ireland in 1957 that Umberto Agnelli, the president of Juventus, took him to Italy. Players didn't have agents in those days, but Kenneth Wolstenholme, the commentator for the 1966 World Cup, acted on John's behalf in the deal. He got a £10,000 signing-on fee – when the limit in England was £10. Italy felt like another world in those days, let alone another country. By then, Italian coaches had discovered *catenaccio* – man-for-man marking – and it was very hard to score over there. Yet John played 155 games for Juventus and scored 93 goals, an incredible achievement. The most amazing aspect of it is that he often spent half the game in defence. If John gave Juventus the lead, they would often then move him to centre-half to shore up the game. Manchester United would do that with Duncan Edwards, too, but in youth matches, not Serie A, arguably the strongest league in the world at the time. For this reason, John was considered by many the best player in the world. His transfer was a world record fee and, even recently, I saw he was still voted the best foreign player at Juventus – ahead of Michel Platini and Zinedine Zidane.

How good was he? Well, Nat Lofthouse said he was the best defender he played against, and Billy Wright said he was the best striker he ever faced. He managed to be incredibly delicate on the ball, and devastating in a shoulder charge a minute later. Jack Charlton called him a one-man team, the most effective player he ever saw. There were others from that era who might have been more skilful, but none who could do a job for the team like Charles. I know Jack also said John didn't close his eyes when he headed the ball. That usually happens automatically, but his stayed open. He was 6 ft 2 in anyway, but had such a leap that his chest was often resting on the shoulders of the defender when he scored.

And a gentleman? How about this? An Italian friend of mine says that John is alone in being as admired by supporters of Torino as Juventus. In his first Turin derby game, he bustled past a Torino defender but accidentally caught the player with a trailing arm and laid him out. No foul was given, but John saw what had happened and kicked the ball out of play for him to be treated, even though he was clean through on goal. The rival fans have never forgotten that gesture. My friend says that 20 years after John had left Italy they were still using one of his goals in the introduction of Italy's equivalent of *Match of the Day*.

Despite playing at centre-half John never got a booking throughout his career. It was a brutal game back then, particularly in Italy. John thought a lot of the tackling powder puff compared to England, but there were some real nasty sorts. He played with a little Argentinian forward called Omar Sívori, who was a great player, the nearest thing to Diego Maradona in those days, and in one game a centre-half did John with his elbow. So the next time the ball was loose, Sívori went over the top and broke the guy's leg. As he hit him, the other centre-half came in and snapped Sívori in two. So both players are on the floor, screaming, with King John in the middle of it, completely bemused. He could look after himself on the pitch – everyone had to in those days – but he was never dirty or gratuitous. Giampiero Boniperti was his other forward partner, and did a lot of his dirty work. If John got kicked he would turn to his team-mate. 'You do something to them – I can't,' he would say.

I think the one thing all of the players in my Fifties XI have in common is that they were also great fellas. Down to earth, all of them, and not flash, despite their incredible ability. I know the media coverage was different and the money, too, but they were connected with the people, they mixed with the fans – they weren't up the West End spending £300 on bottles of champagne. I can remember meeting John Charles at a party in, of all places, a block of flats in Canning Town. He was mates with Ken Brown and John Bond and had come up from the West Country with them – and there he was, the colossus of Italian football, one of the greatest players in the world, just having a beer at a house party in East London. My friend Frank McDonald reminded me of it the other day. Another time, I was down at Swansea City with Bournemouth for a youth game, and he was there. It was a miserable night, teeming down with rain, but he came over and had a cup of tea and a chat. Footballers belonged to the people then. Better, wasn't it?

THE FIFTIES: THE TEAM

**BERT
TRAUTMANN**

Manchester City

**ALF
RAMSEY**

Tottenham
Hotspur

**BILLY
WRIGHT**

Wolverhampton
Wanderers

**DUNCAN
EDWARDS**

Manchester
United

**ROGER
BYRNE**

Manchester
United

**DANNY
BLANCHFLOWER**

Tottenham
Hotspur

**BOBBY
COLLINS**

Everton

**JOHNNY
HAYNES**

Fulham

**STANLEY
MATTHEWS**

Blackpool

**TOM
FINNEY**

Preston North End

**JOHN
CHARLES**

Leeds United

CHAPTER TWO

··

THE SIXTIES

I was fortunate to spend the sixties working for one of the greatest football minds this country has ever produced: Ron Greenwood. It is no exaggeration to say that Ron changed the game in England, and his influence went right through it, from the day-to-day training at clubs to that magnificent afternoon in 1966 when England won the World Cup. I remember watching that game, and all of England's matches through that tournament in fact, and was able to pinpoint the moves and tactics that were straight from the Chadwell Heath training ground of my club, West Ham United. This is taking nothing away from Sir Alf Ramsey, but there were three West Ham players on the pitch that day in July, including the captain Bobby Moore, and it showed. West Ham fans like to boast, only half tongue-in-cheek, that their club won the World Cup – but in a way we did. The passes that Bobby played into Geoff Hurst, Martin Peters's near-post runs, the way the full-backs overlapped – those ideas came straight from West Ham's famous academy. People talk about master coaches in football and I'll be frank and say I haven't seen too many; but Ron was among the few. I signed for West Ham straight out of school when I was 15, and I knew right away it was a special club with different ideas because of Ron.

We had just left an era when the technical side of the game was almost disparaged by many managers. There were some great players, of course, but it was as if they were left alone to sort out their problems. Some managers had a terrible attitude. Don't give them the ball – they'll want it more on Saturday. They thought coaching was running a team around a cinder track or up and down the steps of the terraces, and no sooner had I joined West Ham when the apprentices were packed off to Lilleshall in Shropshire, which was the Football Association's national training centre. About 13 of us went from West Ham, plus hundreds of other good kids from clubs all around the country. I was put in a group run by Johnny Hart, who had been a top-quality inside-forward with Manchester City, and whose son Paul went on to be a very good footballer and manager, too. We would train and then have practice matches against the other groups. The first time we played, I got the ball from one of our midfield players and then motioned to him to come round me on the overlap. I did it with the full-backs as well. 'Come past me,' I said, 'and we'll go two on one against them.' Jack Mansell, who played as a defender for Brighton and Hove Albion, Cardiff City and Portsmouth, was in charge of this session. He blew the whistle and stopped it. 'What are you doing, son?' he asked. 'What are you doing there?'

I'd been at West Ham for five weeks, pre-season. I don't know where Ron had got it from, whether he came up with the idea himself or had seen an innovation abroad, but he had arrived back that summer, 1963, with a whole new approach to wide play. Before, when the winger had the ball, he was on his own and it was up to him to get past his man and cross. It was one versus one, you against him – and if the opponent was better or quicker than you, the move broke down. Ron didn't like those odds. We spent the entire month pre-season working on overlapping play; the midfield player coming round the winger, the full-back bolting upfield to receive the pass on the inside. The plan was to double up on the opposition's wide defender. As he went towards the winger, the ball would be played to the overlapping full-back or midfielder – he couldn't keep an eye on both of them, and his team-mates would not know what was about to happen so would not offer sufficient support. All of West Ham's wide players – John Sissons and Trevor Dawkins, too – were being schooled that way. But I didn't realise what we were doing was so different, until I went to Lilleshall. Alf Ramsey had come nearest to changing the full-back role at Ipswich Town, but Ron was taking wing play in a new and radical direction. Everything we were doing at West Ham was designed to create two versus one. That night at Lilleshall the coaches had a meeting. The following day, every one of their coaching sessions worked on overlapping wide play. It was if the penny had dropped – they had seen the future. That was Ron Greenwood's doing.

Danny Blanchflower invented the wall at free-kicks, Dick Fosbury invented the Fosbury Flop that revolutionised the high-jump technique by flipping over backwards, and Ron Greenwood laid the ground for the wonderful overlapping full-backs we see today. He changed the game, committed defenders in ways others had not imagined. He was always thinking, always one step ahead. The way England got Hurst and Peters to get across defenders at the near post – I would credit Ron for that. The goals that England scored in 1966 were no accident. I used to watch Ron work for hours with the pair of them – when to pull away, how to time the return run. The old way was to wait behind the defender and try to out-jump him. It was Ron who wanted them getting across the face of the marker into that near-post area. And then you see Bobby Moore put the ball down, Hurst come across and – bam. Maybe Ron was too easy with the lads and that was why West Ham did not experience the success they deserved in that time – but he was always forward thinking, a true football brain and a fantastic coach.

I don't want to be disrespectful to modern coaches – after all, I've been one – but having worked with Greenwood and seen how clever he was and how much impact his ideas had, I get a bit sceptical when I hear that this one or that one is so great. I have thought that way ever since I left West Ham – after my very first move as a player, down to Bournemouth with John Bond. John had a fantastic reputation as a coach at the height of his career, but anyone from West Ham who saw him work first-hand would have known straight away that most of what he did was taken from Ron. Every ex-West Ham player was influenced by him, including me. Ron was a visionary. In that era, much of the coaching was ordinary. Clubs all did the same stuff, with a sprinkling of the manager's personality on top. It is a bit like that now. One coach plays 4–2–3–1, then the whole world plays 4–2–3–1. Ron wasn't like that. These were original ideas, innovative and insightful. A lot of what Ron did stands up today: how to make a yard, the areas to target with the ball, the movement in the box. John Bond took Ron's ideas, but added a bit of discipline. You couldn't get away with stuff under John as you could with Ron. But the rest of it, the technical side, the nuts and bolts – nothing changed. I'm not ashamed to admit that I still use lessons from Ron Greenwood today.

Alf Ramsey made the bold decision to pick Geoff Hurst for the World Cup final ahead of Jimmy Greaves, but it was Ron Greenwood who turned Geoff from an average midfield player into a fantastic striker. Ron taught him his movement, so that as soon as Bobby Moore put the ball down his first thought was, 'Where's Geoff? Is he switched on? Is he ready?' We all know what used to happen next. The same with Martin Peters. He was famously described as being 10 years ahead of his time, but it was Ron, as much as Martin, who was a decade in front.

Looking ahead for a moment, one of the sensations of English football in the seventies was Ted MacDougall at Bournemouth, who ended up signing for Manchester United. He still holds the record for individual scoring in the FA Cup – nine goals in a tie for Bournemouth against Margate in 1971 – and in season 1970–71 he had 16 league goals by October. The goal that might have clinched his move to the top division was a spectacular diving header away to Aston Villa. They were a Third Division team at the time, but there were still 48,000 at Villa Park and the game was shown on *Match of the Day*. Everyone was talking about it, but it was a textbook Ron Greenwood/West Ham goal from years earlier. MacDougall played the ball out to Tony Scott and then got across his defender for a magnificent diving header from Scott's right-sided cross. I immediately knew where I had seen that move before. In fact, when I went down to play for

Bournemouth in 1972, it was like stepping back in time. John Bond would be there with Ted, 'Pull away, pull away, pull away, take them away with you. You are pulling away and now they are backing off you. Now you can get in front of them.' I thought Ron Greenwood had followed me down. John was like his echo.

Football was much more open in the sixties; and less predictable. I can remember when I was still an apprentice professional West Ham had back-to-back matches against Blackburn Rovers. They played at home on 26 December 1963 and away at Ewood Park two days later, 28 December. The Boxing Day game ended West Ham 2, Blackburn 8; two days on, the score was Blackburn 1, West Ham 3. Work that out. The only change Ron made between the games was that he brought Eddie Bovington in for Martin Peters and used him as a man marker. That was unheard of, too, in those times. The Italians had invented *catenaccio*, but nobody in English football used it.

People remember the sixties as an era of brutality in football, but it never felt that way playing in it. We knew no different. A player brought up in today's game would be appalled, but that was just how the game was played as far as we were concerned. Looking back, the sheer physicality of it does surprise me now, particularly when you consider the consequences of injury. A broken leg could end a career, yet people still took that risk every week, flying into tackles or in some cases trying to inflict serious harm. It is amazing there weren't more bad injuries, really – not least because the physiotherapists were usually unqualified ex-players. A bloke would come out, put a sponge on your leg and that was the extent of his knowledge done. No one complained. We didn't know any different, we just got on with it. There were no agents to stir up a fuss. Contract negotiation was non-existent. The manager called you into his office and gave you another £2 a week and you went home delighted. Nobody asked for a fiver, and it didn't matter who you were – at West Ham, even Bobby Moore got the same cold treatment as the rest of the team. You made your appointment to see the manager at the end of the season and were usually in and out in two minutes. It wasn't a negotiation as such. These days a player sits down to discuss his contract with the club and three months later they're still talking. Back then the deal got signed that minute, or forget it. You could count on the fingers of one hand the players who acted up. When a teenage Graeme Souness asked to leave Tottenham Hotspur, and told Bill Nicholson he was the best player at the club, it caused a real stir. Players just didn't talk like that to the manager in those days.

The game was harder then, but it certainly wasn't faster. There was more space about, too, with players dropping off. Now pressing has come into the game and everybody is on you at 100 mph. The balls are lighter, the boots are lighter, there is more speed in football; players run faster, jump higher. You see the difference in what players could get away with back then, though. Games would finish 10–10 on penalties these days, looking at some of the things the referees let go. I was watching the 1970 FA Cup final replay the other day between Chelsea and Leeds United, and how that was still 11-a-side by the end I'll never know. There is one moment when Peter Osgood comes in from behind on Jack Charlton, and Jack just turns around and kicks him as hard as he can. Nothing sly, no pretence – and not even a booking for either of them. There is another incident when Eddie McCreadie catches Billy Bremner in the throat – no exaggeration – with a tackle and the referee waves play on. It wasn't just the Leeds team that knew how to look after itself.

It was Bobby Collins that instilled that attitude in them – if somebody is going to get hurt it won't be us – and then Bremner and Johnny Giles carried it forward. Not every team had a nasty streak, but most had one or two players who could put it about, and no matter how high you went in, Leeds would always go higher. Even so, my favourite team from that era? Leeds, without a doubt. I think that hard edge has led to them being underestimated. Take that away and, as footballers, they were a perfect balance; from the full-backs, Paul Reaney and Terry Cooper, through the centre-halves, Jack Charlton and Norman Hunter, to the midfield with Giles and Bremner who were rock solid. Then there was Peter Lorimer with his rocket shot, Eddie Gray, a genius on the wing, and Mick Jones working non-stop for Alan Clarke up front. That team just had a lovely feel. And, yes, they were tough. I imagine they had to be – you wouldn't have survived training with that lot if you couldn't look after yourself. But once on the pitch they were as one, I've never seen a team so unified. Hurt one, and you had to deal with the whole mob.

Yet anyone who thinks they were one-dimensional, all aggression without the technique to match, didn't see them play. There is a famous game against Southampton that they won 7–0, and some of the football that day was quite magnificent. Little flicks, wonderful crossfield passes, glorious goals. And that was a useful Southampton side – Jimmy Gabriel, Denis Hollywood, John McGrath, Ron Davies; they had some hard men who wouldn't have taken kindly to being made to look like fools.

Denis Hollywood was a Scottish full-back and a real handful. I remember Jimmy Gabriel telling me he had a fancy-dress party around his house one Sunday afternoon and Denis came dressed as a schoolboy. He had a drink then for some reason decided he wanted to cycle to his home about seven miles away with his little school uniform and cap on. Halfway there some bloke cut him up. Denis pedalled like a maniac, caught him at the lights and dragged him out of his car into the street. Unbelievable. The bloke must have thought they had some tough schools in Southampton.

Yet that was the culture of football at the time. There were good players and good teams but also a pub mentality that didn't really leave English football until the influx of the foreign players. From the great Liverpool team to the World Cup-winning England team and the King's Road lot at Chelsea, just about every club liked a night out. Most of the teams were made up of local boys and they all got on great. At West Ham we mucked in together and roughed it when we had to. I remember the terrible winter in 1963, clearing the snow off the forecourt at Upton Park with the rest of the players so we could train. Job done, we would play on it for two hours in silly little plimsolls, sliding everywhere. These days, the medical staff would have conniptions about the damage you could do to your calf muscles – but nobody knew, or cared, about that side of the game then. Even Bobby Moore trained on the forecourt at Upton Park. I remember as a junior we had to wait for the main group to finish, sitting inside looking through the steamed-up windows because all the training pitches were under snow. It was a terrible winter; our first team played one game – away at Sheffield United – between December 29 and March 2. It was either the forecourt or up and down the steps in the stand just to keep our fitness up – until Ron found a little gymnasium in Harlow in Essex.

We drove out there, which seemed like miles, in the worst winter ever, snow all over, and we were slipping and falling over because the gym only had a little wooden floor. We'd play four-a-side – there was no room for anything else – then do some ball skills until it was time to let the next lot on. Eventually we found a place in Forest Gate that took eight-a-side – and we all thought that was luxury compared to the slog out to Harlow. These days, if a training pitch isn't like Wembley, the players complain. Modern players moan about everything. They'll walk into a room with £200,000 of equipment and find some fault to pick at – no bananas in the fruit bowl or the temperature isn't right. We used to spend a month running through forests, dodging cars on the Epping New Road. That was our pre-season. Get back on the coach with everybody cramping up. Nobody had heard of stretching exercises. We didn't even warm up. The first time we saw the pitch was when the bell went to signal two minutes before kick-off. We might take the odd shot against the goalkeeper if we were feeling adventurous. There was no such thing as a warm-up. We thought a warm-up was standing by the radiator in the dressing-room on a cold day.

That doesn't mean there weren't some wonderful players about in that time, though. Here's 11 of them.

GORDON BANKS
(LEICESTER CITY)

I know there has been a lot of revisionism of late about That Save. But for my money, it's still one of the most amazing things I have seen on a football field, and it sets Gordon Banks apart from his contemporaries. There were some great goalkeepers from that era – Peter Bonetti, Pat Jennings, the young Peter Shilton, who played his first game for Leicester City as Gordon's understudy in 1966 – but even without winning the World Cup for England, I'd say Gordon was the man. And That Save, from Pelé at the 1970 World Cup? Even now, I don't know how he does it.

Brazil versus England, 7 June 1970, Guadalajara. Carlos Alberto breaks down the right and feeds the ball to Jairzinho, who skins Terry Cooper, gets to the byline and crosses. Pelé jumps higher than anybody from about 10 yards out and heads the ball downwards into the bottom-left corner. Somehow, Banks scrambles across and, with his right hand, scoops the ball up and over the bar, even though it appears to be behind him. 'The save of the World Cup,' David Coleman calls it, immediately. I watched it again, recently, and none of the England players even make a fuss, though. And that is what is special about Gordon. That type of brilliance was almost expected of him. Pelé, I'm told, actually shouted, 'Goal!' Banks says that the only comment was from Bobby Moore, who told him he must be getting old. 'You used to hang on to those, Gordon,' he said.

The greatest save of all time, as some have called it. Who can say for certain? Double saves always look the most spectacular. Jim Montgomery for Sunderland against Leeds United in the

1973 FA Cup final, or Jerzy Dudek for Liverpool against AC Milan in that epic 2005 Champions League win. Colombian goalkeeper René Higuita's scorpion kick from a shot by my son Jamie against England at Wembley must take the prize for sheer panache, but what Gordon does stands out because it is so matter-of-fact, yet so remarkable. He tracks the ball all the way over from right to left, so is just in the perfect place when Pelé makes his header. The ball bounces in front of him, making it awkward, but Banks adjusts and uses the upward momentum to push it even higher to safety. Everything happens in a split second, and looks so instinctive, but there is incredible wisdom there, the sight of a man who has worked so hard to master his craft making the exceptional look easy. I've seen Peter Schmeichel make great saves with his star jumps learnt in handball games in Denmark, but there the ball strikes his arm. Gordon's save is no accident. He is completely aware of where he must be and what he must do, from beginning to end. Maybe other factors have helped it live in the memory, too: it was a wonderful game, in a brilliant World Cup against the best team, and player, there has ever been. It was the first World Cup in colour, too, and we were all watching. Yet even discounting this, there is one unarguable fact: Pelé wrote in his autobiography that it was the best save anyone had made from him. And he would know.

Gordon came from a generation that didn't have the support system of modern footballers. He was a coalman's mate and a bricklayer before being spotted by Chesterfield – and was once let go by an amateur club after letting in 15 goals in one game. He could only turn professional after doing two years' national service with the Royal Signals Regiment. Yet he stood out from the start and only had one full season at Chesterfield before Leicester City signed him for £7,000. One game in particular stands out, the 1963 FA Cup semi-final: Leicester City 1, Liverpool 0. I think the official figures are that Liverpool had 34 shots at goal to Leicester's one. Gordon says it was the best performance of his career. He made his debut for England that same year. He lost his first game against Scotland and I know he thought his second would be his last, because Sir Alf Ramsey gave him such a bollocking for conceding a 30-yard free-kick from Pelé. By the time 1966 came around he was the best in the world. Gordon didn't let in a goal from open play in that tournament until the final. Before that, he had only been beaten from the penalty spot, by Eusébio.

What happened after 1966 seems incredible, even by the crazy standards of football clubs. Within eight months of winning the World Cup, Leicester put Gordon on the transfer list. They had this young kid called Shilton and they fancied him more. These were the days when teams couldn't just use the loan system as they do now. If that situation occurred these days, Shilton would merely be loaned out to get experience. Back then, Leicester had a decision to make. They had arguably the best two English goalkeepers of all time – and they went with youth.

Ron Greenwood at my club, West Ham United, was in the market for a goalkeeper that year, too. He paid £65,000 for a lad called Bobby Ferguson from Kilmarnock when he could have got Banks for less. Ferguson became the world's most expensive goalkeeper at the time. Gordon went to Stoke City for £50,000. I'm told Ron didn't fancy his wages, which were £50 a week higher than Bobby's – but it seems a strange decision looking back. Bobby was a good young goalkeeper but he was no Gordon Banks. And he can't have been much bigger than 5 ft 10 in. Gordon went on to make more fantastic saves for Stoke – and he cost me a Wembley appearance in the 1972 League Cup final.

There were no penalty shoot-outs to decide cup ties in those days – we played until we dropped, replay after replay, and our tie with Stoke lasted four matches and a total of seven hours. We were hot favourites to go through. Tony Waddington had built a good Stoke team, but a lot of the players were experienced – a nice football term that is a polite way of saying old – and we won the first leg at their place 2–1. Bobby Moore was magnificent that night and Geoff Hurst scored our first goal from the penalty spot. Geoff only had one penalty style. Blast it towards the top corner out of the goalkeeper's reach. Gordon got his fingers to it, but could not keep it out. I made our second goal for Clyde Best from the left wing. We were halfway to Wembley. The second leg was played on 15 December 1971, and Stoke scored late in the second half to level the tie on aggregate. For the last minutes of the game we were all over them. I was getting round their full-back Mike Pejic and, sensing danger, Gordon came out and bundled me over. Penalty. Up stepped Geoff again. If he scored we would be 3–2 up with seconds remaining and on our way to Wembley. I don't think the penalty was as good as his first, but it would still have beaten 99 per cent of goalkeepers. Not Gordon. It wasn't quite where the last one had gone, but he adjusted in mid-air and got both hands to it. We couldn't believe it. Gordon told me that was the best penalty save of his career – it turns out that our £50 a week wasn't such a saving after all.

As a winger, your first priority was always to keep the ball away from Gordon. He was very athletic, very determined. He had a strong mind and he made it up early, so anything in his radius he could come and collect. That was always Ron Greenwood's instruction to me: corners, crosses, keep it away from Banks. He was brave too, quick off his line and not scared about getting hurt. Goalkeepers had more protection then than in the fifties, but it was still a physically hard job. Against Leeds United, Jack Charlton would stand on the goalkeeper and obstruct him – like Sam Allardyce's teams do now. Leeds were probably the first to have a plan like that.

So after Banks saved Geoff's penalty, we played extra time, then a 0–0 replay with extra time at Hillsborough. We had to toss a coin to decide the next venue. We wanted a game in London – so our fans didn't have to travel north again – Stoke were proposing Old Trafford. Ron Greenwood called, and lost. When we got out we discovered some nutcase had poured sand into the petrol tank of the team bus and we had to wait for another one to arrive and take us back to London. Ron wasn't best pleased, to say the least. We finally lost the fourth game 3–2 – and everyone remembers that match for Bobby Moore going in goal when Bobby Ferguson went off the field for treatment for about 20 minutes. He saved a penalty in that time, too – but couldn't do anything about Mike Bernard following up for the rebound.

It was only a few months later that Gordon had the car crash that cost the sight in one eye and forced his retirement from the game in England. That was such a terrible shame. He did play on for Fort Lauderdale Strikers in America, but I don't think he enjoyed it. He thought it was too much like showbusiness – Gordon is very down to earth. In one game, he and a few other players had to carry a coffin into the middle of the pitch. Out jumped their manager, dressed as Dracula. 'Tonight, The Strikers are coming back from the dead!' roared the stadium announcer. Gordon said they had only lost two games.

Recalling Gordon's performances over those League Cup ties, though, it seems astonishing that Leicester ever let him go. Certainly, there was never any doubt about him for England, and no doubt about his place in history either. He was the best there has been – even if he did stop me playing in a Wembley final.

PAUL REANEY
(LEEDS UNITED)

There can be no greater praise for Paul Reaney than George Best saying he regarded him as his most difficult opponent. George fancied himself against anybody, but Reaney had a way of putting the shackles on unlike any other full-back of the time. For a start, he was lightning fast. And as George put it, he liked to get stuck in. They all did at Leeds. Reaney was a London boy, but he fitted in with that team perfectly. He was a good technical footballer, an excellent athlete and could put it about. I know George rated him, and Manuel Sanchís at Real Madrid, very highly. They were similar players – quick, physical, uncompromising defenders. I think if you'd asked 99 per cent of the wingers from those days, they would have named Paul Reaney as their least favourite opponent. There was no messing with him. You were going to get a kicking all game, and you knew it.

George Cohen was the right-back for England at the 1966 World Cup, but Reaney came into his own in the late sixties. It shows the talent around at the time that he only played three games for England, but he also had terrible luck. Leeds were fighting for the treble in the 1969–70 season when Paul broke his leg in a match at West Ham. It was 2 April 1970. Leeds were halfway through a European Cup semi-final with Celtic, had beaten Manchester United to reach the FA Cup final and were trying to chase down Everton for the title. They were nine points adrift going into the match with West Ham, but had two games in hand. A young kid we had got from Walthamstow Avenue, Keith Miller, was making his full debut for us. He had come on a couple of times as a substitute, but had not started a game. Reaney was 25 and at the peak of his career, a certainty to be on the plane to Mexico with England. And then it was all gone. There was no malice in the challenge, it was a simple collision, but it broke Reaney's leg and he didn't play again until next season. One minute it was all there in front of him; the next, nothing. I felt almost as sorry for Keith really. He was just starting out and it was a completely fair challenge. We knew that it was no foul by the reaction of the Leeds players. Had Keith taken a liberty, let's just say we would all have known it. There would have been murders – I don't know a team that was more protective of one another than Don Revie's Leeds. Anything in it and they would have all been after Keith, and the rest of us. But it was an accident, and they knew that. It probably affected them, though, because they drew that match 2–2 and their season faded away. Everton won the league, Celtic knocked them out of the European Cup and Chelsea won the

FA Cup. Keith Miller never played for West Ham after that day. He was sold to John Bond at Bournemouth for £10,000, did very well and went on to captain the club. And Keith Newton played right-back for England in the 1970 World Cup finals.

So it feels a little bold, leaving out a man who won the World Cup, George Cohen, and Keith Newton who kept Reaney out of the England team for much of his career – but Reaney, for me, was the pick of them all. He was such a fantastic player, hard as nails and very aggressive. Joe Jordan has told me stories about the way he would target Best when Leeds played Manchester United. He would always get very tight, right up his arse, kicking him, kicking him, all game. That was how Reaney marked, never more than a yard away, a real hard nut. He was a very good tackler too, very clean in the way he took the ball. César Azpilicueta at Chelsea reminds me of him in that way. He is very difficult to play against, too – even though he is used on his opposite side. I was a winger, so full-backs were the enemy, but I could always appreciate the art of the best ones, the guys that were all over you like a rash. I never saw Reaney get a chasing, either. If George Best couldn't outwit him there weren't too many others who could have.

It would be very easy for me to just pick England's World Cup-winning team for my Sixties XI, but I always felt Reaney had the edge on Cohen. George was a different player. Attacking, quick, you wouldn't have seen anyone run him, but Reaney was better technically and the best on the ball.

Defensively, too, he played almost as a man-for-man marker. Against Best, he would be leathering him, whacking him with every tackle. George got treatment like that all the time. He could ride a tackle like no player I have ever seen. Exceptional.

Yet Reaney found a way of stopping George that eluded other players. His physical approach, obviously, was important – but his timing and positioning were faultless, too. I was quite lucky, really, because wingers in those days didn't tend to change sides, so I was up against Terry Cooper when we played Leeds, who could not have been more different to Reaney. What made Leeds special was that they were both great attacking players who would bomb forward at every opportunity. But Terry was probably the nicest bloke in the team. A great competitor, but fair.

BOBBY MOORE
(WEST HAM UNITED)

I'm going to start moaning again about the way Bobby was treated after he retired if I'm not careful, so I'll start with one of my favourite stories about him. We had been up in the West End, Bobby and I, with a few mates including Bill Larkin, who had made millions out of roasted peanuts. We were on our way back to the Baker's Arms in Stratford, one of our regular boozing haunts owned by Alan Wheeler, a former welterweight boxer who fought out of West Ham. Bill was at the wheel and well oiled. He had been on it since early afternoon. Terry Creasey, another of our pals, was in the back, and he noticed we were being followed by a police car. He told Bill he needed to be careful. 'Don't worry,' said Bill, full of bravado, 'I'll lose them down the back doubles, I'll shake them off.' He promptly turned sharp left into a dead end, and the police were now blocking us off.

Drink driving wasn't the offence it is now, but with the state of Bill we knew we were in trouble. 'Good evening, sir,' said the officer. 'And where are you off to?' Whatever Bill said in reply obviously didn't make much sense because the copper then started saying that Bill appeared to have had too much to drink, and it was all getting pretty serious. Bobby was in the back, keeping his head down, as the policeman asked Bill to step out of the car. 'Get out, Bob, let them see you,' we were pleading. Bobby did as we asked. Suddenly the mood changed – from 'You're nicked' to 'Hello, Bobby, how are you doing?' and 'Bloody hell, Bob, can I have an autograph?' These days it would have been a selfie on a mobile phone, of course. Bobby duly obliged and now we were all good pals. 'We going to win on Saturday, Bob?' said one of the policemen. 'Who else have you got in there?' He took a look in the car and we were all packed like sardines. There must have been about seven of us. 'Look, fellas,' he said, 'two of you are going to have to get out. You might get stopped again and you're overloaded.' So Terry Creasey, our team-mate Brian Dear and another of our friends, Frankie Macdonald, said they would walk the remaining distance. They set off, but the police must have had a change of heart because a minute later the same squad car pulled up again. 'Where are you going, lads?' the police driver said. When they said the Baker's Arms the coppers said they would drop them off. They did – and ended up staying with us in there until about three in the morning. They were knocking them back and dancing with the girls behind the bar. They had a great time. That is the effect Bobby could have on people. They just wanted to be around him.

Another time the chief of police took us on a pub crawl. He was the top man in the area, including Upton Park. I don't quite recall how it happened but we ended up in his company after one match, and went on a big night out around Bethnal Green. He was driving, too, and by the time we left the last place he really wasn't in a fit state. I think he forgot that red lights meant stop. We were in the car hanging on for grim death. It's got to be about the only time I was actually hoping to get stopped by the police.

But Bobby Moore the footballer? After devoting a chapter to him in my last book, I don't really know what else I can say about Bobby. Perhaps that I don't think he is given enough credit for the way he changed the position of centre-half in this country. Franz Beckenbauer is acclaimed for inventing the sweeper role, but I don't think any English central defender played the ball out of the back in quite the same way until Bobby came along. Centre-halves were all about heading it and kicking it clear. And then Bobby showed there was so much more to the role. He was the antithesis of the English centre-half really. Is he quick? No. Can he head it? No, he's not very strong in the air. No wonder West Ham nearly said no thanks. Yet Malcolm Allison saw something special in Bobby as a youth player and made sure the club kept him on.

I met Matthias Sammer, the great German sweeper-midfielder, a while ago and we were talking about the way the Germans changed their own defensive roles by switching to three at the back. They put their best passer, Beckenbauer, into defence from midfield, and he would break from there, where no one could pick him up. It was an incredibly original tactic. And they have used it many times since. Lothar Matthäus made the switch, so did Sammer – they were both great midfield players who went deeper into the sweeper role. And Bobby could certainly have operated as a sweeper had any team in England been interested in playing that way. With his reading of the game he would have been perfect with two quicker central defenders ahead, but once again English football missed a trick. Here was a player who was always in the right position at the right time, an incredible football brain and brilliant passer, who was sharper than anybody else but lacked pace. It would be wrong to say we didn't make the most of him – we won the World Cup – but Bobby's presence did not change English football the way Beckenbauer altered the culture in Germany.

Bobby's understanding of the game was incredible. I always come back to that passage of play against Jairzinho of Brazil at the 1970 World Cup. He was running everyone ragged, yet Bob just took him down a blind alley and then claimed the ball. He held him up, didn't dive in, just pushed him into an area that was safe. That was Bobby's great gift; because he was slow you would think you could run him, but the next thing you knew you'd be heading away from goal into a dead end. I'm not saying everybody could have played like Bobby Moore, but English football missed an opportunity in not getting players to at least think like him. He wasn't the greatest athlete, but the way he compensated for that was what mattered. There should always be a place in football for a man who can make the game look simple, and that was Bobby's great attribute. Rather than playing someone who is quick yet always ends up making a last-ditch lunge, sliding or blocking, why not have someone who has read the situation as it develops, and is there waiting for the centre-forward without any great drama?

A forward marked by Bobby might jump and flick it on, but he would drop and be there to let the ball fall and catch it on his chest. Other centre-halves would be nutting the forward in the back of the head, but Bobby almost used to let him have it, let him think he'd won it in the air and then step back, scoop it up, and go off and play. At throw-ins, he would step in front of his man. The opposition would be taking a throw into the box, and generally defenders would mark their opponent from behind. The striker would back in, almost trapping the defender in his place, and then the ball would come in and they would hold it, almost at the six-yard box. So Bobby started stepping in front. When he did that, the striker would think he had to reclaim his territory, so would step in front of Bob; and then Bobby would do it again. And this would carry on until the striker was 10 yards farther away from our goal. Nearly 50 years later, I am still telling my centre-halves to do that. Only the other day, with Clint Hill at Queens Park Rangers, we went through how to avoid getting pinned by the centre-forward – and it boiled down to the trick Bobby used with West Ham in the sixties. A tactic nobody had taught him, which he had worked out using nothing more than his nose for the game.

I sometimes wonder whether Bobby would have come through the ranks in modern football. Not strong enough, not quick enough – athletic prowess counts for so much these days. But then I think of his determination, his intelligence and strength of character, and I feel he would surely have forced his way through. I can't imagine that there wouldn't have been one coach – like Allison at West Ham – who could see how special he was, one that looked at what he could do, and saw that it more than compensated for his deficiencies. I think progress purely depends who is coaching the kids. As a manager you hope that you have youth team coaches capable of recognising the all-round talent of a young player. But a kid must still have that work ethic. That is what is often forgotten about Bobby; how hard he worked at his game, how much he listened to advice, how much he studied. Some people you can tell a hundred times, a thousand times, and it doesn't go in, but Bobby had a real brain for football. Tell him once and he had it. He must have been a dream to coach.

He wanted to learn, too, wanted to move his game on. Malcolm Allison helped devise what we now know as Bobby's style of play: knowing when to collect the ball off the goalkeeper, how to clip it to a forward or into a forward channel. Bobby absorbed that information, put it to work and then it was just wasted by the English game. We didn't seem to want intelligence on the football field at that time; we didn't want to think too hard about our play. Basically, we weren't as open-minded as the Germans and have been playing catch-up ever since. It was 30 years after the 1966 World Cup, with Terry Venables and then Glenn Hoddle, that we started thinking differently about the way the England team played. All those years, wasted.

JACK CHARLTON
(LEEDS UNITED)

There are plenty of contenders for the other centre-half in this team. Liverpool had Ron Yeats, a big Scotsman they got from Dundee United. When he signed, Bill Shankly told the journalists to go into the dressing-room and walk around him, to see how big he was. He'd just come out of the shower, and stood there stark naked with all those sports writers peering at him. But what a good player. He was club captain within six months of signing and led Liverpool throughout that era as they won promotion and became one of England's strongest teams. Shankly used to say that as long as they had Yeats they could play Arthur Askey in goal. Liverpool changed their strip to all red under Shankly because he thought a block of one colour looked more imposing – and which player did he get to model the new strip? Yeats, of course.

I've heard he was also the only player to beat Shankly in a penalty shoot-out. Bill used to challenge one of the first-team players every Friday, and one week it was Yeats's turn. He had never taken a penalty and Shankly was apparently a master at it – he hadn't lost all season. The goalkeeper was Tommy Lawrence, who Shankly was always having a go at for being overweight. Shankly's first two went flying in, but Lawrence saved his third. 'I got lucky there, boss,' he said. 'Yes, you did, you fat twat,' said Shankly, with all the players crying with laughter. The story goes that Big Ron then scored his first two with his eyes shut, but hit an absolute cracker into the top corner with his last to win the day and cost Shankly a tenner. Bill went straight over to poor Tommy Lawrence, while the goalkeeper was still prone on the floor. 'If it had been a fucking meat pie you'd have caught it,' he spat.

Frank McLintock at Arsenal was another fine centre-half. Arsenal were a hard team – Ron 'Chopper' Harris used to call Peter Storey the bastards' bastard – but Frank was a touch of class. He was another, like Bobby Moore, who nearly didn't get his chance. Frank's manager at his first club, Leicester City, didn't fancy him at all, but one day they had so many injuries there was no option but to put him in the team. The last person he wanted to pick was Frank, apparently, but he was never off the team sheet after that. Leicester had a good side in those days and Frank had an excellent half-back pairing alongside either Colin Appleton or Ian King. He went on to Arsenal and captained the double-winning team. But Frank was a very different kind of centre-half to Jack Charlton and many others from that time. I think all they had in common was the attitude of their teams. Leeds and Arsenal were quite similar in their aggressive approach. If one of their number got kicked, they were straight in, both of them. They'd all come over, all start poking at you. Other teams were intimidated by them.

Jack wasn't the best footballer but, by God, he was effective. I first saw him play when I was very young, about 15, for Leeds against Tottenham Hotspur. Frankly, I couldn't believe he was Bobby's brother. There was Bobby, one of the most graceful footballers who ever lived, poetry in motion just the way he moved – drop a shoulder, glide the other way, hit a 35-yarder into the top corner, all on the run. And there was Jack, who couldn't trap a bag of cement. I remember thinking, 'My God, how bad is he?' Yet he could head it, he could tackle, he could organise; he was perfect for Bobby Moore at England level really. Jack would attack the headers, Bobby would drop off. They were good cop and bad cop. Jack the aggressive, hard one who would do anything to win; Bobby his cool companion. I was too young to understand it that day, but Jack was just a really good, old-fashioned centre-half. He knew the game as well as Bobby; he just couldn't play it like him.

I found that out much later on doing my coaching badges at Lilleshall. Jack would be there, too, and half the day would be taken up with him rowing with the coaches over what we had been told. He was usually right as well. Just as Bob's understanding of the game overcame his lack of pace, so Jack's reading of it made up for his lack of technical ability. Jack wouldn't be exposed for lack of pace, but he could be caught out other ways, so he got himself into the right positions and focused on his strengths. He was great in the air, great at barking orders and getting that Leeds team set up, and he took that into his management style. His Republic of Ireland team hardly played the Leeds way, but they were very powerful, well drilled and difficult to beat.

That was Jack. He was one of the first central defenders to score goals from set plays – 9 in 34 league matches in 1961–2 and 7 the season before – and defensively he always made sure there was a screen in front of the back four. He got people at it, got them tackling and working. That is how I remember him, shaking his fist at people in his own team, bullying them into grafting harder. He wasn't the captain, but he was very much in the mould of Tony Adams or John Terry. Barking his instructions, always a leader even without an armband.

You used to hear him from all over the field. He was a big, blunt bugger, who didn't give a shit. He wouldn't mess about, he was always to the point – and he was no different on those coaching courses. There is one I particularly remember. Everything was wrong. That's wrong. This is wrong. You're wrong. He's wrong. You don't mark like that. If you want to play like that, then you can't do this. He just took over. A lot of the coaches were glorified schoolteachers and Jack would just overpower them. He was too much for all of us, really. He knew his stuff and he was a big bloke; in the end, they didn't argue with him.

The one time I did see someone get the better of Jack was on 21 November 1964 – West Ham 3, Leeds United 1. Johnny Byrne destroyed him that night in a way I never saw, say Paul Reaney, get completely outclassed by his winger. Budgie was only 5 ft 8 in, but he weighed over 11 stone and could look after himself. Jim Stannard, our goalkeeper, was pumping balls upfield and Budgie was backing into Jack, battering him and catching them on his chest. Sometimes he would volley one out to Peter Brabook and then turn and run for the return. Johnny was a fantastic player and the way he held Jack off, and his movement, was masterful. Leeds lost the league title on goal average that season, but West Ham absolutely ripped them to pieces. It could have been six. And no one would have envisaged that the centre-half who was left so exposed would be winning a World Cup medal with England two years later.

That is the other incredible element of Jack's career – how late he came to international football and what he then achieved. He had made over 300 appearances before he got his first England call-up, and two Leeds managers had already come close to selling him, including Don Revie. It is testament to his perseverance that he achieved so much in the game. That 15-year-old in the crowd at White Hart Lane in 1962 got it wrong. No, Jack Charlton wasn't at all like Bobby Charlton. But he was never trying to be.

RAY WILSON
(HUDDERSFIELD TOWN)

If Paul Reaney was George Best's most troublesome opponent, Denis Law used to say that Ray Wilson was the most difficult defender he had ever faced – and that was just in practice sessions at Huddersfield Town. It seems faint praise to call Ray a great left-back – but that is what he was. Uncomplicated, efficient, he would be 7/10, minimum, every game – the way Ashley Cole is now. He was quick as lightning, maybe not the greatest on the ball by modern standards, but his crosses were accurate and he loved to get on the overlap.

I think it says most for Ray's consistency that the mistake he made in the World Cup final – a weak header that fell to Helmut Haller to give West Germany the lead – sticks in the memory. It was so out of character, so uncommon for Ray to give the opposition a sniff. When the great defenders make a mistake everyone remembers it because it is so rare, and Ray was famous for just doing his job. I didn't see too many get past him, and while he could bomb forward when necessary, he always knew his first task was to defend. He wasn't spectacular, but every successful team needs men like Ray Wilson. He was probably the least known of that 1966 team, but that didn't mean he wasn't absolutely vital. Without good full-backs in those days, you were stuffed.

Huddersfield was a breeding ground for a lot of good players back then. Wilson and Law, obviously, but Frank Worthington came out of there too, and some decent full-backs such as Chris Cattlin, who went on to play eight seasons in the First Division for Coventry City, and Derek Parkin, who still holds the record number of appearances for Wolverhampton Wanderers. Huddersfield were more of a feeder club by then, sadly. They didn't keep any of their stars. Just before the World Cup, Ray Wilson was transferred to Everton. He was probably the best left-back in the world by that time, too.

There were a few contenders. Nílton Santos of Brazil had been the top man – and some people think the finest left-back of all time – but he retired in 1962. Wilson's only rival by the time of the 1966 World Cup would have been Giacinto Facchetti, who captained the winning Italy team in the 1968 European Championships. He played all his life for Inter Milan, and even ended up president of the club. Facchetti was a brilliant player, but I can't help thinking that when Wilson was winning the World Cup, his Italian team was going home having been beaten by North Korea. Remembering Jairzinho's performance against Italy in the 1970 World Cup, I think Ray just had the edge as a defender, too.

As I've said before, the sixties were the time when full-backs became as fast as wingers, and Ray was a product of that thinking. He wasn't an overly aggressive player, he wasn't nasty or vicious, or swearing at you the whole match; he was just quick and difficult to beat. Ray would have been faster than many wingers and it would have been interesting to see how Sir Stanley Matthews would have coped had he been up against players like that throughout his career. Stan had a good run against slower full-backs, and by the time the game changed he was coming to the end and not as much was expected of him. It would have been interesting to see Stan deal with the likes of Tommy Smith or Terry Cooper – and he never played against Wilson at his absolute peak.

Ray was certainly one of the toughest I ever faced, and there was plenty of competition at the time. Eddie McCreadie was an outstanding opponent at Chelsea, fast, with an excellent sense of timing in the tackle. I remember a goal he scored against Leicester City in the League Cup. He must have run the length of the field and, when everyone thought he might panic, he just slotted it past Gordon Banks. Very cool. Eddie was an incredible bloke. He managed Chelsea when he retired and one of his first acts was to take the captaincy away from Ron Harris and give it to an 18-year-old kid, Ray Wilkins. So he was clearly a very good judge. They won promotion under him, but he only lasted two seasons and he was gone. The rumour at the time was that he wanted a club car because the manager of Fulham, Bobby Campbell, had one. The chairman, Brian Mears, refused so Eddie quit. Then Mears decided he could have one but Eddie felt he couldn't go back on his word. I suppose there was probably more to it, but it seems incredible to give up a great job like that. The last I heard of Eddie he was a born-again Christian living in America. I don't think he has seen anyone from his old football days in years. I know Chelsea invited him to come to one of the games when they toured America recently, but he refused. He has a new life and good luck to him.

I think one of the big differences back in the sixties was that great players could come from anywhere, not just a small group of elite clubs, as today. Wilson was from Huddersfield and Eddie was signed from East Stirlingshire, who were in the Scottish Second Division at the time – and he went straight into Chelsea's first team. Cyril Knowles was another excellent left-back at Tottenham Hotspur, and he came out of Middlesbrough. Cyril was class on the ball and made that step up with no problem. If you go through that first great Liverpool team there are players from Motherwell, Dundee United, Preston North End. There was so much talent around in the lower divisions, and Scotland, whereas now it is very hard to find. Good players move much earlier, almost in their teens, so very little comes out of there. Often a kid will get picked up, move to a bigger club and then disappear in a reserve group that is full of foreign imports. He loses his way in the game, and vanishes or drops down through the divisions. When I played, every First Division team had two or three good Scottish players, now there might be ten in the entire Premier Division. I hope that is beginning to change now because there are some good reports coming out about young players in Scotland. Maybe they are getting the chance to play again – in recent years the top of the Scottish league became too focused on foreign players. It would be good to get back to the days when a great international footballer could come from almost anywhere – and Huddersfield produced as many as Manchester United.

GEORGE BEST
(MANCHESTER UNITED)

So where would I put George Best in my list of the greats? Simple. I regard him as the best footballer the British Isles has ever produced. A genius. We've never had another like him.

I can remember reading the account by Harry Gregg, Manchester United's goalkeeper, of the first time he met George. Great man, Harry – pulled semi-conscious injured team-mates out of a burning plane on the tarmac at Munich. That's bravery. These days a midfielder receives the ball with a man marking him and we say he's brave. He was also a hard man who almost used to bully opponents. He came out fast and aggressively in one-on-one challenges, and sometimes made the forward's mind up for him. Harry was not the sort of chap that a young kid fresh over from Belfast should be messing with.

The first training session George had at United ended with a practice match. George, just over 5 ft 8 in and no more than seven stone at the time, got the ball, ripped through the defence and made to shoot. Gregg went one way, and George casually took the ball past him and rolled it into the net. Harry consoled himself with the thought that it was a mistake, that he had sold himself too early and made up this kid's mind. Next attack, George went through on his own again – out came Harry, and the same thing happened. He dived one way, George went the other and tapped into an empty net. 'Do that to me again, son,' Harry warned, from his position on the seat of his pants, 'and you won't be playing tomorrow.' Yet George just laughed it off. That was what made him so magnificent. There is a fantastic clip of George playing against Chelsea. He is going through the defence, the mud is ankle deep, yet somehow he is travelling on, when Ron Harris comes across and tries to cut him in half. It is an incredible tackle by today's standards, absolutely brutal, yet he rides it, carries on and slots the ball in. George went out every game knowing there were players whose job was to hurt him. Not scare him or intimidate him, just stop him by any means necessary. He always suspected there were a couple who actively tried to break his legs. Yet they never stopped him demanding the ball, never stopped him running with it. I haven't seen anybody as brave as George. He was a one-off.

When great players retire often a myth builds up around them, but I know what George went through from experience. I grew up in the same era as him – George was the year above my West Ham United youth team that won the FA Youth Cup – and it could be really intimidating playing against these hard-nut defenders. Yet it never seemed to bother George. He never stopped wanting the ball, never stopped taking players on – too much so, some of his Manchester United colleagues thought, but if you've got that unique talent why wouldn't you use it?

Sometimes you hear a buzz about great young players because of their achievements at junior level, but there was nothing like that with George. He was fresh off the boat and straight into the first team. He didn't really bother with youth football. The player we all knew from United's junior team was Willie Anderson, a lad from Liverpool who played in George's position. George just flew straight past Willie and never looked back. Willie ended up as George's understudy, going nowhere, and signed for Aston Villa for £20,000. Sometimes that happens. Willie was a useful player and must have thought he was going to have a good career at Manchester United. Then this wonder kid from Northern Ireland comes over and that's his lot – it was a pity really, but how could they resist George? He had everything. He could dribble, shoot, he was strong in the air, a good tackler. He was the ultimate street footballer, really. That was where he'd learnt to play the game, not from any coach. Lionel Messi reminds me of him, the way he would run with the ball tight to his foot. Tap, tap, tap. He would take the ball up to defenders like that, and then swivel and go past them. You almost need to create a fresh way of measuring talent to assess George. There were so many great players in that Manchester United team but, even then, George stood tall.

He had plenty of good games against West Ham, but one stands out. We had gone up to Old Trafford to play them near the start of the 1971–2 season and I got talking to David Sadler, their centre-half, before the game. He told me there had been uproar earlier that day. 'George didn't turn up at the hotel, Harry,' he said. 'He missed the team meeting, he's been out all night. Been off with a bird, had no sleep, look at the state of him.' I must admit, the figure warming up across the other side of the pitch did look a bit dishevelled. I went straight back to our dressing-room, keen to pass on this juicy gossip. 'This is handy, lads,' I told the group. 'I've just found out that Best's been out all night on the piss. He's just turned up at the ground now, missed the team bus, missed the meeting, they're only playing him because they've got no one else.' We went out that afternoon full of confidence, and you can imagine what happened next. George scored a hat-trick and we lost 4–2. He got a header for his first goal and a fantastic shot on the turn in the middle of a penalty-area scramble for his second. For the last goal, United got a corner and George went out towards it, telling John Aston he would score from there. John played it short and George took it past about four of us from this acute angle, bomp, bomp, bomp, made to shoot, left Bobby Moore on his arse and stuck it in the far corner. I don't think I've seen a better goal. The rest of the players were looking at me as if to say, 'Thanks for that tip, Harry.' But he just had this incredible, natural ability. I should have known that one late night in a thousand wasn't going to affect George.

There were some wonderful players in that era, real crowd-pleasers like Peter Osgood, but George was the only one who could add 10,000 to a gate the way Tom Finney or Stanley Matthews had previously. Certainly, that was the deal when he came to Bournemouth late in his career. Brian Tiler, the managing director, did a deal where the away team would pay a percentage of his wages as long as we put George in the starting line-up; I really don't know how we got away with it because there must have been regulations against that type of thing. Everyone was happy, though, because a gate of 4,000 would suddenly become 14,000 with the news George was playing.

Despite this, he was always just one of the lads. I think a lot of the best players are like that. It's the ones who get the money without the ability that tend to become flash little twerps. I never hear a bad word said about Paul Gascoigne by any of his team-mates, and I was once told that it was the same with Diego Maradona. The rest of the dressing-room loved him. He didn't care that his ability was carrying the team; he just mucked in. George was like that. I imagine some people might think he was a right flash bastard, but that was never the case. He trained as if he was an ordinary player, even in America with Los Angeles Aztecs. He had his mate out there with him, Bobby McAlinden, who was his best man when he married Angie; he got him a contract with the club and they shared a house, but that was the only time I can recall George getting star treatment. McAlinden never made it as a player – he was part-time with Stalybridge Celtic when he went to America – but George liked him, and the franchise wanted to keep George happy.

How I like to remember him, though, is in front of a full house at Old Trafford in his prime. He had a style, a swagger when he played that I don't think I've seen since. And he changed football. Girls screaming at him, boys trying to dress like him. Sometimes, with all the celebrity trappings, it is easy to forget how good he was. The best: simple as that.

BILLY BREMNER
(LEEDS UNITED)

It is hard to separate Billy Bremner and Johnny Giles. They were both so integral to the midfield of the great Leeds United team that it seems unthinkable to imagine them apart. But there is no way I won't find room for Dave Mackay, so it comes down to a straight choice between Bremner and Giles – and I am going for Bremner. Billy was the captain; Billy was the driving force behind that team. They were two great players, without a doubt, but Billy edges it for me. He never seemed to get injured, no matter how much he gave, and for his size his contribution to the game was just incredible. It was not unusual for him to sleep for 13 hours after a match because his effort had been so great, and while I had my run-ins with him, it never clouded my appreciation of him as a player.

It was hard to get sent off in the sixties, but I managed it against Leeds. Looking back, I am sure they knew what they were doing that day. I was having a good game – I always fancied my chances against Leeds because the left-back, Terry Cooper, was so attack minded that I often got an opening – and after 15 minutes I knew this was going to be my day. I was getting past Cooper time and again, and heaven knows how the score was still 0–0. I went on another run, got to the byline and won a corner. Bremner started complaining that it should have been a goal-kick. 'Stop moaning,' I told him. 'You're always fucking moaning.' Billy clearly didn't appreciate that because as we lined up for the corner, he stamped on my foot. I pushed him away. Then he raked his studs down my shin. I gave him a kick and he went down as if felled by a sniper's bullet. The next moment the whole Leeds team, bar Billy and the goalkeeper, Gary Sprake, were crowding in on me, hands around my throat, jostling me, pushing me back. Billy Bonds, bless him, was the only West Ham player who came to my aid – the rest just looked on. Bremner escaped, I was sent off, and as I walked past Bobby Moore, who was still in West Ham's defensive half of the pitch, the look on his face was a picture. He had his arms folded and gave a brief shake of the head, as if to say, 'Harry, son – how did you fall for that?' Yet that was the Leeds way. They were cute, often plain cynical. They won 2–0 that day, from a direct free-kick by Peter Lorimer and a penalty by Giles. 'Fouls, imagined and actual, were so frequent that I stopped counting them,' wrote the reporter from the *Yorkshire Post*. Getting played for a mug was costly in those days, too. I had to serve a suspension, and back then that meant a week with no pay. Billy Bonds organised a whip-round for me and even asked Ron Greenwood, our manager, to chip in. He didn't like confrontation, so agreed. He must have been fuming, though, coming to the rescue of a player who had cost his team the game.

Still, no hard feelings. Bremner was just trying to do the best for his team, driving them on in whatever way he could, as always. I think Giles was the brains of the midfield, but Bremner was its engine. Giles could really play. He had come to the club from Manchester United, and letting him go may have been the biggest mistake that club ever made. People think Eric Cantona being allowed to leave Leeds for Manchester United was a serious error, but to my mind that was merely the equaliser after the earlier sale of Giles to Leeds. He was such a fantastic footballer, a right-winger at Manchester United, but desperate to be given the chance to play in the middle. Even at Leeds he had to wait his turn behind Bobby Collins, but once he got it he never looked back. His touch on the ball was absolutely superb and he had a lovely passing range. Everything happened so deftly. The ball would come in and he would kill it and pass it, all in one movement. He saw everything from that central position, and with Bremner beside him they were such a great pair.

I think Billy set standards as a leader at Elland Road. Don Revie had a unique way of managing, demanding that the team stayed tight and that nothing upset his boys. Billy was instrumental in that. When Gordon McQueen signed for the club from St Mirren it was said he fancied himself a bit. Billy would have made it his business to ensure nobody's ego got in the way. 'Side before self, every time' was his motto. Even by the standards of the day he was tiny: just 5 ft 5 in. He grew up in Scotland playing against men and learning that the only way to be big enough was to act big enough – he flew into tackles harder than any player from that era. A lot of those boys could put it about but Billy was, if you like, the pound-for-pound champion. For his size, a tackle from Billy felt like being hit by a six-footer. Yes, he was nasty, but he could also play. He always wanted the ball, and always tried to run the game. He often succeeded. His passing was as well developed as his wicked streak, so no wonder the fans and his manager loved him. Whatever way you wanted to play, Billy could play. If you wanted a tear-up, he was ready to roll; if you wanted a football match, he was the best player on the field.

A few years back I watched the film *The Damned United* about Brian Clough's short time at Leeds. I know it isn't intended to be historically accurate throughout but, even so, the portrayal of Bremner was a disgrace. They made him look like a little fat sod, with a pot belly. If that was the player that was chasing midfielders all around the pitch for almost 800 games, I don't think Revie's Leeds would be regarded as one of the greatest teams of all time. At one stage they showed him smoking a cigarette waiting for Clough to come out. Shirt and shorts on, and a fag. I was so surprised I even asked Joe Jordan about it. I couldn't repeat what he said about the way that Leeds team was portrayed. I don't know why they did that. They made them look like a Sunday league team. It was nonsense – like the scene where Clough is the manager of Derby County and he doesn't even watch one of his biggest games of the season. Peter Taylor, his assistant, tells him the score. I'm sorry, I can't see that happening. Like Bremner with a beer belly, anyone who was around in those times knows it just isn't true.

I know Billy was very loyal to Revie and preferred his methods, and that he stood up to Clough. There is a story that Leeds had a pre-season game away at Aston Villa and Clough decided to give the team talk on the grass bank of a dual carriageway. It started to pour down with rain, and some of the players got up to leave. Clough asked them where they thought they were going. 'You stand up when I say you can,' he said. It was Billy who led the mutiny. 'If you think we're sitting in the rain, you must be joking,' he said, and walked off. It is no surprise that it didn't work out for Clough. They were all experienced players. They didn't have to take that.

The quote that best sums Billy up is that he was 10 stone of barbed wire. He was a warrior, a ball-winner and the scorer of the odd great goal. He had a lovely reverse pass that could wrong-foot some of the best midfielders, and he embodied the spirit of the sign that hung on the wall of the home dressing-room. 'Keep fighting,' it said. I think they always left the door half open to make sure you saw it when you visited Elland Road. It was their equivalent of the 'This Is Anfield' sign over the tunnel at Liverpool – reminding you what you were up against. I know Leeds played Chelsea the weekend after Billy died, and it was rather fitting because they had two men sent off, but still managed a 0–0 draw. The fans were singing about having 'nine men – and Billy'. He would have loved that.

It is almost impossible to overstate what he did for that team, and that club. I played Leeds in my second game for West Ham on 28 August 1965 and we beat them 2–1. I didn't think they looked much cop, yet from there they just went from strength to strength and Billy was so important in pulling the team together. A sports writer once told me a story about Billy and that spirit at Leeds. He said they were in Eastern Europe for the away leg of a European tie and they were all out after the game – players, some of the press boys, the way it used to be. The bill arrived for the night, and it was clear they were being ripped off. They'd had a good go at it, but this place must have thought they were millionaires. There was an almighty row and the next thing they knew the exit door was blocked by a big gang of heavies. Billy didn't mess about. He turned to the players and the press corps. 'Pick up a chair, lads,' he said. 'We're leaving.'

DAVE MACKAY
(TOTTENHAM HOTSPUR)

Bill Nicholson said Dave Mackay was his greatest signing, and selling him was his greatest mistake. If you look at the talent Bill brought to Tottenham, that is some statement. Dave was the manager's player, the player's player, the fan's player, the complete footballer really. Every major club he represented regards him as a legend – from Hearts in Scotland, through Tottenham, to Derby County. He won every domestic honour north of the border before coming to England, and played in a Hearts team that scored 132 league goals in one season – which at the time was a British record. Dave was a warrior, but another one of those players who could take the game in whatever direction he fancied. He could give you a war all right, but he also had incredible skill and ability. On the ball he was magnificent; off it he was a ferocious competitor and tackler, the strongest you've ever seen. Jimmy Greaves said he was the best player ever to wear a Tottenham shirt, and I wouldn't argue with that. George Best thought he was the hardest player he ever faced – but he didn't mean hard in a sneaky or dirty way. Just tough. It's a huge testament to Dave's standing among his fellow professionals.

I remember watching Dave when I was a junior at Tottenham. I followed them through all the European games and at weekends whenever I could. The team had a big Scottish contingent at the time: John White, Bill Brown, who was the goalkeeper, and Dave. They had all arrived within a few months of each other in 1959, which for those days was quite a bold move from a manager. Nicholson was proved right, though, and the Scots were essential to Tottenham's double-winning team. White never missed a game, Brown missed one and Dave missed five – but Mackay was still the pick of the bunch. He was a powerhouse, making tackle after tackle. It was just incredible to watch. I remember one game from that season against Aston Villa, which Tottenham won 6–2. I was 13 at the time. Villa weren't a bad team and they had a tough little nut playing at right-half called Ron Wylie, who went on to be manager of West Bromwich Albion. Wylie had the ball when Mackay tackled him and the poor sod must have gone eight foot up in the air. The ball came down to another Villa player, but before he knew it Dave had hit him as well, with the same result. That was Mackay. He would just plough through a midfield, tackle after tackle. You could never imagine he would come out second best.

He must have done, on occasions, because Dave had terrible luck with injuries. He broke his left leg in a tackle with Noel Cantwell of Manchester United in a European Cup-Winners' Cup tie in 1963, came back nine months later and, four games in, did it again against Shrewsbury Town reserves. Dave always says he didn't break his leg, other players broke it for him. I got to know him via Jim Smith when Jim was manager of Derby, and I know Dave believes that on at least one of those occasions he was deliberately targeted and fouled.

That is also the story behind one of the most famous photographs in football. A furious Mackay is in mid-stride, marching over and grabbing Billy Bremner by his collar, almost picking him up, as his team-mate Terry Venables looks on and referee Norman Burtenshaw dashes over frantically blowing his whistle. It was taken on 20 August 1966, the first day of the new season. Dave had returned from his second broken leg the previous campaign, his resilience merely adding to his legend. A broken leg could end a career in those days, let alone two within nine months, and while many thought this proved Mackay was indestructible, he must have felt very vulnerable when he stepped on to the field. Within the opening minutes, Bremner had hit him with a naughty one – but that wasn't why Dave was so furious. He thought Bremner had avoided tackling his right leg – the leg that had the ball – and instead had gone for his left. He thought he had set out to either break his leg again or at least make him fearful. I think you can see from the photograph that Billy quickly realised he had made a big mistake. They were two of the great competitors of the sixties, but even Billy knew that you didn't mess with Dave. The referee prevented the confrontation from coming to blows but, had it done, judging by the look on Dave's face there would only have been one winner. I'm told Dave hates that image because he thinks it makes him look like a bully – although he wasn't much taller than Billy, only 5 ft 8 in – but every football man I know loves it. Sir Alex Ferguson even had it up in his office at Old Trafford.

Everyone who played with Dave, or knew Dave, has a story about his skill. He was good and he knew it, and liked to show off. Sometimes Eddie Baily would take the training at Tottenham. He never had much time for players and would sometimes devise drills just to put them in their place. They had a wall with coloured lines on it at the training ground. The players were convinced Baily would make these sessions up as he went along. 'Right you lot,' Eddie would say. 'Get a ball each. Now,

I want you to chip it against the blue line, get it back, shoot it against the red line, take it on your chest, let it drop, back against the yellow line, keep it high, then on your head this time, head it back against the green line, wait for it, side-foot against the white line, volley up to the black line, trap it and stop.' The lads would be looking at him as if he was mad. They couldn't even remember the exercise let alone perform it. At which point, Dave would get his ball – chip, blue line, shoot, red line, chest, drop, yellow line, back, header, green line, side-foot, white line, volley, black line, back, trap. 'Like that, you mean, Ed?' he'd ask.

Phil Holder, who was a trainee at Tottenham as Dave was coming to the end of his career there, says he used to watch him in the gym repeatedly volleying the ball against the wall from 20 yards, one shot after another, left foot, right foot, never letting it drop. Graeme Souness says he saw the same. That is an incredible skill to perfect. I don't know another player who could do it. Mackay's feet were amazing.

Another memory is of that barrel chest. Dave always seemed to have mud on his hands from a slide tackle. The pitches were conducive to it then and he'd start in at the opponents from about five yards away, go right through him and always come out with the ball. He'd get up and wipe his muddy hands on the front of his shirt. It was his trademark. There was a lot of the showman about Dave. When Tottenham ran out he would kick the ball as high as he could, and then kill it on the way down with the deftest touch. It was his way of showing the opposition the technical level they were up against. 'Can you do that, lads?' he was asking. He was just this wonderful combination of brawn and brain. When he went in for a tackle, he got the ball, and once he had the ball he could do anything with it – power past people, hit a pass, hit a thunderous shot from 30 yards straight on goal. He had everything. Even after the broken leg he still went crunching into tackles, and after Bill sold him to Derby, he turned them around and won promotion playing almost as a sweeper. Anyone who pigeon-holes him as just a hard man doesn't know the player. He was a fantastic technician, too – and a member of one of football's most ferocious drinking schools at Tottenham, adding to the legend.

That team didn't just win the double, they sunk quite a few of them too. A friend of mine says he went to a match at White Hart Lane back then without a ticket, hoping to pick one up from a tout outside. He was waiting for Stan Flashman when he saw a chap he knew getting out of a taxi with Dave Mackay. Dave hurried into White Hart Lane, but his mate said the pair of them had been out at a party that weekend and Mackay hadn't been to bed since. Bill Nicholson was going to be furious. In the end, my mate got his ticket and went inside. Tottenham won. Man of the match? Dave Mackay. He was probably straight up the Bell and Hare pub or The Corner Pin with Jimmy Greaves after the game, too.

BOBBY CHARLTON
(MANCHESTER UNITED)

On 6 May 1967, Manchester United came to Upton Park in search of the league title. They were three points clear of Nottingham Forest with two games remaining – just two points for a win in those days of course – so could still be overtaken.

Their last two games were at West Ham and then at home to Stoke City, two mid-table clubs. Forest had to play away against Southampton and Fulham, both of whom had only just avoided relegation. Manchester United were the favourites, but still – might they slip up? As if. They beat us 6–1 – and I don't think I've ever seen a classier performance than Bobby Charlton gave that day. The picture on the front of the book is from that game.

We were a raw side, with a lot of youth, and Manchester United annihilated us. It was the great team – Best, Law and Charlton – and all got on the scoresheet, but it was Bobby who gave United the lead after two minutes, and Bobby whose quality and passing guided the win. He was class personified, gliding past people, the most graceful mover I have seen on a football field, able to shoot from anywhere once within the 40-yard range. He was just the most perfect striker of a ball. He would drop his shoulder and, bang, top corner. And fast. Because he was so skilful, people forget the speed Charlton had. What I remember that day is that in United's first attack Law and Nobby Stiles burst through, Law's shot was blocked and our full-back Jack Burkett made to clear. Before he got the chance, Charlton was upon him. It was like watching a gazelle taken down by a cheetah. He came from nowhere, first time shot, 1–0. It was a masterclass in taking an opportunity in the blink of an eye. One minute Jack was about to play it safe, the next we were behind. After that, United showed why they were the best team in the land. Our goalkeeper was my old friend from the Burdett Boys team, Colin Mackleworth, and he had a terrible time of it. I know he dropped a cross for their third goal but it hardly mattered – the game was only 10 minutes old when that was scored.

Bobby was the man of the match. A midfield genius at a time
when there was plenty of competition. Markers couldn't control
him, couldn't kick him, couldn't get near him. His passes were
always so clean, his technique so faultless, and the way he switched
the play was devastating. He would take half the opposition out
with one pass, and did so countless times that day. What a player,
and what a man. Not aggressive, not dirty, always gentlemanly
in his conduct. I must admit I was in awe of him. Most young
players of the time were, and perhaps that day it showed.

It makes such a difference to have a player like that in your
team. I had that at Tottenham with Gareth Bale. He would get
the ball, 25 to 30 yards out and – bang – find the top corner.
I watched him do it for Real Madrid last season, too. All the
football around the world, all this talk about possession, nothing
beats the direct approach of a great player like Bobby Charlton or
Bale. A team can have 28 passes to create a shooting opportunity,
but a player who can hit the target from 30 yards out – that cuts
straight to the heart of the game. We were raving about Bale in
his last season in England, but Bobby was doing exactly that 40
years ago: the same driving runs, the same spectacular finishes.
When you think what the man went through at Munich, it can't
have been easy. To lose all your friends, particularly in a sports
team, must have made playing very difficult. So many memories
every time he stepped on the field, what must he have been
thinking? How did he overcome that, seeing those ghosts? To
come back and become the player he was – I think that's why he
is such an icon in English football. Bobby is the only one who
spans the three most seismic events in our game: the Munich air
disaster, winning the World Cup in 1966 and the first European

Cup win by an English club, Manchester United in 1968. As a director, one could even say he was part of United's treble in 1999, too.

I can't say I know him very well personally, but the way he carried himself was important, too. He might have been involved in all those events and turned into a horrible bastard, but instead Bobby was a gentleman and a great ambassador for football, an ambassador for the best in the game: skill and grace and commitment. Bobby Charlton represented football played the right way as a player and a man, which is why I think he holds a special place in its history.

I was 19 when England won the World Cup and watched the match on the Burdett Estate with my mum and dad. I was in the West Ham first team by then and felt very proud because three of my team-mates were in the starting line-up, but I didn't have a ticket. Bobby Moore was a big friend of mine, but I wouldn't have dreamed of asking him to sort me out. He had far too much on his plate to be bothered hunting down tickets for me. Anyway, it was great to watch the game with Dad. We still had a black-and-white television in those days, despite my successful career. I can't remember getting a colour set for quite a few years after that. I think by the time the Redknapps came into the modern world I was married to Sandra and we had our first son, Mark.

Actually, our quest for a colour TV belongs in an episode of *Only Fools and Horses*. I was in the Dallas café opposite Upton Park station with my team-mate Roger Cross when a chap came in. He must have recognised me from the West Ham team and knew I might have a bit of spare cash. 'Harry,' he said, 'do you

fancy buying a colour television?' He explained that he had a
couple to sell – we didn't ask too many questions about how and
why – but he needed to let them go as a pair because he wanted
them off his hands. We should have smelled a rat from the start.
Roger had just got married and was very keen. 'They're £110
each,' the man said. That was a lot of money – more than a
week's wages. I wasn't sure, but Roger said he could have a
word with his mum and borrow the cash. She had a sweet shop
in Katherine Road, so was always regarded as having a few quid
compared to the other parents. I thought it was expensive but
in the end was persuaded. This bloke was a good salesman and
told us this was a top-of-the-range piece of equipment, well in
advance of most of the sets you would find in the shops. He said
he would bring it round that night.

Eight o'clock, as arranged, he arrived. 'I'm sorry, Harry,' he
said, 'one of the sets has got a little damaged in the van. Nothing
serious, but it's got a scratch on the side.' 'Roger can have that
one,' I said. 'I'll have the good one.' He brought it in, and made
a big show of putting it in the middle of the room. His legs
were buckling with the weight and he placed it very carefully to
make sure there was no damage. 'Right,' I said. 'We'll switch it
on.' 'Oh no, Harry,' he countered. 'You can't just switch a set
like this on. It needs an expert, someone to do all the tuning.
You might mess it up if you turn it on without knowing what
you're doing. It's very sophisticated. Highly technical. You'll
need help.' And, pocketing the money, off he went to deliver
Roger's, with the scratch.

As luck would have it, I knew a bloke in Chelmsford who
worked in television repair, and asked him to come round. The

following day he arrived and we all sat down to watch the launch of the colour era in our front room. Nothing. Not a flicker. He seemed mystified. In the end, he went round the back and unscrewed the panel. 'Harry,' he said, 'is this *Candid Camera*?' There was nothing inside. Not so much as a loose screw. I had bought an empty wooden cabinet with a screen on the front. My first thought was what a mug I had been letting Roger have the one with the scratch, but we went round there and his was the same. We had been done, good and proper. Of course, we never saw our mates from the Dallas café again.

Still, that night in July 1966, Mum and Dad's black-and-white set was good enough for me. Bobby and the boys gave the East End of London one of the best nights out it had ever seen.

JIMMY GREAVES
(TOTTENHAM HOTSPUR)

We were at the training ground with Queens Park Rangers last season and Sky Sports News was showing a goal by Lionel Messi. He got into the penalty box, took his time, waiting for all the defenders and goalkeeper to commit themselves, and then just rolled it into the corner. The players were in rapture about it. I told them Jimmy Greaves scored one like that every weekend, and frequently more. He was a genius. Without doubt one of the greatest goalscorers of any era. When he got the ball in the penalty box, the world stopped; it was like somebody had hit pause on the television screen. The action around him carried on, but Jim appeared to be operating in another dimension; slower, calmer, making his mind up oblivious to the surrounding frenzy.

The centre-half would come flying across; Jim would make out as if to shoot. The centre-half would throw himself into a desperate slide to try to block; Jim would stop the ball. The centre-half would go whizzing past; Jim would switch it to his other foot. The goalkeeper would anticipate the direction and dive full-length; Jim would place the ball, gently, into the other corner. As it nestled, just about reaching the back of the net, there would be bodies lying everywhere. It was just amazing.

Jimmy could side-foot one with the same devastating effect others got from a 30-yard shot. Strikers often want pace on the ball to get it past the goalkeeper, but Jim never seemed to worry about that. His accuracy did the work: moving the ball half a yard to manoeuvre it around the blocking player, always finding the corner. So cool.

It was said Jimmy didn't take the game seriously. God knows what he'd have been like if he did take it seriously then, because he was that good. I saw his debut at Tottenham. He had returned from half a season at AC Milan and there was speculation about whether he could adjust back to English football, would he be the same player, would he score? I'll never forget it: 16 December 1961, I would have been 14. He scored a hat-trick, the first a fantastic scissor kick. It was as if he had never been away. He scored in torrents of goals. Hat-tricks, fours, even fives. He scored more than 20 league goals a season in each of the first 12 years of his career – and that includes the opening campaign with Tottenham that didn't start until December. There was once a question-and-answer session with Jimmy and someone in the audience asked if he would have scored more had he not been lazy. Frank Blunstone, one of Jimmy's team-mates at

Chelsea, was on the stage and he cut in and told this bloke that nobody scored five goals against Billy Wright's Wolverhampton Wanderers if they were lazy.

Jimmy's debut matches were phenomenal. Nigel Clarke, a sports writer from the *Daily Mirror*, told me he saw his first game for Chelsea against Tottenham. He said when he scored his first goal there was almost a pause before the cheer, like an intake of breath, because the fans were gasping at what they had seen. Jimmy was just 17 but the crowd instinctively knew this was a special talent. In his last season as a Chelsea youth team player, Jimmy had scored 114 goals. A year into his first-team career, on 30 August 1958, Chelsea beat the champions Wolves 6–2 and Jimmy scored five. He destroyed the great Billy Wright that day, while still a teenager – ripped him to pieces. The numbers are amazing: five against Wolves, five against Preston North End, five against West Bromwich Albion, four against Newcastle United, four against Nottingham Forest – and that was just for Chelsea. Even his time at AC Milan was successful in terms of scoring – he got 9 goals in 10 Serie A matches, an incredible return for the time.

Jimmy only went to Italy for the money, and he never liked it. He wasn't one for tactical talks or hard training and hated the discipline that was expected from Italian players at that time. He said he paid out so much in fines he had to get his win bonus just to break even. He even got fined for not supporting his team-mates in a punch-up with the Inter players during the Milan derby. My favourite story concerns some girls who used to hang about outside Milan's training ground. Jimmy thought they were fans, so one day, seeing them walking up the lane towards the camp, he offered them a lift in his Jaguar to come up and meet the players. It turns out they were all prostitutes. Jimmy says that misunderstanding cost him a fortune.

Jimmy was another player who operated completely on instinct. He would have learnt his dribbling on the school playground or in the street, not from any coach. He certainly didn't think about it. If you thought about some of the goals he scored you wouldn't be able to pull them off. There is a famous one against Manchester United for Tottenham in 1965 and it is almost like watching a kid playing against his mates. Greaves turns, takes two out of the game, glides past another, runs past – not around – the goalkeeper and taps it into the net. There is such confidence in that goal, such simplicity. It is not something that could have been learnt from a coaching session. I went to the same Chelsea sessions that Jimmy would have attended. They took place in a car park, same as at West Ham – and even if the coaches had been the greatest, most innovative, in the world it would have made no difference. You cannot coach what a Best or Greaves did. You can't coach a player to pick up the ball and beat four men.

This was probably the last era in which the best footballers were allowed to play with complete freedom of expression. The last era when the streets were not full of cars and when every bloke who took a kids' team on a Sunday didn't fancy himself as José Mourinho. Last season, I went to watch my little grandson play at a park where there are lots of small pitches, side by side. I was watching his game and, when there was a break in play, I'd turn and look at the other game. One side had a goal-kick and the whole team dashed up the field to the halfway line and waited as the goalkeeper kicked it as hard as he could. At the end of the game, their coach came over. 'Harry, can we have a picture with you and the kids?' he asked. 'Of course,' I said. So I started talking to these kids. 'I saw a bit of your game, boys,' I said. 'Look, goalie, when you get the ball, pass it. Give it to one of your defenders. Then they get the ball and pass it to another defender. Then try to pass it forward, go forward by passing the ball to each other. Don't just kick it as far as you can. Pass it, then you'll all be involved, passing to each other. Am I right, coach?' 'Yeah, yeah,' he replied, but his expression said, 'Fuck off, Harry, we only wanted a photograph for the clubhouse wall.' But I wanted to make my point. 'Pass the ball,' I told them, 'don't worry if you make mistakes, it doesn't matter. If you make a mistake, you learn. But you've got to try to get the ball and play football. And sometimes when you get the ball, try to beat a man. Have a go, try to dribble.' Will it make any difference? Probably not. It's a shame what happens in kids' football these days. The coaches give up their time, and that's wonderful, but I think they are more bothered about winning than trying to get the kids to play. I'm not sure how much anyone learns or improves that way. It's all about winning, clearing your lines, booting it. You see a kid start dribbling and the other parents are shouting to get rid of it and stop being greedy, all because he hasn't passed to their little Johnny. It's frightening. The goalkeeper kicks it to this wall of bodies on the halfway line. Yet you can tell the naturals, the street footballers, a mile off. That's why Wayne Rooney stood out straight away, that's why Luis Suárez was a revelation in the English game.

Yes, when Messi went to Barcelona he obviously learnt more about the game; but when he gets the ball and goes past three men, that's him, that's his instinct. It was how we all learnt in the fifties and sixties. Keep it tight to your boot and off you go, and Jimmy Greaves was just a natural at that. Nobody taught him to feint to shoot and then delay – he worked that out before he came to Chelsea. He worked that out in the park. It was his gift. The pity is that if a player like Jimmy came along now, with all his natural talent, he would be told to hassle their holding midfield player, and if he didn't do it to the coach's liking, that brilliance would count for nothing and he'd be out. The best players are no longer left to play.

I'm not sure Jimmy even worked too hard on his partnership with Alan Gilzean at Tottenham. He just knew where he needed to be when Gilzean had the ball. Suárez strikes me like that. At times he will make a run that you know is straight from the streets of Uruguay – a player operating purely off his wits, as Jimmy did.

When Robbie Fowler broke into the Liverpool team he drew some comparisons with Greaves, and the *Sun* newspaper thought it would be a good idea to get the two of them together. It was a priceless interview. At one stage Jimmy asked Robbie if he did his work – did he get back, did he cover his man? Robbie, who was a diligent player anyway, gave him the answer he thought he wanted to hear. 'Oh yes, Jim,' he said. 'I always do my work, stop their defenders coming out.' 'Don't do that!' Jimmy exploded. 'You've got nine other players on the pitch for that. How are you going to stay fresh and ready to make a run and score, if you're knackered from chasing the left-back fifty yards? Let them do that, and you wait to score. They can't do your job, that's why they play where they do.' I imagine Robbie's face would have been a picture – but that was how Jimmy saw the game.

He did score goals with 50-yard runs – I remember one against Newcastle – so he wasn't interested in chasing all over the field defending. He stopped playing for England because he wasn't getting picked by Alf Ramsey and just wasn't interested in being a squad player and listening to the tactical talks. Jimmy loved playing, and only playing. I don't think he really cared for football much beyond that. He is more of a cricket and rugby-union man. I know that, when Jimmy retired, he had the opportunity to write a coaching book on how to score goals, but told the publisher he didn't have a clue how any of it happened. 'I turned up and the ball turned up,' he said. 'I don't know why I was there.' Malcolm Macdonald got the job instead. He was a brilliant goalscorer, too, but one who worked far harder on his game – to the extent of keeping notes on opponents. That wasn't Jimmy's style at all. I remember seeing John Bond work with Ted MacDougall at Bournemouth and Ron Greenwood with Geoff Hurst at West Ham. Approach runs, getting across defenders, pulling away – but the bottom line was that neither of those players were in Jimmy's class. They needed direction, they needed instruction; but even then they still couldn't score goals like Jimmy. You could have spent every morning with him and it wouldn't have made any difference. He came into football fully formed.

I got to know him when he came to West Ham in 1970 – two goals on his debut away at Manchester City, same as always – and by then he was past his best. He was no longer part of the England squad and was a heavier drinker than most. Even then, however, you could still see flashes of that old magic. What I remember most about Jimmy was his pre-match ritual. He'd still

111

be in his suit 15 minutes before kick-off. He'd then disappear to the toilet, have a fag, come back and put his kit on. Warm-up routines were not as they are now – some clubs didn't even bother with them at all – but Jim didn't even have oil rubbed into his legs like the rest of us. He'd put his boots on, tie them up, then stand by the door. I can see him now, kicking his feet out, 10 times each leg, ready to go. No running, no stretching. Just go out and score a couple of goals. It was all so matter-of-fact, as if this was what he was supposed to do and everything else was unnecessary. When they were at Chelsea together, Jimmy used to give the young Terry Venables a lift to games, as they lived on the same side of London. Terry says that they would stop for a pre-match meal and Jim would have a full roast dinner, everything you are not supposed to eat before exercise, and then go out and score another hat-trick. I think that's what other players loved about him. He was so laid back, so natural, so completely his own man. We all thought he was great at West Ham, even though, looking back, he was heading for trouble. He was a world-class footballer, but a world-class bloke as well. We all loved being around him.

With hindsight, knowing Jimmy became an alcoholic, it is easy to recognise the signs. Even by the standards of the famous West Ham drinking school, he was hitting it big time. He would go up to the Slater's Arms pub opposite Romford dog track after training, and stay there until the landlord, Jack, called time. A session might start at one in the afternoon and last all day. We didn't know about alcoholism then – we just thought Jimmy liked a drink a bit more than the rest of us. We thought he had everything. A lovely wife, a huge house with seven bedrooms, a successful business – he had a lot more going for him than many footballers – as well as being a great player. We didn't know his drinking was at another level. We had some guys who could really put it away in our team – Frank Lampard, Bobby Moore – a lot of days or nights would end up in the pub, so Jimmy's habits didn't seem particularly unusual. Every club had the odd player whose reputation preceded him. We just thought Jimmy fell into that category.

One of the things I most admire about Jimmy, actually, is the way he has fought back from those days. He became disillusioned with football, and then had problems with addiction, but he fought it and hasn't touched a drop since 28 February 1978. In that time he has been a television personality, a newspaper columnist and now conducts entertaining one-man shows. And just like Jimmy the player, he does it all in his own inimitable way.

DENIS LAW
(MANCHESTER UNITED)

One place left, but it isn't going to either of the forwards that won the World Cup final with England. I should explain why. Roger Hunt was an excellent striker for Liverpool. He wasn't a natural goalscorer, but he was a hard worker, very determined – the sort that was most appreciated by those he played with. Bobby Moore spoke very highly of him, while acknowledging he didn't have the skill or guile of, say, Jimmy Greaves. He was a great player in a great Liverpool team, and was their top goalscorer eight years in a row – but it was an era with a lot of extraordinary players, and I don't think Roger was ever quite in the class of the very best. He was a great team man, but lacked that individual skill that sets a player apart. Geoff Hurst was also a fantastic striker and nobody has equalled his feat of scoring a hat-trick in a World Cup final – and maybe nobody ever will. Yet as special as that performance was, Geoff had to work so hard to become that player. The strikers I have chosen – Jimmy Greaves and Denis Law – were geniuses. Geoff took his chance like no man in history, but he didn't have the ability of Jimmy or Denis, he didn't bring that guarantee of goals. Jimmy, for me, was the pinnacle, but Denis wasn't far behind him and both men could turn a bad performance into a win. Jim didn't score every time, but if you got three chances he would put two away, and Denis was the same. George Best said that Denis didn't need half a chance – he needed a hundredth. That is what gives these two the nod from me.

Denis was a class act around the box. Lightning-quick reactions, razor-sharp thinking. His most famous goal, the back-heel for Manchester City against Manchester United, is proof of that. Denis saw opportunities that others didn't, and he knew it. There was a swagger about him, a cockiness. He came from a poor family, didn't have shoes until he was 12, didn't have football boots until he was a teenager, and people from that sort of background learn to live by their wits. That is what Denis did as a footballer, too. A sniff of a chance and he would go for it, with no thought of danger. Sir Matt Busby said Denis scored the bravest goal he ever saw, for Manchester United against Everton. He said they had a left-sided corner, which Bobby Charlton took and swung in towards the near post. There was a giant Everton defender there looking to hoof it clear, but with his great big boot at the top of its backswing and about to come down, this little figure in red darted in and scored with a diving header. He could have got his teeth kicked in, or his skull, but he didn't care. That was Denis. Brave as anything. He was 5 ft 8 in but was fantastic in the air, often out-jumping big brutes of centre-halves.

He showed promise instantly. Andy Beattie, who was the manager of Huddersfield Town when Denis went for a trial, said he was the most unlikely looking footballer he had ever seen. He was skinny and scrawny and had NHS spectacles and a squint. But Andy said he knew he could be great, the moment he saw him kick a ball. Sir Matt Busby felt the same. He was trying to recruit Denis from the day he witnessed his talent in Huddersfield's youth team, destroying a Manchester United side that included some of his famous Babes. Another good judge reckoned Denis from the start, too – my dad. He saw Denis play for Huddersfield at the age of 19, in an FA Cup replay against West Ham. The game took place in the afternoon because there was another replay on in the evening, Arsenal at home to Rotherham United. My dad went to both games – but the player he was raving about when I came home from school the next day was this kid called Law. The pitch was frozen solid, but he was outstanding and Huddersfield won 5–1. 'I saw a proper player yesterday,' Dad told me. 'He had everything – his balance was amazing.' He must have made a big impression because I've heard the same from other people who were there or were told the same story by an older relative. The whole of the East End was talking about this kid called Denis Law after that, and he signed for Manchester City two months later.

Like Jimmy Greaves, Denis went to Italy to play for Torino, but didn't like it, and that was when Matt Busby finally got him for Manchester United. I think that is the Denis that everyone remembers. Sleeves pulled down and the white cuffs clasped in his hands, like he was freezing. At the start, they had to tell him to stay high up the pitch because he wanted to be involved in everything. He would sometimes almost tackle a team-mate because he thought he knew a better way to get a move started, and in the end Busby banned him from the Manchester United half. I think that was the season he scored a goal a game and ended up the European Footballer of the Year. He was magnificent in that period of his career. Not a dribbler, but a live wire nonetheless. He'd be the player the dribbler would look for at the end of his run, the player most likely to finish the move. The way he arrived in the box showed the most brilliant timing, and he was non-stop, always on the move, always causing problems. He had that electricity around him and when he got the ball everything came alive. At any other club, George Best would have overshadowed everybody, and I suppose it is a tribute to the players around him that we still refer to Best, Law and Charlton. It shows you how fantastic Denis was, to be acknowledged in that company.

He wasn't the typical striker of the time, either. Although neither of my selections, Greaves and Law, were tall men, the fashion was for big imposing strikers. Ron Davies was a particular favourite of mine. He had a tremendous scoring record wherever he played – Chester City, Luton Town, Norwich City and then Southampton – and whenever you headed down to The Dell, Southampton's old ground, your defenders knew they were in for a real battering from Ron. I remember one game in 1971. Ron Greenwood, my manager at West Ham, decided we would get the train from Waterloo rather than stay overnight. We got on board late morning, with a big long carriage almost to ourselves. It was Ron's idea that we could have our pre-match meal on the train, eggs or tea and toast, walk from the station to the ground to stretch our legs and still be in the dressing-room by two o'clock. This was going to be the way forward. It was all going nicely until the railway waiter came out with a boiling hot pot of tea, just as the train made a sudden lurch to the left. Over went the tea, straight on to about four players, including our goalkeeper Bobby Ferguson. They all got scalded, they were all screaming and Rob Jenkins, our physio, was having to rush around with balms and cold flannels. People had bandages on their arms and legs, great big patches full of cream and soothing ointments. It had taken about 10 minutes to sort it out, when this bloke appeared with a replacement pot of tea. Another lurch, to the right this time, and he did it again – now all over the lot on the other side of the carriage. Ron went mad. 'Get out, get out, you bloody idiot!' he shouted, and then there were eight of the team looking like they've just come home from the Great War. God knows how we must have appeared as we hobbled off the train, players covered in bandages, creeping along because the material from their suits was now rubbing on the scalded areas. What a fantastic preparation that was – half the team had second-degree burns. Somehow, we went 3–0 up that day – but Southampton came back to draw 3–3. Ron Davies was up front with Mick Channon, and what a handful they were as a pair.

Andy Lochhead at Burnley was another that could always guarantee you a tough game. I think he was probably Bobby Moore's least favourite opponent. A big Scotsman with a bald head, and as hard as nails. He was at you from the start. I remember one game up there, we kicked off and knocked the ball back to Bobby. Lochhead started chasing him down like a lunatic. Bobby didn't fancy that, so he laid it to our other centre-half, John Cushley, but Lochhead wouldn't give up. Now he began charging at Cushley, who thought, sod that, and played it as quick as he could out to John Charles. Again, Lochhead carried on and just as John was about to play it down the line he launched himself at him from about five yards away. It was like he was competing in the long jump. He hit John about knee height and just left him in a heap. Today it would have been the quickest sending off of the season. He'd have been gone within 30 seconds of kick-off. Back then, it was just regarded as setting the tone for the rest of the game. Let them know they were in for a tough match. And being Scottish, Lochhead always had it in for Bobby, too. It was the joke of the dressing-room that Bobby used to get it from the Scots because he was England captain. That was probably the one thing Lochhead and Law would have had in common.

I think Denis described it as the worst day of his life when England won the World Cup. I can't understand that. I know there is rivalry in football between our countries, but some of the England players would have been his mates. How could you want your mate to lose the biggest game of his life? I know Denis thought Jimmy Greaves was the best striker he ever saw, so he must have had respect for English players. I was really disappointed when I read how Denis felt. He said he went out to play golf while the game was on, and threw his clubs into the locker in disgust when he heard the result. Don't worry, Denis. You might not have loved us, but we loved you.

THE SIXTIES: THE TEAM

**GORDON
BANKS**

Leicester City

**PAUL
REANEY**

Leeds United

**BOBBY
MOORE**

West Ham
United

**JACK
CHARLTON**

Leeds United

**RAY
WILSON**

Huddersfield
Town

**GEORGE
BEST**

Manchester
United

**DAVE
MACKAY**

Tottenham
Hotspur

**BILLY
BREMNER**

Leeds United

**BOBBY
CHARLTON**

Manchester
United

**JIMMY
GREAVES**

Tottenham
Hotspur

**DENIS
LAW**

Manchester
United

CHAPTER THREE

. . . .

THE SEVENTIES

For me, the 1970s begin with the best World Cup I can remember: Mexico 1970. I think that was probably the finest England team – yes, better than 1966 – and certainly the greatest Brazilian side we have ever seen. They may be the best national team ever. They won every match they played, from the qualifying group to the World Cup final – a run of 12 straight victories. Played 12, won 12, scored 42, conceded 9. Some record. On the way to lifting the trophy they beat Paraguay, Colombia and Venezuela (all twice), plus England, Romania, Czechoslovakia, Peru, Uruguay and Italy. No minnows in that lot, really – and every opponent from either South America or Europe. They had two 1–0 wins, against Paraguay, when they had already qualified, and England, and apart from that never scored fewer than two goals in any game. And like many people, I'd put Carlos Alberto's goal – Brazil's fourth – in the final against Italy as the best the competition has seen. The passing, the movement, that slow build, the vision of those players knowing precisely where their team-mates are, and then that explosive finish.

It truly is a thing of beauty. Tostão works hard, tracks back, mops up, and then Brazil play four short passes around the back waiting for their forwards to get in position. Clodoaldo goes on a little run in his own half, beats about four Italians and lays the ball to Rivelino, who pushes it down the left side to Jairzinho. He passes it inside for Pelé, who spots Carlos Alberto arriving like an express train on the right, waits until just the perfect moment and slips the ball inside to him and – first time – wham! Enrico Albertosi in Italy's goal had no chance. Nobody did, really, against that team.

England came as close as anybody, though, and I think that is part of the reason why the 1970 team is rated so highly. Even though we lost, the match against Brazil felt like a new era was beginning in English football and it is a terrible shame that it was not pursued. There were so many good technical teams at that tournament – Italy were outplayed in the final, but they had some great players like Luigi Riva and Sandro Mazzola. Their semi-final against West Germany that ended 4–3 is recalled as the Game of the Century. It had everything. A last-minute equaliser for Germany and five goals in extra time. Back home, we all thought England should have been in that game, though. We were 2–0 up against Germany in the quarter-finals and lost 3–2. That was probably the beginning of the end for Sir Alf Ramsey. He went after England failed to qualify for the 1974 World Cup, but there was an increasing backlash after losing the Germany game. We had played so well to go two up through goals by Alan Mullery and Martin Peters, and Alf plainly thought the match was won. England's defence had only conceded a single goal in the tournament group stage – and that was against Brazil. The

Keeper Bert Trautmann, who came over here as a German prisoner of war and then stayed. I don't think he could do that now, what with all the media attention and the way fans act now, but back then we appreciated what a great player he was, and he became one of us.

Roger Byrne (*far right*), pictured a year before his death in the Munich air disaster, with Busby and the other babes. They're celebrating winning the Division One League Championship. What an extraordinary, magical team.

Here's Leeds United's Bobby Collins in 1962 re-studding his boots with his son. It's a wonder they used to play such great football with the equipment they had in those days. Most had big hard toe-caps and studs banged in at the bottom with the nails coming through!

Johnny Haynes, Fulham's golden boy, on crutches in 1962 after the car crash that effectively ended his England career.

The legendary Stanley Matthews, Duncan Edwards and Billy Wright warming up on England duty with a jog around Highbury in 1957. In those days they had very unsophisticated training regimes – a few times around the cinder track, or up and down the steps of the terraces for fitness.

Tom Finney taking off his boots for the last time at Preston North End in 1960. We set different standards for success then – he played for one club his whole career even though they never won anything, which never counted against him. He was still the best – and everyone acknowledged that.

John Charles – King John, as they called him, or The Gentle Giant – a lovely man away from the pitch but a monster on it, fearless and strong, a real powerhouse. I'd say he was one of the best all-round footballers to come out of Britain.

Danny Blanchflower and
his Tottenham team in the
dressing room, celebrating
winning the Division One
Championship in 1961.
At first Danny clashed with
manager Bill Nicholson,
but together they were
behind the best team
Tottenham have ever
produced. Bill's in the
centre in the bowler, with
Danny sitting on his left.

The great Gordon
Banks, who used to be
a coalman's mate and a
bricklayer before being
spotted by Chesterfield,
is congratulating Bobby
Charlton here on playing
his 100th International
in 1970.

The Charlton brothers on England duty in 1965. I was about 15 when I first saw Jack play, and I couldn't believe he was Bobby's brother. Bobby was so graceful, poetry in motion; Jack was aggressive and would do anything to win. But they were both great players in their own way, and each deserve a place on my team.

I regard George Best as a genius – the best footballer to have come from the British Isles. He had everything, and he changed football forever. Here he is before Denis Law's testimonial in 1973. Best always said about Law that he didn't need half a chance to score, he needed a hundredth. That's what gives him the nod from me.

One of the most famous photographs in football. Dave Mackay had just returned from his second broken leg when Billy Bremner hit him with a naughty one. I think you can see from the photograph that Billy quickly realised he'd made a big mistake.

Bobby Moore and Jimmy Greaves. Bobby wasn't the best athlete, but he more than compensated for that – his determination and understanding of the game was incredible. On the other side of the coin was Jimmy, who people said didn't take the game seriously. God knows what he'd have been like if he did. He scored goals in torrents – hat-tricks, fours, even fives.

Training on the terraces 60s style. It was brilliant being part of that West Ham side. As well as playing with Bobby Moore and Jimmy Greaves, there were so many legends – John Charles, Geoff Hurst and Billy Bonds, amongst others.

myth, however, is that he makes two substitutions and Germany score three goals – that wasn't the way it happened at all. He was already preparing to take Bobby Charlton off when Franz Beckenbauer scored in the 69th minute – and I suppose his mistake was carrying through with that decision. Yet Germany had already equalised through Uwe Seeler when he removed Peters. He wasn't trying to save him for the semi-final as is widely claimed – he just thought he was exhausted and wanted Norman Hunter to shut Germany down in midfield. Gerd Müller won the game for Germany in extra time and I don't think Alf ever recovered his standing.

He had my sympathy. We've all been there. Every manager has tried to shore a game up, or win one, from the substitutes' bench, always with the best intentions. We all have our reasons, but when things go wrong, if you were winning and you lose, you are the biggest fool in the world and every change you made was the wrong one. Sometimes a substitution will not have had the slightest impact on the game, yet you win and get praised. That's how it goes. Everyone thinks you are a genius if you win – but the substitution has often made no difference. And look at it another way: if the substitute has won the game, why didn't you start him? If the manager was such a bright spark, surely he would have kicked off with the XI that ended up winning the match? I heard last season that one of the reasons Norwich City sacked Chris Hughton was that his substitutions didn't make enough impact. What rubbish. One of the reasons subs don't much make impression at Norwich is because they're Norwich. If the player can't get into Norwich's team, how good is he likely to be? You'll find your substitutions make a lot more impact when you're Manchester City manager and Sergio Agüero or Edin Dzeko is coming off the bench. Funnily enough, Norwich's substitutions didn't seem to make too much impact after Chris left, either. So maybe there was more to it than that.

Whatever the reason England lost in 1970, that was still a fine team, and I think it is a pity that English football was then overwhelmed by the Charles Hughes era, when it was all about scoring with less than five passes and direct play was considered the way to go. Hughes was a former PE teacher who became the assistant director of coaching at the Football Association in 1964 and rose to a position of great power and influence in the game. Under him, we missed an opportunity, thinking we could teach the Brazilians about football rather than the other way around. We told ourselves that Brazil were getting it wrong with all these passes, when there really was a chance to come home from Mexico and try to take our football forward – keep our strengths but try to add some of that Brazilian flair. I think the 1970s changed English football – it is the beginning of the game we see now with so many foreign players. At the start of the decade, we were the reigning world champions and able to hold our own against anybody. By the end, Ossie Ardiles, Ricky Villa, Arnold Mühren and Frans Thijssen had come to our game, and it is the beginning of the thought process that leads to foreign players doing the skilful jobs because our own players are considered not up to it. We were too slow to change. Even now, there are very few British coaches bold enough to try to play a very technical game. The long ball, the quick fix, will always be easier.

Yet I remember 1970 as a real highpoint for football in the country. It was a cracking summer. All day you looked forward to the football at night, and we had a World Cup panel on the television for the first time, which was good fun. It was something new. Malcolm Allison, Derek Dougan, Paddy Crerand and 'beautiful' Bob McNab were the first ones, on ITV. I don't know where Bob's beautiful tag came from – and he was probably the quietest of the lot. Malcolm, typically, was the most outspoken. After England lost to Germany he said Alan Mullery was unfit for international football, and Mullery was so incensed that when he came back to England he insisted on joining the panel. The pair had a tremendous row and Mullery threw one of his England caps at Malcolm. Can you imagine that happening now?

'I am a better player than you ever were,' Mullery told him. 'You're entitled to your opinion, but you never, ever change your mind, you see.' 'If you're going to compare yourself with Overath and Beckenbauer and Ball and Bell, I don't think you're as good a player as them,' Malcolm replied. 'I think you're a good passer of the ball, a good one-paced player – but no acceleration. And I don't think you're good in the air.' 'Is that a problem, no acceleration?' Mullery counters. 'There are stacks of midfield players with no acceleration. I'm as quick as Bally is. I'm not as good a player – but I'm as quick as he is, any day.'

Malcolm was the manager of Manchester City at the time. It would be like having Brendan Rodgers in the studio last summer and having him going at it hammer and tongs with Frank Lampard. It just wouldn't happen now. But football on television was completely different back then. When Brian Clough was sacked by Leeds United, they had his predecessor Don Revie waiting in the studio for him that very night. Incredible. It would be like setting up a live interview with David Moyes the

night he was sacked by Manchester United and having Sir Alex
Ferguson sitting there – if Moyes and Ferguson hated the sight
of each other that is. The whole thing lasted 25 minutes and
for the last 10 of them Austin Mitchell, the interviewer, could
barely get a word in as the two went at each other. Even now, it
is a remarkable piece of television – not least because Revie was
the England manager. Can you imagine the Football Association
letting their man do that now?

Revie hated Clough and wanted Johnny Giles to get his job.
Clough had taken over, got the sack, and clearly inside Revie
was doing cartwheels. Obviously, he had been talking to his old
players all through Clough's time; they would have been ringing
him every minute of the day: 'You'll never guess what this
fucking idiot's done now.' You can feel the crackle in the air in
the studio the moment that red light goes on. They even call each
other 'Clough' and 'Revie', not Don and Brian. Clough talks
directly into camera, but it is Revie that is the more aggressive.
Now, everything is so slick. These days there would be a team
of PR people advising against a studio head-to-head – yet in the
interview, Revie actually admits he rang Mitchell and wanted to
come in sooner to dispute a statement Clough had made a few
weeks previously. Television was a new medium. Everyone was
finding out how it could be used. And it was great for the rest of
us because we had really interesting coaches like Malcolm Allison
or a great manager like Clough analysing the games.

Now, so much of what is said is sanitised. Back then, we loved
television's new relationship with the game. Before, no one had
ever come on and talked about matches like that – you were used
to watching with just a commentator and it was all very staid.

So we loved hearing the panel and guys like Malcolm sounding off – we looked forward to ITV's coverage for that as much as the football itself. I don't think I've ever enjoyed a World Cup so much, and that last goal in the final to cap it off felt like the cherry on the cake. It was a privilege to watch that Brazilian team, and I think we were all rooting for them by the end. If England couldn't win it, then we wanted Brazil because they literally played fantasy football: fantastic skills, fantastic ability, fantastic goals, everything about them was special.

We'd never seen anyone do the Roberto Rivelino move before. He would take the ball up to an opponent put his foot on the inside as if to go outside him and then, at the last moment, step over it and move off in the opposite direction. We couldn't believe what we were seeing. Defenders were going six yards the wrong way, and everyone at home was asking the same question: how did he do that? I can remember the panel slowing the footage down so they could study how it was done. Now everybody tries it – Ronaldinho, Lionel Messi, Cristiano Ronaldo – but Rivelino was the first to do the flip-flap, as he called it. This really was a great, great World Cup.

Even footballers try to imitate the greats. I think when we reported back for training that summer, everyone was trying, secretly, to see if they could do the stepover like Rivellino. I mastered it in the end, but not at the speed he managed it, so I'm not saying I used it in too many matches. I think the greatest coaching vehicle in the world for anyone – particularly kids – is to observe good players and see what they do. All the coaching in the world is sometimes not as valuable as watching a good player in his position. My grandson Harry plays right-back for Bournemouth's youngest academy team, so when we go to Bournemouth together I get him watching the right-back, to see where he plays, where he stands, where he goes. We might not be watching the best right-back in the world, but even if he just learns what the job of the right-back is, that's a good coaching lesson. Suddenly, little Harry knows about forward runs and overlaps, and how to position himself around the other defenders. The better the players, the better the lesson. I remember as a youth player, Ron Greenwood, the West Ham United manager, would get us tickets to go to all the big games. He wanted us to watch Arsenal, Tottenham Hotspur, Chelsea – if there was a game on in London he encouraged us to be there. 'Go and watch the good players,' he would say. I remember in 1963 he took a few of West Ham's best kids to see the European Cup final between AC Milan and Benfica at Wembley. Benfica had a brilliant right winger called José Augusto who became a legend at the club, and all through the match Ron was talking to the four of us about the players that were in our positions. There were some real greats on show that night: Cesare Maldini, Gianni Rivera, José Altafini, Eusébio, Mário Coluna. Milan won 2–1, but to watch them all play was an education in itself. As was the journey home. Ron cut up a lorry by mistake and the driver caught us at the next traffic lights. Suddenly, we were exposed to a whole new vocabulary. 'You fucking stupid cunt, I'll break your fucking neck,' the driver was shouting. Ron looked mortified as the cream of his youth team heard this. To us, he was still Mr Greenwood.

Yet everyone came back from that World Cup and into coaching pyramids that were basically run by schoolteachers. When you went on a course at Lilleshall it was all run by men like

Charles Hughes. There was no flair – it was football as taught by PE instructors. Some had been out to Brazil but the material they returned with didn't make any sense. I remember one day when we were being told that Brazilian footballers hone their skills on the beach. That was where they learnt to control a football and it was how we should do it, too. Where the manager of, say, Derby County was going to find a beach when his training ground was about 70 miles inland, I don't know. I'll never forget there was a silence as we digested this brilliant insight, and some years later I heard it repeated in the company of Jim Smith. 'The beach?' he said. 'In that case, why aren't Torquay, Southend and fucking Brighton and Hove Albion top of the league?' They had no answer to that.

Instead of a great leap forward, we came to the end of an international era, with nothing to replace it. Bobby Charlton retired at the end of the 1970 World Cup; Bobby Moore played his last game for England in November 1973; Alf Ramsey was sacked in May 1974. It was clear we were falling increasingly behind. England won their qualifying group for the 1972 European Championships, but were completely outplayed by West Germany in the play-off game at Wembley and lost 3–1. Günter Netzer was the star of that night – he ran the midfield in a way no English player could – but the German team were shockingly superior in every way. They did things that had never occurred to us. Their full-backs, Horst-Dieter Höttges and Paul Breitner, switched. Franz Beckenbauer played as a *libero*, orchestrating the play from behind the defensive line. They played a 20-year-old, Uli Hoeness, as a deep-lying forward. The manager who came up with this innovation was Helmut Schön,

129

who would go on to win this tournament and the 1974 World Cup. 'England seem to have stood still in time,' he said. 'They gave us a fight, but we were far superior technically.' How often have we heard that since?

The rest of Europe was moving towards total football, and we were going into an era when we stopped trusting our most skilful players. Alan Hudson (2 caps), Tony Currie (17 caps), Stan Bowles (5 caps), Rodney Marsh (9 caps), Peter Osgood (4 caps) – England had players that, technically, could have made any team in the world. We just didn't pick them. I cannot think of a bigger waste of talent in English football than Hudson's two caps or Osgood's four, although knowing Alan, I can imagine why he wasn't picked. If you look at the men that managed England through his era – Ramsey, Joe Mercer, Revie – they were a type. They wouldn't have liked his lifestyle and they wouldn't have liked him. Alan could be his own worst enemy. He could have an argument anywhere and if he didn't respect a manager he wouldn't hide it. I can't think Alan would have had much time for Revie, and the feeling would have been mutual. I do recall, though, that one of his two appearances was in 1975 and ended in a 2–0 home win over West Germany, who were the reigning world champions. Hudson was magnificent that night. So maybe Revie should have persevered.

Alan was a world-class player with a list of flaws a mile long. At Chelsea, he used to have big rows with Dave Sexton, who was one of the nicest men in football and a great coach. Alan was a maverick. He could easily have walked out of the England team hotel the night before a match and gone to the pub, if that's what he fancied. In terms of ability he was second to none, and he had a natural level of fitness that was quite astonishing considering his lifestyle – but no England manager was going to stand for that.

I took Alan to Seattle Sounders with me in 1979 when he was only 27. He was an Arsenal first-team player but had fallen out hugely with Terry Neill, their manager. I met the two of them at Heathrow Airport to get the forms signed before I returned to Seattle. The signature on the paper and deal done, Terry put his hand out to Alan to wish him all the best in his new career and got the worst abuse I've heard in my life. It started with 'fuck off' and went from there. 'Shake hands with you?' Alan said. 'You ain't got a fucking clue, mate.' Terry was the perfect gentleman – he just stood there and took it, didn't say a word – but I can remember thinking, 'Oh Lord, what have I done?' Alan looked as if he was going to be a whole load of trouble – but nothing could have been further from the truth. He was a brilliant player for us, but a brilliant drinker, too. World class in fact. He could go for two days without sleep, or food, and still be the best trainer. I've never seen anyone quite like Alan.

We might play on a Tuesday. He'd be the best player on the pitch, run the game, then go back to his house drinking, and have a party. That would go all night – Sandra and I wouldn't stay because we had a young family back then – but Alan's crowd would only be warming up. A little group of them would then go down to the lake the next day for a barbecue. Alan would buy a gallon of gin, vodka, Coca-Cola and sit there drinking all day. They'd go for a swim, have a bite to eat – not much for Alan, as I recall – and then go straight out for the night, drinking hard again. The following morning we'd be back in for training, so he'd have a few hours' kip and then run harder than anybody. He'd been drinking for two days but no one could keep up with him. At first I organised heavy running sessions specifically to keep Alan fit, because I knew how big his drinking was, but really there wasn't any need. We had a running track at the training ground and Alan could do 200 metres and 100 metres faster than anybody. Then he would go out when training was finished and repeat the session. I'd watch him sometimes and he didn't used to run, he'd glide. He wouldn't have eaten for two days – a pure liquid diet – but there was not an ounce of fat on him and he could run and run. Of course there were rows – Alan could be hard work at times – but they were usually over very quickly and I think his reputation went before him a bit, like a few from that era.

Tony Currie was another. He was a beautiful footballer and if he'd been German he would probably have had three times as many caps; he might even have been our Netzer. Tony had great control, scored fantastic goals and could play a killer pass. He had a great feel for the ball, was a real master of it, and I think could be more disciplined than guys like Hudson or Bowles. He would beat two or three players, look up and see the pass or curl the shot, but I'm not sure he had the defensive mindset that managers of that period wanted. He scored the Goal of the Season in 1978–9, for Leeds United against Southampton, a beautiful low bending shot that was typical of his style.

Ramsey had more faith in him that most other England managers, and it was Tony who absolutely peppered Poland's box in 1973 when we were looking for that winning goal to take us to the World Cup. Revie clearly didn't fancy him as much, and Ron Greenwood picked him at first but then preferred

Trevor Brooking, who had similar ability but forged a unique understanding with Kevin Keegan. In most countries at that time Tony would have been the stand-out player in the national team, but we went through a spell when everybody became obsessed with the other side of football – what does he do when he hasn't got the ball? Guys like Tony and Alan were probably marked down for their defensive work. It was madness really.

I'm sure Tony lived life to the full, as Alan Hudson did – but there was probably less opportunity for mischief in Sheffield than the King's Road. They were proper lads, Hudson's Chelsea team. Big characters like Osgood, Charlie Cooke, Dave Webb – they needed a lot of controlling. You now realise how good a side like Leeds United must have been back then, though, when you go through the individuals in that Chelsea team and realise they never won the league. Maybe there were just too many mavericks for it to work – but every team seemed to have them, including Queens Park Rangers.

Rodney Marsh and Stan Bowles succeeded each other at Loftus Road. They were brilliant footballers – but completely unpredictable. We always imagine the best ball players to be small, but Rodney was a giant for his time, over six foot, yet with a great ability to go past people. I've always felt it was a shame he is associated with that failed transfer to Manchester City – he doesn't deserve to be tagged as the man who cost a team the championship. City were four points clear and coasting when Rodney joined them from QPR in March 1972 – and they ended up in fourth spot. Rodney, by his own admission, didn't play well, but one player alone isn't responsible for such a significant drop in form. Rodney is still a hero at Rangers. He inspired the team through two promotions, reaching Division One, and they won the League Cup as a Third Division side. He really had a special talent but, like Hudson, always found a way of talking himself into trouble. Rodney is credited with one of the most famous one-liners in football – and it may even have cost him his England career. In one game, Alf Ramsey told Rodney he would be watching him particularly closely in the first half, and if he wasn't working hard enough, he would pull him off. 'Bloody hell, Alf,' said Rodney, 'at City they only give us an orange.' I've heard that tale a thousand times, with a thousand different culprits, but I'm told Rodney was the one. (And it was Ray Parlour who sat down with Glenn Hoddle's spiritual healer, Eileen Drewery, and asked for a short back and sides – although I've heard that credited to Robbie Fowler and Paul Gascoigne, among others.) When Tony Book took over at Manchester City, Rodney was in open rebellion. It got back to Book that Rodney had described him as fucking useless. 'If you think I'm fucking useless, this is never going to work,' Book said. 'Do you want to take it back?' 'Actually,' Rodney replied, unrepentant, 'I don't think you're as good as that.'

As players Marsh and Bowles, who both played number 10 for QPR, were quite similar. Fantastic one moment, and then fading out of the game. That is the most frustrating type of player for any manager – and I had another one exactly like that last season in Ravel Morrison. If he'd played consistently at his best, he might have gone to the World Cup; on his bad days you wouldn't have put him in our reserve team. Maybe it's something about QPR. They seem to have had a long line of mavericks here.

There is another story about Rodney at Manchester City, when they were due to play Valencia in the UEFA Cup. They met up for the away leg, everyone in their club gear, and Rodney arrived wearing jeans, a T-shirt with a toothbrush in the top pocket and sandals, carrying a pair of football boots. 'Where do you think you're going?' said one of the coaches. 'Spain,' said Rodney, and carried on walking. He was a real one-off.

Stan was no different. I remember seeing him play for Crewe Alexandra at Brentford back in 1971 and, although he finished on the losing side, he looked different class. You could see then that he would be a top player – but like a lot of those with the most ability in that period he never got the international recognition he deserved. He is still idolised at Loftus Road, but he lives back in Manchester now so we don't see much of him. I don't know if he bets as much as he once did, but his gambling was legendary. He would play snakes and ladders for £50 a corner in the days when that was real money – the most Stan earned in his career was £600 a week. He would be watching the racing at five to three when everyone else was preparing to go out and play – but once he was on that pitch, what a player.

I think these guys had real personalities, and that's why the fans loved them. They were characters. I can remember the first time I met Frank Worthington, who was playing for Huddersfield Town against West Ham. He can only have been about 17 but he came bowling straight up to Bobby Moore. 'All right, Mooro?' he said. 'Here, sign this for us.' And handed him an autograph book. That took some front – particularly as he then went out and played superbly against him. Bobby loved it. 'Class, wasn't he, Harry?' he said. 'Had a bit of style.' And he did. Frank had a unique way and a prolific scoring record at clubs that were never fashionable. And, typically, won a paltry eight caps. He also scored one of the greatest goals ever, for Bolton Wanderers against Ipswich Town in 1979. It is worth seeking out on YouTube. Sam Allardyce takes a long throw from the left, which is flicked on at the near post and comes to Frank with his back to goal on the edge of the penalty area. It is an April pitch, very springy, and the ball bounces up. Frank controls it with his head, and then plays two keepy-ups before, with the third, flicking it over his head, taking four Ipswich defenders out in one move, running round and meeting it on the volley to shoot low into the bottom corner. Apparently, Terry Butcher had been giving Frank a hard time all game, very niggly, and after he scored that goal, Frank couldn't resist a little dig. 'You should have been sitting up there,' he said, pointing to the stand. 'Why?' Butcher asked. 'Because you'd have had an even better view of it from up there,' said Frank.

I just don't think those guys fitted in with the England managers of the time. They certainly wouldn't have appealed to Alf, and while the guys at Leeds could be a bit lively, Revie would have had control over them in a way he wouldn't over Alan Hudson. I think there was a distrust of some of the Southern players from the Northern managers, too, so that wouldn't have helped. I can't imagine Revie being a big fan of any of those Chelsea boys. And then Frank with his cowboy boots – they were just different, those guys. People talk about Brian Clough being a maverick sort of England manager, but I'm not sure he would have changed in this attitude to the tearaways. People forget he took Bowles to Nottingham Forest and they fell out almost instantly. Stan had only been there five days when Clough said to Trevor Francis, 'What are you doing mixing with people like him? I thought you had more class and sense than that.' Stan thought he was joking – but there was no smile, and no punchline. He lasted six months and was sold to Leyton Orient. Clough barely played him.

Looking at this team I've picked from the 1970s, it's striking that there are no Arsenal players in there. They won the double in 1971, the first club to do so since Tottenham in 1961, yet when I go through that team now I am even more impressed by their manager Bertie Mee's achievement. It's a good team, but not a great one. I'm looking at players like Peter Storey, Pat Rice, Peter Simpson, even Charlie George, and I wouldn't have any of them ahead of the ones I've picked here. I think two of the Arsenal players that came along later, Liam Brady and Graham Rix, would have been the stars of that double-winning team. I suppose it shows the value of the team as a unit. I'd still back my lads all day, though.

PAT JENNINGS
(TOTTENHAM HOTSPUR)

I first saw Pat playing in the Northern Ireland youth team in what we called the Little World Cup, against England at Wembley in 1963. The competition had a real name – the UEFA European Youth Tournament – and only countries from one continent were involved, but we weren't as familiar with international football then and it felt like a World Cup to us. I went to all the games that England played, and Northern Ireland made the final.

They beat the Republic of Ireland, Belgium, Czechoslovakia, and drew with Sweden and Bulgaria to get there. There were no penalty shoot-outs, so they went through in the semi-final against Bulgaria by drawing lots, which seems ridiculous now. England won 4–0, but I remember everybody being impressed by this big lad in goal for Northern Ireland. A week later Pat signed for Watford.

I got to know him a few years ago when I was managing at Tottenham and he was coaching there. At first he told me didn't want to come over to England. He didn't want to leave his parents in Newry. Pat was a quiet man then, so I can imagine what he must have been like as a teenager. Bill McGarry was one of his managers at Watford and he reckoned the last word Pat ever spoke was 'Goodbye' when he left his parents' house. He wasn't as bad as that, but he certainly wasn't an outgoing type, just very softly spoken, calm and sensible. He was a class act off the field as well as on it, and chatting with Pat was one of the reasons I used to look forward to going to work at Tottenham. He used to come in two or three days a week to work with the goalkeepers, and it was always a pleasure to talk football with him. He doesn't shout his mouth off, but his views about the game are spot-on and I always valued his opinions. He kept goal the same way. He never made a fuss, he was never showy, but what he did, he did magnificently. For a time he was probably the best goalkeeper in the world.

That Northern Ireland youth team of 1963 wasn't bad. As well as Pat there was Dave Clements, who had a big career at Coventry City, but it was just too early for George Best. I think it's a real shame that players like George and Pat never got to play a real World Cup at their peak. Pat did make it to Mexico with Northern Ireland in 1986 and played their three group matches, but he turned 41 on the day of the last one, against Brazil. It was a fitting end to his international career – but what a pity he couldn't have been part of it, say, 12 years earlier when he was at the height of his powers with Tottenham. Even so, it must have been more fun managing Northern Ireland through those years than it is now. Best up front, Jennings in goal – you might get away with that combination. I think they would certainly have qualified had the World Cup been in its present, 32-team, format. These days they are too far down the rankings to get much luck when the draw is made. They always seem to be up against West Germany or one of the really big boys. Maybe they'll have more chances now the European Championship is up to 24 teams – but they haven't got many around like Pat any more.

Pat's background was in Gaelic football and I think that gave him a disregard for getting hurt. He was very brave in the way he came for the ball, and very athletic, always throwing himself about. Not in a dramatic way – but Pat wasn't scared of taking a tumble or going in where it hurt. Gaelic is a very hard game, so Pat probably didn't think too much of getting the odd bang on the football field. Bill Nicholson took him to Tottenham in 1964 as part of a big rebuilding process when the double team began to fade. Alan Mullery, Cyril Knowles, Alan Gilzean – they all joined at around the same time. Pat was the replacement for Bill Brown, who was another double winner and a local hero. It took about two seasons, but by 1966 Pat was Tottenham's first-choice keeper. It would have been hard because there was huge expectation at Tottenham after what had gone before, but they won the FA Cup in 1967 and Pat was a huge part of that. He wasn't very big by modern standards – about 5 ft 11 in – but he looked big, and acted big; he was the first goalkeeper I remember that really dominated his area. Anything near that six-yard box and you knew Pat was coming for it. When I met him later in life I said that I couldn't believe he wasn't 6 ft 4 in. He always seemed huge to us, and was famous for being able to pull a cross out of the air with one hand. He made it all look so easy. Never flapped. Never got ruffled. I remember a game against Liverpool at Anfield in the 1972–3 season when he got cheered off by The Kop having almost cost them the league title. He was brilliant, Tottenham got a draw and at the time it looked as if he might have handed the prize to Arsenal. Liverpool came through in the end – but it shows the sort of man Pat was, that the Liverpool fans could still appreciate him, despite the cost to their team. I'm not sure it would happen now.

In fact, I think it shows how highly Pat was regarded that in 1977 he left Tottenham for Arsenal without there being a lasting feeling of resentment towards him at White Hart Lane. Sol Campbell did it and got slaughtered – and it seems he'll be hated by Tottenham fans for evermore. Yet there is a lounge named in Pat's honour at White Hart Lane now; he is a coach at the club and a match-day host. And he always strolls into any supporters' list of Tottenham legends.

Selling Pat to Arsenal must rank as one of the biggest transfer mistakes Tottenham have ever made – and there's quite a list. I think the club thought his best years were behind him – so it must have come as quite a surprise to see him still holding a place in Arsenal's first team six years later, as he became the first player in English football to pass 1,000 senior appearances. Pat reached the FA Cup final in three consecutive campaigns with Arsenal, winning once, and saved a penalty from Mario Kempes in the final of the 1980 European Cup-Winners' Cup, but sadly ended up on the losing side because Liam Brady and Graham Rix missed.

Manchester United, Aston Villa and Ipswich Town were all in for Pat when he left – but, unsurprisingly, a typical piece of Tottenham politics pushed him the way of Arsenal. Pat knew he was leaving but still went to the ground to say goodbye to the rest of the team, who were departing for a pre-season trip to Sweden. The directors were going, too, and Pat says that as they passed him, one by one, they all blanked him. It was then he decided to consider an offer from Arsenal. Until that point he had resigned himself to commuting up and down the motorway – but getting such cold treatment after 13 years at the club drove him to sign for Tottenham's big rivals. He is very straight about it – he did it for convenience and in the hope of embarrassing the Tottenham bigwigs. Over the next eight years he did just that – yet he still got applauded every time he went back to Tottenham. The fans never blamed him for what happened.

The negative reaction to former players is something quite new in football. There was plenty of bad behaviour among fans in the seventies, but players did not seem to be targeted the same way. The crowd fought each other and obviously some grounds were livelier than others, but there never seemed to be that animosity towards those who played the game. When Pat left Arsenal he even came back to Tottenham to keep himself fit and ready for the 1986 World Cup.

I know Bob Wilson, who Pat replaced at Arsenal, says he was the best of all time. He puts him ahead of Gordon Banks or Peter Shilton. The one I feel sorry for, really, is Ray Clemence. In any other era he would have been England's number one, but at either end of his career he coincided with the two greatest goalkeepers this country has had. I do remember Ray was coach at Tottenham, though, when Ian Walker broke into the team as goalkeeper and in one of his first games took a cross with one hand, Pat Jennings style. It is fair to say the views Ray expressed on the subject that day indicated he too thought there could only ever be one Pat Jennings.

PHIL NEAL
(LIVERPOOL)

Until Ryan Giggs came along I cannot imagine too many would have matched Phil Neal for medals: eight title wins, four European Cups, four League Cups, the UEFA Cup and UEFA Super Cup. He is still the most decorated English footballer in history, but holds a record even more fantastic than that. Between 23 October 1976, when he played in a 1–1 draw away at Leeds United, and 24 September 1983, a 1–0 defeat at Manchester United, Phil Neal did not miss a single Liverpool game in any competition: a run of 417 consecutive matches. He then lost three games to injury, after which he did another 127 in a row. I can safely predict that in these days of squad rotation we will never see that record broken by an outfield player at an elite club.

Phil seemed indestructible – he certainly behaved as if he was. Derby County had a telegraph pole of a centre-forward around that time called Roger Davies. He had come through the non-league ranks, worked as an apprentice engineer, and had been picked up by Derby for £12,000. He wasn't the most subtle or technically gifted player, but he was always difficult to play against and in one game caught Phil with an elbow and broke his cheekbone. The injury was so bad it needed an operation to realign Phil's face, and the specialist said he should rest for a month – yet four days later he played for the club again, having told Paisley he was fine. And no protective masks back then, either. He just marched out and, fingers crossed, hoped he would get away with it. On another occasion he broke a toe – the fifth metatarsal that ruined Wayne Rooney's World Cup in 2006 – but played on with a tiny plaster cast made by Ronnie Moran. He went up a boot size and a half and could barely walk in normal shoes, but somehow Phil played on. He had injections into the damaged area to enable him to kick a ball and tackle. There are very few players in the modern game who would go through the pain barrier like that.

Liverpool nearly missed out on him, too. On Paisley's last scouting trip to see Phil play for Northampton Town, he took along a director, Sidney Reaks, probably to convince him that he was worth the money. Just 20 minutes into the game, the Northampton goalkeeper got injured and Phil spent the rest of the night in goal. Fortunately, the men had already seen enough and Paisley paid £66,000 for Phil as a replacement for Chris Lawler at right-back. He could have played left-back, too, and within days started the Merseyside derby. Back then, players could take those dramatic steps up, and Liverpool were the best at judging it. They just had the knack of pulling players from the lower leagues and turning them into superstars. They scouted Phil and saw in him a cultured, classy full-back, far superior to his surroundings. Phil was good on the ball, passed nicely, took penalties and scored so many important goals the Liverpool players nicknamed him Zico.

He was another of those 7 out of 10 players. He wasn't one for cavalier charges up field, but as a manager you recognise the type – and guys like him are often the first names on the team sheet. If you think back to the Liverpool team of that era, so much of their strength came from the back. Phil Neal, Alan Hansen, always unruffled, never under pressure, always composed on the ball. Just passed it and passed it. You never saw Neal panic and whack it anywhere, there was always a ball into a channel, something the rest of the team could work from. Liverpool simply had an air of calmness, and that stemmed from Neal and those players at the back. He always looked composed, playing the game as if he was completely in control.

I always thought it was a shame for Phil that to a certain generation he is remembered for the documentary about Graham Taylor's ill-fated World Cup campaign as England manager. Phil Neal is Taylor's coach and comes across in the film as a bit of a yes man, always agreeing with his boss, seconding his opinions or parroting what has just been said. I know Phil thinks he was misrepresented at the editing stage but, whatever the truth, it is never easy fulfilling the assistant-manager role, because the boss it always going to back his hunch in the end. In the first high-profile job that I had, with West Ham United, Frank Lampard was invaluable to me because he had strong opinions that he wasn't afraid to share. You don't want to be rowing every two minutes, but you do want your assistant to speak up if he spots something going wrong, and if you ask him about a substitution, for instance, you want his call, not what he thinks you want to hear. You're looking for genuine feedback, not just agreement – and my guess is that there was more to Phil's partnership with Graham than what we saw. Frank was someone I could bounce things off all the time, even during the games. He is a wealthy individual, invested wisely during his playing days, and didn't have to be nice to anybody to stay in a job. It made a difference. He didn't stay in football long after West Ham because what appealed was working for me, and at Upton Park. I'm sure Graham got Phil in as the type of coach that would be admired by the team for his achievements as a player, and he should have felt confident enough to use that experience. If Phil read the game as a coach as well as he did as a player he could have been tip-top.

PHIL THOMPSON
(LIVERPOOL)

Wimbledon's Crazy Gang were never the greatest respecters of reputations, but even by their standards full-back John Kay was relentless, and known for a vicious sense of humour. One tackle by Kay on Peter Haddock, a defender playing at Leeds United, left manager Howard Wilkinson saying his leg looked like it had been run over by a tractor. After that, Kay revelled in the nickname 'The Tractor'. He moved from Wimbledon to Sunderland in 1987 and in one game against Birmingham City broke a leg – his own this time. Despite being in terrible pain, Kay sat up on the stretcher and pretended to row it off the pitch and down the tunnel. It's fair to say he was a nutcase. And it was Kay who during one of the first matches between upstarts Wimbledon and the mighty Liverpool is said to have taken a distinct interest in Phil Thompson's pronounced features while waiting for a corner to be taken. 'Do you know what, mate?' Kay told the Liverpool captain. 'Walt Disney couldn't draw your fucking face.'

Wimbledon's attitude was the reason they made such an impact on the top division, so I'm not knocking it – but Phil Thompson deserved a little more deference than that. We are talking about one of the great centre-halves in one of the great teams. He might be craggy, he might have a famously prominent hooter, but he was also a leader, a winner and a serious competitor. I don't know if Kay got the last word that day, but if I know Phil, there was an elbow in the gob waiting somewhere along the line. He could play, but he was aggressive too. They were a beautiful team, Liverpool, but they also had a knack of finding or producing some real hard cases – Tommy Smith, Ron Yeats, Emlyn Hughes, Phil, they could all look after themselves. Mark Lawrenson was a lovely footballing centre-half, but there are plenty in the game who will vouch for the fact he was the hardest tackler, too. In some ways those Liverpool players were like Brazil stoppers. They were up against great strikers every day in training – Kevin Keegan, John Toshack, Ian Rush, Kenny Dalglish – and they could be made to look pretty silly if they weren't at the top of their game. It's the same in Brazil – growing up playing against some of the finest footballers in the world, no defender wants to be made to look a mug. People are often surprised that Brazilian players are quite cynical – but playing against the likes of Ronaldo or Rivaldo, wouldn't you be? The alternative is getting a chasing.

Phil started off as a central midfield player and only moved back to centre-half after his first season. He was physically strong, but not a big man and far from a routine defender. Hughes and Alan Hansen, his two main partners, were more conventional in their approach, while Phil played it like a continental. Bob Paisley thought he was one of the best readers of a game that he saw, and he was very comfortable on the ball. Graeme Souness told me that Thompson was actually a better technical footballer than Hansen and, as he played with both, I'm not about to disagree. He was an organiser, too, and different class when the pressure was on; you never saw that generation of Liverpool players rattled. In the 1978–9 season, he was part of a defence that let in only 16 goals in 42 matches.

A lot of people of my generation remember the 1974 FA Cup final as one of Phil's greatest matches: Liverpool 3, Newcastle United 0. Kevin Keegan scored twice, but before the game all the talk had come from Malcolm Macdonald, who had scored in every round and was promising to do all of that and more to Liverpool. Bill Shankly, in his last competitive game as Liverpool manager, put the 20-year-old Thompson on him, and Phil marked him out of the match. Malcolm did get some tiny revenge, though. Sometime later they were on an England trip together and sitting down at dinner he discovered that Thompson couldn't stand the smell of garlic. A dish with a strong garlic smell came to a table nearby and Thompson was extremely uncomfortable. After that, the story goes, Macdonald would eat cloves of garlic before every match against Liverpool, and breathe on Thompson the moment he got near. He claimed to have an extra half-yard through the rest of his career using this method. Makes you wonder how Phil was so good in Europe, though.

I think what also sets Phil Thompson apart in Liverpool folklore is that he was a local lad from Kirkby who had stood on The Kop since he was a kid. Liverpool had a brilliant scouting network at that time – in fact, I've never seen one better – and just had a way of spotting these players in the lower leagues and bringing them through. They would go to Bury and get a player like Alec Lindsay or Northampton for Phil Neal; and while Emlyn Hughes came from Blackpool, who were then a top division club, Bill Shankly bought him after only 28 appearances.

These players would go straight into the team, too. It makes me think that maybe English players could still do it, given the opportunity. There were no foreign players in the English game back then, so you had to rely on your instincts and make these promotions. Given the opportunity, belief and support from the manager, and the comforting environment of a good team, English players showed they could make the step up from the lower leagues to, in some cases, the European Cup final.

One of the unsung heroes of Liverpool's success is Geoff Twentyman, the chief scout for close to 20 years, whose discoveries ranged from Neal to Alan Hansen (£100,000 from Partick Thistle) and Ian Rush (£300,000 from Chester City). Twentyman was a player at Carlisle United when Bill Shankly became manager there. He moved on and had a modest career with Liverpool, and he left just as Shankly was arriving as manager in 1959. It wasn't until 1967 that the pair reunited, when Shankly offered him the position of chief scout. Liverpool were a very different club then and Twentyman's brief was to find the best players that they could afford, not established stars on huge wages. He and Shankly had very similar ideas on what constituted a Liverpool player, and there are stories of Geoff ending a scouting mission having watched only the warm-up because he wasn't happy with his target's level of professionalism. Another factor was what Twentyman and Shankly called a Northern soul – they didn't like Southerners – and it wasn't until Paul Walsh joined Liverpool in 1984 that Twentyman recommended a Londoner join the ranks. Excluding such a large swathe of the populace didn't harm Liverpool's fortunes, though. Twentyman's strike rate was nothing short of astonishing: Kevin Keegan, John Toshack, Steve Heighway, Ray Clemence – and he was always in on the ground floor, so Liverpool were bidding when other clubs were just waking up to the news of a young prospect at Scunthorpe or Skelmersdale United. Liverpool bought Gary Gillespie from Coventry City, but Geoff was already monitoring him at Falkirk. Not every trip ended in success, though. Twentyman's first recommendation to Shankly was Francis Lee, but Liverpool could not afford him; nor did they follow up Geoff's interest in Andy Gray, Trevor Francis or Martin Buchan. Yet his strike rate was phenomenal.

Liverpool looked at players differently. Often they had already come to a conclusion about a player's technical ability and were more worried about character. Does he take the warm-up seriously? Is he a bit flash? Paisley wouldn't sit with the managers or scouts if he was watching a player. He, or Twentyman, would buy a ticket and stand behind the goal, get talking to the local fans, ask what a certain player was like. These days managers are so famous that this could never happen. Imagine José Mourinho turning up at Southend United and trying to remain incognito. He would be mobbed. Not that Chelsea would be buying players from Southend any more, of course. Scouting has completely changed in the modern era.

I still go to watch players and it makes me laugh, sometimes, sitting with those old boys. Half of them spend the match gossiping – what is going on at this club, who's getting the sack, who's been tapped up, who is going where. Then there is usually a moan about the facilities, about how you always used to get nice sandwiches here at half time, but now they don't even lay out a plate of biscuits. Then, 15 minutes before the end, they all get up and go to beat the traffic. In the meantime, most of the big money scouting is done on video via agents. If you need a right-back, an agent comes on and tells you he has a 20-year-old from Estonia, who is going to be the best full-back in Europe. He sends a link, you go into the club cinema and a minute later everything you need to know about him is up on screen – the games he's played, the goals he has scored, match footage, the lot. You can go from never having heard of a player to watching him play a full game in the time it takes to make a cup of tea.

It has changed so much. When I started playing, club scouts were at every big schoolboy game in the area: East London Boys, Ilford Schools, Hackney Boys, Barking Schools, Dagenham Boys, they would be there on the touchline, grafting, talking to the parents if they thought the kid was good enough. The next week, they would be round the house, chatting them up over a cup of tea, because a good kid might have six clubs chasing him. Scouts were real grafters in those days.

When I was a youth team coach in the mid seventies, during my playing days at Bournemouth, one of my smartest moves was to appoint one of the best youth scouts. How did I come to be coaching? John Benson was the manager at the time and we had a youth team but no coach. The old kit man was doing the best he could; the kids would arrive in the morning and he'd oversee matches, eight-a-side, six-a-side, depending on how many were available, but it was very unorganised. I said to John, 'Those kids, they're wasted. They never get any instruction – why don't I take them?' We had a fantastic scout working for us called Reg Tyrell, who had been at Ipswich Town and discovered players like Clive Woods and Trevor Whymark. A lot of people reckoned Reg as the best in the country. He was a great character, always laughing. He used to wear a little trilby hat.

Reg drove Bill McGarry, the manager of Ipswich, mad. In the end, Bill used to draw a line in the grass at the training ground. 'Reg, if you cross that line, I swear I'll fucking boot your arse.' John Bond had persuaded him to come down to Bournemouth as our chief scout in the early seventies, and I ended up getting him involved with youth development as well. We ended up with about six young players who had good careers, like Steve Gritt who played 435 games for Charlton Athletic – and a couple of England internationals, Kevin Reeves and Graham Roberts. Reg found them all just by watching Sunday-morning parks games. They weren't schoolboy superstars. He got them in the old-fashioned way, standing in his cap in the rain on a touchline. That was what it was about back then: going to these out-of-the-way places, scouting and having the balls to back your judgement. Imagine spotting Phil Neal playing for Northampton, and thinking he'll have the ability to play a European Cup final in front of 57,000 people three years later – and the guts to take a penalty to wrap the game up. But he did. Go back to that 1977 Liverpool team – scouted from Scunthorpe, Northampton, Wrexham, Blackpool, Skelmersdale, Bury – what an incredible achievement to see the potential in all of those boys. There was no sitting on the fence, no uncertainty about making the step up. The scout had to go to Shankly, or Paisley, and put his neck on the line. He had to say that Scunthorpe's goalkeeper wouldn't let us down in a European Cup final against Real Madrid. And he was right – Ray Clemence was superb when the moment came.

There must have been real pleasure in making those discoveries, though – a satisfaction you just won't get from watching tapes in a dark room. Imagine the night Bobby Gould, then manager of Coventry City, first saw Stuart Pearce play for Wealdstone in the old Gola League. That rarely happens now, that feeling of revelation. I can picture Bob sitting there now, watching this six-foot, marauding left-back, who can score goals one minute and boot the right-winger into the stand the next. It wouldn't have taken a genius to see what he saw in Pearce – but he must have felt like he'd just found a diamond lying on the pavement. He made a £30,000 bid the next day and put him straight in Coventry's team. I remember Dave Webb getting Nigel Spackman from Andover's bench. He couldn't even make their team, but went on to captain Liverpool and Glasgow Rangers. Jim Smith paid £15,000 for Les Ferdinand at Queens Park Rangers after spotting him playing for Hayes.

Cyrille Regis was another great centre-forward who came from Hayes. I remember David Pleat saying there was a real buzz around this kid Regis playing in the Isthmian League, and on one particular night there was no other game in town and it seemed that every club in the country was there, watching him. Regis did nothing. All the managers and scouts were looking at him, shrugging their shoulders; nobody was impressed. With about 10 minutes left to play, one of them made a move to go, and one by one they all started to follow him, down the wooden stairs at Hayes's Church Road ground. With that, Hayes's wide player put in a cross and Cyrille jumped three feet higher than anyone on the pitch – bang, straight in the corner. Everyone froze in mid-step. That was what they had all gone there to see. If a goalscorer can do that one thing better than any other player, he'll make it. West Bromwich Albion were the first on the telephone the next day. The directors weren't sure about paying so much for a non-league player, but Albion's scout, Ronnie Allen, was so sure he offered to cover the £5,000 fee himself.

Sometimes you just have to trust people. Stuart Morgan, my assistant manager at Bournemouth in the eighties, went to watch Efan Ekoku at Sutton United. He came into my office the following morning. 'Harry,' he said, 'I've seen a player – he's something special. Different class. He's got pace, he's got ability, he's so fucking strong. We've got to take him.' Their next game was the following Tuesday night, so I said I'd go with Stuart and watch him play. If he had wanted to, he couldn't have performed any worse. I don't remember him doing a single thing right in 90 minutes. I said to Stuart, 'Have you gone mad?' 'I'm telling you, Harry,' he said, 'I've watched him twice and he's been amazing. If he isn't any good, you can sack me.' He was going to cost us £40,000. We asked Sutton if he could train with us for a week. If we liked him, they had their £40,000. Seven days later, it was still touch and go – but Stuart was insistent. In the end we took him and he was brilliant for us. We sold him to Norwich City for £500,000 – and they moved him on to Wimbledon for £900,000. He had a good Premier League career. And that was all down to Stuart backing his judgement and being trusted – because if it had been left up to me I would have walked out at half-time.

You don't get stories like that these days – unknowns straight into the first team at elite clubs. Daniel Sturridge is looked upon as a revelation at Liverpool, but it wasn't as if he came from nowhere. He was a Manchester City player, a big signing at Chelsea, and then Liverpool paid £12 million for him. If anything, it was a surprise that Chelsea let him go. He was ripping into teams from that right-sided position, coming in on his left foot. We played against him at Tottenham, and a lot of our defensive work all week was built around stopping Sturridge. He could dart in towards goal, he could go outside and get it across the face of you; he really looked a player. He didn't track back enough, though, and André Villas-Boas bombed him out. Liverpool got lucky, really. It wasn't as if they discovered him in the wilderness. Liverpool were outstanding for a lot of last season, but it wasn't a team built up like in the old days. Luis Suárez was Uruguay's striker, and a World Cup player. The only one whose arrival compares to that Twentyman era really is Raheem Sterling, who came from Watford. But he didn't walk straight into the team as players used to.

Yet that great Liverpool team wasn't just about the signings. Shankly was a real visionary when it came to scouting and recruitment. Players like Thompson came through after being spotted at a young age, and that's not easy when you have a team as big as Everton across the way. In 1968, Shankly appointed the first Youth Development Officer in English football, Tom Saunders, and the club were still getting use from him when my Jamie went there in 1991. He was an ex-schoolteacher, a wily old boy, and I think Kenny Dalglish and then Graeme Souness leaned on him a lot. He did all their overseas scouting missions in Europe, going to these places inside the Iron Curtain where they definitely didn't want you. The story goes that for one match at Anfield, the manager of Dinamo Tbilisi came over to create his scouting report, so Liverpool thought they would show how hospitality to the opposing club should be done. They invited this bloke down to the famous boot room, where he got stuck into the Guinness with Bob Paisley and the boys. By the end of it, he could hardly stand. They virtually had to carry him to his car and I doubt he remembered much.

ROY McFARLAND
(DERBY COUNTY)

Here we go again. Roy McFarland was one of the greatest central defenders in one of the finest defensive partnerships this country has produced, and Derby County took him for £24,000 from Tranmere Rovers. Apparently, Liverpool were also sniffing around, but Brian Clough and Peter Taylor went to his house and refused to leave until he joined Derby. Then they paired him with Dave Mackay and he never looked back. He was a footballing centre-half. He was strong in the air, but would get the ball down and play as well, little one-twos out of the area. Colin Todd, who succeeded Mackay, was under instructions not to cross the halfway line, but Roy had more freedom. He says the greatest piece of advice Clough ever gave him was that he couldn't bring the ball out of defence every time; sometimes it had to end up in the back of the stand. The key to being a great defender was to know when was the right time for each move, Clough said – and only he could work that out. Very true.

I admit, I have had to agonise long and hard over this one. I really wanted a place for Todd in this team, too, but I prefer McFarland, and there is no way I won't find room for Phil Thompson. Yet Todd was a quite outstanding player, and captained Derby at their peak. He was very quick, could bring the ball out and was difficult for attackers to compete with because, basically, he was built like them. He didn't have the stereotypical defender's frame at all – he was squat, with a low centre of gravity and good ball skills. He could read the game and played magnificently off McFarland, but he was tough, too – just like his son, Andy.

It shows how times have changed that Todd was an integral part of the Sunderland team that won the FA Youth Cup in 1967, coached by Brian Clough, yet also made 30 first-team appearances that season. It just wouldn't happen now. Once a young player has made the senior team, he wouldn't demean himself playing with his youth team-mates any more, and the manager wouldn't want him risked at a lower level. Yet in those days tournaments like the FA Youth Cup were there to be won, and clubs would put out the best-qualified team regardless of the players' status. I wonder if we haven't lost something there.

The most impressive aspect of Clough's Derby team is the football they managed to play on that pitch. The Baseball Ground was comfortably the worst in the country, yet they played some marvellous stuff. Not a blade of grass on it after about two months, and then like a beach in April, but it never seemed to stop them. Alan Hinton and Kevin Hector were terrific centre-forwards, and they had Terry Hennessy in a defensive midfield role, stepping up from centre-half, ahead of his time. That Derby team could all play. They moved the ball beautifully and that was down to Clough. Just getting Dave Mackay in was a genius move, and judgement calls like that happened too often with him for it to be luck.

Frank Clark was a free transfer for Clough's Forest from Newcastle United, who'd probably thought he was at the end of his career. Clark was talking to Stan Anderson, the manager of Doncaster Rovers in Division Four, when Clough got in touch. Clark signed the next day. From Birmingham City he took Kenny Burns, who was known as a bit of a thug, and turned him into the Footballer of the Year; and he took Larry Lloyd, who everybody thought had enjoyed his best years at Liverpool.

It was a pity that, later in Clough's career, some of that brilliance deserted him and what was left could be a bit difficult. During the summer in 1991, my chairman at Bournemouth called and said he'd had Brian Clough on the phone wanting to buy our centre-half, Shaun Teale. Shaun was a player I had bought from Weymouth for £50,000 two years earlier and he was going right to the top. He reminded me of Colin Todd: similar size, great spring, fast, aggressive, a good left foot. The chairman said he had told Clough to speak to me about any deal and had given him my number. 'He's going to ring you,' he said, so I waited for the call. It was a beautiful day and we were heading out to Salisbury races. I waited but heard nothing. Then, in the car on the way there, the mobile burst into life. The voice was unmistakable.

'Harry, it's Brian Clough.'

'Hello, Brian, how are you doing?'

'Yes, I'm fine. Very good, actually. Now, listen, I'm interested in your man Teale. He's one of your cockney boys, is he?'

'No,' I said. 'He's from Southport.'

'Is he?' he said. 'And how big is he?'

I said: 'He's about five foot eleven or six foot, Brian. He's not a giant for a centre-half, but he can jump like he's six foot four, he's fantastic in the air, a great header of the ball, beautiful timing.'

'All right,' he said. 'How much do you want for him?'

I told him the price was £500,000. 'I'll not give you that,' he said, 'but I'll give you £499,999.'

This was his little game. He always said he paid £999,999 for Trevor Francis because he didn't want the tag of being the first £1 million player going to his head. By now I had pulled the car over. I didn't have to think for long. 'We won't fall out over a pound, Brian,' I told him. 'You've got a deal.' 'Have a word with the boy and we will get it sorted,' Clough said. So I got hold of Shaun and he came down to our ground to await instructions on the next step of his big move. Nottingham Forest had just lost to Tottenham Hotspur in the FA Cup final and were still in the top half of Division One at that time. Three hours passed, we hadn't heard a thing from Clough. I called the club, got through to his secretary. 'I'm sorry, Mr Redknapp,' she said, 'Brian's gone to Majorca for two weeks and he's not contactable.' We never heard another word.

In the end, Shaun signed for Ron Atkinson at Aston Villa, who had also never seen him. I bumped into Ron on holiday in Spain. By then, we'd gone a month without hearing from Forest, so I knew the deal was dead. 'Who is the best centre-half in your division?' Ron asked me. 'Shaun Teale,' I said. 'Who's he play for?' said Ron. 'Bournemouth,' I told him. 'No, seriously,' he repeated, 'who's the best centre-half? Don't try to sell me your player, I'm asking you a sensible question.' 'And I'm giving you a sensible answer,' I told him. 'Shaun Teale – check him out.' I came back and three days later Ron rang me. 'I've checked him out,' he said. 'You were telling the truth, he is a good player. But I'm told he might be short of a yard of pace.' 'Whoever told you that isn't a judge, then,' I told him, 'because he's like lightning.' So Ron took him and he made close to 200 appearances for Villa. I think Clough was the loser that day.

But that was Brian. Many years earlier he did the same to Kevin Bond, who was supposed to sign for Nottingham Forest from Manchester City. John Benson, his manager, said the deal with Forest was done, so off he went. Kevin arrived at the ground at 9am as arranged and was told to wait outside Mr Clough's office. He sat there for an hour and a half. Brian's secretary kept telling him that Clough was busy. Suddenly, he came out, stopped and looked at Kevin. 'The first thing you need to do, young man, is get your hair cut,' he said. And on he walked, straight past him. Kevin, waiting another hour or two, thought, 'What am I doing this for?', got up and went back to Manchester City. He never heard another word.

It's hard to tell with Brian how much was psychological masterstroke, and how much was random acts caused by his problems with alcohol. There is a story in a book about Clough that concerns the party after Derby had won the league in 1972. Everybody was having a wonderful time, when Clough suddenly rounded on Colin Todd. 'Toddy,' he said, 'I don't like you, and I don't like your missus, either.' Todd walked out. The next day everybody got flowers and the whole thing was smoothed over, and the take on it is that Clough thought Todd was too nice for a defender and too quiet for someone he thought might captain the club. He wasn't a drinker, a smoker, a gambler, a womaniser – Clough couldn't work him out, so wanted to get a reaction from him. And maybe that is true. Todd says Clough might kick him in training too, just to get him wound up. He obviously doesn't bear a grudge, but you wonder how much was intended. It's sad, but I think Brian's problems got worse through his career.

Every manager has a different way of handling players. Rafael Benítez is known for being very cold, very sparing in his praise. When Liverpool won the Champions League in Istanbul, Steven Gerrard thought he might finally get a 'well done' out of him, after the game of his life. They had the giant trophy in pride of place on the top table, and all night Steve kept edging towards it thinking that he would ultimately get a pat on the back from his manager. Eventually he got there. Gerrard, Benítez and the trophy all within touching distance. 'Not bad that, eh, boss?' said Steve, eyeing the cup. 'Yes,' said Benítez, 'but ...' And he started bollocking him for mistakes he made in the first half. I think everybody needs to hear 'well played'. Even Bobby Moore used to secretly hope for more praise from Ron Greenwood.

I can remember talking to Stuart Pearce about the way Clough operated when we were at West Ham United together. I think all managers are fascinated by him because there was so much innovation in what he did, and so many myths have grown around him since. 'He was amazing,' Stuart told me. 'We wouldn't see him all week, and then he'd come in on Friday and walk his dog. We were playing five-a-sides one day and he said to [Forest full-back] Brian Laws, "You're wasting your time doing this – take my dog for a walk." And Brian did – twice around the training ground, while Clough watched the five-a-side.' Unbelievable, isn't it?

Last season, Chelsea beat Fulham 3–1 and José Mourinho said the first half was their worst performance of the season. He claimed that he said nothing to them at half-time, just walked in and walked out. That is straight out of Clough's handbook. It is what he's said to have done with his players when they were losing 1–0 to Southampton in the 1979 League Cup final. 'You lot got yourselves into this, you can get yourselves out of it,' he said. As a manager, you've only got 15 minutes to try to influence the game once it has begun. It takes some guts to do that.

Alan Hill, who was Clough's assistant, is a good friend of mine and he told me how Clough used to simplify the game. 'Goalkeeper, your job is to save goals. Right-back, left-back, stop their wingers. You tackle, you win the ball. You, centre-halves, you head it out of the box. Ball comes in, your job is to clear it out, your job is to get there, win headers, win tackles. You get it, give it to people who can play. Midfield players, get on the ball, make us play. Get it out to your wingers. Give them the ball, we play with two wingers, give it to them. Every time you've got it, I want that ball supplied to the wingers. Wingers, you get down the line, you get crosses in. That's your job. Beat the full-back, get the ball in the box. You two up front, your job is to score the goals. Centre-forwards score.' And that was it. He played 4–4–2, nothing else, but his observations within that framework, Alan tells me, were so clever. Little pieces of information he would come out with, like his advice to McFarland about not expecting to bring the ball out of defence every time. He must have just had a gift for football thinking, and the way to motivate players. However difficult he may have been to deal with at times, you can't achieve what he did by accident. You can't take Derby to the title and Nottingham Forest to the European Cup just making it up as you go along. There was always a philosophy there. He may have couched it very simply, but we all remember how a Brian Clough team played. The same with Sir Alex Ferguson, José Mourinho, and younger managers like Brendan Rodgers and Roberto Martínez. They have a plan. I'm not saying it always had to be the beautiful game. Wimbledon had a plan under Dave Bassett and Bobby Gould, and while if might not always have been pretty, it was effective, and they came through four divisions and won the FA Cup, so I don't think anyone can criticise it. And that was Clough's greatness, too. You knew what you would get from his teams, but his players were so good and his ideas so clearly visualised that, at its best, nobody could cope with it.

TERRY COOPER
(LEEDS UNITED)

For a time, Terry Cooper was quite simply the best left-back in the world. He had turned up with his boots in a paper bag at

Leeds United one day and just asked for a trial. He wouldn't get past the security guard at the gate at any of the top clubs now, but imagine what they would have lost. I remember first seeing Terry as a left-winger. I didn't think he was much cop at all. He was very average; no top club would have looked at him twice. As I've said before, it was hard for wingers in the sixties. You were stuck out there, the right-back booting you up in the air every time you got the ball. A lot of wingers were being made to look very ordinary by the changes in the game, including Terry. But Don Revie must have seen something in him because he switched him to left-back and suddenly it was a different ball game. That was a masterstroke by Revie, really. Now he was coming on to the ball, running forward with it, so he'd have a head of steam by the time the full-back was arriving. Terry changed the way full-backs played. He wasn't the first to go on the overlap, but he took it to a new level. His combination with Eddie Gray on the left for Leeds was just devastating.

The full-back position evolved very quickly from the fifties to the seventies. Roger Byrne, captain of the Busby Babes, liked to get forward, but more typical was a player like Tommy Banks at Bolton Wanderers, who was fast and physical and would put a winger in the stand at the first sign of danger. Ray Wilson took full-back play on, and Alf Ramsey and Ron Greenwood were both coaching players to get on the overlap, but the first player to fully exploit the potential of the role in this country was Cooper. He was our version of Nílton Santos, the great Brazilian, so eye-catching in the 1958 World Cup. Cooper was the first Englishman to play the full-back position in a way that kids watching football today would recognise. He was the forerunner of all the greats – Kenny Sansom, Stuart Pearce, Ashley Cole. And no, he wasn't the greatest defender, but full-back hasn't been a solely defensive position for close to 50 years now. After Cooper at Leeds it was never the same.

My second game for West Ham was against Leeds, on 28 August 1965. Willie Bell was their left-back that day, I played well against him and we won 2–1. Terry was the left wing. I can remember thinking that if *he* could make a career in Division One, I wouldn't have a problem. He was frighteningly bad. The next year when we played them, he was transformed. He was picking it up deep and running at us – I thought he was the best I saw all season.

For a spell he was the best around, certainly on the attack. He could dribble, he had real pace, he could hit a great cross and he had the skill and imagination to cut inside and join up with the midfield action. We all remember his wide interplay with Gray, but he could be as effective linking up with Johnny Giles. And while the defensive side of the game wasn't natural for him, he picked up tips from players like Norman Hunter, Paul Reaney and Jack Charlton, and he could certainly get by.

Having started as a winger, the aggression that most defenders had was not really part of Terry's game. He could tackle all right, but it was going forward that Terry was most effective, even scoring goals, like the volley that won the 1968 League Cup final at Wembley against Arsenal – the first major trophy of the Revie era. It was a pity that a broken leg sustained in 1972 kept him out for almost two years and altered his long-term prospects. Until then, Revie had never employed a reserve left-back, using Paul Madeley, who was a utility player across the defence, whenever Terry was injured. That had to change after the broken leg, and eventually he lost his place to Trevor Cherry. By then, every team had full-backs who were trying to play like Terry – but I'm not sure too many of them ever managed it.

LIAM BRADY
(ARSENAL)

I first saw Liam Brady in the Arsenal youth team playing West Ham at Chadwell Heath. Everybody was talking about him even then, this little Irish kid with an amazing left foot. Arsenal had a couple of outstanding players coming through at the time; the other was Graham Rix, who was in the same mould as Liam, another fantastic footballer, but a bit younger. Liam's team won the FA Youth Cup and South-East Counties League that season, 1970–71. Rix was in the next batch off the production line, and they both got into Arsenal's first team within a few years of each other. Later they combined for the winning goal scored by Alan Sunderland in the 1979 FA Cup final – that Arsenal team probably under-achieved considering the talent at its disposal.

Liam could cross with his right, but it was all about the left for him really. He had a left foot like a magic wand; he was a real artist with the ball. My old man absolutely loved him. Dad was still an Arsenal man at heart and he would put Brady right up there with the best he had seen. I was in America then, so he was back watching Arsenal and every week I'd get a call from him raving about something Brady had done. It's just a pity for the club that many of his best years were spent with Juventus in Italy; but it shows how good he was that he was probably our first player since John Charles to truly look at home there. He only left Juventus because they bought Michel Platini. It's a bit hard to argue with that.

When people look back at the great players from that era, I don't think they give Liam the recognition he deserves. Arsenal fans do – they watched him every week – but the rest of us barely got to see him before he was gone. He was only 24 when he went to Italy, and his only honour won in the English game was the FA Cup. We tend to think of Leeds and Liverpool players from that era, and clubs like Arsenal get forgotten. Liam came into the Arsenal team just as the Bertie Mee era was drawing to a close, and it was quite difficult for Terry Neill and Don Howe. Italy was the place to be then, though, and it shows how good Liam was that he was chosen as the player from English football that could end a pattern of quite negative publicity around our players. John Charles was a legend there, but Jimmy Greaves and Denis Law couldn't settle, and after that they seemed to lose interest in us. Liam changed that. He showed that a top player from the Football League could adapt, and paved the way for Ray Wilkins, Trevor Francis and Graeme Souness, among others.

In the seven full seasons Brady played at Arsenal, the club did not finish higher than fourth and even spent two campaigns in the bottom half of the table, so most of the great memories of Brady are restricted to individual big games rather than consistent displays over the season. The highlight for many Arsenal fans, for obvious reasons, is a 5–0 win against Tottenham Hotspur at White Hart Lane, on 23 December 1978. Alan Sunderland scored a hat-trick that day, but what people remember above all is Brady's fourth goal, 20 minutes into the second half.

Peter Taylor turned into him, but Brady was too quick in the tackle, nicked the ball and took two or three strides towards goal. He hit a left-foot banana shot from 25 yards that Mark Kendall, the goalkeeper, didn't even try to save. Then there was his performance in the 1979 FA Cup final against Manchester United. Undoubtedly, he was man of the match. Arsenal were leading 2–0 with five minutes to go but, to the amazement of all, Manchester United scored twice. Arsenal kicked off, lost the ball again, got it back and Sammy Nelson played a long pass up to Frank Stapleton. He fed it to Brady and it was his run, with Rix on the overlap outside, that inspired the winner, Rix crossing for Sunderland to score. Sadly, that was the beginning of the end for Brady in an Arsenal shirt. The win put the club in the European Cup-Winners' Cup the following season, and they were paired with Juventus in the semi-final. Brady was so magnificent over the two legs of the tie that the Italian club bought him that following summer, 1980.

Juventus had little answer to Brady at Highbury. They decided to try to kick him out of the game and Marco Tardelli was sent off. The match ended 1–1 and Juventus attempted to defend that away-goal lead by getting a 0–0 draw at home – a plan ruined when Brady crossed for Paul Vaessen to score a winner late in the game. Pat Jennings told me that as they walked past the Juventus dressing-room after the final whistle it was completely silent because their players were so stunned. Juventus had only lost one home game in Europe since 1968. I know Liam considers it the greatest display by an Arsenal team in his time there.

I think the impact of playing in Italy is probably lost on the modern generation. These days, Adel Taarabt gets relegated with

Queens Park Rangers and then goes off to play for AC Milan. Back then, only the greatest went to Serie A. Even the lesser known players from the exodus in the sixties – Gerry Hitchens and Joe Baker – were outstanding players in their time. A lot of those moves did not work out and it went quiet for close to 20 years before Juventus went for Brady. He was a trailblazer, really, because life in Italy was so different when compared to the standards and professionalism in England.

Graeme Souness told me a story about when he was at Sampdoria. He said they played a game pre-season against a village team, up in the mountains, in front of about 6,000 people. It was a nothing match, just preparation for the new season, and a bit of a public relations exercise because Sampdoria were in a camp down the road and were leaving to go back to Genoa the next day. Graeme said it must have been about 85°C and as he was leaving the club after the game he grabbed a small, cold bottle of Peroni from the bar to take on the coach. He got on and sat at the front, beer in hand, and it was like one of those Wild West saloons where everything falls quiet as the stranger enters. The players were all staring; the manager boarded and stared; then the president, too. He looked at Graeme coldly. 'Monday morning, in my office,' he said. That day, the president absolutely slaughtered him. 'Do that again, and you'll be out of the club,' he was told. All for having one cold beer because it was hot. He said he got no support from the players, either. Their looks had said it all. 'Oh my God, what are you doing?' Italy was a different world, then, for a British-based footballer.

I know one of the things that drove Jimmy Greaves mad about the Italian system was that you didn't get to go home after the game. There was the team camp the night before the match, and the team camp the night after. They would all go back to the training ground, stay over, warm down the following morning and have massages, and only then get to go home. Yet Liam fitted in with the Italian regime immediately. He won back-to-back titles with Juventus, the first playing some beautiful football. The second time, he took the penalty that clinched the league, even though he knew he was being replaced by Platini. It shows how much the coach trusted him – but then Chippy, as he was known at Arsenal, was always a class act. (And, by the way, he was called Chippy not because he had a lovely way of chipping the ball – but because he loved chips. I bet that too had to end when he went to Italy.)

GERRY FRANCIS
(QUEENS PARK RANGERS)

Okay, as manager of Queens Park Rangers, I might be biased, but Gerry Francis is one of the unsung heroes of English football in the 1970s. He was captain of a great QPR team that came within a whisker of winning the league, he was captain of England at the age of 23, he won Goal of the Season for 1975–6, and if he hadn't suffered a back injury at the peak of his career, I am sure he would be remembered as an England great. He reminds me a little of Bryan Robson – a player whose individual talent was undermined by the failure of his team. Gerry didn't even get a chance to play in a World Cup. He came into the England team set-up after they had failed to qualify for the 1974 tournament and his international career was over before the qualification process for 1978 began. He only made 12 international appearances but 8 of them were as captain and he scored 3 goals – not bad for a central midfield player. It is a faster strike-rate than Steven Gerrard, for instance.

Every time I come to work I walk past a photograph of that QPR team. It's on the wall at the training ground – what a set of players: Phil Parkes, Dave Clement, Ian Gillard, Dave Webb, Frank McLintock, John Hollins, Mick Leach, Don Masson, Stan Bowles, Don Givens, Dave Thomas – and Gerry, the captain. He scored 12 goals in 36 league games, 1 in 3 from midfield. He scored more goals that season than Bowles. They started the campaign with a 10-game unbeaten run, defeated Liverpool 2–0 at Loftus Road, went to Derby County, who were the reigning champions, and won 5–1. Later in the season they won 11 out of 12 matches, drew the other and were top the second week of April. They lost 3–2 at Norwich City but went back to the top again on the last official day of the season – but Liverpool had a game in hand at Wolverhampton Wanderers. These days, they make sure all the matches kick off at the same time to maintain credibility, but it wasn't like that back then. Rangers had to wait 10 days for Liverpool to play. Wolves went 1–0 up and the dream looked like becoming reality, but Liverpool equalised and went on to win 3–1. They took the league by one point – it was their first title under Bob Paisley.

Rangers played some lovely football that season, though, and a Francis goal against Liverpool epitomised it. McLintock played it into Bowles, he back-heeled it through his legs to Gerry, a lay-off to Givens, back to Gerry and he finished it quite superbly on the angle past Ray Clemence. They won't have seen too many like that at QPR. Gerry is still a big hero at the club and all the players from that team speak very highly of his ability. You don't end up England captain at 23 without being special. He scored a lovely goal against Scotland in the Home Nations match in 1975, just five minutes in at Wembley, batting through midfield and hitting an absolute screamer from 30 yards. The goalkeeper, Stuart Kennedy, didn't even move. England ended up winning 5–1.

There were a lot of fantastic maverick midfield players in that time – Alan Hudson, Tony Currie, Bowles – but I just think that Gerry was a more modern midfielder, a real up-and-back guy, and his forward runs from that position were the best. He always seemed to have space, always seemed hard to pick up. He wasn't aggressive in the tackle like, say, Bryan Robson, but he did his work and it was such a terrible shame when he got that injury in 1976. He was never the same after that, never played for England again, and he was only 32 when he drifted into management at Exeter City.

It was probably just as well that he had so many interests outside of football. Gerry always had a head for business – antiques, property, theatre shows. I think one of his companies has the rights to the musical *Buddy*. And, of course, he always had his pigeons. Gerry's whole family were into pigeon racing and breeding – though his dad was also a professional footballer – and I know Gerry had quite a successful side career as a pigeon fancier. It would seem strange to hear that about a professional footballer now. They all seem much more one-dimensional in their interests these days. Birds, yes. Pigeons, no.

GRAEME SOUNESS
(LIVERPOOL)

If English football struggled through the 1970s, Scottish football thrived – maybe that is why there are so many Scots in this team. Graeme Souness, though, would probably make the starting XI in any era. What a player. Also he just had an aura about him. He said to me that he would never go into the players' bar after a game. All the time he played for Liverpool he shunned it because he wanted to keep a barrier between himself and the opposition players. He thought if he went in and had a drink, suddenly his guard would come down and he couldn't be the Souness they feared on the pitch any more. And he was feared. Players thought he was evil. No chance of that if he was in among them, laughing and having a drink at the end of a game. He must have been one of the first players to think about image, to actively try to shape the way he was perceived by others. Keeping that aura was very important to Graeme. Any unwinding would be done in private, and with a glass of champagne, if I know him. Deep down, he isn't a miserable type at all, really. He just knew his own ability, and liked intimidating people. That was part of his job.

He always had faith in himself. It takes some guts to tell Bill Nicholson you are the best player at Tottenham Hotspur – when still a teenager who can't get in the team – but that is what Graeme did. He had been there since the age of 15 but wasn't making any headway, so he told Bill that he wanted to leave. Bill was one of those old-school managers whose attitude was, if you didn't want to play for him, stuff you, and off you went – so he sold Graeme to Middlesbrough. I still think it was an audacious statement on Graeme's part, though. Imagine having the confidence to say that, at 19, to a manager who had won the double?

Coming down from Edinburgh, it was hard for Graeme, and I know he thinks some of his experiences at the club helped toughen him up. An old team-mate of his, Phil Holder, does some scouting for me at Queens Park Rangers, and he was a young player coming up through the ranks with Graeme. Steve Perryman was Phil's big mate and they were inseparable at Spurs. Phil's only a little guy but he's a South London boy and there's no bullshit with him. That's why I like him as a scout – he tells it as it is. Last summer we were at a do with a lot of old friends near where I live, and Phil was there. The sun was shining, a singer was performing Frank Sinatra songs, and everyone was mingling and having a good time, when who should walk in but Graeme Souness. He had been in the restaurant the night before and his wife had left her mobile telephone there. I told him there was someone here he might remember from the old days – and brought him over to see Phil. I couldn't believe his reaction. He gave him a big hug, and then all the old memories started coming out. 'You and Stevie, you fucking slaughtered me every day,' he said. 'Dear lord, what a pair of lads you two were. No one messed with you.' I can imagine that of Phil as well, because he hasn't changed. Graeme said it was a huge part of his education. He had come down from Scotland, Billy Bigtime, but Phil was about a year older, as hard as nails too, and wasn't going to take any old nonsense. Steve Perryman was the same – he never took any prisoners as a player and he was going to sort anyone out who he thought was a bit flash. I can't imagine there were too many got the better of Graeme later in his career – but he said coming across Phil and Steve at Tottenham was the making of him. He loved them to bits. They were all in the same Tottenham team that won the FA Youth Cup in 1970.

Graeme knew his worth by then. He was going to be a top player. That is why he went to see Bill Nicholson when he had only made one appearance in the first team by the end of the 1971–2 season. Graeme said he was better than any of the players in the first team and if he wasn't getting picked he wanted to leave. 'That's your opinion,' Bill told him – but as the manager who had let Dave Mackay go, he wasn't about to be told what to do by some kid. I think Graeme met his match that day because Nicholson was as stubborn as anyone in football. Once confronted there was only going to be one winner – so Graeme ended up at Middlesbrough, in the Second Division, where he came under the influence of the great Bobby Murdoch, a member of the 'Lisbon Lions' Celtic team that won the European Cup in 1967. Murdoch had been Jack Charlton's first signing when he took over at Middlesbrough, and I know Graeme believes he was a formative influence on him as a footballer. Jock Stein said Murdoch was the best player he had ever managed, and he only sold him because he ran out of challenges at Celtic. They had lost the European Cup final to Feyenoord in 1970. When Stein was asked when they might win it again, he replied: 'When Bobby Murdoch is fit.' Middlesbrough won promotion in Jack's first season and Murdoch's influence was crucial, according to Graeme. He said his experience settled the team down, and he had an excellent attitude, as well as being a fantastic passer. 'He would always pull me to one side to pass on advice or to tell me when he thought I was acting wrongly,'

Souness said. He was a hard man, too, which is probably how Graeme learnt to look after himself.

By the time he came to Liverpool, Graeme was nearly the finished article. The transfer fee, £350,000, sounds like a snip but it was a record for a move between two English clubs in 1978. The time with Murdoch had added real steel to go with that glorious talent. He was the same type as Bremner and Mackay – whatever way you wanted to play it, he was happy. A pure football match, and he was the best player on the field. A tear-up, and he would be nastier than anybody. He seemed to have a particular problem with Peter Nicholas, a Welsh midfielder who played for Arsenal. In one game, Nicholas went in high on Graeme, and soon afterwards Souness put him out of football for two months. He needed six stitches on a knee injury. Willie Young, Arsenal's giant centre-half, came tearing over and Graeme thought there was going to be a punch-up. What he didn't know was that Young hated Nicholas almost as much as he did. 'Oh, come on, big man, you know he deserved it,' said Souness as Nicholas lay on the ground. 'I know,' said Willie. 'I was coming to congratulate you.' There was another match between Scotland and Wales in 1985 when the two clashed and Souness appeared to rake his studs down Nicholas's face, almost causing a riot. That was Graeme. He could be wicked if provoked, but people only went at him like that because, left alone, he could do the lot. He lives down near me on the South coast now and we have the odd game of golf. He hasn't changed – he's so competitive, it's ridiculous. I like him a lot.

And get him talking about football after, and you're certainly in for a good night. What you see on Sky television isn't the half of it. His favourite word is bluffer. This manager's a bluffer; that manager's a bluffer – and it doesn't matter who he's talking about. I know he sometimes does it for effect, just for the sake of argument. Arsène Wenger: bluffer. Pep Guardiola: bluffer – thinks he's reinvented football. He does it just to get us all going, and then sits back laughing.

I know he thinks his Liverpool team was the best, and maybe he is right. They were a fantastic side, and I think anyone of that generation remembers tuning in to *Sportsnight* in midweek, watching grainy footage from somewhere like Bulgaria, with a lousy picture you could barely see – it was half-time before the smoke from the pre-match flares had cleared – but Liverpool were the best in Europe and I think we all felt very proud of them. Graeme was a hit at Liverpool from the start. I remember he scored a cracking goal against Manchester United in one of his first games for the club, and when he was made captain in 1981, his inspiration turned the season around. They had lost to Manchester City on Boxing Day and fallen to 12th place, when Bob Paisley gave the armband to Graeme. I know it made things awkward with the existing captain, Phil Thompson, but I don't think Graeme is the sort to be bothered by that. John Toshack's Swansea City were top at the time, but there were bigger clubs in the chase, like Manchester United and Bobby Robson's Ipswich Town. Driven on by Graeme, Liverpool reeled them all in: they hit the top by the end of March and never looked back. They were four points clear of Ipswich by the end – and had won the League Cup, too.

Graeme was always best under pressure. He was immense in the 1984 European Cup semi-final second leg away to Dinamo

Bucharest, when he was targeted by a hostile crowd on account of an incident in the first match that left their captain, midfielder Lica Movila, with a broken jaw. The incident happened off the ball, and off camera, but it must have been one hell of a blow. Naturally, the Romanians were not best pleased and the reception in Bucharest was ferocious – Kenny Dalglish later wrote that he'd 'never been in such a war zone'. But the louder they got, the better Graeme played. He almost revelled in it. Stayed calm, stayed focused, let that negative energy wash over him and steered his team to the final. Just brilliant. It was the same in the final, against AS Roma at their home stadium in Rome. It was Souness's idea, as captain, to lead the team out on to the pitch to get used to the atmosphere, provoking an inevitable tirade of boos and jeers. Having shown the home crowd that they were not afraid, Liverpool won the match. That was Graeme's thing: show no fear.

I remember we were all having dinner in Spain once – myself, Jim Smith, Trevor Francis and Graeme – and Trevor brought up the name of Claudio Gentile, the notorious Italian hard man, who did such a horrible man-marking job on Diego Maradona at the 1982 World Cup. 'He scared you, Gentile,' Trevor said. 'I remember he waited for you down the tunnel – ' But Graeme didn't even let him finish the story. 'No, he didn't,' he snapped. 'Not a fucking chance.' He really had the hump about it.

He managed as he played, too. He was a brave, bold influence on Rangers – and it would have taken real guts to challenge and change the culture of that club by signing Mo Johnston, a very high-profile Catholic player. I don't think another manager would have done that – and so much of Rangers's success during

Graeme's time and after he left was built on this new freedom. Fans were burning season tickets in the street when the deal was announced, but that wouldn't have bothered Graeme in the least. The only person I know he's scared of is his wife, Karen.

JOHN ROBERTSON
(NOTTINGHAM FOREST)

Bill Shankly said he could pass the ball with the accuracy of a snooker player potting the black, but John Robertson was on his way out at Nottingham Forest when Brian Clough and Peter Taylor arrived. He was the most unlikely professional footballer anyone had seen. He was overweight, smoked liked a trooper and, in Clough's words, was living out of a chip pan. He ate all the wrong foods, wasn't interested in staying fit, wasn't interested in football really – and dressed scruffily, which Clough hated. Yet he must have seen something, a glimmer, in training because Clough decided it was worth persevering with him if he could clean his act up. Peter Taylor delivered the message, as I understand it. He took Robertson to one side and just slaughtered him – told him everything Clough had said about him in private. Taylor concluded: 'It's clear you have problems – but we think you can play.' Robertson knew it was his last chance to sort himself out or his career would be over. And what a player he became.

Clough's description of him in his autobiography sums up the incredible transformation that occurred. 'John Robertson was a very unattractive young man,' he said. 'If, one day, I felt a bit off colour, I would sit next to him. I was bloody Errol

Flynn in comparison. But give him a ball and a yard of grass, and he was an artist, the Picasso of our game. He became one of the finest deliverers of a football I have ever seen – in Britain or anywhere else in the world – as fine as the Brazilians or the supremely gifted Italians.' People remember Clough buying players like Trevor Francis or Peter Shilton, but the bulk of his signings involved taking incredible gambles on players that were not in the least household names. Robertson wasn't a signing, but he was evidence of the unique way Clough thought about football and footballers. No matter his talent, had he just given up on Robertson he would not have been the first. Even a great manager like Sir Alex Ferguson has sometimes just decided a player simply has too many problems to handle, and washed his hands of him. Paul McGrath, one of the greatest central defenders of the modern era, fits that category. Alex didn't think he was worth the trouble. Yet Clough persevered with Robertson and won two European Cups. He scored the winner in one, and made the winner in the other. Apparently when he signed Francis he told him to get the ball to Robertson and the rest would look after itself.

I think once people saw what Clough had done with Robertson, everyone wanted a winger like that. Not necessarily a flying machine, but intelligent with the ball. He was Forest's playmaker but he started wide – that was what made him special. Even at Bournemouth we were trying to replicate what Forest had. I took a little winger called Mark O'Connor on a free transfer from Bristol Rovers because he reminded me of Robertson in lots of ways. He's the under-21 coach at Bristol City now, but before that he was with Tony Pulis. Tony took him everywhere – Gillingham, Portsmouth, Plymouth Argyle, Stoke City. I wouldn't be surprised if he ended up at Crystal Palace, too. Mark was a clever player, he knew exactly where he should be, like Robertson. He could toy with defenders, get it, roll it in front of them; he joined the play very quickly. He was quick enough over 10 yards, but not lightning, so it was the way he used to work the ball that made things happen – and Robertson was the same, just a step up in class. He had a fantastic football brain, and it showed in the way he orchestrated Forest's attacks.

John was one of the first playmakers we saw that would start wide and come in to link up with the front man. It was a real thinking formation. A lot of the great players in recent times have done that – Gheorghe Hagi, Zinedine Zidane, Lionel Messi, Thierry Henry – but when John did this it was revolutionary. Clough gets a lot of credit for intuition and psychological ploys, but not so many people talk about his coaching – yet he did a quite wonderful job with Robertson. He wanted him to play with the whole game in front of him, side on, so that when he got the ball he had the complete picture. Too many people these days come and get it off the full-back and they are moving towards the ball with their back to the game. They should be side on, so when it comes to them they can see the full-back, their own team, who is in the best position, everything. If it's tight they can turn it round the corner first time, if it's not they can hold it, and they don't even need a call because they have the game right there, in vision. Clough got Robertson playing like that and coached him to be the most influential winger in Europe.

The minute Forest got the ball, John would hit the touchline and then all you could hear Clough shout was, 'Show me your arse, show me your arse!' He wanted him heels on the touchline, backside facing towards the stand and the dugout. He didn't want him facing back or forwards, he had to play sideways on so he could see the game. I remember watching Manchester United's game against Olympiakos last season – the away leg that they lost 2–0 – and seeing Ashley Young receive the ball blind, with his back to the opposition goal, and back-heel it straight into touch. Clough would have gone spare. It showed so little awareness, not only of where he was on the field, but of where the rest of the players were, too. Had he been side on he could have made the smart decision, the way Robertson would. Body position is so important in football. Robertson still got up and down the field, but he did so showing Brian Clough his arse because that way, when he received, Forest began to play immediately.

He was a great character, too. In season 1979–80, Nottingham Forest played Liverpool five times: twice in the league, in the FA Cup and over the two legs of the League Cup semi-final. Liverpool won the title that season and Forest won the European Cup, and matches between the teams were always big events. Forest won the home league game, lost in the FA Cup, but had knocked Liverpool out over two legs of the League Cup, with Robertson scoring from the penalty spot in each match. The Anfield league game was scheduled for seven days after the second League Cup tie and as Forest were warming up, The Kop were given them all kinds of stick. Someone threw a tennis ball at John, who did no more than trap it in the air and play keep-up with it to the penalty spot. He then put it down gently, and in front of the Liverpool crowd, rolled it gently into the corner, just as he had done in the cup ties. What a reply.

John was always a bit of lad, though. He did start trying to live right, but the Forest boys always hit the town on Wednesday if there was no match, and I don't think he ever stopped smoking. There is a story about one trip away with Scotland when he spent ages chatting up this girl at the hotel. In the end, she told him her room number and he arranged to call later. He knocked at around midnight but couldn't get a reply, so he went back to his bunk and tried to get through on the telephone. He asked to be put through to the room number she had given. 'Why do you want to call Jock Stein at this hour?' the night porter asked. Luckily for John, Scotland's manager was a heavy sleeper – or there could have been real trouble.

KEVIN KEEGAN
(LIVERPOOL)

I was watching a game down at Bournemouth when I first saw Kevin Keegan in action, and my first instinct was to telephone Ron Greenwood at West Ham and recommend him. I knew Bournemouth wouldn't be able to afford him and he was obviously destined for greater things. 'Scunthorpe have got this kid, Ron,' I told him. 'He's fantastic – you should have a look at him.' Kevin was playing in midfield then, often on the right, like me, and maybe Ron thought West Ham were well staffed in that department. I don't know if he ever acted on a word I said, really – our relationship wasn't the best by that time. Kevin joined Liverpool at the end of that season, so maybe West Ham made an inquiry and were told it was too late. I can't see how Ron wouldn't have seen the promise in Kevin at that time. Still, it is all about opinions. The other player I recommended to West Ham was David Speedie during his time at Darlington – and he didn't end up at Upton Park, either. I was the manager of Bournemouth by then and we had tried, and failed, to sign him. Darlington wanted £30,000, which was too rich for us, but he would have been a snip for West Ham, where John Lyall was now the manager. Never mind – just add it to a list of ones that got away.

I was right about Keegan, though. What a player – and what a career. Brilliant at Liverpool, brilliant in Germany with Hamburg, won the European Cup, twice European Footballer of the Year – he turned into a truly amazing player. I know he took something Bill Shankly said to heart. 'Even if I was a road-sweeper,' Shankly told him, 'I'd have the cleanest street in town.' And that was Kevin's attitude to football. He threw himself into every job he ever had, particularly his role at Liverpool. Once he had been spotted – by Geoff Twentyman, naturally – the work he put into his game was just phenomenal. It is said Kevin made himself a great player, and some might find that a little disrespectful, but he was at Scunthorpe for a reason and I think it's perfectly feasible that the great player we now recall bears no relation to the one that came into football at the age of 17. He went for a trial at Coventry City and didn't make it, so he must have worked very hard to improve from that point. Scunthorpe spotted him playing for his works team, Pegler, a plumbing manufacturing company in Yorkshire.

So Kevin wasn't a player that was born with silky skills. He wasn't like Kenny Dalglish, for instance. I saw Kenny play at 14, and everyone there instinctively knew we were watching someone destined to be one of the great players in British football. Kevin was different. Obviously, earlier in life, professional clubs had looked at him and thought he came up short. In the same way I can remember seeing Jamie Carragher as a young player for Liverpool and not rating him at all. He is another who worked extremely hard to get to the top.

By the time I saw Kevin for Scunthorpe the player we know was beginning to form. He was busy, busy, busy – a threat all the time. Bournemouth's defenders couldn't get to grips with him, couldn't mark him, and it was easy to see why Shankly took one look and decided to make him a forward. Central defenders at that time were used to having people that stood up against them, and suddenly there was this little lad who was always on the move, buzzing everywhere, causing problems. Did I think he would be the European Footballer of the Year? Frankly, no. But I could see he was way better than Scunthorpe and could probably make it at a First Division club – by then Kevin's energy alone set him apart.

The idea at Liverpool was that Keegan would replace Ian Callaghan on the right side of midfield. Ian had been a wonderful player but was coming to the end of his career and was injury prone. Liverpool sorted out the Keegan transfer while preparing to meet Arsenal in the 1971 FA Cup final. The story goes that they were going to bring him through gradually, but Shankly played him in a practice match against the first team the following season and he created such havoc, he went straight into the starting line-up; and 12 minutes into his debut, he scored.

If I had to compare Kevin to a modern footballer, it would probably be Luis Suárez. Not in terms of his technical ability, because Suárez's skill level is quite amazing, but in terms of his work-rate and the way his threat as a goalscorer never ceases.

He was a pest, the way Suárez is a pest; the test was constant because he was always on the move, a perpetual motion machine for 90 minutes. It is the same with Suárez: defenders do not get a second's rest. You don't know where he is because he never stands still, constantly changing positions, wanting the ball, playing it and spinning, impossible to mark. Again, it was a wonderful bit of scouting from Geoff Twentyman – Liverpool seemed to pluck players from thin air in those days.

Of course, it must have been hard to go there and not do well for someone like Shankly. He was such a strong character. I was told he wouldn't even talk to injured players, would just ignore them completely until they were fit again. Brian Clough was the same. He wouldn't even have injured players at the ground. Liverpool's training was legendary, too. It didn't change in close to 30 years. They would have a warm-up and play nine-a-sides. Before European matches foreign coaches would come to watch them in open sessions, go away disappointed, and then sneak back in the afternoon, thinking they could peer through the fence and all the secrets would be revealed. There was nothing to see but an empty training ground. They weren't hiding anything at all. There were no secrets; they really did just play nine-a-side. And it hadn't changed from Shankly's time to when Kenny Dalglish was manager. When my son Jamie signed for Liverpool I was fascinated to hear what Liverpool did to produce such wonderful teams. 'What did you do this morning?' I'd ask. 'Nine-a-side,' he'd say. 'No, before that,' I'd press, 'you must do something else.' 'No, Dad, it's the same every day,' he would insist. 'Two-lap warm-up, nine-a-side. Kenny plays, Ronnie Moran plays, all the coaches play. We have proper games, Dad. Good games. But that's it.' And that is how Keegan would have trained 20 years earlier, too. I don't imagine it changed that much until Gérard Houllier took over.

Key to Keegan's greatness is that he formed one of the great forward partnerships with John Toshack. It was a classic pairing, really, the big 'un and the little 'un. Toshack, strong and fearless, winning the headers; Keegan buzzing around him, feeding off those scraps. As a model, there's not too many better than that – it was a perfect combination then and, really, it still is. Look at Burnley in the Championship last season – Sam Vokes, the big Welsh striker, knocking it down to the quicker and more mobile Danny Ings – or go right back to Jimmy Greaves and Alan Gilzean, or John Radford and Ray Kennedy at Arsenal. If you can get a partnership like that going you've got a chance.

Kevin was the bridge between the era when fans and players still felt connected and the modern era when players are superstars, living in gated mansions and earning money that is beyond the imagination of the ordinary man. He was probably the first footballer to work carefully on his image, and although he was a household name he was rarely in the newspapers for the wrong reasons. He wasn't like George Best – there was never any scandal around Kevin. He made Liverpool's number seven shirt famous – although the next player to wear it may have been even better.

KENNY DALGLISH
(LIVERPOOL)

I go back a long way with Kenny Dalglish. In 1966 I used to take him to training when he came in for a trial at West Ham. I've read that he was rejected by Ron Greenwood, but I don't think that's true. Ron would have loved to sign him, but knew we had no chance. Every club in Britain was clamouring for Kenny's signature by that time.

Kenny would have been 15 when he came to us for two weeks, and was staying in digs about a minute up the road from our training ground in Chadwell Heath. I had a little green Austin 1100 and would collect him and another Scottish lad, Jimmy Lindsay, who had come down from the same Scotland Schools team and ended up signing for us. The boys were both forwards – Jimmy eventually played as a midfielder – and had good reputations. Scotland had put a strong team into the Victory Shield, the schoolboy equivalent of the Home Nations tournament. One Saturday morning during Kenny's brief time at West Ham we had a practice match and Ron Greenwood played him in with the first-team players. One of the lads laid a ball to him and it was like fast forwarding through the next 20 years of British football – he took it perfectly, dropped a shoulder, turned and curled it into the far corner of the net. Our reserves didn't know what had hit them. Both sets of players just stopped and applauded. I can remember talking to Ron about him after that game. 'Will we get him?' I asked. 'No chance,' he said. 'We've tried. Everybody wants him, but he's going to Celtic.' He was right. Kenny signed as a professional there a year later.

I don't remember him being very talkative then, but I'm not sure I would have understood a word anyway. The strength of Kenny's Glasgow accent is legendary. When Liverpool wanted to sign my son, Jamie, Kenny rang up to speak to us about it. I could hear my wife, Sandra, on the phone but I didn't know who she was talking to. 'I'm sorry,' she kept saying. 'I can't understand your Scouse accent.' She must have said it about four times. In the end, I heard her say the name Kenny. I took the phone, just in time to hear Kenny saying in the broadest Scottish tone you'll ever hear, 'Can ye nae understan' me?' That's my missus. She's got to be about the only person who doesn't know Kenny Dalglish is from Scotland. 'I thought he was from Liverpool,' she said. 'No, he manages Liverpool – he was born in Glasgow,' I replied. We got there in the end.

Kenny was just a fantastic player. Absolutely world class. He could hold the ball as well as any man twice his size; he could bring team-mates into play or take it on himself. He didn't have pace, but that didn't matter. His pace was in his head. He was the attacking equivalent of Bobby Moore, in that he read the play better than anybody. And, despite his size, he was so strong. David O'Leary, who was an outstanding defender with Arsenal, said it was impossible to get the ball off Kenny at his peak. He said Kenny would almost crouch over it with his legs spread and his elbows poking out, so that whatever angle the defender came in from, he'd have his backside in the way of the ball. Bob Paisley said Dalglish was the best player he ever worked with at Liverpool, and praise doesn't come much higher than that. There were some great strikers around in that era, but I'd say Kenny was the pick of them.

Trevor Francis was the first £1 million footballer – whatever Brian Clough says – at Nottingham Forest, but I'm not sure he was ever better than in his earliest years at Birmingham City. He was this country boy, from Plymouth in Devon, but he broke into the first team at the age of 16 and had scored four goals in a game against Bolton Wanderers before his 17th birthday. He scored 15 goals in 22 games in his first season – a phenomenal feat for a youngster. He could pack a ground like the greats of the 1950s – over 50,000 at St Andrew's in 1972 when they won promotion. He was so prolific in those first seasons that one edition of BBC's *Sports Report* began with the news that he *hadn't* scored. He was fast, brave and prolific. Talk to him now about that game at Bolton and he'll still say that he came off injured and his replacement missed a sitter. 'I should have had five,' he'll moan. I've talked quite a bit in this chapter about scouting in this era, and I think the chap who discovered Trevor for Birmingham should get his own statue at St Andrew's. No, I don't know who it was either. That's my point. Those blokes worked in anonymity back then, digging out these gems of players from obscure parts of the country, regions where nobody was expecting to find the next Jimmy Greaves. How did Birmingham get him and not Plymouth? How did Plymouth miss the one true great to be born on their doorstep?

I find it amazing that England failed internationally through the 1970s, because I do believe it was a golden age for strikers: Kevin Hector, Alan Clarke, Martin Chivers, Mick Channon, Malcolm Macdonald – these are players that would walk into most teams today. Can you imagine if Roy Hodgson had that lot to choose from in Brazil last summer?

Yet Dalglish, I feel, stands alone in his generation. Liverpool must have wondered how on earth they could replace Kevin Keegan, but Dalgish turned out to be an upgrade. Liverpool played Keegan's Hamburg in the UEFA Super Cup shortly after the change had been made and won 6–0, which I think says it all about his ability to slot straight into a successful team. He came down from Scotland, but there was no talk of needing to adapt. It was as if they knew, and he knew, that there was only one man for the job. He scored 30 goals in his first season, including the winner in the European Cup final. It allowed them to maintain this fantastic period of dominance in the English game. Somehow they could always identify goalscorers that were perfect for the Liverpool way – Ian St John, Roger Hunt, Keegan, Dalglish and then Ian Rush. In the second phase of his Liverpool career, Dalglish turned from the best goalscorer to the most imaginative goal provider – so the next decade belonged to Liverpool, too.

THE SEVENTIES: THE TEAM

PAT
JENNINGS

Tottenham Hotspur

PHIL NEAL

Liverpool

PHIL THOMPSON

Liverpool

ROY McFARLAND

Derby County

TERRY COOPER

Leeds United

LIAM BRADY

Arsenal

GERRY FRANCIS

Queens Park Rangers

GRAEME SOUNESS

Liverpool

JOHN ROBERTSON

Nottingham Forest

KEVIN KEEGAN

Liverpool

KENNY DALGLISH

Liverpool

CHAPTER FOUR

THE EIGHTIES

The eighties was the last decade before the Premier League and probably the last time there was room to fail in football. Not consistently, obviously. Managers would still get sacked if they regularly fell below expectations. But there would be time to build a team, and one bad season didn't end with a P45. John Lyall managed West Ham United from 1975 to 1989. There were good years and bad years. One season the club got relegated – but John's vision fitted West Ham's own and they gave him time to get it right. Eventually, he brought them back up. Now, lose five games and you're under threat. Get relegated and the whole regime changes – players, coaches, scouting staff. People say that the money has changed football – but it was still a business even then. I think the culture has changed. Once one chairman sacks a manager, they all want to sack a manager because they want to be seen to be doing something. Yet West Ham's board were doing something under Lyall. They were buying players and trying to improve the team that way. That's action, just the same.

I think chairmen are terrified, literally terrified, of relegation now. The Premier League is football for such big stakes and everybody thinks they cannot afford to be out of it. Plus there are more foreign owners, billionaires from around the world who have never known anything but success and cannot understand why they are not winning the league. Listen to them and everyone is going to be in the Champions League or Europe in the next few years, no matter how ropey the team is. I'm not sure owners talked like that 30 years ago – and the league was a lot more open with considerably more movement. Now, nobody seems happy. Everyone should be doing better, getting greater value for the fortune they have invested. And, yes, it is a fortune – but if it's only one tenth of what Sheikh Mansour has spent at Manchester City, the chances are you'll have one-tenth of the team. I do fear one day we will be lucky to have any clubs that are locally owned, and that is going to make it difficult for our domestic game, for our managers and players to thrive.

Looking at the other teams I've picked for this book, this is the last one that does not include a foreign player. Once the Premier League begins, everything about our domestic game changes. Foreign players, foreign coaches and foreign wages to keep up with the biggest clubs in Europe. I'm not knocking that – suddenly managers are earning as much as the top players, but has the quality gone up? I'm not convinced. If you look back at the achievements of men like Brian Clough and Bob Paisley, I don't understand why owners suddenly lost faith in British managers.

Should Brian Clough have been England manager during this period? I think so. I feel his record at Derby County and

Nottingham Forest should have been enough to promote him, instead of either Ron Greenwood in 1977 or Sir Bobby Robson in 1982. Sadly, he didn't fit the bill. Appointing Don Revie was probably as bold as the Football Association were ever going to get, considering the controversy around his Leeds United side, and when that backfired, Clough's chances were almost certainly over. From there, until the appointment of Terry Venables in 1996, I think they were after a safe pair of hands. I'd love Clough to have managed England, but knowing the type of FA people he would have had to deal with, it seems an impossibility looking back. On his first day, he would have cancelled all the free trips for the blazers, on his second he would have questioned why they needed to be at matches at all, and before the first game he would have been kicking them off the chartered plane. It would never have worked – but what a wonderful manager. He really knew how to put a team together, how to match players up, get them working as a unit. That is what he was best at, the simple stuff. Get players doing what they are good at, and in that way get the best out of them.

Bob Paisley was another who would be in any list of the greatest managers of all time. When Carlo Ancelotti won his third Champions League title last season with Real Madrid, it was good that a younger generation were reminded whose record he was equalling. Liverpool had a unique style and was run in a unique way back then. There are a lot of coaches, players and owners who wouldn't recognise it as an elite club in the modern sense, considering the way it just ticked over, built on wonderful traditions. Every day the same, every training session the same, the ball zipping about in those famous nine-a-sides, great players like Alan Hansen and Ian Rush taking it as seriously as any game. A warm-up and then half an hour each way.

What was their secret formula? Good players. They kept producing them, kept finding them, putting them in the right positions, and then that Anfield atmosphere made them feel 10 feet tall. The managers just carried on the tradition of the boot room – the same philosophy handed down from Bill Shankly. It went right through the club – and modern managers like Kenny Dalglish carried it through. Yet Liverpool was ahead of its time, too. For all the tradition it had a continental set-up because Peter Robinson, the chief executive, conducted all the football business. Bob and later Joe Fagan ran the football team, and made the football decisions, but Peter was in charge of the club. When my son Jamie signed for Liverpool, Kenny Dalglish met us – but Peter Robinson did the deal, and Kenny still addressed him formally in front of us as Mr Robinson. At a lot of clubs the manager would have been weighed down with the business, but Liverpool knew how to compartmentalise the club. They trusted the scouts to find players, the chief executive to sign players, the coaches to guide players and the players to play. It was a winning formula, and every successful club since has deployed a version of it.

This was also the last decade when the prizes were spread around, particularly the FA Cup. Between 1978 and 1988 there were 9 different winners of the FA Cup in 11 seasons; in the next 19 years, 17 of the FA Cup finals were won by four clubs (Liverpool, Manchester United, Arsenal and Chelsea) with Tottenham Hotspur and Everton – who probably make up the big six – accounting for the other two. I am pleased to say my club, Portsmouth, broke that stranglehold in 2008 – and Wigan have also managed it. You look at some of the clubs that won the FA Cup in the eighties and wonder whether they will pass that way again: Wimbledon, Coventry City, West Ham United. It's a shame. It isn't healthy when football loses its uncertainty. Everybody fielded their best team in the FA Cup then, too. You didn't toss the cup off because relegation wasn't the death sentence it has become now. The league was important but it wasn't all-consuming, and the cups mattered. These days, many people think fourth place is akin to winning a trophy, and small clubs associate a cup run with relegation. If Sunderland or Hull City had gone down last season everyone would have blamed it on getting to Wembley, which is ridiculous.

It was also the decade in which football was touched by tragedy. On the day of the Heysel Stadium disaster, 29 May 1985, I was playing cricket in a charity match with Alan Ball and a few other ex-players. We were doing it to raise money for the family of a policeman who had died in the line of duty. We would play the game and then go back to the police clubhouse to watch Liverpool versus Juventus in the European Cup final. We got there and saw it all unfold on television. 'Someone's been killed,' said one of the club members. We didn't believe him at first. Then you saw the footage and realised how terrible it was. I still can't believe they played the game, or that Michel Platini celebrated Juventus's goal. They must have had an inkling something was wrong, even if they were unaware there were so many dead.

Bournemouth were at home to Stoke City on 15 April 1989, the day of the Hillsborough disaster. We lost 1–0 but that is about all I remember of the match. I think everyone in football felt numb with shock. We knew the game couldn't be the same

again. It felt that way after the Bradford City stadium fire in
1985, too. Bradford were in the same league as us, Division
Three, and I can remember the silence on the coach as we drove
back from Leyton Orient, having heard the news. Terrible times.

It was a decade when football was beginning to change in
every aspect and I witnessed the new wave arriving, first-hand, at
Lilleshall. Bobby Robson had brought two Dutch players over to
Ipswich Town, Arnold Mühren and Frans Thijssen, and Mühren
in particular was a disciple of a Dutch skills coach called Wiel
Coerver. He had developed a pyramid method of instruction by
studying the best players in the world, and it was the first time
anyone had really applied academic techniques to basic skills.
I'm not saying it was going to turn anyone into Lionel Messi,
but it would certainly improve technical levels. We were all at
Lilleshall, just about every young coach in the country, when
Coerver came over – and it was the most fantastic couple of
days. 'Tomorrow we have a man arriving from Holland,' we
were told. 'He teaches dribbling skills and he is going to put
on a session for us.' I think Bobby was instrumental in getting
him in because his Dutch players spoke so highly of him. It was
a revelation. Coerver turned up with some Dutch kids in tow.
He was older than most of us, but looked super fit. He laid out
loads of balls and all these boys started doing stepovers. Then
they speeded it up. Double stepovers. Passing people on the run
and doing it. He had them playing games where the skill level
was just mind-blowing – then he asked for volunteers. That was
my favourite part. George Graham was straight up there – he
fancied his chances. The kids would do a skill and then Coerver
would ask us to replicate it.

There were some sights that day. I had my assistant manager, Stuart Morgan, with me. He was a good coach but as a player let's say skill wasn't his strong point. If Coerver had a course entitled 'Clumping the striker off the ball at corners', Stuart would have been his man. Stepovers, not so much. As for Jimmy Sirrel, the old manager of Notts County, his stepover was so slow I think the half-time whistle would have gone by the time he completed it. We were in tears of laughter watching some of the guys – people were stepping on the ball and falling over. Yet the one thing we all agreed on was that here was a way forward for English football. All the different skills that were shown to us that day could be applied in the game. The plan was that we would all be given videos to take back to our clubs and use as the basis for youth training. Instead of running them into the ground, the kids would learn new skills and could then go away and practise in their back garden or over the park, just as they do in Holland. Of course, it didn't happen. There was a big argument over the rights and the videos never got ordered. So the only people exposed to the brilliant coaching of Wiel Coerver were a load of middle-aged football managers, not the next generation of young players.

Yet I'll never forget those kids that he brought over. It is no coincidence that the Dutch produce wave after wave of beautiful footballers when they are working with coaches like that. The skills they had – they were sending people five yards the wrong way with a twitch of the foot, doing drag-backs at full pelt. And none of it got used. It was so hard to introduce new ideas into Football Association courses back then. Up at Lilleshall all the lads would have a chat and talk about different ideas, but there were very few new techniques to be learnt. I can remember us all asking if Wiel could stay another day because everybody loved it so much – and the second session was as good as the first. Then he disappeared from our game. It was as if he had been smuggled away for letting the cat out of the bag. What a waste. His methods should have been put to all the clubs in this country. Take it or leave it. Here's what you do with the kids, here's what you show them; give them a ball each so they get hundreds of touches in training. You could have taken his methods anywhere, even into Sunday league clubs, and the kids would have loved it. Yet we had our own ways and, sadly, there were too many PE teachers without the imagination to understand what Coerver was doing. So many of the coaches at Lilleshall came through the same route, and a lot of it involved non-league football. Basically, our coaches were being taught by people who couldn't play – and that cannot be healthy.

I know I say skill is mostly natural, but that doesn't mean coaching is worthless. You can definitely put Wiel Coerver's methods into a session; you would certainly improve any kid by doing that for 30 minutes each day. I introduced it at Bournemouth as soon as I returned. Each time I took a coaching session, instead of warming up without the ball running round the pitch, I would tell them to have a little stretch, then spend about half an hour with a ball each. Stepover. Take it away with you. Stepover. Take it away to the right. Double stepover – bang, bang. Every morning. I don't think we spend enough time like that – or we hadn't done, until Coerver opened some minds. I used to go and watch our kids every Tuesday and Thursday night and they might be doing doggies and fitness work for two hours.

They're young, fit men. They can run anyway. Skill is what the game is about – as the players in my next XI would know.

PETER SHILTON
(NOTTINGHAM FOREST)

Peter could have made my team of the decade for the sixties, seventies or eighties, really. He was that good. I know Ron Greenwood couldn't make up his mind between Peter and Ray Clemence, but Shilton just had the edge for me. Brian Clough thought him the better man in every aspect, but I think that's harsh on Ray. Clemence only suffers in comparison to one of the greatest goalkeepers of all time – maybe the best there has been. It is a myth, though, that Peter and Ray alternated throughout Ron's time in charge as England manager. Ray was his first choice for most of it and played over half of Greenwood's 55 games in charge. Joe Corrigan, another excellent goalkeeper, played in eight. Peter was only capped 19 times by Ron, and 5 of those were the last matches of his reign, when he finally made Peter his number one at the 1982 World Cup. Before that tournament Ray had played twice as many England matches under Ron for England. In many ways, it shows how good he was that, for a time, he kept Shilton out of the England team. Without Ray, I don't think Peter's caps record could ever be broken. It stands at 125 – but imagine how many he could have got.

Peter had a presence about him. He was a goalkeeper who was just dedicated to his craft, an exceptional worker, an exceptional trainer, absolutely obsessed with his game. I'm not saying he was perfect. He liked a drink, he liked a bet – he'd be the first to admit that. But when he was about his business he could be quite fanatical – that probably comes from growing up as the understudy to Gordon Banks. He studied Gordon and his game expanded from there – he couldn't have had a better start in life, really. As I've said, you can have all the schooling in the world but to go in every day and see the greatest goalkeeper in the world, as Banks was at that time, is the best education around.

I think everybody knew Peter was destined for greatness from an early age. At West Ham, we had a young goalkeeper called Steve Death. He wasn't big but he was a real prospect, and he was the second-choice England schoolboy goalkeeper when Peter was number one – poor Steve couldn't get a look in. It just shows you the gulf in class, really. Steve was a great kid, but he couldn't get in the team at West Ham ahead of Bobby Ferguson either and ended up going to Reading, where he had a fantastic career and played well over 500 games. He held the record for the longest time without conceding a goal – 1,074 minutes – before Edwin van der Sar broke it in 2009. Bit of difference between going that long at Manchester United and at Reading, though. Yet while Steve couldn't break through at West Ham, Shilton displaced Gordon Banks at Leicester City. It shows you how good he must have been.

Shilton was exactly six foot but looked much bigger. He managed to give that impression by spreading himself and working the angles brilliantly. He had a way of setting himself that made him appear hard to beat and, apart from Diego Maradona, I don't remember too many besting him in a race to the ball. He was very quick off his line.

I remember watching the game against Argentina at home in 1986. Like the rest of the country, watching it in real time I had no idea he'd handled it. I just couldn't believe Shilton had been beaten from there – it was so unlike him. It looked like a fantastic, incredible jump and it was only when the replay was shown that we all thought, 'Hold on.' I know Terry Butcher wanted to strangle Maradona after the game, and I don't think Peter has ever forgiven him. Maybe I've led a sheltered life but I'd never seen anything like that before – a player get away with punching the ball into the net. I believe Peter has had the opportunity to meet Maradona since, to shake his hand and forget it, but he won't. He thinks he should have apologised – which he never has.

And, yes, I can understand why people think the attitudes in the professional game are strange at times. It isn't the handball that Peter objects to, but the lack of an apology. If Maradona had said sorry it would have been okay. Do I get that? I guess so. Professionals are trained to win at all costs and if someone gets away with one, we tend to think that all's fair in love and war. Just own up – admit it in the bar later. Maradona never did that. He acted as if what he did was some sort of divine intervention, and that sticks in the throat a little more. It was as well he scored one of the greatest World Cup goals to effectively win the match soon after, otherwise I think the bitterness would have lasted even longer.

The one thing I cannot comprehend, though, is when people say it was an instinctive reaction. Handball is a foul in football. How can sticking your hand up be instinctive, then? Every instinct as a footballer should be telling you to get your hand out of the way. I won't accept that it was instinctive. Maradona knew what he was doing, and he intended to cheat to try to score. A slip fielder wouldn't try to catch a hard cricket ball with his foot – so why would a footballer attempt to divert a ball with his hand? I saw the same excuse made for Rafael of Manchester United last season, and I thought it was rubbish then, too. He's just rash, that's his problem. He hasn't got instincts any different to the rest of us. I had his brother, Fabio, at Queens Park Rangers and he was the same. He'd rush in and kick a player up in the air after the ball had gone. It seemed to be his greatest talent.

I know Brian Clough credited Peter Shilton with winning the league for Nottingham Forest – he reckoned he was worth 12 points a season – but the relationship between the manager and the goalkeeper was unconventional to say the least. On one occasion, Clough was due to meet John Holmes, Peter's agent, and his partner Jeff Pointon. He kept them waiting outside his office and then his secretary announced that Clough was ready to see them. They entered the room and both went flying head over heels. Clough had rigged a squash racquet handle up by the door to trip them over as they came in! On another occasion, before the 1980 European Cup final – which Nottingham Forest won – Peter complained that the training pitch in Madrid wasn't suitable for his practice routines. Clough announced he knew just the place and instructed Peter Taylor to take Shilton there. They ended up on the grassy centre of a large roundabout, surrounded by chaos and tooting traffic horns. Clean sheet the following night, mind you.

It is a shame that, after retiring from football, Peter has had financial problems. The gambling took a toll. In 1996, after Peter left Leyton Orient, he was with me at West Ham for a spell as a back-up goalkeeper. He must have been 47 by then, and things weren't easy. I got him a little club car because he didn't even have transport to get him back and forth to training. He was borrowing a motor from somebody at the time. He didn't play for us but I enjoyed having Peter around, working with our goalkeepers along with Les Sealey who was my goalkeeping coach. I'm glad to see he's getting back on his feet now. I often see him at charity dinners or fund-raisers and the like. It's easy to tell us apart – he's getting paid and I'm not.

I'm a real sucker for that stuff. I just find it so hard to say no. I'll ring a bloke back and hear his story and the next thing I know I'm driving home from Ipswich at two in the morning, or stuck at the worst hotel in living memory, because I think I should do something to help. And once you've said yes one time, they've got you. The League Managers Association must see me coming. Every time they have a function I get roped in to speak. I wouldn't mind if it was shared around – but you never seem to see Arsène Wenger there. Just me. Would you do a dinner for 20 people, Harry, they'll give a lot to the charity if they could meet you? Of course. Then you get to the dinner, and they say they're having a raffle. First prize: dinner with me. But they're at a dinner with me! Oh no, this is a more intimate one – only five people. And on it goes. I swear, if I don't learn to say no soon, I'll end up having to go round and cook somebody breakfast one day.

David Armstrong, the old Middlesbrough and Southampton player, is one of the worst for calling in a favour. He's always hitting people up for prizes and he gets hundreds of people to his events. I can remember doing one when I was manager of

Bournemouth. I went down there with my mate Jimmy Gabriel, another Southampton old boy who, like Peter Shilton, hadn't been doing so well and was struggling to find work. David got me up on stage with Lawrie McMenemy to draw the raffle. Everyone had to sign a tenner, and the first prize was a weekend for two at the five-star George V hotel in Paris, flights included. Dave could get prizes off anybody. He could get you a night out at Buckingham Palace if he put his mind to it. Jimmy was at a table with a lot of his old Southampton team-mates – Denis Hollywood, John McGrath, Hugh Fisher, all good lads. Dave had put all the £10 notes in a big barrel, and I thought it was an opportunity to do my mate Jimmy a turn. A weekend in Paris would be lovely for him and his wife, Pat – she had been quite ill and they could probably use a holiday. I pulled out a tenner at random. 'Great news,' I said, 'it's one of your favourite players of all time at Southampton – Jimmy Gabriel!' And I made sure to chuck the £10 straight back into the barrel, where it couldn't be seen. The crowd went mad. They were all singing his name: 'Jimmy! Jimmy! Jimmy!' Meanwhile, Jimmy was at the back of the room waving his arms at the stage. 'No, no,' he was shouting, 'it's a mistake – I didn't have a ticket.' Oh my God. What was he playing at? He did me like a kipper. Now, I had to improvise. Fortunately, nobody could hear Jimmy's protests above the noise – and I still had the microphone. 'What's that you say, Jimmy?' I said. 'What a fantastic gesture, ladies and gentlemen, Jimmy wants to have the prize re-drawn. Round of applause for Jimmy Gabriel.' I could see Jimmy looking puzzled and I was trying to catch his eye and mouth to him 'shut up'. In the car on the way home, the first thing he said was, 'I don't

206

know what happened there, Harry. I didn't have a ticket.' 'I know you didn't have a fucking ticket, Jim,' I hissed. 'I just made out it was you because I thought then you could take Pat away for a weekend because she hadn't been well. I thought it would be nice for you and her to go to France.' 'Oh,' he said. 'That would have been nice. I would have liked that.' What can you do?

There was another occasion when I went down to Southend, in Essex, because some people I knew who had a casino in London were opening a new club down there and they wanted me to visit on opening night. I was the manager of West Ham at the time and when I arrived it turned out Lester Piggott was also a guest. Being a horse-racing man I was pleased to meet Lester and we all went up to the Mayor's office for a reception, which wasn't really my cup of tea, or Lester's. We were clinging to one another a bit by this time and the plan was to drive to the new place in a horse-drawn carriage along the seafront. The owners wanted to put on a bit of a show, and the council and Mayor's office were clearly all behind it. Off we went, with a big black horse up front like they have for funerals. Lester and me, the Mayor and Lady Mayoress. She was loving it, acting very regally, waving at people like the Queen. Suddenly I spotted a gang of kids running alongside the carriage and I could see they had these giant water pistols, the huge ones that look like machine guns. It was early evening during the summer school holidays and they looked like proper scallywags, too. By now, Lester had also seen them and we both leaned back into the carriage to escape the inevitable barrage. Not the Lady Mayoress. She was enjoying her moment too much and the poor woman copped the lot.

Her hair collapsed like a bad soufflé – it was as if someone had doused her with a bucket of water, which in a way they had. I'm sorry, but Lester and I were struggling to control our laughter. We didn't know where to look. These little sods ran off hooting and hollering, too. In the end, Lester got out and just lit a cigar. What could you do? The whole plan was a bust.

It was good to meet one of my racing heroes, though. I was always a huge fan of Lester's – he was the greatest jockey and, in my opinion, there is no one quite like him. Alan Ball had a few horses and it was always his dream for Lester to ride one. In the end, he booked him for a race at Salisbury with one he thought was a real prospect. The horse finished way down the field and by the time Alan had scurried over to the unsaddling enclosure, Lester had dismounted and was walking over to his next ride. Alan chased after him, desperate to hear the wisdom and insight of racing's greatest pilot. 'Lester, Lester,' he said, finally getting his attention. 'What do you reckon?' Without breaking stride, Piggott looked at Alan and in his sneering nasal tone uttered one word. 'Glue,' he said, and walked on. Not another sound. That was the end of Alan's little dream. I dare say his Southampton team-mate Peter Shilton backed a few like that, too.

STEVE NICOL
(LIVERPOOL)

'Where have you been all my life?' Alan Hansen's words to Steve Nicol, apparently, after their first match together. It's the same old story. Liverpool spot a kid at Ayr United, buy him for buttons – £300,000 – and turn him into one of the most versatile players in Europe. Steve was a right-back who could also play on the right or in the centre of midfield. He was the butt of the jokes in the Liverpool dressing-room, apparently, but it was no laughing matter when the game started. He was a serious player: powerful, fast, imposing, technically outstanding. He had a reputation for not being the brightest, but he certainly didn't lack intelligence with the ball at his feet. I read Kenny Dalglish's description of his arrival at Anfield in 1981. It bears repeating.

'Until then, the three Scots already at Anfield, Alan Hansen, Graeme Souness and me had been pretty well able to look after ourselves. We had built up an understanding that the Scots were the master race. We would quote historical facts to the English players to prove it. Some of the most important inventions and discoveries in the world came from Scots, the television, the telephone, penicillin, the steam engine and tarmac. Their names are part of history – John Logie Baird, Alexander Graham Bell, Alexander Fleming, James Watt. Not to mention those other wonders of the world, golf and whisky. Per heads of population, the Scots are the most educated race in the world. We did well flying the flag of Scottish supremacy, until Nicol came. Everything we had built up, he destroyed in ten minutes.'

He had all sorts of nicknames. Chico after one of the Marx Brothers, and Chopsy because he liked chips, which in his broad accent were pronounced 'chops'. The Liverpool lads from that time said he had the worst diet of any footballer they'd seen. Endless packets of crisps, chips with everything – and he smoked, which drove Kenny Dalglish mad. This was probably the last era in the English game in which a player could live unhealthily and get away with it. The next decade saw the arrival of the Premier League and the influx of foreign players. It all changed from there.

Yet, no matter how he prepared, Nicol was never found wanting as an athlete. He had size 12 feet that would pound the right flank like no other player of his time. When you think of the other players about in that era, Mike Duxbury at Manchester United, Gary Stevens at Everton, I think Steve was in a league above. Certainly his versatility set him apart. He ended up in central midfield and was outstanding in that role, too. He was two-footed, a strong presence in the air and a very courageous defender. When Phil Neal was at right-back he played on the right wing, and at one time he deputised for Hansen at centre-half when he was out injured for a spell. Hansen said that when he returned to the side he felt as if he could play with a cigar on when Nicol was to his right.

Was he as daft as they make out? Well, he held down a manager's job with the same club in America, New England Revolution, for nine years, and now has a good number with ESPN over there, so he can't be that stupid. I think every club needs one guy who hasn't got the guile of the others – there are always some pretty sharp lads in football dressing-rooms – and messing them around is good for team spirit as long as it doesn't go too far. When my son Jamie was at Liverpool, Jason McAteer was in the Steve Nicol role. There are so many stories about Jason – although I have no idea how many, if any, are true – footballers like a good story. One day, away with the Republic of Ireland team, the players were out at a local Italian for a bonding exercise. They were all ordering pizzas. 'Do you want yours cut in four or eight?' the waitress asked Jason. 'Four, definitely,' he said. 'There's no way I'll eat eight.' Another one, which Neil Ruddock swears is true, has Jason filling in a credit-card application form and getting to the line that says 'position at company'. 'What should I put?' he asks earnestly. 'I'm usually a midfielder, but he keeps playing me at right wing-back.'

Graeme Souness swears that Nicol turned up for his first away trip with a teddy bear tied to the top of his travel bag, which must have kept the lads going for a few months, but he was most certainly one of the boys once he settled in and was even known to sneak a fag on the team bus on the way home after a game. These days, players have often come through an academy system and are therefore attuned to the professional way of life from a young age. But Steve had been a building-site labourer back in Scotland and only played for Ayr part-time. He smoked, liked a drink, enjoyed his chips and his fatty snacks like any other working-class lad. And he wasn't going to stop that just because he now played for Liverpool.

I think sometimes that experience of life outside the game makes a character stronger. Although Steve Nicol missed Liverpool's first penalty the night they won the shoot-out for the European Cup against AS Roma, what impresses me is that he wanted to take one at all. Here was a kid, on as a substitute for Craig Johnston, having played just over 20 matches for Liverpool, and he volunteered to take the first penalty against Roma in their own stadium. They don't make them like that any more.

Picking this Eighties XI, and other teams from the Premier League era, I notice this one is the last to include Scottish players, and I think that's a real shame. Nicol and Hansen, maybe Gordon Strachan, were probably the last of the greats – the last truly magnificent Scottish players to operate at the pinnacle of the English game. Looking back through the other teams, there are Scotsmen at the heart of it all – Souness, Dalglish, John Robertson, Denis Law, Dave Mackay, Billy Bremner, Bobby Collins – but the driving force in the Scottish game begins to dwindle at the end of the Football League era. It surprised me that it dropped off so quickly. We went from every good team being built around a Scottish influence to a time when Darren Fletcher of Manchester United was probably alone as a Scotland international in a top English side. It can't have been prejudice on the part of the coaches – not with men like Sir Alex Ferguson around. I think their league simply became overstuffed with second-rate foreign players and their kids just couldn't get through. Once that happens, people stop putting such emphasis on looking and scouting. The production line has never stopped in terms of Scottish managers, but for a time nobody searched north of the border for players any more.

That's a pity because there was a raw talent in some of those Scottish lads that you won't always find at academies. I'm thinking of another Scottish right-back from around that time, Ray Stewart at West Ham. He came from Dundee United, who were a reasonable team, but even so there was something untutored in the way he used to smash his penalties as hard as he could off a proper run. The West Ham fans called him Tonka because, like Tonka Toys, they reckoned he was indestructible. West Ham, in particular, seemed to have a good connection to Scotland once Ron Greenwood signed Bobby Ferguson and John Cushley in 1967. We were a team of London boys at the time and at first with their accents it was like they came from another planet, but they soon fitted in. Like Liverpool, West Ham had a long tradition of Scottish players: Neil Orr, Don Hutchison, Frank McAvennie, Christian Dailly, even a goalkeeper called Alan McKnight, whose name sounded a little too much like McNightmare – and he did have a few. Yet where are the Scots in Sam Allardyce's team now? Where are they for Brendan Rodgers? I would love to see a resurgence of Scottish players in our game – and I just hope the sort of men who unearthed Nicol and Hansen haven't given up.

ALAN HANSEN
(LIVERPOOL)

Reading the game, understanding the game, always in the right place at the right time, Alan Hansen was just a class act. What you have seen on *Match of the Day* for the last two decades or so was how he played. Never rushed, always cool, very laid back. No matter how frenetic the match, Alan looked like he had time. He was a centre-half who could play, could pass, could come out with the ball and build the attack. Again he was player that Liverpool picked up from an inferior level of football, yet put straight in the team. Hansen won promotion with Partick Thistle, played one season in Scotland's Premier Division and came to Anfield. He signed in the summer and was in the starting line-up the following September. He didn't play every game of that 1977–8 season, but he was regarded highly enough to start in the European Cup final against FC Bruges of Belgium that Liverpool won. In the end, he took over from Emlyn Hughes. In season 1978–9, Liverpool conceded just 16 goals in 42 matches – only 4 at Anfield – and kept 28 clean sheets.

Goalscoring partnerships are important, but no more so than getting the centre-halves right, and Liverpool have had some fabulous pairings over the years. Hansen and Mark Lawrenson are two of the best there have been at any club in the world. Liverpool broke their club transfer record to sign Mark from Brighton and Hove Albion, and I think that shows the sweeping changes in our game now. It is unthinkable that a signing record would be created with a move like that in the modern era. At the end of last season, in the entire Premier League, only one club, Crystal Palace, still had a lower league player as their record signing – Dwight Gayle from Peterborough United for £4.5 million. That record is bound to fall, too. The rest are either expensive foreign imports – and not always successful ones, if you consider Dani Osvaldo at Southampton and Erik Lamela at Tottenham Hotspur – or established Premier League players like Andy Carroll, Darren Bent or Peter Crouch. I doubt very much if the modern Liverpool are hunting for the next Lawrenson at Brighton, either. And is their defence better for it? Not on last year's evidence.

I think the talent is still there in the lower divisions, but people just haven't got the time to make it work, or the freedom to take a risk. When so many managers are losing their jobs they will go for the tried and tested, the comfort blanket of a big foreign name with proven success. There aren't the opportunities in the modern game because everybody is looking over his shoulder. If there was more space to breathe, managers would bring some of those players through and we would see that the talent is there. It might take time, but given the opportunity I still believe talent exists in the lower leagues. I remember going to West Ham from

Bournemouth and taking little Matthew Holmes with me for £40,000. He did great, and was runner-up in our Player of the Year Awards in his first season; we used him all over the place and ended up selling him to Blackburn Rovers for £1.2 million. So they are out there, but if I hadn't gone to West Ham as manager, who would have taken a chance on Matthew? He'd have been in the lower divisions all his career.

If managers are constantly under pressure they are not going to gamble. They'll always look for the instant fix. I'm not advocating picking up second-rate players from second-rate leagues, but either clubs like Partick, Brighton and Ayr United have just stopped producing players overnight – which seems unlikely – or we've stopped looking; because those guys came in and won European Cups.

It was a great pity that Liverpool didn't win the league last season with the number of English players they had in the team. We've been told for so long that English footballers aren't good enough, and then suddenly there were six of them – plus Joe Allen, who is Welsh – at the top of the table. I know Manchester City have a long-term project with their academy, but Manuel Pellegrini, their current manager, doesn't seem too interested in developing English players. Half of the English lads at the club spent all summer trying to get away. I really fancied Liverpool at one stage last season, particularly at home. Once they had beaten Manchester City, with Vincent Kompany struggling to contain them, it really looked possible. In the end, though, what they missed was steel at the back. The modern team used Luis Suárez the way the great Liverpool side used Kenny Dalglish, and they have Steven Gerrard where the great team had Graeme

Souness – but what they don't have is Hansen, Lawrenson, Steve Nicol, the great defenders that got them over the line in so many matches. The best Liverpool teams only needed one goal because their back four were not going to leak. That makes life so much easier.

There were some good defenders around at that time. Terry Butcher was a fantastic competitor and Mark Wright had a lot of style, but I don't think anyone had the aura or control of Hansen. As a manager, sitting there watching him you would have felt comfortable. In fact Bob Paisley said he gave him more heart attacks than any other player because he would insist on playing the ball out when others would just have lumped it clear, but all I remember is his air of calm. There was never any panic, no last-ditch tackles. He reminded me of Bobby Moore. I never saw Bob throw himself into a diving header or make a lunging tackle because he'd seen the danger ages earlier and was in the right place. Hansen was the same. He would cut out a pass or a cross, fill in the space at the near post and catch it on his chest, like Bobby. And play from there. And that's what he is like away from football, too. He's an easy person, a wonderful golfer – three handicap – and very laid-back company. Jamie goes golfing with him in Florida every year, and I was with him at the World Cup in 2010, working for the BBC. He's a good chap.

We were based in Cape Town, which was lovely, but then England had to play Germany in Bloemfontein. What a strange, hick town that was. I don't know where Alan was – somewhere classy, no doubt – but I ended up staying in a bungalow with a pal of mine, Clive Tyrell. Clive's just like his dad, Reg, who I worked with at Bournemouth – he always makes me laugh. He was an apprentice at Chelsea as a kid but it didn't work out. I lost my licence for six months for speeding and Clive was my driver in that time. I ended up taking him to South Africa to say thanks. We played a lot of golf, had a great time. In Cape Town it was marvellous. Lovely big hotel suite – he had a bedroom, I had a bedroom. Perfect. So on we went to Bloemfontein, where it is fair to say conditions were somewhat different. When we pulled up outside this bungalow I couldn't quite believe it. 'Sorry,' said the chap from the BBC, 'there are no hotels.' That night the temperature must have dropped 15 degrees and, try as we might, we couldn't find the heating. It went from lovely during the day to freezing. I don't think I've ever been colder. The result the next day didn't do much to warm us up, either. Hansen wouldn't have stood for it, I know that. And he wouldn't have got beat by four, either.

PAUL McGRATH
(MANCHESTER UNITED)

What a player he was, but what a player he could have been. Without the injuries, without the drinking, who knows what he would have achieved in his career. Ron Atkinson rated him as better than John Terry and Tony Adams – put together. I don't know about that, but he was a quite exceptional footballer. He had incredible pace and was equally at home in a back four or running midfield, as he did later in his career with Aston Villa. He was a great player – but we probably never saw how good he could have been because of the way he lived his life. When I tell stories about lads who liked a drink, it is usually with fondness because those days were fun, and most of the lads could handle it. Paul was different; twice he tried to kill himself and on one occasion he consumed a bottle of Domestos. There was little merriment here. Paul, sadly, was a man with serious problems.

He was brought up in orphanages around Dublin at a time when they were not many black faces about: a hard life. He didn't touch a drop of alcohol until he was 18 but then discovered a real taste for it. Like a lot of alcoholics he used it to give himself confidence and to escape reality. He admits there were times when he played while still drunk, even falling over the ball once in a pre-season friendly. Yet when he was right, and his game was right, there was no one to touch him. I think by the time Sir Alex Ferguson came to Manchester United he was almost beyond help, and Alex just associated him with a poisonous drinking culture that was ruining the club. He sold him to Aston Villa where, for all his troubles, he became a club legend. He played every game in the 1992–3 season when they just missed out on the title. He was magnificent on occasions for Villa – inspired, I think, by a determination to prove Ferguson wrong. Aston Villa beat Manchester United in the League Cup final during his time there and Paul was exceptional that day. I know Alex never stopped admiring him as a player, but he couldn't control the man – and at that time what he had to do above all at United was establish control. Players like McGrath and Norman Whiteside had to go.

The way Paul lived would have made his injury problems worse, no doubt of that. Tony Cascarino roomed with Paul for Villa, and on Ireland trips, and he says he was one of those fellas

Here's Pat Jennings, who I got to know a few years ago when I was managing at Tottenham and he was coaching there. His background was in Gaelic football which gave him a complete disregard for getting hurt. Here he is with his Arsenal teammate Liam Brady, who my dad really used to rate. He'd put Brady right up there with the best he'd ever seen.

Liverpool defenders Phil Neal and Phil Thompson, celebrating their 1981 European Cup victory. Liverpool through and through, Thompson was a local lad from Kirkby who'd stood on the kop since he was a kid, while Neal holds a record for playing in 417 consecutive matches for them, never missing a game in almost seven years.

Two legendary managers, Brian Clough and Bob Paisley, at the Manager of the Year lunch in 1978. If you look back at the achievements of men like these two, I don't understand why owners suddenly lost faith in British managers. They're both on my list of the best managers of all time.

I remember the first time I saw Kevin Keegan in action, down at a game in Bournemouth. I knew he was destined for great things. He just threw himself into every job he ever had and the work he put into his game was just phenomenal.

Liverpool's Graeme Souness, Alan Hansen and 'King Kenny' Dalglish celebrate their championship win in 1983 with champagne in the dressing room. Graeme told me he never went into the players' bar in the whole time he was at Liverpool, because he wanted to keep a barrier up between himself and the opposition – he wanted to be feared. It's nice to see him here enjoying a drink!

John Robertson and Peter Shilton. John was the most unlikely footballer anyone had ever seen when he started out – he was overweight, he smoked, wasn't interested in staying fit. But what a player he became. Peter was so good he could have made my team for the decade of the sixties, seventies or eighties.

Alan Hansen with the FA Cup in 1986. What you have seen on *Match of the Day* for the last two decades or so was how he played. Never rushed, always cool, very laid back. No matter how frenetic the match, Alan looked like he had time.

Paul McGrath, who suffered with alcoholism but was a genius with the ball, and Bryan Robson, the man Paul Gascoigne rates as the best English footballer he ever saw. Here they are with Sir Alex at Old Trafford.

Gary Lineker and John Barnes after a European Championship qualifier in 1987 against Turkey where they scored five between them. John was such a versatile player and was brilliant for Liverpool, although I don't think he ever performed for the national team as well as he did for the Reds. Gary was such a great finisher – he always found space. It was like a psychic ability.

Poor Gazza, unable to hold back the tears after England's penalty shoot out defeat to Germany. I'd say at this time he was close to being the best player on the planet.

The two great warrior-midfielders and famous rivals, Arsenal's Patrick Vieira and Manchester United's Roy Keane. It took Keane a long time to get his break as a player, because apparently he was a bit timid. For anyone who saw his set-tos with Vieira, that's pretty hard to imagine.

I've selected many players from the Manchester United 1999 treble-winning team for my two premiership teams – Roy Keane, Gary Neville, Paul Scholes, Ryan Giggs and Peter Schmeichel. All fantastic players, who brought about one of the most incredible feats in the history of the game.

It's hard to say who is the best English team of all time, but I'd say the game to decide it would have been Manchester United's treble-winning team versus Arsenal's Invincibles, the team that went the entire 2003-4 season unbeaten. They were only five years apart, but sadly never really met. That would have been a fascinating battle.

John Terry, a fantastic centre-half and a great leader, with Rio Ferdinand who I tipped at 16 to be the greatest centre-half in Europe – for a while, he was just that.

Having a laugh with Stuart Pearce. I managed him at West Ham when he was 37, and he was fantastic for us, but I have to say I wish I'd worked with him in his prime. He was a ferocious competitor, and I think if you asked any right-sided player for his least favourite opponent, Stuart's name would be top of the list.

Everyone knows Gareth Bale is good, but I think until you've worked with him you might not realise how good. People see him as a flying machine, but he's so much more. He wins game after game for you, and I think he'll go on to be an all-time great.

Holding the FA Cup trophy with Sol Campbell in 2008. Sol was a great captain for Portsmouth – he'd been there and done it all and the players looked up to him. He had such a strong, imposing physique – he was a monster of an athlete really.

that could be out every night, no matter where they were in the world. If they were in a hotel in Norwich on a Tuesday, Paul had somewhere to go; and the same in Oslo on a Monday. He always knew the places, but that lifestyle takes its toll.

At Villa, they had a physiotherapist, Jim Walker, who devised a way of nursing Paul through the week with his knee problems. He would do a bit of bike work, have a bath and a massage, sometimes collect the balls from behind the goal, just to be involved with the team. Paul reckons he would have retired four years earlier if it wasn't for Walker – in fact, Manchester United's first plan before they sold him was to have him quit and claim the insurance. He was only 29, but his knees were that bad. Yet more than five years later he was playing for Ireland at the 1994 World Cup finals and marking Roberto Baggio of Italy out of a game.

Paul just had everything. He was a big lad. Strong, quick, powerful. Ledley King was similar some years later. A lot of the same attributes, and terrible problems with injury. He couldn't train all week, either, and the day after he played his knees looked like you had inflated them with a bicycle pump. In the end, he didn't train at all through the week. I think that shows amazing commitment and discipline – not to train, and then still play at the level Ledley and Paul McGrath achieved.

I was close to taking Paul at the end of his career. He came in to train at West Ham, but he was struggling with injury. He worked hard and tried to get fit for us, and he still had that pace, even with the dodgy knees. Not many could get the better of him in practice matches, but in the end he had to face the truth. To be fair, he was completely honest. He called me up. 'I don't think I can do it now, Harry,' he said. 'I don't want to let you down.' So that was that – but he was as good as gold in the brief time we were together.

Of the other central defenders from that time, Des Walker had fantastic pace as well, but I don't think he had Paul's technical ability. When they did away with the back-pass rule in 1992 it made a huge dent in Des's game. He would use his speed to nip in front of the striker, mop up the ball and knock it back for the goalkeeper to pick up. Then they changed the laws so that the keeper couldn't handle it from a back pass and that was a real problem for Des. Suddenly, he was being required to play his way out of trouble, and that wasn't his style at all. A man like McGrath was far more comfortable in that position, and that gives him the edge.

KENNY SANSOM
(ARSENAL)

They used to call him 'White Shorts' at Arsenal because Kenny often left the pitch as spotless as he went on it. It wasn't that he lacked the courage for a tackle, more that his timing and reading of the game were so perfect he did not need to go flying in. He carried on where Terry Cooper left off really, as a great marauding left-back. Stuart Pearce took over from him, and then Ashley Cole – it's a position where English football has been strong for a few decades now. They had a very good left-back at West Bromwich Albion at the time called Derek Statham, but he couldn't get a look in. He only made three appearances for England, which shows you how strong Kenny, who made 86, was in that role. He was just a fantastic player and I can remember the coaches at Crystal Palace raving about this kid they had discovered. Every now and then you find one and think, 'If we can't make him a footballer we should pack up.' They felt like that about Kenny at Palace. I know Sir Alex Ferguson did about Ryan Giggs at Manchester United, Arsenal did with Jack Wilshere and I did with Joe Cole at West Ham. Kenny was a certainty, apparently. He was a brilliant trainer, came back in the afternoon, worked non-stop on his game, always striving to be the best. I can remember seeing him in those early days – he stood out a mile. He had a low centre of gravity, was great going forward and you couldn't get past him. Strong in the air, too, for a small guy. Now he's battling alcoholism. With a guy like Kenny you really do wonder where it all went wrong.

In his book he says he didn't have a drink until he was 21 and then he couldn't leave it alone. He was a big gambler, too. Maybe it's the punter in me, but I look at an ex-player like Kenny and wonder what I could do to help him. Could you help him? Could he change? I don't know. Maybe he is beyond help, but I have never understood why a great club like Arsenal doesn't get hands-on in situations like this. Get him involved with community projects, give him something permanent in his life. It's sad to see a player who has done so well left to fade away like that. We see it with Paul Gascoigne and a lot of others from this era. Looking at this team now, a lot of these players have had problems – Peter Shilton, Paul McGrath, Kenny, Paul Gascoigne, even Bryan Robson. I think the next generation made more money from the game, so could ride it. If you look at a player like Tony Adams, he's had his troubles with addiction, but he has stayed relatively comfortable. I don't think everybody will end up that way, but at least they have a little more protection. You look at Kenny now, and he's got nothing. I'm not saying that isn't his fault. There are plenty of players from the same period like Gary Lineker or Ian Rush that have been successful. Yet not everybody has a future as a television presenter, and clubs could do more to help their ex-players. I think it's easy for people to say, oh it's his fault, he's lost his money gambling. I'm a gambler, too, but I'm a lucky one because I have been able to control it. I love a bet, it gives me a buzz. I enjoy a glass of wine, too. But when I see boys who have lost all their money, or have drunk their lives away, I don't feel superior. Addiction is an illness. Even now, with all the money being earned, I still think there will be lots of players who will end up potless. One of my old Portsmouth players, David James, was declared bankrupt this year and he was a fine professional.

I don't think Kenny would have been a heavier gambler than some of the lads these days – he just didn't have the same level of income. He might have earned £300 a week and lost that in the betting shop by the time he got home on Friday night. And, with football, that financial lifeline gets cut at a very young age. Kenny had a good career but he was still only 36 when it was all over. Suddenly, he didn't have a job. What is he going to do? What does he know? What's the next move? There is nothing out there beyond coaching or the media. It would even take three years to learn to be a taxi driver in London. You hear about chaps taking pubs, but I've always seen that as the road to ruin. A lot of the boys I know went in that direction and it turned out to be a marriage breaker. They start drinking, telling all the old tales – that turns into too many late nights, and in the end the wife packs up and leaves. Not ideal.

Yes, I know, somewhere along the line you have to do something for yourself. It's no good expecting a testimonial or a handout every year. But some people just do need help more than others. Players like Kenny Sansom and Paul Gascoigne are clearly higher maintenance than some of their contemporaries. They need more direction in life, a greater sense of purpose. They need a proper job in football. Not something part-time or just on match-days, a job that they get up to every morning.

I've never worried that my own betting was getting out of hand because, throughout my life, I've only gambled what I could afford. I have never been in a situation where the family was affected, nor do I bet amounts that are going to change my life. I'm a heavier gambler now than I used to be because I'm earning more – but what I'd call a good bet, and what was a good bet to Kenny, are probably two different things. I tell my players that football is a window of opportunity in which a fortune can be made if you're good enough – but look after your money because when it's finished there is no second chance. I'm not saying everyone listens. I saw John Hartson lose just about everything during his time at West Ham.

I think footballers live on the adrenalin of big matches and that gambling is a way of maintaining that buzz. They say the reason drugs are so prevalent in the music industry is that there is a rush associated with performing, and when the concert is over a rock star wants to find a way of maintaining that high. Obviously, professional sportsmen can't take drugs without risking severe punishment, so gambling fulfils that function for them. They replicate that excitement by having a bet.

I don't get to the races as much as I used to. I loved it as a day out, but these days you get some people who won't leave you alone. It's different if you're in a hospitality box, but to go walkabout – I'm afraid I can't do it any more. I prefer a quiet life. But I'll still have my bets – on golf, cricket, anything I'm watching really. They're changing the rules now to ban all football betting because of some recent scandals, but I think that is an over-reaction. What harm is there in me having a bet on a game in Serie A or the Champions League? It won't spoil my enjoyment – I can watch football without having a bet – but I just think it's a stupid rule. Banning bets on matches that take place in my league, I can understand. But why shouldn't a Premier League player be able to place a bet on a match in League One, or a lad at Bournemouth pick a winner between Arsenal and Chelsea? When I see new rules like that being made I am glad I am not at the start of it. The people in charge haven't a clue – particularly as all of football's governing bodies now have betting partners themselves.

If they are going to benefit from those commercial deals maybe they could use the money to help out guys like Kenny Sansom, by putting the proceeds into an addiction centre or rehabilitation. That would make more sense than banning gambling one minute, and teaming up with bookmakers the next.

GLENN HODDLE
(TOTTENHAM HOTSPUR)

Glenn Hoddle was such a beautiful footballer. The scorer of spectacular goals, and a simply fantastic passer. At Tottenham he had a great understanding with his fellow midfield players, like Ossie Ardiles, and again with striker Clive Allen. The game always seemed to unfold at his pace, he had a way of appearing to have time on the ball and always knew where the other good midfield players were. It was as if he had pictures in his head, he saw what was on and knew where the ball was going before it arrived. He reminded me a bit of Johnny Haynes. Glenn would hit a pass and everybody would be thinking, 'How did he see that, how did he know that player was there?' He never seemed to be obviously searching for it, either. He would look up – he always played with his head up – but it was never as if he was hunting a pass. He knew what the next move was before the ball even came. That is how the best play – and Glenn was one of the greatest midfielders this country has produced.

Some of the goals he scored, the little free-kicks and the clever things he did are evidence of an outstanding football brain, and it is a real pity that there is a generation that will remember him only for the controversies around his time as England manager. Even then he was on the right lines – but the off-the-field stuff surrounding his beliefs did for him.

I worked with Steve McClaren at Queens Park Rangers last season and his contribution was excellent. I think it is a real pity that failure in the England job taints a manager almost for life. Steve should never have been my temporary coach at QPR. He was too good for that, as he then showed with Derby County. But at the time he was glad of the work, just to get his foot through the door. A lot of clubs still wouldn't touch Steve because the fans would have been up in arms, and it needed one like Derby, where he is still highly regarded from his time as a player, to show that faith in him.

Glenn had been out of league football for eight years before I took him to QPR – how had we lost a football mind like that? It isn't right – and it makes the England job increasingly an older manager's game. The downside is so great these days that it's now becoming a position you take at the end of your career when you can't be tainted and aren't really looking for more work. For a young man, while it may seem irresistible, it may also come to be considered too great a risk. Unless you do very well – and even the quarter-finals wasn't considered good enough for Sven-Göran Eriksson in the end – people are going to be on your case, and it might render you unemployable. Why would a bright young coach take a chance like that?

Roy Hodgson is old enough not to be affected by this now. He isn't thinking of going too far from here. He's managed Liverpool and Inter Milan, as well as Switzerland, he's taken Fulham to a European final – he's had a fine career. He's not looking to get the Sunderland job when he stops working for the Football Association. In fact he probably sees this as his last managerial role in football. It's different for a younger guy, and I think it took a lot for Steve to get over the fall-out of managing England and failing to get to the European Championship. He had to go to Holland and work with Twente Enschede to escape the negativity at home – and ended up winning the Dutch league. So he's clearly no fool. It is a job that has chewed up two of our best young coaches in recent years and that is not right.

I'm not saying Glenn didn't get his chances after England. He did a very creditable job at Southampton, and also took charge of Tottenham and then Wolverhampton Wanderers – but he deserved those jobs because it wasn't as if he flopped as England manager. Steve did fail to get England to the European Championships in 2008, but Glenn qualified for the 1998 World Cup and was unlucky to lose to Argentina on penalties. I'm sure he would have got us to the 2000 European Championships, too, given time. Statistically he was one of the most successful

England managers ever. Yet every job he went to after England there seemed to be a stigma attached. Tottenham were a mid-table team, with middling investment, and Glenn's league finishes suggest this – but somehow it wasn't enough. How could the club show so little patience with a man who as a player pretty much *was* the club for 12 years?

Glenn was another player who was wasted by England really. In the 1979–80 season he scored 19 goals in 41 league games from midfield – yet only started 4 games for England. Even then, he scored two goals – but never kept his place. That seemed to be the story for Glenn. No England manager ever really showed enough faith in him, and it was as if he constantly had to prove himself. He played 53 games for England but it was a stop-start career. He made his debut against Bulgaria, started, scored, England won 2–0, and he then had to wait four matches and six months for his next game, against Wales. Then another three games before he was used again, then another three. He played his first game on 22 November 1979, and his fifth on 25 March 1981 – and in that time England played 15 matches. He was at the top of his game. It was a terrible waste of a great player.

I feel we've squandered Glenn's insight as a manager, too. In many ways, he pre-dated Brendan Rodgers and Roberto Martínez with the approach he took to players in the lower leagues. What Glenn did at Swindon Town, the belief he showed in getting those guys to pass their way to promotion rather than just hoof it, was ground-breaking. We need more people like Glenn in the game, more coaches with his philosophy. I think we'd produce better players in this country, better technical players. Look at what Brendan has done and Roberto Martínez – Glenn was years ahead of his time. From the start at Swindon, he had a clear idea of how he wanted to play – with a sweeper, coming out of the back, passing their way through midfield and always trying to play. He was influenced by what the Germans had done with Franz Beckenbauer, Matthias Sammer, Lothar Matthäus, and he thought that was the way England should go. He was very unlucky because in the end he wasn't sacked over football matters.

Glenn probably got the England job too early, too. He hadn't really let go of his playing career. There are stories of clashes on the training field with players like David Beckham, when Glenn wanted him to replicate certain of his own skills. I think it's difficult if the manager is still angling to be the best player, too, and I'm sure he would do things differently second time around. I have always found Glenn a nice guy, with good ideas on how the game should be played, and it was just a shame he didn't get a proper run at it. I feel certain he would have developed into one of the best England managers we have had, and I'm very happy to have him back involved again with us at QPR. He's definitely got something special to offer, and he's been out of the game for too long.

PAUL GASCOIGNE
(TOTTENHAM HOTSPUR)

There should be an inquiry into Paul Gascoigne one day. How did it end up like this? How, when we could all see the trouble ahead, did his decline just happen, like a slow-motion car crash? What could we, as people in football, have done to help him?

It would be an inquiry with one difference, though. When a great player like Gascoigne falls on hard times, former clubs, old friends and team-mates often rally around in support. So the people I'd want to hear from, right at the start, are his agents, his accountants, his lawyers, all the people that made fortunes from the industry that was Paul Gascoigne. What do these people actually do to help when the money stops coming in? I'm sure there are one or two agents who care beyond that final payday, but a lot of them are only interested in the loot. They are hanging about for their percentage, and when you're skint they move on. Who is looking after Paul Gascoigne now? At one time you never saw him without an agent by his side. Now he's out there, it seems, totally alone. We shouldn't be surprised, I suppose.

Mel Stein was Gascoigne's first agent, although in those days he preferred to be called his lawyer. Either way, his services won't have come cheap. In the aftermath of the 1990 World Cup, with offers pouring in every day, can you imagine how many hours he could justifiably say he'd spent working for his client? The pair fell out in the end – which is not much of a surprise either.

I am sure Gascoigne's many advisers did their best, but in another way they are lucky that he became an alcoholic, because that way everyone blames Paul for his problems and forgets that he had a legion of experts who were supposed to look after him – lawyers, accountants, commercial and marketing gurus, PR people. Everyone looks at him and thinks he's pissed his money up the wall, and nobody asks questions beyond that. Yet not every agent has the best intentions. A lot of people who make fortunes – bankers, investors – have money as their business. So for most people earning at that level, managing their accounts is not much different to their nine-to-five job. Sadly, in terms of numbers and accounts, footballers don't know what day it is. Some footballers earn £300,000 a week. How many people pull that in, without any financial knowledge? Sports people, pop stars, film stars. Unless the people around them are honest, they are vulnerable, an easy target. I'm not exempting myself from this; as my court case showed, I'm near the top of any list for naivety.

Of course, owners are always moaning about agents, too, but they forget how players used to get ripped off before they came along. You'd walk into the manager's office, get given an extra fiver and be told to send the next one in – there was no negotiation, no bargaining. We were just boys who had wanted to play football from the age of six – while the bosses had all the power. Sure, there will always be the odd book-smart lad – but most of us weren't interested in anything beyond playing football. The school work comes a poor second. I'm not saying footballers are thick. There are plenty that are what might be termed street-wise, but they are not going to have an A* in Further Mathematics. In the old days they accepted what they were given, and now they sign up with agents and put complete trust in them instead.

I met a chap in Dubai a few years back who had built two new houses near Chelsea's training ground in Cobham. He sold one but was struggling to find a bidder for the other. The bank was on his back, and then he heard about a player signing for Chelsea for a lot of money – an English lad. He got hold of the player's agent and offered him £100,000 if he could persuade his client to buy the second house. And he did it. Took the lad there and convinced him to do the deal – and I bet the lad didn't know his friend, the one who was supposed to be looking after him, was on a six-figure kickback to make the sale happen.

Should clubs take greater responsibility, get more involved in their players' lives and welfare? Definitely. I know Sir Alex Ferguson was very keen on the junior players getting some coaching qualifications, so that if they were let go by Manchester United and couldn't get a club, they at least had something to fall back on. That's a good idea. All those years ago at West Ham, Ron Greenwood did the same. He encouraged us to take our basic coaching badges young, and we then got paid to coach at the local schools. We didn't get our full badges, but we got the next best thing, which was called a premium – but I don't know how many clubs would bother encouraging that now.

I also like the way some clubs link their academies to good schools in the area – like Crystal Palace do with Whitgift in Croydon. Colin Pates, the former Chelsea captain, and Steve Kember are teachers there, and having those connections ensures the boys get a good education, academically as well as in football. Victor Moses came through there, and if you look at the choices he has made throughout his career, you can see he's been using common sense rather than chasing the money. I read that when Moses went to the European Under-17 Championship in Belgium, a condition of his release from the school was that the Football Association paid for a teacher to travel with him and help him revise every day, because it was in the build-up to his GCSEs. Moses got three goals, helped England reach the final, won the Golden Boot – and came home and got five GCSEs. I think what is key here is that the school insists on treating the academic side seriously, too – the young footballers are not just there to win trophies for the school football team. Yes, they'll strengthen the first XI – but they'll also have a good education. I think that shows what can be achieved – but obviously not every club has the money to send its star prospects to private schools. And not every boy would be suited to that environment, either. But at least the ones that are have more of a chance.

I just don't think the advice is there, even now. This is what to do with your money. This is how to avoid going skint. For all the advances in other areas of the game, I still think players are left to rely solely on their agents.

I had Ravel Morrison at Queens Park Rangers last season. Sir Alex Ferguson said he was the most naturally gifted player he has seen at Manchester United since Paul Scholes – and then sold him because he could do nothing with him. He'd been at West Ham, scored one of the goals of the season against Tottenham, but they, too, found it hard to control him. He'd already had one loan spell at Birmingham City, but ended up with me. The kid can really play. He goes past people and makes them look silly. He's like Alan Hudson. He doesn't run, he glides.

By the time we came to the end of the season, though, he couldn't get in our starting line-up. I left him out in the second play-off match against Wigan Athletic and the play-off final against Derby County when we won promotion. Yet all season Barry Silkman, his agent, was telling everybody he's better than Gareth Bale. 'Harry,' he said to me, 'he's on a different planet to Bale.' And yes, Barry, Ravel is a very good player. But Gareth Bale? He as good as scored the winning goal for Real Madrid in the Champions League final on the day Ravel couldn't get in QPR's team. Scary, isn't it? All year I heard Manchester City might take him, Liverpool might take him – and he's an amazing talent. But his attitude makes you think about where he will be in six years' time. By then Morrison will be 27 and we may still be wondering if someone's going to get a grip on him.

There was one game last season. We had all the ball in the first half but conceded a goal from a corner, lost confidence, and were getting pegged back on the edge of the penalty box. Half time came, saved us, and I decided we couldn't go out for the second half the same way. I introduced a second striker and said to Ravel that I wanted him to play off the left. Start left, but come inside when we have the ball. His face fell into a petulant pout. The whole team were looking at him. We were losing 1–0 and, deep down, I wanted to call him every name under the sun for playing up. In the end I pulled him away from the rest, took him outside and explained as patiently as the time allowed.

'Ravel, we are losing the fucking game,' I said. 'I just want you to play there and do a job for the team. We have to win the game. It's not about you, Okay? It's about the team. People look at your face in there when I've asked you to do something, and they will all go away and think you are a big-headed bastard, because your attitude stinks. That's what people say about you. You've come here, you've done well and I treat you like a million dollars. I keep telling you how good you are, I pick you, now I've asked you to do something for me and you fucking do that. I'm not asking you to play on the left or play wide. When they get the ball, go out there, because they are playing with three at the back, so they have a right wing-back. Once we have the ball, you come inside and the only one who is going to come against you is their big, slow, right-sided centre-half. That's all I fucking want you to do.' Second half he was absolutely different class. He ran the game, everything good we did came from him, and we were all watching it thinking, 'What a talent.' You looked at that performance and thought he could get us promoted on his own if he put his mind to it. It was like watching a player with Bale's class in the Championship. He would get the ball, beating three or four players like little kids in the playground, and have a shot at goal. The keeper had the game of his life to keep him out.

The trouble is, you could imagine him getting in the England team, being asked to do a job, and reacting in exactly the same way. Ravel should look at the fact that Will Keane still has a contract at Manchester United and he doesn't. We had Will on loan last season and he's a decent player, but in terms of pure ability he couldn't lace Ravel's boots – yet United would rather have Keane on the staff than Ravel. That should be a wake-up call, no matter what he is hearing from elsewhere.

Lee Clark, the Birmingham City manager, said to Ravel that he was the best player since Gazza. His response: 'Who's Gazza?' Should that surprise us? Admittedly that World Cup in Italy is 24 years ago now, and Ravel Morrison is 21, but however long ago it was, I think he can be expected to know who Paul Gascoigne is. But it does show you that when you've gone, when you've had your day, nobody cares.

All young players should be familiar with Gascoigne's story – first as inspiration, because he was such a great footballer, but then as a warning of how quickly the fun can turn to tears. I've been lucky. I've always been in a position where I've earned really good money over the years, as a manager. Paul earned great money as a footballer – but then it was over. He was a recovering alcoholic by the time he was at Everton, and he was only 34 when he played his last game for that club.

I remember crying with laughter one night with Walter Smith, who managed him at Rangers as well, telling stories about the stuff he used to get up to. Some of it was madness. He used to go out with his air rifle and would give his mate Jimmy Five Bellies £100 to use his backside as a target. He would send Jimmy up the end of the range, get him to drop his trousers and bend over, and every time he got hit on the arse he would give him £100 compensation. He hit him on the same place twice once. Walter says you could hear the screaming from the centre of Glasgow – and also Gazza laughing about it. He once played a wicked trick on Ally McCoist, who had just bought a big and expensive new car. Gazza had been fishing, so he hid a giant salmon in Ally's motor, under the floor of the boot where the spare wheel goes, then put it all back exactly as it was. It drove Ally mad – it was the height of summer and his car stank of rotting fish. Eventually, he took it back to the dealer and they found it. What he didn't know was that Gazza had a pal who was a mechanic, and he had actually hidden a second one in the engine somewhere it couldn't be found – just like in the film *The French Connection*. Every time Ally put his air conditioning on, he got another blast of decomposing salmon. Walter said you could smell Ally coming before you could see him. He wanted to strangle Gazza.

He was hyperactive, that was the problem. He couldn't sleep. Jamie told me that during the European Championships in 1996, he might get a call at 2am and Gazza would ask if he fancied a game of table tennis. In the 1991 FA Cup, Portsmouth played Tottenham in the fifth round. Terry Venables, the Tottenham manager, was at breakfast on the day of the game when one of the players approached him, very worried. 'There's something you should know, boss,' he said. 'Gazza couldn't sleep. He's been up since 3am playing squash.' 'Thanks,' said Venables, 'but who was he playing against?' It turned out to be Paul Walsh. Terry dropped Walsh from the team, but started

Gascoigne – knowing one had the metabolism to handle it, and the other would be dead on his feet. Tottenham won 2–1, and Gascoigne scored both goals. He had an energy level that was berserk – but what a footballer. He is another one who didn't look coached. It all seemed so natural with him – the dribbling, the way he could go past people and open the game up, the fantastic goals he scored.

Considering his talent, some of the moves he had at the end of his career were heartbreaking, though. Kettering Town, Gansu Tianma in China, near the Gobi desert, Boston United. There is history over the years of players with great talent finishing up in these career dead ends. George Best was with Brisbane Lions and Nuneaton Borough; Jimmy Greaves played with Chelmsford City, Barnet and Woodford Town. They are not making the right decisions, not getting the right advice.

Yet when Paul was at his peak before the bad injury there was no one like him. At the World Cup in 1990, I think he was close to being the best player on the planet. Diego Maradona was still around, so it would be difficult to say for sure, but he was certainly the best player England had, the way he could run with the ball, putting his arm out, beating people off as he went. It is great to see people that can just go past players and do something special, who can open the door in a way others can't. In the modern game, I'd put him alongside Lionel Messi, Luis Suárez, Sergio Agüero, because he had flair that was almost South American. All the top teams are searching for that figure now, the individual who can change the game. Modern defences are so packed, defensive midfields so organised, that everyone is searching for a Gascoigne type to unpick that lock. When Ross

Barkley came into the Everton team, straight away there were comparisons with Gascoigne. We're desperate for another one to open the game up. We all loved him, whatever his weaknesses as a person.

I think the difference between Gascoigne and a lot of the players I've heard mentioned in the same breath since is that he went out there and actually did it. He didn't leave us wondering. Until the injury he sustained in the 1991 FA Cup final, every week we saw evidence of his brilliance. He went to the World Cup and was arguably the best player; he turned major matches on his own. He won an FA Cup semi-final against Arsenal in 10 minutes, having been told that he might last 35, maximum. That was a quite incredible performance. Gascoigne had a hernia operation after the quarter-final with Notts County and had only played half the midweek match against Norwich City before the Arsenal game. The medical advice was that he would last little more than 30 minutes, and Venables decided to start him and told him to see what he could do in that time. He won the game in 10. Tottenham got a free-kick 30 yards from goal and Gary Lineker's advice was just to smash it. Gascoigne did. He took a run-up like Michael Holding from the boundary and absolutely leathered it past the Arsenal goalkeeper, David Seaman. Soon after, he played a beautiful little pass inside to Paul Allen, who set up Gary Lineker for Tottenham's second goal. They won 3–1, and in the end Gascoigne lasted around an hour. My favourite story from that day is what he is supposed to have said to Venables on Tottenham's bench after the free-kick went in. 'Did you see that silly bastard in the goal?' Gascoigne asked. 'He only tried to save it.'

I see Paul reasonably often because he lives in Bournemouth now, and he always stops and has a chat. He's good as gold really. He's someone I'd love to find a spot for somewhere, if I could. If he actually wanted to come and do it, I'd like to help, get him doing something with the youth team, get him back in the game again. Yet, really, shouldn't Tottenham be prioritising that now? I can understand that clubs might not want him to coach academy kids – there could be worries about parent reaction because of his run-ins with the police – but surely there is a way of finding work for him? Would he turn up? I would hope so.

When people make wild claims about some of the young players I'm often sceptical about their credentials. Better than Bale? The next Gazza? Okay, prove it. Where are the Wembley winners? Where are the performances that people will still be talking about nearly 25 years on? I think the pity with Gascoigne is that in the end the desire to define those big occasions just overwhelmed him. In the 1991 FA Cup final against Nottingham Forest he was hyped up to an unhealthy degree and ended up with a self-inflicted injury that changed the course of his career. He damaged his ligaments and was lucky he did not do worse to Gary Charles. I think he always knew he wasn't quite the same player after that, and it really hurt him. He couldn't help himself, though.

BRYAN ROBSON
(MANCHESTER UNITED)

And now to the man Paul Gascoigne rates as the best English footballer he ever saw. I think one of the reasons Liverpool would have been popular Premier League champions last season is that a lot of people wanted to see Steven Gerrard win the league. I know many felt the same way when Bryan Robson finally got his hands on the trophy in 1993. He wasn't an integral part of the team – in fact, he only featured in 14 league games that season, and 15 when Manchester United retained it the following year – but it was considered a long overdue reward for a player regarded as so much greater than the team in which he played. What Robson truly deserved was to be in a successful England team and at the beating heart of Manchester United when they dominated English football. It wasn't to be. Robson was approaching the end of his career when Sir Alex Ferguson won the first of 13 Premier League titles, but he still got to play a part. Alex speaks very highly of him, as a man and a player, and I am glad to see United have given him a role at Old Trafford as an ambassador of the club.

If Robson had the same medal collection as Ryan Giggs it would not have been unmerited. He was a fantastic player, and a great signing from West Bromwich Albion. Ron Atkinson had inherited him at West Brom and, when he left to take over Manchester United, made sure that Robson followed him. It was a record transfer fee in 1981, £1.5 million, but Ron knew exactly what he getting. Robson could do the lot. He was a world-class box-to-box midfield player, he scored goals, he would run through a brick wall – it is no surprise that his replacement at Manchester United was Roy Keane. It would have taken a player of Keane's calibre to fill Robson's shoes. He was a proper leader as well, a warrior, the type of player that would drag his team back into the game, and that comes across off the field as well.

He's a good lad, the sort of bloke people enjoy being around. Whenever I've been in Bryan's company, I've always liked him.

I think it is a testament to Bryan's ability that Alex always puts him in his best Manchester United XI because he didn't even work with him that long as a first-team regular. There have been other central midfielders who had longer or more successful careers, yet he always finds room for Bryan. He would have been worth his weight in gold to Manchester United under David Moyes – they wouldn't have finished seventh if he had been in the heart of midfield.

When major tournaments came around we always seemed to be praying for Robson to get fit, which was a pity. The way he threw himself into games didn't help – he was a bit like Wayne Rooney in that – but I think once a player becomes injury prone it is very much a downward spiral. One injury leads to another, taking the stress off one muscle puts greater pressure on muscles elsewhere, and had he been a little more robust who knows what he might have achieved. He missed the 1983 League Cup final, the 1992 League Cup final and, having scored two goals in the 3–0 comeback against Diego Maradona's Barcelona side in 1984, missed both legs of the European Cup-Winners' Cup semi-final with Juventus, which United lost. He was chaired off the Old Trafford pitch by the fans after the Barcelona win – they always recognised his contribution, even if injury meant he didn't play more than 30 league games for United in any of his last five seasons.

Bryan could have been the first player to score an FA Cup hat-trick in 30 years when, having already nabbed two against Brighton and Hove Albion in 1983, United got a penalty. But

Robson stood to one side and let Arnold Mühren, the regular taker, do his job. Robson was always a class act. When he scored after 27 seconds against France at the 1982 World Cup, he was rewarded with a gold watch for the fastest goal of the tournament, and he wanted to sell it so the money could be divided among the team.

He was a proper lad, too. He was in the Peter Shilton-era England team and that was a hard school. Drinking, gambling, cards, they must have taken a bit of controlling. No wonder things sometimes got a little confused. There is a lovely story about Sir Bobby Robson bouncing down to breakfast one morning. Bobby was never the best with names, but this time he excelled himself. Spotting Bryan Robson in the lobby he offered a cheery wave. 'Morning, Bobby,' he said. Bryan looked up and explained carefully. 'Boss,' he said. 'I'm Bryan – *you're* Bobby.'

People knew what they had in Bryan. Although there are many stories about those sessions with Manchester United and England, it is interesting that he was one player to whom Alex turned a blind eye. He got Norman Whiteside and Paul McGrath out of the club, but he tolerated Robson. Maybe Bryan reined it in a little, too, but that Manchester United team were certainly famed for their fierce spirit. I remember one year when they won the title in midweek without playing – another result had gone their way – and Steve Bruce, who had succeeded Bryan as captain, rang all the team about 10.30 at night, got them to his place to celebrate, and they all went into training the next day straight from the party. That sort of togetherness is hard to find now, and Robson would have helped build it at United. He may not have been around for all of the good times, but he certainly deserves the accolades for helping to get them started.

JOHN BARNES
(LIVERPOOL)

What strikes me about a lot of the players in this team is the versatility. Steve Nicol could play in the full-back role, at centre-half or across midfield; Paul McGrath played centre-half or could step into midfield; Glenn Hoddle was a brilliant midfield player who late in his career moved to sweeper; and when a recurring Achilles tendon injury robbed John Barnes of his pace on the left, he became a fine central midfielder, controlling the game and schooling the younger players around him. They were all British or Irish, these players, too. We think of total footballers, the ones who can play anywhere on the pitch, as being the property of the Dutch, or the Hungarians back in the 1950s, but it shows that we can do it, too, if required. I find the way John Barnes adapted to his changed circumstances hugely impressive. Some players with his injury problem would have slowly dropped through the leagues, but he never gave up. Roy Evans created this new role for him in Liverpool's midfield, and John played it to perfection, even getting back in the England team as a central midfield player under Terry Venables.

John was so much more than just a wide man. He was an all-round footballer, with a good football brain and lots of intelligence. His goalscoring record from left wing alone suggests he could have been a striker, too, had Liverpool not had Ian Rush, John Aldridge and later Robbie Fowler to play that role. As a winger, John had real strength. He was a big, powerful lad who could pick it up and just drive through people. The moment he dropped into a midfield role, however, he showed there was such subtlety to his play – what Ryan Giggs brought to Manchester United late in his career, Barnes brought to Liverpool. He dictated matches the way a real top midfielder does. It was as if he had played there all his life.

His is a remarkable story really, because he was playing as a centre-half for his boys' club in Paddington when Watford spotted him. He joined the club in 1981 and they put him in their youth team against Leyton Orient, still at centre-half. Suddenly he brought one down on his chest and volleyed it in with his left foot, and that was the beginning of his career as a forward. Watford were on the rise through four divisions under Graham Taylor, and John came in on the end of that. Everybody was swept away by his talent, obviously, and Watford's success continued – in 1982–3 they finished second to Liverpool in the league, which is an incredible feat for a club of that size, especially in their first season in the top flight.

But it was when Kenny Dalglish signed him at Liverpool prior to the 1987–8 season that his career really took off. He was offered to Manchester United first but Sir Alex Ferguson turned the deal down, something I know he regretted until Giggs came through. That was the season Liverpool beat Nottingham Forest 5–0 in April in what must rank among the finest performances seen at Anfield. Barnes's part in that is immense. It is his lovely one-two that sets up Ray Houghton for the first, his speed of thought from the corner that creates the third for Gary Gillespie, and for the fourth he nutmegs Steve

Chettle out on the wing, rides another tackle superbly and cuts the ball back for Peter Beardsley's shot. Without doubt at the time he was among the best players in the world. When you spoke to the greatest players in his position, men like Sir Tom Finney or George Best, they used to rave about him. The only surprise that day was that he didn't score. John was prolific at Liverpool, for a wide man – 17 goals in his first season, a tally only beaten by Aldridge, and club top scorer in his third with 28 goals in all competitions including 22 in 34 league games. All from left wing.

They still talk about one of his goals at Queens Park Rangers. It was in his first season for Liverpool, and he nicked the ball off Kevin Brock in the centre circle and went on a run through the middle, all the way to the penalty area. Terry Fenwick dived in, but he rounded that tackle, landed on the other side, changed direction and somehow stuck it in with his left foot. It is hard to see how he stayed upright, but he had such incredible balance. John says it was the best goal he scored – better than that one in the Maracana Stadium, he reckoned.

I'm not sure. I think what made that particular goal special was that it was scored against Brazil, and in a Brazilian style. We were ready for one of their players to do that to us – we weren't expecting one of ours to do it to them. The slalom run, the poise, the courage to keep taking the ball on, it was a special moment. The expectation level around John for England after that probably stifled him at international level. He won a lot of caps, but I don't think he ever performed for the national team as he did for Liverpool. Maybe Liverpool were just a better side at the time, too.

Injuries troubled John from 1992 onwards, and it was Roy Evans's promotion to manager in 1994 that led to his swansong as a central midfield player – the career change that I feel sets him apart from his contemporaries. It showed how well he read the game. He didn't need to beat half the team as he did in the Maracana. He could take them out of the game with a sly little pass. He had my Jamie and Steve McManaman around him, and I know they learnt so much from watching him play. He was an exceptional footballer and I think it's a pity he's not more involved in the game today. He had a few spells in management and it never worked out, but if you listen to him he talks a lot of sense on the game. I think he could be a great influence on young players, talking to them about the need to adapt, to be versatile, to open their minds to playing different positions. A player like Ross Barkley, for instance, could learn a lot from John.

I think it is so important to have that variety in your game. At Liverpool now, Glen Johnson is one who I think could switch roles. He can play right-back, and also further forward, but I know Glen has the ability to operate as a centre-half as well. If he could get the ball and bring it out he would be fantastic, because when he's on the ball he's like a Rolls-Royce, so smooth. I had Glen at West Ham and we thought he had it all. He was a centre-half back then; it was his first position with us and he played there for England Schools, too. He's not the tallest, but neither is Javier Mascherano – and he has shown what can be done at Barcelona. Glen was quick, he had a good spring, he was strong in the air – and I've always felt he had the ability to play anywhere if he was encouraged. He certainly has the quality on the ball. Luke Shaw is another. He looks as if he could play further forward, as Gareth Bale did. A lot of coaches are switching the left-back and left-wing roles now. Danny Rose came to Tottenham Hotspur as a left-winger, but now he's at left-back. Stuart Pearce certainly liked him on the wing with the under-21s, but I think he just lacks the little bit of magic to thrive there. He's better coming on to the ball from deep, just like Terry Cooper. It would be great to see John Barnes involved with the younger England players, showing them how to make the changes to their game. I know how good he was with Jamie and I think he'd have a lot to offer.

IAN RUSH
(LIVERPOOL)

We'll get on to the goals in a minute. Everyone knows about the goals. What many managers equally admired about Ian Rush was his phenomenal work-rate. Jimmy Greaves said there was no point in strikers doing their defensive work because they would be too exhausted to go out and score – but Rush was the forward who proved it was possible to do both. He is Liverpool's all-time top goalscorer – no mean feat considering the calibre of some of their players – but was also the first line of their defence. Joe Fagan described him as an example to the rest of the team, and he didn't mean the goals but his willingness to work back and tackle. Seeing Rush do that so successfully, Joe thought, gave the rest of the team a psychological boost.

I know what Jimmy would have said about that, but he's never been a manager. Rush was the envy of every other coach in the league. He is the example we would all use if we thought our forwards were being lazy and not helping their team-mates. 'Go home and watch Ian Rush. He's the best goalscorer in the league. If he can do it, why can't you?' The game was changing and Rush changed with it. It was no longer acceptable for forwards to just stand around waiting to be brought into the game, and as soon as Liverpool lost the ball, Rush would chase the full-back or the centre-half down, as Luis Suárez does now. He was the first line of defence, with a fantastic work-rate. Now there are strikers who seem to get picked purely for shutting the opposition down – scoring goals is the secondary aspect of their game. Yet Rush had it all. He could do the donkey work – but he was also the greatest finisher.

Rush was one of the last players to be discovered by that great old Liverpool scouting network. They got him from Chester City and had to make him the most expensive teenager in British football – but what a bargain that £300,000 turned out to be. Rush didn't settle in well at first, barely played in his first season and didn't score, and it only turned around for him after he went to see Bob Paisley asking for a chance in the first team – or permission to leave. Paisley said he would alert clubs, Rush went away and redoubled his efforts in the reserve team to get a move – and started scoring regularly, which is what Paisley wanted all along. Given a chance in season 1981–2, he never looked back. Indeed, from that point until 1987 when he left for Juventus, his scoring aggregate was two goals every three games. Anyone who saw the first live midweek league game on the BBC, Aston Villa versus Liverpool, on 20 January 1984, will never forget Rush's hat-trick that night. It was a frozen pitch and everyone was finding it difficult, but Rush's poise in front of goal made it look like Wembley in the spring. It was what is called a perfect hat-trick – left foot, right foot, header – so delicate, but also lethal. I know it is generally felt that Manchester United were a more entertaining team when they came to dominate English football – but looking back at the goalscorers Liverpool have had over the years I'm not sure that is true. Ian St John, Roger Hunt, John Toshack, Kevin Keegan, Dalglish, Rush, John Aldridge, Michael Owen, Robbie Fowler, Fernando Torres, Luis Suárez and Daniel Sturridge – incredible. I don't think any club loves its strikers quite like Liverpool. Not even Newcastle United.

Torres has his critics now, but he was magnificent there. When Liverpool signed him, Sir Alex Ferguson thought they had made a mistake. 'We watched him and I don't fancy him,' he told me. 'I don't think he's got the bottle. When we play them we'll steam into him and he won't want to know.' He took a year to settle in, but the following season Liverpool went to Old Trafford and won 4–1. Torres scored the first goal and Nemanja Vidić couldn't handle him. He ended up getting sent off. He always seemed to struggle against Torres after that.

I think the reason a lot of people didn't see the great Liverpool teams as cavalier and entertaining was because they knew how to shut up shop, too. Against United, opponents always felt they had a chance to score – but if Liverpool went 2–0 up their defence was so strong and players like Rush so tireless that the game was over. If you tried to chase it, they just picked you off on the counter-attack; but because of their solidity people overlooked how wonderful they were going forward. At their best, they were a complete team. The guile of Dalglish and then John Barnes, the finishing of Rush and this rock-hard defence. It would be hard to find a weakness in Liverpool back then.

GARY LINEKER
(EVERTON)

Why Lineker and not Andy Gray? If you were going to pick an Everton striker from the eighties, surely it would be Gray, whose goals under Howard Kendall took the club to the pinnacle of the English game. And, yes, I can see that argument. But it's simple, really: just look at the goals Lineker scored in his one season at Goodison Park. It really is one of the most underrated turns of recent years.

Football is a results business, and that is why Gray and Lineker are recalled differently. Andy Gray scored 22 goals in 68 games for Everton in all competitions – an average of one goal every 3.09 matches. Lineker scored 38 goals in 52 games – an average of one every 1.36 matches. Yet who do the Everton fans remember? Gray, of course – because his goals helped win the FA Cup in 1984 and then the league title and European Cup-Winners' Cup a year later. Lineker was considerably more prolific and without doubt a better player – but Everton won nothing in his time at the club. They lost the FA Cup final and came second in the league, so Evertonians tend to forget what a special season he had.

I think Gary's record was exceptional because he wasn't always with the best teams. He scored 51 goals in his last two seasons with Leicester City, and even in his final year with Tottenham

Hotspur before going to Japan he scored 35 times. I'm grateful to Jamie Carragher for pointing out the anomaly about Lineker's time at Everton, and how poorly he is recognised, considering his performances. It is no coincidence that after one season he was snapped up by Barcelona, where he scored 41 goals in his first two seasons until Johann Cruyff, the coach, switched him to a wider role. Jamie grew up as an Everton fan, and he said all he ever heard was Andy Gray this and Andy Gray that – but when he looked at his record it was good, but not great. Lineker's was exceptional. It just goes to prove that only winning matters. Graeme Sharp had a better scoring record than Gray, too – 159 in 426 games, an aggregate of one goal every 2.67 matches.

Gary was, plain and simple, just a fantastic finisher. He wasn't a dribbler, he wasn't a special link-up player like Gray or Sharp, but give him half a chance in the box and the ball was in the net. He was razor sharp, with probably the best poacher's instinct of any player from his generation. He was one of those players like Gerd Müller, the great West German striker. I can't remember a goal Müller scored from outside the penalty area, and I'm not sure I saw too many from Gary either. If I was arranging all of the players from all the teams I have picked for this book on grounds of pure technical ability, Gary would be pretty near the bottom. Yet when you have his knack for getting goals – which is the point of the game after all – that doesn't matter. It didn't for Müller either. When he signed for Bayern Munich, the coach, Zlatko Cajkovski, told the club president: 'I will not put this bear among my racehorses.' Yet it was Müller's 35 goals that drove the club out of the Oberliga Süd into the recently formed Bundesliga in 1965 – and they have not been out of it since.

Müller was never regarded as the most fluent footballer, but his record in the international game is unsurpassed in modern times – 68 goals in 62 appearances. He wasn't a fast runner over distance, but was typical of the sort of athlete with fast-twitch muscle reflex, because his bursts over the shortest distances were exceptional. Franz Beckenbauer said nobody stood a chance against him in training.

That wasn't quite true of Lineker who, despite possessing the same razor-sharp reactions, hated training and refused to work on his game. It is amusing to see Gary looking so fit now because during his peak years as a player his aversion to practice sessions was famous throughout football. He was a terrible trainer. He just liked to come in on Saturday and play. I know Gary's explanation is that he was superstitious about using up his luck and thought that spending all week banging in goals would somehow dry up the amount of chances he might get on a Saturday. He wanted to save his sharpness for when it mattered. Fair enough, but that doesn't make sense to me – and I have heard an alternate version.

It goes like this. Despite his magnificent scoring record, Gary was far from the cleanest striker of the ball. His goals were often scruffy, and he didn't like having to finish in training with the whole team looking at him. He thought it harmed his reputation if the rest of the players saw these shots that were hardly pristine. On Saturday, it wouldn't matter. He would get the goals and nobody would care how cleanly the ball went in – but training was different. All eyes were on him and he felt the pressure. It made him quite self-conscious, so he came up with a lot of excuses to miss training. I don't know if that is true, but if so I sympathise. With Gary's technique, in a typical shooting session from 20 yards he wouldn't have been the one pinging them into the corner, lovely and clean. Clive Allen is the sort of player who excelled at that. I worked with Clive as a coach at Tottenham and, even now, he could put it in the top corner, clean as a whistle, all day. Clive could hit the ball beautifully, showing the other strikers how to do it. I can't imagine Gary being like that. He was a darter, an instinct player. He found space, he knew where it was, almost on a psychic level. I imagine you could take him on to a pitch blindfolded and he would be able to point to where the goals were. That was why his partnership with Peter Beardsley for England worked so well. Beardsley was the schemer, the craftsman, and Gary gave his work that cutting edge.

THE EIGHTIES: THE TEAM

PETER
SHILTON
Nottingham Forest

STEVE   **ALAN**   **PAUL**   **KENNY**
NICOL   **HANSEN**   **McGRATH**   **SANSOM**
Liverpool   Liverpool   Manchester   Arsenal
                                     United

GLENN   **PAUL**   **BRYAN**   **JOHN**
HODDLE   **GASCOIGNE**   **ROBSON**   **BARNES**
Tottenham   Tottenham   Manchester   Liverpool
Hotspur   Hotspur   United

            IAN   **GARY**
            RUSH   **LINEKER**
         Liverpool   Everton

CHAPTER FIVE

PREMIER LEAGUE I

When we first heard about the Premier League, we all thought it was just a change of name, really. Division One was now going to be called the Premier League – what a load of rubbish. It was the same when Division Two got renamed the Championship. More crap, really. You're at Bournemouth playing Darlington and suddenly that's a League One fixture? We all knew the reality was Division One, Division Two, Division Three, Division Four. We considered the rest mere window-dressing – and I don't think anyone in football realised just how big the plans were for this new competition, or what it would become. The first weekend, the referees were in green shirts so the goalkeepers had to wear a different colour – it all seemed so trivial and unnecessary.

The changes were huge, though. The money coming in from Sky Television, the influx of foreign players – we all had to learn to adapt very quickly. Everybody's thinking had to change, if not overnight, then certainly within one or two years. Suddenly, we were dealing with foreign players that were brought up differently, that were totally professional in the way they lived. They weren't into the drinking culture that pervaded English football. Those nights out were part of our game – even the most successful teams had their Tuesday drinking clubs. But Italian players didn't go out getting hammered and acting stupid. They looked after themselves, they went to bed early, they were in great shape. That made a real difference to the fitness regimes. These players had higher expectations. They wanted fitness coaches, and foreign coaches too. The English guys had to change their ways. The days of walking in, shouting and screaming and throwing teacups at players were gone. There is no point effing and blinding at a player who can hardly speak English. You had to talk to them, slowly, reasonably. An awful lot of British coaches ruled by fear and bullying, and the foreign players wouldn't accept that. They weren't used to being talked to like that, being embarrassed or humiliated in front of their team-mates.

Levels of athleticism rose, too. I remember Paolo Di Canio brought his fitness coach to West Ham United. He requested we engage a guy from Milan that he knew well, and he changed so many things at the club. Players were stretching properly; times were set aside for conditioning routines. The food at the training ground changed, too. Lunches at Chadwell Heath had barely altered since my day – steak and kidney pie, loads of potatoes, anything you could get. By the end of that first season with Paolo's man everyone had their own tailored, balanced food intake, and a special dietitian supervised that regime. English football changed dramatically. Before we didn't even have goalkeeping coaches; now a player could see an acupuncturist if the fancy took him. In that first season, the Premier League clubs didn't have a fifth of the backroom staff they have got now.

Prozone is one of the biggest changes. Last season, when Queens Park Rangers were due to play Blackpool, our most recent scout's report had them operating with four at the back and two holding midfield players. In the old days, that would have been all that was available. Now we've got machines that can call up game after game, personnel, the most detailed statistics, changes in the gameplan – so we knew that for most of the season they had played three centre-halves, and pushed the full-backs on – and that would be how they intended to play if everyone was fit. The aids for a manager are incredible now. When I began, we might have one report on the opposition. That aside, you just played – sorted your own team out and went from there. If they had a player you fancied was good you might tell one of the lads to watch him, give him an idea of what to expect – but there was no detail. Don Revie at Leeds United was the only one who went into depth, and his dossiers were the talk of football. Other managers were still not convinced that they were a good idea. Play your own game, that was the mantra. You set your team out the way you liked and that was how you played – no managers changed their team to accommodate the opposition. Nobody mirrored formations. These days, if the England manager is caught out tactically he gets slaughtered; but, even a few years before the Premier League, if the same man came in and said the other team were using wing-backs so he would probably go with a back three, too, and flood midfield, he would have been called a coward. What are we worrying about them for? We're England – let them worry about us!

I must admit, I find the point of Prozone baffling at times. Yes, you've got it – but so has the team you are playing. So while you're watching them, they're watching you, and while you're changing to deal with them, they're doing the same. We all go along with it, but where's the edge? I can call up statistics on every opponent we'll face on Saturday. How far they've run, how many touches they've had, who eats what for breakfast. But I know my opposite number will be doing the same with my players. So we're back to square one.

The arrival of Arsène Wenger in 1996 certainly heralded a change in English football. He was very successful very quickly, and suddenly all the talk was about his revolutionary new training methods. He only trains for an hour ... does everything on the stopwatch ... the players are wearing heart monitors at training ... he gives them supplements ... There is always some new idea that is meant to hold the secret. There will be another one along soon, you watch.

What certainly altered was the way you tried to build team spirit. The old methods were very simple – bonding sessions, getting the lads to go out for a drink or have a day at the races. Everybody laughs, falls about, gets into a few scrapes. A typical jolly boys' outing. The foreign players didn't want to know about that. I can remember during my time at Tottenham Hotspur I took the lads to the Cheltenham races. I thought we'd have some fun, relax together, come back a bit tighter as a unit – you would have thought I'd took them on a prison visit. We got on a coach at the training ground, a lovely coach with nice food available, and we had booked a hospitality box along the home straight. We weren't in with the crowd, we had a great view, a lovely lunch overlooking the course – and the moment we arrived I knew I had made a mistake. About eight of them were looking at their watches after half an hour. What are we doing here? Why have you brought us here? Roman Pavlyuchenko never moved out of his seat all day. Just sat there, waiting for the time to get on the coach and go home. All of the atmosphere of Cheltenham, all of the spectacle, he wasn't interested. I thought it was a failure of imagination, to be frank. To have so little fascination with the world around you that you don't even want to come to the balcony, peer over and see what all the cheering is about. I know he is from a different culture, but if you went to Russia and the locals took you to a carnival day – which is basically what Cheltenham is – surely you would be interested, surely it would be a tale you would want to take back home? Not Roman. Wouldn't watch a race, wouldn't have a bet, just not interested in joining in.

I never went anywhere greatly exotic as a player, but I did spend some time in Seattle. One day a year, the people at the club would take us all out salmon fishing in Puget Sound on a giant barge. I remember Geoff Hurst knocking me up at 5am in the apartments where we lived. It was freezing cold, so we all wrapped up warm, but when the sun came up it was glorious. I'd never been sea fishing in my life – but that was the fun. We caught giant salmon, all of us, but they would only allow you to bring three home. That night, though, we were all cooking the catch and the whole apartment area smelled of barbecued fish. It was something I had never done, and something I will never forget. I can understand the new standards of professionalism, but they shouldn't prevent you embracing new experiences. In the end, it has been the English footballers that have had to change because at most clubs now they are isolated. It is a different life for them now; they can't go in the Black Lion after a game, as we could, and I'm not sure they could even go out to some of the nicest places without being bothered. Their level of fame is completely alien to anything we experienced. George Best was famous. The rest of us could walk into any pub in London without a fuss being made. And we were East End boys, not West End boys. A night up town was a big occasion for us; usually we would hang around the pubs in the local area. The captain of England would be drinking in the Baker's Arms in Stratford. Yet none of the players in my team of the first Premier League era would be seen dead there. Well, maybe the odd one.

PETER SCHMEICHEL
(MANCHESTER UNITED)

Sir Alex Ferguson called Peter the bargain of the century, and I'm not about to argue with that. He cost £505,000 from Brondby in Denmark in 1991 which, when you consider West Ham paid £565,000 for Phil Parkes in 1979, does make Schmeichel rather cheap. Not that Phil wasn't a good goalkeeper, too, but in an inflationary market Alex did rather well. He hasn't always been that lucky with goalkeepers – anyone remember Massimo Taibi, 'The Blind Venetian'? – but in Schmeichel he found a gem.

He was a rucker, as we might say in East London. He used to ruck people – really have a go at them. He was always on at his defenders, and anyone else that got in his way. On one occasion he even turned on Alex, who had criticised him after United lost a 3–0 lead at Liverpool, and a lesser goalkeeper might have been out of the club. But Alex knew what he had and, once Peter apologised to him and the team, they straightened it all out.

He had a fantastic presence, a great size and physique. He used to wear XXXL shirts apparently – which shows you another way football has changed. The goalkeepers of my day, even the best ones, were not much different in stature to the rest of us. But Schmeichel came to Manchester United at a time when goalkeepers simply had to be big. Chris Turner was Ferguson's first goalkeeper when he arrived in 1986 and he was only 5 ft 10 in – that couldn't happen now. Modern goalkeepers are a different physique, and Schmeichel had a way of coming out and spreading himself that made him look huge.

As well as being a brilliant organiser, he had a very unique style, which stemmed from playing handball. It's not a big sport over here, but it's massive on the continent and, from what I've seen, goalkeepers don't have much chance one on one. If you think how accurately an outfield player can place a ball with his foot, imagine being able to throw it. The only option a goalkeeper has is to make himself as big as possible by spreading all four limbs – it's called the star jump. Peter introduced that into football and it was very effective. He even used it on the line if there was a header from close range. The chances of reacting to an opportunity in that split second are small, so Peter's star jumps enabled him to cover as much of the goal as possible. Typical goalkeeper, really. It is a very singular role, so they are often the most clearly defined individuals within the team group – the ones most likely to conjure something from left-field.

Some of his saves were simply outstanding. There was one in the Champions League against Rapid Vienna in 1996 that Peter regards as his greatest. It is a downward header from close range, and Peter scoops it up and over the bar much like Gordon Banks did against Pelé in 1970. He doesn't have to come as far across the line as Banks did, and it is probably nearer his body to begin with, but it is still an exceptional effort. There is another from John Barnes in his Newcastle United days that is almost as good – a well-positioned header that should have crept in by the post, but somehow Schmeichel got a hand there. I think the fans voted it the save of the decade in the Premier League's first 10 years.

Great goalkeeping must run in the family because his son, Kasper, is very good, too. He came up with Leicester City last season but I don't think it will be long before he is signed by one of the biggest clubs. He was at a lot of different places on loan and then Notts County and Leeds United, but he has really improved in the last year or two and now looks ready to make a real step up.

Manchester United, like his dad? Probably not at the moment, as David De Gea looks to be finally coming into his own at the club, but Alex has never had the easiest time with goalkeepers and until Edwin van der Sar arrived I think he really struggled to find an adequate replacement for Peter. He left Manchester United in 1999 – and talk about going out on a high. He was captain when they won the Champions League final against Bayern Munich to claim the treble.

I think the rest of the Premier League managers were quite glad to see the back of him while he was at Sporting Lisbon. We rarely used to get a shot at him when I was at West Ham, and when we did, he probably saved it. Most of my memories are of being on the receiving end and getting beat up rather than forcing any heroics from Schmeichel. In fact, there's one particular game against United from that era that stands out for me – not because we caused Schmeichel a lot of problems but because our own goalkeeper, Ludek Miklosko, outshone him.

It was 14 May 1995. Blackburn Rovers and Manchester United were battling it out for the title. Blackburn were two points clear going into the final day, but United had a much superior goal difference. If Blackburn dropped points at Anfield and United won, the title would go to Old Trafford. Few thought it would happen because Blackburn were managed by Kenny Dalglish. Liverpool wouldn't want to deny an Anfield hero the prize and let it go to Manchester United, surely? Yet it was one of those days that restores faith in football's honesty. Liverpool won – with a winning goal scored by Jamie – meaning that if Manchester United took three points against my West Ham team, they would be champions.

What a game. Michael Hughes scored for us in the first half, from a cross by Matty Holmes, and then Brian McClair equalised for United after half time. As the news came through that Blackburn were not winning, United absolutely battered us, but we hung on. I think Ludek must have made about 20 saves in as many minutes – he had the game of his life. Alex seemed to throw on every forward that he had at the club. By the end of the game he was playing Andy Cole, McClair, Mark Hughes and Paul Scholes, with Lee Sharpe bombing on and his centre-halves in the mix for every set play. And then he got the hump because with two minutes to go I brought on Simon Webster as an extra defender. He was going bananas on the touchline, as if we were doing something tricky. He was the same when Billy Bonds was in charge and West Ham beat Manchester United, having already been relegated. He called the effort the players showed that day 'obscene' – because they hadn't played like that before all season. I don't know what else he expected opposing players to do. Roll over and let United win the title? Did Liverpool do that for Blackburn? I thought it was a fantastic day for football: a real gutsy performance from my lads, a master class from our goalkeeper, and Liverpool probably going against the wishes of their own fans to beat Blackburn and almost cost Kenny the title.

As it was, because we drew with United, Blackburn still won the league even though they lost the match. And Alex quickly calmed down. Within a minute or so he was in my office asking if I knew what had won the big race at Lingfield – but still moaning about my extra defender.

GARY NEVILLE
(MANCHESTER UNITED)

Gary Neville said he expected to be asked to leave Manchester United's academy each year of his young life from the age of 11 onwards. He would turn up 45 minutes early for training every day and practise furiously in an attempt to survive in the same company as the teenage Paul Scholes and Nicky Butt, local lads who were regarded as the cream of the crop. Then the batch from outside Manchester arrived: David Beckham, Keith Gillespie and Robbie Savage. Neville redoubled his efforts to keep pace. He feared that any week could be his last, ending with a tap on the shoulder and the polite order not to return. Yet Neville played over 600 games and was a quite exceptional full-back for his country. Don't be fooled by the negativity and cynicism often directed at him, and his brother Phil. Nobody plays that number of games for the biggest club in the country without deserving it. The partnership Gary Neville established with his friend David Beckham on the right is also among the most devastating this country has produced.

Gary was a class act, good on the ball, and deserves an enormous amount of credit for the way he worked with Beckham. He had a great understanding of his role in that partnership: when he needed to overlap or come inside, when he needed to play Beckham back in, or when he should be available to receive it. You wouldn't look at Gary and say he was particularly big or physically imposing, and although no slouch he didn't have blistering pace either. Yet, every week, he was a 7 out of 10 man – very steady, never rattled, knew what he was doing, knew when to play or when to make a pragmatic defensive decision. These were great Manchester United teams, yet there was never a thought of replacing Gary. He made the right decision 99 per cent of the time and was always smooth, never rash or erratic. He ended up as Ferguson's captain as well, succeeding Roy Keane, so that says a lot about his strength of character. You can't be a flapper and lead Manchester United.

So much of the play in the modern game comes from the full-backs. I don't think you can get away with not having a good technical footballer there any more, and Gary is a classic example. He was a much better passer than he got credit for, and I always felt there was a real sense of enjoyment in his partnership with Beckham. They had grown up together, had come through the ranks at United, liked each other a lot, and it showed.

Gary got into the England team very young. He had only played 27 matches for Manchester United when he was picked for the squad for the Umbro Cup held the year before the 1996 European Championships. People think international friendlies are a waste of time, but if you look at that competition – games against Japan, Sweden and Brazil – it ended up solving one of England's biggest problems. At that point England's right-backs were Rob Jones of Liverpool, who was very injury prone, and Warren Barton of Wimbledon, who was probably just short of international standard. But after Gary was picked to play against Japan and Brazil, he didn't miss an England game until the semi-final of the European Championships with Germany the following summer. Apparently, when Terry Venables, the England manager, asked Ferguson about Gary Neville, he tried to steer him in the direction of his brother, Phil. A lot of people believed Phil was going to be the better player at the time – but he was younger and had played even fewer games, just three by the end of the 1994–5 season. Venables decided against taking Alex's advice and picked Gary (although Phil was also in the squad by the time of the 1996 tournament) and his hunch was proved right. It wasn't only age that got Gary in Manchester United's starting line-up more frequently than his brother.

Sometimes a player doesn't develop the way you predict. Phil never was quite as good as Gary, as it turned out. Even the greatest managers can make mistakes. It wasn't so long ago that Alex was comparing Phil Jones to Duncan Edwards, which was a very bold statement. It's fair to say he has a way to go yet. Sometimes we're not as clever as we think – and the career Gary Neville mined from his talent, and from the hard work he put in from his beginnings at the academy to his 600th game, surprised us all.

TONY ADAMS
(ARSENAL)

Tony Adams was one of the finest captains there has ever been in this country. He was a great leader, a great organiser, and everything I have heard about him throughout his playing career sets him apart. Jamie said to me that at the 1996 European Championships England almost didn't need a manager. They had a great one in Terry Venables, but Tony was such an influence that he as good as ran the dressing-room.

As a manager I think what you look for in a captain is someone you can talk to, that you can involve in important matters such as team selection. Your captain is close to this group – so what does he think? You will have the final say, but you value his input. Beyond that you want somebody who can go out and organise the players and make decisions for you in the heat of the moment. You can't keep shouting from the touchline all day. Often you can't make yourself heard, so the captain has to be someone that you trust to carry out your wishes out on the football field. And strong characters like that are getting harder and harder to find now. There are a lot more quiet footballers, not as many real personalities as there used to be. If you can find a good one, you are very lucky.

George Graham said there were occasions at Arsenal when the bullets were flying and he would look out there, see Tony Adams in the thick of it, and think, 'Thank God he's my captain.' Most managers will know what he means. I would imagine Brendan Rodgers says that about Steven Gerrard, and José Mourinho about John Terry. Teams that are going well usually have an inspirational skipper, whether it is Bobby Moore, leading by example, or Tony Adams, who was more of an 'up and at 'em' type. Tony had presence and took responsibility – and I noticed that from the moment I saw him.

He would have been about 16, playing for Arsenal in a youth team game. I don't think I have ever seen any player of his age prepared to be the boss in that way. He was ordering everybody about – 'Fucking get it out, squeeze up, push in, tuck in here, play it there.' People talk about Tony as if he was under George Graham's control, but at his age that level of leadership comes from within. He was the sort of player that you didn't need to tell twice. Obviously he had been coached on how a defence should be organised, but there was nobody passing on instructions from the sidelines. This was his team and he was taking care of it. He knew what was expected and he had the will and confidence to carry it out.

I remember a couple of years ago a friend of mine went to an Arsenal game and saw Kieran Gibbs, their young left-back, coming forward to join an attack. The ball was being switched left to right, as happens with Arsenal, but now Gibbs was involved in the pattern of play. With that, Bacary Sagna, the right-back, went on an overlap but Gibbs continued following the ball. It ended up with Arsenal's two full-backs standing on the same wing, up by the opposition penalty area. Madness. My friend saw Lee Dixon, the great Arsenal full-back, after the game and asked him what Graham would have said had that roving wantonness occurred during his time as manager. 'George wouldn't have had to say anything,' Dixon replied. 'Tony Adams would have threatened to knock me out as I was making the diagonal run across the pitch. I would have heard this voice: "Come here – where do you think you're going?" Tony worked even harder than George at keeping us organised. He would almost bully you in the changing-room before the game.'

Tony was a complete defender. If you were up against him there wasn't much that you could tell your forwards about how to get around him. He wasn't short of any particular quality and I never saw him get a chasing, even though he wasn't the fastest. It was simply a fantastic back four, with Steve Bould as his partner, and later Martin Keown. The two full-backs were amazing as well. Nigel Winterburn came to West Ham later in his career and was as good as anybody I have ever seen at closing players down. He wouldn't just do it the conventional way; he got after people, like he was going to assault them, really. Stuart Pearce was the same. Lots of the very modern full-backs, they stand five yards off. Nigel was on you, like Dixon. David Ginola says Dixon was like a pitbull when they played against each other. I think Arsène Wenger was very lucky to take over that back four with David Seaman in goal. George had organised them so well, the machine almost ran itself. I'd say that could probably also be said of Roberto Martínez at Everton after David Moyes left.

Yet Tony was the pick of it. He was so committed, so brave with his headers – absolutely fearless. It sounds as if he lived that way off the field at the time, too, judging by some of the stories Paul Merson tells. A lot of the Arsenal players from that era talk about the Tuesday Club. Wednesday was always a day off, so Tony used to lead these huge sessions on the Tuesday, involving players like Dixon, Winterburn, Merson, Ray Parlour and Perry Groves. When Paul talks about some of the stuff that went on it was amazing they could play so well, year on year. Apparently, everyone had sobered up by Thursday morning training, though, so George Graham didn't mind. It all changed when Arsène Wenger took over – and Tony changed, too. He announced he was an alcoholic in 1996 and, from there, was a different person. It's funny – when Paul Merson admitted his alcoholism in 1994, Tony says he was sceptical. He said he was going around telling people, 'There's no way he's an alcoholic – I drink more than he does.' He reckons it took him another two years to work out that was the problem. It is amazing a player like Tony could live life as he did and still play well, week in, week out in the Premier League.

I ended up adding Tony to my staff when I was at Portsmouth because I had heard so many good reports about his leadership qualities. I liked Tony, but he was on a different path by then. He has done brilliantly in confronting his demons, but it has brought out the quieter, more introverted side of his character. He wouldn't come away with us on a Friday night, and wouldn't travel with the team, because he didn't want the temptation of having dinner and being with the staff when they were getting on the wine. I had a lot of respect for him over that. He's had his problems and he's come through.

SOL CAMPBELL
(ARSENAL)

I first saw Sol at Tottenham Hotspur, playing in the youth team. He was another kid who had come from that fantastic East End production line, Senrab FC. I can't think of a goalkeeper they have produced, but you could make up one hell of an outfield team from ex-Senrab players. How's this? Ugo Ehiogu, John Terry, Ledley King, Sol Campbell, Ashley Cole, Ray Wilkins, Lee Bowyer, Vince Hilaire, Jermain Defoe, Bobby Zamora. There's plenty of others, too, like Muzzy Izzet, David Kerslake and Paul Konchesky – there's not been another boys club in the South of England like it.

When I watched Sol he was a 16-year-old striker. He converted to centre-half later. He was already becoming the player we remember from his professional days – lightning fast, strong, imposing physique, just a monster of an athlete really. He was heading them into the goal as powerfully as he was heading them away from it later in his career, a real handful. If he had persevered I'm sure he could have made it as a goalscorer, too. I suppose what attracted Tottenham to him as a defender was that he was so hard to break down. We had a lively striker at West Ham in John Hartson, but you always knew your man had to be at his best if he was up against Sol Campbell. He moved from Tottenham to Arsenal, and having better players around him just brought that strength out even more. He was part of a team that won the double and another that went a season unbeaten, and you've got to say a record like that stems from the defence. Sol made a good team into a great team under Arsène Wenger and I think those were his peak years.

After he left Arsenal in July 2006 I took him to Portsmouth. It was an incredible deal, really. He told the club he wanted a new challenge and they agreed to cancel what was left on his contract – about two years. I think the feeling was mutual – he wanted out and they wanted him out, but it was remarkable because he was walking away from a deal worth in excess of £10 million. He was on massive money and took a £3 million-a-year pay cut to join us, about half of what he was earning at Arsenal. I arranged a meeting and I couldn't believe it came off, particularly once I knew the figures involved. It wasn't even as if he took a rest – he left Arsenal and a month later came to join us. It was really strange and I wasn't sure quite what to expect – but he was as good as gold. Arsenal had a state-of-the-art training ground and were moving to the Emirates Stadium; we had Third Division facilities and a stadium that was falling to bits. But he never complained. Well, only once. Then I reminded him of where Senrab used to play, on Wanstead Flats. I told him I knew where he'd come from – where I'd come from, where so many of us had come from, in fact. And he never said another word after that. I partnered him with Sylvain Distin and they were as hard as nails as a duo. Distin was fast and powerful as well – we made it hard for anybody to break us down.

I made Sol my captain, too, and I know there's been some controversy recently around this issue. Sol said he should have been England captain, and that he didn't get the job because he was black. He's entitled to his opinion but I don't agree. I don't think Sol was overlooked because he was black – maybe the England managers had more options than I did at Portsmouth. I liked Sol, I thought he was a good lad – but he was a far bigger fish at Portsmouth than he would have been at international level. He'd been there and done it all and players looked up to him. With England there were a lot of players that had Sol's CV and commanded the same respect, and there were many who had his quality and presence on the pitch. I was surprised that

Sol felt the way he did because I could not imagine any England manager ignoring his captaincy claims because he was black – all the years I have been in football I haven't heard of anyone doing that. The manager picks the captain, not the Football Association, and managers go with the best man, always. Are we to believe that Kevin Keegan and Sven-Göran Eriksson are racists? I don't think so. It never enters your mind whether a player is black or white when you make those selections.

I think it is more likely that the managers thought Sol was a quiet lad, which he is. He has a presence, an aura about him, and you only had to look at him and you wouldn't want to mess with him. He was a real big, strong, powerful guy – but he wasn't about to shout and scream. He would organise, but he was never as vocal about it as Tony Adams, for instance. With Sol, I think it depends on the team. He could captain Portsmouth and did a fine job – and he did captain England on occasions. But generally I would say there were people in the England team who were more vocal, more in tune with the manager and perhaps more forthcoming within the group. Thinking of the team I had at Tottenham – Sol would be captain. At Arsenal last season – Sol would be captain. Yet he wouldn't necessarily be captain at Liverpool in front of Steven Gerrard, or Manchester City ahead of Vincent Kompany, or Chelsea before John Terry. He'd certainly be captain of Portsmouth now, though – in fact, if he fancied it, he might even be able to play up front again.

Looking back, I had a lot of experienced players in that team – a lot of potential captains. Lassana Diarra certainly wanted the job, and guys like Distin, Patrik Berger, Glen Johnson, Hermann Hreidarsson and David James were all contenders, but Sol had the edge. Glenn Hoddle always said that your captain should be your best player. If he is leading out the team in Italy, say, he is the guy the fans see first and he needs to be impressive. They should be a little worried by him, a little daunted, they should be fearing having to overcome him in the match – and, for us, Sol had a little of that. He wasn't a match-winner like Hoddle's England captain, Alan Shearer, but I imagine people might have looked and wondered how they were going to get round him.

There were some fine central defenders around in that era, too – not least Colin Hendry at Blackburn Rovers and Steve Bruce and Gary Pallister at Manchester United. Bruce was a great competitor. I had been telling everyone about him at Gillingham before he went to Norwich City, but he made a strange first impression. He wasn't a great mover, he wasn't fast – he was a bit of a funny shape. I can see why people turned him down. Yet he ended up a wonderful player for United – and he's still going strong as a coach with Hull City. I made Tony Pulis and Steve the managers of the year last season. Even if he hadn't reached the FA Cup final with Hull he would have been in with a shout for it. Looking at that team, I thought he would do well to keep them up. I bumped into him on holiday before the season began, told him that, and he agreed.

I hear Sol is doing his coaching badges now. I'd like to see him get into it. I had a lot of time for Sol when he was with me, and maybe coaching will afford him the respect and the acknowledgement he thinks he should have been given as captain of England.

STUART PEARCE
(NOTTINGHAM FOREST)

I think if you asked any right-sided player for his least favourite opponent, Stuart's name would be top of the list. He had the lot – powerful, strong, aggressive, but skilful when he needed to be. I tried to take him to West Ham when he left Nottingham Forest in 1997, but my chairman, Terry Brown, said no way. 'He's too old,' he told me. 'He's finished.' He was 35, but that didn't stop Kenny Dalglish signing him at Newcastle, where he played 34 matches in his first season, including games in the Champions League against Barcelona and Dynamo Kiev. Newcastle reached the FA Cup final, losing to Arsenal, and Stuart would have been involved considerably more the following season too, had he found favour with new coach Ruud Gullit. So when he was finished at Newcastle, I persuaded Terry Brown to change his mind and signed him at the second time of asking. By then Stuart was 37, but despite his age he was fantastic for us and ended up playing 50 games over two seasons. In 2001, he was named Hammer of the Year.

Stuart was one of those players that made me wish I had worked with him in his prime. He was such a ferocious competitor – ferocious runs, ferocious ability to boot people up in the air, just an intimidating presence on that flank. I worked with Julian Dicks at West Ham, too, who was probably the only left-back in Stuart's league at the time. If anything, Julian might have had a fraction more technical ability. He could have played for England but he didn't have Stuart's control. Stuart had a way of directing his energy, while with Julian it often turned nasty, which was unhelpful. He got sent off in one of his early performances for England's under-21 team, and when it looked as if he was under consideration again, he got banned for three matches for stamping on John Spencer of Chelsea – but not before he had been sent off for the eighth time in his career for a foul on Ian Wright of Arsenal. Stuart was a hard man, too – but in the end more reliable. I'm not saying he was an angel – he got sent off five times in his career, too – but for the most part he was hard and fair. Occasionally, hard and not fair – but I don't know a defender who isn't.

Someone once asked me, as a winger who played on the right, how I would handle coming up against Stuart Pearce. I told them I'd change wings. I don't know how you would handle him, really, because he was on a search-and-destroy mission from the start. The first time the ball came to you, he was going to smash you, run all over you, chip you into the stand and then take the ball, run forward and shoot. Then he'd get back just as fast as he got up. He was a dream left-back, really, exactly what any manager would want from a player in that position. I can't remember him ever getting a roasting or being turned inside out.

He was also a player you could trust. On the odd occasion, he would ask me if he could stay home, because he still lived in the Midlands and he found driving to London every day a chore. He always promised to do some fitness work over the park – and I know for a fact that when he made that promise, he kept it. Even on Christmas Day, so his wife said. He always trained Christmas Day, even during his non-league career, and one year I let him have 25 December at home. And off he went, training over the park as promised. He said he wouldn't be able to look me in the eye if he had said he'd gone and it was a lie.

He was such a team man, too. There is a great story about Stuart getting headbutted by Basile Boli of France in the European Championship. It opened a big cut on his chin, but the referee didn't see it. Stuart knew it was Boli, but instead of having it out with him, he went straight over to the little winger he had been marking and blamed him – because he knew this lad would be absolutely terrified of retribution and wouldn't be able to focus. Sure enough, he spent the next 20 minutes protesting his innocence and went completely off his game.

Nobody ever ran rings around Stuart. The new way is to play a winger on the wrong flank – a right-footer on the left, left-footer on the right – and I've seen players like Arjen Robben causing havoc that way. I think Stuart would have handled it. There was a lot more intelligence to his game than many realised.

He worked in warehouses as an electrician, and I think that kind of experience may help in producing a stable character. It is what I would call an old-school upbringing. You appreciated being a footballer; you loved it. Stuart said he never used to dream of playing professional football because when you are in some big shed in Stonebridge it doesn't feel like it is something that will ever happen. I think there was a lot to be said for the old way. Even the lads who were on the books at football clubs had their feet on the ground. You cleaned the boots, you got the kit ready, and come Friday you went back in the afternoon and polished the brass at Upton Park. Nobody does that any more. You mustn't clean the boots, you mustn't clean the ground. Suddenly they are all 17, driving big cars, and have agents claiming they're as good as Gareth Bale. Yet if you do come across boys who haven't had all that, they tend to be the ones that appreciate it the most. Ian Wright was like that, and Alan Devonshire who was a fork-lift truck driver. It happens less and less now. Can you imagine a player from Southall going straight into West Ham's first team these days?

It was Bobby Gould who spotted Stuart playing for Wealdstone, and Bobby who probably gave him the lesson that defined his career. When they were at Coventry City together, before a game with Tottenham, Bobby took their striker Terry Gibson to one side and, in front of Stuart, asked him, 'Who do you prefer going up against in the Tottenham team, Terry? Graham Roberts or Paul Miller?' Terry said he preferred playing against Miller. 'Why?' Bobby asked. 'Because Graham Roberts kicks me all over the place,' Terry replied. Bobby looked at his new signing, the former electrician from Wealdstone. 'There you are, son,' he said. I don't think Stuart ever forgot that.

MATT LE TISSIER
(SOUTHAMPTON)

Matt Le Tissier's 10 greatest goals would stand alongside those from any of the greatest goalscorers in the world – Lionel Messi, Cristiano Ronaldo, even Diego Maradona or Pelé. Le Tissier at his scoring peak would not look out of place. As for the Premier League, if you collected the 20 best goals over its 22 years, he would be responsible for a quarter, at least. Off the top of my head, there is the chip over Peter Schmeichel against Manchester United in 1996, the incredible long-range shot against Blackburn Rovers in 1994, the ball that bends from the middle to the top corner against Coventry City, the run against Newcastle United that begins with him back-heeling the ball from behind and over his head on the run, before he beats one player, lobs the centre-half, meets it on the other side and slots its past Mike Hooper – and, in the same game, the winning goal that he takes on his thigh and volleys in from 25 yards, as cool as you like. I'm sure there are plenty more that I've missed and would be contenders. He had such ability with the ball that he used to shoot from corners.

The goal against Blackburn is possibly his greatest. Tim Flowers, Blackburn's goalkeeper, had a Union Jack towel that he used to hang from the stanchion at the top of the goal. Le Tissier and Flowers were old friends from Southampton and before the game Matt kept teasing Tim, saying he was going to hit that towel with a shot. When the chance arose he did not disappoint. He picked up the ball inside the Blackburn half, broke forward and struck a right-foot shot from a good 30 yards. At first it appeared to be floating, almost like a chip, but then it just gathered pace and by the time it crossed the line it was going like a rocket – bang, against the stanchion and Tim's towel. There are not many players who could do that, and I think Le Tissier would have been famous worldwide had he not been content to stay with Southampton throughout his entire career. He had offers – Terry Venables wanted him at Tottenham Hotspur, and Matthew Harding, the late Chelsea director, used to say it was his life's ambition to bring him to Stamford Bridge. Yet Matt was happy where he was. His last goal for the club was the last goal ever scored at The Dell on 19 May 2001. Matt didn't start that day, but came on as a substitute and says he felt that goal was his destiny. It was a beauty, too – a pinpoint shot on the turn to win a game against Arsenal. A perfect Le Tissier moment.

He was a one-man band there for a lot of the time, like Sir Tom Finney had been at Preston North End, and because he came from Guernsey and wanted to stay close to home, I think some people had him down as a bit of a country bumpkin. Why is he stuck down there? Why isn't he playing for Manchester United? Yet anyone who knows Matt will tell you he is far from dumb. He was just happy to be at a club he had known since he was 16, happy to be 30 minutes away from his family in the Channel Islands. I think he would have been brilliant at a club like Arsenal, but just because he didn't make that jump doesn't mean he's not smart. He was just one of those great natural footballers from a real football family – all of his brothers played and are still involved in running teams on Guernsey – and he got his buzz from the game itself and his contribution to it, not from constantly pursuing wealth and prizes. He once said that later in life, when all the ex-players are reminiscing at the bar, there may be some that will be able to say they won more trophies but there won't be too many who can say they were better footballers. Matt says that is good enough for him, and more power to him for that.

I can say with confidence that Matt is a natural because I've seen him play other sports. There isn't any effort in it at all – as he played football, that's how he is at golf, for instance. We're both members at Remedy Oak in Dorset and the last hole there is a 365-yard par four with a dogleg right. Everybody drives down to the fairway – not too far as there's a devilish bunker if you're too long – and then hits across water to the green. Not Matt. He takes a short cut, up and over the trees, over the water and on to the green for one. They're massive, those trees, but it doesn't bother Matt. He hits the ball an absolute mile and with near enough the same accuracy that he strikes a football. No wonder he's a five handicap. Another day a Bournemouth XI played a Southampton XI in a charity cricket match. Matt walked in and started flipping balls for sixes. There was no effort in it at all. Clip – six. Flip – six. His hand-eye co-ordination was as good as anything I had seen. He's a very natural all-round sportsman.

Like the maverick players from the 1970s, there should have been more caps for England. He only won eight and it was a shame the way that soured his relationship with one of his heroes, Glenn Hoddle. Glenn was Matt's idol growing up and they had many similarities as players – but I think Matt feels Glenn made him a scapegoat for the defeat by Italy in 1996 and their relationship deteriorated after that. Having heard his after-dinner speeches, I think it is fair to say that this episode still rankles with Matt. He should definitely have had more opportunities at international level – and it seems strange that Venables tried to get him for Tottenham, but rejected him for England.

Terry played him in the game against the Republic of Ireland that was abandoned in 1995, and he didn't start him again after that. He must have felt he had seen enough in those 20-or-so minutes. Glenn later gave him a surprise start against Italy, but lost faith very quickly and didn't pick him in his extended World Cup squad of 30 in 1998, despite a hat-trick for the B team. It was a shame that throughout his career Matt was regarded as a left-field selection, even though we all knew what he could do.

Something Sir Alex Ferguson said sticks in my mind. He said he wouldn't put Le Tissier in his own team – but he was never happy to see him lining up against Manchester United for Southampton. That sums up the contrasts. Venables, I'm told, thought Matt's best position was in the centre of forward midfield, but he wasn't mobile enough to play there at the highest level as he would simply be picked up by any man marker.

Venables thought that if he named Le Tissier, a thinking coach would simply put a man on him. Fine, if Le Tissier was willing to drag that man about left and right, creating space for others to run into, but if he remained static the game would simply become 10 against 10, with England losing a playmaker and the opposition a crude destroyer – which wasn't a fair exchange. I can understand that but, surely, there was a way of accommodating him, a way of setting the team up to highlight what Matt could do, rather than his weaknesses. He could score goals, he could take free-kicks, corners, penalties. There was always an end product to him – and out of nowhere he would turn a game. You could ask what happens if we don't get a free-kick or penalty, but Matt usually had a way of involving himself in a game. He was very confident in his own ability. He certainly didn't stay at Southampton because he was shy.

I know he liked Alan Ball, who took over from Ian Branfoot as Southampton manager in 1994. Branfoot didn't appear to trust Le Tissier's talent and often left him out, but Alan made it clear he thought Matt was Southampton's best player and he would build the team around him. He scored six goals in Alan's first four games, and eight in the last six of the season to keep Southampton up. He chipped in like that year on year, with the vital goals to avoid relegation. Like Preston and Finney, Southampton were relegated relatively soon after Le Tissier retired. I think Alan gave him the love he needed. He would tell him how great he was – and wouldn't be slow in telling the others to get the ball to him, either. Matt would have responded to that, I'm sure – it shouldn't have been so hard to work out how to handle him.

He's a player I would have loved to have in my teams because at any time you could be struggling, or even outclassed, and he could turn the game in your favour. At West Ham I had one like him in Paolo Di Canio, and he always made you think you had a chance. We could be playing Arsenal and they might be stronger and better than us, but Paolo would do something and the game would change in that one moment. Matt could pick it up from 25 yards and – pow. Make as if to shoot, drag it past in the other direction and chip it over the goalkeeper's head. He made The Dell an intimidating place to visit. It was never the same once they moved to St Mary's – but that was partly because Le Tissier was missing. You knew you didn't have him around to hurt you, either. They have had some real aggressive teams down there, but with Matt it was aggression of a different kind. It was a rundown stadium, and the crowd were on top of you, but Matt gave it a different edge – a feeling of the unknown. You could be playing your best football of the season but that wouldn't matter if he got the ball in the right spot. It didn't even have to be the right spot, really – goals came out of nowhere. And that is a daunting thought for an opposition coach.

I can remember the day Manchester United were getting such a beating at The Dell that they changed the strip at half-time. They were wearing grey, and the players said they couldn't find each other in the crowd. That's when you know it's got to you. The greatest manager in the world on the touchline and he had no other answers beyond blaming the kit. A player like Le Tissier can send you loopy.

Of course, by picking Le Tissier in this team I'm leaving out David Beckham. I know some people will think I've gone mad. But David was a fantastic player in a fantastic team, whereas Matt was performing heroics that built a football club. Without him, Southampton couldn't have stayed in the top division for so long, and without that they would not have been able to build their new stadium and its fabulous academy. He was paid a £2,000 bonus per goal after 1997, but in reality those goals were worth millions when you consider the way they moved that club forward. Think how many of Southampton's young academy players have now been told about Le Tissier by their dads or mums. For me, that loyalty to a small club at a time when it simply wasn't done sets him apart.

David was a brilliant technical player, a great crosser of the ball and scorer of phenomenal goals and free-kicks. In the end, though, I decided that what Le Tissier meant to Southampton was extra special. You talk to the fans down there and they haven't got as many idols as Manchester United, but what they have got is Le Tissier – Le God, as they called him. So this is one for the small clubs and the men who keep them going. I realise I'm probably blowing any chance I've got of managing Beckham's new club in Miami. Maybe Matt will put in a word for me at Guernsey FC instead.

ROY KEANE
(MANCHESTER UNITED)

Our scout in Ireland told me about Roy Keane's start in football. He said Keane was the only kid in their national schoolboy team that didn't have a club – the other 15 had all got fixed up. He called Barry Lloyd at Brighton and Hove Albion, who were struggling for young players, and recommended Keane. Barry wouldn't go with that alone, but he said he would come over and watch Ireland's youth game the following Tuesday. So the scout went to see the schools manager and explained the situation – that this was Roy's big break and he could become an apprentice at Brighton if they liked the look of him. 'He's been in every squad, but he hasn't played a minute of any game,' he said. 'Can you make sure he is involved on Tuesday?' The coach said no. 'We're not here to showcase kids, we are here to win football matches,' he said. Keane never played and Brighton didn't take him – they probably don't realise the poor turn that youth manager did their club to this day. Keane ended up working as a hospital porter and playing part time for Cobh Ramblers. That was where he was spotted by Nottingham Forest scout Noel McCabe in an FAI Youth Cup match against Belvedere, from Dublin.

My friend Alan Hill, Brian Clough's assistant manager, told me what happened next. They invited three Irish kids over for trial and they couldn't train because of the snow – so the trial was rearranged, but this time only one lad, Roy Keane, could make it. They took him on a trip to a tournament with the youth team and he wasn't bad – even Brian liked him – so they signed him. The following season, after a pre-season tour, Clough wasn't happy with the make-up of the squad. On the day they came back there was a reserve fixture in the evening. Clough had been sitting in his office having a few whiskies. 'Is the Irish fellow playing tonight?' he suddenly asked. 'Come on, let's go and watch.' So Brian and Alan jumped in the car and drove to Mansfield Town. Alan went to find out the starting line-up from Archie Gemmill, the reserve coach, while Brian took a seat at the back of the stand. He wasn't happy with the news. 'He's not starting,' Alan told him. 'Who's playing instead?' Clough demanded to know. 'Archie's boy, Scot,' Alan told him. 'That fucking little Scots bastard,' Clough exclaimed. At half time, he told Alan to go to the dressing-room and tell Gemmill to put Keane on. Alan duly did as he was told. They came out for the second half, but no change had been made. Keane was still in his tracksuit on the bench. 'Fucking hell,' said Clough. 'I'm not having this.' And he climbed over the rows of empty wooden seats, over the perimeter fence and marched straight on to the pitch. 'Referee, referee, stop the game,' he insisted. The play was halted 'Right,' said Clough. 'Gemmill: off. Irishman: on.' And he stood there waiting while Keane got his gear on and only when the substitution had been made did he take his place again in the stand. That was the beginning of Keane's career at Nottingham Forest. He started him in the second game of that season, 1990–91, away at Liverpool and he never looked back.

And do you know why it took so long for Roy Keane to get his break? He was a bit timid. Unbelievable isn't it? But those were the words of our Irish scout, and he knew him inside out. He was a right-winger at the time, and they thought he was a bit soft. It is amazing how people change. Brian Tiler, my best pal who died in a car crash in Italy in 1990, came across Norman Hunter playing with Rotherham Schoolboys and said the same about him. 'A timid little left-winger' was how he described Norman. He ended up the fiercest centre-half in the country. 'Norman bites yer legs' as he was known.

As for Keane, he was another player who just had a marvellous presence – another type like Graeme Souness, really, with a bit of the devil in him. I think even his own team-mates were in awe of him – or maybe just intimidated by his intensity. He was the driving force behind that great Manchester United team, the treble winners, and I think it is a real shame the way it ended between him and Sir Alex Ferguson at Manchester United. When he'd been been such a great captain and won so much, it is a pity that relationship could not be patched up and there was no place for Keane at Old Trafford. I know that he went too far in his criticism of team-mates by the end, but I wonder if that could have been reined in earlier. It seems such a waste to have a man of that stature outside the club. Would Manchester United have come seventh last season if Keane had been around to pull the players up? He would have been after them as he always was – in the peak years when there were no short-cuts at United and those messages were passed from Ferguson, through Keane.

There is a story of him laying into Mark Bosnich, the goalkeeper, for turning up late on his first day of training. Bosnich said he got lost. Keane's point was that on his own first day at the club, he got up early, hired a taxi and followed it to the training ground in his car to ensure he arrived on time. He had these incredible professional standards and expected the same of everybody. It's great to have a player like that in your team. Every manager wants a Tony Adams, John Terry or Roy Keane really – we all want someone who will have a go, fighting the manager's battles and those of the team, too. I imagine the treatment meted out to Ryan Giggs and David Beckham by the opposition might have been a lot harsher if they didn't think they would be answering to Keane.

I know he had a reputation for being high maintenance but I never found him that way. He was as good as gold as a manager and if you asked him about players you always got excellent, straight opinions. I've appeared on television with him, too, and he was absolutely different class. There are too many stories for him not to have a bit of an edge, and he can obviously lose it, but every time I've been with him I have absolutely loved his company. John McDermott is the academy manager at Tottenham and he says the same. John takes a lot of the Pro Licence courses for the Football Association and told me of all the players he has taught, Roy Keane had the most presence when he was coaching. I know he's been with Sunderland and Ipswich Town and it hasn't always worked out for him, but John thought he was excellent.

PATRICK VIEIRA
(ARSENAL)

It is impossible to write about Roy Keane without mentioning that other great warrior-midfielder from the start of the Premier League era, Patrick Vieira. Gareth Southgate tells a story that links the two, even in retirement. Keane hadn't long started his career as a pundit with ITV and they were covering a Manchester City match away in Europe. ITV have this set-up where the experts stand around a raised table pitch-side before and after the game and at half time, but on this occasion the presenter told Roy there was a special guest coming to see them – someone he might remember from his playing days. With that, Gareth could see Patrick Vieira walking towards them, in his new role as Manchester City ambassador. Roy could see him too, and Gareth says the change in his demeanour was terrifying. His mood darkened, his eyes narrowed, he stiffened and his grip on the table was almost white knuckle. The presenter was now wittering on, oblivious to the fact that at the very sight of Patrick, nearly 10 years after they had last played each other, Roy had gone into battle mode. Gareth said it was like being transported back into that tunnel at Highbury in 2005. Anything could have happened from there. The others around the table were looking at Roy's face and beginning to take a step back. His eyes had just glazed over. Patrick was completely unsuspecting, approaching the table with a big smile ready to reminisce. It looked as if it could backfire horribly, except the first words out of Patrick's mouth were so complimentary towards Roy it just diffused the situation. He was asked about big nights in Europe and he said none of them were the same as playing against him, pointing at Keane. They were the best nights of his life because Roy was such a fabulous competitor. Keane couldn't be anything other than pleasant after that; the glare disappeared, the muscles relaxed and the other guests breathed a small sigh of relief. Business as usual – but it shows you how much it means to the very top players. Even all those years later.

Quite how Vieira has ended up on the staff of Manchester City – he has moved on to running their Elite Development

Squad now – I do not know. Shouldn't he be at Arsenal? I can't understand why when you have such a leader on the pitch, you don't follow that through and get them leading your backroom staff, too. At Bournemouth I got my captain Tony Pulis on board as a coach for that reason, and had I stayed at Tottenham I would definitely have found a role for Ledley King. Patrick was a fantastic signing for Arsenal and I find it a little bizarre to see him now in a Manchester City blazer representing a club he only played for 46 times.

Vieira was the ultimate box-to-box footballer. He was a lean giant of a man, 6 ft 4 in tall, and the power behind Arsenal's Invincibles. He is still a legend at the club – but what people don't know is that he almost signed for me at Tottenham. It was before the 2009–10 season, my first full campaign at White Hart Lane, and he was not being picked by José Mourinho at Inter Milan. I thought it was an incredible decision to want to come to us when he'd been such a hero at Arsenal. I met him at his house in Hampstead and he had no fear about what people would think or what reception he would get. He had enough confidence in his ability to just brush it away.

I remember talking to Daniel Levy, our chairman, about him. He said the crowd would be hostile. I knew that – but if he had enough bottle to want to put on our white shirt after all that had gone before, I thought it said something about the man. I can imagine what it would have been like for him at Tottenham previously. Our fans would have been slaughtering him because he was captain of Arsenal, and he would have been winding them up because Arsenal would have been, almost certainly, winning. If he had the nerve to put it all to one side and come to us, it shows what character he had. I was expecting him to run a mile, to be honest. Not a bit of it. In the end, his circumstances changed and he decided to stay in Italy, but he was definitely up for the move that summer. When we spoke, Patrick was convinced that Inter wanted to get rid of him – and then José suddenly named him in his squad. When Patrick rang to tell me he sounded completely surprised. It was a shame because by the time he did become available – the following January – our needs had changed and Manchester City snapped him up.

Patrick is the player Arsenal have never really replaced. He could run with the ball in that long, loping style, but he was powerful, too, and aggressive – he could take care of himself, even against the toughest opponent. I think every major club would like to have a Patrick Vieira now – certainly Arsenal could do with one. Arsène Wenger doesn't really discover players like that any more. In recent years, Arsenal signings have been well-established stars like Olivier Giroud, Mesut Ozil or Lukas Podolski. People forget how original his ideas were when he first arrived. Nobody had heard of Vieira or Emmanuel Petit – these French names seemed like a big gamble, but proved very successful. Vieira and Petit were great signings, and great additions to the English league – two six-foot midfield players absolutely dominating the centre of the park. They operated like pistons pumping, one forward, the other back, never caught out, always in the right place. It isn't as easy to pull off as it looks – think how hard we tried to get Steven Gerrard and Frank Lampard working together like that for England. Vieira and Petit were a special partnership, really, as valuable as any pair of strikers or central defenders. They were dangerous at set plays, strong going forward, fearless defensively; they could both head the ball and were impressive technically. Everyone talks about Arsenal's passing, but at goal-kicks they were on that second ball faster than anybody. They walked over teams, really, just trampled over them in the middle of the park.

It is ironic that so many associate Arsène with the beautiful game, yet his Arsenal teams did as much as anybody to introduce real physical power into the modern Premier League. Teams got bigger to compete with Arsenal because they were so strong. To go a season unbeaten, as they did in 2003–4, is a quite incredible achievement. They were up there with any of the great post-war teams, I think – the Busby Babes, Tottenham's double-winners, Revie's Leeds United, the great Liverpool teams, Manchester United under Sir Alex Ferguson – they deserve to be mentioned with any of them. Players like Vieira or Thierry Henry would have got into any team in the world.

I would say Tottenham's first double-winning team was the best – until Leeds came along, because Revie had them so finely balanced. I think the game that would decide it, though, would be Arsenal's Invincibles against the Manchester United treble-winning team of 1999. They were only five years apart, but the teams never really met. Remarkably, eight of the regular starting XI from the Invincibles were not even in Arsenal's first team when Manchester United won the treble (Vieira and Dennis Bergkamp were the only regulars, while Freddie Ljungberg played 14 games) and by the time Arsenal went through the season unbeaten only four regulars from United's treble season (Keane, Gary Neville, Paul Scholes and Ryan Giggs) plus Phil Neville (who had a lesser role behind Denis Irwin in 1999) remained. It would be

RYAN GIGGS
(MANCHESTER UNITED)

Here we go again with the story of another unsung hero from the world of talent-spotting. Harold Wood was a local newsagent in Manchester who used to work part-time as a steward at Manchester United's training ground. He was the man who first told Manchester United scouts that there was a young lad training with Manchester City who was regarded as exceptional. His name was Ryan Wilson and he was the son of Welsh rugby-league player Danny Wilson, who was at that time playing second receiver for Swinton. The young Wilson, Wood said, was a Manchester United fan and would prefer to play for the Reds. Nobody followed up on his advice, so he repeated it, this time to Alex Ferguson. He immediately dispatched Joe Brown, who had briefly been manager of Burnley after a playing career mostly spent at Bournemouth, to check this out. Brown offered a positive report and a trial was quickly arranged. On first sight, Alex needed no further encouragement. 'If we can't make that one a player we might as well give up,' he is believed to have told Brian Kidd. Giggs (he used his mother's surname) certainly was exceptional as he fast-tracked his way through United's academy.

What a player. Will we see his like again? Probably not. Retiring only last summer after 24 seasons in the Premier League with Manchester United, Giggs stands out as *the* footballer of the Premier League era. He burst on to the scene as a flying teenage winger, and left it as a cultured central midfield player, trusted to run the team as caretaker coach after David Moyes was sacked. Right to the end he maintained his ability and intelligence and was capable of turning in great performances. He was just a natural athlete. He kept himself fit and found ways of extending his career beyond any reasonable expectation. He looked after himself for longer than most players are prepared to, really. In the end, they get bored with the demands of a fitness regime, but he never did. There wasn't an ounce of fat on him, even at the very end. I think everybody knew when he was 17 that he was going to be special – but nobody could have imagined how special. Sir Alex once said that 20 years on the wing for Manchester United would never be done again – and he went on another four years beyond that.

I remember Paul Merson telling me how all those years ago George Graham used to sit him down when they were together at Arsenal and order him to watch videos of Ryan Giggs. George has now been away from Arsenal for 19 years, Paul Merson went into management 10 years ago – and Giggs was still going strong until the summer, so he may have been on to something. George loved the way Ryan tracked back and wanted that level of commitment from Paul. Good luck with that, by the way.

Ryan just had an athlete's physique. He could run all day. The only other player I've seen like that was Billy Bonds. He was all bone really, a real tin ribs. He never blew up in the summer, never put weight on year to year, and that was Giggs too. I remember when he took his shirt off after scoring that wonder goal against Arsenal in the FA Cup semi-final replay in 1999 – there was nothing of him, really. He was muscular, yes, but you'd think a powerful full-back would be able to bash him up. They couldn't. I think every Englishman wishes he could have played for us because we had a real problem on the left throughout the 1990s, but his family is all Welsh. He played for England Schoolboys, but the moment it came to senior football he could only represent Wales.

It could have solved so many issues had he been able to play for England because we ruined a succession of players out on that left flank: Paul Scholes retired because he kept getting stuck out there; Joe Cole made a decent fist of it for a while; they even tried my lad Jamie out there in one game. It's a scary position if it is not yours by right because it is so hard to get in the game. Ryan was born there; he had pace, he could cross, come inside or go outside. Alex has had any number of players on the right side for United – but until recently it has only been Giggs on the left. He helped build a modern club and defines a style of play. I can remember Peter Schmeichel talking about the famous goal against Arsenal. He said that, seeing it, United felt invincible. And with Giggs in full flow they were, on their day.

DENNIS BERGKAMP
(ARSENAL)

Thierry Henry said he was a dream of a striker, and he was certainly the best number 10 of the Premier League era. He linked up, scored great goals, made the final pass, but was always clever, clever, clever. He always had his head up, so he saw the game in a way others do not. It was as if he played with telepathy, but really it was about vision. Every young player should be made to study Dennis Bergkamp, the way his head was always on the swivel, taking it all in, so that when the ball came it would go out again so quickly, and with such precision. He didn't watch the ball, he watched the play, so he was a step ahead of the rest. It was like seeing a ballroom dancer in motion, he was so smooth, so classy; there really was no one like him.

I think the number 10 role is one of the great losses in the modern game, so thank heavens the Dutch, in particular, still produce them. I had Rafael van der Vaart at Tottenham, and I think Ravel Morrison has the wit to play the position, too, if he is willing to channel his energy, but the bottom line is you have to score goals from there or make telling final passes, otherwise it turns into an ego-trip. I think the reason the role has increasingly faded from the game is that there were too many players who were simply not effective in it. It is no good the number 10 dropping deep and looking pretty – you've got to be up there, weighing in, otherwise your striker is utterly isolated and the position is wasted. It is about intelligence, and Bergkamp had a football IQ at genius level. The way he would take up positions between the centre-halves or in between midfield and defence, and pull teams apart with his movement, was extraordinary to watch. When you see 10 played well it's a great position because there are the gaps to exploit if you think about the game. It is not like being the centre-forward, up there with two hairy-arsed central defenders sticking the boot in. You drop into little pockets, play between the lines – but you need to be smart.

One of the great flaws in English football over the past decades is that we don't produce enough artistry. We miss out on the Bergkamp type of player. Even now, with a lot of the promise around the England team, there isn't a great number 10 coming through. Raheem Sterling can play through the middle, but is more of a winger, and Ross Barkley is clever enough for it, but we need to see if he makes the role his own. Wayne Rooney has not been allowed to play there, even though it is probably his best position – there have always been coaches wanting to shunt him into a wide forward role or play him as an out-and-out striker. Matt Le Tissier was probably the nearest we've had to it recently and, like Bergkamp, he scored great goals from that position. Matt was one for the long range, though, whereas Dennis was more intricate. He scored wonderful goals, but they would be full of lovely one-twos, chips and flicks. Exquisite. His play always seemed very delicate – there was nothing nasty in the way he performed, and no big shows of strength.

Dennis could hit them – as Bolton Wanderers and Southampton among others will testify – but replaying his greatest moments in my head it is the stunning close control in the penalty area that I recall. Drag-backs, flicks and audacious keep-ups that found the net against Leicester City, Tottenham Hotspur and Newcastle United, or perfectly executed chips against Derby County, Sheffield United and Bayer Leverkusen. Trying to work out how to play against Dennis was always a puzzle. What you needed was a deep holder in midfield and maybe a cluster of three eating up his space, because if you sent the centre-half out to deal with him Arsenal were going to rip you to shreds. You had to keep them squeezed up and you certainly didn't want the back four dropping off – because if he found space and there was a nice hole for him, he was going to kill you. Arsenal were so difficult to work out, in their prime. The forwards would all disappear, Henry to the left, Bergkamp upfield, Robert Pirès and Freddie Ljungberg to wide midfield, and your centre-halves would be standing there with no one to mark when, suddenly, there was a stampede and they were all breaking at you from every angle. Fans get frustrated if you play one up sometimes, but if you have the right players it can be so effective. West Ham United played 4–6–0 at Tottenham last year, and ended up winning 3–0. I remember being at Portsmouth in a match with Reading. We had one fit striker, Benjani, who hadn't scored in about five years. Actually, that's not true. He'd scored one goal the previous season against Wigan Athletic in April. We were hoping he might nick another one against Reading and we could get away with it. He finished up getting a hat-trick and we scored seven. The final score was 7–4. I'd told everyone beforehand that we were setting out to be hard to beat because of circumstances and it could be a dour game. Scored seven, let four in. It was like playground football. The highest scoring game in the history of the Premier League.

There is a statue of Bergkamp at the Emirates Stadium now, and so there should be. Players like him won't come around too often, and Mesut Ozil, all £42 million of him, can only dream of filling Bergkamp's shoes at present. Chelsea should put up a statue to Gianfranco Zola, too. He was another genius little number 10, who changed the dynamic of his club. He was hugely important to the development of Chelsea, and if it wasn't for Bergkamp he would walk into this team.

ALAN SHEARER
(BLACKBURN ROVERS)

Alan wasn't a clever player like, say, Thierry Henry, but he was a proper English striker. As an opponent you knew you were in for an afternoon's work if Shearer was in the team. He came to prominence at the time the Premier League began and I remember the first game he played for Blackburn Rovers, away to Crystal Palace. He had signed from Southampton for £3.6 million that summer, which was the British transfer record, and everyone thought Kenny Dalglish had taken a bit of a gamble at that price. He scored twice at Selhurst Park in his first game, two absolute stunners from long range, and then got the winner at home to Arsenal three days later. He just looked an old-fashioned centre-forward, but with a cherry on top because he could score goals from anywhere. A player like Gary Lineker was expert from close range, and Matt Le Tissier was a danger from long range – but Alan scored from all over. He got the little sniffer's goals and the ones that got the stadium on its feet. And he was relentless. He scored 11 hat-tricks in the Premier League because once he got two there was no way he wasn't hunting down that third. He could be selfish – yet his partnership with Chris Sutton at Blackburn was one of the best the Premier League has seen.

They had such a great understanding. There is one goal that is just a succession of one-twos between the pair of them, working their way from the centre circle to the penalty box. Sutton made great channel runs and took defenders away, and Shearer came charging into that space. He didn't have electric pace, but he was fast and once he got in front of the target he rarely missed. Neil Ruddock, who was an ex-team-mate of his at Southampton, used to have a standing bet with him. He would give Shearer £10 a goal, but Alan had to pay £20 every time he played a match and did not score. Neil thought this was such a good deal, but he always ended up out of pocket. Shearer was a goal machine – he got his headers in, he picked up the bits and pieces, and he had an incredibly powerful shot. I think his career represents the passing of an era in the English game, too, because he won the league with Blackburn Rovers, which may be the last time a club from outside the elite achieves such a feat, and then he chose his hometown club, Newcastle United, over Manchester United. He wanted to go back there when he was still at his peak, rather than as a favour at the end of his career. We won't see that too often, either. People think he must regret not signing for United, but I'm told he doesn't. He did everything that he wanted with his career, and I admire that.

Jack Walker was a wonderful man for Blackburn and the team he allowed Dalglish to build is underrated. To do that, from scratch, at a club with no pedigree is very difficult, particularly when you have a club with the clout of Manchester United as your main rival. People talk about Blackburn at that time as being like Manchester City now, but the sums involved are tiny by comparison. They were still getting beaten in terms of salary and transfer fees by clubs like Liverpool, whereas nobody could outbid City in a straight fight for a player now.

Alan's time as England's striker also coincided with a real upsurge in standards for our game. Terry Venables decided very early on that he was going to be his number nine at the European Championships in 1996, despite competition from Robbie Fowler, Les Ferdinand and Andy Cole. Then Alan went on a terrible run with England – he didn't score for 12 games. Venables wanted to rest him more often to give the others a chance, but he knew that if he did that when Alan hadn't scored, it would be perceived as him being dropped – and the negative headlines might harm his confidence. So Venables kept him in. The moment he scored he was due to be out – but Shearer went 21 months, a 12-game run, without finding the net prior to Euro 96. I think it shows Alan's fantastic strength of character that he never lost faith – and that Venables didn't lose faith in him – and it paid off because he began scoring the moment the serious business started. He ended up top goalscorer of the championship with five – and made UEFA's team of the tournament.

For a striker who was supposedly selfish, there was another great partnership, forged with Teddy Sheringham for England. Teddy was a smart number 10, the perfect foil for a conventional striker like Alan. He could lead the line or drop out of the front two; he wasn't quick but he caused you constant problems. I can remember going to Old Trafford as West Ham manager, and Manchester United smashed us to pieces. Teddy came short, Andy Cole made runs in behind him – our centre-halves didn't know what to do. You had to really think about the way you controlled Teddy back then, or he would murder you, and I think England's 4–1 win over Holland in the Euro 96 tournament is the best I have seen our team play in the modern era. I know we won 5–1 in Munich under Sven-Göran Eriksson, which is an incredible result, but the Germans were having a sticky patch at the time. Getting a point in Italy to qualify for the 1998 World Cup under Glenn Hoddle was also impressive because nobody really fancied us in the Olympic Stadium in Rome. Yet, as positive as the result was, the game was still drawn. Fabio Capello's wins over Croatia were also impressive – but the Croatians aren't really a force in world football. To beat Holland 4–1, and to play them off the park as we did that year, is the stand-out result in this time for me. Venables should have been England's manager for years after that. He was doing a great job, and you've got to wonder how the Football Association managed to blow that one

– it says everything about the running of English football, really. That was a genuinely good, balanced team – and to see them slaughtering Holland shows what can be achieved with proper coaching and direction. We knew what we were about at that tournament – we had a way of playing that brought the best out of our players. It certainly got the best out of Shearer – he was outstanding that summer.

He had to be, really, because if he had flopped a lot of questions would have been asked about Fowler being overlooked. In any other era Fowler would have won a lot more caps for England, but he was unfortunate to come along at the same time as Shearer, the way that Ray Clemence was unlucky to be fighting against Gordon Banks and then Peter Shilton.

It was after the tournament that Alan signed for Newcastle, and it is a pity he couldn't replicate the revolution at Blackburn in his hometown. It was written in Alan's contract that he had to wear number nine, and I think that shows there was a romantic element to the move. He wanted to follow in the tradition of Newcastle's greats – Hughie Gallacher, Jackie Milburn and Malcolm Macdonald. Some people think it flopped, because he didn't win a trophy, but I can't agree. In his first season with Newcastle he was top goalscorer in the Premier League for the third year in succession, and players are still chasing his record of 260 goals in the Premier League. That's good enough for me.

PREMIER LEAGUE I: THE TEAM

PETER SCHMEICHEL
Manchester United

GARY NEVILLE
Manchester United

TONY ADAMS
Arsenal

SOL CAMPBELL
Arsenal

STUART PEARCE
Nottingham Forest

MATT LE TISSIER
Southampton

ROY KEANE
Manchester United

PATRICK VIEIRA
Arsenal

RYAN GIGGS
Manchester United

DENNIS BERGKAMP
Arsenal

ALAN SHEARER
Blackburn Rovers

CHAPTER SIX

. . . .

PREMIER LEAGUE II

I sometimes get asked whether, if I'd had my career in modern times as a Premier League footballer, I would still have gone into management, as I did at Bournemouth in 1983. The answer has to be no. I didn't have a bad career. I played seven seasons in the first team at West Ham United, made close to 200 appearances, played for an ambitious lower league club, and played in the United States earning reasonable money. These days that would have been enough. A lot of modern players talk about wanting to get into coaching, but when the reality presents itself, it's not the job they thought it would be. Take Frank Lampard. Now he's finished at Chelsea, would he really want to take a job at, say, Gillingham, the way I worked at Bournemouth? He might have earned three times as much in one week as the Gillingham manager would in one year. The financial imperative that players of my generation faced simply will not be a part of Frank's life.

Let's face it, if you've been earning £200,000 a week, are you going to take a job for £80,000 a year that involves going out every night watching inferior games and inferior players on the off chance of finding a gem? The chairman is driving you mad because he wants success just the same, whether it is League Two or not, and you're commuting to a rotten training ground in the middle of winter, with players who aren't in the same class as the lads you've played with all your career. Mark Lawrenson left Oxford United because he got tired of giving ordinary footballers the same training ground lesson day after day – in Mark's Liverpool team nobody needed telling twice – and believe me the standard hasn't got better. If you have been brought up around world-class players it is going to be very difficult, and I greatly admire anyone from the modern generation who fancies putting themselves through that.

It's different if a top player is going to walk in and manage Chelsea. But in years gone by that didn't happen. Kenny Dalglish's appointment as Liverpool manager came as a huge surprise. Everyone else took the same, less glamorous route – with your coaching apprenticeship starting low down the leagues as soon as you had finished playing. We all did it. Even Bobby Moore, England's World Cup-winning captain. He ended up at Southend United, while Sir Bobby Charlton got a job at Preston North End. It made no difference then that you were a great player. Kenny's path was the exception. As for the rest of us, was it for the best? I think so. Kenny was a natural and had an outstanding backroom staff at Liverpool who filled in the gaps in his education. Mere mortals have a lot to learn: the basics of working with players, finding a way to win and how to rough it away from the five-star lifestyle. For the great players now, the top players, it is going to be hard for them to just walk in and do a job, without serving that lower league apprenticeship. They are missing so much by not learning the ropes the old way because there is still so much to understand. Also, if you are successful, that grounding will make you appreciate those moments more. I can't see too many of today's successful professionals wanting to do it, if they don't need to.

I look at the make-up of the television panels these days, and there are some of our brightest minds and best players sitting in the studio, guys that could really have made a difference. But they don't need the money, so do they want the hassle? I even ask myself that question from time to time. In the end, I think all of our young British coaches will end up being ex-players from the lower divisions. If you look at League One and League Two now – even the Championship to some extent – the overwhelming majority of managers are former players who did not have particularly successful careers. There is the odd exception – Nigel Clough at Sheffield United, James Beattie at Accrington Stanley – but I don't see guys like Sol Campbell rushing to take a post in the lower divisions.

It's hard work down there. To do the job at Southend properly you've got to be out every night of the week, looking for talent, as I was at Bournemouth. You've got to become a regular at non-league grounds and get used to not seeing your family in midweek. You've got to like travel – but not of the exotic kind. As a lower league manager you spend a lot of time on motorways at midnight in the rain – you embark on a lot of fruitless missions, devote time you will never get back to watching a player on the merest whisper of recommendation. The modern millionaires won't do that. I had no retirement money when I came out of the game – I had no idea what to do with my life. The only option for me was to have a go at being a coach. If you've spent your career at Tranmere Rovers, that won't have changed. Different if you had 10 seasons at Chelsea in the Roman Abramovich years. Those lads won't get out of bed for what the manager of Exeter City gets paid.

Take Ryan Giggs. It was never even considered that he might follow the Bobby Charlton route and end up at Preston. If he was entering coaching it was going to be at Manchester United, or nothing. If Stockport County had phoned him up I think it would have been the shortest conversation of all time. Steve Bruce has been around some smaller clubs, and was he even considered for the Manchester United job? No, because a few times in his career, it hasn't worked out. Yet that would be true of Louis van Gaal, too, if he had spent his managerial life at the likes of Sheffield United, Huddersfield Town – or even Hull City. Van Gaal couldn't have done a better job with Hull than Bruce did last year. Yet has that made a ripple at Old Trafford?

So Giggs has not taken that risk – why would he test himself against a guy like Steve Evans at Rotherham United? Evans will never get a Premier League job, but his record as a lower division manager is outstanding. He gets in a lot of trouble over his comments to referees and officials, but he has won promotion with Crawley Town and Rotherham in two of the last three seasons. Would Giggs know what he was doing in a lower division, up against him? Evans knows where to look for the players, he's obviously out grafting all the time, and he knows how to put a League Two or League One team together. Giggs wouldn't have a clue by comparison. These guys are specialists in their own way, just like the lads Bobby Moore and I came up against during our brief time at non-league Oxford City. They would be part-time coaches working in the meat market by day, but they were familiar with every player in that league. What was the captain of England going to know about the Isthmian League? Brian Clough wasn't a non-league expert either, but he knew that I was during my time at Bournemouth – so when he read that I was about to sign a player from Runcorn called Ian Woan, he did a bit of research and hijacked the deal. Would Giggs, or any Premier League player, know who is the sharpest boss for that market now, who has a good track record of taking lads from outside the league? Would he know who to follow, which of the guys have a clue? Would he even know what gets a team out of League Two?

I've been around plenty of Premier League dressing-rooms and I don't hear too many players talk about watching matches lower down. I don't see John Terry going over to take in a game at Leyton Orient. The modern players are as likely to want to be media men or agents as run a team. I don't blame them. A player like Jamie Carragher, who was used to being involved in the big European nights with Liverpool, will still yearn for that taste of the Nou Camp or the San Siro. He can't get out on the pitch any more, but at least he can be around the big game, in the stadium, soaking up the atmosphere, seeing other ex-players, adversaries and friends that are in the same position now. If he's the manager of Leyton Orient he'll be playing the same night as the Champions League, and on a coach back from Milton Keynes someone will tell him Liverpool have just beaten Barcelona 2–1. He's out of it – and dealing with players who aren't a patch on the ones he used to play alongside. I still watch lower league football, but my wife Sandra is in better condition than some of the players I see there now. They're a different shape to the guys in the Champions League. Cristiano Ronaldo takes his shirt off and he looks like Mr Universe. He lives differently. If you are used to those professional standards it would be too frustrating to start in League Two and work your way through.

But how many of this generation of English footballers will be able to find a job higher up? That is the big question now. Foreign players, foreign coaches, foreign owners. It is not just the continental influence on the pitch that has come to define the second decade of the Premier League, but the influence of foreign chairmen. There is barely an elite club that is in the hands of a local businessman or diehard wealthy fan these days – Bill Kenwright is the exception at Everton, but even he would sell if he received the right offer, I'm sure – and this has changed the culture of the English game forever. Despite all our best efforts to encourage homegrown talent I can only see the opportunities for English coaches and players getting fewer – there seems to be a lack of trust in our own football people, which started at the top when the Football Association appointed Sven-Göran Eriksson as England manager, and later Fabio Capello.

At club level the foreign owners come in and, obviously, they only know big names. So it's big names they want – they are not interested in delving into the Championship to give somebody a chance. There are only two ways an upcoming young English manager gets a job in the Premier League these days: he gets promoted, like Sean Dyche at Burnley or Nigel Pearson at Leicester City, or he takes over a club that looks doomed, as Tony Pulis did at Crystal Palace, and somehow stays up. And it is not just the top clubs that have foreign owners. Even Bournemouth and Derby County are owned abroad these days.

So the whole dynamic around English football has altered. I know that during one of their rows, Roy Keane accused Sir Alex Ferguson of having changed. And I know Alex's response. 'Of course I've changed,' he told him. 'How could I have survived this long if I hadn't changed?' He's right, of course. We've all had to change to deal with the demands of modern football. It's not just that players have agents – it's that those agents sometimes have a better line of communication to the chairman than the manager. And it's not just that the players know who the chairman is – it is that they are on first-name terms and think nothing of putting in a call if they are unhappy with anything from team selection to training.

I've got a great relationship with Queens Park Rangers's owner Tony Fernandes – and I'm too old to be a creep, so believe me, I mean it – but not every manager is as lucky. The chairman talks to current players, he talks to ex-players, he talks to agents, to a ring of yes-men – and then he comes away thinking he knows more than the manager. Sometimes a foreign coach gets the benefit of the doubt, but British managers are increasingly coming under particularly harsh scrutiny. Did Steve Clarke really deserve the sack at West Bromwich Albion? Was Pepe Mel truly the better man?

Then there's Chelsea. Unless Lampard or Terry gets the job, do you really see Roman Abramovich appointing an Englishman or even a British manager? He's had enough chances in 11 years now and hasn't done so yet. Brendan Rodgers? Maybe – but would he leave Liverpool for Stamford Bridge? Either way, it's hardly a big list – just one name. I don't see anybody on the horizon, either, and that is worrying. Even if you look at the England team, who is the next manager after Roy Hodgson? Who jumps out at you? Gary Neville? He's never even managed a club. He's not done his apprenticeship, even on the coaching staff at Manchester United. Gareth Southgate is in charge at under-21 level, but I think he should go off and do well in club football before he gets that chance.

When you manage it's a different ball game. It's fine being a coach, you can be friends with everybody. Take a bit of training in the morning, have a laugh with the boys; you're not picking the team, everything's lovely. Then try it the other way – leaving them out, letting them go, even playing them in a position they don't like. Suddenly, they hate you, their wives hate you, their mates hate you. And the England job is the most demanding of all. The pressure of the country is on you, the press are on you. Fail and there's no escape.

I think it was a blow for British managers that David Moyes did not do better at Manchester United, although I always thought whoever got that job would find it hard succeeding Sir Alex Ferguson. I didn't think it would go as badly as it did, mind you, but it was still a setback for the managers here. It will be different for van Gaal. They can see the team needs rebuilding now, and are doing so with some urgency.

I was desperate to see Liverpool win the league last season, just for the fillip it would give the domestic game, with so many English players and a British coach – but increasingly the team with the biggest wage bill wins the league. That's the modern game, sadly. It used to be about having the best players, or the best manager – now it's often down to the best or richest owner. You can buy a successful team. Take over Leicester tomorrow and, if the owners have the money and want to spend it on world-class players, you are going to be up there challenging. Roberto Mancini, Manuel Pellegrini, Yaya Touré, Sergio Agüero – they've all played a part. But the bottom line is that Manchester City have come from where they were because of Sheikh Mansour.

Keep throwing the money at it and, eventually, you'll be all right. Yet will this new breed of owner give English coaches a chance? No, I don't think they will. Here's my final team of the decade.

PETR CECH
(CHELSEA)

Not long ago I had a call from my old friend Harry Gregg, the great Manchester United goalkeeper of the Busby Babes era and beyond. I always look forward to speaking to Harry; he talks so much sense about the game. We were just chatting away and the subject of goalkeepers came up. 'Harry,' he said, 'where have they all gone? Where have the British keepers gone? What's happened?' And he's right – there is such a shortage at the top level these days, particularly in England. Joe Hart has come through, but compared to the days when we had Peter Shilton and Ray Clemence fighting it out with Joe Corrigan and Phil Parkes, what has gone wrong? I like Hart, but I think he would have a serious challenge on his hands if any of those lads were about today. Yet, beneath him, there is nothing. My goalkeeper at Queens Park Rangers, Rob Green, was as good as any of the lads that went to the World Cup to understudy Hart, and I think it is a real pity that England managers seem to ignore the Championship division completely these days. It means that any player with international ambitions has to leave if his club is relegated from the Premier League. That is another of the big changes in the game. If you look at the players in the early chapters of the book, even some of the greatest among them spent time outside the top division. Nowadays that would be career suicide. You play in the top league, and for a top club, or you are nowhere. Even a career outside the Champions League is not enough for a lot of them.

Harry Gregg was right, though. There is a shortage of great goalkeepers across the board. I don't want to damn Petr Cech with faint praise here, because he has had a marvellous career with Chelsea and has definitely been the pick of the bunch in the modern Premier League era, but I can't help viewing him as the best of a pretty ordinary lot. Is he better than Gordon Banks? No. Pat Jennings? No. Peter Shilton? No. Peter Schmeichel? No. Is he better than some of the second best goalkeepers from previous decades like Ray Clemence or David Seaman? No. If I'm honest I haven't always been Cech's biggest fan. I can think of great saves he has made – and he is a strong, imposing presence in the penalty area – but there have also been times when I've been disappointed in him and I can see why Chelsea have been so anxious to develop the young Belgian goalkeeper Thibaut Courtois.

Maybe in a few years' time we will look back on Hart's career and place him on a par with some of England's greats from previous campaigns, but he is not there now. I thought Manuel Pellegrini handled him very well when he left him out of Manchester City's team for a while last season. A degree of over-confidence had crept into his game, and that short spell on the bench seemed to bring him down to earth.

I just don't think you see as many great goalkeepers as you used to. Some of the best ones from previous years were behind ordinary defences, too, whereas Cech has benefited from having some outstanding protection at Chelsea. I think he did well to recover from the serious head injury he sustained against

Reading in 2006 – he was brave in the way he came rushing out that day, and I haven't noticed any change in him after he recovered. Then again, Harry Gregg was pulling people out of a plane that was about to blow up in Munich, so I suppose with goalkeepers a casual disregard for danger goes with the territory.

It is amazing that goalkeeper has become a problem position, really, because there has never been more coaching and instruction available for them than there is now. Every team has at least one specialist goalkeeper coach, and usually more, yet when you think back to the heyday of Banks and Shilton there was no such thing. Goalkeepers arrived in the morning and went off and practised kicking balls at one another down the field. Then the manager would call them over to go in goal while the rest of us worked on our shooting – and that was it. They didn't get separate coaching. They didn't go off with a specialist for detailed work. Goalkeeping coaches are a new thing. Banks would have done no more than face daily shooting drills – yet Hart will get all the training in the world. So where have the English goalkeepers gone? I don't understand it.

I suppose the influence of foreign goalkeepers will have played a part. A young English midfield player isn't as vulnerable to being shut out of the team because he has a variety of options. There might be a foreign player blocking his way on the right, but he could be used on the left or in central midfield. The same for all outfielders, really. But if Arsenal have a foreign goalkeeper, there is no way through. It is a unique position and if that place is filled there is just nowhere to go. I think it will become an increasing problem for the England manager in the future. An injury to Hart, and then what? There isn't much out there.

PABLO ZABALETA
(MANCHESTER CITY)

Zabaleta came in from Espanyol in 2008 and when I first saw him I wasn't sure. He looked full of energy but I was dubious about his discipline. He seemed like one of those players who is all over the place and very committed, but lacks direction and focus. I've changed my mind since, obviously. He's a real leader, another of the type you can mark down for 7 out of 10 as a minimum, even before the game starts. He's up and down, he's committed, and you never really see him get slaughtered by any winger. I know Micah Richards has had a lot of injuries recently, but when he first came into the game he was tipped for big things – he was in Steve McClaren's England team after just 28 appearances, for instance, and was the youngest defender to play for England, beating Rio Ferdinand's record – so to keep him out of the Manchester City team, as Zabaleta has done, is a big achievement. There is no longer even a debate about the best right-back at the club, and that is testament to Zabaleta's consistency and determination.

Speaking as a manager, he just looks the proper sort. He's tenacious and he knows his job. I think right-back has been a difficult position for England since Gary Neville came to the end of his career and, much as I like Glen Johnson, I think Zabaleta would get into our team right now. Glen is outstanding going forward, but so is Zabaleta. His crossing, in particular, is very accurate and I think he has more to his defensive game than Glen. He reminds me a little of Stuart Pearce, one of those guys that runs backwards almost as quickly as he runs forward. He is capable of getting into great attacking positions, but always seems to be able to recover with enough time not to get caught out. He's quite an English style of right-back really – he's tough and aggressive, not a nutter, but he can put it about. All of our best full-backs would fit that description.

I know he has captained Manchester City on occasions, and I think the fall-out they had with Carlos Tevez would have been a big proving ground for him. The players of one nationality tend to stick together at clubs and, if you lose one, the chances are his mates will follow. I imagine City might have expected the issues with Tevez and Roberto Mancini to spread to the other Argentinians within the club, but Zabaleta didn't get dragged into it, and as a result it didn't then influence Sergio Agüero. That was the leader in him coming through; he kept his head down and carried on doing his job. I bet there was a fair amount of pressure to take sides with Tevez but it shows you how professional he is that he didn't let the club down. He's 29 now, and I think it was a good move when City went for Bacary Sagna in the summer to take some of the strain off him. Even so, he looks as if he has got a few years left in him yet. He is the type of player that survives managerial upheaval, too – because we all want a Pablo Zabaleta in our team.

JOHN TERRY
(CHELSEA)

The modern Tony Adams – I can't pay him a higher compliment than that. John Terry embodies the same qualities I saw in Tony Adams all those years ago. He has the same organisational skills, he's a leader on the pitch and a player who would run through a brick wall. Simply a fantastic centre-half. After Queens Park

Rangers were promoted last season, I remember saying that if we could take Terry from Chelsea I would feel very confident, just with that one signing alone, that we would stay up. He is that influential. He's one of those players that change a club. He gets people at it, he's a talker, he takes charge of the dressing-room. I know that off the pitch he has had his problems, like Tony – but I think managers are prepared to overlook that because he is a real voice within the team. I could imagine him in a Rangers shirt heading balls out of our box and making everybody else defend properly. No one would shirk with John around.

You don't get talkers these days, you don't get organisers. I don't know why, but it is so hard to find a player that is prepared to speak his mind, that uses his mouth the way great leaders from past generations did. I'm thinking of some of the characters I've written about in this book – Bobby Collins, Danny Blanchflower, Dave Mackay and Bobby Murdoch. Those players, those days, are gone. You won't find them like that any more; they're not coming through in the same way. Maybe it is the coaching. A friend of mine who rides horses in event meetings said that accidents are on the increase because the animals are now so highly trained they respond completely to rider instruction and no longer trust their own instincts. In times past, if a horse was approaching a fence at the wrong angle because the rider had made a misjudgement, it would simply stop and refuse. It knew it couldn't make the jump, so it didn't jump. Now, the horses have been so highly trained they override their natural common sense, jump, fall and everyone gets hurt. Maybe it is the same with footballers. They get told what to do, so they don't think for themselves – and now they don't know how to tell others, either. Everyone is waiting to receive information; they all exist in their own little worlds. They don't talk to each other off the pitch or on the coach. Everyone's sits there with headphones, looking at an iPad or playing a computer game. Is it any wonder modern players lack communication skills?

So Terry is a throw-back in the way he bosses a team. I've got a lot of time for John, even though I know his career has not been without controversy. I just think we only hear one side of a story sometimes. I saw a documentary on television earlier this year in which John spent time with this little kid who was seriously ill, and he looked a genuine guy to me. People will say he was acting up for the cameras, but looking at the way he was affected by this poor boy's problems, I don't agree. He gave up his time, came in before the game, after the game – he really looked like he cared. I already liked him as a player, but when I saw that he went up in my estimation.

To see what an influence he can be you only have to look at what he did for Gary Cahill at Chelsea. His partner became an international defender just by being around John. Nothing else changed in Gary's approach other than he was suddenly alongside Terry. He taught him the game. Some people may think John is a dubious role model, but I would have no hesitation in saying to any of the young academy defenders at QPR: go and watch Chelsea tonight, go and watch Terry, study him all game. If they pay attention they will learn more in that 90 minutes than in a month of training sessions. It's still the best way – watch Terry, see what he does, how he organises people, how he pulls them in, keeps it tight. To play alongside him must have been a fantastic education for Cahill, and I think he's even come out of himself more now; you can see that he talks more. He's a different defender because of Terry.

Maybe he won't ever be as influential as John, but that vocal confidence is either in you or it isn't. I could never coach a player to be a talker. If someone isn't happy communicating, no amount of encouragement from me will change that. John is a natural, like Tony Adams. Standing with Frank Lampard senior watching the teenage Tony Adams run a youth team game like no kid we had ever seen is a memory that will stay with me for all time. It was so unusual, almost unreal. I know his dad ran his boys' team in Dagenham, but even so. He might have been able to tell his son how to defend, but he couldn't have taught him to be such a forceful personality. That comes from within.

I also think John is a much better passer than he is given credit for. Adams only proved himself in this area once he was with England and Terry Venables encouraged him to play. George Graham, at Arsenal, was never too keen on the centre-half bringing the ball out from the back, but it was an integral part of Venables's plan at the 1996 European Championship; he encouraged Tony and it worked. I'm sure he found it quite liberating after years of being told to play in a more conservative style. John on the other hand was always good with the ball, and showed it. Jamie Carragher said he thought John was actually a better passer than Rio Ferdinand.

Rio was great with the ball at his feet, running with it, working it out of defence, while John was a fantastic long passer. He's a very clean striker of the ball.

It is so important to have good distribution from the back. Not long ago my son Jamie was with Roberto Martínez, the Everton manager, and he was talking about his time at Wigan Athletic. He told Jamie about Emmerson Boyce, who Martínez inherited when he went there in 2009. We played Wigan in the play-off final and Boyce is a good passer now, but Martínez said when he first met him, he just didn't want the ball. He wouldn't accept it or show for it because successive managers hadn't trusted him in possession and had told him just to kick it. They even told his team-mates not to pass to him. Roberto said he spent hours with him every day, working on getting the ball, passing the ball, becoming comfortable on the ball. He'll never be Franz Beckenbauer, or even John Terry, but it just shows how you can improve people, given time. It happens too often in the English game that the centre-half is just there to boot the ball up the pitch. It makes me even more of a John Terry fan. If Chelsea ever lose faith in John, I'd take him like a shot.

RIO FERDINAND
(MANCHESTER UNITED)

A tough one this, choosing between two great centre-halves at Manchester United. I loved Nemanja Vidić – he was just such a great competitor. I don't think it was United's decision to let him go to Inter Milan at the end of last season and, although he was approaching the end of his career, I still think he will be a big loss. He was the backbone of the team, and I knew he would be a player the first time I set eyes on him alongside Dejan Stefanović. I went to watch Serbia play to have a look at Stefanović when I was Portsmouth manager – Vidić caught my eye that night, too, but he was very young and we were looking for someone with more experience, and cheaper. He went to Spartak Moscow soon after that and then on to Manchester United, and he was everything you wanted in a centre-half – strong, good in the air and a real tough character.

Yet there is no way I can leave Rio Ferdinand out of this team because I tipped him at 16 to be the greatest centre-half in Europe and I think, for a time, that is exactly what he was. Vidi'c was a tank, but Rio was a Rolls-Royce. You could see it from day one. He had pace, absolutely electric pace, and was so comfortable on the ball. He could have played in midfield, without a doubt. In fact, I used him there against Wimbledon one night when he was about 18 and he ran Vinnie Jones ragged. He was drifting by him, drifting by all of them actually, running half the length of the pitch with the ball, laying it off. He had that natural, long-legged running stride, and once he hit it he was gone.

I think it is one of the consistent failures in our game that we haven't realised the potential in some of the players we have at centre-half. We tend to go for the hero types, the ones who head it clear and hoof it out, who just defend and nothing more. Yet the game has changed now. Everything starts from the back. The full-backs push on and centre-halves split and those players must be able to play because you can't get going if your centre-halves can't pass. If you see a goalkeeper booting it downfield all game these days it means only one thing: the centre-halves can't play. All of Rio's teams could build from the back because he was such a smooth footballer. He used to roll it into Paul Scholes in midfield and away Manchester United would go. Rio was fantastic, and United's best times of late always seemed to coincide with his good spells. I never doubted for one second that he would go on to become a top player and achieve so much in the game. From the day he walked into West Ham we knew he was special. Nothing he has done since has surprised me.

Now it's come full circle and I'm lucky enough to have Rio at QPR showing he's a class act, with that touch and that leading of the game, still there after all these years.

ASHLEY COLE
(CHELSEA)

I think there have been a few times when English football could claim to have the best left-back in the world – and Ashley Cole is the most recent player to hold that unofficial title. Fantastic energy, fantastic ability, just up and down, run after run after run after run. Even the greatest in the game, like Cristiano Ronaldo, couldn't get the better of him. I was amazed when Chelsea let him go last summer. What a free transfer he was: Manchester United, Real Madrid, Barcelona, they should all have been in for him. As far as his non-selection for England at the World Cup in Brazil goes, that was less of a surprise. I thought Leighton Baines had come to the fore, certainly in Roy Hodgson's mind, and he also had the opportunity to take Luke Shaw, who is young but is going to be a top player. I could see his reasoning on that, more than I could understand Chelsea's decision.

Ashley is a Stepney boy, like me, but he didn't play for the famous local club, Senrab, like John Terry and Ledley King. He was with Puma, their big rivals, who also played on Wanstead Flats. He was a striker and came to Arsenal's attention because he scored 100 goals in one season. When I saw him he was in the Arsenal youth team playing wide left midfield in a cup final against West Ham; our lads won but he certainly looked a player. He had the low centre of gravity that a lot of naturally quick players have and he worked really hard. I know he has had a playboy image at times in his career, but you don't have Ashley's stamina and physique without really putting it in on the training pitch. Whatever distractions he might have had, it never really affected his performance. He was always consistent, always a match for the best players. His attacking energy was perhaps the best of any player I have seen. I would imagine his weekly Prozone statistics would have been incredible in terms of the ground he covered. All of the greatest full-backs are players who want to run, but I think Ashley took it to a new level. He was relentless. Towards the end of the game you are still looking at your full-backs to make those runs, particularly if you are chasing the game, but by then even the best ones are sometimes too knackered. They don't want to attack because that means chasing back twice as hard if the move breaks down. Yet Ashley would go, time and again. He was a machine. After Chelsea's first game with Atlético Madrid in the Champions League last season, the statistics showed that Chelsea's two most forward players over the 90 minutes were the full-backs, Cole and César Azpilicueta, who played on the right. Azpilicueta is 24; Cole is 33. I think it shows he still has his appetite for the game – and his fitness.

I've always said football has two disciplinary codes – one for players who can play, and another for the rest. Ashley is proof of that. The episode with the air rifle at Chelsea in 2011 – when he brought the gun to the training ground and accidentally shot a 21-year-old student, there for work experience – is evidence of that. I imagine a lot of people would have been sacked by their employers for that – and a lot of footballers, too. Yet Chelsea let it ride, with an apology and a disciplinary hearing. If that was a player they wanted out he would have been gone the next morning. But Ashley survived. That's when you know they rate you.

Is Cole the best left-back England have had? I'd say yes, though it's difficult. Kenny Sansom and Stuart Pearce would both have claims, and for a while I thought Stuart was right up there, even with Paolo Maldini. Yet Cole at his peak was close to faultless – he was cleverer than Stuart on the ball, as powerful and strong as Sansom, and he had the attacking instincts of a left-winger. He was the top man, for me.

CRISTIANO RONALDO (MANCHESTER UNITED)

Sandra and I were at the Hotel Pitrizza in Sardinia last year and Cristiano Ronaldo was there with his family. I made sure not to sit too near to him on the beach, obviously, but what a lovely man. He must have had 20 of them out there with him, including his girlfriend, who looked like Miss World, and his little mum, a widow, who was always in black from head to toe. They looked typical working-class Portuguese, but every day they made their way back from the most exclusive shops in the town of Porto Cervo absolutely laden with gear. They had so many bags hanging off them they could hardly walk – Gucci, Prada, the best designer labels in the world – and he was paying for it all, obviously. They stayed two weeks in one of Europe's finest hotels and he looked after everything. A lot of footballers treat their families like that. It's a side that people don't see, and he just looked really happy to be back with them all again. He had quite a few little cousins or nephews out there and you could spot them a mile off because they were tiny Cristiano clones. Same hair, same cheeky grin – it was really nice to see. Each day he would stop and have a chat with us. He seemed really down to earth, for all his wealth, success and fame.

In the Messi versus Ronaldo debate I've always just about been in Lionel Messi's camp – until the last year. Not because I met Ronaldo and he was a genuine bloke, but because he has stepped up to a new level in that time, and I very much supported the vote that won him the prize as the World Footballer of the Year. I like the way Messi and Ronaldo are constantly inspiring each other, driving one another on.

Jamie Carragher wrote an article in which he made a great point, saying it helps that they genuinely don't seem to like one another. That adds to the rivalry, in the way it did for Alain Prost and Ayrton Senna, or even Don Revie and Brian Clough. If Messi and Ronaldo were great mates it wouldn't have that edge – and what makes their duel so compelling is that they seem genuinely concerned about out-doing one another. If Messi scores two goals on Saturday, Ronaldo wants to get three on Sunday – and don't tell me Ronaldo wasn't inspired by the desire to break Messi's record when he went in search of the greatest number of Champions League goals scored in one season. He did it, too. I just hope that at the end of their careers they realise that they were both fantastic for each other and make up.

An extraordinary thing about Ronaldo is that he has almost invented a new way of kicking a football. I know there are innovations in sport all the time, but to find a fresh way of doing something so utterly basic is, to me, quite astonishing. The way he makes the ball dip and then rise when he hits a free-kick has got players trying to imitate it in training like the old Rivelino stepover. After Ronaldo did it, Gareth Bale worked and worked until he could do it, too – but Ronaldo was the first. I suppose it was like watching Jonny Wilkinson take those penalty kicks and conversions in rugby union for the first time. One minute, he had a unique style and then suddenly everyone was trying to copy him.

Messi's trademark is that lovely little dink over the goalkeeper – the way, when he is through one on one, he just lifts it up and over as the goalkeeper goes to ground. He reminds me of the best kid in the school playground. The other boys are trying to kick lumps out of him, but they can't get near him because he's 10 times better. I saw a game when I thought Atlético Madrid were going to kill him, but he kept skipping around them, time and again. I also love the way he is prepared to stop in the middle of a game, and think about what he is going to do next. Then it is always an intelligent move, a dart into a gap, an angle that nobody has considered. He makes space just by standing still. He's not running in there where all the bodies are, he comes out of the crowd and works out a better route. Very few are brave enough to do that, and fewer still have the intelligence to make it work. They think if they stop they will just lose momentum – yet Messi never does. We are privileged to see this duel, really, because I cannot recall a time in the game when two players of such wonderful ability went head to head like this. Pelé and Diego Maradona were not contemporaries, and the peak years of Johann Cruyff bridged the gap between the two of them. Yet when you think Ronaldo scored 17 goals in the 2012–13 Champions League campaign to break Messi's joint record of 14 set in 2011–12, it shows you what a magnificent contest this is.

Ronaldo is an amazing footballer. He can do the lot – his dribbling is sensational, his shots are unstoppable and he heads the ball with the bravery and power of an old-fashioned centre-half up for a corner. He scores a quite ridiculous amount of goals, particularly when one considers that those 17 in the Champions League haven't been scored in routs against the champions of Luxembourg, as they were in the old days. He has an incredible physique for such a nimble player. He's 6 ft 1 in and, as I've said, when he takes his shirt off he looks like Mr Universe.

He has scored so many great goals but one of his headers stands out, the first goal in a Champions League tie for Manchester United against Roma. The cross comes in from Paul Scholes and Ronaldo isn't even in the picture when the ball leaves Scholes's boot – he arrives at full speed, off a quite astonishing spring and the ball goes in like a rocket from a good 14 yards out. In mid-air Ronaldo gets clipped by a defender and goes down heavily, but his injury could have been far worse. If one of the Roma players had also gone in with his head he could have got his teeth knocked out or his face smashed in, but he had no thought for that – only for the goal. He has got a lot more substance to his game than people think.

When Ronaldo first came to England, some people were saying he was a show pony, all tricks and flicks, and he would never make it in our game. I thought they were mad. He wasn't dancing around the ball. He was using incredible skill to move past people in a way we didn't often see in England. You knew that sooner or later those shots were going to start crashing in the top corner and he was going to be unstoppable. And that is exactly what happened. I think Manchester United's 3–0 win over Millwall in the 2004 FA Cup final changed a lot of perceptions of him because he was absolutely mesmerising that day – but I always thought he was the real deal.

STEVEN GERRARD
(LIVERPOOL)

Roy of the Rovers. It's surprising to me how often people have used this tag as a criticism of Steven Gerrard and his all-action playing style. He wants to be everywhere … he deserts his position … he can't play in the middle because he'll leave a gap. What nonsense. Roy Race was a comic book hero and Steven Gerrard is a real-life one. He's been the driving force behind Liverpool for more than a decade now and I think all true football fans were disappointed when last season he could not realise his dream of leading them to a first title of the Premier League era.

I saw him when he first broke into the Liverpool team in 1998 and I had no doubt then that we were seeing the beginning of a truly great player. Why? Well, he played like Roy of the Rovers! It was as if he was taking the game on, one against 11. He covered every blade of grass, he drove the team on despite being the youngest there, he made great passes, he wasn't scared to shoot – he looked a real player. You could see he was going to end up their captain. When I was Portsmouth manager we tried to man mark him with a player called Richard Hughes. Richard was a big, strong lad – a very dogged type who had done that kind of job for us before. He couldn't get near him. Gerrard just ran all over him, and us, and by the time he was taken off with 16 minutes to go they were winning 3–0. It was the full repertoire – box to box, shooting from 30 yards, he did everything bar score. Now he has changed his role and is playing as more of a holding midfielder, but at his peak he could play anywhere. I've seen him play right-back in an emergency, and I know England managers who have considered using him as a right wing-back because he is so versatile.

To be fair, my son Jamie was even quicker on to Steven's quality than I was. I can remember him calling me after Liverpool training one day to say that they brought a 16-year-old over to play with the first team and he was absolutely outstanding. When Jamie struggled with injury in the 1998–9 season it was Steven who took his place in the team. He just got on with it, as he always does. I know Steven says that, looking back, he was very nervous in his earliest games but he has always been hyper-critical of his own game. If he was below par in those days it was only by his own, impossibly high, standards. I've always found Steven very honest and knowledgeable about football. I think it is one of the positives about the top players of his generation that they are all good lads, and proper football people. If I wanted an opinion about a player at Liverpool I knew I could pick up the phone to Steven or Jamie Carragher, ask a straight question and get a straight answer. They wouldn't put you wrong. Even a player they liked as a lad, if they thought he was struggling with injury or his heart wasn't in it any more, they would tell the truth.

So, Roy of the Rovers? Even if he was, what is wrong with that? He is a more disciplined presence now because he has no choice, but in the days when he could be in his own box one moment and over by the opposition corner flag the next, why not? I've heard that managers like Rafael Benítez thought he lacked discipline, but Benítez also won two major trophies at Liverpool – the 2005 Champions League and the 2006 FA Cup – that he wouldn't have got anywhere near without Steven, so I'm pretty sure he did more good than harm. I think that if he was one of the two in midfield, it was up to the coach to make sure a dedicated holding midfielder covered for him. I would never have tried to take that energy away from Gerrard because the goals he scored and the games he dominated poured that same energy back into the team.

So no place in my team for Frank Lampard. I know – I'm not going to win any uncle of the year awards, am I? I picked Frank at West Ham and was accused of nepotism every week, so at least here I've avoided that charge, but the fact is my faith in Frank has been borne out 100 per cent. Frank has had the fantastic career I predicted many years ago and, even now, I don't think people realise the lengths he went to in order to become a professional footballer. He remains the most dedicated professional I have ever come across, overcoming weaknesses in his game and even a period during his teenage years when he became so obsessed with getting his weight down that his late mum, Pat, feared he had become anorexic. He was like a bag of bones and we had to get help for him. Luckily he pulled through and became one of the greatest players in this modern Premier League era. I think Frank has the edge on Steven for his goals, but Steve is a better all-round player – by a whisker. A better passer, perhaps; defensively so strong and aggressive. I wish I had room for them both – but there is no way I am leaving this next lad out.

PAUL SCHOLES
(MANCHESTER UNITED)

You'd try to tie Paul Scholes down when you played against Manchester United but it was impossible. You just couldn't balance your team up to get anywhere near him. I tried having someone sit on him, but he always found a way to get space. As for his passing, he had eyes in the back of his head, and his instinct for goal was exceptional. One of the highlights for me was the two he scored for England in Scotland in the 1999 European Championship play-off – goals that show his stunning reading of the game and his ability to define matches, even with his head. The first goal is a cross from Sol Campbell that Scholes meets on the run, jumping up and taking it on his chest to go past Colin Hendry and tuck it past Neil Sullivan. The next is a header from a David Beckham free-kick, ghosting in between taller men the way Martin Peters once did. He is only about 5 ft 7 in, but he took those goals like a man a head taller.

He saw everything on the football field – where his team-mates were, where you were as you tried to stop him. That's why Manchester United did all their best work through him. He'd come deep, pick it up, run off the back of you, get in the box. He was a master, and yet at the same time a completely unassuming guy. Speak to Brazilians about England's players of the last 20 years, and Scholes is the one they rave about. They saw him as one of their own, and Socrates said he would have got into any Brazilian team. The boy with the red hair and the red shirt, he called him. I saw an interview with Xavi in which he too said Scholes was his favourite player. 'He was my role model,' he said, 'the best central midfielder I've seen in the last fifteen or twenty years. He's spectacular, he has it all: the last pass, the goals, he's strong, he doesn't lose the ball, he has vision. If he'd been Spanish he might have been rated more highly. Players love him, too.' Pep Guardiola said Scholes was the best midfielder of his generation, and Thierry Henry said he was the Premier League's finest player. That's some line-up of fans.

He won plenty with Manchester United, but can you imagine him in Xavi's Barcelona side? Sir Alex Ferguson said he was the one player that he never got an offer for – because it was well known all over Europe that he would not consider leaving Old Trafford. Even so, we can dream. Scholes was playing tiki-taka football when nobody in England knew what it was. He was another of those players, like Denis Law or Bobby Moore, who at the age of 15 probably looked as if he wouldn't make it. Too small, you would think – can't run, dumpy little ginger nut – but then the ball would come to him and he would dazzle you.

Out of all that great Manchester United team I'd put Scholes right at the top. Roy Keane would be the driving force, and Ryan Giggs had the greatest career, but Scholes was the best footballer, for me. He played in the middle, and that's where you've really got to know your stuff to survive in the modern game. When the ball arrived, he knew everything, he already had the information and he never gave it away. If he had 90 touches in a game there would be 89 successful passes – and one diabolical foul, of course. I never bought that one, the idea that Paul Scholes couldn't tackle. Oh, really? So he can play the greatest passes you'll see, score the most beautiful goals, but a skill as basic as tackling eludes him? Do me a favour. He knew exactly what he was doing with every one of those fouls. He knew when to break the game up and when to get an opponent back, too. And he didn't care what people thought, either – which seems to be his attitude when it comes to giving his opinion now he has retired from the game.

I was out with Paddy Power just before the World Cup – yes, he does exist, his father David was one of the co-founders of the business – and he said, 'Harry, you'll never guess who we've signed up as a columnist. It's so left-field. It's a guy that nobody has ever heard speak.' I guessed straight away: Paul Scholes. If no one has heard him talk, people will be interested in what he has to say – that was their logic, and they were proved right. Paul was an excellent World Cup columnist – outspoken, forthright in his opinions about England and invariably right. He called it just as he used to play it – he saw all the angles, eyes in the back of his head.

GARETH BALE
(TOTTENHAM HOTSPUR)

I'm so pleased with the way Gareth's first season in Madrid has gone. I'll admit: I was worried for him. I thought he might shrink into the shadows a bit around a big personality like Cristiano Ronaldo, but those two goals – against Barcelona in the Copa del Rey and Atlético Madrid in the Champions League final – have made him. They've proved what a fantastic talent he is, and now that the Real Madrid public believes in him, he could go on to be an all-time great, even at a club of that size. He's like Ronaldo mark II – he's a supreme physical specimen, he can dribble, he can shoot, he takes great dead balls and, as they now know, he scores headers, too. Fantastic stamina – he can run all day. Tottenham Hotspur thought they had done good business, but losing a talent like that was always going to take a toll.

The moment I saw it I knew the goal against Barcelona would be the making of him. It was just a wonderful moment of athleticism. The Barcelona defender, Marc Bartra, tries to knock him off the pitch but he just runs around him – and from there his pace over 80 yards is electric. His ability to run long distances without slowing reminds me of Ronaldo. Some wingers drop off as they get near the penalty area, but Gareth almost seemed to get stronger. The power is so impressive, but then the finish is so subtle. He may end up the best winger in the world – but Gareth could have stayed at left-back and been the best at that, too. Wherever he had played he was destined for greatness. There is one particular game I remember, against Benfica in a pre-season friendly in 2010, that has to rank among the best individual performances I've seen. He made a goal for Peter Crouch, which was disallowed, and in the end he scored the only goal of the game – but what I most clearly recall is the number of forward runs he made from left-back. The length of the field, it seemed, something like 40 times. It was one of the games that persuaded me to move him to left wing.

Yet Gareth could play anywhere in forward midfield. I switched him to the right and I played him through the middle. The crowd didn't like it. 'Gareth Bale, he plays on the left,' they used to sing because all they wanted him to do was go flying up that wing, whereas I could see the advantages of him on the right coming inside and having a shot, or playing off the striker as he did against Norwich City one night. He ran amok. Plays on the left? He plays where he wants to play – that's how it should be. That's what the great ones do: Messi, Ronaldo, Suárez, Bale – let them have their freedom.

I'm so happy that he looks to be enjoying his football in Spain. Having an English coach at Real, Paul Clements, will definitely have helped, and Carlo Ancelotti has always struck me as a lovely guy. I think Paul said he knew Gareth was good but he didn't realise how good, and I think a lot of people who haven't worked with Gareth won't have appreciated that yet either. They will see him as a flying machine, but he's so much more. He wins game after game for you, and I don't think even Tottenham were fully aware of that when they took Real Madrid's money. Buying half a team for £100 million having sold one player sounds a good deal, but you can't replace him as a match-winner. Looking at Madrid in the Champions League final, there were two ex-Tottenham men, Bale and Luka Modrić, who were worth all of Tottenham's subsequent signings put together. Tottenham have nobody capable of influencing the game like that pair.

The next two years could be very big for Gareth. The increased numbers of qualifiers for the 2016 European Championships in France have given Wales a better chance of getting there, and although they have a tough group with Belgium and Bosnia-Herzegovina in there, with even the third-placed team going into a play-off they will never get a better chance. Wales have got a few decent players at the moment – Aaron Ramsey of Arsenal, Ashley Williams, his former team-mate Neil Taylor at Swansea City, and I know Crystal Palace think very highly of their young midfield player Jonathan Williams, too. It would be another huge achievement if Gareth could inspire those lads to their first major tournament since 1958.

THIERRY HENRY
(ARSENAL)

The first time I saw Thierry Henry he was playing on the left wing for France's under-21 team against Norway. I was on a scouting mission to look at John Carew, who had been recommended to me, and while Henry looked as if he had plenty of skill, it wasn't immediately obvious that he was going to become one of the Premier League's great goalscorers. Norway won and it was Carew who looked the best bet, creating havoc in the French defence. He went on to have a good career with, among others, Valencia and Roma – but he couldn't dream of scoring the exquisite goals that Henry conjured up. It shows how even the greatest players mature with age.

What a signing Henry was for Arsenal. On his day, he was one of the few strikers that were simply unplayable. He could rip you to pieces and there really was nothing you could do. He was that modern phenomenon – the highly skilful player who was also a good size and a physical handful. Didier Drogba is an even greater example of that. He had a delightful touch, but before using it would give you an absolute battering. Henry wasn't quite as combative as Drogba – but he still presented a physical challenge to any opponent. On their best days, the Arsenal of Henry and Dennis Bergkamp asked more questions of you than any other team in recent memory. Bergkamp dropping in, Henry going beyond and making runs – what hope did defenders have, apart from prayer? We had a good back line at Portsmouth in particular but, even so, it was very difficult. What do you do? If you drop off, Henry picks it up deep, turns and runs at you. If you get tight, he'll turn and run in behind you – and he had astonishing pace. He found these pockets of space all over the pitch and the moment your move broke down Arsenal counter-attacked at demon speed.

What makes Henry and Bergkamp's success all the more surprising is that, basically, these two players destroying Premier League defences were both on the rebound from failed careers in Italy. Bergkamp couldn't cut it at Inter Milan and Henry was a flop at Juventus, where he was used mostly wide. They were bold signings by Arsenal, really, because they could easily have come here low on confidence and disappeared again. Bergkamp did have a slow start, initially; but Henry, definitely, fitted in straight away. Wherever he has been since, Arsenal has always felt most like his home to me. The crowd fell in love with him instantly, and as he lifted the club his confidence grew. They just fitted – and he fitted with Bergkamp, too. They were magnificent together. Henry was so smooth, I sometimes used to go to Highbury just to see him – and managers don't tend to get involved like that. If I didn't have scouting on and I was near London, I'd watch him almost like an Arsenal fan again, for the sheer fun of it. If Arsenal were in trouble there was sometimes a moment when you could see him switch on – as if he had decided, 'Right, I've got to do something about this.' And then he'd go out and win the game on his own.

Wayne Rooney? It was a tough call leaving him out – but I think Henry was consistently a better player. There were never any real problems with Thierry, whereas Wayne has been high maintenance at times and that has led to him losing his way and his form occasionally. For me, Henry has the edge.

LUIS SUÁREZ
(LIVERPOOL)

Despite all that has happened in his career since, one of the biggest regrets of my life in management is not taking Luis Suárez to Tottenham Hotspur when we had the chance. We were looking for a striker and he was one of the players recommended to us. I asked around and Ruud Gullit, in particular, fancied him for his life. 'You've got to take him, Harry,' he said. 'He's fantastic.' Yet all of our scouts' reports said that at Ajax he played wide off a striker, whereas we were looking for a proper front man. We had lots of support players – Gareth Bale, Aaron Lennon, Rafael van der Vaart – but no forward target. Every time another report came in saying Suárez didn't play through the middle I became less certain. I think the last man to go and see him was Tim Sherwood. The reports were all positive but Tim, like everyone else, wasn't convinced that he could operate in a defined central role. There were doubts about his character, too, and even in Holland not everybody was convinced he was worth taking a chance on for the money, which was £15 million. And then, just when I was on the verge of taking the plunge, the price went up. Ajax must have had Liverpool in at that point and knew they had a market. In the end he was sold for £22.8 million. We wouldn't have paid that.

It didn't take long for me to realise what I had missed. Can he play through the middle? Absolutely. He can play anywhere he likes – and he never stops. He's a perpetual motion machine in the style of that other Liverpool great, Ian Rush. I put it down to that will to win that the greatest players have. He works and works because he so hates losing. He's a pest, a defender's nightmare. Never gives you a minute's peace. He's got all the ability in the world. When he has the ball he runs at you, and when he gets near to an opponent, the tricks start. He'll nutmeg you, or play it off your legs, or hands. He improvises all the time like the great street footballers, showing the opponent the ball and then nipping it past him. He is another like Paolo Di Canio: when he is in the team you have always got a chance because he can suddenly conjure a goal from thin air.

His work-rate is such an important quality because, when the best player in the team is putting himself about like that, the rest of them cannot stop either. Team-mates take their lead from him and you can't stand and watch while the best player in the team runs around like a lunatic. Last season he inspired Daniel Sturridge doing the same, putting a real shift in, leading by example. Steven Gerrard is similar in that he sets an example to the rest of the team. Suárez and Gerrard were arguably Liverpool's two best players in that season – and the hardest working, too. You can tell there was a bond between the pair, and I'm told Suárez was a very popular guy in the dressing-room. They could see that he always wanted the best for the team and it's not just about him.

He reminded me a little of Wayne Rooney, too. The way he runs, it looks as if he just loves playing football – and Rooney also has that quality. Rooney reminds me of the first kid out into the playground at lunchtime – the one who couldn't wait to get through the classroom door and start playing. Suárez is the same. Brendan Rodgers, the Liverpool manager, says that's the way he trained like that every day, and I'd say until this last outrage he was not far off being considered for World Footballer of the Year. Cristiano Ronaldo was the top man last season, obviously – it was a pity he was injured in the World Cup – but with Suárez in the Champions League this season, it was his crown to win. If he scored at the rate he did in the Premier League, anything was possible. Now he has ruined that chance.

I always had a feeling he could leave Liverpool after the World Cup, but I believed it would be his form in the competition, not another controversy, that would secure his move to Spain. Having appeared to make great personal improvements, the circumstances around his departure came as such a shock. I'm not going to pretend I understand biting an opponent even once – but to have done it on three occasions? That is beyond belief. When Suárez bit Giorgio Chiellini, at first, I wasn't sure what I had seen. England were playing Costa Rica at the same time as Uruguay's game against Italy, but we had already been knocked out after two matches by that time, and our game was dull and meaningless. I kept flicking over to see how we were getting on through a sense of loyalty really, but if I am being honest the match I wanted to see was Uruguay and Italy – because both teams were playing for their lives to get through to the second round.

I saw Suárez put his head towards Chiellini and my instinct was that he had tried to head-butt him. 'Funny sort of head-butt – in the shoulder,' I thought. 'What was the point of that?' As the replays were shown it became clear it was a bite. Another bite! It didn't make sense. Is he mad? How does he think he will get away with this stuff? It isn't like the old days. When I played, someone could throw a right-hander and nobody – apart from the bloke on the receiving end – would know. Even the players were clueless about half the stuff that went on. These days there are television cameras everywhere, at every game. The bigger the match, the more footage there will be. The level that Suárez plays at, he is always going to be found out. He must have a screw loose.

I've been a manager a long time now. We all know players can do irrational things. Tackles that are beyond the pale, handball, spitting, diving, saying despicable things in the heat of a moment. I don't condone it, but I understand that it happens. And thankfully, the worst behaviour is usually a first, and last, offence. Make it clear in no uncertain terms that spitting at another player is unacceptable and it never happens again. I really don't know where a manager goes with a player like Suárez who insists on reoffending. Liverpool must have been at the end of their tether dealing with the fall-out. They must have felt they had already done so much.

His behaviour seemed to have improved, too. Given the choice between having a shot and biting someone he now seemed to prefer having the shot. Professionals are always seeking an edge, but sometimes they look for it in the wrong places and that is what Suárez tended to do. And then he regressed. What I cannot work out is what he thinks he gains from this behaviour. I don't agree with diving, but I can see why players do it. We all know games that have been won, goals that have been scored, because a player has dived in the penalty area and fooled the referee. It's wrong – but I do see the benefit. But biting? Can anyone tell me a goal that was scored by a brilliant piece of biting? Why would any player do that?

If Suárez at last channels that energy into a more positive enthusiasm he can be as big an asset at Barcelona as he was at Liverpool. His partnership with Lionel Messi is one we will all want to watch. Without a doubt, he is an impact player, and as good as drove Liverpool into the Champions League last season. Brendan has done a great job at Anfield but I'm sure he will admit that to walk in and have a player of Suárez's calibre at the peak of his game was the biggest bonus. My fear for the club now is that Suárez will be like Gareth Bale was for Tottenham Hotspur last season – and prove impossible to replace. Liverpool threw a huge amount of money at rebuilding, but what Suárez brought was unique and over a season we may increasingly realise that. I would certainly place him up there with the true Liverpool greats, like Rush, Kenny Dalglish and Kevin Keegan, for all his faults. He may not have their same qualities as a person, but as a player he sits beside any in the modern era, and he will leave a big hole in our game.

I know there are a lot of players in this last team who have been accused of diving throughout their careers – Ronaldo, Bale and Suárez in particular – but I'm not about to get on my high horse about it here. Frankly, there are a lot of managers who worry more about diving than they do about a player going over the top and trying to break someone's leg – my old friend Tony Pulis is on a permanent campaign about diving, but when one of his players gets away with it, this doesn't seem to be such an issue. Look, it happens – and frankly I feel sorry for the referee. It's the hardest decision in the world to call, in my experience. I've refereed games in training where I've given a penalty and all the players have started laughing. 'What's wrong?' 'He didn't touch him, boss.' 'Are you sure? He looked like he did to me.' I've seen incidents on television 20 times over and even then still can't make my mind up. Sometimes momentum carries a player over and he gets the blame. And even some of the most blatant dives look like fouls in real time. There was a horrendous dive by James McClean of Wigan Athletic against us in the play-off finals last year – a real rotten one because he was trying to get our goalkeeper, Rob Green, sent off as well as win a penalty. In slow motion it looked really poor. In real time? I thought it was a penalty and Rob was a goner. I don't know how the referees do it sometimes.

And I'll be on the touchline again this season, trying to work out how to stop some of the other names I've mentioned in this book. The last time Suárez came to Loftus Road he destroyed us – we were beaten by four and it could have been double that. So I'd be lying if I said I was looking forward to seeing him again.

You want to know the truth? When it was announced that he was banned, the first thing I checked was whether any Rangers matches against Liverpool were included and when I found out one was, I had a big smile. Now he's gone, I'll miss his input to English football, but not the task of trying to stop him. When any manager says he is looking forward to the challenge of pitting his wits against the greatest players, he's kidding you. Do you think any of us wants to have to deal with George Best or Tom Finney or Matt Le Tissier or Luis Suárez? Sir Alex Ferguson had the best defenders in the league, but by his own admission he was never happy when he saw Le Tissier's name on the team-sheet. He would much rather have played Southampton without him. I wasn't wishing for serious harm to befall Suárez but that ban suited me just fine. And if Brendan Rodgers wants to rest Steven Gerrard for a big Champions League game the next time we play, he can be my guest. I've loved every second of watching these guys; trying to beat them is another matter. You need to be lucky – and good. I'll keep trying, and hoping we can be a bit of both.

PREMIER LEAGUE II: THE TEAM

PETR
CECH
Chelsea

PABLO ZABALETA	**JOHN TERRY**	**RIO FERDINAND**	**ASHLEY COLE**
Manchester City	Chelsea	Manchester United	Chelsea

CRISTIANO RONALDO	**STEVEN GERRARD**	**PAUL SCHOLES**	**GARETH BALE**
Manchester United	Liverpool	Manchester United	Tottenham Hotspur

THIERRY HENRY
Arsenal

LUIS SUÁREZ
Liverpool

PICTURE CREDITS